# VEDIC TANTRISM

M. S. BHAT

# VEDIC TANTRISM

*A Study of Ṛgvidhāna of Śaunaka with Text and Translation*

CRITICALLY EDITED IN THE ORIGINAL SANSKRIT WITH AN INTRODUCTORY STUDY AND TRANSLATED WITH CRITICAL AND EXEGETICAL NOTES

MOTILAL BANARSIDASS
*Delhi Varanasi Patna Madras*

*First Published* **1987,1998**

MOTILAL BANARSIDASS
Bungalow Road, Jawahar Nagar, Delhi 110 007
*Branches*
Chowk, Varanasi 221 001
Ashok Rajpath, Patna 800 004
120 Royapettah High Road, Mylapore, Madras 600 004



ISBN: 81-208-0197-0

PRINTED IN INDIA
BY JAINENDRA PRAKASH JAIN AT SHRI JAINENDRA PRESS,
A-45 NARAINA, PHASE I, NEW DELHI 110 028 AND PUBLISHED BY
NARENDRA PRAKASH JAIN FOR MOTILAL BANARSIDASS, DELHI 110 007.

# PREFACE

It is a great pleasure to me to present before the scholarly world a critical edition of the *Ṛgvidhāna* with a translation and critical and exegetical notes, to which a thorough study of the same work is prefixed. So far as I know, the text of the *Ṛgvidhāna* with a Latin introduction was brought out by R. Meyer in 1878 and a translation of the same text with notes by J. Gonda in 1951. Another work of Śaunaka, viz., *Bṛhaddevatā* was critically edited and translated by Prof. A.A. Macdonell in 1904. Under the circumstances a new critical edition of the *Ṛgvidhāna* based on the hitherto unutilized manuscript material of the text and the commentary available in all the parts of India was highly desirable, nay positively welcome.

The *Ṛgvidhāna* of Śaunaka enjoins the aspirant to utilize the Mantras of the *Ṛgveda* for the attainment of 'the four aims of human life' (Puruṣārtha) and promises quick results, rather magical, without resorting to the elaborate and tedious sacrifices. The analysis of the contents and the subject-matter of the *Ṛgvidhāna* yields a fairly good picture of the superstitions, taboos, religions and magical practices of that post-Brāhmaṇa period of which we have, unfortunately, few records.

Acknowledgements are due to the authorities of the Bombay University Library, Baroda Oriental Institute and Tanjore Sarasvatī Mahal Library for permitting me to utilize the manuscripts in their possession.

I must express my gratitude to my late revered teacher Dr. N.J. Shende, M.A., Ph.D., D. Litt. who was a source of inspiration to me for a fairly long period.

M.S. BHAT

# CONTENTS

# PART

# I

## *Ṛgvidhāna : A Study*

# INTRODUCTION

It is perhaps difficult to exaggerate the importance of the *Ṛg-vidhāna* attributed to Śaunaka from the point of view of the ritual literature in general and the Vidhāna literature in particular. The Vidhāna texts are important in the history of Vedic literature for more than one reason. They mark a new period of literature and a new outlook in the religious life of India, since they were written with a practical object in view, to wit: the simplication of the complicated and burdensome ceremonies treated in the Śrauta and Gṛhya Sūtras, and this was achieved by adjusting the matters, with the help of magic, in such a way that observances became easier in practice. Śaunaka and Kātyāyana who are mentioned as the authors of the *Ṛg-* and *Yajur- Vidhānas* respectively have distinguished themselves in branches of the Post-Vedic literature, particularly in the Anukramaṇīs and Prātiśākhyas. Finally these works which serve as a connecting link between the Brāhmaṇism and the Purāṇic Hindu Religion contribute to our knowledge of that age of literary activity among the Brāhmaṇas which preceded the rise of Buddhism.

*Ṛgvidhāna* describes the magical effects produced by the recitation of hymns of the *Ṛgveda.* The *editio princeps* of this work was brought out by Dr. Rudolf Meyer in 1878. It was published at a time when Sanskrit scholarship in Europe was making a headway into the Vedic literature. The bulk of the Vedic Saṁhitās and Brāhmaṇas was no doubt available in print. But the case was entirely different with the secondary works like the *Bṛhaddevatā*, the *Pariśiṣṭas* of the *AV* etc. which were accessible in manuscripts only. The existence of the Kashmir Collection of Ṛgvedic Khilas was not known. Taking these facts into consideration Dr. Meyer's achievement is remarkable. But it is, however, obvious that a work edited under such circumstances hundred years ago shows some defects. First of all, his materials—the three Berlin MSS.—from which the text was prepared were extremely faulty. Secondly, the then prevailing method of textual criticism was possibly responsible for the introduction of an element of eclectism in his edition. In Dr. Meyer's text, there is practically no distinction between the additional passages in the longer recension and those passages whose authenticity is open to doubt, since both of them are put within brackets. This practice of Dr. Meyer is misleading and he himself realised the difficulty later on.[1] Thirdly, a formidable number of emendations in his text. There are, according to my reckoning, about forty-eight emendations, many of which are unnecessary.

The editions of the *Ṛvidh* which appeared later are useless from the textual point of view, since the editor of the Bombay edition did not mention the manuscript or manuscripts utilised in the constitution of his text and the editor of the Lahore edition gave a Devanāgarī version of Dr. Meyer's text.

Of recent years the position has changed. The MSS of the *Ṛvidh* are now available in some of the best manuscript libraries in India. Further, the discovery of a unique commentary on *Ṛvidh* by Mātṛsūnu has provided us with further means for the critical examination of the *Ṛvidh*. Finally, we have the parallel or abridged versions of the *Ṛvidh* in the *Viṣṇudharmottara-* and *Agni-Purāṇas*. The availability of so much fresh material makes a new edition of the *Ṛvidh* both possible and highly desirable. I have on these grounds undertaken to edit the *Ṛvidh* afresh.

Lately, the translation of the *Ṛvidh* by Prof. Gonda has been made accessible to scholars. As I had an occasion to consult it, I must record my impression of that rendering here. His rendering, on the whole, is inaccurate and at times absurd. The translation which I have given is meant to be a close one in which every word of the text is accounted for. To the text and the translation I have prefixed a study which discusses all aspects of the *Ṛvidh*. It is for the first time such an exhaustive study on the *Ṛvidh* has been undertaken.

The present work consists of two parts: the first contains the study dealing with various aspects of the *Ṛvidh*; the second, the Sanskrit text, the *apparatus criticus* and the translation with notes which discuss many difficulties of the text.

First Part is divided into the following six chapters:—

1. *Ṛvidh.* Praefatio, p. viii.

*Chapter* I traces the beginnings of the Vedāṅga literature in the Brāhmaṇas. Next it takes up the six Vedāṅgas, one by one, giving out at the same time some of the important works which represent them. Then it takes up the Anukramaṇīs and the Vidhānas briefly indicating the relationship which exists between them on one hand and with the Vedāṅgas on the other hand. Finally, it treats of the extant Vidhānas, their characteristic features, the relative chronor logy of these works etc. and this brings us to the end of the Chapter I.

*Chapter* II takes up the characteristic features which the *Ṛvidh* shares in common with other Vidhānas. This is followed by detailed analysis of the contents and of the subject-matter of the *Ṛvidh.* The analysis of the contents treats of the three parts into which the *Ṛvidh* can be divided on the basis of the actual presentation of the matter. They are: the introductory part, the main body of the work and the concluding part. The introductory part consists mainly of classification of Vedic mantras along with their magical properties and objects, followed by an enumeration of purificatory hymns, austerities and vows. The main body of the work relates to the employment of Ṛks for all sorts of magical and superstitious purposes. The concluding part treats of Vāstuśamana and Dakṣiṇā followed by Phalaśruti, the apocryphal character of which is self-evident. The analysis of the subject-matter treats of various charms and rites which are prescribed for obtaining various objects of desire. The last section is devoted to mythology of the *Ṛvidh.*

*Chapter* III takes up the peculiarities of the language of the *Ṛvidh.* They are considerable and very remarkable also. They are classed under six heads: I Phonology: II Euphonic Combination; III Morphology; IV Syntax; V Vocabulary; and VI Metre. The *Ṛvidh* has not got much to offer under the head Phonology, but in the case of others we have enough words and forms which are both against Vedic usage and against Pāṇini's rules. The occurrence of so many irregularities in so small a treatise as the *Ṛvidh* is, proves clearly that Śaunaka did not follow Pāṇini's grammar and makes it very unlikely that he ever knew it at all. On the linguistic grounds it seems to me that Śaunaka cannot be placed later than fifth century B.C.

*Chapter* IV discusses the problem of authorship and of the date on the basis of external and internal evidence. A short account of Mātṛsūnu, the commentator of *Ṛvidh*, is given at the end of this Chapter.

*Chapter* V is devoted to the description of manuscripts and other materials upon which my edition of the *Ṛvidh* is based. To the text and the commentary manuscripts which I have directly collated, I may add the three manuscripts collated by Dr. Meyer and three more manuscripts collated by Prof. Gonda. Thus directly or indirectly, the evidence of altogether ten manuscripts was available to me in the constitution of the text. Next it takes up the external evidence bearing on the text of the *Ṛvidh*. Finally, the emendations carried out in the text and the sources utilised by the author of the *Ṛvidh* are treated.

*Chapter* VI is a reśumé of the results hitherto gained.

CHAPTER I

# VIDHĀNA LITERATURE

The remarkable thing about Śaunaka's literary activity is the unity of purpose that underlies all of them. They have been written with the express purpose of preserving the Ṛgvedic tradition. Śaunaka's *Anukramaṇīs* give details about seers, deities, metres, Anuvākas and Sūktas. His other two works, viz. *Bṛhaddevatā* and *Ṛgvidhāna* give respectively the legends concerning the deities and the magical effects produced by the recitation of Ṛgvedic hymns or verses. All these works are intimately connected with the Vedāṅga literature which had its germs in the Brāhmaṇas.

## 1. *The Brāhmaṇas and the Vedāṅgas*

The Brāhmaṇas have been variously defined.[1] The tradition[2] distinguishes their twofold contents: *vidhi* and *arthavāda*; but this gives only an incomplete picture of these works. The Brāhmaṇas originated from scholastic controversies or opinions of individual Ṛṣis, some of which relate to the description of the rites; and some to the verses of the Saṁhitās; and the texts which have come down to us are rather the last series of such works, the earlier ones being either entirely supplanted and effaced or lost.[3] Suffice it to say that they represent one of the early attempts in the direction of a dogmatic commentary on the Saṁhitās to which they belong. The main purpose of the Brāhmaṇas, then, is to explain the Ṛk, the Yajus, or the Sāman as the case may be and to enjoin the procedure of the sacrificial ritual by indicating the connection between the Ṛk, the Yajus etc. and the ritual. An example or two will illustrate this.

(a) "Yajñena yajñam ayajanta devā [*RV*.1.164.50a = 10.90.16a] ityuttamayā paridadhāti, iti / yajñena vai tad devā yajñam aya-

1. Müller, *ASL* (Reprint), 1926, pp. 179 ff.
2. Sāyaṇa's intro. to the *RV* (*VSM*), Vol. I, p. 9.
3. Winternitz, *HIL*, Vol. I, p. 189.

janta / yad agninā' gnim ayajanta te svargaṁ lokam āyan, iti / "tāni dharmāṇiprathamāny āsan / te ha nākaṁ mahimānaḥ sacanta yatra pūrve sādhyāḥ santi devā" [*RV*.1.164.50bcd = 10.90.16 bcd) iti, iti / chandāṁsi vai sādhyā devās te' gre'gninā' gnim ayajanta te svargaṁ lokam āyan, iti / ādityāś caivehā'sann Aṅgirasaś ca te' gre' gninā' gnim ayajanta te svargaṁ lokam āyan, iti / saiṣā svargāhutir yad agnyāhutir yadi ha vā apy abrāhmaṇokto yadi durukto yajate'tha haiṣā" hutir gacchaty eva devānna pāpmanā saṁsṛjyate, iti / gacchaty asyā" hutirdevān nāsyāhutiḥ pāpmanā saṁṣrjyate ya evaṁ veda iti //[4]

(b) "Agnir deveddha" [*RV.Kh*.v.5.1] iti śaṁsaty asau vā agnir deveddha etaṁ hi devā indhata etam eva tad etasmiṁ loka āyātayati, iti / "agnir manviddha" iti śaṁsaty ayaṁ vā agnir manviddha imaṁ hi manuṣyā indhate' gnim eva tad asmiṁ loka āyātayati, iti / "agniḥ suṣamid" iti śaṁsati vāyur vā agniḥ suṣamid vāyur hi svayam ātmānaṁ samindhe svayam idaṁ sarvaṁ yadidaṁ kiñca vāyum eva tad antarīkṣaloka āyātayati, iti / "hotā devavṛta" iti śaṁsaty asau vai hotā devavṛta eṣahi sarvato devair vṛta etam eva tad etasmiṁ loka āyātayati iti / "hota manuvṛta" iti śaṁsaty ayaṁ vā agnirhotā manuvṛto' yaṁhi sarvato manuṣyair vṛto' gnim eva tad asmiṁ loka āyātayati, iti / "praṇīr yajñānām" iti śaṁsati vāyur vai praṇīr yajñānāṁ yadā hi prāṇity atha yajño'thāgnihotraṁ vāyum eva tad antarīkṣaloka āyātayati, iti / "rathīr adhvarāṇām" iti śaṁsaty asau vai rathīr adhvarāṇāṁ eṣa hi yathaitac carati rathīr ivaitam eva tad asmiṁ loka āyātayati iti / "atūrto hotā" iti śaṁsaty ayaṁ vā agnir atūrto hotemaṁ ha na kaścana tiryañcaṁ taraty agnim eva tad asmiṁ loka ātātayati, iti / "tūrṇir havyavāḍ" iti śamsati vāyur vai tūrṇir havyavāḍ vāyur hīdaṁ sarvaṁ sadyas tarati yad idaṁ kim ca vāyur devebhyo havyaṁ vahati vāyum eva tad antarīkṣaloka āyātayati, iti / "ādevo devān vakṣad" iti śaṁsaty asau vai devo devān āvahaty etam eva tad etasmiṁ loka āyātayati, iti / "yakṣad agnir devo devān" iti śaṁsaty ayaṁ vā agnir devodevān yajatyagnimeva tad asmiṁ loka āyātayati, iti / "so adhvarā karati jātavedā" iti śaṁsati vāyur vai jātavedā vāyur hīdaṁ sarvaṁ karoti yad idaṁ kiṁca vāyum eva tad antarīkṣa loka āyātayati, iti //[5]

4. *AB* 1.3.5.
5. *AB* 2.5.2.

These above extracts from the *AB* are sufficient to show that there is much valuable information to be gathered from this work. Being primarily intended for the Hotṛ-priest whose duty it was to form a Śastra out of the hymns or verses of the *RV*, the Brāhmaṇas of the *RV* do not strictly adhere to the sequence of the hymns as they occur in the *RV*. But the Brāhmaṇas of the other Vedas and especially those of the Yajus school closely follow the ritual, being based upon Saṁhitās which are more or less adapted to the proper order of the ritual. Thus the first nine books of the *Śatapatha-brāhmaṇa* can be considered as a running commentary on the first eighteen sections of the *Vājasaneyī-Saṁhitā*.[6] Besides paraphrases of verses, we notice the prevalance of remarkable comparisons, or a web of identifications, symbolism of figures, etymological explanations and the mystical explanations of metres in the Brāhmaṇas. An example under each head will suffice.

(a) Ghṛte caruṁ nirvape ta yo'pratiṣṭhito manyeta, asyāṁ vāva sa no pratitiṣṭhati yo na pratitiṣṭhati / tad yad ghṛtaṁ tat striyai payo ye taṇḍulās te puṁsas tan mithunaṁ mithunenainaṁ tat prajayā paśubhiḥ prajanayati prajāyati / prajāyate prajayā paśubhir ya evaṁ veda //[7]

(b) saptadaśa sāmidhenīr anubrūyāt / saptadaśo vai prajāpatir-dvādaśa māsāḥ pancartavo hemantaśiśirayoḥ samānena tāvān saṁvatsaraḥ saṁvatsaraḥ prajāpatiḥ / prajāpatyāyatanābhir evā'' bhīrādhnoti ya evaṁ veda //[8]

(c) Āhūtayo vai nāmaitā yad āhutaya etābhir vai devān yajmāno hvayati tad āhūtīnām āhūtitvam iti / ūtayaḥ khalu vai tā nāma yābhir devā yajamānasya havam āyanti ye vai panthāno yāḥ srutayas tā vā ūtayas tā u evaitat svargayāṇā yajamānasya bhavanti, iti //[9]

(d) Atho pañcavīryaṁ vā etac chando yad virāṭ / yat tripadā tenoṣṇihāgāyatryau yad asyā ekādaśākṣarāṇi padāni tena triṣṭub yattrayastriṁśad akṣarā tenānuṣṭumnavā ekenākṣarenacchaṁdāṁsi viyanti na dvābhyāṁ yad virāṭ tat pañcamam / sarveṣāṁ

6. Winternitz, *op.cit.*, p. 192.
7. *AB* 1.1.1.
8. *Ibid.*, 1.1.1.
9. *Ibid.*, 1.1.2.

chandasāṁ vīryam avarundhe sarveṣāṁ chandasāṁ vīryam aśnute sarveṣāṁ chandasāṁ sāyujyaṁ sarūpatāṁ salokatām aśnute' nnādo'nnapatir bhavaty aśnute prajāyā'nnādyaṁ ya evam vidvān virājau kurute, iti //[10]

Finally, the Brāhmaṇas contain cosmogonic myths, ancient, legends, and narratives which though unconnected with the ritual are brought in connection with the explanation or justification of some sacrificial ceremony or other. Thus the Brāhmaṇas which carry discussions on matters of etymology, metrics, grammar, etc. along with the explanations of the ritual matters presuppose the beginnings of the Vedāṅga literature.

## 2. *The Vedāṅgas*

In the preceding section we have seen that most of the Vedāṅgas had their origin in the Brāhmaṇas, and we may rightly include the Āraṇyaka portions of those Brāhmaṇas where along with the theosophical and philosophical explanations of the sacrifice, we find discussions on Saṁhitā, Pada- and the Krama-pāṭhas, Śikṣā, etc.,[11] which in course of time were pursued more independently and systematically as Vedāṅgas. *Ṣaḍviṁśa-brāhmaṇa* refers to the four Vedas and the six Aṅgas without enumerating them.[12] The oldest enumeration of the six Vedāṅgas occurs in the *Muṇḍaka-Upaniṣad*,[13] where the Aparāvidyā is said to consist of *Ṛgveda*, *Yajurveda*, *Sāmaveda*, *Atharvaveda*, Śikṣā, Kalpa, Vyākaraṇa, Nirukta, Chandas and Jyotiṣa. The exegetical Vedāṅgas, viz., Śikṣa, Vyākaraṇa, Nirukta, and Chandas are meant as aids to the correct reciting and understanding of the Vedas, whereas the ritual Vedāṅgas, viz. Kalpa and Jyotiṣa deal with the public and domestic rites as well as with the customary law and the proper time for performing them. Now, I shall take up these, one by one, in the above order.

### (a) *Śikṣā*

Several brief treatises bearing the title Śikṣā have come down to us; but they are only late productions of the post-Vedic period.

10. *Ibid.*, 1.1.6.
11. *Vide AĀ* 3; *TĀ* 7.1.
12. *Ṣaḍ-Br* 4.7.
13. *Mu Up* 1.1.5.

These works contain directions for the recitation and correct pronunciation of the Vedas. If compared with the Prātiśākhyas, these texts represent a stage of intense popularisation. The treatises which really represent the Vedāṅga Śikṣā are the Prātiśākhyas.[14] As is well known, the *Aitareyāraṇyaka*[15] is aware of the three principal modes in which the Veda is recited, viz. the Saṁhitā-, the Pada-, and the Krama-pāṭhas. The main object of these Prātiśākhyas is to determine the relation of the Saṁhitā and Pada-pāṭhas to each other, to teach how to form the Pada-pāṭha out of the Saṁhitā-pāṭha and *vice versa*, and to lay down definitions of technical terms and rules in regard to quantity etc. They furnish us with a systematic account of Sandhi and metrics. These texts are of utmost importance for the linguist and for the interpreter of the Vedas.

### (b) *Vyākaraṇa*

Unfortunately, the Vedāṅga text on grammar has not come down to us and its place might have partly been usurped by the Prātiśākhyas which though connected with the correct recitation of the Vedas, also deal with the grammar proper to some extent. The tradition has raised the grammar of Pāṇini to the status of a Vedāṅga text which it hardly deserves since it superficially treats of the Vedic language and moreover it does not belong to any Vedic school.[16]

### (c) *Nirukta*

The Vedāṅga Nirukta is represented by one work, the *Nirukta* of Yāska. It is in reality a Vedic commentary[17] and is based on the Nighaṇṭus "glossaries", a collection of rare or obscure words which occur in the hymns of the *RV*. The Nighaṇṭus consist of five lists of words which are divided into three sections, viz. the Naighaṇṭuka-kāṇḍa, the Naigama-kāṇḍa and the Daivata-kāṇḍa. The first three lists constitute the Naighaṇṭuka-kāṇḍa, in which groups of synonyms are found. The Naigama-kāṇḍa which is also

14. Winternitz, *op.cit.*, p. 285.
15. *AĀ* 3.
16. Winternitz, *op.cit.*, p. 289.
17. *Ibid.*, p. 69.

known as Aikapadika-kāṇḍa contains a list of isolated and specially difficult words, while the Daivata-kāṇḍa gives a classification of the Vedic gods. The work of Yāska is a series of etymological analyses of the words given in these lists and while analysing he adduces as examples a large number of Ṛgvedic verses in which those words occur. The first Adhyāya which is a sort of introduction deals with the principles of grammar and Veda-exegesis. The second and the third Adhyāyas comment on the Naighaṇṭuka-kāṇḍa; Adhyāyas IV-VI, on the Naigama-kāṇḍa; and Adhyāyas VII-XII on the Daivata-kāṇḍa. The Vedāṅgas so far treated supply a good deal of information on the growth of the grammatical science in India.

### (d) *Chandas*

Allusion to metres are fairly common in the Brāhmaṇas. The Brāhmaṇas have developed a mysticism of the syllable and of the verse to such an extent that it is next to impossible to find a systematic account of metres in them. However, we have some chapters on metre at the end of the *Ṛgvedaprātiśākhya*[18] and one section of the *Śāṅkhāyanaśrautasūtra*[19] is also devoted to metres. The Sūtras of Piṅgala, the *Chandaḥsūtra*, on metrics existing in two slightly different recensions is regarded as a Vedāṅga on metre of the *RV* and *YV*. The Vedic portion of the *Chandaḥsūtra* lays down the rules of prosody, expounds "the metres of the gods" and "the metres of the Asuras" etc. and treats of the seven normal metres and several others which have either complex or aberrant forms. Though claimed as a Vedāṅga it is a late supplement which reflects ancient teachings on the subject. For the metres of the *SV*, we have the *Nidhāna-sūtra* which treats metrics and other component parts of the *SV*.[20]

### (e) *Kalpa*

The Vedāṅga on Kalpa is represented by a vast literature on ritual and is the most complete amongst the Vedāṅgas. During the Brāhmaṇa period, the ritual has grown to very large propor-

18. *RV Prāti*, Paṭalas, 16-18.
19. *ŚŚS* 7.27.
20. Winternitz, *op.cit.*, p. 288.

tions and naturally with the ritual the sacrificiants officiants had increased until sixteen or seventeen are enumerated as taking part in the principal sacrifices.[21] The sacrifice which was originally supplicatory in character has now given rise to a belief that it, if properly done, exercises compulsion over the gods to grant the wishes of the worshipper. The profound and beneficial efficacy of these elaborate ceremonies had a peculiar charm to the people of that age and a need to condense and systematise the ritualistic contents of the Brāhmaṇas was felt and the result of all this was the Kalpa-sūtras. The Kalpa-sūtras are divided into (a) The Śrauta-sūtras which present us in the rationalised form, the great sacrificial rites, at which a number of priests were employed; (b) the Gṛhya-sūtras which deal with the household rituals and other duties performed by the householder with or without the assistance of a priest; and (c) the Dharma-sūtras which deal with the customary law prevalent at that time. The ritual literature does not come to an end here, for, we find numerous other works like Śrāddha-kalpa, Pitṛmedhasūtras, Pariśiṣṭas, Prayogas and Kārikās.[22]

### (f) *Jyotiṣa*

Of the Vedāṅga Jyotiṣa we possess only texts of rather late date.[23] However, the two recensions (both metrical: 36 ślokas in that of the Ṛk-school and 43 in that of the Yajus-school) which have come down to us belong to the *Ṛgveda* and *Yajurveda* respectively. It has its beginnings in the Brāhmaṇas where allusions to astronomical subjects are fairly frequent. A need for drawing up a ritual calendar to fix proper seasons for sacrifices was felt very early, though no work representing astronomy has survived from the Vedic period. The work which is before us gives the position of the moon and the sun at solstices and other related matters. A work bearing the title of *Ātharvaṇa-Jyotiṣa*[24] exists. It sets forth the divisions of time, the names of Nakṣatras, etc. and gives auspicious time for conception.

21. Keith, *RPV*, Part I, p. 298.
22. Winternitz, *op.cit.*, pp. 280-281.
23. Winternitz, *op.cit.*, p. 283.
24. *ĀJ* Edited by Bhagavad Datta, Lahore, 1924.

### 3. *The Anukramaṇīs and the Vidhānas*

Intimately connected with the Vedāṅgas and yet a distinct class of literature are the Anukramaṇīs and the Vidhānas. The Anukramaṇīs give lists of the hymns, the seers, the metres and the deities in the order in which they occur in the various Saṁhitās and the only ones which are well known are those of the *Ṛgveda.*[25] Out of the five Anukramaṇīs which are ascribed to Śaunaka, only three have been preserved.[26] The *Ārṣānukramaṇī* gives the seers of the *RV*. The *Chandonukramaṇi* enumerates the metres in which the hymns of the *RV* are composed. The *Anuvākānukramaṇī* gives the Pratīkas of each of the eightyfive Anuvākas of the *RV* and the number of hymns contained in them. The MSS of the *Devatānukramaṇī* and the *Sūktānukramaṇi* are no longer extant, though some quotations from the former work are embedded in the *Vedārthadīpikā* to the *Sarv* (1.165). The *Sarvānukramaṇī* of Kātyāyana, a more systematic work in the sūtra style, combines the data contained in the Anukramaṇīs treated above. For every hymn in the *RV* it gives, first of all, the Pratīka, then the number of its verses, as well as the Ṛṣi, the deity, and the metre, even for single verses.

The distinctive peculiarity of the style of Śaunaka if contrasted with that of Kātyāyana lies in the fact that the work ascribed to the former are composed in mixed Śloka and Triṣṭubh metres, whereas the works of Kātyāyana are written in aphoristic prose. Mention is to be made here regarding Śaunaka's *Bṛhaddevatā* which bears the most manifest traces of Śaunaka's style and which has superseded to some extent his own *Devatānukramaṇī*.

Śaunaka and Kātyāyana who are mentioned as authors of the Anukramaṇīs and Prātiśākhyas stand out also as authors of the Vidhāna texts. It may be remarked now as to what is the relation between the Vidhānas and the Anukramaṇīs as well as their connection with the Vedāṅga literature which was barely hinted earlier. The Vidhānas insofar as they, in spite of numerous omissions, follow the sequence (Anukrama) of the traditional text of the Saṁhitās[27] to which they refer, can be regarded as part and

25. Winternitz, *op.cit.*, p. 286.
26. Macdonell, *Sarv*, Preface, pp. v-vi.
27. cp. *Ṛvidh* i.2: Mantrebhyo mantradṛgbhyaś ca.

parcel of the Anukramaṇī literature with this difference, viz., that the former, while giving the Pratīkas of hymns or parts of hymns, employs the hymns or even single verses for some tangible purpose, whereas the latter gives only a table of contents. Exception is, however, to be made in the case of Kātyāyana's *Sarvānukramaṇī* which by its very title suggests that it is a "catalogue of all things" (including to some extent the Viniyoga of some ṛks) for the *RV.* Although the Anukramaṇīs and the Vidhānas form no part of the Vedāṅga literature, still they are inseparable from the auxiliary literature of the Vedas on account of their close relation with the Kalpa.[28]

4. *The Vidhānas*

The term *vidhāna* is interpreted in two ways: it means "sacred precept" and is synonymous with *vidhi.* We often find *vidhāna* used in the sense of *vidhi* in the *Ṛvidh*[29] and in one instance the latter has replaced the former.[30] Baudhāyana[31] refers to *ṛgvidhāna* in a passage which is not likely to have been interpolated, but it is not known whether he refers to the well-known work of that name or he means simply "a prescription consisting of a Ṛk". For our present purpose it will suffice if we state that the use of the *vidhāna* in the sense of *vidhi* is attested not only by the *Ṛvidh* itself but also by Baudhāyana. Secondly, it can also mean "sorcery practice", a sense which is strictly Atharvanic.[32] The fact

---

samāmnāyānupūrvaśaḥ /
karmaṇām ṛṣidṛṣṭānāṁ
vidhiṁ provāca Śaunakaḥ //

28. Cp. the beginning of the *Sarv.*: Atha Ṛgvedāmnāye śākalake sūktapratīkaṛksaṅkhya ṛṣidaivatacchandāṁsy anukramiṣyāmo yathopadésam / na hy etaj jñānamṛté śrautasmārtakarmaprasiddhiḥ //

29. (a) i.26cd: tataḥ śeṣaṁ vidhānena śucir bhuñjīta vāgyataḥ //
(b) iii.28cd: anenaiva vidhānnea ṣaḍbhir varṣair pramucyate //
(c) iii.155cd: vakṣye Puruṣasūktasya vidhānaṁ tvarcanaṁ prati //
(d) iii.161cd: yathā dehe tathā deve nyāsaṁ kṛtvā vidhānataḥ //
(e) iii.230cd: muktyaikamārgapratibodhanāya dṛṣṭvā vidhānaṁ tviha Nārōdoktam //

30. Phalaśruti st.13: Tuṣyanti devatāḥ sarvāḥ saṁpadyante vibhūtayḥ / durādhayaḥ praṇaśyanti nityam Ṛgvidhi-pāṭhinām //

31. *Bau DS* 1.7.10.

32. Cp. Vidhānakalpa, one of the names of the Āṅgirasakalpa *vide* Bloomfield, *Hymns of the Atharvaveda* (SBE XLII) intro. p. xix.

that we find some such practices in the course of our work leads us to assume that the *Ṛvidh* partakes of both the characteristics, viz., the characteristics of a *vidhi* as well as of *Vidhāna*. In this connection, it is worthwhile to quote Barth who observes:[33] "A whole class of writings, the vidhānas, the origin of which is besides very ancient, have no other object than to direct in the observance of a kind of cultus at a reduced rate, which should procure the same advantages as the great sacrifices."

To the *RV* belongs in the first place the *Ṛgvidhāna*[34] composed in the mixed Śloka and Triṣṭubh metre. There are two recensions of this work: the shorter one, which is also incidently the earlier, is entitled the *Kaniṣṭha-Ṛgvidhāna* or simply *Ṛgvidhāna* and the longer one in the typical Purāṇic style is entitled the *Jyeṣṭha-* (or as some MSS style it *Bṛhad-*) *Ṛgvidhāna.*[35] The shorter one with which we are concerned here consists of four Adhyāyas. It describes the magical effects produced by the recitation of hymns or even single verses of the *RV*. It is ascribed to Śaunaka. Corresponding to the above *ṛcāṁ vidhānam* we have *sāmnāṁ vidhānam*, to wit: the *Sāmavidhāna-brāhmaṇa*[36] which, in spite of its erroneous title "*Brāhmaṇa*", belongs to the Vidhāna literature. It consists of three Prapāṭhakas and is somewhat similar to the above mentioned *Ṛvidh*. To the *Śuklayajurveda* belongs the *Śuklayajurvidhānasūtra*[37] of Kātyāyana. It consists of seven Adhyāyas in the best recension preserved of that text. The earlier edition of this work was unfortunately designated as *Yajurvidhāna-śikṣā* and was included among Śikṣas,[38] There is no corresponding work to the *Atharvaveda*. The *Kauśikasūtra*, which deals with the magical and other practices in addition to the Śrauta and Gṛhya ceremonies can be regarded as representing the Vidhāna text proper for this Veda.

33. *Religions of India*, tr. by Rev. J. Wood, 5th Ed., 1921, pp. 96-97.

34. The *editio princeps* of the *Ṛvidh* was brought out by Rudolf Meyer and published at Berlin in the year 1878.

35. For this see Keith, *Catalogue of Skt. & Prakrit Mss in the Library of India Office*, Vol. II, Part I, No. 4254; *Des. Cat. of Skt. Mss.* in the *TMSSML*, Vol. III, Nos. 1727-30. Printed at Ganpat Krishnaji Press, Bombay, 1890.

36. Edited with Sāyaṇa's commentary by A.C. Burnell, London, 1873.

37. *Yvidh* with the commentary entitled "Yajurmañjarī", ed. by Aṇṇāśāstri Vāre, Bombay, 1943.

38. "A Collection of Sikshas by Yājñavalkya and others" ed. by Pandit Yugalakiśora Vyāsa, Benares, 1893, pp. 327-361.

### 5. *Commentaries on the Vidhānas*

The Vidhānas were made the subject of commentaries in the course of the Medieval Period. The earlier ones, if existed, have not come down to us. We are happily in possession of an unique commentary entitled the *Ṛgvidhāna-pada-pañcikā* on the *Rvidh.* It is written by Mātṛsūnu about whom we know next to nothing. Mātṛsūnu has commented creditably on the first few stanzas, but his comments become shorter and shorter as the work advances. The existence of this commentary was known as early as 1925,[39] but it has not so far attracted the attention of the scholars. The *Sāmavidhāna-brāhmaṇa* was commented upon as early as the later half of the fourteenth century A.D. by Sāyaṇa.[40] A commentary entitled *Yajurmañjarī* on the *Yvidh* has been published.[41] It is claimed to have been written by Mahārāja Mahībhuj[42] with the assistance of Kālanātha-bhaṭṭa,[43] son of Svayambhū-bhaṭṭa. We have as yet no means to determine the date of either Mātṛsūnu or Mahārāja Mahībhuj, though in the case of latter we possess a long genealogical list of rulers who possibly ruled some parts of Punjab during the thirteenth century A.D.[44]

### 6. *Parallel or abridged versions of the Vidhānas and other late Compendia*

The Vidhāna texts treated so far do not exhaust the literature on the Vidhānas for, we find some chapters devoted to the *Ṛg-*, *Yajur-*, *Sāma-* and *Atharva- vidhānas* in the *Viṣṇudharmottara-* and *Agni-Pūraṇas.*[45] It is more than likely that most of these versions, as I call them, are based on homonymous works, some of which have not survived. In the case of *Ṛvidh* we find that the versions

39. *Descriptive Catalogue of Mss. in the Central Library*, Vol. I: Vedic, Baroda, 1925, p. 24.

40. *Vide supra* f.n. 36.

41. *Vide supra* f.n. 37.

42. Cp. the final colophon: iti śrī Vāgharakulabhūṣaṇamahārājamahībhujā kṛtinā / viracitāyām ajani Yajurmañjaryāṁ pallavas turīyo' yam //

43. Cp. the introductory St. 25: vivicya bhāṣyān vividhāṁś ca kālānetasya toṣāya mudā vyatānīt / bhaṭṭasvayambhūtanayo'tra vidvān Śrīkālanāthaḥ sahakāribhāvam //

44. *Yvidh.* pp. 51-54. See Ep. Indo. Mos. 1913-14, p. 41.

45. *Viṣṇudharmottara-Purāṇa*, Khaṇḍa II, Chapters 124-127, *Agni-Purāṇa*, Chapters 259-262.

preserved in the *Viṣṇudharmottara-* and *Agni-Purāṇas* are, more or less, successive abridgements of the original *Ṛvidh*. More of this later. The *Ṛvidh* is followed up by a number of works bearing titles like *Ṛgvidhānakārikā*,[46] *Ṛgvidhānasaṁkṣepa* and *Ṛgvidhi*.[47] These works are, at best, late compendia.

## 7. *The Contents*

If now we take a comprehensive view of the class of literature which we have just examined, we find some characteristic features in them. All these works begin with the description of various penances, expiatory practices etc. and the individual vidhāna texts differ only in matters of detail or scope. Thus the description of the preparatory restraints or austerities in the *Ṛvidh* is somewhat more detailed than the *Svidh* which contains few of them, but the latter work has a number of expiatory practices which are totally absent in the former. The *Yvidh* stands on a different footing altogether for it[48] merely alludes to penances without so much as elucidating them. All these works relate in the strictest manner to Vedic Saṁhitās to which they belong and from which they draw Mantra-material in the form of Pratīkas. The pratīkas, then, along with the rules (Vidhāna) and the desired results (Phala) constitute another characteristic feature of these works. The rules (Vidhāna) formulate Japa or Homa or both. Finally the sum and substance of these works is to lay down in respect of each hymn or verse, the Kāmya ceremonies i.e. ceremonies which are intended to secure the attainment of various benefits and which are mostly of a magical nature.

## 8. *The Date*

It is no more possible to date the *Ṛvidh* than the other Vidhānas. If account is taken of internal indications, borrowings, linguistic features etc., the relative chronology of the Vidhānas can be fixed

46. *Descriptive Catalogue of Govt. collections of Mss. deposited at the Deccan College*, Poona, Vol. I, 1916, p. 44.

47. *Alphabetical Index of Skt. Mss. in the University Mss. Library*, Trivandrum, Vol. I, 1957, p. 104.

48. Tatra karmakaraṇe tulāpuruṣacāndrāyaṇakṛcchrādibhiḥ pūtaśarīreṇa karmāpekṣayā dvadaśarātraṁ ṣaḍrātram trirātram ekarātram iti karmāṅgāni prāyaścittāni karyāṇi / *Yvidh*. pp. 1-2.

with some certainty. The *Ṛvidh* is older than all the other known Vidhāna texts because it does not presuppose any of them. That *Ṛvidh* preceded the *Svidh* is proved by the fact that the former[49] is aware of the Amṛtā, Pitryā, Vāsavī, Raudrā, Ādityā and Vaiśvadevī Saṁhitās, whereas the latter[50] knows of the Mādhucchandasī, Vaiṣṇavī, Vaināyakī and Skāndī Saṁhitās, besides Amṛtā, Pitryā and Raudrī Saṁhitās. Moreover, some of the ceremonies of the latter work betray its late character.[51] Comparing the linguistic features and the style of the *Ṛvidh* with the *Svidh* we find that the former definitely appears to be an older work.[52] The *Yvidh* is definitely more recent as its author, Kātyāyana, was a grand disciple of Śaunaka according to Ṣaḍguruśiṣya. There is every likelihood that these works must have been composed between 500 and 300 B.C.

Having determined the position occupied by the Vidhānas in the Vedic literature, it remains for me to state the possible origin of these works. The following hypothesis may, however, be advanced. It was the pious duty of every Brāhmaṇa to learn the Veda and its Aṅgas.[53] The Anti-Vedic scepticism of Kautsa and others who derided the Vedas as mere conglomeration of words without any sense may have led to a reaction among the orthodox to meet the new challenge.[54] Śaunaka as a champion of the orthodox school wrote numerous works to preserve the Ṛgvedic tradition. The *Ṛgvidhāna* in particular was written by him with the purpose of proving the efficacy of the Ṛgvedic mantras in the accomplishment of various objects of desire with least effort. In the next chapter these are examined in detail.

49. *Ṛvidh* iv. 127-131.

50. *Svidh* i.4.12-20.

51. Cp. *Svidh* 2.6.11 which lays down the procedure for the vaśikaraṇa of prostitutes and (Buddhist?) nuns. For the *Svidh*, Burnell has assigned a date between 5th century B.C. and 7th century A.D. (vide *Svidh*, intro. p. x).

52. Meyer, *Ṛvidh*, Preface, p. xi.

53. Vide Sāyaṇa's intro. to *RV* (VSM), Vol. I, p. 21: brāhmaṇena niṣkāraṇo dharmaḥ ṣaḍaṅgo vedo' dhyeyo jñeyaś ca tad vidhiḥ /

54. *Nirukta*, 1.15.

## Chapter II

# CONTRIBUTION OF THE *ṚGVIDHĀNA* TO THE RITUAL LITERATURE AND MYTHOLOGY

In Chapter I, I have dealt with the characteristic features which the extant Vidhāna texts share in common. In this chapter I propose to give detailed analysis of the contents and of the subject-matter of the *Ṛgvidhāna*. The analysis gives us an insight into superstitions, taboos, religious and magical practices of that early period of which we have, unfortunately, few records.

### 1. *Analysis of the Contents*

The *Ṛvidh* is divided into four Adhyāyas and each Adhyāya in its turn is divided into Vargas generally of five Ślokas.[1] Adhyāya I has thirty-one Vargas; Adhyāya II, thirtyfive Vargas; Adhyāya III, fortythree Vargas; and Adhyāya IV, twentyseven Vargas. Adhyāya IV is followed by the Phalaśruti, consisting of three Vargas or thirteen Ślokas, called Adhyāya V in Dr. Meyer's edition. From the point of view of the actual presentation of the matter we can divide the *Ṛvidh* into three parts: the introductory, the main body of the work and the concluding part.

The work, which is before us, begins with an invocation addressed to the self-existent Brahmā, the protector of the World, and to the seers of Mantras. It promises to expound the ancient precept concerning the Ṛks in the order of the Samāmnāya i.e. the *Ṛgveda* and refers to the precept of rites which were formerly determined by the Ṛṣis and which relate to pacification (Śānti) and prosperity (Puṣṭi). More of this later on. This leads us to the categories *Stutyādayaḥ* which are barely hinted at in our work and which are further incorrectly designated as modifications (Vikārāḥ). Fortunately for us, the *Bṛhaddevatā*[2] has preserved

1. *Vide* Appendix A.
2. *BD* i.35-39ab.

them. They are *stutiḥ* (praise), *praśaṁsā* (laudation), *nindā* (blame), *saṁśayaḥ* (doubt), *paridevanā* (plaint), *spṛhā* (desire), *āśis* (prayer), *katthanā* (boasting), *yācñā* (request), *praśnaḥ* (question), *praiṣaḥ* (summons), *pravalhikā* (enigma), *niyogaḥ* (commission), *anuyogaḥ* (injunction), *ślāghā* (vaunt), *vilapitam* (lament), *ācikhyāsā* (narration), *saṁlāpaḥ* (conversation), *pavitrākhyānam* (purifying narrative), *āhanasyā* (lascivious verses), *namaskāraḥ* (obeisance), *pratirādhaḥ* (obstacle), *saṁkalpaḥ* (resolve), *parlāpa* (prattle), *prativākyam* (reply), *pratiṣedhaḥ* (prohibition), *upadeśaḥ* (admonition) *pramādaḥ* (intoxication), *apahnavaḥ* (denial), *upapraiṣaḥ* (invitation), *saṁjvaraḥ* (agitation), *vismayaḥ* (wonder), *ākrośaḥ* (abuse), *abhiṣṭavaḥ* (eulogy) *kṣepaḥ* (invective) and *śāpaḥ* (curse). To these categories *Ṛvidh* adds *arthavāda*.

Next it refers to the fourfold objects of desire, viz., *āyus* (long life), *svargaḥ* (heaven), *draviṇam* (wealth) and *sūnavaḥ* (sons) and states that hundreds of desires are incidently indicated by sages who praised the gods. The mantras when perfected by the correct method and employed according to the precept impart the desired result to the Brāhmaṇa. Truth, self-control, tranquillity, endurance, freedom from envy and equanimity are the means of achieving them. A twice-born person is asked to engage himself in muttered prayers (Japa) and burnt-offerings (Homa) which are the only means of overcoming miseries in his case. Next it gives a further list of objects, viz., *vidveṣaṇam* (the causing of hostility), *saṁvananam* (propitiating), *viṣaghnam* (counteracting poison) and *roganāśanam* (removing of disease). A twice-born person is also asked to perform the Prājāpatya-kṛcchra before undertaking the commencement of the Vedic study and he is further requested to cut the hair on his head, beard and body, to trim his nails, to take a bath and to stand during the day and sit during the night. He must mutter the purificatory verses, the Vyāhṛtis, the syllable *oṁ*, the famous verse addressed to the Sun (*RV* 3.62.10), the hymn beginning with Āpo hi ṣṭha (*RV* 10.9) and the other hymns i.e. *RV* 1.89.6 or 5.51.11-15; 7.35; 8.95. 7-9; 9.1-67 or *RV Kh* iii.10; and *RV* 10.190. He must perform *tarpaṇa* to the *ācāryas*, the seers, metres and deities and must wait upon the god Rudra with hymns addressed to him. A consecrated person must not talk with non-Aryans, Śūdras, censured people, menstruating woman, outcasts, low-born people, nor with those who dislike gods, Brāhmaṇas, *ācāryas*, elders and parents. After a period of twelve days, he should offer *sthālīpāka* to Agni, Soma, Agni-Soma, Viśvedevāḥ, Rudra, Avasānasya Pati, Anumati, Dhanvantari, the Gandharvas, the Apsarases, Brahmaṇaspati, Brahmā, Sarasvatī, Viṣṇu and Agni Sviṣṭakṛt accompanied by the preliminary and terminal oblations of clarified butter. He must feed the Brāhmaṇas and partake of the remnants.

We come now to the enumeration of Kṛcchras[3] followed by an eulogy of Kṛcchras.[4]

1. Prājāpatya Kṛcchra.[5] It consists of four periods of three days each following the other in which there is respectively eating once only in the morning, once only in the evening, eating once only without asking for it and observing complete fast.
2. Atikṛcchra.[6] This penance is constituted by eating only one morsel of food for three days in the morning only, for three days in the evening only, for three days eating one morsel got without asking for it and observing a complete fast for the next three days.
3. Sāṁtapana Kṛcchra.[7] It lasts for two days: on the first one drinks cow's urine, dung, milk, curds, ghee and kuśa water, and on the second day fasts altogether, whereas the Mahāsāṁtapana lasts for 21 days, each of the six ingredients being taken for three days and a fasting being observed for three days. The Śiśusāṁtapana[8] consists in fasting for seven days. Possibly the latter is same as the Mahāsāṁtapana in *Yāj* 3.315. It consists in drinking separately for six days in succession the six ingredients and fasting on the next day i.e. in all 7 days.
4. Taptakṛcchra.[9] It comprises four periods of three days each. In this one drinks hot water, hot milk, hot ghee, for three days each and then for three days there is a complete fast when he inhales hot vapour.

3. *Ṛvidh* i.27-28ab.
4. *ibid.*, i.28cd-32.
5. *ibid.*, i.33.
6. *ibid.*, i.34.
7. *Ṛvidh* i.35.
8. *ibid.*, i.36.
9. *ibid.*, i.37.

5. Yatikṛcchra.[10] It is same as the Prājāpatya Kṛcchra, water being substituted for food.
6. Parāka Kṛcchra.[11] This penance is constituted by not taking any food for twelve days while one controls one's senses and remains vigilant.
7. Cāndrāyaṇa Vrata.[12] There are two varieties. If one begins the Vrata on the first lunar day of the dark fortnight, then one must reduce one morsel on the 1st. i.e. takes 14 morsels on that day, 13 on the second lunar day and so on. On the 14th of the dark fortnight one must eat one morsel but on the Amāvāsyā one must not eat anything. Then on the first lunar day of the bright fortnight one must take one morsel and goes on increasing the intake till on the Paurṇamāsī one takes 15 morsels. The second one is as follows: on the first lunar day of the bright fortnight only one morsel of food is taken, on the second lunar day two and so on. On the Paurṇamāsī 15 morsels are taken but on the first day of the dark fortnight 14 morsels, one being reduced on each succeeding day. So on the fourteenth lunar day of the dark fortnight one morsel is eaten and on the Amāvāsyā day there is a complete fast.
8. Śiśucāndrāyaṇa Vrata.[13] It consists in eating four mouthfuls in the morning and four after sun-set.
9. Yaticāndrāyaṇa Vrata.[14] It consists in eating eight mouthfuls of sacrificial food only once in the noon.
10. There is another Cāndrāyaṇa Vrata[15] which consists in eating 240 morsels of sacrificial food in a month of 30 days distributing them according to one's own inclination.
11. Yāvaka [kṛcchra].[16] It consists in partaking of barley gruel for one week. The performer has to mutter purificatory verses and must remain standing during the day and sitting during the night.

10. *ibid.*, i.38.
11. *ibid.*, i.39.
12. *ibid.*, i.40-41.
13. *Ṛvidh* i.42.
14. *ibid.*, i.43.
15. *ibid.*, i.44.
16. *ibid.*, i.46.

12. There is yet another Kṛcchra[17] which consists in consuming consecutively broken grain, cil-cake and butter-milk.

Śaunaka states that the rites that are declared henceforth are meant for a person who has duly purified himself with these penances. A fast for three days or eating food at night for three days must invariably be undertaken before the commencement of all rites. When this has been finally disposed off, in vss 53-55, we come again to those purificatory verses which have already been dealt with above but which are here meant to be muttered in a forest after a bath with clothes on. Then it provides for varying numbers (3, 6, 8 and so on upto a hundred) of Prāṇāyāmas and finally extols the value of Prāṇāyāma in the removal of blemishes.

From now onwards the rules regarding the commencement of Vedic study follow. One must commence the Vedic study after mentally revolving the syllable *oṁ*, the three Vyāhṛtis and the famous verse addressed to Savitṛ (*RV* 3.62.10) and must recite it in a low tone in the morning, in a high tone at midday and in the afternoon. One is further asked to get up at the hour sacred to Brahmā, to immerse in water thrice and to recite the Veda after having resorted to the mode of reciting in a medium speed, neither too quickly, nor too slowly. Besides, one must perform the morning, the midday and the evening Saṁdhyā and must not utter a word, nor desist from the recitation of the Veda. Exception is, however, to be made in the case of a Brāhmaṇa who has arrived at one's house, but the Vedic study must immediately cease at the approach of a Śūdra. With this we come to the end of the introductory part of the *Ṛgvidhāna*.

The main body of the work, commencing with the sixtysixth stanza of the Adhyāya I, treats of charms and rites intended to produce some benefit or other to the performer by means of the recitation of each hymn or even of single verses of the *RV*. It follows a definite order. First, we have the Pratīka, i.e. the first words of the Ṛgvedic hymn, then the *vidhāna* which consists in Japa or Homa and finally the Phala, i.e. the desired result. As a rule, the Pratīka and the *vidhāna* of the hymn precede those of its Ṛks,[18] but once it is otherwise.[19] At one place[20] we have the Pra-

17. *Ṛvidh* i.49.
18. *Ṛvidh.*, i.99-104; 127-128; ii.4-9ab.
19. *ibid.*, ii.10cd-11.
20. *ibid.*, ii.78.

tīka and the *vidhāna* without any Phala whatsoever and at another[21] we have Phala only. Quotations of Ṛgvedic hymns or verses are made in 4 ways: 1, by quoting the first words in the hymn (e.g. Āpo hi ṣṭheti sūktam, *Ṛvidh* i.16) and in few instances the first words are abbreviated (e.g. Ānobhadrīya, Asyavāmīya etc. *Ṛvidh* i.108, 141); 2, by mentioning the seer or the deity addressed (e.g. Aghamarṣaṇam, Raudraṁ mantragaṇam etc. *Ṛvidh* i.16, 19); 3, by indicating the key-words with possessive suffixes (e.g. Śuddhavatyaḥ, *Ṛvidh* i.55)., by mentioning the subject dealt with (e.g. Pāvamānyaḥ, *Ṛvidh* i.16, 55). An attempt is made in the following pages to examine whether there is any connection between the charms and rites prescribed by the *Ṛvidh* and the respective hymns either by way of similarity of word, sound or idea.

1. *RV* 1.1-11. Hymn 1 is addressed to Agni and is ascribed to Madhucchandas. Its contents are: Agni, the domestic priest, the shining ministrant of sacrifices, is asked to conduct the gods to the sacrifice (vss 1-2); one obtains wealth and heroes only through Agni's good offices (vss 3-4); Agni, the invoker, the true, the shining guardian of order, is asked to come with the gods and to abide with the worshipper for his well-being (vss 5-9): Hymn 1 forms the Gāyatrī portion of the Agni section and is used at the Prātaranuvāka (*ĀŚS*.4-13; *ŚŚS*.6.4.1); at the Agniṣṭut ekāha (*ŚŚS*.14.52.1); and at the Adhyāyopākaraṇa (*ĀGS*.3.5.6; *ŚGS*.4.5.6).

Hymn 1 is intended to secure the attainment of wealth (*Ṛvidh* i.66); and it reappears in the Agni-sādhana (*Ṛvidh* i.79-83). There is hardly anything in the hymn itself to indicate that it is meant for such a purpose.

Hymn 2 consists of three tristiches: the first addressed to Vāyu, the second to Indra and the third to Mitra and Varuṇa. Like the preceding, this hymn is also ascribed to Madhucchandas. Its contents are: Vāyu, Indra and Vāyu, Mitra and Varuṇa are alternatively asked to come and drink libations of the Soma juice and they are further requested to vouchsafe strength and action (vss

21. *ibid.*, i.153cd-154ab.

1-9). Hymn 3 consists of four tristiches: the first addressed to Aśvins, the second to Indra, the third to the Viśvedevas and the fourth to Sarasvatī. Its contents are: Aśvins are asked to accept the prayer and the pressed Soma juice (vss 1-3); Indra is likewise asked to do the same (vss 4-6); the Viśve devas, who protect, cherish and reward men, are asked to accept the Soma draught (vss 7-9); Sarasvatī is praised as the goddess of sacred speech in vss 10-11 and as the river-goddess in vs 12. Hymns 2-3 are used at the Praüga-Śastra of the Agniṣṭoma (*ĀŚS*.5.10; *ŚŚS*.7.10.9), and of the Abhiplava-ṣaḍaha (*ŚŚS*.11.9.3).

In *Ṛvidh*, hymns 2-3 are intended to secure the attainment of numerous benefits (i.84); further with Hymn 1 they are directed to be muttered before the partaking of a meal (ii.165-166).

Hymn 4 is addressed to Indra and is ascribed to Madhucchandas. Its contents are: Indra, the doer of fair deeds, is asked to come and partake of the Soma draught so that the worshipper may get acquainted with his innermost benevolence (vss 1-3); Indra is the best friend and protector, let others say what they like (vss 4-6); the worshipper wishes to obtain wealth through the help of Indra (vss 7-10). Hymn 5 is addressed to Indra and is ascribed to Madhucchandas. In this hymn, Indra is invoked to stand by the worshipper in the hour of his need and to protect him (vss 1-10). Hymn 6 is addressed to Indra and the Maruts. In this hymn, Indra surrounded by the Maruts is invoked to help the worshipper (vss 1-10). Hymn 7 is addressed to Indra. In this hymn he is invoked to raise the sun in heaven, to break open the mountain for the sake of cows, to help the worshipper in the mighty battles as well as in the lesser ones and to rule over the five-fold race (vss 1-10). Hymn 8 is, like the preceding, addressed to Indra. In this hymn, he is invoked to bestow wealth, to assist in battles, to conquer foes, and to protect the worshipper with his mighty powers (vss 1-10). Hymn 9 is also addressed to Indra. In this hymn, he is invoked to bestow manifold bounty, fame etc. (vss 1-10). Hymn 10 is addressed to Indra and is ascribed to Madhucchandas. In this hymn Indra is invoked to bestow wealth, abundant kine and thousandfold aid in battles and to prolong the life of the worshipper (vss 1-12). Hymn 11 is addressed to Indra and is ascribed to Jetṛ, the son of Madhucchandas. In this hymn, Indra is invoked to sustain every sacred rite and to bestow precious gifts in thousands (vss 1-8). At the Abhiplava-ṣaḍaha, hymns 4-10 are inserted for the sake of over-recital by the Brāhmaṇācchaṁsin-priest at the morning pressing of Soma (*ĀŚS*.7.5). Hymns 1-10 with the Mahānāmnī-verses at the end are regarded by *Ṛvidh* as constituting the Amṛtā-saṁhitā, by means of which the gods attained immortality (iv.127cd-128). Cp. *Svidh* 1.4.8. Hymns 1-11, which are vaguely referred to by the *Ṛvidh* as representing the whole *Ṛgveda*—of which they are the beginning—are intended to secure the attainment of the Ṛgveda-saṁhitāphala and of various other benefits (i.67-69). In all these applications there is nothing that suits the real character of the hymns.

2. *RV* 1.18.6. This verse is addressed to Sadasaspati and is attributed to the seer Medhātithi. Its paraphrase would be: the worshipper waits upon the wondrous Sadasaspati who is Indra's lovely friend and who gives wisdom (Medhā) with a prayer. This verse is used in the Dhiṣṇyopasthāna (*ŚŚS* 6.13.3) and in the Anupravacanīya-homa (*ĀGS* 1.22.13; *ŚGS* 2.8.1). *Ṛvidh* directs it to be muttered by one desiring wisdom (i.85).
3. *RV* 1.22.15; 22.17-21. The verse 15 is addressed to the goddess Pṛthvī, who is invoked to spread wide and to vouchsafe a broad and sure shelter for the worshipper. It is used on the Mahānāmni-vrata, whilst touching the earth (*ĀŚS* 8.14) and in the Pratyavarohaṇa ceremony (*ĀGS* 2.3.7; *ŚGS* 4.18.5).

Used by the *Ṛvidh* in a charm for obtaining large tracts of land (i.86) and in another for obtaining release from the Bhūmipāśa (ii.149).

Verses 17-21 are addressed to Viṣṇu and their paraphrase would be: Viṣṇu strode through all this world planting his foot thrice and none can deceive him (vss 17-18); Viṣṇu's works and holy ways are to be visualised by the worshippers: [then] they will perceive the most sublime abode of Viṣṇu (vss 19-21). The verse 17 is employed as an inviting-verse at the Vaiṣṇavopāṁśuyāga and at the Darśapūrṇamāsa (*ĀŚS* 1-6; *ŚŚS* 1-8-8). It is also used in the consecration of ponds (*ŚGS* 5.2.6).

In the *Ṛvidh*, verses 17-21 accompany the plunging of the thumb into the food in a Śrāddha ceremony (i.87), and further the vs 20 is meant to expiate the sin of eating forbidden food (i.88). All these applications are evidently imposed upon these verses from the *RV*, not contained in them.

4. *RV* 1.23.16-24. These verses are addressed to the waters. They are asked to speed forth the worshipper's sacrifice, to accept oblations, to protect the worshipper, to remove sins, evils etc. and to give offspring and a long life (vss 16-24). At the Agniṣṭoma, vss 16-17 are used in the Aponaptrīya rite (*ĀŚS* 5.1); vs 22 in the sprinkling ceremony of a sacrificial victim (*ĀŚS* 3.5) and in the final purificatory bath (*ĀŚS* 6.13). Vss.16-19 are reckoned by *Kauś* (7.14) to the *apāṁ sūktāni*, applied (19.1) in a healing rite for sick kine and (41.14) in a ceremony for good fortune.

*Ṛvidh* regards vss 16-24 as sprinkling verses which are conducive to long life and health (i.89) and further vss 22-24 are meant to expiate the sin of cohabiting with forbidden women (ii.153).

5. *RV* 1.24-30. Hymn 24 is addressed to Agni, Savitṛ and Varuṇa. It is ascribed to Śunaḥśepa. Its broad contents are benevolence of Agni and Savitṛ (vss 1-5); Varuṇa's might (vss 6-8) which is followed by a request for release from sins and fetters (vss 9-15). Vs 11 is employed as an offering-verse at the Varuṇapraghāsa (*ĀŚS* 2.17) and vss 14-15 are employed as the inviting- and offering-verses in the final purificatory bath (*ĀŚS* 6.13). Hymn 25 is addressed to Varuṇa. In this hymn, Varuṇa is invoked to condone the violations committed daily by the worshipper, to prolong the worshipper's life and to unloosen his bonds (vss 1-21). At the Abhiplava-ṣaḍaha this hymn is inserted at the Hotṛkaśastra (*ĀŚS*. 7.5). Hymn 26 is addressed to Agni. In this hymn, Agni is invoked to officiate at the sacrifice, to hear the songs and to find pleasure in the sacrifice offered by the worshipper (vss 1-10). Hymn 27 is also addressed to Agni. In this hymn, Agni is invoked to bestow gifts on the worshipper, and to protect him in battles (vss 1-13). Hymn 26-27 constitute the Gāyatrī-portion of the Agni-section and are used at the Prātaranuvāka (*ĀŚS* 4.13). Hymn 28 is addressed to Indra and its broad contents are: Indra is asked

to drink with eager thirst the Soma-droppings which are shed by the mortar (vss 1-4); the praise of mortar and pestle (vss 5-8); the Soma remnants are taken into the vessels and then filtered (vs 9). *AB* (7.17) employs vss 1-4 in the Añjaḥsava and the rest in the Abhiṣava. Hymn 29 is also addressed to Indra. In this hymn, Indra is invoked to bestow thousands of horses, kine etc. on the worshipper (vss 1-7). At the Pṛṣṭhya-ṣaḍaha, this hymn is inserted at the Hotṛkaśastra (*ĀŚS* 7.11). Hymn 30 is addressed to Indra, Aśvins and Uṣas and its broad contents are: Indra is asked to heed to the worshipper's call and to bestow various benefits on him (vss 1-16); the Aśvins are invoked to give riches to the worshipper (vss 17-19) and finally the goddess Uṣas is also requested to give riches to the worshipper (vss 20-22). Vss 17-19 of this hymn forms the Gāyatrī-portion of the Aśvin-section and are used at the Prātaranuvāka (*ĀŚS* 4.15). Likewise vss 20-22 form the Gāyatrī-portion of the Uṣas-section and are used at the Prātaranuvāka (*ĀŚS* 4.14). Further, Sāyaṇa understands that hymns 24-30 are meant to be communicated to the newly consecrated king on the Abhiṣecanīya-day of the Rājasūya and quotes *ĀŚS* 9.3 and *AB* 7.18.

In the *Ṛvidh*, hymns 24-30 are directed to be muttered by a person desiring release from fetters, diseases, etc. (i.90) and further hymns 28-29 are directed to be repeated by one desiring permanent benefits (i.91).

6. *RV* 1.32. This hymn is addressed to Indra and is ascribed to Hiraṇyastūpa Āṅgirasa. In this hymn, Indra's deeds like slaying the dragon, releasing the waters, etc. are recapitulated in a vivid manner (vss 1-15). At the midday pressing of Soma this hymn is used as an intercalatory Nivid-hymn at the Niṣkevalyaśastra of the Agniṣṭoma (*ĀŚS* 7.15; *ŚŚS* 7.20.8) and further is used in the Viṣuvant (*ĀŚS* 8.6).

Used by *Ṛvidh* (i.92) in a charm for driving away the enemies.

7. *RV* 1.35.2.11. The hymn is addressed to Savitṛ and is ascribed to Hiraṇyastūpa Āṅgirasa. The paraphrase of Vs 2 is: advancing through the dark space, laying to rest the immortal and the mortal, on his golden chariot god Savitṛ comes seeing all

creatures. The paraphrase of vs 11 is: thine ancient path, O Savitṛ, the dustless, the well-established in the air [going] by those paths easy of travel, protect us today and speak for us O God! On the fourth day of ihe Abhiplava-ṣaḍaha, this, intercalatory Nivid-hymn meant for Savitṛ is recited at the Vaiśvadeva-śastra (*ĀŚS.* 7.7).

*Ṛvidh* employs vs 2 in a ceremony for health and long life (i.93-94) and vs 11 while setting out on a journey and further it is intended to secure a healthy housewife (i.95).

8. *RV* 1.42. The hymn is addressed to Pūṣan and is ascribed to Kaṇva Ghaura. In this hymn, Pūṣan is invoked to drive away wolf, robber etc. to make the path pleasant and fair to tread upon and to lead the worshipper to grassy meadows (vss 1-10). It is directed to be recited by a person setting out on a dangerous way (*ĀGS* 3.7.10). But *KGS* (i.18.4) employs it in the Niṣkramaṇikā ceremony.

*Ṛvidh* (i.96) designates it as "adhvanya" (the speeding up of the journey) and regards it as a destructive charm against robbers.

9. *RV* 1.43. The hymn is addressed to Rudra and is also ascribed to Kaṇva Ghaura. In this hymn, Rudra is invoked to grant health to steeds, rams, ewes, men, women etc. (vss 1-9). Used by *ŚŚS* (4.20.2) in the Śūlagava ceremony and by *ĀGS* (4.9.21-22) to accompany the homage to quarters in sacrifices offered to Rudra.

*Ṛvidh* employs it in a rite for appeasing Rudra's anger (i.97) and further in a Kāmya-rite by one desiring power (i.98).

10. *RV* 1.50. This hymn is addressed to Sūrya and is ascribed to Praskaṇva Kāṇva. Its broad contents are: bright rays bear Sūrya up aloft so that all may look on him and the constellations pass away before the all-beholding sun (vss 1-2); Sūrya's rays are seen afar and he illumines all the radiant realm (vss 3-4); Sūrya looks upon the race of men and further sees all things that have birth (vss 5-7); Sūrya has yoked seven

steeds to his chariot and goes forth (vss.8-10); Sūrya is invoked to remove the heart-disease and to transfer it to parrots, starlings, etc. (vss 11-12); and the worshipper finally requests Sūrya to hand over his enemy to him (vs 13). Vss 1-9 of this hymn constitute the Gāyatrī-portion of the Sūrya-section and are recited at the Āśvina-śastra (*ĀŚS*.6.5). Used by *ŚGS* (4.6.4) in the Utsarga ceremony. *Sarv* (i.50) designates vss 11-33 as "rogaghna upaniṣat".

*Ṛvidh* understands the complete hymn to be destructive of heart-disease (i.99); further vss 11-13 are directed to be muttered for the sake of health (i.101); vs 13cd is designated as "dviṣad-dveṣa" and is employed as a charm to make an evil-doer odious (i.100, 102-104); and further the same half-verse reappears in a sorcery-rite (iv.52).

11. *RV* 1.65-73. These hymns are addressed to Agni and are ascribed to Parāśara the son of Śakti. Hymns 65-67 treat of the flight of Agni and are, besides, full of comparisons which at times are unintelligible. In hymn 68, Agni is invoked to vouchsafe wealth and progeny to the worshipper (vs.1-5). In hymn 69, Agni is invoked to grant audience to chieftains and to remember the worshipper always (vss 1-5). In hymn 70, Agni is asked to regulate the acts of worship and to protect the worshipper (vs 1-6). In hymn 71, Agni is invoked to prosper the worshipper, to protect cattle and not to break the ancestral friendship between him and the worshipper (vss 1-10). In hymn 72, Agni is invoked to grant all immortal bounties, to guard the life of plants and cattle and to send abundant food to the worshipper (vss 1-10). In hymn 73, Agni is invoked to give food, to prosper the worshipper's dwelling, to grant a long life to the rich worshippers and to lead the worshipper on to riches (vss 1-10). *ĀŚS* (8.12) designates hymns 65-70 as "dvaipadam" and directs them to be recited at the Vaiśvadeva śastra on the tenth day. Hymns 71-73 forms the Triṣṭubh-portion of the Agni-section and are used at the Prātaranuvāka (*ĀŚS* 4.13).

In the *Ṛvidh*, hymns 65-73 are intended to destroy enemies, but no sufficient indication of such value is to be found in these hymns.

12. *RV* 1.84.16,18. These verses are addressed to Indra and are ascribed to Gotama Rāhūgaṇa. The fact that these verses are in the form of questions may perhaps explain their designation "ādhyātmikīḥ" and their inclusion in the *Ṛgvidhāna.* In the Iṣṭi entitled Sarvapṛṣṭha, vss 16 and 17 are respectively used as the inviting- and the offering-verses of the oblation for Prajāpati (*ĀŚS* 4.12). Used by *Svidh* (1.8.1) among expiatory rites.

In the *Ṛvidh,* these verses are intended to secure the attainment of the highest abode (i.107).

13. *RV* 1.89. This hymn is addressed to the Viśvedevās and is ascribed to Gotama Rāhūgaṇa. In this hymn, the Viśvedevās are invoked to lengthen the worshipper's life, to grant felicity and to promote the increase of wealth (vss 1-10). In the Agniṣṭoma this intercalatory Nivid-hymn (except vs 10) meant for the Viśvedevās is recited at the Vaiśvadeva-śastra (*ĀŚS* 5.18; *ŚŚS* 8.3.16). It is also used in the Viśvajit (*ŚŚS* 11.15.9) and in the Vājapeya ;*ŚŚS* 15.3.1).

*Ṛvidh* declares that this hymn to be conducive to long life (i. 108) and further vs 6 of this hymn is designated as and included among "Svastimatyaḥ" and is used at the beginning and end of all rites (i.16,53).

14. *RV* 1.90.6-8. This hymn is also addressed to the 'Viśvedevās'. The worshipper implores wind, rivers, etc. for remaining always sweet. Used by *ĀGS* (1.24.14) in the respectful reception of Ṛtviks.

But *Ṛvidh* (i.109) employs them in the Śrāddha ceremony.

15. *RV* 1.91. This hymn is addressed to Soma. In this hymn, Soma is invoked to guide the worshipper, to guard him and to bestow milch-cow, steed, etc. (vss 1-23). Vss 1 and 2 of this

hymn form the inviting-verses of *vapā* and *puroḍāśa* respectively to the victim immolated to Soma (*ĀŚS* 3.7). The first verse alone is used for a similar purpose in the Prāyaṇīyeṣṭi (*ĀŚS* 4.3; *ŚŚS*.5.5.2).

In the *Ṛvidh*, this hymn is intended to secure the release from three-fold miseries (i.110-111) and the attainment of the abode of the moon (i.112)—all artificial uses, having no relation to the above hymn.

16. *RV* 1.92. This hymn (except vss 16-18 which are addressed to Aśvins) is addressed to Uṣas and is ascribed to Gotama Rāhūgaṇa. In this hymn Uṣas and Aśvins are invoked to bestow all felicities, strength etc. on the worshipper (vss 1-18). Vss 1-4 of this hymn form the Jagatī-portion of the Uṣas-section and are used at the Prātaranuvāka (*ĀŚS* 4.14; *ŚŚS*.6.5.9-12); further vss 5-12 form the Triṣṭubh-portion of the Uṣas-section and are used at the Prātaranuvāka and Āśvina-śastra (*ĀŚS* 4.14); further vss 13-15 constitute the Uṣṇiḥ-portion of the Uṣas-section and are used at the Prātaranuvāka and Āśvina-śastra (*ĀŚS* 4.14); and finally vss 16-18 form the Uṣṇiḥ-portion of the Aśvin-section and are used at the Prātaranuvāka and Āśvina-śastra (*ĀŚS* 4.15).

Used by *Ṛvidh* (i.113) in a charm for obtaining wealth.

17. *RV* 1.94. This hymn is addressed to Agni and is ascribed to Kutsa Āṅgirasa. In this hymn, Agni is invoked to prolong the life of the worshipper and to release him from every sin (vss 1-26). Vss 1-14 of this hymn form the Jagatī-portion of the Agni-section and is used at the Prātaranuvāka and Āśvina śastra (*ĀŚS* 4.14); further this intercalatory Nivid-hymn meant for Jātavedas is recited at the Āgnimārutaśastra (*ĀŚS* 7.7; *ŚŚS* 10.8.15) and further this hymn is used in the Anvādhāna rite (*ŚŚS* 4.2.10).

Used by *Ṛvidh* in a rite for prolonging life and for surmounting adversities (i.114-115ab).

18. *RV* 1.97. This hymn is also addressed to Agni. In this hymn,

Agni is invoked to bestow wealth, fields etc. and to chase with his brilliance the sin of the worshipper (vss 1-8). Used by *ŚŚS* (4.2.9) in the Anvādhāna rite. The *ĀGS* (4.7.18) uses it in the Pretakarma, whereas the *ŚGS* (4.17.5) employs it in the Pratyavarohaṇa rite. This hymn is designated as "apāgham" and is used in the Strīkarma (*Kauś* 36.22), in an expiatory ceremony for seeing bad sights (42.22) and in the Pretakarma (82.4).

But *Ṛvidh* designates it as "aghāpaham" and employs it in a expiatory ceremony (i.115cd-117ab).

19. *RV* 1.99. This hymn which consists of one single verse is ascribed to Kaśyapa Mārīca. Its paraphrase would be: Agni is invoked to consume the slanderer's wealth and to help the worshipper to surmount all his troubles. On the second and other series of sacrificial days this verse is recited at the Āgnimāruta-śastra before the intercalatory Nivid-hymn to Jātavedas (*ĀŚS* 7.1).

This verse is used in *Ṛvidh* (i.117cd-118ab) as a benediction while setting out upon a dangerous path; it is also directed to be muttered when one is in dangerous situations (i.118cd-119) or when one sets out on a business journey or when one sees evil dreams (i.120-122).

20. *RV* 1.101.1. This verse is addressed to Indra. In this verse, Indra is invoked to drive away dark aborigines (Kṛṣṇagarbhā) and to remain in friendly terms with the worshipper. On the ninth day of the ten-day-period, the complete hymn, except perhaps the last verse, is used at the Marutvatīya-śastra (*ĀŚS* 8.7; *ŚŚS* 10.11.6). The first verse of this hymn is designated as "garbhaśrāviṇyupaniṣat" by *Sarv* (i.101).

*Ṛvidh* (i.123) employs it in a charm for safe delivery. This application has nothing to do with the text of the verse, except for the word Kṛṣṇagarbhā which occurs in the latter and which possibly misled both *Sarv* and *Ṛvidh*.

21. *RV* 1.105. This hymn is addressed to the Viśvedevās. In this

hymn, the seer Trita implores Heaven and Earth for releasing him from distress (vs 1-19). Not noticed in any of the ritual texts of the *RV*.

*Ṛvidh* directs it to be muttered when one is in difficulties or when one desires all kinds of benefits (i.124ab).

22. *RV* 106. This hymn is addressed to the Viśvedevās. In this hymn, the Viśvedevās are invoked to aid the worshipper and to rescue him from distress (vs 1-7). Not noticed in any of the ritual texts of the *RV*.

Used by *Ṛvidh* (i.124cd-125ab) in a rite for securing release from all distress.

23. *RV* 1.112. This hymn is addressed to the Aśvins. In this hymn, Aśvins are invoked to rescue the worshipper just as they did in the case of Rebha, Vandana, etc. and to protect him always (vss 1-25). This hymn is used at the laud (Abhiṣṭava) in the Pravargya ceremony (*ĀŚS* 4.6; *ŚŚS* 5.9.24). Moreover, it forms the Jagatī-portion of the Aśvin-section and is used at the Prātaranuvāka (*ĀŚS* 4.15; *ŚŚS* 6.6.12).

*Ṛvidh* designates it as "Śaṁtātīya" and employs it in a rite for obtaining prosperity as well as for obtaining release from infirmities (i.125cd-126).

24. *RV* 1.114. This hymn is addressed to Rudra. In this hymn, Rudra is invoked to remain gracious to the worshipper, to repel the anger of the gods and to grant protection, shelter, etc. (vss 1-11). Used by *ŚŚS* (4.20.2) in the Śūlagava ceremony and by *ĀGS* (4.9.21.22) to accompany the homage to quarters in sacrifices offered to Rudra. *ŚGS* directs it to be muttered when a disease has befallen to someone (5.6.2).

In the *Ṛvidh*, this hymn is intended to secure the attainment of long life, knowledge, wealth, progeny and a healthy housewife (127, 129-130); further vss 7-8 are employed in a remedial rite to counteract impurity of one's own self perpetrated on heroic sons, grandsons and cowpen (i.128).

25. *RV* 1.115. This hymn is addressed to Sūrya. In this hymn Sūrya is invoked to deliver the worshipper from trouble and dishonour (vs 1-6). This hymn is recited at the Āśvina-śastra just before the actual sun-rise (*ĀŚS* 6.5; *ŚŚS* 9.20.21). Vss 1-3 of this hymn are respectively the inviting-verses of the *vapā*, *puroḍāśa* and *havis* for the victim immolated to Sūrya and further vss 4-5 are respectively the offering-verses of *vapā* and *Puroḍāśa* (*ĀŚS* 3.8; cp. *ŚŚS* 11.13.9).

In the *Ṛvidh* this hymn is intended to secure the attainment of wealth and long life (i.131-132).

26. *RV* 1.120.12. The wealth of a rich man is compared to a dream. *Sarv* (i.120) designates it as "Duḥsvapnanāśinī'. Used by *ŚGS* (1.4.2) in the Utsarga ceremony.

In the *Ṛvidh*, this verse is intended to avert the bad effect of dream and the fear by reason of fasting (i.133).

27. *RV* 1.133. This hymn is addressed to Indra who is invoked to drive sorceresses, to strike demons and to bestow wealth on the worshipper (vss 1-7). Not noticed in any of the ritual texts of the *RV*.

In the *Ṛvidh*, this hymn is intended to destroy demons, rivals, etc. (i.134).

28. *RV* 1.139.11. The paraphrase of this verse is: the thrice eleven gods living respectively in heaven, earth and waters are requested to accept the sacrifice with pleasure. On the sixth day of the ten-day-period, this verse is the second one in the tristich addressed to the Viśvedevās and is used at the Praüga-śastra (*ĀŚS* 8.1). Used by *ŚGS* (2.14.16) in the Vaiśvadeva ceremony.

In the *Ṛvidh*, this verse is intended to secure the attainment of all objects of desire (i.135).

29. *RV* 1.154.1-3. These verses recapitulate the deeds of Viṣṇu.

At the third pressing of Soma, this hymn is recited for the sake of over-recital by the Acchāvāka-priest (*ĀŚS* 7.9); further vss 1-2 are the inviting and the offering verses in the Ātithyeṣṭi (*ŚŚS* 5.7.3); and further the complete hymn is recited over the victim immolated to Viṣṇu (*ŚŚS* 6.11.5). Used by *Kauś* (59.19) in a Kāmya-rite by one desiring all kinds of benefits.

In the *Ṛvidh*, these verses are intended to secure the attainment of dharma, knowledge, etc. and the eternal abode (i.136-137).

30. *RV* 1.158.5. The paraphrase of this verse is: the rivers are asked not to devour the worshipper who is thrown into them. Not noticed in any of the ritual texts of the *RV*.

In the *Ṛvidh*, this verse is intended to repel incendiaries, tigers, etc. (i. 138-140)—an artificial employment, having no relation to the above verse.

31. *RV* 1.164. The hymn consisting of fifty-two verses is rather an enigmatic one in the form of questions, doubts, etc. and is, besides, addressed to various deities. The major part of this hymn is used in the Mahāvrata (*ŚŚS* 18.22.7; cp. *AB* 5.3.2). Used by *Kauś* (18.25) in a ceremony for prosperity.

In the *Ṛvidh*, this hymn is meant to expiate the sin of stealing gold (i.141) and further it is intended to secure the attainment of a kingdom (i.142).

32. *RV* 1.165. This *saṁvāda* hymn is ascribed to Agastya who brings about a reconciliation between Indra and the Maruts (vss 1-15). In the Saṁsava and in the Caturviṁśa day, this hymn is recited at the Marutvatīya-śastra before the intercalatory Nivid-hymn (*ĀŚS* 6.6; 7.3; *ŚŚS* 13.5.15; 11.2.4).

In the *Ṛvidh*, this hymn is meant to expiate the sin of calumny (i.143).

33. *RV* 1.179.5-6. The paraphrase of these verses is: the wor-

shipper asks Soma for forgiving his sins (vs 5); Agastya nourished both Kāma and Tapas and won fame thereby (vs 6). Not noticed in any of the ritual texts of the *RV*.

In the *Ṛvidh*, these verses are intended to secure the attainment of all objects of desire (i.144).

34. *RV* 1.187. In this hymn, food is invoked to protect the worshipper (vss 1-11). Not noticed in any of the ritual texts of the *RV*. *Sarv* (i.187) designates it as "annastuti".

Used by *Ṛvidh* (i.145-148ab) as a charm against poison and diseases arising out of food.

35. *RV* 1.189. In this hymn, Agni is invoked to lead the worshipper along good paths, and to protect him always (vss 1-8). It forms the Triṣṭubh-portion of the Agni-section and is used at the Prātaranuvāka and Āśvina-śastra (*ĀŚS* 4.13). Vss 1-4 are used by *ĀGS* (2.1.4) in the Śravaṇā-karma.

*Ṛvidh* directs the hymn to be muttered by a person when he loses his way or when he commits an ignominious deed (i.148cd-150ab).

36. *RV* 1.190. In this hymn, Bṛhaspati is invoked to punish the spiteful and to bestow kine and horses on the worshipper (vss 1-8). On the third day of the Pṛṣṭhya-Ṣaḍaha, this hymn is meant for the Brāhmaṇācchaṁsin-priest (*ŚŚS* 12.12.8); further vss 2 and 7 are respectively the offering-verses of the *vapā* and *puroḍāśa* for the victim immolated to Bṛhaspati (*ĀŚS* 3.7).

In the *Ṛvidh*, this hymn is intended to secure the attainment of heroes, wealth and high fame (i.150cd-151ab).

37. *RV* 1.191. According to *Sarv* (i.191), this hymn is said to have been recited by Agastya when he suspected that he had been poisoned. Vss 4 and 9 are used by *Kauś* (31.8) in a remedial rite against demons; further vs 16 is used by *ĀGS* (3.5.7) and

*ŚGS* (4.5.8) in the Adhyāyopākaraṇa and Utsarga ceremonies. The complete hymn is used by *Ṛvidh* (i.151cd-153ab) in a remedial charm against venomous bites of snakes etc. and poison.

38. *RV* 2.12. In this hymn which is ascribed to Gṛtsamada, Indra's deeds are recapitulated and he is, finally, invoked to aid the worshipper in his battles (vss 1-15). In the Saṁsava and on the third day of the Abhiplava Ṣaḍaha, this hymn is recited at Niṣkevalya-śastra before the intercalatory Nivid-hymn (*ĀŚS* 6.7; 7.7; *ŚŚS*.13.5.16; 11.9.5).

Used by *Ṛvidh* (i.153cd-159ab) with *RV* 2.21.6, in an extended rite for obtaining dharma, intelligence, etc.

39. *RV* 2.23. In this hymn, which is also ascribed to Gṛtsamada, Bṛhaspati is invoked to chase revilers, to crush enemies and to prosper the worshipper's progeny (vss 1-19). Used at the laud in the Pravargya rite (*ĀŚS*. 4.6; *ŚŚS*.5.9.18).

In the *Ṛvidh*, this hymn is intended to secure the destruction of enemies and the attainment of wealth, prosperity and all kinds of benefits (i.159cd-161ab).

40. *RV* 2.28.10. The paraphrase of this verse is: Varuṇa is invoked to afford protection from a threatening friend or a kinsman, wolf or robber seen in slumber. Used by *ŚGS* (1.4.2) in the Svādhyāya ceremony.

But *ĀGS* (3.6.6) and *Ṛvidh* (i.161cd-162ab) employ it in a rite to avert the bad effect of dreams.

41. *RV* 2.32.4-8. In these verses, Rākā and other female deities are invoked to give a heroic son, wealth and progeny to the worshipper. Vss 4-5 and 6-7 are respectively the inviting and offering verses in the Patnīsaṁyāja-offerings (*ĀŚS* 1.10; *ŚŚS* 1.15.4). *ĀGS* (1.14.3) employs vss. 4-5 in the Sīmantonnayana ceremony, whereas *ŚGS* (1.22.12) prescribes vss.4-6 in the selfsame ceremony.

In the *Ṛvidh*, these verses are intended to procure the birth of a magnificent progeny (i.162cd-164ab).

42. *RV* 2.33. In this hymn, Rudra is invoked to prolong the life of the worshipper, to ward off all attacks of mischief-makers, to bestow healing and blessing on the worshipper and to remain merciful to his children and descendants. (vss 1-13). Regarding the ritual use of this hymn see under (9) above.

Used by *Ṛvidh* (i.164cd-167ab) in a remedial rite against a fatal disease.

43. *RV* 2.41.16. In this verse, Sarasvatī is invoked to bestow renown on the worshipper. On the first day of the ten-day-period, this verse is used at the Praüga-śastra (*ĀŚS* 7.11).

*Ṛvidh* directs this verse to be muttered by a person who has been accused falsely (i.167cd-168ab).

44. *RV* 2.42-43. In these hymns, Indra who has assumed the form of a Kapiñjala is invoked to bring happy tidings and to proclaim good luck in all directions.

Hymns 42-43 are employed in *ĀGS* (3.10.9) and *Ṛvidh* (i.168cd-170) against birds of ill-omen, and further they reappear in a charm for successful home-return in the latter work (ii.1-2).

45. *RV* 3.26.7. According to *Sarv* (iii.26), this verse as well as the next are designated as "ātmastutīḥ". In the Agnicayaṇa, this verse is employed while praising a kindled fire (*ĀŚS* 4.8). Used by *Ṛvidh* (ii.3) in a remedial charm against diarrhoea.

46. *RV* 3.33. This hymn which is a dialogue between the sage Viśvāmitra and the twain rivers, Vipāś and Śutudrī, has no liturgical significance.

However, *ŚGS* (i.15.20) directs vs 13 to be muttered while crossing a river, whereas *Ṛvidh* (ii.4-6) prescribes the complete hymn for selfsame purpose. Further in the latter work, vs 5 is directed to be muttered while crossing a swollen river (ii.7ab); vs 9, while in the midst of waters (ii.7cd-8ab); and vs 13 while crossing the river with a chariot (ii.8cd-9ab).

47. *RV* 3.45. In this hymn, Indra is invoked to bring wealth for

the worshipper. Vs 1 is employed in a laud for Ṣoḍaśin draught of Soma (*ŚŚS* 9.5.9): further on the third day of the Abhiplava-ṣaḍaha vss 1-3 are the corresponding tristich for the Hotṛkas (*ŚŚS* 12.9.11). The first verse of this hymn is found as a single-versed hymn in *AV*.7.117 and is used by *Kauś* (59.14) in a rite for welfare. The first verse of this hymn is employed by *ĀGS* (3.10.5) in the Samāvartana ceremony.

*Ṛvidh* directs this hymn to be muttered while setting out on a business journey (ii.9cd-10ab). Cp. *Svidh* 2.4.1.

48. *RV* 3.53. In this hymn, Indra and Parvata are invoked to drink a draught of well-pressed Soma and to give Pramagandha's wealth to the worshipper and incidentally goddess Sasarparī is also invoked to dispel ignorance and to bestow new vital power on the worshipper. The later part of this hymn however, deals with the consecration of chariot and its different parts and the last four verses contain a strongly-worded imprecation against an enemy. In *ĀGS* (2.6.7), vs 17 accompanies the touching of the various parts of a chariot in the Rathārohaṇa rite and further vs 19 is used by *ŚGS* (1.15.10) in a rite to repair the damage caused to a chariot.

In the *Ṛvidh*, the complete hymn is intended to secure the attainment of long life and wealth (ii.11cd); further vs 14 reappears in a charm against a miser (ii.10cd-11ab); vss 15-16 in a rite for the retention of knowledge (ii.12-13); vss 17-20 are directed to be muttered while travelling in a cart (ii.14); vss 19-20 recur in a rite to repair the damage caused to the axle (ii.15); and finally vss 21-24 reappear in a witchcraft ceremony against enemies (ii.16-20).

49. *RV* 3.55. In this hymn the mysteries of the godly rule are clothed in a sundry, unusual allegory and paradox. Possibly this fact explains the reason of its inclusion in the *Ṛvidh*. In the Vājapeya, hymns 54-55 which are designated as "honeycomb-cell" are employed at the Vaiśvadeva-śastra after intertwining them (*ŚŚS* 15.3.2).

*Ṛvidh* designates hymn 55 as "ādhyātmika" and employs it in a charm for obtaining all benefits (ii.21).

50. *RV* 3.62.4-18. This hymn consists of six tristiches: the first addressed to Indra, the second to Bṛhaspati, the third to Pūṣan, the fourth to Savitṛ, the fifth to Soma and the sixth to Mitra and Varuṇa. Here we are not concerned with the first tristich which is addressed to Indra. Contents: Bṛhaspati, beloved of all gods, the bull among men, who can change his shape at will, is invoked to bestow wealth and power on the worshipper (vss 4-6); Pūṣan is invoked to protect the worshipper (vss 7-9); Savitṛ is invoked to stimulate the prayers and bestow prosperity on the worshipper (vss 10-12); Soma is invoked to give salutary food to bipeds and quadrupeds (vss 13-15); and finally Mitra and Varuṇa are invoked to take their seats in the sacrificial assembly (vss 16-18). Vs 4 is the inviting-verse in the Soma rite connected with Cayana (*ŚŚS*.9.27.2). In the Agnihotra, vs 10 accompanies the pouring out of libations into the Dakṣiṇāgni (*ŚŚS*.2.10.2); further it is the inviting verse to Savitṛ in the Prāyaṇīyeṣṭi (*ŚŚS*.5.5.2); and further it is employed in the Sāvitrānuvacana (*ŚGS* 2.5.12), in the Anuvācana (*ŚGS* 2.7.19) and in the pacificatory rite (*ŚGS* 64.8). On the second day of the Abhiplava-ṣaḍaha and Pṛṣṭhya, vss 10-11 which form the first two verses in the beginning tristich are used at the Vaiśvadeva-śastra (*ĀŚS* 7.6) and further on the sixth day of the ten-day-period, vss 10-11 which form the second and third verses in the beginning-tristich are used at the Vaiśvadeva-śastra (*ĀŚS* 8.1). On the fifth day of the ten-day-period, vss 10-12 are the Anucara-tristich and are used at the Vaiśvadeva-śastra (*ŚŚS* 10.6.17). Vss 13-15 are employed in the Agnisomapraṇayana (*ĀŚS* 4.10; *ŚŚS* 5.14.15). In the morning of the Agniṣṭoma vss 16-18 are the laud-tristich and are employed at the Maitrāvaruṇa-śastra (*ĀŚS* 5.10; *ŚŚS* 7. 11.2). Vss 16-18 are used by *Svidh* (2.2.23) in a Kāmya-rite.

Vss 4-18 are used by *Ṛvidh* (ii.22-24) in a rite for obtaining gems, progeny, cattle, festivities and a long life. Vs 10 is employed in a number of rites: as a purificatory verse (i.15, 18); in the introduction to the study of Veda (i.61); in a pacificatory rite for obtaining prosperity, wealth, etc. (i.72-74); in a sorcery rite for the death of one's enemies (i.75-78); and finally in the various Kāmya-rites for those intended to secure the attainment of various benefits (ii.25-62).

51. *RV* 4.4. In this hymn, Agni is invoked to transfix the fiends, to vouchsafe a dominion to the worshipper, and to destory Rakṣas (vss 1-15). Vss 1-5 are used at the laud (Abhiṣṭava) of the Pravargya ceremony (*ĀŚS* 4.6; *ŚŚS* 5.9.11).

In the *Ṛvidh* it is intended to destory enemies and Rakṣas (ii. 63).

52. *RV* 4.9.8. In this verse, Agni is invoked to protect the worshipper. At the Āgnyādheya, this verse is employed in the Agnyupasthāna (*ŚŚS* 2.12.7).

In the *Ṛvidh*, this verse is intended to secure protection from Agni (ii.64).

53. *RV* 4.25. In this hymn, Indra is invoked to drink the pressed dregs of Soma and to protect the worshipper (vss 1-8). At the midday-pressing of Soma on the fourth day of the ten-day-period, this hymn is inserted for the sake of over-recital at the Maitrāvaruṇa-śastra (*ĀŚS* 7.12).

In the *Ṛvidh*, this hymn is intended to secure boons from Indra (ii.65).

54. *RV* 4.31. In this hymn, Indra is invoked to approach the worshipper with hundred aids, and to bestow kine, steed, etc. on the worshipper (vss 1-15). At the midday-pressing in the Agniṣṭoma, and in the Caturviṁśa day, vss 1-2 are the Stotra-tristiches for the Maitrāvaruṇa-priest (*ĀŚS* 7.4; cp. *ŚŚS* 7.22. 2); further vs 1 is the inviting-verse of the oblation to Prajāpati in the Varuṇapraghāsa (*ĀŚS* 2.17). *ŚGS* (1.16.6) employs vss 1-3 in the post-marriage rite to accompany the touching of bride's tresses. *Svidh* designates this hymn as "Kayānīyā" and directs its use in expiations (1.6.7; 8.8) and in Kāmya-rites (2.3.3; 4-5).

Used by the *Ṛvidh* (ii.66) as a benediction for the night.

55. *RV* 4.40.5. In this verse, Sūrya is compared to Haṁsa dwel-

ling in light, the Vasu in the mid-air, the priest near the altar, the guest in the house, the dweller in the noblest place amidst men, in Ṛta, in sky, etc. At the third-pressing on the third day of the the ten-day-period it is used at the Maitrāvaruṇa-śastra (*ĀŚS* 8.2); but *ŚŚS* (11.14.14) employs it in the Viṣuvant. Used by *ŚGS* (1.4.2) in the Brahmayajña.

In the *Ṛvidh*, this verse is intended to secure the highest abode of Brahmā (ii.67).

56. *RV* 4.57. In this hymn, Kṣetrapati 'Śunāsrīra' and Sītā are respectively invoked to provide nourishment to kine, to sprinkle the earth with heavenly milk and to bless the worshipper. In the Aptoryāma, vss 1-2 are the closing-verses at the Atiriktokthya and are recited before the Āśvina-śastra (*ĀŚS* 9.11); further vs 3 is the closing verse at the Atiriktokthya for the Brāhmaṇācchaṁsin-priest (9.11); and further vss 5 and 8 are the inviting- and offering-verses of the oblation to 'Śunāsīra' in the Śunāsīrīya rite (2.20; cp. *ŚŚS* 15.8.18). The complete hymn is employed in the Kṛṣikarma (*ĀGS* 2.10.4; *ŚGS* 4.5.8). Vss 4-8 are found in the *AV* 3.17.4-8 with a changed verse-order and are used by *Kauś* (20.1 ff) in a rite for success in ploughing.

*Ṛvidh* (ii.68-72) employs vss 4-8 in a sacrifice to deities whose characteristic marks are found in them; further vss 1-3 are intended to secure the attainment of a pre-eminent field (ii.73). All these rites are followed by a feeding of the Brāhmaṇas and by expiations (ii.75-77).

57. *RV* 4.58. *Sarv* (iv.68) offers a choice of deities: Agni or Sūrya, waters, cow or Ghṛta, but the contents reveal that it is in praise of Ghṛta. It is the Ājya-sūkta in the Viṣuvant (*ĀŚS* 8.6; *ŚŚS* 11.13.11). *ŚGS* (4.18.4) employs vs 1 in the Sarpabalikarma.

*Ṛvidh* (ii.78) fails to give the Phala. Mātṛsūnu understands it to be "the attainment of all desires."

58. *RV* 5.2.9. In this verse, Agni is invoked to conquer the godless, to ward off enchantments and to destroy Rakṣas.

Used by *Ṛvidh* (ii.79) in a rite for obtaining good fortune and wealth.

59. *RV* 5.4.9-10. In these verses, Agni is invoked to help the worshipper to surmount all woes and dangers, and to vouchsafe high renown. Vs 10 is used in the Putrakāmeṣṭi (*ĀŚS* 2.10) and in the Anvādhāna (*ŚŚS* 4.2.9).

In the *Ṛvidh*, these verses are intended to overcome adversities and to secure renown (ii.80).

60. *RV* 5.24. In this hymn, Agni is invoked to give wealth to the worshipper and to keep him away from the sinner (vss 1-4). In the Mahāpitṛyajña, this hymn it muttered by Ṛtviks while proceeding towards the Āhavanīya fire (*ĀŚS* 2.19); and further at the third-pressing in the sixth day of the ten-day-period vss 1-2, & 4 are the Stotra-tristich for the Maitrāvaruṇa-priest (*ĀŚS* 8.2; cp. *ŚŚS* 12.11.2-3). Used by *Svidh* (i.8.13) in an expiatory rite.

In the *Ṛvidh*, this hymn is intended to secure the attainment of wealth and long life (ii.81).

61. *RV*.5.38. In this hymn, Indra is invoked to bestow splendid wealth and heroic strength on the worshipper (vss 1-5). Used by *ŚŚS* (18.18.7) in the Mahāvrata.

In the *Ṛvidh*, this hymn is, intended to secure the attainment of manifold wealth and inherent power (ii.82).

62. *RV* 5.46.7-8. In these verses, the wives of gods are invoked to grant protection to the worshipper and to bestow progeny on him. These verses form the inviting- and offering-verses in the Patnisaṁyāja-offerings (*ĀŚS* 1.10). Verses occur as a separate hymn in *AV* 7.4.9. *Kauś* ignores this hymn.

According to Mātṛsūnu on *Ṛvidh* (ii.83-85ab), these verses are employed in a Kāmya rite by one desiring progeny.

63. *RV* 5.50-51. In these hymns, the Viśvedevās are invoked to

drive away the foes, to afford shelter to the worshipper, to drink the pressed Soma juice, to keep the worshipper away from calamity and to bestow prosperity on him. Vs 1 of hymn 50 is the beginning-tristich at the Vaiśvadevaśastra on the first day of the Pṛṣṭhya and Abhiplava-ṣaḍaha, but in the latter it is also used for a similar purpose on the second, fourth and sixth day (*ĀŚS* 7.6); and further it is the beginning-tristich at the Vaiśvadeva-śastra on the second day of the ten-day-period (*ŚŚS* 10.3.11). In the Agniṣṭut ekāha vss 1-3 of hymn 51 constitute a tristich for the Viśvedevās at the Praüga śastra (*ŚŚS* 14.52.5). On the sixth day of the Pṛṣthya-ṣaḍaha, vss 11-13 are used at the Vaiśvadeva-Śastra (*ĀŚS* 8.1); and further in the Bṛhaspatisava, these verses are inserted at Vaiśvadeva-śastra (*ĀŚS* 9.5). Vss 13-15 are inserted at the Vaiśvadeva-śastra in case a Dīkṣita is sick on that day (*ĀŚS* 6.9) and the same verses are inserted at the end of the Vaiśvadeva-śastra on the sixth day of the ten-day-period (*ŚŚS* 10.8.17). Vss 11-15 are designated as "Svastyātreya" and are used by *ĀGS* (3. 11.2) in the Sarvatobhaya-homa, whereas *ŚGS* employs them in the Svādhyāya (1.4.2) and in the post-marriage rites (1.15. 12).

*Ṛvidh* designates hymns 50-51 as "Svastyātreya" and directs them to be muttered for the sake of a friend or a relative who goes forth (ii.86); further it designates vss 11-15 of hymn 51 as "Svastimatyaḥ" and employs them as purificatory verses at the beginning and end of all rites (i.16, 53; cp.*ĀGS* 2.3.12, where, according to the commentary, they are also designated as "Svastyayanāni"); and further it employs vs 15 of hymn 51 as a benediction while setting out on a journey (ii.87ab).

64. *RV* 5.78.5. In this verse, the rescue of Saptavadhri by Aśvins is recapitulated. Not used in any of the ritual texts of the *RV*.

Used by *Ṛvidh* in a charm for driving away one's enemy (ii. 87cd-89ab) and in a charm for safe delivery (ii.89cd-90ab).

65. *RV* 5.83. In this hymn, Parjanya is invoked to lay the seed of germination in plants, to smite the trees and the wicked and

to pour down the flood of rain (vss 1-10). Used by *ĀŚS* (2.13) in the Digupasthāna at the Kārīrī sacrifice.

*Ṛvidh* (ii.90cd-92) employs it in a Kāmya-rite by one desiring rain.

66. *RV* 6.2.11. In this verse, Agni is invoked to bring weal from heaven and to help the worshipper to overcome the foe's malign oppressions. Not used in any of the ritual texts of the *RV*.

Used by *Ṛvidh* as a charm for conquering enemies and for surmounting difficulties (ii.111).

67. *RV* 6.28. In this hymn, cows are invoked to bring prosperity to the worshipper (vss 1-8). Used by *ĀŚS* (8.10) in a homage to cows. The first seven verses occur in *AV* 4.21 and are used by *Kauś* (10.1) in a rite for sick kine and further in a rite for the prosperity of kine (21.8ff). *ĀGS* designates this hymn as "āgāvīya" and directs it to be muttered when cows return from pasture. Used by *ŚGS* in the Goṣṭha-karma (3.9.3) and in the Āśvayujī-karma (3.16.3).

Used by *Ṛvidh* (ii.112) in a charm for obtaining cows.

68. *RV* 6.46. In this hymn, Indra is invoked to bestow kine, steeds, manly powers, etc. and to protect the worshipper and his family (vss 1-14). Vs 1 of this hymn is the laud-Pragātha in the Niṣkevalya-śastra (*ĀŚS* 5.15; *ŚŚS* 7.20.4).

Used by *Ṛvidh* (ii.113) in a rite for obtaining wealth.

69. *RV* 6.47.29.31. In these verses, the presiding deity of the kettle-drum is invoked to drive enemies and to assign strength and vigour to the worshipper. These verses occur in *AV* 6.126 and are applied by *Kauś* (16.1) in a battle-rite. *ĀGS* (3.12.7) directs these verses to be muttered while consecrating the kettle-drum.

Used by *Ṛvidh* (ii.114) in a charm for obtaining vigour and strength and for destroying enemies.

70. *RV* 6.48. In this hymn, various deities are invoked to bestow wealth, and to protect the worshipper (vss.1-22). Vs.1 of this hymn is the laud-Pragātha in the Āgnimāruta-śastra (*ĀŚS* 5.20; *SŚŚ* 8.6.5).

Used by *Ṛvidh* (ii.115-17) in a charm against Rakṣas, Dasyus and enemies.

71. *RV* 6.51.16. In this verse, the Viśve-devās are invoked to help the Ṛṣi in evading robbers and in collecting wealth. *ĀŚS* (2.5) directs it to be muttered by one who has returned from abroad, whereas *ŚGS* (3.6.3) prescribes it for one who goes forth.

*Ṛvidh* directs this verse to be muttered while setting out on a business journey (ii.118).

72. *RV* 6.52.15. In this verse, the Viśve-devas are invoked to vouchsafe a long life to the worshipper. It is the offering-verse to the all-gods in the Āgrayaṇa-rite (*ĀŚS* 2.9) It is also the offering verse to the victim immolated to the Viśve-devas (*ŚŚS* 6.10.6).

Used by *Ṛvidh* (ii.119) in a rite for prolonging life.

73. *RV* 6.53. In this hymn, Pūṣan is invoked to bring wealth to the worshipper to scatter enemies and to bestow kine, horses, etc. on the worshipper (vss.1-10). *ŚŚS* (3.5.7) directs the first verse to be muttered by one going abroad, whereas *ĀGS* (3. 7.8) prescribes the hymn to be muttered by one setting out on a business journey.

In the *Ṛvidh*, this hymn is intended to secure the attainment of wealth (ii.120).

74 .*RV* 6.54. In this hymn, Pūṣan is invoked to guide the worshipper to recover lost articles (vss.1-10). *ĀGS* (3.7.9) directs it to be muttered when something is lost or has strayed.

Used in *Ṛvidh* (ii.121) in a charm for recovering lost things, either a cow, men or wealth.

75. *RV* 6.61. In this hymn, Sarasvatī is invoked to bestow prosperity, to guard the worshipper from hate and to guide him to glorious treasure (vss.1-14). On the sixth day of the Pṛṣṭhya-ṣaḍaha vss.1-3 which constitute a tristich to Sarasvatī are used at the Praüga-śastra (*ĀŚS* 8.1) and further the same verses are used for the above purpose on the fourth, fifth and sixth day of the ten-day-period (*ŚŚS* 10.5.4; 6.6; 8.3).

In the *Ṛvidh*, this hymn is intended to secure the attainment of eloquence (ii.122).

76. *RV* 6.69. In this hymn, Indra and Viṣṇu are invoked to grant riches to the worshipper (vss.1-8). On the third-pressing of the Ukthya, the hymn is used at the Acchāvāka-śastra (*ĀŚS* 6.1; *ŚŚS* 9.4.6).

Used by *Ṛvidh* (ii.123) in a charm for obtaining all benefits.

77. *RV* 6.73. In this hymn, Bṛhaspati's deeds like rending asunder the mountains, breaking of forts, etc. are recapitulated. On the third pressing of the Abhiplava-ṣaḍaha and Ukthya, this hymn is recited for the sake of over-recital at the Brāhmaṇacchaṁsi-śastra (*ĀŚS* 7.9; cp. *ŚŚS* 9.3.3).

In the *Ṛvidh*, this hymn is intended to destory enemies (ii.124).

78. *RV* 6.74. In this hymn, the twin deities Somā-Rudra are invoked to drive away sickness, to provide medicines and to release the worshipper from Varuṇa's fetters (vss.1-4). Not employed in any of the ritual texts of the *RV*.

In the *Ṛvidh*, this hymn is intended to secure release from wickedness and from Varuṇa's fetters (ii.125-126).

79. *RV* 6.75. Its broad contents are: the first verse praises the coat of mail the second, the bow; the third, the bow-string; the fourth, the ends of a bow; the fifth, the quiver; the sixth, the charioteer and the reins; the seventh, the horses; the eighth, the chariot; the ninth, the chariot-attendants; the tenth, vari-

ous deities; the eleventh and twelfth, the arrow; the thirteen, the whip; the fourteenth, the brace; the fifteenth and sixteenth, again the arrow; the seventeenth, the battle-ground; Bṛhaspati etc.; the eighteenth, the coat of mail, Soma etc.; and the nineteenth, the gods. Used by *ĀGS* (3.12.3-11) in the Rājasaṁnāhana-rite.

*Ṛvidh* (ii.127-129) employs the hymn to accompany, the consecration of chariot-parts, chariot horses, etc. in a battle-rite.

80. *RV* 7.1. In this hymn, Agni is invoked to bestow wealth of wisdom, wealth of brave sons, etc. to drive away pain and sickness and to pour blessings and ample riches on the chiefs and nobles (vss.1-25). In the Viśvajit and on the fourth day of the Caturvīra sacrifice this hymn is used at the Ājya-śastra (*ĀŚS* 8.7; 10.2) and further the same hymn is used at Ājya-śastra in the Mahāvrata (*ŚŚS* 17.8.2). Used by *Svidh* (3.7.9) in a rite for success in subduing spirits, etc.

Used by *Ṛvidh* in a Kāmya rite by one desiring progeny, long life, etc. (ii.130); and further it is directed to be muttered before the partaking of a meal (ii.165).

81. *RV* 7.5-7. In the hymn 5, Agni Vaiśvānara is invoked to rend asunder castles, to drive Dasyus and to bestow riches on chiefs and nobles (vss.1-9). Not employed in any of the ritual texts of the *RV*. In hymn 6, Agni's deeds like destroying of forts, chasing Dasyus, etc. are recapitulated. On the fourth day of the ten-day-period this hymn is used at the Āgnimāruta-śastra (*ŚŚS* 10.5.24). In hymn 7, Agni is invoked to come and help the worshipper and to bring food to singers and nobles (vss.1-7). Not employed in any of the ritual texts of the *RV*.

Used by *Ṛvidh* (ii.131) in a charm against Rakṣas, besides it is intended to secure the attainment of wealth.

82. *RV* 7.32.22-23. This verse contains a praise of Indra. This verse is a laud Pragātha and is used at the Niṣkevalyaśastra in the Jyotiṣṭoma (*ĀŚS* 5.15; *ŚŚS* 7.20.3).

In the *Ṛvidh*, these verses are intended to secure the attainment of good fortune, wealth and long life (ii.132).

83. *RV* 7.35. In this hymn, the Viśve-devās are invoked to remain favourably disposed towards worshippers (vss.1-15). Used by the Ā*ŚS* (8.14) in the Mahānāmnīvrata and further vs.1-13 of this hymn are used in a healing rite (*ŚŚS* 16.13.6). *Sarv* (vii.35) designates the hymn as "Śāntiḥ" whereas *ĀGS* designates it as "Śaṁtātīya" and employs it in Vāstukarma (2.8.11; 9.7) and in the Śūlagava sacrifice (4.8.39, 43). Used by *ŚGS* (5.10. 3) in expiatory rites.

*Ṛvidh* designates it as "Śaṁvatyaḥ" and directs it to be muttered at the beginning and end of all rites (i.16,53) and further it reappears in a charm against Rakṣas, Bhūtas and diseases (ii.133).

84. *RV* 7.41. In this hymn, various deities are invoked to guide the worshipper, to bestow wealth on him and to shower all abundance (vss.1-7). It occurs in *AV* 3.16 and is used by *Kauś* (10.24) in the Medhājanana and in certain other ceremonies.

Used by *Ṛvidh* (ii.134) in a charm for obtaining a Niveśa (settling in life).

85. *RV* 7.46. In this hymn Rudra is invoked to heal all sickness, not to harm the worshipper's sons or progeny (vss.1-4). Regarding the ritual use of this hymn see under (9) above.

A person who mutters this hymn suffers no harm in respect of progeny, wealth and self (*Ṛvidh* ii.135).

86. *RV* 7.49. In this hymn, waters are invoked to protect the worshipper (vss.1-4).

*Ṛvidh* directs this hymn to be muttered while crossing a stream (ii.136). Cp. *ŚGS* 4.14.5.

87. *RV* 7.51-52. In these hymns, the Ādityas are invoked to declare the worshipper sinless, to protect him, to release him

from every bond, and to afford protection to his seed and offspring. Vs.1 of hymn 51 is the inviting verse of the *Vapā* of a victim immolated to Ādityas (*ĀŚS* 3.8); and further the same verse is inviting-verse of the Soma draught for Ādityas (5.17). Hymn 52 is not employed in any of the ritual texts of the *RV*.

Used by *Ṛvidh* in a charm against enemies and diseases (ii.137).

88. *RV* 7.54. In this hymn, Vāstoṣpati is invoked to bring prosperity to men and animals (vss.1-3). Used by *ĀGS* (2.9.9) in the Vāstuśānti and by *ŚGS* (2.14.5) to accompany the offering to Vāstu in the Vaiśvadeva ceremony.

*Ṛvidh* directs this hymn to be muttered after the Vaiśvadeva ceremony (ii.138).

89. *RV* 7.55. Its broad contents are: Vāstoṣpati is requested to remain friendly with the worshipper (vs.1); Saramā's son is asked to retrace his steps and to go to sleep (vss.2-4); the rest a sleep-charm (vss.5-8). The first verse of this hymn is used by *ŚGS* (3.4.8) in the Gṛhapraveśa ceremony. Vss.5-8 occur in *AV* 4.5 and are used by *Kauś* (36.1 ff) for putting to sleep a woman and her attendants in order to approach her safely. *Sarv* (vii.55) designates this hymn as "prasvāpinyupaniṣat."

In the *Ṛvidh*, the complete hymn is intended to put all living beings to sleep (ii.139); and further vss.2-8 are directed to be muttered in case of distress in any inaccessible defile, etc. (ii.139-141ab). But Śaunaka holds that the complete hymn should be muttered even in the aforesaid instances (ii.141cd).

90. *RV* 7.59.12. In this verse, Rudra is invoked to release the worshipper from death. Not employed in any of the ritual texts of the *RV*.

*Ṛvidh* employs this verse in a rite to prolong life (ii.142-143).

91. *RV* 7.66.16. In this verse, Sūrya is invoked to prolong the life of the worshipper. In the Pitryeṣṭi, *ŚŚS* (3.17.6) directs

this verse to be muttered while looking at the sun. Used by *ŚGS* (3.8.7) in the Āgrayaṇa-rite and in the pacificatory rite (6.6.1).

In the *Ṛvidh*, this verse is intended to prolong long life (ii.144).

92. *RV* 7.75-80. In these hymns, Uṣas is invoked to vouchsafe manifold and splendid riches; to grant food and bounty rich in chariots, kine etc. to being wealth that keeps the worshipper happy; to distribute treasures to the pious; and to shine forth with wealth of kine. Hymns 75-80, which constitutes the Triṣṭubh-portion of the Uṣas-section are used at the Prātaranuvāka and Āśvinaśastra (*ĀŚS* 4.14).

In the *Ṛvidh*, these hymns are intended to secure the attainment of manifold wealth consisting in gold etc. kine, horses, corn, etc. (ii.145-146).

93. *RV* 7.88. In this verse, Varuṇa is invoked to unite the bond that binds the worshipper, Not employed in any of the ritual texts of the *RV*.

In the *Ṛvidh*, this hymn is intended to secure release from all fetters. (ii.147-148).

94. *RV* 7.89.5. In this verse, Varuṇa is invoked not to punish the worshipper for whatever offence he, as a human being, might have committed against the heavenly host. In the Devasū-offerings, this verse is the offering verse of the Havis to Varuṇa (*ĀŚS* 4.11). Used by *ŚGS* (5.2.6) in the consecration of ponds, etc.

In the *Ṛvidh*, this verse is meant to expiate the sin of cohabiting with forbidden women (ii.150-152) and in (ii.153) it is used along with *RV* 1.23.22-24 for the above purpose.

95. *RV* 7.99-100. In these hymns, the deities Indra and Viṣṇu are invoked to accept the offerings and to bestow splendid wealth and spacious dwellings. Vs.1-3 of hymn 99 form respectively

the offering-verse, the inviting-verse and the offering-verse of the Puroḍāśa, Vapā and Havis to the victim immolated to Viṣṇu (*ĀŚS* 3.8). In the Ukthya, hymn 100 is recited at the Acchāvāka-Śastra (*ĀŚS* 6.1).

Used by *Ṛvidh* (ii.154) in a rite for obtaining power. This application is evidently imposed upon the hymns, not contained in them.

96. *RV* 7.101-102. In these hymns, Parjanya is invoked to vouchsafe triple shelter to the worshipper and to provide pasturage for the worshipper. Hymn 101 is not employed in any of the ritual of the *RV*. In the Anvārambhaṇīyā-iṣṭi for Vaiśvānara and Parjanya, vs. 1 of hymn 102 is the inviting verse of the Caru to Parjanya (*ĀŚS* 2.15; *ŚŚS* 3.13.4).

Used by *Ṛvidh* in a charm for obtaining rain (ii.155-156).

97. *RV* 7.104. In this hymn, the deities Indra and Soma are invoked to destroy demon foe, evil beings, an adversary who accuses the worshipper, etc. and to cast their weapon at fiends and sorcerers (vss.1-25).

In the *Ṛvidh*, this hymn is intended to secure release for a person who is either seized or falsely accused by enemies (ii.157-158).

98. *RV* 8.11. In this hymn, Agni is invoked to guard the sacred rites and to come and help the worshipper in battles (vss.1-10). This hymn (except the last verse) constitutes the Gāyatrī-portion of the Agni-section and it used at the Prātaranuvāka (*ĀŚS* 4.13); and further vs.1 of this hymn is the inviting verse to Agni Vratapati (*ĀŚS* 3.13; *ŚŚS* 2.4.8).

In the *Ṛvidh*, this hymn is meant to expiate the sin arising out of a breach of vow (ii.159). Cp. *ŚGS* 5.1.91.

99. *RV* 8.16. In this hymn, Indra is invoked to give happiness, to fight foes and to lead the worshipper towards felicity (vss.1-12). In the Atirātra, this hymn is used at the second Paryāya (section) of the Acchāvakaśastra (*ĀŚS* 6.4).

*Ṛvidh* (ii.160-161) uses the hymn in a charm for overcoming an adversary in a dispute and for overthrowing enemies.

100. *RV* 8.18.9. In this verse, the worshipper implores Agni to bless him, Sūrya for warming him, Vāta for moving auspiciously and for chasing foes. Not employed in any of the ritual texts of the *RV*.

Used by *Ṛvidh* in a charm or obtaining relief from a great calamity (ii.162).

101. *RV* 8.21.18. This verse is in praise of Citra's liberality. Not employed in any of the ritual texts of the *RV*.

In the *Ṛvidh*, it accompanies the offering of rice-mess to the King of Moles (ii.74). For the story of Citra, see *BD*v i.58-62.

102. *RV* 8.30. In this hymn, the Viśvedevās are invoked to defend the worshipper and to give wide protection to him (vss.1-4). On the ninth day of the ten-day-period, vs.1 of this hymn is employed at the Vaiśvadeva-Śastra (*ŚŚS* 10.11.8).

Used by *Ṛvidh* (ii.163) in a charm against fear.

103. *RV* 8.32-45. In hymn 32 Indra's deeds are recapitulated and further he is invited to drink the pressed Soma-juice and to afford wide protection (vss.1-30). In hymn 33, Indra is invoked to come and drink the Soma draught (vss.1-19). In hymn 34, Indra is invoked to bestow riches in hundreds and thousands, but vss.16-18 of this hymn celebrate the munificience of Vasurocis.

In the *Ṛvidh*, vss.16-18 are intended to secure the attainment of all conceivable objects of desire (ii.164).

In hymn 35, the Aśvins are invoked to drink the Soma draught, to bring strengthening food, and to bestow vigorous strength on the worshipper (vss.1-24). In the Aptoryāma this hymn is the additional laud of the Hotṛ-priest (*ĀŚS* 9.11).

Used by *Ṛvidh* (ii.168-169ab) in a charm for obtaining supreme power, wealth, etc.

In hymn 36, Indra is invited to drink the pressed Soma-juice and to help the worshipper (vss.1-7). On the fifth day of the ten-day-period, this hymn is used at the Marutvatīyaśastra (*ĀŚS* 7-12; *ŚŚS* 10.6.9). In hymn 37 also, Indra is invoked to bring success (vss.1-7). In the Mahāvrata this hymn is used at the Niṣkevalya-śastra (*ĀŚS* 7.12), but *ŚŚS* (10.6.16) employs it on the fifth day of the ten-day-period. In hymn 38, Indra and Agni are invoked to hear the hymn of praise and to bestow felicity on the worshipper (vss.1-10). At the morning pressing of the Pṛṣṭhya and Abhiplava-ṣaḍahas, this hymn is inserted at the Acchāvākaśastra (*ĀŚS* 7.5) and further vss.1-3 of this hymn are the Stotra-tristich for the Acchāvāka-priest on the sixth day of the ten-day-rite (*ŚŚS* 12.1.5). In hymn 39, Agni is invoked to deck the thirty-three gods and to bestow all vital power etc. on the worshipper (vss.1-10). Not employed in any of the ritual texts of the *RV*. In hymn 40, Indra and Agni are invoked to aid the worshipper, to guard him with triple shelter and to bestow a store of riches on him (vss. 1-12). In the Mahāvrata, this hymn is used at the Niṣkevalya-śastra (*AĀ* 5.3.1). In hymn 41, Varuṇa is invoked to guard the worshipper's thoughts and to support the world of life (vss.1-10). At the mid-day-pressing on the Caturviṁśa day vss.3-5 or vss.4-6 of this hymn are recited at the Maitrāvaruṇa-śastra before the Ārambhaṇīyā-rite (*ĀŚS* 7.2). In hymn 42, Varuṇa and the Aśvins are invoked to vouchsafe protection (vss.1-6). Vs.11 of this hymn is the offering-verse of the Havis to the victim immolated to Varuṇa (*ĀŚS* 3.7). In hymn 43, Agni's deeds are recapitulated and he is further invoked to bestow choicest wealth. This hymn as well as the next one constitute the Gāyatrī-portion of the Agni-section and are used at the Prātaranuvāka (*ĀŚS* 4.13; *ŚŚS* 6.4.1) and Āśvinaśastra (*ĀŚS* 4.13). In hymn 44, Agni is invoked to bring the gods and to prolong the worshipper's life (vss.1-30). For the ritual use, see under the preceding.

*Ṛvidh* (ii.169cd-170) employs hymn 44 in a rite for obtaining long life and unequalled success.

In hymn 45, Indra's deeds are recapitulated and further he is invoked to destroy enemies and to bestow wealth on the worshipper (vss.1-42).

In the *Ṛvidh*, hymn 45 is intended to destroy rivals (ii.170cd-171ab). Hymn 32-45 with others are directed to be muttered before the partaking of a meal (ii.164-166).

104. *RV* 8.46-47. In hymn 46, Indra is invited to drink the Soma juice, to bestow wealth, excellent treasures, etc. on the worshipper and to stir his thoughts (vss.1-33). Vss.1-20 of this hymn are used at the Niṣkevalya-śastra in the Mahāvrata (*AĀ* 5.2.5). *Svidh* employs the complete hymn in a Kāmya-rite by one desiring long life (2.1.5). In hymn 47, Ādityas are invoked to afford protection in the earlier verses, but in the later ones Uṣas, is invoked to remove the bad effects of dreams (vss. 1-18). Vs.1 of this hymn belongs to the isolated verses and is recited during the twelve-day-period (*ŚŚS* 12.2.14).

In the *Ṛvidh* these hymns are intended to regain health (ii.172 cd); and further vss.14-18 of hymn 48 are intended to avert the evil dreams and to destroy sins (ii.173ab).

105. *RV* 8.48.4-5. In these verses Soma is invoked to lengthen the worshipper's life. Vs.4 is directed to be muttered while touching the heart after the partaking of the Soma dregs from the bowl (*ĀŚS* 5.6; *ŚŚS* 7.5.15).

*Ṛvidh* (ii.173cd-174ab) employs these verses to accompany the touching of the heart in a charm for prolonging life.

106. *RV* 8.61.13-18. In these verses, Indra is invoked to give the worshipper, security from whichever [object or direction] he is afraid of and to protect him from all directions. At the midday pressing on the Caturviṁśa day vss.13-15 are optionally the Stotra-tristich at the Acchāvākaśastra (*ĀŚS* 7.4), and further the same verses are used in the Dhiṣṇyopasthāna (*ŚŚS* 6.13.3). Vss.13-18 are used by *ĀGS* (3.11.2) in the Sarvatobhaya-homa, but *ŚGS* employs vs.13 only in the Brahmayajña (1.4.2).

*Ṛvidh* (ii.174cd-176ab) employs these verses in a ceremony against danger from any direction.

107. *RV* 8.64. In this hymn, Indra is invited to drink the Soma-juice and to drive off enemies (vss. 1-12). Used by *Svidh* (3.6.6) in a battle rite.

*Ṛvidh* (ii.176cd-177ab) employs it in a witchcraft rite against enemies.

108. *RV* 8.67. In this hymn, the Ādityas are invoked to release the worshipper from fetters, to rescue him from wolves, etc. and to dispel sins (vss.1-21) In the Consecration of the high altar, vs.1 of this hymn is the inviting verse of the Havis to the Ādityas (*ŚŚS* 9.24.3).

In the *Ṛvidh*, this hymn is intended to secure release from imprisonment (ii.177cd-178ab).

109. *RV* 8.70.5-6. In these verses, Indra is invoked to help the worshipper to win a stable full of kine. On the third day of the ten-day-period, vss. 5-6 are the Stotra-pragāthas at the Niṣkevalya-śastra (*ĀŚS* 7.10); and further the same verses occur in the corresponding-tristich of the Marutvatīya-śastra (*ŚŚS* 11.13.22).

In the *Ṛvidh*, these verses are intended to secure the attainment of fame and all objects of desire (ii.178cd-179ab).

110. *RV* 8.71. In this hymn, Agni is invoked to guard the worshipper from malignity and to bestow wealth, kine, precious gifts, etc. (vss.1-15). Vss.1-9 of this hymn constitute the Gāyatrī-portion of the Agni-section and are used at the Prātaranuvāka and Āśvinaśastra (*ĀŚS* 4.13).

Used by *Ṛvidh* (ii.179cd-180ab) in a rite for winning wealth through the Agni's assistance.

111. *RV* 8.81. In this hymn, Indra is invoked to help the worshipper to gather the spoil (vss.1-9). Vss.1-3 of this hymn are the Stotra-tristich in the middle-round of the Maitrāvaruṇa-śastra (*ĀŚS* 6.4; *ŚŚS* 9.12.1). Used by *Svidh* (i.4.18) in a rite for obtaining all benefits.

In the *Ṛvidh*, this hymn is intended to secure the attainment of wealth (ii.180cd-181ab).

112. *RV* 8.91. In this hymn, Apālā implores Indra to drink the

Soma-juice out of her mouth and to unite with her and the rest of the hymn describes the boons given to her by Indra (vss.1-7). Not employed in any of the ritual texts of the *RV*.

Used by *Ṛvidh* (ii.181cd-182ab) in a healing charm against skin-disease. For the story of Apālā, see *BD* vi.99-107.

113. *RV* 8.93.4. In this verse, the greatness of Indra is extolled. In the Aptoryāma, this verse as well as the succeeding two verses which form the Stotra-tristich are recited by the Maitrā-varuṇa-priest for the sake of over-recital (*ĀŚS* 9.11). Used by *Svidh* (2.4.8) in a blessing ceremony.

*Ṛvidh* (ii.182cd-183ab) employs it for destroying sin and for subjugating the world.

114. *RV* 8.95.7-9. In these verses, Indra is glorified with a pure Sāman and he is invoked to drink the pure milky draught and to enrich the worshipper. Used by *Svidh* (1.5.13) in an expiatory rite.

*Ṛvidh* designates these verses as "śuddhavatyaḥ" and directs them to be repeated at the beginning and end of all rites (i.16, 55.)

115. *RV* 8.110.10-11. In these verses, Goddess Vāk is invoked to yield food and vigour. Vs.10-11 are respectively the inviting and offering-verses of the Vapā and Havis to the victim immolated to Vāk (*ĀŚS* 3.8; cp. *ŚŚS* 9.28.6). Vs.11 is used by *ĀGS* (3.10.9) in a rite against the disagreeable voices of birds.

In the *Ṛvidh*, these verses are intended to secure the attainment of polished speech (ii.183cd-184ab).

116. *RV* 8.101.11-16. Their broad contents are: the greatness of Sūrya and the far-spreading unconquerable light is extolled (vss. 1-12); Uṣas clothed in red colours is seen advancing towards the ten regions of the world (vs.13); mortal generations, past and present are described (vs.14); goddess cow who is identified with Aditi, etc. is invoked not to injure the sinless (vs.15)

and finally goddess cow speaks of herself as skilled in eloquence (vs.16). With vss.11-12 the Hotṛ priest, desiring to recite Āśvina-Śastra, offers oblations into the fire (*ĀŚS* 6.5).

In the *Ṛvidh*, vss.11-12 are meant to avert the consequences arising out of uttering falsehood (ii.184cd-185ab). *Ṛvidh* (ii.185cd-186ab) employs vs.13 in a charm for splendour and also for good eyesight; vs.14 is intended to cbtain release from rebirth (ii.186cd).

Vs. 15 is used by *ŚŚS* (4.21.24) and by *ĀGS* (1.24.32) at the respectful reception to a guest.

*Ṛvidh* (ii.187ab) employs vs.15 in a charm for obtaining kine.

Vs.16 is the offering-verse of the Havis to a cow (*ŚŚS* 9.28.15).

*Ṛvidh* (ii.187cd) employs vs.16 in a charm for gracious speech.

117. *RV* 9.1-67. In hymn 1, Soma is invoked to flow onward to Indra who after drinking it pours wealth on the worshipper (vss.1-10). In hymn 2, Soma is invoked to rush to the purifying cloth and then into Indra who wins kine, heroes, etc. for the worshipper (vss.1-10). In hymn 3, Soma is asked to settle down in the vats of wood and then flow to the straining-cloth. Soma is invoked to bestow rich gifts on the worshipper (vss.1-10). In hymn 4, Soma is invoked to win heavenly light, strength, etc. to drive away foes, and to better the lot of the worshipper by bringing wealth in steeds (vss.1-10). In hymn 5, Soma is requested to send forth his rays on every side, to shine mightity and to anoint the sacrificial stake (vss.1-11). In hymn 6, Soma is asked to flow on to the woollen sieve and to flow onward to Indra (vss.1-9). In hymn 7, Soma is asked to flow for the upkeep of Law, and to win wealth, treasures etc. for the worshipper (vss.1-9). In hymn 8, Soma is invoked to bestow heroic strength on the worshipper and to drive his enemies (vss.1-9). In hymn 9, Soma is invoked to bestow high renown, kine, etc. on the worshipper (vss.1-9). In hymn 10, Soma is requested to bring about the union between the gods in heaven and the worshipper (vss.1-9). In hymn 11, Soma is invoked to bring wealth, flow on to Indra who wins spoil for the worshipper (vss.1-9). kine, etc. (vss.1-9). In hymn 12, Soma is requested to bring wealth to the worshipper (vss.1-9). In hymn 13, Soma is asked

to flow on to Indra who wins spoil for the worshipper (vss.1-9). In hymn 14, Soma is asked to come as a faithful friend of the worshipper and to bestow treasures on him (vss.1-8). In hymn 15, Soma is invoked to bring forth abundant food (vss.1-8). In hymns 16-17, Soma is requested to flow into the sieve and then hasten to the pitchers (vss.1-8). In hymn 18, gods are invoked to come and drink Soma (vss.1-7). In hymn 19, Soma is invoked to bring wondrous treasure to the worshipper and to bring down the might of the foe (vss.1-7). In hymn 20, Soma is invoked to subdue enemies and to bestow lofty glory on the worshipper (vss.1-7). In hymn 21, Soma is asked to drive away foes and to bestow vital force on the worshipper (vss.1-7). In hymn 22, Soma is asked to bring the niggard's wealth in kine (vss.1-7). In hymn 23, Soma is requested to bring wealth of the miser (vss.1-7). In hymn 24, Soma is asked to flow onwards to Indra and to rule the mankind (vss.1-7). In hymn 25, Soma is requested to flow on to gods and to shine with them (vss.1-6). In hymn 26, Soma is invoked to support the heaven and to flow on to Indra (vss. 1-6). In hymn 27, Soma is asked to flow to the purifying cloth and then to Indra (vss.1-6). In hymn 28, Soma is asked to run to the woollen straining-cloth and then to the wooden vats (vss.1-6). In hymn 29, Soma is invoked to win precious things and to protect the worshipper "from the godless" (vss. 1-6). In hymn 30, Soma is invoked to bestow heroic sons on the worshippers (vss.1-6). In hymn 31, Soma is asked to give wealth and might to the worshipper (vss.1-6). In hymn 32, Soma is invited to bestow illustrious fame on the worshipper (vss.1-6). In hymn 33, Soma is asked to give riches to the worshipper (vss.1-6). In hymn 34, Soma is requested to flow onwards to Indra and other gods (vss.1-6). In hymn 35, Soma is invoked to bestow abundant wealth on the worshipper and to aid him in subduing enemies (vss.1-6). In hymn 36, Soma is invoked to bestow all treasures of the heaven, earth and the mid-region on the worshipper (vss.1-6). In hymn 37, Soma is asked to run forth to the luminous realm of heaven (vss.1-6). In hymn 38, Soma is asked to rush through the woollen filter and then to Indra (vss.1-6). In hymn 39, Soma is invoked to consecrate the worshipper who is unconsecrated and to bring a store of food to him (vss.1-6). In hymn 40, Soma is asked to bestow heroic strength and riches on the worshipper (vss. 1-6). In hymn 41, Soma is invoked to drive the black skin, to quell the riteless Dasyu and to bestow wealth in kine, etc. on the worshipper (vss.1-6). In hymn 42, Soma is asked to bring all desirable things, abundant store of food, etc. (vss.1-6). In hymn 43, Soma is invoked to bestow heroic power on the worshipper (vss.1-6). In hymn 44, Soma is invoked to win strength and high renown for the worshipper (vss.1-6). In hymn 45, Soma is asked to flow onwards to Indra for his drink (vss.1-6). In hymn 46, Soma is asked to strengthen Indra and to bestow opulence on the worshipper (vss.1-6). In hymn 47, Soma is invoked to win riches for the worshipper (vss.1-5). In hymn 48, Soma is invoked to gladden the worshipper, to crush the bold ones, to rule with a mighty sway and to destroy a hundred forts (vss.1-5). In hymn 49, Soma is asked to bestow a ample store of wholesome food on the worshipper and to drive off the Rakṣasas (vss.1-5). In hymn 50, Soma is requested to flow on to the fleece and then to Indra for his drink (vss.1-5). In hymn 51, Soma is invoked to give strength and fame to the worshipper (vss.1-5). In hymn 52, Soma is requested to bring down the vigour of foes (vss.1-5). In hymn 53, Soma is invoked to crush the fiends and to chase the foes (vss.1-4). In hymn 54, Soma is compared to the sun (vss.1-4). In hymn 55, Soma is invoked to bestow all felicities on the worshipper (vss.1-4). In hymn 56, Soma is requested to slay the fiends and to guard the worshipper from distress (vss.1-4). In hymn 57, Soma is asked to bring all the treasures of heaven and earth (vss.1-4). In hymn 58 Soma is repeatedly invoked to rescue his worshippers from sin (vss.1-4). In hymn 59, Soma is asked to bring wealth with progeny to the worshipper (vss.1-4). In hymn 60, Soma is requested to flow onwards to Indra as his drink (vss. 1-4). In hymn 61, Soma is invoked to flow to different gods, to bestow blessings on kine, to kill foes, to win booty, to strengthen Indra in order to kill Vṛtra and to guard and worshipper from every foe (vss.1-30). In hymn 62 Soma is invoked to bring all felicities and to bestow glories and heroic strength on the worshipper (vss.1-30). In hymn 63, Soma is invoked to vouchsafe renown to the worshipper, to find wealth for him, to drive away Rakṣasas and to bestow all desirable boons on the worshipper (vss.1-30). In hymn 64, Soma is invoked to pour forth all treasure from heaven, earth, etc. on the worshipper and to guard him (vss. 1-30). In hymn 65, Soma is invoked to bring might and speed to the worshipper (vss.1-30). In hymn 66, Soma is asked to bring food and to bestow splendour and heroic strength on the worshipper (vss.1-30). In hymn 67, Soma is invoked to bring wealth in steeds, cattle, etc. to drive away danger and to strengthen the solemn rite (vss.1-32). In *ŚŚS* (4.15.3). hymn 4 accompanies the ablution of the bereaved persons in the funeral ceremonies of a Āhitāgni. Hymn 5 is an Āprīsūkta attributed to Kaśyapa (*ĀŚS* 3.2.com). Vs.4 of hymn 8 is used by *ĀŚS* (5.12) in a laud to the pressing-stones. Hymn 8 is used by *Svidh* (2.6.6) in a charm to subdue a woman and to make her docile. Hymn 37 is used by *Svidh* (2.1.5) among Kāmya-rites. Vs.1 of hymn 54 is used by *ŚŚS* (2.11.2) in the Agnyupasthāna during the Agnyādheya. Hymn 58 is used by *Svidh* (2.1.7) among Kāmya-rites. *ĀŚS* (5.12) possibly designates hymns 1.67 as "pāvamānyaḥ" inserts them in a laud to the pressing stones and directs them to be recited before Arbuda's hymn (i.e. *RV* 10.94).

*Ṛvidh* also designates them as "pāvamanyaḥ" and directs them to be muttered at the beginning and end of all rites (i.16,55). Moreover, they are intended to secure the attainment of Brāhmā's abode and to conquer the fear of death (iii.1-6, 12-14ab). *Ṛvidh* designates, hymn 11 as "trivṛtā ṛcaḥ" and includes among Āyuṣya rites (i.53); further it designates hymn 58 as "taratsamandīya" and directs its employment in expiatory practices (iii.7, 14cd-15ab); and lastly it (iii.10-11) directs hymns 66-67 to be muttered by one incapable of reciting the complete text of the Pāvamanī-verses (i.e. *RV* 9.1-67).

118. *RV* 9.83. In this hymn, Soma is invoked to flow on to Brahmaṇapati's filter which is spread in the heaven, to sustain all living beings, to guard the generation of the gods and to accomplish the sacrifice (vs.1-5). Vss.1-2 of this hymn are used as a laud (*ĀŚS* 4.6). In the *Svidh*, this hymn is intended to secure the attainment of various desires (1.4.19).

*Ṛvidh*, however, designates it as "ādhyātmikaṁ sūktam" and employs it in a rite for prosperity and for attainment of a favourite refuge (iii.17cd-18ab).

119. *RV* 9.112-115. In hymn 112, the seer states that thoughts, plans and ways of mankind are diverse, though all strive for wealth and follow desires like a cow (vss.1-4). In hymn 113, Soma is invoked to flow on to Indra, to place the worshipper in that deathless undecaying world and to make him immortal in that realm (vss.1-11). In hymn 114, Soma is invoked to guard the worshipper in a such a way that no malignity nor any evil may harm him (vss.1-14). Vs.4 of hymn 114 is used by *ĀGS* (3.5.7) and by *ŚGS* (4.5.8) in the Upākaraṇa ceremony.

*Ṛvidh* directs hymns 112-114 to be muttered by one desiring highest abode and immortality (ii.18cd-19ab); and further the complete ninth Maṇḍala is directed to be muttered whilst holding a bunch of Darbha and a gold piece in hand (ii.188).

120. *RV* 10.1-5. In hymn 1, Agni is invoked to come along with the gods (1-7). In hymn 2, Agni is asked to fix rites and seasons and to correct the faults and failings of the worshipper (vss.1-7). In hymn 3, Agni is invoked to bestow ample wealth on the worshipper (vss.1-7). In hymn 4, Agni is invoked to protect the worshipper's children, descendants, etc. (vss.1-7). In hymn 5, Agni is identified with all beings, particularly with the Sun and Prajāpati (vss.1-7). Hymns 1-5 (as well as the succeeding hymns 6-8 after omitting the last tristich of hymn 8) form the Triṣṭubh-portion of the Agni-section and are used at the Prātaranuvāka and Āśvinaśastra (*ĀŚS* 4.13) but *ŚŚS* (6.4.5) prescribes hymns 1-7 only and further vs. 1 of hymn 2 is the inviting-verse for Agni Sviṣṭakṛt (*ĀŚS* 1.6; *ŚŚS* 1.91).

*Ṛvidh* directs hymns 1-5 with others to be muttered before partaking of a meal (ii.165).

121. *RV* 10.9. In this hymn, waters are invoked to bestow energy, health, etc. on the worshipper and to remove whatever sin or evil committed by him (vss.1-9). Vss.1-3 fof this hymn are

used at the Āgnimārutaśastra (*ĀŚS* 5.20; *ŚŚS* 8.6.7). Vss.1-3 of this hymn are used by *ĀGS* in the Vāstukarma (2.8.12;9.8) and in the Pretakarma (4.6.14). *ŚGS* designates this hymn as "Āpohiṣṭīya" and employs it in the Saptapadi ceremony (1.14.8) and in the Samāvartana rite (3.1.5). The first seven verses of this hymn occur in *AV* 1.5-6 and are used by *Kauś* (43.12) in the house-building ceremony. *Svidh* (1.2.5) prescribes its use in the preliminary restraints.

*Ṛvidh* designates this hymn as "ābvatyaḥ" and employs it at the beginning and end of all rites (i.16, 55); further it directs its use in the expiation of Brahmahatyā, and other Pātakas (iii.19cd-33) and finally in a charm for obtaining rain (iv.127ab).

121. *RV* 10.14. In this hymn, Yama is invoked to lead the departed one to the abode of the fathers, to bestow a place of rest and a long life amongst the gods (vss.1-16). In the Mahāpitṛyajña, the vs. 1 of this hymn is the inviting verse in the Yamayāga (*ĀŚS* 219), but *ŚŚS* (15.9.5) employs vss.1-5 at the midday-pressing in the Yamayāga.

*Ṛvidh* (iii.34-38) employs this hymn in a rite for long life.

123. *RV* 10.18. In this hymn, Mṛtyu is invoked not to touch the offspring nor to injure heroes (vss.1-4); then Dhātṛ is invoked to fashion the lives and deaths of mankind in such a way that men born later will not die before those born earlier (vs.5); then Tvaṣṭṛ is invoked to lengthen the days of existence for all beings (vs.6); the next three verse deal with women and with the removal of a bow from the hand of the departed one (vs. 7-9), and finally Earth is invoked to preserve the departed one (vss.10-14). Vss.1-4 and 8 are used by *ĀGS* in the Pretakarma (4.6.10; 2.18).

In the *Ṛvidh*, this hymn is intended to secure the attainment of long life and success in controlling death, diseases, etc. (iii.39-42) and further vs. 8 of this hymn is used in the Niyoga (iii.43-44).

124. *RV* 10.20.1. In this verse, Agni is invoked to bestow a good

and a happy mind on the worshipper. Not employed in any of the ritual texts of the *RV*.

In the *Ṛvidh*, this verse is intended to secure the attainment of mental peace, benefits and supernormal powers (ii.45-48).

125. *RV* 10.30. Its broad contents are: a priest is asked to approach the celestial waters and Adhvaryus are asked to be ready with oblations for worshipping Apāṁ napāt (vss.1-3); Apāṁ napāt is invoked to bring waters rich in mead (vss.4-7); the rivers are invoked to hear the worshipper's call and Sarasvatī in particular, is invoked to grant a full life to the worshipper (vss.8-12) and finally waters are asked to bestow wealth on the worshipper (vss.13-15). The Complete hymn (except vs. 12) is used in the Āponaptrīya-rite (*ĀŚS* 5.1; *ŚŚS* 6.7.1).

Used by *Ṛvidh* (iii.49) in a charm for obtaining water in a desert.

126. *RV* 10.34. *Sarv* (x.34) describes the hymn as follows: Akṣa-kṛṣi-praśaṁsā cākṣakitavanimdā ca. This hymn which is secular in character is not employed in any of the ritual texts of the *RV*.

Used by *Ṛvidh* (iii.50-53) in a charm for success in gambling.

127. *RV* 10.35-36. In these hymns, all-gods are invoked to bestow felicity, to keep the worshipper free from distress and to bestow gracious favour, victorious, wisdom, fame, etc. In the Abhiplava-ṣaḍaha, hymn 35 is used at the Vaiśvadeva-śastra (*ŚŚS* 11.9.7) and hymn 36 is also meant to serve the same purpose (*ĀŚS* 7.7; *ŚŚS* 11.9.10).

*Ṛvidh* (iii.54ab) employs them in a blessing ceremony.

128. *RV* 10.37. In this hymn, Sūrya is invoked to guard the worshipper on all sides, to drive away disease, evil dreams etc., to to bestow varied riches, to vouchsafe protection to bipeds, quadrupeds etc. and to condone sins committed by the worshipper (vss.1-12). *AŚS* (6.5) and *ŚŚS* (9.20.23) direct it to be recited when the sun has arisen.

Used by *Ṛvidh* (iii.54cd) possibly for a benedictory purpose and further vs.12 of this hymn is used in a rite for obtaining release from sin (iii.55).

129. *RV* 10.45. In this hymn, Agni is invoked to bestow supreme fortune, glory, etc. on the worshipper and gods are requested to give wealth with heroic children to him (vss.1-12). This hymn (except vs.12) with hymn 4 is used at the Prātaranuvāka and Āśvinaśastra (*ĀŚS* 4.13).

Used by *Ṛvidh* (iii.56) in a charm for obtaining religious faith.

130. *RV* 10.57. In this hymn, the Viśve-devās are implored to help the worshipper in keeping to the right path and fathers are invoked to return to the lifeless one, the spirit of his which wandered to the other world, so that he, be blessed with long-lived children (vss.1-6). *ĀŚS* directs it to be recited by one setting out on a journey (2.5).

*Ṛvidh* prescribes the hymn for a person who has gone astray and for obtaining happiness (iii.57).

131. *RV* 10.58. *Sarv* (x.58) designates this hymn as "mana āvartanam" i.e. recalling the mind or spirit. In the Puruṣamedha, vss.1-3 of this hymn are addressed to the consort of the sacrificer while she rests near the victim (*ŚŚS* 16.13.14).

In the *Ṛvidh*, this hymn is employed with *RV* 10.9 in a rite for long life for a friend whose life is drawing to a close and also for others possibly with *RV* 10.59.4 and *RV* 10.60.7-12 (iii.58-61).

132. *RV* 10.61.1. This verse is intentionally and most successfully obscure and this fact alone explains its inclusion in our work. I append here the English rendering of Prof. Oldenberg's German translation: "This *Brahman* filled with the essence of Rudra is duly performed through his insight by the famous speaker at the competition about the priestly ability, which *Brahman* staying effectively in the sphere of generosity may bring to its goal on the day of trial, his fathers and seven

hotṛs". On the sixth day of the Pṛṣṭhya-ṣaḍaha, the complete hymn as well as others are used at the Vaiśva-deva-śastra instead of *RV* 10.36 (*ĀŚS* 8.1).

Used by *Ṛvidh* (iii.62-67) among Kāmya-rites or those intended to secure the attainment of various desires like, food, wealth, etc.; further, that verse accompanies the preparation and binding of an amulet made of three metals, iron, copper and gold in a ritef or obtaining a thousand followers (iii.68-69).

133. *RV* 10.63. In this hymn, the Viśve-devās are invoked to protect the worshipper from malignant injury and to vouchsafe blessings to him (vss.1-17). On the third day of the Pṛṣṭhya- and Abhiplava-ṣaḍahas, this intercalatory Nivid-hymn for the Viśve-devās is used at the Vaiśvadevaśastra (*ĀŚS* 7.7; cp. *ŚŚS* 11.9.14).

Used by *Ṛvidh* in the blessing ceremony for a Snātaka and in a charm for obtaining heaven (iii.70).

134. *RV* 10.71. *Sarv* (x.71), describes this hymn as follows: bṛhaspate bṛhaspatir jñānaṁ tuṣṭāva navamī jagatī. Its broad contents are: Vāk's first and early utterances lead to the creation of the language (vss.1-3); Vāk favours few wise people, but a laggard wanders on in the profitless illusion (vss.4-6); the value of learning and duties of the four sacrificial priests (vss.7-11); vs.1 of this hymn is the inviting-verse for Bṛhaspati at the Devasū-offerings (*ĀŚS* 4.11).

In the *Ṛvidh*, this hymn is intended to secure the attainment of knowledge and good fortune (iii.71).

135. *RV* 10.73.11. In this verse, the sages implored Indra for dispelling darkness and releasing them from snares. In the Agniṣṭoma, this intercalatory Nivid-hymn is used at the Marutvatīya-śastra (*ĀŚS* 5.14). This verse is meant to expiate the sin of adopting a Vaiśya livelihood (*Svidh* 1.7.13).

Used by *Ṛvidh* (iii.72-74) in a charm for warding off misfortune and for attaining good fortune.

136. *RV* 10.82.7. In this verse, the creation of Viśvakarman is extolled. Not employed in any of the ritual texts of the *RV*.

In the *Ṛvidh*, this verse is intended to secure the attainment of Brahmā's world (ii.75).

137. *RV* 10.83-84. In these hymns, Manyu is invoked to aid the worshipper in conquering Ārya and Dāsa tribes, to chase foes, to slay them and to give their wealth. In the Ajira sacrifice, these intercalatory Nivid-hymns are employed for the sake of success in witchcraft (*ĀŚS* 9.7), and further in the one-day-sacrifices: Vinuti, Abhibhūti and Vajreṣu, these hymns are recited at the Marutvatīya-and Neṣkevalya-śastras (*ĀŚS* 9.8; cp. *ŚSS* 14.22.4-5). These hymns occur in *AV* 31-32 (transposed with few variants) and are used by *Kauś* (14.26ff) in the ceremonies for success in battle, etc.

In the *Ṛvidh* (iii.77-78), these hymns accompany the binding on of an amulet made of iron and are also used in a rite of sorcery for the death of one's rivals.

138. *RV* 10.85. According to the *Sarv* (x.85), vss.1-5 are addressed to Soma, vss.6-16 are a self-praise of Sūryā regarding her wedding; vs.17 is addressed to gods ; vs.18 to Soma and the Sun; vs.19 to the moon; vss.20-28 are marriage-mantras; vss.29-30 are intended to avert evil consequences arising out of touching a bride's garment; vs. 31 is directed against consumption; and finally vss.32-47 are addressed to Sūryā. In *ĀŚS*, vs.19 of this hymn is the offering-verse in the sacrifice to the moon (9.8); and further vs.24 accompanies the ungirding rite of the sacrificer's wife (1.11). In *ĀGS*, vs.26 is directed to be muttered when the bride mounts a chariot in the post-marriage ceremony (1.8.1); vs.27 is employed in connection with the bride's entering her new abode (1.8.8); vs. 32 is directed to be muttered when the bridal train starts off from home (1.8.6); vs.36 accompanies the seizing of bride's hand in the marriage ceremony (1.7.3; *ŚGS* 1.13.2); vss. 43-46 are used in a sacrifice to accompany the bride's stepping forward into the house (1.8.9); and vs.47 is used in the post-marriage ceremony when

the spouses eat the curds or when they anoint one another's hearts with the residue of an oblation (1.8.9).

A marriageable girl is made to hear the complete hymn in order to obtain a suitable husband (*Ṛvidh* iii.115cd-116ab); further vs. 45 is intended to attain a long life for both the spouses (iii.116cd-117ab); and further vs.46 is a charm to command respect from parents-in-law, brother-in-law-etc. (iii.118cd-119ab).

139. *RV* 10.86. According to the *Sarv* (x.86) this hymn is a dialogue between Indrāṇī and Indra who assumed the form of a Vṛṣākapi. On the sixth day of the Pṛṣṭhya ṣaḍaha this hymn is used at the Ukthya-śastra by the Brahmaṇāchaṁsin-priest (*ĀŚS* 8.3; *ŚŚS* 12.6.13ff).

Vss.1-9 of this hymn are used by *Ṛvidh* (iii.124cd-125) in the sprinkling ceremony of a bride, further the complete hymn (except vss.16-17) accompanies bridal bath (iii.119cd with 126cd) and finally vss.16-17 are used in a charm for restoring virile power (iii. 127ab).

140. *RV* 10.87. In this hymn, Agni it invoked to protect the worshipper from evil and to destroy demons, Yātudhānas, etc. (vss.1-15). This hymn (except vss.24-25), occurs in *AV* 8.3 and is reckoned by *Kauś* (8.25) to the Cātana hymns and is employed in the Vaśāśamana ceremony (44.16).

Used by *Ṛvidh* (iii.127cd-129ab) in a rite against Rakṣas.

141. *RV* 10.88. In this hymn, Agni is invoked to sustain the world, to drive away darkness, etc. and the rest of the hymn deals with the paths of fathers and gods and other matters of mystic import (vss.1-19). On the fifth day of the ten-day-period, this intercalatory Nivid-hymn for Agni Vaiśvānara is used at the Āgnimārutaśastra (*ĀŚS* 8.8; *ŚŚS* 10.6.19).

In the *Ṛvidh*, this hymn is meant to expiate the sin of eating forbidden food (iii.129cd-130) and is also intended to secure the attainment of supernormal power and Vaiśvānarī-vidyā (iii.131-132).

142. *RV* 10.89. In this hymn, Indra's deeds are recapitulated at first and he is invoked to aid the worshipper in battles, to slay the Vṛtra etc. (vss.1-18). In the one-day-sacrifice Sūryaśtut this intercalatory Nivid-hymn is used at the Neṣkevalyaśastra (*ĀŚS* 9.8; *ŚŚS* 14.24.4).

In the *Ṛvidh*, this hymn is intended to destroy enemies (iii.133).

143. *RV* 10.90. This hymn is addressed to Puruṣa, the Primordial Being, by sacrificing whom as a victim the world came into being (vss.1-16). Used by *ŚŚS* (16.13.1) in the Puruṣamedha. This hymn (except vs.16) occurs in *AV* 19.6 (with a different verse order) and is employed by *Vait* (37.19) in the Puruṣamedha to accompany the release of a human victim.

Used by *Ṛvidh* in a Kāmya-rite by one desiring progeny (iii. 134-148); in the Viṣṇu-worship (iii.149-173) and in one for obtaining the highest bliss and all benefits (iii.186-223).

144. *RV* 10.97. In this hymn, herbs are invoked to release the patient from disease, pain, grief, curse etc. and to subject the evil-doer to the worshipper's control (vss.1-23). This hymn accompanies the sprinkling of the consecrated persons (Dīkṣitas) in case they fall ill (*ĀŚS* 6.9). Vs.1 and 10 are respectively the inviting-and the offering-verses for herbs in the Anubandhyā-rite (*ŚŚS* 9.28.7).

Used by *Ṛvidh* as a benediction (iii.231), in a rite for curing diseases in general and diarrhoea (iv.1) and in one for obtaining herbs from an enemy's herbal field (iv.2-3).

145. *RV* 10.98. In this hymn, Bṛhaspati and other gods are invoked to send rain, to bestow lucid and vigorous speech on the worshipper etc. and Agni is invoked to drive away foes, troubles, etc. (vss.1-12). Not employed in any of the ritual texts of the *RV*.

Used by *Ṛvidh* (iv.4-5) in a rite for obtaining abundant rain.

146. *RV* 10.103. In this hymn, Indra's deeds are recapitulated side

by side with an invocation for aid and victory in battle (vss. 1-13). When the fire is being carried around, this hymn is recited by the Brahman-priest who accompanies it at the south-side (*ĀŚS* 1.12; 4.8). Most of the verses (except vss. 10 and 12-13) occur in *AV* 19.13. *Vait* designates it as "Apratiratha hymn" and directs the Brahman-priest to recite it (1.18). Used by *ĀGS* (3.12.13) in the Rājasaṁnāhana-rite.

*Ṛvidh* employs it in a battle-rite (iv.6-8) and further it is directed to be muttered at the benediction for the path (iv.9).

147. *RV* 10.106. In this hymn, the Aśvins are invoked to taste banquet, and to bestow vigour, kine, etc. on the worshipper (vss.1-11). In the Aptoryāma this hymn is used at the over-recital by the Acchāvāka-priest (*ĀŚS* 9.11).

Used by *Ṛvidh* (iv.10-16ab) in a ceremony for obtaining progeny.

148. *RV* 10.117. *Sarv* describes this hymn as follows: Na vā u bhikṣur dhanānnadānapraśaṁsā dve jagatyau. Not employed in any of the ritual texts of the *RV*.

*Ṛvidh* directs it to be muttered by one desiring food or release from sin (iv.16cd-18ab).

149. *RV* 10.125. *Sarv* (x.125) describes this hymn as follows: Aham aṣṭau vāgāṁbhṛṇī ātmānaṁ tuṣṭāva dvitiyā jagati. For a victim immolated to Vāk, vss.1-3 of this hymn are respectively the inviting-verses for the sacrifice of the omentum, of the cake, and of the animal offering (*ŚŚS* 6.11.11). It occurs in *AV* 4.30 and is used by *Kauś* in the Medhājanana rite; further in the same rite as forming part of the Upanayana ceremony (57.31), and finally in the Utsarjana ceremony (139.15).

Used by *Ṛvidh* (iv.18cd-19ab) in a Kāmya-rite by one desiring eloquence.

150. *RV* 10.126. In this hymn, the Viśve devās are invoked to

guard the worshipper, to help him in surmounting troubles, foes etc. (vss.1-8). Not employed in any of the ritual texts of the *RV*.

In the *Ṛvidh* intended to secure the attainment of the abode of the Viśve-devās (19cd-20ab).

151. *RV* 10.127. In this hymn, goddess Night is invoked to protect the worshipper from the wolf and the thief (vss.1-8). Used by *AĀ* (3.2.4) in a rite to avert evil dreams. For the victim immolated to the goddess Night, vss.1-3 are respectively the inviting-verse for the sacrifice of the omentum, of the cake, and of the animal offerings and vss.4-6 are the offering verses for the same occasion (*ŚŚS* 6.11.6). Used by *ŚGS* in a rite to ward of the evil consequences of bad dreams.

Used by *Ṛvidh* (iv.20cd-28) in an intricate rite for obtaining release from rebirth and sins.

152. *RV* 10.128. In this hymn, the Viśve-devas are invoked to assist the worshipper in battles, to bestow riches and freedom on him and to drive away his foes (vss.1-9). In the Saṁsava, this hymn is used at the Vaiśvadeva-śastra (*ĀŚS* 6.6; *ŚŚS* 13.5.17); further in the Samāvartana ceremony, it accompanies the laying of fuel by the prospective Snātaka (*ĀGS* 3.9.2) and further in the Brahmayajña, vs.1 of this hymn is used *ŚGS* 1.4.2). All verses of this hymn occur in *AV* 5.3 (with a different verse-order) and is variously employed by *Kauś* in the Parvan sacrifices (1.33); in rites for glory (12.10) and for prosperity (22.14), etc.

In the *Ṛvidh*, this hymn is intended to secure the attainment of all benefits (iv.29).

153. *RV* 10.129. In this hymn, the origin of this world as evolution of the existence from the non-existence is explained. Not employed. in any of the ritual texts of the *RV*.

In the *Ṛvidh*, this hymn is intended to secure the attainment of Prajāpati's abode (iv.44cd-45ab).

154. *RV* 10.137. In this hymn, the Viśvedevās are invoked to restore again to life the man who has committed sin, to drive away disease and to heal the diseased person (vss.1-7). In the Puruṣamedha this hymn with others is used by *ŚŚS* (16.13.4) in the healing ceremony of a sacrificer who has been instrumental to man-slaughter. All verses (except vs.6) occur in *AV* 4.13 and is used by *Kauś* (58.3.11) in the ceremonies for long life that follow the initiation of a Vedic student.
Used by *Ṛvidh* (iv.45cd-48) in a remedial rite against a disease.

155. *RV* 10.141. In this hymn, the Viśvedevās are invoked to bestow wealth on the worshipper, to aid him and to urge the donors to bestow their wealth on the worshipper (vss.1-6). Not employed in any of the ritual texts of the *RV*. But all verses occur in *AV* 3.20.2-7 and is used in *Kauś* in the Nirṛti-karma (18.13); again in the Agnyudvāsana (40.11); and with others in a rite for success in winning wealth.

Used by *Ṛvidh* in a Kāmya rite by one desiring wealth (iv.49-51) and with *RV* 1.50.13cd in a rite of sorcery to bring about the death of one's enemy in order to obtain his wealth (iv.52.53).

156. *RV* 10.142. In this hymn, Agni is invoked to keep away his destructive flame from the worshipper and to spare his house from conflagration (vss.1-8). Vs.7 is used in the Pavitreṣṭi (*ĀŚS* 2.12). Vss.7-8 of this hymn occur in *AV* 6.106.1-2 and is used by *Kauś* (52.5) in a rite for preventing conflagration of the house.

Used by *Ṛvidh* in a rite against fire (iv.54) and further vs.7 is directed to accompany the carrying of a continuous stream of water around the thing to be protected (iv.55-56ab).

157. *RV* 10.145. *Sarv* (x.145) designates this hymn as "Sapatnibādhana" i.e. a charm intended to get rid off a co-wife. Not employed in any of the ritual texts of the *RV*. But this hymn occurs in *AV* 3.18 and is used by *Kauś* (36.19-21) in a charm for outwitting a rival.

Used by *Ṛvidh* in a rite for getting rid of one's co-wife and for winning exclusive affection of the husband (iv.56cd-69ab).

158. *RV* 10.146. This hymn addressed to the goddess Araṇyānī unfolds the feelings of a person stranded in a darkening forest. Not employed in any of the ritual texts of the *RV*.

In the *Ṛvidh*, this hymn is intended to secure release from a wild forest (iv.59cd-70ab).

159. *RV* 10.151. In this hymn, the value of religious faith (Śraddhā) is extolled. Not used in any of the ritual texts of the *RV*.

*Ṛvidh* directs it to be muttered by one desiring Śraddhā (iv. 70cd); further it is used with *RV Kh* 4.8 in a rite for obtaining Religious faith, intelligence etc. (iv.71-75); and finally it accompanies the first feeding of a new-born infant (iv.96ab).

160. *RV* 10.152. In this hymn, Indra is invoked to drive away Rakṣasas, foes, etc. (vss.1-5). Used by *ĀGS* (3.12.13) in the Rājasaṁnāhana-rite. It is variously employed by *SGS*: in the Samāvartana ceremony (3.1.13) to accompany the mounting of a chariot; in the Utsarga ceremony (4.6.5) to accompany the homage to quarters by throwing mud-balls in four directions; and finally vs.1 accompanies the homage to eastern direction in the pacificatory rite (6.5.6). Verses of this hymn occur in *AV* 1.20.21 and are with *AV* 1.19 reckoned by *Kauś* (14.7) among the battle hymns.

*Rvidh* (iv.75cd-77ab) in a battle-rite for victory over a hostile army and for destroyingen emies.

161. *RV* 10.155. *Sarv* (x.155) designates this hymn as "Alakṣmīghnam". In this hymn Bṛhaspati is invoked to drive away malevolent she-fiends etc. (vss.1-5). Not employed in any of the rituals texts of the *RV*.

Used by *Ṛvidh* (iv.77cd-80) in a rite against misfortune.

162. *RV* 10.161. *Sarv* designates this hymn as "Rājayakṣmaghnam". In the Puruṣamedha, this hymn with others is used by

*ŚŚS* (16.13.4) in the healing ceremony of a sacrificer who has been instrumental in causing manslaughter. Used by *ĀGS* (3.6.4-5) in a rite for relief from disease, consumption etc. Verses of this hymn occur in *AV* 3.11 and 8.1.20 and are used by *Kauś* in a general healing ceremony (27.32-33); and in a rite for length of life (58.11).

*Ṛvidh* (iv. 81-85) employs it in a remedial rite against consumption.

163. *RV* 10.162. *Sarv* (x.162) designates this hymn as "Garbhaśrāve prāyaścittam". In this hymn, Agni is invoked to drive the evil malady that has attacked the womb in labour that which kills the baby at birth, and that which destroys the progeny. Used by *ŚGS* (1.21.2) in the Garbharakṣana-rite to accompany the offering of cooked rice-mess into the fire.

Used by the *Ṛvidh* in a remedial rite against abortion, still-births, etc. (iv.86-88) and in one for successful delivery of a male child in which the binding on of a triple amulet made of Nyagrodha-shoot accompanied by Svastyayana ceremonies is prescribed.

164. *RV* 10.163. *Sarv* (x.163) designates this hymn as "Yakṣmaghnam". In the Puruṣamedha, this hymn with others is used by *ŚŚS* (16.13.4) in the healing ceremony of a sacrificer who has been instrumental in causing manslaughter. Used by *ŚGS* (1.21.3) in the Garbharakṣaṇa rite to accompany the anointing of limbs with clarified butter. Most of the verses of this hymn occur in *AV* 2.33 and are used by *Kauś* (27.27) in a healing ceremony.

*Ṛvidh* (iv.98cd-101ab) employs it in a remedial rite against consumption.

165. *RV* 10.164. *Sarv* designates this hymn as "Duḥsvapnaghnam". Its broad contents are: the spirit of evil dreams is asked to depart and to vanish far away (vss.1-2); Agni and Bṛhaspati are respectively asked to drive all evil doings to dis-

tant places and to prevent the foes from troubling the worshipper (vss.3-4); evil thoughts are asked to take possession of a person who hates the worshipper (vs.5). Used by *ŚGS* in the Brahmayajña (1.4.2).

In the *Ṛvidh*, this hymn is intended to ward off evil dreams (iv. 101cd).

166. *RV* 10.165. *Sarv* (x.165) designates this hymn as "Kapotopahatau prāyaścittam". It is meant to expiate the pollution brought about by a dove, owl etc. (*ĀGS* 3.7.7; *ŚGS* 5.5.2). Verses of this hymn occur in *AV* 3.27-29 and are used by *Kauś* (46.7) in a rite against birds of ill omen.

*Ṛvidh* (iv.102) directs it to be muttered when a dove excretes on a house.

167. *RV* 10.166. *Sarv* (x.166) designates this hymn as "Sapatnaghnam". In this hymn, Vācaspati is invoked to put down foes and rivals and to help the worshipper in excelling others in thought and strength (vss.1-5). It is directed to be muttered whilst attacking an opponent in an assembly (*ĀGS* 2.6.13).

In the *Ṛvidh*, this hymn is intended to destroy rivals (iv.103ab).

168. *RV* 10.169. This hymn is addressed to the cows. Its broad contents are: Vāta, Rudra and Parjanya are respectively nvoked to send healing wind over the cows, to be gracious towards them and to vouchsafe protection to them (vss.1-2). Cows have offered their bodies to the gods (vs.3); Prajāpati is invoked to bestow auspicious cattle on the worshipper (vs.4). In *ĀGS* (2.10.5), vss.1-2 accompany the consecration of cows proceeding to pasture but in *ŚGS* (3.9.5), the complete hymn accompanies the consecration of cows proceeding to cowstall, and further in the latter work, the hymn is used in the Vṛṣotsarga ceremony (3.11.15).

Used by *Ṛvidh* (iv.104cd-105) in the Goṣṭhakarma to accompany the blessing ceremony for cows.

169. *RV* 10.173. In this hymn the king is asked to remain steadfast and to hold the kingship in tact (vss.1-4). Indra and Agni are asked to keep the realm steadfast (vss.5-6). Used by *ĀGS* (3.12.2) in the Rājasaṁnāhana rite when a king as about to mount a chariot. Verses of this hymn occur in *AV* 6.87-88 and are used by *Kauś* in a Kāmya rite by one desiring fixity (59-13); and in a rite of expiation for earth-quakes (98.3).

Used by *Ṛvidh* (iv.106-114) in the consecration ceremony of a king.

170. *RV* 10.177. *Sarv* (x.177) designates this hymn as "Māyābhedam". In the Pravargya-rite vss.1 & 3 of this hymn are used at the laud (*ĀŚS* 4.6) and vs. 2 is the inviting verse for the sacrifice of the cake to the victim immolated to Vāk (3.8). The complete hymn is used by *ŚŚS* in the Pravargya-rite (5. 9.14) and in the Viṣuvant (11.14.17).

In the *Ṛvidh*, this hymn is intended to destroy sorcery and illusions (iv.115-116).

171. *RV* 10.178. This hymn is addressed to Tārkṣya. On the second and the subsequent series of sacrificial days, this hymn is recited before the hymns belonging to the Niṣkevalyaśastra (*ĀŚS* 7.1) but in the Viṣuvant this hymn is recited at the end of the hymns belonging to the Niṣkevalya-śastra (8.6) (ŚŚS 11.14.28), however, inserts this hymn before *RV* 10.177 in the Viṣuvant. Vs.1 of this hymn which forms a single-versed hymn in *AV* 7.85 is reckoned to Svastyayana-gaṇa and is employed by *Kauś* (59.14) with *AV* 7.86 & 117 in a rite for general welfare. Used by *Svidh* among Kāmya-rites (2.1.5) and in one for attaining sovereignty over three worlds (3.9.3).

*Ṛvidh*, however, employs it in the blessing ceremony (iv.117ab).

172. *RV* 10.184. *Sarv* (x.184) designates this hymn as "Garbhārthāśīḥ". Vs.1 of this hymn is used by *ŚGS* (1.22.12) in the Sīmantonnayana ceremony. Vss.1-2 of this hymn occur in *AV* 5.25 and are used by *Kauś* (35.5) in the ceremony for conception of a male child.

In the *Ṛvidh*, this hymn is intended to ensure conception for a woman advanced in years (iv.117cd-118ab).

173. *RV* 10.185. In this hymn the Ādityas are invoked to bestow heavenly favour and eternal light on the worshipper (vss.1-3). Used by *ĀGS* (3.10.7-8) in the Sīmantonnayana ceremony but used by *Svidh* among the Kāmya-rites (2.1.5).

In the *Ṛvidh*, this hymn is directed to be muttered at the benediction for the path (iv.118cd).

174. *RV* 10.186-191. In hymn 186, Vāta is invoked to give strength and to prolong the days of his worshipper's existence (vss. 1-3). In the Puruṣamedha this hymn is used in the healing rite of the sacrificer who has been instrumental in causing manslaughter (*ŚŚS* 16.13.4). Used by *Svidh* (3.5.4) in a rite against various portents. In hymn 187, Agni is repeatedly invoked to overcome the worshipper's enemies (vss.1-7). This hymn as well as the next one constitute the Gāyatrī-portion of the Agni-section and are used at the Prātaranuvāka and Āśvina-śastra (*ĀŚS* 4.13) and further *ŚŚS* employs hymn 187 in the Āgnyupasthāna (4.2.10) and at the Prātaranuvāka (6.4.1).

In the *Ṛvidh*, hymn 187 is intended to do away with enmity (iv.119ab).

In hymn 188, Agni Jātavedas is invoked to promote the sacrifice (vss.1.3). For the ritual use of this see under the preceding. In hymn 189, Sūrya or Sārparājñī is referred to (vss.1-3). This hymn is used in the funeral ceremonies of a consecrated person (*ĀŚS* 6.10; *ŚŚS* 13.11.2.5). Found in *AV* 6.31 and is used by *Kauś* (66.14) in the Savayajñas.

*Ṛvidh* (iv.119cd) uses hymn 189 in a rite against serpents—an artificial application imposed upon the hymn.

In hymn 190, the creation is explained as emanating from Tapas (vss.1-3). Used by *ŚGS* (1.4.2) in the Brahmayajña.

*Ṛvidh* directs hymn 190 to be repeated at the beginning and end of all rites (i.16,55) and further it is intended to destroy all sins (iv.120-122ab).

In hymn 191, Agni is invoked to bring all good things and the subject of the rest of the hymn in unanimity (vss.1-4). Verses of this hymn occur in *AV* 6.63-64 and are used by *Kauś* (12.5) in a rite for harmony.

*Ṛvidh* (iv.123cd-124ab) uses hymn 191 in a rite for concord. Hymns 186-191 are directed to be muttered before the partaking of a meal (ii.165).

It is evident from the foregoing that the *Ṛvidh* presupposes the vulgate text of the *RV*, because of the overwhelming majority of the hymns of this Saṁhitā are quoted in Pratīkas. Now I shall take up the Khila hymns treated in the *Ṛvidh*. At the outset, I may state that the term Khila does not occur in the *Ṛvidh*, but there is every likelihood that the Khilas were regarded as simply Sūktas[22] or Ṛks[23] and that were not differentiated from the regular Sūktas or Ṛks of the *RV*. A definite position is, however, accorded to these Khila hymns in the text of the *RV*. Normally it is indicated in the Kashmir Khila collection by the appended Pratīka of the Ṛgvedic hymn which immediately follows. Of the total of twenty-six Khilas treated in our work, the eleven Sauparṇa-Khilas occur after *RV* 1.73; the Śrīsūkta and the Khila "Agniretu" occur at the end of the fifth Maṇḍala; the Khila "Śaṁvatīḥ" after *RV* 7.34; the Khila "Pāvamānīḥ" after *RV* 9.67; the remaining eleven being scattered through the latter half of the tenth Maṇḍala.

175. *RV Kh* i.2-12. Hymn 2 is addressed to the Aśvins and other deities and is ascribed to Suparṇa, son of Tārkṣa. Hymn 3 is also addressed to the Aśvins and is ascribed to two seers, Niṣat and Upaniṣat, sons of Brahmā. Hymn 4 is addressed to the Aśvins and other deities and is ascribed to Bharadvāja. Hymn 5 is addressed to the Aśvins and is ascribed to Kṛśa. Hymn 6 is addressed to Indra and Varuṇa (= RV 8.59). Hymn 7 is addressed to the Aśvins and is ascribed to Retṛ, son of Gaṅgā. Hymn 8 is addressed to the Aśvins and is ascribed to Yamunā's son. Hymn 9 is addressed to the Aśvins and is ascribed to Yajñavatsa. Hymn 10 is addressed to the Aśvins and is ascribed to Gauravīti. Hymn 11 is addressed to the Aśvins

22. *Ṛvidh*, i .106; ii.110; iii.110; iv.43, 71, 96.
23. *ibid.*, ii.93-94; 96-98, 100.

and is ascribed to Cākṣuṣī. Hymn 12 is addressed to the Aśvins and it ascribed to Apadoṣa. The patronomic of most of these seers is, of course, Suparṇa. The Pratīka: "*upa*" at the end of the hymn 12 indicates the relative position occupied by these hymns, to wit: between hymns 73 and 74 of the first Maṇḍala of the *RV*. Hymn 3 is used by *ĀGS* (3.12.14) in the Rājasaṁnāhana ceremony. Hymn 6 is reckoned among the Hotṛka-Śastras (*ĀŚS* 8.2; *ŚŚS* 12.11.17).

According to *Ṛvidh* (i.106) hymns 2-12 are intended to secure the attainment of sons, cattle, wealth, heaven and unimpaired eye sight.

176. *RV Kh*. ii.6. In this hymn, goddess Śrī is invoked to destroy misfortune and to bestow fame, wealth, etc. on the worshipper. Not employed in any of the ritual texts of the *RV*.

The complete hymn is used by *Ṛvidh* in a Kāmya-rite by one desiring fortune (ii.93-96ab; 103cd-109); further vs.3 is used in a rite for obtaining a kingdom (ii.98-99); vss.5-6, in one for obtaining eternal and everlasting fortune (ii.100-103ab); vs.7 accompanies the sprinkling ceremony of a king (ii.96cd); and finally vss.10 and 11 respectively used in a Kāmya-rite by one desiring cattle and progeny respectively (ii.97).

177. RV Kh ii.11. This hymn is addressed to Agni and Varuṇa and is ascribed to Jīvaputra. The Pratīka: Tvam hyagne prathamo manotā (*RV* 6.1.1) at the end of this hymn indicates that this hymn as well as the preceding one were inserted at the end of the fifth Maṇḍala. Used by *ĀGS* (1.13.6) in the Puṁsavana ceremony.

*Ṛvidh* employs it in a rite for obtaining excellent progeny (ii. 110).

178. *RV Kh* ii.13. The *Khilānukramaṇī* designates this hymn as "Śāntiḥ". The Pratīka: Śaṁ na indrāgnī bhavatām avobhiḥ (*RV* 7.35.1) at the end of this hymn indicates that it is inserted after *RV* 7.34.25. Not employed in any of the ritual texts of the *RV*.

Used by *Ṛvidh* with *RV* 7.35 as a charm against Rakṣas, Bhūtas, etc. (ii.133).

179. *RV Kh.* iii.10. This hymn is designated as "Pāvamānīstutiḥ" by the *Khilānukramaṇī.* The Pratīka: Pra devam acchā madhumanta (*RV* 9.68.1) at the end of this hymn indicates that it is inserted after *RV* 9.67.32.

This hymn is possibly used by *Ṛvidh* in a rite for obtaining release from sins (iii.15cd-17ab).

180. *RV Kh.* iii.15. This hymn which is addressed to the 'Viśvedevās is ascribed to Hṛdya, son of Prajāpati. The *Khilānukramaṇī* designates it as "Vivahārthāśiḥ". Vs. 1 of this hymn is used in the Upanayana ceremony (*ĀGS* 1.21.7; *ŚGS* 2.4.1).

Used by *Ṛvidh* in a long and intricate rite for bringing various types of individuals under one's control by making his image of sand, offering oblations over a metallic image, etc. (iii.79-97ab); again, in a healing rite for calf, kine etc. (iii.97cd-100ab); further in a rite to gain control over a woman by making an image of her with the rice-meal, anointing it with sesamum oil, piercing the various limbs of her image, etc. (iii.100cd-104) and finally in a charm for bringing a low woman under one's control (iii.105-110).

181. *RV Kh* iii.16. This hymn which is addressed to Agni is ascribed to Parākadāsa. The Pratīka: Satyenottabhitā bhūmiḥ (*RV* 10.85.1) indicates that this hymn as well as the preceding one were inserted after *RV* 10.84.7. Not employed in any of the ritual texts of the *RV.*

Used by *Ṛvidh* as a charm for bringing women and men under one's control (iii.111) and further with the text designated as Dveṣyam in a rite of sorcery against kinsmen and for death of one's enemies by making an image of sand or husk, piercing it with a Khādira-pin, fighting a mock-battle with it (iii.112-115ab).

182. *RV Kh* iv.5. The *Khilānukramaṇī* designates it as "Pratyaṅkṛtyānāśanam". Not employed in any of the ritual texts of the *RV.*

In the *Ṛvidh*, this hymn is intended to counteract witchcraft (iv.30-33); again, it is used in the blessing ceremony and in other ceremonies with which it has no apparent connection (iv.34-35); further in a rite against witchcraft in which preparation and binding of an amulet made of gold is prescribed (iv.36-37); it also accompanies the preparation and binding on of an amulet made of equal parts of five metals, the consecration of the tops of standards, musical instruments, etc. at the time of hostile encounters (iv.38-39); and finally it is intended to secure release from all misfortunes (iv.40-42).

183. *RV Kh* iv.6. The *Khilānukramaṇī* designates this hymn as "Hiraṇyātmastutiḥ" and ascribes it to Sanaka, Sanāka, etc. of Dakṣa's family. The Pratīka, "Nāsad āsīn no sad āsīt (*RV* 10.129.1) at the end of this hymn indicates that this hymn as well as the preceding one were inserted after *RV* 10.128.9. It accompanies the Samāvartana ceremony in which the binding on of an amulet is prescribed (*ĀGS* 3.8.21). *ŚGS*, however, employs the tying on of a gold necklace with it (3.1.7).

In the *Ṛvidh*, this hymn is intended to secure the attainment of long life, splendour, etc. (iv.43-44ab).

184. *RV Kh* iv.8. The *Khilānukramaṇī* ascribes it to Medhā, a daughter of Manu. The pratīka: Śāsa itthā mahāṁ asi (*RV* 10.152.1) at the end of *RV Kh* iv.9 indicates that this hymn as well as the next one were inserted after *RV* 10.151.5. The vs.2 of this hymn is used by *ĀGS* (1.15.2) in the Medhājanana ceremony to accompany the first feeding of a new-born infant.

*Ṛvidh* employs it with *RV* 10.151 in a rite for success in obtaining religious faith, intelligence, etc. (iv.71-75ab); and further it is used with *RV* 10.151 in the Medhājanana ceremony to accompany the first feeding of a new-born infant (iv. 96-98ab).

185. *RV Kh* iv.11. The *Khilānukramaṇī* designates this hymn as "Śivasaṁkalpa" and ascribes it to Manu's son. The Pratīka: Tubhyedam indra pariṣicyate madhu (*RV* 10.167.1) indicates that this hymn is inserted after *RV* 10.166.5. Not employed in any of the ritual texts of the *RV*.

In the *Ṛvidh,* this hymn is intended to secure the concentration of mind (*Ṛvidh* iv.103cd-104ab).

186. *RV Kh* iv.13. The *Khilānukramaṇī* ascribes it to Nejameṣa, a son of Prajāpati. The Pratīka: "mahī trīṇām avo'stu" (*RV* 10.185.1) indicates that this hymn is inserted after *RV* 10.184. 3. It is used in the Sīmantonnayana ceremony (*ĀGS* 1.14.3; *ŚGS* 1.22.7).

In the *Ṛvidh,* this hymn is intended to secure conception for a woman advanced in years (*Ṛvidh* iv.117cd-118ab).

187. *RV Kh* v.1. The *Khilānukramaṇī* ascribes this hymn (except vs.5) to Saṁjñāna, son of Kaśyapa. Possibly this hymn comes after the tenth maṇḍala.[24] Used by *ŚŚS* (3.6.3) in a rite for harmony when relations are in mutual disagreement; further vs. 5 of this hymn is used in the Upākarma (*ĀGS* 3.5.9; *ŚGS* 2.11.13).

In the *Ṛvidh,* this hymn is intended to being about reconciliation among kindred (iv.124cd-125ab); and further vs. 5 of this hymn is used in the blessing ceremony (iv.125cd).

188. *RV Kh* v.2. The *Khilānukramaṇī* describes it as 'Sapatnaghnaṁ senādāraṇam" and ascribes it to Nirhastya. According to *Ṛvidh* (iv.122) this hymn comes after Aghamaraṣaṇa's hymn (RV 10.190), but according to *BD* it is the fourth hymn from *RV* 10.190. See, however, under (187) and note. Not employed in any of the ritual texts of the *RV.*

Used by *Ṛvidh* (iv.122cd-123) as a charm for splitting an army.

24. *RV* (*VSM*), Vol. IV, p. 976 and the footnote. From the fact that the *BD* (viii. 93) treats of Saṁjñānam (*RV Kh* v. 1) immediately after *RV* 10.190 and the *Ṛvidh* (iv. 122) does likewise the hymn Nairhastyam (*RV Kh.* v. 2), one can rightly assume that the position of these hymns was not, at any time, fixed; but, in the case of the *BD*, the *Ṛgvedasaṁhitā* would have ended with the verse: Tacchaṁyorā (*RV Kh* v. 3.7), whereas in the case of the *Ṛvidh* it would have ended with the verse: Tachaṁyorā (*RV Kh* v. 1.5) with this difference viz. that the hymn Prādhvārāṇām (*RV Kh* v. 3), except the vs. 7, formed a part of the hymn Nairhastyam (*RV Kh* v. 2). Cp. Mātṛsūnu's commentary to *Ṛvidh* iv. 122. *Pro contra*, Macdonell *BD*, Part II, p. 320.

189. *RV Kh* v.4. *ĀŚS* (7.12) designates the first nine verses of this hymn as "Mahānāmnyaḥ" and the rest as "Puriṣapadāni". On the fifth day of the Abhiplava ṣaḍaha, the first nine verses are used as the Stotra-tristich when the Śākvarasāman is the Pṛṣṭha-stotra (*ĀŚS* 7.12).

According to the *Ṛvidh* the Mahānāmnī-verses mark the proper end of the *RV* and further they with the syllable oṁ, the Vyāhṛtis, and the first ten hymns (*RV* 1.1-10) constitute the Amṛtā saṁhitā by means of which immortailty is attained (iv.126, 127cd-129ab).

190. *RV Kh* v.22. According to the *Khilānukramaṇī* this hymn consists of ten verses and is described as "Hotṛpratigaritroḥ saṁvādaḥ" (cp. however, *ĀŚS* 8.3). *ŚŚS* designates these ten verses as "Āhanasyā ṛcaḥ" (12.24.1).

Used by *Ṛvidh* (iii.126ab) in the sprinkling ceremony of a bride who is likely to go astray.

The topics discussed in the third or the concluding part are not at all very important from any point of view as it is, more or less, a glorification of the work. We are told here that the syllable *oṁ*, the Vyāhṛtis, the first ten hymns of the *RV* and the Mahānāmnī-verses at the end constitute the Amṛtā-saṁhitā by means of which the gods attained immortality. By inserting hymns addressed to Fathers in the aforesaid collection we have the Pitryā saṁhitā and the likewise Vāsavī-Raudrī-Ādityā-and Vaiśvadevī-Saṁhitās can be compiled. This is followed by the procedure of the *Vāstuśamana* or *Vāstuśānti* which is to be performed every year in the midst of cow-stall with flowers, sandalwood paste, etc. and in which Vāstoṣpati and Bṛhaspati are to be worshipped with rice-mess boiled in milk and '*balis*' are to be offered to the eight presiding deities of quarters and sacrificial fees to priests. Then the threefold classification of Vedic deities and the means of pleasing them, the success in such matters being instantaneous in the case of Ṛṣis. Finally, the eulogy of the sacrificial fee and the work. The Phalaśruti which consists of thirteen stanzas extols the value of the *Ṛgvidhāna* and further recommends its recitation for pleasing the gods, for attaining powers and for destroying mental uneasiness.

## 2. *Analysis of the Subject matter*

In the preceding pages, I have dealt with the analysis of the contents of the *Ṛvidh* and incidentally I have discussed in detail the citations from the *RV* occurring therein. In the above analysis, it can be seen that the employment of the hymns of the *RV* in the *Ṛvidh* for the purposes shown therein has a broad justification. The hymns themselves do not seem to be primarily intended for these purposes. Their employment is arbitrary. I take up now the magical results obtained either by the recitation of the *Ṛgvedic* mantras or by the offering of a sacrifice to the accompaniment of mantras. As to the purpose to be attained by the magical charms or rites, it covers the field of possible desires: pacification, prosperity, long life, heaven, wealth, progeny and several others, most of which have been indicated by Śaunaka himself in the introductory part of the *Ṛvidh.* According to him the essence of the magical operation consists in Japa and Homa and to some extent in the practices of Yoga and of asceticism. In the Puruṣasūkta-vidhāna, for example, we come across an altogether different atmosphere from that of the *Ṛvidh* proper, though the former, as it is at present, forms a part of the latter work. The prominent features of the former are devotion and worship of a personal god. I describe now the essential features of the tenets of the *Ṛvidh.*

### 1. *Japa*

The *Ṛvidh* asks a twice-born person to engage himself with Japa (i.8ab) and he is further told that adversities can be surmounted by muttered prayers and burnt-oblations (i.91). The purificatory hymns or verses such as *RV* 1.89.6, 3.62.10, 5.51.11-15, 7.35, 8.95, 7-9, 9.1.67, 10.9 and 190 with the syllable *oṁ* and Vyāhṛtis are directed to be muttered at the beginning and end of all rites (i.15-17). Japa is to be performed sitting on a seat of Kuśa grass and the Japa prescribed in the case of commencement of Vedic study is the famous Gāyatrī (*RV* 3.62.10) with syllable *oṁ* and Vyāhṛtis i.59.61). Japa is of three kinds: *mandra* (uttered in a low tone), '*upāṁśu*' (inaudibly uttered) and '*mānasa*' (mentally revolved); each succeeding one being ten times superior to each preceding one (i.71). Further on, we are told the Gāyatrī verse must be muttered three hundred thousand times before performing any rite (ii.27-28). Subsisting on five products of a cow for one day, fasting the next day and eating the food offered by a Brāhmaṇa is Gāyatrījapa (ii.58). As a matter of fact the Japa plays an important part in the *Ṛvidh*, since almost all hymns or parts of hymns are directed to be muttered for the sake of some benefit or other and rarely does the *Ṛvidh* prescribe a sacrifice for the same purpose. The benefits which accrue by means of the Japa will be treated later on (p. 96 onwards), but at present I am concerned with those special benefits which are few in number to merit a separate treatment.

(1) The muttering of the first eleven hymns of the *RV* confers Saṁhitā-phala (i.67cd). (2) The muttering of the Gāyatrī verse whilst subsisting on the five products of a cow confers the recollection of previous births (ii.45cd). (3) A person becomes a *siddha*, if he subsists on curds, milk and ghee and mutteres the Gāyatrī verse two million and five hundred thousand times (ii.57). (4) The *RV* 6.48 is directed to be recited with grass in hand in order to attain the desired fruit of the hymn (ii.115). (5) The *RV* 8.101. 14 is directed to be muttered for the sake of release from rebirth (ii.186cd). (6) The recitation of *RV* 9.1-67, the recollection and the retention in memory of the same are considered meritorious and knowing them in reality one attains the highest abode of Brahmā. Among the preceding three, whatever is subsequent is more effective. By recitation one becomes pure, by recollection one remembers the highest and by retention in memory one attains oneness with Brahmā and remains in His abode (iii.2cd-5ab). (7) The muttering of *RV* 10.45 and 151 is prescribed for the sake of religious faith (iii.56; vi.70cd-71ab). (8) A person who considers himself as if covered by mental blankness or engrossed in the self with misfortune is asked to mutter *RV* 10.71.2 (iii.73). (9) The *RV Kh* iv.11 is directed to be muttered for the sake of mental ease (iv. 103cd-104ab). (10) The muttering of *RV* 10.177 destroys illusion (iv.115ab).

## 2. *Homa*

The *Ṛvidh* asks a twice- born person to engage himself with the Homa (i.8ab) and to surmount adversities by means of it (i.9d). As the Homa is necessary in some rites, few preliminary remarks are called for. These rites consist mainly of small sacrifices with simple ceremonial in which the offerings are usually rice-mess. The basis of the offering is *ājya*,[25] *ghṛta*,[26] or *sarpis*[27] i.e. melted and clarified butter and when no particular substance is specified the offering into the fire is to be clarified butter. But in the case of Ābhicārika and propitiatory rites, the use of mustard oil and oil of the Vibhītaka-wood is frequent. The number of *āhutis* may be 100, 1000 or as many as are expressly specified. All are similar in outline: the principal oblation (*sthālīpāka*[28] or *caru*)[29] is accompanied by the usual preliminary and terminal oblations of ghee offering (*ājyāhuti*).[30] The oblation is thrown into the fire as the verses of the *RV* are recited and the remains of the oblatory butter are collected in a vessel (*saṁpāta-bhājana*).[31] The method of offering an oblation is to repeat the Mantra, to put the oblation into the fire and to exclaim 'to such a such deity' with *svāhā*[32] at the end. The fire is maintained by means of logs, *samidhs*, and sometimes by means of cow-dung cakes.[33] The principal trees for *samidhs* are *aśvattha*,[34] *udumbara*,[35] *khādira*,[36] *palāśa*,[37] *bilva*,[38] *rohitaka*,[39] and *śamī*[40] but the *samidhs* of *rājavṛkṣa*,[41] *vibhītaka*[42] and *vyāghāta*[43] are used only in the Ābhicārika rites. The utensils are confined to two spoons:

25. i.85, 94, 98, 125, 129, 163; ii.93, 110, 119, 130, 154, 159, 175; iii.16, 55, 145; iv. 29, 79, 82, 86, 88, 98, 102.
26. i.116, 149; ii.23, 30, 45, 78, 169, 176, 179; iii.63, 66, 77, 89, 91, 172
27. ii.100, 102, 106, 142; iv. 49.
28. i.22, 25; ii.68, 95, 101; iii.26, 34; iv.11, 22.
29. i.81, 98, 163, 165; ii.74, 83-84, 142; iii.97, 134, 136-137, 169, 172, 214, 220, 222; iv.23, 25, 96.
30. i.25, 114, 166; iii.128, 129.
31. iv.83.
32. iii.37, 221.
33. ii.34; iv.105.
34. iii.144.
35. iii.63-64; iv.51.
36. ii.30, 32; iii.78, 112; iv.50, 84.
37. ii.31, 53; iv.51, 133.
38. ii.17, 53, 55, 100-101, 106-107, iii.85; iv.51-55.
39. iv.51.
40. ii.53.
41. ii.18.
42. ii.49; iii.50, 93; iv.52.
43. i.77.

one for dipping (*sruva*) and the other for offering (*sruk*), and a *camasa*, all of which are made of *udumbara* wood in the case of Kāmya rites, but in the case of Ābhicārika rites, the *sruk* is made of Vibhītaka wood (i.77). A slight modification to the ordinary ritual results in Abhicāra (i.75-78). Now let us examine these ceremonies and rites in which the Homa forms an integral part, leaving aside for the present those which are meant for Ābhicārika and propitiatory purposes.

(1) The offering of a *sthālīpāka* with preliminary and terminal oblations of ghee offering to Agni, Soma, Agni and Soma together Viśvedevās, Rudra, Avasānasya Pati, Anumati, Dhanvantari, the Gandharvas, the Apsarases, Brahmaṇaspati, Brahmā, Sarasvatī, Viṣṇu and Agni Sviṣṭakṛt is prescribed in a ceremony before the commencement of Vedic study (i.22cd-25ab). (2) A Homa must invariably be performed with Gāyatrī verse for the accomplishment of all objects of desire (i.74). (3) The offering of a *caru* dedicated to Agni with the oblation of clarified butter is prescribed in the Agnisādhana (i.82-83ab). (4) The oblations of *ājya* are offered by means of *RV* 1.18.6 for securing intelligence (i.85cd). (5) The oblations of clarified butter are offered by means of *RV* 1.35.2 for prolonging life (i.94). (6) The offering of a *caru* dedicated to Rudra with the oblations of *ājya* is prescribed in a rite for acquiring power (i.98). (7) The oblations of clarified butter are offered by means of *RV* 1.94 for prolonging life (i.144). (8) The oblations of ghee are offered by means of *RV* 1.97 for securing ritual purity (i.116). (9) The oblations of clarified butter are offered by means of *RV* 1.106 for securing release from sin (i.124cd-125ab). (10) The offering of *udumbara* fuel-sticks purified by curds, honey and *ājya* with the preliminary and terminal oblations of clarified butter to the accompaniment of *RV* 1.114.7, is prescribed in case of impurity of one's self perpetrated on heroicsons, grandsons, cow-stalls and evil dreams (i.128-129). (11) The offering of clarified butter by means of *RV* 1.189 is prescribed for a person who has lost his way or has committed an ignominous deed (i.148cd-149). (12) The offering of a *caru* boiled in milk with oblations of *ājya* by means of *RV* 2.32.4-8 is prescribed for the sake of progeny (i.163). (13) The offering of a *caru* with oblations of clarified butter by means of *RV* 2.33 is prescribed in a rite for conquering death and for securing release from diseases (i.164cd-167ab). (14)

The offering of ghee into the fire kindled with the *khādira* wood to the accompaniment of the Gāyatrī verse confers thousandfold gain (ii.30). (15) The offering of fuel-sticks of *palāśa* wood anointed with ghee to the accompaninment of the Gāyatri verse at the conjunction of Rāhu and Sūrya confers thousandfold gain (ii.31). (16) The offering of red sandalwood and ghee into the fire kindled with the *khādira* wood to the accompaniment of the Gāyatrī verse at the conjunction of Rāhu and Sūrya confers a thousand gold pieces (ii.32). (17) The offering of barley corns confers horses; sesamum seeds, elephants; barley meal, she-buffaloes; and the offering of *śāli* grains, a virgin wife (ii.35). (18) The offering of flowers and fuel-sticks of *jātī*, *caṁpaka*, *rājārka*, anointed with ghee to the accompaniment of the Gāyatrī verse confers clothes (ii.36). (19) The offering of water into the orb of the sun reflected in the water confers a thousand gold pieces and the same when offered into that of the moon confers silver pieces (ii.37). (20) The offering of food into the fire confers much food (ii.46cd). (21) The offering of *bilva* fuel-sticks anointed with ghee into the fire confers a fortune (ii.55). (22) The offering of a *caru* to the wives of gods by means of *RV* 5.46.7-8 is prescribed for the sake of progeny. The *caru* must be boiled in the milk of a cow having a calf of the same colour (ii.83-85ab). (23) The offering of a *sthālīpāka* into the fire kindled with *bilva* fuel-sticks is prescribed for a person desiring a fortune (ii.101). (24) The offering of oblations of clarified butter to the accompaniment of *RV Kh* ii.11 is prescribed for the sake of progeny (ii.110). (25) The offering of oblations of *ājya* to the accompaniment of *RV* 6.52.15 is prescribed for the sake of long life (ii.119). (26) A Homa with *RV* 6.74 is prescribed for the sake of securing release from Varuṇa's fetters (ii.126). (17) The offering of oblations of clarified butter into the fire to the accompaniment of *RV* 7.1. is prescribed for the sake of everlasting happiness (ii.130). (28) The offering of an oblation of rice boiled in milk in honour of Tryambaka Mahādeva to the accompanment of *RV* 7.59.12 is prescribed for the sake of long life (ii.142-143). (29) The offering of oblation of *ājya* into the accompaniment of *RV* 8.44 is prescribed for the sake of success and long life (ii.169cd-170ab). (30) The offering of oblations of ghee to the accompaniment of *RV* 8.71 is prescribed for the sake of wealth (ii.179cd-180ab). (31) The offering of a *sthālipāka* into the fire is prescribed in the expiatory rite for a Brāhmaṇa killer (iii.26). (32) The offering of a *sthālipāka* to Yama to the accompaniment of *RV* 10.14 is prescribed for the sake of long life (iii.34-36ab). (33) The offering of oblations of ghee at the cross-roads to the accompaniment of *RV* 10.61.1 is prescribed for one desiring food (iii.66). (34) The offering of a *Caru* to Viṣṇu to the accompaniment of *RV* 10.90 is laid down for the sake of progeny (iii.134-136). (35) The offering of rice-mess consisting of self-procured wild grain is prescribed for the sake of supernormal vision, countless objects of desire and long life (iii. 220.223). (36) The offering of a *sthālipāka* to Aśvins together with *pāyasa*, *kṛsara*, meat, porridge, curds, barley meal, sour gruel, dish of parched grains, fruits, garlands, fragrances and other foods and drinks is prescribed for the sake of progeny and for obtaining all objects of desire (iv.11-16ab).

### 3. *Pūjā*

In the beginning of this section I have referred to the atmosphere which prevails in the Puruṣasūktavidhāna (p. 87). Here we find the worship of Viṣṇu for the first time. Considering the fact that the whole of the Puruṣasūktavidhāna belongs to the later stratum of the *Ṛvidh*, it is not to be wondered if we find the worship of Viṣṇu described therein has its correspondence in the Purāṇic Hindu Religion.

Now let us see as to what our text has to say about the worship of Viṣṇu. The highest beatitude is attained by the performance of Viṣṇupūjā (iii.149). Hari is present in water, fire, heart, sun, altar and in idols. For the ritualists, Hari is present in fire; for the intellectuals, in the heaven; for the dull-witted ones, in idols; and for the yogins, in the heart. Since water is considered to be Hari's abode, He is always present in it and by reason of His omnipresence He is present in the altar. The whole universe consisting of movable and immovable beings is adored by him who offers flowers or water by means of *RV* 10.90, the deity of which is Puruṣa, the Ṛṣi Nārāyaṇa and the metre Anuṣṭubh (iii.150-154). With whatever object one mutters this hymn or performs a sacrifice, Japa and Naivedya that object becomes fulfilled. Superiority among kindred, wealth, fame, highest refuge and deliverance from sin are some of the objects which can be attained by means of *RV* 10.90 (iii.213-125). The wise regularly worship Hari by means of a burnt-offering into the fire, by means of offering flowers into the water, by means of meditation in the heart and by means of muttered prayers in the orb of the Sun. Hari is pleased with the offering of a *bilva*, *śamī*, *bhṛṅgāraka*, Jasmine, *Kuśa* and lotus. When anything is not readily available one must at least meditate on him for everything turns out well by the grace of Viṣṇu. All are asked to intensify their efforts for obtaining release from births and deaths (iii.226-229).

The *Ṛvidh* lays down the Pūjā first then Homa, Stotra and Japa. I shall take up these, one by one, in the following paragraphs.

After bathing one must face the east and perform the Aṅganyāsa with the sixteen verses of the *RV* 10.90 in the following way: One must direct the first verse towards the left hand; the second towards the right hand; the third towards the left foot; the fourth towards the right foot; the fifth towards the left knee; the sixth towards the right knee; the seventh towards the left hip; the eighth towards the right hip; the ninth towards the interior of the navel; the tenth towards the heart; the eleventh towards the throat; the twelfth towards the left arm; the thirteenth towards the right arm; the fourteenth towards the mouth; the fifteenth towards the eyes and the sixteenth towards the crown of the head. In the same manner, one must perform the Nyāsa on the deity and then commence the worship proper. One must adore the Puruṣottama with the *ṣoḍaśopacāra*, viz., *āvāhana, āsana, pādya, arghya, ācamanīya, snāna, vastra, yajñopavīta, anulepana, puṣpa, dhūpa, dīpa, naivedya, namaskāra, pradakṣiṇā* and *dakṣiṇā* with the sixteen verses of the *RV* 10.90. One must invariably offer water for sipping after *snāna*, *vastra* and *naivedya* and make an offering of hymn-recital to Him after muttering it (iii.155-167).

On the right side of the deity, one must prepare a Kuṇḍa or an altar whilst muttering the very first verse of the Puruṣasūkta (*RV* 10.90); sprinkle around it with water whilst muttering the second verse; deposit the fire whilst muttering the third verse; kindle it whilst muttering the fourth verse; heat the clarified butter and cook the rice-mess whilst muttering the fifth verse. Then one must meditate on the chief god amongst gods in the midst of fire and offer sandal wood paste, flower, incense, lighted lamp and food-offering. After taking leave of the principal deity, one must offer fuel-sticks sprinkled with clarified butter by means of the seventh and subsequent verses of the Puruṣasūkta (*RV* 10.90) and finally take leave of Agni (iii.168-173).

In the Stotra, Viṣṇu has been addressed as Puṇḍarīkākṣa and Hṛṣīkeśa and has been further declared to be the presiding deity common to gods and demons. He is the creator and the annihilator of the universe. The wise, on attaining His refuge, cross over the ocean of existence. There is no colour, nor form, nor abode for Him, though at times He appears in a human form. The devotee is afraid of Saṁsāra and hence requests Puṇḍarīkākṣa to protect him even in the future births and to give him the necessary discernment (iii.174-185). Towards the end, we have the well-known stanza Dhyeyaḥ sadā etc. addressed to Nārāyaṇa and we are told that whosoever recites this stanza attains the abode of Viṣṇu (iii.224-225).

The Puruṣasūkta is in itself the sacred knowledge of the Soul and the highest knowledge of Yoga. One must mutter it always and must subsist on fruits for one month, fast after eating fruits for another month and subsist on water for the next month: then one sees Self in the self (iii.187). One must remain in a forest, bathe thrice a day, worship the Sun with the Puruṣasūkta, offer oblations with it whilst subsisting on fruits: then one wins heaven within three years. Whoever absorbed in mind by that hymn worships Nārāyaṇa for twelve years, sees Him in person (iii.188-191). Finally one is asked not to lessen one's devotion to the Highest Person, even if one does not fully accomplish one's object (iii.219).

### 4. *Tapas*

The idea of Tapas permeates our work though not explicitly referred to always. We are told that the accomplishment of supernormal attainments are dependent on Tapas (i.4cd) and that a twice-born person should engage himself in Tapas (i.8c). As a matter of fact; all rites prosper only by Tapas and even heaven can be attained only by Tapas (i.10). A Brāhmaṇa who is devoted to Tapas becomes an ascetic in course of time (iii.212). Finally we are told that Tapas in itself is a great power (iv.42d).

## 5. *Yoga*

Asceticism has a certain efficacy, but it is by way of means. Only the knowledge of the godhead assures salvation and this is achieved by means of Yoga disciplines. The regulation of breath (Prāṇāyāma) plays an important part in the removal of blemishes (i.59) and we are told about the number of Prāṇāyamas that must be performed and the sacred text which must be muttered while performing it (i.56-58). The posture also plays an important part in these practices and one is asked to sit in a lotus posture (Padmāsana) whilst muttering the mystic syllable *oṁ* and to fix one's soul and sense-organs in the region of the heart (iii.194-196). One is asked to lead the mind gradually above the heart and fix it in the place between the eyebrows and finally one must cause it to go to the crown of the head which is declared to be the highest abode of Brahmā (iii.119-203). Further, we are told about the steady abstraction of mind and the mode of performing Dhāraṇā on objects like sun, fire, moon, tree-tops, mountain-tops and sea and the means of eliminating external obstacles. The Yogin finds the Highest Self in the crown of the head and the Highest Light there leads him from the crown of the head to the starry path. The Yogin on attaining Viṣṇu, the Lord of Yoga, becomes indifferent to the pairs of opposites (Dvandvas) and sees the Self everywhere (iii.206-210). These facts show that the Vedic tradition was gradually giving way to Yogic practices of varied kinds.

The subject-matter of the *Ṛvidh* is, broadly speaking, Atharvaṇic. By Atharvaṇic we mean those elements in which the desired result is brought about merely by the strength of a muttered prayer or spell and in some cases by a simple sacrifice consisting of an offering of oblation of Ājya, *caru*, fuel etc. into the fire with or without the accompaniment of Mantras. No valid reason appears as to why of all the Vedas, the *RV* was singled out for magical purposes. The following may, however, be stated. Dr. Shende has conclusively proved the important part played by the Bhṛgus and the Aṅgirases in the redaction of the *RV*, *Mahābhārata* and other works.[44] Śaunaka, being a Bhārgava, naturally wanted to pre-

44. (1) *Foundations of the Atharvanic Religion* in BDCRI, Vol. IX.
(2) *Atharvan in the Vedic and Epic Literature* in JUB, Vol. XVII, Pt. 2, pp. 23-44.

serve the traditional knowledge concerning the magical employment of the Ṛgvedic mantras for the sake of Ṛgvedins, who may like to employ its Mantras for obtaining various benefits without recoursing to the *AV* for that purpose. Dr. Shende further points out that "*RV* is not innocent of the magical practices."[45] It was hitherto believed that magic plays an inconspicuous role in the *RV*, since it consists almost entirely of hymns addressed to various deities in which their greatness and their deeds are extolled and all kinds of benefits are prayed for, though they are mainly intended to accompany the Soma sacrifice. About thirty hymns of the *RV* are not addressed to the gods or deified objects. A dozen hymns among these, occurring mostly in the tenth Maṇḍala are concerned with magic, about one half of them being auspicious, the rest maleficent in character. Thus the *Ṛvidh* which practically incorporates most of the hymns of the *RV*, does not radically depart from the Ṛgvedic religion and it emphasises the magical employment of the Ṛks. In this respect, tenets of the *RV* according to the *Ṛvidh* are similar to the *AV*. Now I may recapitulate the Atharvaṇic elements in the *Ṛvidh* following, as a rule, those indicated by Śaunaka himself in the introductory part of the work with such additions as are necessitated by the subject-matter.

### 6. *Charms or rites for bringing about pacification and general prosperity* (*Śāntipuṣṭikarmāṇi*)

These charms or rites are few in number. The Gāyatrī verse plays an important role in these rites (i.72).

(1) The muttering of the very first hymn of the *RV* bestows prosperity (i.66). (2) The pacification in respect of women, men and cattle is sought of Rudra by means of *RV* 1.43 (1.97). (3) The muttering of *RV* 1.112 bestows prosperity (i.125cd-126). (4) The impurity of one's self perpetrated on heroic sons, grandsons and cowpen is removed by means of an offering of *udumbara* fuel-sticks sanctified by curds, honey and clarified butter to the accompaniment of *RV* 1.114 (i.129). (5) The muttering of *RV* 2.12, a hundred times, is prescribed for the sake of prosperity (i.158c).

---

(3) *The authorship of the Mbh* in ABORI, Vol. XXIV, pp. 67-82.

(4) *The authorship of the Rāmāyaṇa* in JUB, Vol. XII, Pt. 2.

45. *Religion and Philosophy of the Atharvaveda*, p. 2.

(6) The muttering of *RV* 2.23 bestows prosperity (i.159cd). (7) The pacification of planetary influences is brought about by the muttering of the Gāyatrī verse (ii.62). (8) The mental recollection of *RV* 10.20.1 confers pacification and mental ease (iii.45). (9) The pacification and ease is brought about by the ritual employment of *RV Kh* iii.15 (iii.88ab). (10) A prosperity-rite by means of *RV Kh* iii.15 is laid down (iii.96cd). (11) *RV* 10.87 is employed in a pacificatory rite (iii.129). (12) *RV* 10.103 is considered to be a pacificatory hymn and is to be employed while marching against an enemy or a country (iv.6). (13) The offering of a thousand fuel-sticks of *khādira*, *bilva*, *udumbara*, *palāśa* and *rohitaka* trees to the accompaniment of *RV* 10.141 is prescribed for the sake of prosperity (iv.50-51). (14) The muttering of *RV* 10.141 bestows prosperity (iv.53cd).

### 7. *Charms or rites for securing long life (Āyuṣyāṇi)*

As is well known, the *Ṛvidh* aims at securing full enjoyment of life extending a hundred years without any disease or distress. In order to attain this ideal, the *Ṛvidh* prescribes a simple ceremonial consisting of an offering of oblations of clarified butter into the fire or an offering of a *sthālīpāka* into the fire to the accompaniment of Mantras.

(1) The muttering of the first eleven hymns of the *RV* (1.1-11) confers long life on a person who fasts and keeps other observances (i.69cd). (2) The water charmed with *RV* 1.23.16-24 when sprinkled over a person confers long life (i.89c). (3) The offering of oblations of clarified butter to the accompaniment of *RV* 1.35.2 confers long life (i.94). (4) The muttering of *RV* 1.50.13 confers long life (i.103cd-104c). (5) The recitation of the eleven Suparṇa hymns (*RV Kh* i.2-12) confers long life (i.106c). (6) The muttering of *RV* 1.89 confers long life (i.108). (7) The offering of oblations of clarified butter to the accompaniment of *RV* 1.94 confers long life (i.114). (8) The muttering of *RV* 1.114-115; 154.1-3 confers long life (i.127c, 132d, 137b). (9) The muttering of *RV* 2.12 a hundred times confers longevity (i.157c). (10) The muttering of *RV* 3.53 confers long life (ii.11cd). (11) The muttering of the Gāyatrī verse a thousand times confers long life (ii.29c). (12) The worship of Vahni with *RV* 5.24 prolongs life (ii.81). (13) The muttering and offering of oblations of Ājya to the

accompaniment of *RV* 6.52.15 is prescribed for the sake of long life (ii.119). (14) The offering of Ājya to the accompaniment of *RV* 7.1 confers long life (ii.130). (15) The worship of Vajrin with *RV* 7.32.22-23 prolongs life (ii.132). (16) The worship of the Tryambaka Mahādeva with *RV* 7.59.12 prolongs life (ii.142-143). (17) The worship of Divākara with *RV* 7.66.16 prolongs life (ii. 144). (18) The offering of Ājya to the accompaniment of *RV* 8.44 is prescribed for prolonging life (ii.169cd-170ab). (19) The muttering of *RV* 8.48.4-5, whilst touching the heart, is prescribed for the sake of long life (ii.73cd-174ab). (20) The muttering of *RV* 9.1-67 confers long life (iii.9c). (21) The offering of a *sthālīpāka* to Yama by means of *RV* 10.14 is prescribed for the sake of long life (iii.34-36ab). (22) The muttering of *RV* 10.18 is prescribed for a person, who remains abstemonious and keeps certain observances in order to conquer death and to obtain release from diseases (iii.39-42). (23) The muttering of *RV* 10.58, a thousand times, is to be undertaken for the sake of rescuing a friend whose life is coming to a close, and further he must be anointed with ghee to the accompaniment of *RV* 10.9 (iii.58-59). (24) The muttering of *RV Kh* iv. 6 confers long life (iv.43ab). (25) The decoction of Śaṅkhapuṣpī, Brāhmī flowers, Śatāvarī and Vacā duly consecrated with *RV* 10.151 and *RV Kh* iv. 8 confers long life (iv.72cd-74).

### 8. *Charms or rites for securing Heaven or Highest Abode*

As is well known, the numerous sacrifices detailed in the Brāhmaṇas aim at securing Heaven. But here a mere muttering of some hymn with or without an offering of oblations of clarified butter brings about the desired result.

(1) Heaven is attained by the recitation of *RV Kh* i.2-12 (i.106d). (2) The Highest Abode is attained by the muttering of *RV* 1.84. 16-18 (i.107). (3) The world of Candra is attained by the muttering of *RV* 1.91 (i.112). (4) The Highest Abode is attained by the muttering of *RV*.1.154.1-3 (i.137cd). (5) The Abode of Indra is attained by the muttering of *RV* 2.12 (i.159b). (6) The Highest Abode is attained by the offering of a hundred thousand oblations of barley corn anointed with ghee to the accompaniment of the Gāyatrī-verse (ii.44). (7) The Abode of Brahmā is attained by the muttering of *RV* 4.40.5 (ii.67). (8) The muttering of *RV* 9.112-

114, when one's death is near is prescribed for the sake of attaining Highest Abode and immortality (iii.18cd-19ab). (9) The muttering of *RV* 10.63 is prescribed for the sake of attaining Heaven (iii.70cd). (10) The Abode of Brahmā is attained by the muttering of *RV* 10.82.7 (iii.75). (11) The Abode of Viṣṇu is attained by the offering of rice-mess boiled in milk on every twelfth lunar day for one year (iii.137). (12) Heaven is attained by the muttering of *RV* 10.90 (iii.186). (13) The Abode of Prajāpati is attained by the muttering of *RV* 10.129 (iv.44cd-45ab).

### 9. *Charms or rites for securing wealth, fortune and glory*

These are quite numerous and do not call for any special remark.

(1) The muttering of the first eleven hymns of *RV* confers *dhanam* (i.69c). (2) The recitation of the eleven Sauparṇa hymns (*RV Kh.* i.2-12) confers *vittam* (i.106c). (3) The muttering of *RV* 1.92, 114-15, 154.1-3, 190 confers *dhanam* (i.113, 127c, 132, 137a, 151d). (4) The muttering of *RV* 2.12 confers *vittam* (i.157a). (5) The muttering of *RV* 3.53 confers *draviṇam* (ii.11cd). (6) The muttering of the Gāyatrī verse, a thousand times confers *dhanam* (ii.29cd). (7) The offering of five products of a cow into the fire to the accompaniment of the Gāyatrī verse confers *dhanam* (ii. 46ab). (8) The muttering of the Gāyatrī verse three thousand times is prescribed for the sake of *dhanaiśvaryam* (ii.52). (9) The offering of flowers and fuel-sticks of *śāmī*, *bilva*, *palāśa* and *arka* to the accompaniment of the Gāyatrī verse is prescribed for the sake of getting *haimam* (ii.53). (10) The muttering of *RV* 5.2.9 is prescribed for the sake of getting *draviṇam* (ii.79). (11) The worship of Vahni with *RV* 5.24 is prescribed for the sake of obtaining *dhanam* (ii.81). (12) The offering of one hundred thousand oblations confers boundless fortune (ii.102ab). (13) The offering of white victuals a hundred times ten thousand confers boundless, uninterrupted and eternal fortune (ii.102cd-103ab). (14) The worship of Śatakratu with *RV* 6.46 is prescribed for the sake of obtaining *dhanam* (ii.113). (15) The muttering of *RV* 6.53; 7.5-7 confers *dhanam* (ii.120, 131). (16) The worship of Vajrin with *RV* 7.32.22-23 is prescribed for the sake of obtaining *dhanam* (ii. 132). (17) The muttering of *RV* 7.46 confers *vittam* (ii.135). (18) The worship of Uṣas with *RV* 7.78-80 is prescribed for the sake

of obtaining manifold wealth (ii.145-146). (19) The muttering of *RV* 8.35 confers (*draviṇam* (ii.169ab). (20) The offering of ghee into the fire to the accompaniment of *RV* 8.71 confers wealth (ii.179cd-180ab). (21) The worship of Puraṁdara with *RV* 8.81 is prescribed for the sake of obtaining *dhanam* (ii.180cd-181ab). (22) The muttering of *RV* 9.1-67 confers wealth((iii.9c). (23) The muttering of *RV* 10.71 and especially verse 2 of that hymn is prescribed for the sake of obtaining boundless fortune ((iii.71-72). Further, the wiping of eyes whilst muttering this verse is also prescribed for the same purpose (iii.74). (24) The muttering of *RV Kh* iv.6 is prescribed for the sake of obtaining ornaments and gold (iv.43). (25) The muttering of *RV* 10.141 is prescribed for the sake of obtaining *dhanam* (iv.49).

### 10. *Charms or rites for securing progeny*

The rites for conception, safe delivery, etc., are treated in the sub-section 19 on rites pertaining to women (Strīkarmāṇi).

(1) The muttering of the first eleven hymns of the *RV* confers sons (i.69c). (2) The recitation of eleven Suparṇa hymns (*RV Kh* i.2-12) confers sons (i.106c). (3) The muttering of *RV* 1.114,154. 1-3 confers sons (i.127c, 137a). (4) The muttering of *RV* 1.190 confers heroic sons (i.151a). (5) The worship of wives of gods with *RV* 5.46.7-8 is prescribed for securing progeny (ii.83-85ab). (6) *RV Kh* ii.6.11 is prescribed in the sprinkling ceremony of a person desiring progeny (ii.97cd). (7) The offering of oblations of clarified butter to the accompaniment of *RV Kh* ii.11 is prescribed for securing progeny (ii.110). (8) The offering of oblations of clarified butter to the accompaniment of *RV* 7.1 is prescribed for securing sons (ii.130). (9) The muttering of *RV* 7.46 confers progeny (ii.135). (10) The muttering of *RV* 9.1-67 confers progeny (iii. 9d). (11) The offering of a *sthālīpāka* to Viṣṇu to the accompaniment of *RV* 10.90 confers a son who is devoted to Viṣṇu and who is fit for lineage. Then follows a list of names: Keśava, Nārāyaṇa, Mādhava, Govinda, Viṣṇu, Madhusūdana, Trivikrama, Vāmana, Śrīdhara, Hṛṣīkeśa, Padmanābha and Dāmodara which are assigned to each of the twelve months from Mārgaśīrṣa to Kārttika and which must be muttered for obtaining all objects of desire including a long-lived son. Then a burnt-offering with preliminary and terminal oblations of ghee is offered. A woman is asked

to partake of the residue before cohabiting with her husband. Then the feeding of Brāhmaṇas. This rite ensures a male child (iii.134-138).

11. *Charms or rites to obtain special wishes* (*Kāmyāni*)

Many of these are not specified but are referred to in a general way. I have included at the end some objects which are not covered by any subject-headings.

(a) *Objects of desire in general*

(1) The muttering of the first eleven hymns of the *RV* confers all desires (i.68). (2) The worship of Indra with *RV* 1.28-29 is prescribed for the sake of obtaining permanent benefits (i.91). (3) The muttering of *RV* 1.105 is prescribed for a person desiring all objects of desire (i.124ab). (4) The muttering of *RV* 1.139.1; 179.5-6 confers all desires (i.135cd, 144). (5) The worship of Bṛhaspati with *RV* 2.23 is prescribed for the sake of fulfillment of all objects of desire (i.160-161ab). (6) The muttering of *RV* 3.55 confers all favourite objects of desire (ii.21). (7) The offering of one hundred thousand oblations of ghee confers all desires (ii. 45ab.) (8) The muttering of *RV* 6.69 confers all favourite objects of desire (ii.123). (9) The muttering of *RV* 8.34.16-18 confers all conceivable objects of desire (ii.164). (10) The muttering of *RV* 1.1-3; 7-1; 8.32-45; 10.1-5, 186-191 is prescribed for the sake of obtaining all desires (ii.165-66). (11) The muttering of *RV* 8.70. 5-6 confers all desires (ii.178cd-179ab). (12) The Puruṣa-sūkta (*RV* 10.90) confers all objects of desire (iii.127). (13) The muttering of *RV* 10.103 is prescribed for the sake of fulfillment of all objects of desire (iv.7cd). (14) The muttering of *RV* 10.128 confers all objects of desire (iv.29).

(b) *Other objects of desire*

(1) The muttering of *RV* 10.117 is prescribed for the sake of obtaining *annam* everywhere (iv.16cd-17ab). (2) The recitation of *RV* 7.41 is prescribed for settling in life (ii.134). (3) The offering of rice-mess with clarified butter to the accompaniment of *RV* 1.43 is prescribed for the sake of obtaining *bhūti* (i.98). (4) The muttering of the Gāyatrī verse a thousand times confers *bhūti* (ii.29c). (5) The offering of oblations of clarified butter to

the accompaniment of *RV* 7.99-100 is prescribed for the sake of obtaining *bhūti* (ii.154). (6) The muttering of *RV* 1.22.15 confers Bhūmi (i.86). (7) The offering of oblations of clarified butter to the accompaniment of *RV* 1.18.6 is prescribed for a person desiring *medhā* (i.85). (8) The muttering of the Gāyatrī verse whilst subsisting on ghee confers *medhā* consisting of much understanding (ii.40cd). (9) The muttering of Medhā-sūkta (*RV Kh* iv.8) confers *medhā* (iv.71b, 74a). (10) The muttering of *RV* 8.101.6 is prescribed for the sake of graceful speech (ii.187cd). (11) The muttering of *RV* 10.125 is prescribed for the sake of eloquence (iv.18cd-19ab). (12) The muttering of the first eleven hymns of the *RV* confers *vidyā* (i.69c). (13) The muttering of *RV* 1.114 confers *vidyā* (i.127c). (14) The muttering of *RV* 3.53.15-16 is prescribed for the sake of acquiring *vidyā* (ii.12-13). (15) The muttering of *RV* 10.71 is prescribed for the sake of knowledge (iii.71). (16) The muttering of *RV* 2.12, a hundred times, is prescribed for the sake of obtaining *siddhi* (i.157b). (17) The offering of one hundred thousand oblations of sesamum seeds anointed with ghee to the accompaniment of the Gāyatrī verse confers *siddhi* (ii.43). (18) *Siddhi* can also be attained by eating *bilvas*, making a shelter under *bilva* trees and offering *bilva* fuel-sticks anointed with ghee into the fire (ii.106). (19) The muttering of *RV* 10.151 and *RV Kh* iv.8 confers *siddhi* (iv.71cd-72ab). (20) The decoction of *śaṅkhapuṣpī*, *brāhmī* flowers, *śatāvarī* and *vacā* confers *siddhi* (iv.72cd-74).

### 12. *Charms or rites for securing prosperity to agriculture and cattle* (*Kṛṣigopuṣṭikarmāṇi*)

Strictly speaking, agriculture and rearing cattle fall to the lot of Vaiśyas, but even Brāhmaṇas are allowed to take up these occupations in times of distress.

(1) A farmer is asked to prepare a *sthālīpāka* and to offer oblations to the following deities, viz., Indra, Maruts, Parjanya, Bhaga, Pūṣan, Dhānya, Sītā, and Śunāsīra by means of *RV* 4.57.4-8. He must further honour them with sandalwood paste, garlands, food offerings, fruits, parched grain and spirituous liquors at the sowing and mowing times. Then his cultivation prospers (ii.68-72). The muttering of *RV* 4.57.1-3 confers a pre-eminent field (ii.73). The offering of rice-mess to the king of moles to the accompaniment of *RV* 8.21.18 and feeding of Brāhmaṇas and others are prescribed

(ii.74-75). Sins committed while breaking the soil, etc. are absolved by the gift of a granary. One-twentieth part of the total grain harvested is to be offered to the *śrotriya* for obtaining release from the guilt of ploughing the earth (ii.76-77).

(2) The offering of cow-dung ball mixed with red sandalwood pieces and ghee to the accompaniment of the Gāyatrī verse confers wealth consisting of cows (ii.33). The worship of cows with *RV* 6.28 is prescribed evidently for multiplying the number of cows (ii.112). The muttering of *RV* 8.101.15 is prescribed for the sake of obtaining cows (ii.187ab). *RV* 10.169 is directed to be muttered at the blessing ceremony of cows (iv.104cd).

### 13. *Domestic rites* (*Gṛhyāṇi*)

In addition to the numerous charms and rites described above, we have some ceremonies or rites which later on came to be associated with Saṁskāras and daily duties of a pious Hindu. We find in our work a reference to the Pañcamahāyajñas (i.135ab) and the Vaiśvadeva-rite is specially referred to (ii.138). In all these ceremonies, *dakṣiṇā* must invariably be given to Brāhmaṇas since no ceremony is complete without it (iv.138cd-140).

#### (a) *Sprinkling and Svastyayana ceremonies*

*RV* 1.23.16-24 and *RV* 10.9 are regarded as verses which are to be muttered at the sprinkling ceremony (i.89ab; iii.19cd-20). The following hymns or parts of hymns are to be muttered at the *svastyayana* ceremony: *RV* 1.99 (i.117cd, 121-122ab); *RV* 4.31 (ii.66); *RV* 5.50-51 (ii.85cd-86ab); *RV* 10.35-36 (iii.54ab); *RV* 10.63 (iii.70ab); *RV* 10.97 (iii.231); *RV Kh* iv.5 (iv.34ab); *RV* 10.178 (iv.117ab) and *RV Kh* v.1.5=V.3.7 (iv.125cd).

#### (b) *Rite for begetting wisdom* (*medhājanana*)

Before the breast-feeding one must cause a child to swallow an oblation consisting of rice-meal mixed with honey and rubbed with gold to the accompaniment of *RV* 10.151 and *RV Kh* iv.8: then that child becomes intelligent, lives for hundred years and acquires the faculty of memory after six months. In order to free that child from consumption one must offer oblations of clarified butter to the accompaniment of *RV* 10.163 and touch the head, ears, eyes, chin and two nostrils with ghee (iv.96-100ab).

(c) *Charms or rites for securing welfare on journey and while crossing rivers*

The following hymns or parts of hymns are directed to be muttered while setting out on journey: *RV* 1.35.11 (i.95); *RV* 1.42 (i.96); *RV* 1.99 (i.120); *RV* 5.51.15 (ii.86cd-87ab); *RV* 6.51.16 (ii.118); and *RV* 10.57 (iii.57). In order to return home successfully, the muttering or the recollection of the following viz., *RV* 2.42-43 (ii.1-2); *RV* 3.45 (ii.9cd-10ab); and *RV* 3.53.17-20 (ii.14) is prescribed. If the axle is broken then in order to remedy it, the muttering of *RV* 3.53.19-20 is prescribed (ii.15). If one loses one's way, the muttering of *RV* 6.54 is prescribed (ii.121). In order to regain the correct path, one is asked to worship Anala and to offer oblations of clarified butter to the accompaniment of *RV* 1.189 (i.148cd-150ab). Further *RV* 10.103 is directed to be muttered for the sake of protection from robbers, evil beings and snakes (iv.9). Finally the muttering of *RV* 10.185 is considered to be a benediction for the path (iv.118cd).

A person intending to cross a river must mutter *RV* 3.33 after throwing a handful of water into the river (ii.4). If the river is swollen, one must mutter *RV* 3.33.5 (ii.7ab). In order to reach the other shore quickly or to get a ford, *RV* 3.33.9 is directed to be muttered (ii.7cd-8ab). A person desirous of crossing a river with chariot must mutter *RV* 3.33.1 (ii.8cd-9ab). Whilst crossing a river one must mutter *RV* 7.49 at the confluence of streams (ii. 136).

(d) *Marriage*

A father is asked to relate *RV* 10.85—which consists of nine sections and which bestows an affable husband and children—to his girl in order to win a suitable husband for her (iii.115cd-116ab, 120ab). A girl is asked to mutter *RV* 10.85.45 whilst touching her navel (iii.116cd). A brother or a father is asked to sprinkle the girl by means of the befitting Mantras culled from *RV* 10.85 in order that she may bear ten sons, etc. (iii.117cd-118ab). A girl will be honoured by her parents-in-law, brothers-in-law and sisters-in-law if *RV* 10.85.46 is muttered while touching her head (iii.118cd-119ab). At the bridal bath, *RV* 10.86.16-17 is to be employed (iii.119cd) A sacrifice is to be performed for Soma, the Gandharvas, Vahni, Bhaga, the Apsarases, Lord of

Yakṣas, Indrāṇī, the wives of gods, Ratī and Pradyumna at a place endowed with aquatic plants (iii.120cd-122ab). In that place the girl must be sprinkled with the decoction of Priyaṅgu, Vaṭa and other fragrant substances and with water kept overnight in order to obviate the effect of evil signs in her body. If she is likely to consorting with others then she is made to bathe whilst muttering *RV Kh* v.22 (iii.122cd-126ab), and *RV.* 10.86.16-17.

(e) *Rite connected with the building of a house*

*RV Kh* iv.5 is directed to be muttered at the time of establishing a real estate, towns, villages and houses (iv.35). A house-holder is asked to perform *vāstuśamana* in the midst of cowpen. He is further asked to scatter flowers, sandalwood paste, garlands, fruits, herbs with seven kinds of grains on the floor of the house. A sacrifice must be offered to Vāstoṣpati and Bṛhaspati with *pāyasa* and with fuel-sticks of *udumbara* and *palāśa* trees. A *bali* must be offered in every direction. A donation must be given to Brāhmaṇas for the sake of well-being in one's house. This rite must be repeated every year (iv.131cd-135).

(f) *Śrāddha*

Whilst plunging the thumb into the food, one is asked to mutter *RV* 1.22.17-21 in order to drive away demons (i.87). The muttering of *RV* 1.90.6-8 at the *śrāddha* is prescribed (i.109). Further on, at the *Pitṛkarma*, the muttering of *RV* 9.1-67 is prescribed for the sake of pleasing the manes (iii.6cd, 8ab).

### 14. *Charms or rites for expiation and release from distress and misfortune*

It will be noticed in sequel that the *Ṛvidh* contains a number of expiatory rites which formed a regular feature of the later Dharma-śāstras.

(a) *Expiations for sins in general*

(1) The muttering of the first eleven hymns of the *RV* is prescribed for the sake of release from all sins (i.68cd). (2) In order to get release from sins, a sprinkling by means of *RV* 1.23.16-24 is prescribed (i.89d). (3) The muttering of *RV* 1.91 is prescribed for the sake of release from misery (i.110-111). (4) The offering

of fuel-sticks to the accompaniment of *RV* 1.97 is laid down for the sake of obtaining release from sins (i.116). (5) The offering of oblations of clarified butter to the accompaniment of *RV* 1.106 is prescribed for the sake of obtaining release from sins (i.124cd-125ab). (6) The muttering of *RV* 1.115 whilst holding fuel-sticks in hand is prescribed for the sake of removing infirmity (i.131-132). (7) The water charmed with the mutterings of the Gāyatrī verse a thousand times, has the power to remove sins (ii.38). (8) The muttering of the Gāyatrī verse a hundred times, while taking a bath, a hundred more while immersed in water and another hundred while sipping water, is prescribed for the sake of release from all sins (ii.59). (9) The muttering of *RV* 6.74 is prescribed for obtaining release from sins (ii.125). (10) The muttering of *RV* 9.1-67 frees one from sins (iii.1-2ab). (11) The muttering of *RV Kh* iii.10 is prescribed for the sake of release from infirmity (iii.15cd). (12) In order to get release from sins, a sprinkling by means of *RV* 10.9 both in the morning and evening is prescribed (iii.32-33). (13) The offering of oblations of clarified butter to the accompaniment of *RV* 10.37.12 is prescribed for the sake of release from sins (iii.55). (14) The muttering of *RV* 10.88, 90 and 117 frees one from sins (iii.132cd, 205, 211, iv.17cd-18ab). (15) The muttering of *RV* 10.126 is prescribed for the sake of destroying all taints (iv.19cd-20ab). (16) The muttering of *RV* 10.127 destroys all sins (iv.28). (17) The muttering of *RV* 10.155 is prescribed for the sake of removing misfortune. Further one is asked to purify oneself by holding a branch of an *apāmārga* and to offer oblations of clarified butter a hundred thousand times by means of the above hymn. The *Cāndrāyaṇavrata* must also be performed in addition in order to remove misfortune of a thousand years (iv.77cd-80). (18) The muttering of *RV* 10.190 destroys all sins (iv.120-122ab).

(b) *Expiations for different sins*

(1) Seeing Śūdras is considered to be a sin for a consecrated person. After seeing them, he is asked to take a bath and to behold auspicious objects like cow, fire, and sun (i.70). (2) The muttering of *RV* 1.22.20 is prescribed as an expiation for the sin of eating forbidden food (i.88). (3) The muttering of *RV* 1.164 is prescribed for a Brāhmaṇa who has stolen gold (i.141). (4) The

sin of calumny is effaced by the muttering of *RV* 1.165 (i.143). (5) The offering of oblations of ghee to the accompaniment of *RV* 2.41.16 is prescribed for a person who has committed an ignominous deed (i.149). (6) The muttering of the Gāyatrī verse releases a killer of a cow, a patricide, a matricide, a killer of a Brahmaṇa, one who drinks spirituous liquor (ii.60), a person who has violated his teacher's bed, a robber of gold and a Brāhmaṇa. (7) The muttering of the Gāyatrī verse is prescribed as an expiation for the sins of sacrificing for an unworthy person (ii.61). (8) The muttering of *RV* 7.89.5 releases one from all sins and it is also intended to expiate the sin of cohabiting with forbidden women, Sagotrā-women and wives of friends (ii.150-152). (9) The offering of oblations of Ājya to the accompaniment of *RV* 8.11 is prescribed for a person who has associated with Vrātyas (ii.159). (10) The muttering of *RV* 9.58 releases one from all sins including drinking intoxicants, accepting gifts that ought not to be accepted and eating forbidden food (iii.7, 14cd-15ab). (11) A Brāhmaṇa-slayer holding a skull and a foot of bedstead in each hand and wearing bark cloth must go about proclaiming his deed for twelve years whilst mentally recollecting *RV* 10.9 without actually muttering it. But after five years he should mutter *RV* 10.9 in thousands with an additional muttering of three thousand everyday. On the completion of twelve years a Brāhmaṇa-slayer becomes guiltless. He must then approach the Brāhmaṇa-pariṣat and declare that he has fully carried out the expiation. After their approval he should offer a *sthālīpāka* to the fire and only after that he recovers the Gāyatrī (iii.21-26). (12) The muttering of *RV* 10.9 is prescribed as an expiation for the sin of appropriating the wealth of a Brāhmaṇa and a preceptor (iii.28). (13) The muttering of *RV* 10.9 is prescribed for a person who attacks a Brāhmaṇa (iii.30-31). (14) The muttering of *RV* 10.88 is prescribed as an expiation for the sin arising out of eating forbidden food (iii.129cd-130). (15) The muttering of *RV Kh* iv.5 is prescribed as a general expiation for all sins (iv. 34cd).

(c) *Charms for removing evil effects of bad dreams and of ominous birds*

The following hymns or parts of hymns are directed to be muttered for the sake of removing the evil effects of bad dreams: *RV*

1.99 (i.122cd); *RV* 1.114.7-8 (i.128f); *RV* 8.47.14-18 (ii.173ab); and *RV* 10.164 (iv.101).

The muttering of *RV* 2.42-43 is prescribed for the sake of averting ominous birds and thieves (i.168-170).

### 15. *Remedial charms or rites* (*Bhaiṣajyāni*)

This consists in expelling diseases and ailments from the body of a sick person. It may be mentioned at the outset that the *Ṛvidh* contains few directions regarding curative spells and it hardly mentions any concrete remedy except in the case of *yakṣmā*. In this connection it is worthwhile to remember that in the *Ṛvidh* even the muttering of simple spells is regarded as effective in curing diseases.

(a) *Against diseases*

(1) The muttering of *RV* 1.50 destroys heart-disease (i.99). (2) The muttering of *RV* 1.114 destroys diseases in general (i.130cd). (3) The muttering of *RV* 1.187 destroys diseases arising from food and poison (i.145-148ab). (4) The muttering of *RV* 1.191 counteracts the poison of serpents, worms, spiders, hyenas and scorpions (i.151cd-153ab). (5) The muttering and offering of rice-mess to the accompaniment of *RV* 2.33 destroys a fatal disease (i.164cd-167ab). (6) The muttering of *RV* 3.26.7 destroys diarrhoea (ii.3). (7) The muttering of *RV* 7.51-52 destroys diseases in general (ii. 137). (8) The muttering of *RV* 9.1-67 is prescribed for the sake of release from diseases (iii.14ab). (9) In order to secure release from fever the muttering of *RV* 10.60.7-12 is prescribed (iii.61). (10) The worship of herbs and offering of an oblation to Rudra are prescribed for the sake of overcoming diseases and other digestive troubles (iv.1). (11) One afflicted with indigestion should mutter *RV* 10.137, offer ghee into the fire, and transfer the residue to another vessel. When there is not enough food and when a person, though competent to eat but cannot do so, should perform this rite after smearing the body with the residue of Ājya. This hymn accompanies the smearing of the body of a diseased peison as well as of a person suffering from indigestion (iv.45cd-48). (12) In order to remove consumption, one should sprinkle a consumptive patient with a bunch of *kuśa* grass to the accompaniment of *RV* 10.161 and offer oblations of Ājya into the fire. A

consumptive patient is made to drink the milk with residues. Further he is to consume ghee and powder of *khādira* wood. Another method is as follows: With water, one should filter the decoction of *khādira* shavings and the patient is made to drink it together with honey and Ājya. The removal of consumption is also brought about by means of *RV* 10.163 (iv.81-85, 100cd-101ab).

(b) *Against fear and danger*

(1) The muttering of *RV* 1.99 destroys all fear (i.118-119). (2) The muttering of *RV* 6.48 destroys fear from robbers, demons and enemies (ii.117). (3) The muttering of *RV* 7.35 and *RV Kh* ii.13 destroys fear from Rakṣas, spirits and diseases (ii.133). (4) In order to protect oneself from danger, the muttering of *RV* 8.30 for two months is prescribed (ii.163). (5) The worship of Indra with sandalwood paste etc., the offering of oblations of *ājya* to the accompaniment of *RV* 8.61.13-18 and the presentation of *pāyasa* and *dadhimantha* destroy fear (ii.174cd-176ab). (16) The muttering of *RV* 9.1-67 wards off violent fear of death (iii.12cd-13). (7) The muttering of *RV* 10.30 is prescribed for a person to whom mortal fear presents itself in a sandy desert (iii.49). (8) When there is a fear from fire, one should mutter *RV* 10.142 after satiating the fire with milk, curds and ghee and lead around a continuous stream of water to the accompaniment of the Ṛgvedic verse (10.142.7) whilst proceeding as much in all four directions as one wishes to protect oneself. That stream becomes, as it were, a pool of water and one possesses the healing power from Agni (iv.54-56ab).

(c) *For regaining health and vigour*

The following hymns are directed to be muttered for the sake of health: *RV* 1.23.16-24 (i.89d); *RV* 1.24-30 (i.90); *RV* 1.35.2 (i.93); RV.1.50.11-13 (i.101); and RV 8.46-47 (ii.172cd). The offering of reddened rice grains, anointed with ghee into the fire by means of *RV* 3.62.10 confers vigour, whereas the offering of cow's milk mixed with honey and *ājya* restores it (ii.50-51). In order to regain virility, the muttering of *RV* 10.86 is prescribed (iii.127ab).

16. *Charms or rites pertaining to royalty* (*rājakarmāṇi*)

These are not numerous and the only ceremony which is given in detail is the coronation of a newly installed king.

The muttering of *RV* 1.164 is laid down for the sake of establishing a kingdom with kinsmen, sons, friends and allies (i.142). The offering of lotuses a hundred thousand times to the accompaniment of the Gāyatrī verse confers a kingdom without a rival and free from difficulties (ii.56). The *RV Kh* ii.6.7 accompanies the sprinkling ceremony of a king (ii.96cd). Likewise the *RV Kh* ii.6.3 accompanies the bathing-ceremony of a person desiring a kingdom. If that person be a Brāhmaṇa then he must sit on an ox hide while taking bath. The tiger skin is alloted to a king, *ruru* hide to a Kṣatriya and goat hide to a Vaiśya. A Homa in which lotuses are offered while muttering *RV Kh* ii.6.5 and *bilva* fuel-sticks while muttering of *RV Kh* ii.6.6 should be performed (ii.98-100). The consecration of battle-drums by means of *RV* 6.47.29-31 is prescribed for the sake of obtaining vigour and strength to the king when he is on the battleground (ii.127-129). A king proceeding for conquest should be consecrated by means of *RV* 10.103: then he will not return without conquering other countries or foes (iv. 6cd-7ab, 8). In order to counteract witchcraft, the priest must prepare for the sake of a king an amulet made out of equal parts of metals (viz. gold, silver, copper, iron and lead) and consecrate it by means of *RV Kh* iv.5. He must also consecrate the tops of standards, musical instruments, seats, couches, and various vehicles at the time of hostile encounters (iv.38-39).

A king should be installed under any of the following asterisms, viz. Tiṣya, Śravaṇā, Revatī, Hastā, Mṛgaśiras, Aśvinī, Rohiṇī, Uttarā Phālgunī, Uttarāṣāḍhā and Uttarā Bhādrā. The priest should offer oblations into the fire by means of verses possessing characteristic marks of royalty. A king, while seated on a stool covered with tiger skin, should be sprinkled with the fine sap of all sorts of herbs and river waters. Then the priest facing the west should mutter the following benediction: "May thou conquer the earth and may thy religious merit increase by protecting thy subjects. May thou prosper unto fortune, prosperity, victory and success and may there be further kings in your lineage." Then the priest should mutter *RV* 10.103. The skin used in this rite must invariably be that of a tiger and the fuel that of an *Udumbara* tree. After anointing the king, the priest should consecrate the large kettle drums. Then the king is to be sprinkled again whilst muttering the following benedictory stanzas: "May the Vasus anoint thee in the eastern quarter for lustre and let the Rudras anoint thee in the southern quarter for success. May the Ādityas anoint thee in the western quarter for prosperity and let the Viśvedevās anoint thee in the northern quarter for auspicious result." Finally the priest should consecrate the king by means of *RV* 10.173 (iv.106-114).

### 17. *Charms or rites for subduing people and for securing harmony*

The propitiatory hymn of Hṛdya (*RV Kh* iii.15) is mysterious and wonderful (iii.79). One must fast for twelve days and mutter *RV Kh* iii.15 during those days. At the end of that period one should prepare an image of man made of sand and tread upon it while muttering *RV Kh* iii.15; then one can win over a rich *Vaiśya* within three days, a Kṣatriya within four days, a king within five days, a Brāhmaṇa within six days and an ascetic after seven days (ii.80-84). Avoiding a low person, as a rule, one should pour the powdered Bilvas duly charmed into a well to bring a person under control and employ *RV Kh* iii.15 on one's own mother, sons, father and friends for the sake of propitiation (iii.85-87). Likewise charming an odd number of fruits of a Mahāvṛkṣa and sparing those forming half of the pairs among them after consuming the other half one should give the remainder to him whom one wishes to bring under control, whilst muttering *RV Kh* iii.15. This is declared to be propitious when given to a friend who has turned out to be an enemy (iii.108-109).

While in a forest, one must purchase the *Pāṭhā* with a handful of barley whilst muttering Mantras—some of which are found in the *Āp GS* (3.9.5)—and cast it along with flowers on a shrub in an open space. One may even mutter *RV* 10.145 while digging the *pāṭhā* and one must have it crushed by a *Brahmacārin* or by a person observing vows, or by a virgin or by a Brāhmaṇa in the morning. A woman should drink it thrice along with ghee in the morning after consecrating it by means of *RV* 10.145; then she wards off a co-wife and her husband will value her highly (iv.56-

63). The husband on his part should drink it together with milk for seven days; then he wards off rivals (iv.64).

The muttering of *RV* 10.191 is prescribed for the sake of harmony. It should be employed when dissensions occur among relatives. But when the dissension is complete the *RV Kh* v.1 should be muttered in order to bring about reconciliation (iv.123 cd-125ab).

### 18. *Charms or rites for causing rain* (*Vṛṣṭikarmāṇi*)

The offering of *vetasa* leaves mixed with ghee into fire by means of *RV* 3.62.10 causes rain to fall over the whole earth (ii.41). A person who has fasted and who has worn wet clothes, should mutter *RV* 5.83 and offer ten thousand fuel-sticks of rattan smeared with milk into fire in order to obtain a heavy rainfall (ii.90cd-92ab). The worship of Divākara with *RV* 7.101-102, while immersed in water upto the mouth is prescribed for the sake of obtaining a heavy rainfall (ii.155-156). A person desiring rain should worship Bṛhaspati with *RV* 10.98 together with food-offering and burnt-offering consisting of rice-mess boiled in milk; then he obtains excellent rain after saluting Parjanya (iv.4-5). The muttering of *RV* 10.9 is prescribed for the sake of obtaining rain (iv.127ab).

### 19. *Charms or rites pertaining to women* (*Strikarmāṇi*)

The *Ṛvidh* contains many charms or rites to secure a woman's love and to attract her mind. It has spells for securing successful conception and for ensuring safe delivery, besides charms against 'still-births'.

The muttering of *RV* 1.101.1 ensures safe delivery for a woman (i.123). The water consecrated by means of *RV* 5.78.5 should be given to a woman who is about to bring forth a child (ii.89cd-90ab). The muttering of *RV* 8.91 is laid down for girls suffering from skin disease (ii.181cd-182ab).

The method of subduing a woman is as follows: One should by means of fire soften the fine particles of rice grains unhusked with nails, over which the residue of one thousand oblations has been poured. With that substance one must prepare an image of a woman and offer, member by member, that image anointed with mustard oil into the fire exclaiming each time *Phaṭ* and after cutting off the heart region of that image, should place it on one's own heart while muttering *RV Kh* iii.15; then one obtains that woman (iii.100cd-104). A Brāhmaṇa should not direct this rite towards married women nor towards faithful and virtuous women. Rather he who acts towards low-caste women must subjugate her husband first, then that woman. One should preserve the remains of milk-porridge secured from vomitting it out, after consuming it first. The powder prepared out of this substance when given to a low-caste woman is declared to be propitiatory (iii.105-107). Further *RV Kh* iii.16 is declared to be propitious for women and men ( ii.111). A woman is warned not to employ roots and Mantras other than the *pāṭhā* and the Mantra, to wit: *RV* 10.145. She may ruin her husband if she employs any other thing (iv.65-66). A woman kind to her husband, whose sole object in life is her husband and whose voice is melodious—this in itself is highly propitious to her husband—after getting an affable husband should drink the decoction of the *pāṭhā* and whoever reproaches such a woman should be considered as the vilest among men (iv.67-69ab).

One should offer a burnt-oblation with Ājya into the fire by means of *RV* 10.162 for the sake of a woman who miscarries. She should be made to anoint herself with the remnant of the Ājya and to drink the same; then her child will be born alive (iv.86-87). If her children die after they are born, then one should offer Ājya into the fire by means of *RV* 10.162, pour the residue of ten thousand oblations on the amulet made out of a sheath of a young bud of a Nyagrodha tree and consecrate it ten thousand times by means of the Sāvitrī verse and *RV* 10.162. A woman, when pregnant, should wear it on the head and in the third month of her pregnancy she should fasten it to her neck. Till menses reappear, a woman together with her young sucking one should remain like a cow having a calf. After the birth of a boy one should fasten the amulet to his neck after honouring the residue of Ājya, anointing the boy with it and offering oblations into the fire to the accompaniment of benedictory verses. Thus a woman brings forth a male issue. The muttering of *RV* 10.184 and *RV Kh* iv.13 is prescribed for the sake of ensuring conception for a woman advanced in years (iv.117cd-118ab).

## 20. *Witchcraft practices* (*Ābhicārikāṇi*)

We have seen above as to how *vidhāna* came to mean both 'a sacred precept' as well as 'sorcery practice'. It is with the latter aspect we are concerned in this subsection. The magical act rests, in a large measure, on a transfer or a symbolic representation. Thus an image of wood, sand, etc. is frequently made and operated upon for the purpose of producing a similar effect on the victim. The most favourable time for the practice of magic is the night and the place selected is, generally, a lonely one. Direction is an important element. The performers of Ābhicārika rites must face the south. The fuel and other materials used in these rites have been referred to above (p. 89).

(1) In the Ābhicārika rites, the Gāyatrī verse is spelled backwards, and the mustard oil is offered into the fire with the offering ladle made of Vibhītaka wood in order to drive away an enemy as well as to kill him (i.75-78). (2) By means of *RV* 1.1 one can cause the fire to appear on a non-combustible material and to burn enemies (i.82-83). (3) By means of *RV* 1.32, one can drive away enemies (i.92). (4) In order to make an enemy odious, *RV* 1.50. 13cd is directed to be muttered (i.100, 102-103ab, 104ab). (5) By means of *RV* 1.65-73, one can kill enemies (i.105). (6) The muttering of *RV* 1.133 is laid down for the sake of destroying enemies. (7) In order to kill a miser and to appropriate his wealth, *RV* 3.53.14 is directed to be muttered (ii.10cd-11ab). (8) On the fourteenth lunar day of the dark fortnight a person, after fasting for three days, should remain on burial ground sloping towards the south. He should wear a red headgear and hold a sword in hand. He should offer mustard oil mixed with salt into the fire kindled with *bilva* and *rājavṛkṣa* fuel-sticks, and should further prepare an image of his enemy with the *śamyāka* wood. Standing on it, he should perform a Homa aiming at the name of the enemy by means of *RV* 3.53.21-24. The enemy will die within seven nights (ii.16-19). (9) In order to remove the fear of theives, fire and wind, one is asked to throw a clod of earth charmed by means of the Gāyatrī verse (ii.39). (10) The offering of hundred thousand offerings to the accompaniment of the Gāyatrī verse causes a Kṛtyā to rise from the water (ii.42ab). (11) The offering of red mustard seeds to the accompaniment of the Gāyatrī verse subdues enemies (ii.47cd). (12) In order to bring a man under con-

trol, one should offer salt mixed with honey by means of the Gāyatrī verse (ii.48ab). (13) The offering of red *karavīra* flowers to the accompaniment of the Gāyatrī verse can cause fever to adversaries (ii.48cd). (14) The offering of the oil of Vibhītaka wood to the accompaniment of the Gāyatrī verse can expel an enemy from the country (ii.49ab). (15) The offering of Nimba leaves to the accompaniment of the Gāyatrī verse can cause hostility among men (ii.49cd). (16) The muttering of *RV* 4.4 destroys enemies and demons (ii.63). (17) In order to bring about the expulsion of an enemy his image made of sand should be trodden upon whilst muttering *RV* 5.78.5 (ii.87cd-89ab). (19) By means of *RV* 6.2.11 one can conquer enemies and surmount difficulties (ii.111). (19) The consecration of battle-drum subdues enemies (ii.114). (20) After muttering *RV* 6.48, one should deposit the grass held in hand in a fire or in an inhospitable region (ii.116). (21) The worship of Bṛhaspati with *RV* 6.73 is laid down for the sake of destroying enemies (ii.24). (22) The muttering of *RV* 7.51-52 destroys enemies (ii.137). (23) The muttering of *RV* 7.55 causes sleep (ii.139). (24) The offering of Ājya to the accompaniment of *RV* 7.104 destroys enemies (ii.157-158). (25) The muttering of *RV* 8.45 is prescribed for the sake of destroying enemies (ii.170cd-171ab). (26) The offering of seasamum seeds and Ājya to the accompaniment of *RV* 8.64 destroys enemies (ii.176cd-177ab). (27) In order to obtain success in gambling, one is asked to perfume the three dices, cover them with flowers and place them in a terrace and then one should remain in an upright position and mutter *RV* 10.34.1 during the night. He should mutter the rest of the hymn after going to the gambling place and touching the opponent (iii.50-53). (28) The muttering of *RV* 10.83-84 destroys enemies. Then the preparation and binding on of an amulet made of iron and the offering of an iron pin into the fire kindled with *khādira* fuel are prescribed for the sake of warding off rivals (iii.77-78). (29) When any propitiatory rite has failed, one is asked to set on fire the image of sand and offer oblations of ghee, if the victim is a Brāhmaṇa; but in the case of a Kṣatriya and Vaiśya, one is asked to offer mustard oil into the fire. Alternatively one should place a metallic image into the fire kindled with Vibhītaka fuel. At midnight, with hairs dishevelled and sitting on three stakes and desiring the death of one's rival, one is asked to prepare a seat full of arrow-heads kept invertedly and offer mustard oil with salt. Then one subdues a person in no time. Optionally one should go on exorcising with spells and offer one's blood; then one brings under subjection a king, a country and a town (iii. 88cd-96ab). (30) A Brāhmaṇa is prohibited from performing any rite connected with murder against a sinless person (iii.97ab). (31) The *RV Kh* iii.16 and the text designated as '*Dveṣyam*' are employed in a sorcery rite against kinsmen. One is asked to fix a *khādira* pin into the heart of an image made of sand or husks and to arrange a mock battle with that image, after charming an arrow, in order to destroy one's enemies (iii.112-114). (32) The muttering of *RV* 10.87 and offering Ājya with it are laid down for the sake of destroying demons (iii.127cd-129ab). (33) In order to see the path leading to gods and to attain the knowledge of the Highest Self, one is asked to mutter *RV* 10.88 after fixing the gaze on sun (iii.131-132ab). (34) The muttering of *RV* 10.89 destroys enemies (iii.133). (35) In order to obtain herbs from the field of detesters, one is asked to worship the herbs with *RV* 10.97 and to offer an oblation to Varuṇa (iv.2.37). (36) In order to counteract Kṛtyā and fierce incantations, one is asked to mutter *RV Kh* iv.5 (iv.30). An expert in Pratyaṅgirasa-text wards off charms cast by an expert in Āṅgirasa-texts, besides he suffers no harm from Kṛtyās and imprecations. As a matter of fact, no evil contacts him when a known or an unknown person curses him or addresses him harshly (iv.31-33). Then the preparation and binding on of a triple amulet made of gold. One is asked to pour the residue of one thousand oblations over it to the accompaniment of *RV Kh* iv.5: then neither evil spirits nor imprecations injure him (iv.36-37). One can ward off enchantments of even Ṛṣi Āṅgirasa himself by means of Pratyaṅgirasa-text (iv.40). In order to obtain release from an unwelcome thing, one is asked to cast a charm on the unhuman Kṛtyās (iv.41). (37) The agent of these practices must be devout, restrained, mild and full of Tapas; then he overcomes everything (iv.42). (38) In order to obtain the wealth of a rich enemy, one is asked to fast for half a month and to offer the fuel-sticks of Vibhītaka and Bilva trees by means of *RV* 1.50.13cd and *RV* 10.141 (iv.52-53ab). (39) In order to destroy rivals and to obtain success in battles, one is asked to mutter *RV* 10.152. It should also be muttered by a person proceeding to a battle in order to drive away enemies (iv.75cd-77ab). (40) The muttering of *RV* 10.166 and offering oblations with it are prescribed for the sake of destroying enemies (iv.103ab). (41) In order to bring about the destruction of sorcery, the muttering of *RV* 10.177 is prescribed. It repels all sorts of sorceries, prevents magic from operating, Śambara or Indrajāla and wards off magic caused by unseen beings (iv.115cd-116). (42) In order to do away with enmity, the muttering of *RV* 10.187 is prescribed (iv.119ab). (43) The muttering of *RV* 10.189 is laid down for the sake of warding off snakes (iv.119cd). (44) In order to split an army, the muttering of *RV Kh* v.2 is prescribed (iv.122cd-123ab). (45) The muttering of *RV Kh* iii.10 destroys rivals (iv.126cd).

Such as above is the nature of the Vidhāna text of the Ṛks. In the *AV* we find employment of magic in its various aspects, such as witchcraft, medicines, domestic rites, statecraft, erotic, blessings and curses. The difference between the Ṛgvedic and Atharvavedic magic is that most of the hymns of the *RV* are not *intended* for this employment while those of the *AV* are primarily intended for this purpose. The employment of the *RV* in these practices is purely artificial. It appears to have been brought in only as the imitation of, or due to the infatuation of the *AV*, or Śaunaka might be recording here tradition preserved in some groups of the Ṛgvedins.

### 3. Mythology

We now turn to the deities referred to in the *Ṛvidh*.

(A) The Vedic and post-Vedic deities that have been referred to in the course of the work are the following, viz. (1) *Indra* (i.91-92, 123, 136, 159; ii.69, 154, 175; iii.218; iv.136). (2) *Viṣṇu* (i.25, 136; ii.136, 154; iii.137, 140, 149, 225, 230); (3) *Agni* (i.22; ii.79, 162, 179; iii.16, 128, 173; iv.136); (4) *Pitaras* (i.26, 109; iii.6, 8, 16; iv.130, 134); (5) *Viśve devās* (i.23, 108, 124; iv.19-20, 58, 113); (6) *Bṛhaspati* (i.150, 150; ii.22, 124; iv.4, 133); (7) *Rudra* (i.23, 127; ii.135; iii.218; iv.1); (8) *Ādityas* (i.45; ii.137, 178; iv.58, 113); (9) *Soma* (22; iii.16, 121; iv.57, 134); (10) *Yama* (iii.34-36, 38; iv.134); (11) *Sūrya* (i.93, 139; iv.134, 136); (12) (iv.20, 22, 24, 26); (13) *Śrī* (ii.92-95); (14) *Vāyu* (ii.162; iv.134, 136); (15) *Aśvins* (ii.168; iv.11, 14); (16) *Brahmā* (i.24; ii.54; iii.218); (17) *Vasus* (i.45; iv.58, 112); (18) *Parjanya* (ii.69; iii.218; iv.5); (19) *Bhaga* (ii.69, 134; iii.121): (20) *Varuṇa* (iv.3, 57, 134); (21) *Sarasvatī* (i.25; ii.122; iii.17); (22) *Maruts* (i.45; ii.69); (23) *Pūṣan* (ii.70, 120); (24) *Vāstoṣpati* (ii.138; iv.133); (25) the *Gandharvas* (i.24; iii.121); (26) *Indrāṇī* (iii.119, 122); (27) *Devānāṁ patnīḥ* (ii.83; iii.122); (28) The *Apsarases* (i.24; iii.121); (29) *Pṛthvī* (i.86; ii. 149); (30) *Avasānasya Pati* (Sadasaspati i.23); (31) *Anumati* (i.23); (32) *Agni Sviṣṭakṛt* (i.25); (33) *Ṛbhus* (i.45); (34) *Ṛtāvṛdhas* (=Mitra and Varuṇa, ii.22); (35) *Śunāsīra* (ii.70); (36) *Nirṛti* (iv. 134); (37) *Dhanvantari* (i.24); (28) *Yakṣādhipati* (iii.121); (39) *Ākhupati* (ii.74); (40) *Pradyumna* (iii.1–2); (41) *Vāk* (iv.18); (42) *Rati* (iii.122); (43) *Dhānya* (ii.70); (44) *Candra* (i.110); (45) *Sītā* (ii.70); (46) *Sūryā* (iii.115); and (47) *Araṇyānī* (iv.70). Out of these, *Dhanvantari, Yakṣādhipati, Ākhupati, Pradyumna* and *Rati* are Puranic deities. *Dhānya* is altogether a new deity.

(B) Synonyms: (i) The following synonyms of *Indra* occur in *Ṛvidh*: *Puraṁdara* (i.91; ii.164, 180, 182), *Śatakratu* (i.155; ii.82, 113), *Śakra* (ii.65; iii.27), *Vajrin* (ii.132, 170), *Mahendra* (ii.171; iv.134) and *Vṛtrahan* (ii.181). (ii) The following synonyms of *Viṣṇu* are mentioned: *Nārāyaṇa* (iii.139, 146, 191-192, 224-225), *Hari* (iii.150-151, 186, 226-227), *Puruṣa* (iii.184, 186, 229-230), *Madhusūdana* (iii.140, 144), *Hṛṣīkeśa* (iii.141, 174), *Puruṣottama* (iii.162, 219), *Puṇḍarīkākṣa* (iii.174, 181), *A*(= *Viṣṇu*, ii.54), *Janārdana* (iii.135), *Keśava* (iii.139), *Mādhava* (iii.139), *Govinda* (iii.139), *Trivikrama* (iii.140), *Vāmana* (iii.140), *Śrīdhara* (iii.141), *Padmanābha* (iii.141), *Dāmodara* (iii.141), *Acyuta* (iii.182) and *Cakrin* (iii.228). A name like Vāsudeva or Kṛṣṇa is conspicuous by its absence. It is possible that identification of Viṣṇu with Vāsudeva had not taken place at the time of *Ṛvidh*: (iii) The following synonyms of Agni occur: *Vahni* (i.83; ii.64, 80-81, 180; iii.121), *Anala* (i.150), *Vibhāvasu* (ii.111) and *Hutāśa* (iii.144). (iv) The synonym of *Bṛhaspati* is *Brahmaṇaspati* (i.24). (v) The following synonyms of *Rudra* occur: *Tryambaka* (ii.54, 143), *Śaṅkara* (i.97, 166), *Īśāna* (i.97), and *Mahādeva* (ii.143). (vi) The synonym of Soma is: *Babhru* (ii.22). (vii) The synonym of *Yama* is *Mṛtyu* (iii.39). (viii) The following synonyms of *Sūrya* have occurred: *Divākara* (i.139; ii.144, 155, 160), *Āditya* (i.99, 131; iii.189), *Bhāskara* (i.131; ii.162), *Arka* (ii.184) and *Savitṛ* (ii.22). (ix) The synonym of *Aśvins* is: *Nāsatyau* (i.126; ii.168; iv.11). (x) The synonym of *Pūṣan* is : *Ajāśva* (ii.22). (xi) The synonym of *Vāk* is: *Gaurī* (ii.183).

Now let us examine the charms or rites in which these deities figure, a couple of legends concerning them and the benefits which can be acquired through their favour. These are taken up in the order of the *Ṛvidh.*

(1) The offering of a *sthālīpāka* with preliminary and terminal oblations of ghee to Agni, Soma, Agni and Soma together, Viśve-devās, Rudra, Avasānasya Pati, Anumati, Dhanvantari and Gandharvas, the Apsarses, Brahmaṇaspati, Brahmā, Sarasvatī, Viṣṇu and Agni Sviṣṭakṛt is prescribed in a ceremony before the commencement of Vedic study (i.22cd-25ab). (2) According to *Ṛvidh* (i.81-83), *RV* 1.1. is employed for offering a sacrifice to Vahni for securing numerous benefits. (3) According to *Ṛvidh* (i.45), Rudras, Ādityas, Vasus, Maruts and Ṛbhus had performed a Cāndrāyaṇa-vrata. (4) The worship of goddess Pṛthvī with *RV* 1.22.15 is prescribed for obtaining landed property (i.86). (5) According to *Ṛvidh* (i.91), Indra is to be praised with *RV* 1.28-29 for obtaining permanent benefits. (6) The hymn *RV* 1.32, which is in praise of Indra's deeds is directed to be muttered for driving away the enemies (i.92). (7) The worship of Sūrya with *RV* 1.35.2 is prescribed for the sake of prolonging life (i.93). (8) According to *Ṛvidh* (i.97), Īśāna is to be praised with *RV* 1.43 for the sake of destroying heart-disease and for obtaining good health (i.99). (10) The hymn *RV* 1.89 which is addressed to 'Viśve-devās' is directed to be muttered for the sake of prolonging life (i.108). (11) The worship of Candra with *RV* 1.91 is laid down for the sake of destroying threefold miseries, for obtaining clothes and for attaining the abode of Candra (i.110-112). (12) When a woman is about to deliver, Indra should mentally be meditated upon with *RV* 1.101.1 for the sake of safe delivery (i.123). (13) According to *Ṛvidh* (i.124cd-125ab), *RV* 1.106 is employed for offering a sacrifice to 'Viśve devās' for securing release from distress. (14) The worship of Nāsatyas with *RV* 1.112 is laid down for the sake of obtaining prosperity and for securing release from infirmities (i.125cd-126). (15) The hymn *RV* 1.114 which is addressed to Rudra, is directed to be muttered for the sake of obtaining long life, knowledge, wealth, sons and a healthy housewife (i.127). (16) The worship of Āditya with *RV* 1.115 is prescribed for the sake of destroying infirmity and for obtaining wealth and long life (i.131-132). (17) The worship of Indra and Viṣṇu with *RV* 1.

154.1-3 is laid down for the sake of obtaining religious merit, intelligence, wealth, sons, health, the increase of Brahman, and the highest abode (i.136-137). (18) The worship of Divākara with hymns addressed to Sūrya is prescribed for the sake of eluding thieves (i.139-140ab). (19) The worship of Anala with offering of oblations of Ājya by means of *RV* 1.189 is prescribed for a person who has lost his way or one who has committed an ignominous deed (i.148cd-150ab). (20) The worship of Bṛhaspati with *RV* 1.190 is laid down for the sake of obtaining heroes, wealth and fame (i.150cd-151ab). (21) The worship of Śatakratu with *RV* 2.12 and *RV* 2.21.6 is prescribed for a person who has fasted for three days and who has performed a hundred Prāṇāyāmas. The hymn *RV* 2.12 must be muttered a hundred times and at the end one must mutter *RV* 2.21.6. In one day one obtains wealth; in two days, highest success; in three days, health; in four days, abundant food; in five days, spiritual lustre; in six days, long life; in seven days, sons and prosperity; and in eight days one obtains fame and goes to the abode of Indra after becoming his favourite (i.154cd-159ab). (22) The worship of Bṛhaspati with *RV* 2.23 is laid down for the sake of obtaining all objects of desire. The hymn must be muttered at both the twilight times (i.159cd-161ab). (23) A person overcome by a fatal disease must fast and offer oblations into the fire, verse by verse, by means of *RV* 2.33 which is addressed to Rudra. Subsisting on sacrificial remnants, he must worship Śaṅkara in order to conquer death and to get release from diseases (i.164cd-167ab). (24) The deities, viz., Bṛhaspati, Ajāśva (=Pūṣan), Savitṛ, Babhru (Śoma), Ṛtāvṛdhs (=Mitra and Varuṇa) are worshipped with five sets of tristiches (i.e. *RV* 3.62.4-18) in order to obtain riches, progeny, cattle, festivities and long life respectively (ii.22-24). (25) A (=Viṣṇu), Brahmā and Tryambaka bestow boons on a person who mutters the Gāyatrī verse a hundred thousand times, after resorting to their respective sanctuaries (ii.54). (26) The worship of Vahni with *RV* 4.9.8 is laid down for the sake of securing all-around protection from Him (ii.64). (27) The worship of Śakra with *RV* 4.25 is prescribed for the sake of obtaining boons (ii.65). (28) A farmer is asked to prepare a *sthālīpāka* and offer oblations to the following deities viz., Indra, Maruts, Parjanya, Bhaga, Pūṣan, Dhānya, Sītā and Śunā-sīra by means of *RV* 4.57.4-8. He is asked to honour them with sandal wood paste, garlands, food offerings, fruits, parched grains and spirituous liquour at the sowing and mowing times. Then his cultivation prospers (ii.68-72). (29) The worship of moles and Ākhupati, the king of moles, with an offering of rice-mess by means of *RV* 8.21.18 (ii.74). (30) The worship of Agni with *RV* 5.2.9 is prescribed for the sake of obtaining good fortune and wealth (ii.79). (31) The worship of Vahni with *RV* 5.4. 9-10 is laid down for the sake of surmounting adversities and for obtaining everlasting fame, and together with *RV* 5.24 for the sake of wealth and long life (ii.180-81). (32) The worship of Śatakratu with *RV* 5.38 is prescribed for the sake of obtaining manifold wealth (ii.82). (33) The worship of Devānāṁ patnīḥ with rice-mess by means of *RV* 5.46.7-8 is laid down for the sake of progeny. One must eat the remnants and hand over the left-overs to one's wife. The rice-mess must be cooked in the milk of a cow having a calf of the same colour. Then one obtains a worthy progeny (ii.83-85ab). (34) According to *Ṛvidh* (ii.92cd-95), *RV Kh* ii.6 is employed for offering a sacrifice to goddess Śrī for obtaining fortune. One must invoke her in a lotus and offer milk, curds and *sthālīpāka* to Her. (35) The worship of Vibhāvasu with *RV* 6.2.11 is laid down for the sake of conquering enemies and for surmounting difficulties (ii.111). (36) The worship of Śatakratu with *RV* 6.46 is prescribed for the sake of obtaining wealth. The hymn should be muttered at midday and at both the twilight times (ii.113). (37) The hymn *RV* 6.53 which is addressed to Pūṣan, is directed to be muttered for the sake of wealth (ii.120). (38) The hymn *RV* 6.61, which is addressed to Sarasvatī, is directed to be muttered for the sake of eloquence (ii.122). (39) The worship of Bṛhaspati with *RV* 6.73 is laid down for the sake of destroying enemies (ii.124). (40) The hymn, *RV* 6.74, which is addressed to Soma and Rudra is directed to be muttered for obtaining release from all sins (ii.125). (41) The worship of Vajrin with *RV* 7.32.22-23 is prescribed for the sake of obtaining abundant fortune, wealth and long life (ii.132). (42) The hymn *RV* 7.41, which is addressed to Bhaga is directed to be muttered for obtaining a Niveśa i.e. settling in life and for securing release from diseases (ii. 134). (43) The hymn *RV* 7.46, which is addressed to Rudra, is directed to be muttered for the sake of progeny and wealth (ii. 135). (44) The hymns *RV* 7.51-52 which are addressed to Ādityas, are directed to be muttered for the destruction of enemies and diseases (ii.137). (45) The hymn *RV* 7.54 which is addressed to Vāstoṣpati is directed to be muttered after the daily Vaiśvadeva ceremony (ii.138). (46) According to *Ṛvidh* (ii.142-143), *RV* 7.59. 12 is employed for offering a sacrifice to Tryambaka Mahādeva for obtaining a long life. (47) The worship of Divākara with *RV* 7.66.16 is prescribed for the sake of long life (ii.144). (48) The worship of goddess Pṛthvī with *RV* 1.22.15 is laid down for the sake of securing release from Bhūmipāśa (ii.149). (49) According to *Ṛvidh* (ii.154), *RV* 7.99-100 are employed for offering a sacrifice to Indra and Viṣṇu for the attainment of power. (50) The worship of Divākara with *RV* 7.101-102 is prescribed for the sake of rain. The hymn must be muttered while immersing in water upto the mouth and facing the east. After five days there would be much rain (ii.155-156). (51) According to *Ṛvidh* (ii.160-161), *RV* 8.16 is directed to be muttered while beholding and worshipping Divākara by one desiring success in a dispute. (52) The worship of Vāyu and Bhāskara with *RV* 8.18.9 is laid down for the sake of surmounting a difficulty. Agni must be praised at first and then the other deities (ii.162). (53) The worship of Puraṁdara with *RV* 8.34-16-18 is prescribed for the sake of obtaining all conceivable objects of desire (ii.164). (54) The hymn, *RV* 8.35 which is addressed to Aśvins, is directed to be muttered, after worshipping Nāsatyas, for the attainment of prosperity, wealth and vigour (ii.168-169ab). (55) The worship of Vajrin with *RV* 8.45. One thereby obtains friendship of Mahendra wand with his help destroys enemies (ii.170cd-171ab). (56) According to *Ṛvidh* (ii.174-cd-176ab), *RV* 8.61.13-18 are employed for offering a sacrifice to Indra for the sake of safety. (57) The hymn *RV* 8.67 which is addressed to Ādityas, is directed to be muttered for securing release from bonds (ii.177cd-178ab). (58) According to *Ṛvidh* (ii.179cd-180ab), *RV* 8.71 is employed for offering a sacrifice to Agni for obtaining wealth. (59) The worship of Puraṁdara with *RV* 8.81 for the sake of wealth (ii.180cd-181ab) and with *RV* 8.93.4 for the sake of destroying infirmity and for subjugating the the world (ii.182cd-183ab). (60) The worship of Gaurī with *RV* 8.100.10-11 is prescribed for the sake of polished speech (ii.183cd-184ab). (61) The worship of Arka with *RV* 8.101.11-12 is laid down for the sake of averting the consequences arising out of speaking falsehood (iii. 184cd-185ab). (62) The worship of Agni, Soma, Sarasvatī, the manes and the Ṛṣis with milk, water, honey and ghee after controlling the breath and muttering *RV Kh* iii.10 is prescribed (iii.15cd-17ab). (63) According to *Ṛvidh* (iii.27), Śakra was previously guilty of Brāhmaṇa-murder, since he had killed Ṛṣi Tvāṣṭra who is said to have been well-versed in the Vedas. Ṛṣi Sindhudvīpa released Śakra from the guilt by means of *RV* 10.9. (64) According to *Ṛvidh* (iii.34-38), *RV* 10.14 is employed for offering a sacrifice to Yama for the sake of long life. The sacrifice is to be performed on the eighth and fourteenth lunar days and a *sthālīpāka* must be offered into the fire together with ghee. It must invariably be performed on the full-moon day of the month of Vaiśākha. One must offer seasamum seeds mixed with water to Yama and his followers, after taking a bath on the two solstices and on the new and full moon days. (65) The worship of Mṛtyu with *RV* 10.18 is laid down for the sake of living one hundred years (iii.39-40ab). (66) The verse, *RV* 10.34.1 which is in praise of dice (Akṣastuti), is directed to be muttered for the sake of success in gambling (iii.51). (67) The hymn *RV* 10.71, which is in praise of knowledge (Jñānastuti), is directed to be muttered for the sake of knowledge and fortune (iii.71). (68) The evolutionary hymn of Sūryā (i.e. *RV* 10.85) is to be communicated to a daughter by her father so that she may get a suitable husband (iii.115cd-116ab). (69) The hymn *RV* 10.86 in which Indrāṇī carries a dialogue with Vṛṣākapi, is employed in the bathing-ceremony of a bride (iii.119cd). (70) According to *Ṛvidh* (iii. 120cd-122ab) a sacrifice for Soma, the Gandharvas, Vahni, Bhaga, the Apsarases, the Lord of Yakṣas, Indrāṇī, the Wives of gods, Rati and Pradyumna, is laid down before the sprinkling ceremony of a bride. (71) According to *Ṛvidh* (iii.128) RV 10.87 is employed for offering a sacrifice to Agni for the destruction of demons. (72) The worship of Janārdana with *RV* 10.90 is prescribed for the sake of progeny. A rice-mess to Viṣṇu should be offered on the twelfth lunar day of the bright fortnight (ii.134-136). (73) *Ṛvidh* (iii.139-142) set out the names of Viṣṇu to be muttered in the months from Mārgaśirṣa to Kārttika: Keśava, Nārāyaṇa, Mādhava, Govinda, Viṣṇu, Madhusūdana, Trivikrama, Vāmana, Śrīdhara, Hṛṣīkeśa, Padmanābha and Dāmodara. These names were declared by Ṛṣyaśṛṅga and they must be honoured for the sake of obtaining all objects of desire. (74) The worship of Hutāśa and Madhusūdana with the offering of *Aśvattha* fuel-sticks to the accompaniment of *RV* 10.90 is prescribed (iii.144). (75) Sages have attained *Brahmanirvāṇa* by the worship of Viṣṇu. Hari is present in water, fire, heart, sun, altar and in idols. For the ritualists, God is present in the fire; for the intellectuals in the heaven; for the dull-witted ones, in idols and for the Yogis in the heart. Since water is Hari's abode He is always present in it and by reason of his omnipresence He is also present in the altar (iii. 149-152). (76) According to *Ṛvidh* (iii.162ab), *RV* 10.90.1 is employed for invoking Puruṣottama. See above subsection on Pūjā for details. (77) The worship of Āditya with *RV* 10.90 is prescribed for conquering heaven (iii.189-190ab). (78) According to *Ṛvidh* (iii.218) Brahmā, Indra, Rudra and Parjanya are present in *RV* 10.90. (79) The worship of Rudra with *RV* 10.97 is laid down for the sake of destroying diseases (iv.1-2). (80) A worship of Varuṇa is laid down for the sake of obtaining herbs (iv.3). (81) According to *Ṛvidh* (iv.4-5), *RV* 10.98 is employed for offering a sacrifice to Bṛhaspati and Parjanya for obtaining abundant rain. (82) According to *Ṛvidh* (iv.10-15) RV 10.106 is employed for offering a sacrifice to Nāsatyas i.e., the Aśvins, for obtaining a long-lived son. (83) The worship of goddess Vāk with *RV* 10.125 is prescribed for the sake of attaining eloquence (iv.18cd-19ab). (84) The hymn, *RV* 10.126 which is addressed to Viśve devās, is directed to be muttered for the destruction of all stains and for the attainment of the abode of Viśve-devās (iv.19cd-20ab). (85) The worship of goddess Rātrī with *RV* 10.127 is prescribed. The hymn is to be muttered during the nights and a *sthālīpāka* is to be offered every day and night. After one year one should offer oblations of rice boiled in milk a thousand times, but after three years oblations of rice with ghee are to be offered. Goddess Rātrī will appear in person and grant the boons asked for (iv.20cd-28). (86) The deities Soma, Varuṇa, the Vasus, the Rudras, the Ādityas and the Viśve-devās are invoked in a charm for getting the herb *pāṭhā* (iv. 56-58). (87) The worship of Goddess Araṇyānī with *RV* 10.146 is laid down for the sake of securing release from forests (iv.69cd-70ab). (88) The Vasus, the Rudras, the Ādityas and the Viśve-devās are invoked for heroic lustre, success, prosperity and auspicious result respectively (iv.112-113). (89) The hymn of

Madhucchandas with the syllable *oṁ* and the Vyāhṛtis at the beginning and Mahānāmnī-verses at the end constitute the Amṛtā-saṁhitā by means of which the gods attained immortality. Likewise hymns addressed to the Pitṛs constitute Pitryā-saṁhitā, those addressed to Vāsava-, Vāsavī-saṁhitā and so on. We have Raudrā, Ādityā and Vaiśvadevī-saṁhitās (iv.127cd-131ab). (90) Finally we have the Vāstuśamana ceremony in which Vāstoṣpati and Bṛhaspati are worshipped with flower, sandal wood paste, garlands and herbs; the Balis are offered to the eight presiding deities of quarters, viz. Sūrya, Vāyu, Yama, the Pitaras, Varuṇa, Nirṛti, Soma and Mahendra. Incidentally, the worship of Agni, Indra, Vāyu and Sūrya with congruous hymns is laid down for the sake of success (iv.131cd-137).

Having arrived at the end of my analysis, it might be interesting to formulate some of the results hitherto gained:

(1) The total number of hymns or parts of hymns occurring in the *Ṛvidh* is 329; for 303 of these, I have been able to trace them in the *RV*. Besides 303 hymns or parts of hymns from the *RV*—many of which occur in the Śrauta and Gṛhya Sūtras, as will be presently shown—there are 26 hymns or parts of hymns which are found in the Khila Collection of the *RV*.

(2) Only 59 hymns or single verses out of 329 hymns or parts of hymns occuring in the *Ṛvidh* are not employed in any Śrauta or Gṛhya-Sūtras of the *RV*. This leads us to infer that hymns or even single verses of the *RV* which have been rubricated in the *Ṛvidh* are those which are familiar enough to any performer of the Śrauta or Gṛhya rites and it is further assumed that he who practises ritual knows these hymns or even single verses by heart.

(3) The fact that the employment of Ṛks in the *Ṛvidh* is arbitrary may lead one to suspect that sufficient indications of such employment are not available in the hymns themselves. Only in the case of 85 hymns or single verses, we find indications of such employment. Majority of the Mantras are either misunderstood or half-understood, or not understood at all.

(4) The *Ṛvidh* does not, in any way, add anything new to our knowledge of the Vedic mythology.

Chapter III

# LANGUAGE AND COMPOSITION OF THE *ṚGVIDHĀNA*

The language of the *Ṛgvidhāna* is, on the whole, good Sanskrit, admitting now and then of various liberties and peculiarities, grammatical, lexical or metrical, part of which is known from the introduction to the *Ṛgvidhāna* by Dr. R. Meyer.[1] An account of these peculiarities is a necessary preliminary not only for determining the question of its date but also for handling many of its textual problems.

Grammatical details, which follow, may seem dry; but are indispensable for a proper study of the *Ṛgvidhāna* text. A few cases of Prakritism or rather few irregular forms caused by the same tendencies as those which affected the formation of the Prakrit language have occurred: *tāṇḍula*, ii.35, without any additional sense;[2] *varṣāpayet*, ii.41; and *utkhāpayīta*, iv.61, are examples of stems having the Prakritic causative form *āpaya*. Prominent instances of Vedism are: *Śam*, ii.126, the indeclinable particle used substantively; *jyok*, ii.174, the adverbial particle of time used with the 3rd sing. opt. part. of *jīv*; and a few more words[3] are used with direct reference to the passages in the *Ṛgveda-saṁhita*. In the exegetical notes appended to each stanza of my translation to the *Ṛgvidhāna*, I have called attention to whatever might

1. *Ṛgvidhānam*, ed. by R. Meyer, intro. pp. viii-xi.

2. The word *tāṇḍula* is neither registered in *MW*, nor in any lexicons, though it could be formed by Pāṇini 4.3.120, still it is not recorded from other literature.

3. These words are collected and given under the heading: V. Vocabulary. Dr. Meyer adds the following Vedic peculiarities: *Sūryāyai*, iii.115; *varcasyam*, iv.43; *Stṛṇute sapatnān*, ii.124, 171; *hās*, iv.20; *ūrjam*, ii.169; *jātarūpamayaḥ*, iv.36; *sumanasaḥ*, iv.59; *virudhaiḥ*=virudbhiḥ, ibid., *sarūpavatsā gauḥ, dhenuḥ*, ii.84, iii.97; *tiṣyena*, iv.106; *śaradam*=year, iv.93. Most of these peculiarities are not exclusively Vedic. The root *hās* does not occur in the *Ṛvidh*. See my notes to *Ṛvidh* iv.20.

seem of interest to the Sanskrit philologists, but for convenience my findings, as a whole will be grouped under the following six headings: I. Phonology; II. Euphonic combination; III. Morphology; IV. Syntax; V. Vocabulary; VI. Metre, and they will be taken up in the order thus indicated.

## *I. Phonology*

### *A. Substitution of Vowels*

Ṛ for RI: *śṛtam*—La Ed i.165—Cr Ed i.163 (śritam). Here *śṛtam* appears to be a hyper-Sanskritized form of *śritam* and its acceptance in the *Ṛgvidhāna* text would spoil the metre.

### *B. Substitution of Consonants*

1. Ṭ for T: *Kīṭalūṭāsu*, Be Ed i.28.2—Cr Ed i.152 (*Kīṭalūtāsu*).
2. Ś for S: *kṛśara-*, Be Ed iv.3.2—La Ed iv.12—Cr Ed iv.12 (*Kṛsara*).
3. Ṣ for S: *anuṣevayet*, Be Ed ii.35.4—La Ed ii.191—Cr Ed ii.185 (*anusevayet*).
4. S for Ś: *srotāṁsi*, Be Ed iii.12.1—La Ed iii.62—Cr Ed iii.61 (*śrotāṁsi*).
5. S for Ṣ: *sisādhayiṣu*, Be Ed i.22.7—La Ed. i.122—Cr Ed i.120 (*siṣādhayiṣu*).

### *C. Shortening or lengthening of a syllable for the sake of metre*

1. Shortening: *abhyupayāt* (for *abhyupeyāt*. so ms D of Prof. Gonda), Be Ed i.4.5; iii.15.3—La Ed i.21; iii.81—Cr Ed i.21; iii.80 (*abhyupayant*); *manyeta*,[4] Be Ed ii.27.2—La Ed ii.147 —Cr Ed ii.141; *maharṣiṇām*, Be Ed ii.32.1—La Ed ii.173—Cr Ed ii.167; *jñātinām*. Be Ed iii.215—La Ed iii.113—Cr Ed iii. 112; *Somagandharvavahninām*, Be Ed iii.23.4—La Ed iii.122—Cr Ed iii.121.
2. Lengthening: *trāyeta*,[4] Be Ed i.26.1—La Ed i.142—Cr Ed i.140; *sidhyate*, Be Ed ii.12.2—La Ed ii.57—Cr Ed ii.57; *jivate*, Be Ed ii.32.4—La Ed ii.176—Cr Ed ii.170; *smarate*, Be Ed iii.1.4—La Ed iii.4—Cr Ed iii.4; *jīveta*,[5] Be Ed iv.19.2+La Ed

4. Observe the use of optative for indicative, *m.c. vide* Hopkins, *The Great Epic of India*, p. 264.

5. As most of the peculiarities in the previous heading are found mainly

iv.98—Cr Ed iv.97; *tuṣyate*, Be Ed iv.27.4—La Ed iv.142—Cr Ed iv.140.

*D. Rare Spellings*

Examples are: *medhyānnamitabhūn*, La Ed ii.27 = Cr Ed ii.27 (*medhyānnamitabhug*); *vāṅmī*, Be Ed ii.23.4; iv.4.4—La Ed ii.122; iv.19—Cr Ed ii.121; iv.19 (*vāgmī*).

## *II. Euphonic Combination*

*A. Hiatus*

1. Inter-pāda hiatus: This is quite freely allowed between *pādas* in the same hemistich. There are, according to my recknoing, about 46 cases of such hiatus, or about one case in every sixteen stanzas. Some of the manuscripts remove the hiatus either by the insertion of a particle or by combining both the vowels into one and thereby leaving the posterior *pāda* a syllable less.
2. Hiatus within a *pāda*: This occurs rather frequently and these occurrences can be reduced to (1) Vedic quotations, e.g. *Ko adya*, ii.65 etc. or (2) *a* or *ā*+*ṛ*, besides hiatus caused by a recent loss of *s* or *y*.

*B. Double-Sandhi*

Examples are: *pra mandineti* (*pramandine iti*), i.123; *amīvaheti* (*amīvahāḥ iti*), ii.139; and *muktyaikamārga*-(*muktyai ekamārga*), iii.230.

## *III. Morphology*

*A. Nominal Inflection*

*(a) Declensional peculiarities*

1. Nominative plural feminine of *ī*-stem in *ayas* for *yas*: *devapatnayaḥ*, ii.83.

---

in the Be Ed and its counterpart Devanāgarī edition printed in Lahore, references are made to them but henceforth I propose to give references to the critical edition only.

2. Accusative singular masculine of *ī*-(or *in*-?) stem: *jñātinam*, ii.86.
3. Accusative plural masculine of *in*-(or *ī*-?) stem: *hastīn*, ii.35.
4. Accusative plural feminine of *ī*-stems in *as* for *īs*: *vyāhṛtayaḥ*, i.15; i.55; *pāvamanyaḥ*, i.55; *mahiṣyaḥ*, ii.35; *devapatnayaḥ* (for *devapatnyaḥ*), ii.83; *vṛddhayaḥ*, iii.18. But we meet with just the reverse in *rauhītakīḥ* (for *rauhītakyaḥ*), iv.51.
5. Accusative plural feminine of *ṛ*-stēm: *lokamātaraḥ*, ii.112.
6. Dative singular of *ī*-stem: *pataye*, i.23.
7. Genitive plural masculine of *i*-(or *in*-?) stem: *jñātinām*, iii.12.
8. Locative singular neuter of *an*-stem: twice the syncopated from *mūrdhni*, iii.160, and 209, but elsewhere the full form, as *mūrdhani*, iii.53.

(*b*) *Stem formation*

1. Feminine stems: *ādhyātmikī*,[6] i.107; *rauhītakī*, iv.51; *bailvakī*, iv.52. These are the only instances of forms in *ī* against normal *ā*.
2. New stems: *agadin*, nom.sing.mas., *agadī*, i.90; but elsewhere normal *agada*, i.93; ii.174. Possibly *agadin* was formed on the analogy of *gadin*, i.90. Again, *jñātin*, acc. sing. mas., *Jñātinam*, ii.86; gen. pl. *jñātinām*, iii.112. Again, *hasti*, acc.pl. mas., *hastīn*, ii.35.

*B. Verbal Inflections*

The abnormalities in verbal inflection concern mainly with "Class" and "Voice."

(*a*) *Change of "Class"*

1. I, Class for II: *ucchvaset*, iii.199 and 202.
2. I, Class for IV: *abhyaset*, i.95.106, 114, 121; ii.115; iii.130-131; iv.2; but normal IV, class, *abhasyet*, iii.198; *nyaset*, iii.93, 157-159; *vinyaset*, iii.157.
3. I, Class for VI: *lopet*, ii.28.

(*b*) *Change of "Voice"*

1. Parasmaipada for Ātmanepada: *anumantrayet*, ii.86; iv.11, 39; *abhimantrayet*, iii.108; iv.111, 114; *ārabhet*, ii.131; *ālabhet*,

6. According to *MW* (*s.v. ādhyātmika*), both forms are admissible.

iii.58; *īkṣet*, ii.67, *upatiṣṭhet*,[7] i.99, 110, 136, 139; ii.184; elsewhere normal *upatiṣṭheta*, i.81, 112, 131; ii.64, 163; *trāyati*; ii.163; *parājayet*,[8] ii.16; *bhuñjīyāt*,[9] i.145, a quite anomalous form,[10] apparently suggested by normal Ātm. form *bhuñjīta*, which occurs in i.126, 147; ii.84; *śaṅket*, ii.136; *samārabhet*, i.51, 53; iii.161.

2. Atmanepada for Parasmaipada: *gaccheta*, ii.129; iii.205; iv.6; *japeta*, i.53, 146; ii.9; iii.20, 231; iv.16, 71; elsewhere normal *japet*, i.15 *passim jīvate*, ii.170; *jīveta*, iv.97; elsewhere normal *jīvati*, ii.19; jīvet, i.93; ii.174; *tuṣyate*, iv.140; *paśyeta*, i.32; elsewhere normal *paśyet*, i.70, 110; *praṇaśyeta*, ii.13; *bhuñjīta*; iii.84; *riṣyeta*, iv.32; *vimṛjīta*, iii.74; *sidhyate* ii.57; *smarate*, iii.4.
3. Causatives: *añjayīta*, iv.48; *utkhāpayīta*, iv.61; *dhārayīta*, iii.207; *vijñāpayīta*, iv.3.26; *śodhayīta*, iv.84, are examples of 3d. sing. opt. Ātm. in *īta* instead of *eta*.[11]
4. Conjunctive particles: *arcya*, ii.168, 175, 179; iii.144; *chādya*, i.60; *dhārya*, iii.202 are instances of gerunds in *ya* from an uncompounded root, but compound gerunds sometimes take *tvā*: *namaskṛtvā*, i.1; ii.124; iii.146; iv.5, 70, elsewhere normal *namaskṛtya*, i.126. Besides *japtvā*, i.15 *passim*, we have a less common form *japitvā*, iii.167, only once, to suit the metre (Anuṣṭubh). Again, *prapīya*, iii.7, a solecism for the grammatically correct form *prapāya*.[12]
5. Derivative suffixes: *vāstoṣpatam* (for *vāstoṣpatyam*), iii.138. We find an action-noun *abhiṣecana* (for *abhiṣecanīya*), i.89; ii.96; used adjectively, but we meet with just the reverse in *nivedana* (for *naivedya*), iii.165, and in *smṛta* (for *smṛti*), iv.98. Further we have *bhaiṣajya* (for *bheṣajya*), i.89, a derivative in *ya* with initial Vṛddhi-strengthening, used adjectively. Finally

7. The Parasmaipada does not express the notion registered by the Vārttika on Pāṇini 1.3.25.
8. The use of Parasmaipada infringes Pāṇini 1.3.19.
9. The root *bhuj* meaning 'eat, enjoy, etc.' takes Atm. terminations, whereas the same root meaning 'control, govern' takes Par. terminations *vide* Pāṇini 1.3.66.
10. *vide* Whitney 688a.
11. *ibid.*, 1043c.
12. *vide* Pāṇini 6.4.69.

we have *bilvodumbara*, (for *bailvodumbara*) iv.51 without initial Vṛddhi-strengthening.

## *IV. Syntax*

From the syntactical point of view, the language of the *Ṛg-vidhāna* is of considerable historic interest, as it retains many of the old idioms side by side with the new ones and in this respect it represents a genuine stage of transition from the later Vedic literature to the classical one. An attempt is made in the following pages to show examples of some uses of cases which, though not always unknown in Sanskrit, are at least not usual in the classical Sanskrit.

### *A. Noun-Syntax*

In regard to syntax, it may be noted that the rules of concord are observed carefully, but the following examples are noteworthy: *satyaṁ teṣāṁ sādhanaṁ saṁyamaś ca śamas titīkṣānasūyā damaś ca*, i.7; *ojas tejas tathārogyaṁ dviṣaddveṣaṁ prakīrtitam,* i.104. Exchange of plural for dual: *śītoṣṇaiḥ*, ii.16; *ripurogaiḥ*, ii.137. Syntactical agreement between the genitive[13] and the accusative is found in iv.105: *yavānāṁ tu ghṛtāktānaṁ...juhuyāt...dadhimadhvājyasaṁskṛtān.*

#### (*a*) *Nominative*

The Nominative is the subject case; and there is hardly anything that goes against the normal usage, but the following may be noted: *uddiśya nāma homo'yaṁ saptarātram na jīvati,* ii. 19.

1. The nominative for the accusative in the object of a sentence: *japed vyāhṛtayaḥ*, i.15; *śaṁvatyaḥ svastimatyaśca japeta,* i.53; *japed dvijaḥ*, *śuddhavatyas tathābvatyaḥ pāvamānyaḥ*, i.55; *mahiṣyo yāvakaiḥ...avāpnuyāt*, ii.35; *yajet...devapatnayaḥ*, ii. 83; *goṣṭhagā lokamātaraḥ, upatiṣṭhet,* ii.112; *vindate ceha vṛddhayaḥ*, iii.18; *japann imam ṛṣiṁ vipraḥ strī vaśaṁ sādhigacchati*, ii.104. Though morphological confusion is apparent in the earlier examples, but the last one is a clear case of syntactical confusion.

13. Interchangeable, of course, with the accusative. See (f) 7 below p. 136.

2. Nominative for instrumental: *yathā yathā prajvalite hūyate jātavedasi, dīptā pratikṛtir vipraḥ tathā sa vaśameṣyati*, iii.91-92, is an instance of a logical subject in the nominative following a passive construction which would require an instrumental.
3. Mixture of cases: *yasya naṣṭaṁ bhavet kiṁcit dravyaṁ gaur dvipadaṁ dhanam*, ii.121, is an instance of an accusative *dvipadam* among the prevailing nominatives.

(*b*) *Accusative*

The accusative is the case of objective construction with verbs, prepositions, etc.

1. The etymological cognate accusative: *yogaṁ yuñjīta*, iii.193.
2. Accusative with verbs: *abhi-car:*[14] *amānuṣīr abhicaret*, iv.41; *grah: yā garbhaṁ na gṛhṇīyāt*, iv.117; *pra-muñc: nārī garbhaṁ pramuñcati* (i.123); *vind: yāvad garbhaṁ na vindati*, iii.147.
3. Accusative with adjectives: *adhvānaṁ prasthitaḥ*, ii.9.
4. Accusative *temporis: tryaham adyād ayācitam*, i.33 etc. and examples need not be multiplied, as its use is quite normal.
5. The accusative denoting a point of space or time: *yāṁ diśaṁ saptajaptena loṣṭena saṁpracāṭayet*, ii.39; *taṁ māsaṁ tasya duḥkhaṁ hi na jātu trividhaṁ bhavet*, i.113; *juhuyād āyasaṁ śaṅkuṁ...caturdaśīm*, iii.78; *dvādaśa dvādaśīḥ...nirvapec carum*, iii.137; *saṁviśet kṣapām*, iii.146. The above examples show that the accusative has replaced the locative to a considerable extent.
6. Accusative for dative: *śunāśīraṁ...hutvā*, ii.70.
7. Accusative with adverbs and prepositions: *tyaktvānyatra bhayāvaham*, ii.116; *brāhmaṇān bhuñjato' grataḥ*, iii.5; *na yoniṁ pratijāyate*, ii.186.

(*c*) *Instrumental*

1. The cognate instrumental: *rāyaspoṣeṇa puṣyati*, iv.50-51.
2. Instrumental with verbs: *abhi-siñc: etābhir abhiṣicya*, iii.27; *stheyābhir adbhiḥ pūrṇena abhiṣiñcet*, iii.125; *sarvauṣadhirasaiḥ ...abhiṣicya*, iv.108; *arc: arcayitvā gandha-mālyaiḥ*, ii.23; *kāmair arcanti*, ii.24; *ava-kir: puṣpair avakiret*, iii.50; *dhṛ: śirasā*

14. For *abhi- car* with the genitive vide (f) 12 below p. 137.

*dhārayed agnim*, i.80; *śirasā dhārayet tu tam*, ii.69; *śirasā dhārayed gurum*, iii.87; *śirasā dhārayet* (*scil.maṇim*), iii.92; *parī-nī: pariṇayet saṁtatodakadhārayā*, iv.55; *prati-kir: puṣpaiḥ pratikiret*, iv.132; *bhāṣ: anāryair na ca bhāṣeta*, i.19; *riṣ: prajayā vittaiḥ...na riṣyati*, ii.135; *vac: mantrair vakṣyāmi*, i.50; *vṛt: haviḥ śeṣeṇa varteta*, i.166: *saṁ-vad: tena saṁvadet*, i.65; *saṁ-spṛś: vrātyairvā saṁspṛśet*, ii.158; *sam-abhivās: gandhaiḥ samabhivāsayet*; iii.50; *sampra-caṭ: saptajaptena loṣṭena sampracāṭayet*, ii.39; *snā: sahasrajaptena snāyāt...jalena*, ii.38; *snātvādbhiḥ*, ii.96; *snāpayed abhirūpaiḥ*, iii.117; *snāpayed āhanasyābhiḥ* iii.126.

3. Instrumental with adjectives and nouns: *sammitā vedaiḥ*, i.73; *rogairgṛhītaḥ*, i.101; *ṛcā dīptam*, ii.111; *āśriyā...āviṣṭaḥ*, iii.73; *gṛhītaṁ yakṣmaṇā*, iv.81; *prāṇāyāmair dagdadoṣaḥ*, i.59; *pāpena vipramokṣaḥ*, iii.215.
4. *Instrumentalis temporis: ekaikaṁ saptarātreṇa punāti*, i.47, and so on, but the following miscellaneous uses of instrumental may be noted.
5. The instrumental for the accusative of time: *māsenāśnan*, i.44; *kriyāṁ tu saptarātreṇa saptakṛtvo' bhyaset*, iv.2.
6. The instrumental denoting the locative of time: *ṣaḍbhir varṣaiḥ pramucyate*, iii.28.
7. The verbs meaning 'be freed from' often governs the instrumental;[15] *pāpaiḥ pramucyate*, i.28; ii.173; *mucyate copapātakaiḥ*, i.29; *pātakaiḥ sarvair duṣkṛtaiś ca pramucyate*, i.30; *tenā'dharmeṇa mucyate*, i.58; *pāpaiś ca parimucyate*, i.68; *malavyādhivināyakair mucyet*, ii.38; *sarvapāpaiḥ pramucyate*, ii.59; iii.2; 132; iv.28; *ripurogaiḥ pramucyate*, ii.137; *mucyate sarvakilbiṣaiḥ*, ii.166.
8. The verb *vi-yuj* governs the instrumental case once: *na ca bhartrā viyujyate*, iii.64.

### (*d*) *Dative*

In the *Ṛgvidhāna*, the dative is replaced by the genitive to a considerable extent and hence its use is much restricted.

1. Dative with verbs: *pra-klp*: *pitṛbhyaśca prakalpayet*, i.26; pra-

15. For normal ablative. See (e) 2 below p. 135.

*pad: prapadyet prayataḥ śriyai*, ii.95; elsewhere normal accusative.

2. The verb meaning 'to employ' governs the dative: *saṁgrāmam abhyudyatāya rājñe caitat prayojayet*, iv.8, but see below (f) 4 p. 136.
3. Dative with adjectives and nouns: *jitaṁ te*, iii.174; *names te*, iii.174.
4. Dative for genitive: *sūryāyai bhāvavṛttaṁ tu śrāvayet kanyakāṁ pitā*, iii.115.

### (*e*) *Ablative*

1. Ablative with verbs: *trā: ekaḥ śatāni trāyeta taskarebhyaḥ*; i.140; *sa trāyati bhayāt svayam, ii.*163; *pari-rakṣ: sarvebhyaḥ parirakṣati*, iv.9; *bhī*: *kilāsatvād bhibheta*, ii.105.
2. The verbs meaning 'be freed from' governs the ablative: *mucyate sarvapāśebhyaḥ*, i.90: *pāpāt pramucyate*, i.117; *tebhyaḥ pramucyate*, i.119; *mucyate, visvasmāt...aṁhasaḥ*, i.125; *tebhya eva pramucyate*, i.138; *mucyeta kilbiṣāt*, i.141; *kṛṣidoṣāt pramucyate*, ii.77; *vāruṇebhyaḥ sa pāśebhyaḥ mucyate*, ii.126; *rogebhyaś ca pramucyate*, ii.134; *bhūmipāśāt pramucyate*, ii. 149; *tasmāt pāpāt pramucyate*, ii. 151; *mahat kṛcchrāt pramucyate*, ii.161; *mucyate bandhanāt*, ii.177; *tasmāt pramocayet*, ii.182; *mucyate pāpāt*; iii.26; *enobhyaḥ pramucyate*, iii.55; *mucyate, sarvato' niṣṭāt*, iv.41.
3. The verb *cyav* governs the ablative: *saṁgrāmāc cyavate*, ii.89.
4. Ablative with adjectives and nouns: *bhraṣṭo vāpi pathaḥ*, i.148; *yatnād yuktaḥ*, ii.109, *vyādhibhyaḥ parimokṣam*, iii.14; *aribhyo bhayam*, i.118.
5. The temporal ablative: *tryahāc chuciḥ*, iii.7, 15; *smṛtam eva tasya syāt ṣaṇmāsāt*, iv.98.
6. In the following instances the ablative carries the sense of the temporal instrumental: *ekāhāl labhate vittaṁ dyahāt siddhim anuttamām*, i.157; *tapasvinaṁ saptarātrāj jayet*, iii.84; *tryahāt siddhiṁ niyacchati*, iv.72.

### (*f*) *Genitive*

The genitive can, rightly, be regarded as the most living case, since it replaces almost all other oblique cases in the *Ṛgvidhāna*.

1. Genitive with verbs: *brāhmaṇasya phalaṁ yacchanti*, i.7; *cak-*

*ṣurdivyaṁ hotur dadāti saḥ*, i.221, are instances of indirect objects being put into the genitive. Sometimes both the objects are put in the genitive: *etat* (*scil. karma*) *phalasyāsya prayacchati*, iii.65.

2. The root *prakāś* seems to take the genitive: *bhaktānāṁ tvaṁ prakāśase*, iii.178.
3. The verb meaning 'to be pleased with' governs the genitive: *prīyate' sya yamo rājā*, iii,36.
4. The verb meaning 'to employ' governs the genitive: *saṁgrāmaṁ tu prayātasya rājñaś caitat prayojayet*, ii.128; *saṁgrāmaṁ vijigīṣataḥ prayoktavyam*, iv.75-76.
5. The root *ud-yam* governs the genitive: *brahmaṇasya ruṣodyamya*, iii.30.
6. Genitive for nominative: *agniṁ prajvālya juhuyād ghṛtena brāhmaṇo yadi, kṣatriyasya tu tailena sārṣapeṇa viśām api*, iii. 89, is an instance in which the nouns of the second hemistich, introduced by *yadi*, are put in the genitive instead of the nominative.
7. Genitive for accusative: *pālāśasamidhāṁ...hutāśane...hutva*, ii.31; *guṭikānāṁ...hutvā*, ii.34; *jātīcaṁpakarājārkakusumānāṁ ...hutvā*, ii.36; *raktānāṁ taṇḍulānām...hutāśane hutvā*, ii.50; *puṣpāṇaṁ samidhāṁ caiva, hutvā* ii.53; *brāhmaṇasya ruṣodyamya*, iii.30; *etat phalasyāsya prayacchati*, iii.65; *khādirīṇāṁ hi samidhāṁ juhuyāt*, iv.50; *yavānāṁ tu ghṛtāktānāṁ...juhuyāt*, iv.105.
8. Genitive for instrumental: *tṛtīyāṁ ca tayoḥ saha*, i.22; *na ca sādhyo' si kasyacit*, iii.179; *japyam eva syāt saṁgrāmaṁ abhigacchataḥ*, iv.76; *tatrāsya bhojanīyaṁ syāt*, iv.83.
9. Genitive for dative: *siddhasyaś ca tapomūlāḥ śraddadhānasya kurvataḥ*, i.4; *brāhmaṇasya phalaṁ yacchanti*, i.7; *gandharvāpsarasām api*, i.24; *tathā viṣṇoḥ*, i.25; *agnir vratānte' syopatiṣṭhati*, i.82; *durge pathi prayātasya nāsyāribhyo bhayaṁ bhavet*, i.118; *juhvatas tat praśāmyati*, ii.51; *hutvā tu pṛthag etāsām*, ii.70; *saṁgrāmaṁ tu prayātasya rajñaścaitat prayojayet*, ii.128; *pūrvāhne japato nityam arthasiddhiḥ parā bhavet*, ii.167; *etat phalasyāsya*[16] *prayacchati*, iii.65; *svastyayanaṁ snātakasya vidhīyate*, iii.70; *strīṇāṁ saṁvananaṁ caitat puṁsām api vidhīyate*,

16. *phalasyāsya=phalam asmai.*

*dveṣyaṁ tu jñātinām eva,* iii.111-112; *kartavyo' tra tathā yāgaḥ somagandharvavahninām...apsarasām...devapatnīnāṁ ratipradyumnayoḥ tathā,* iii.121-122; *agnau kriyāvatāṁ devo divi devo manīṣiṇām, pratimāsvalpabuddhīnāṁ yogīnāṁ hṛdaye hariḥ* iii.151; *bhaktānāṁ tvaṁ prakāśase, iii.*178; *sa sa kāmaḥ samṛddhaḥ syāc chraddadhānasya kurvataḥ,* iii.213; *hotur dadāti,* iii.221; *athāsya varadā devī rātrir bhavati,* iv. 26; *saṁgrāmaṁ vijigīṣataḥ, prayoktavyaṁ tu śucinā,* iv.75-76.

10. Genitive with adverb: *tayoḥ saha,* i.22.
11. Elliptic genitive: *tad vratasya mahātmanaḥ,* i.83.
12. Genitive absolute: *nāsya kaścid avadhyo' sti japato juhvato' pi vā,* ii.20; *tasyābhicarataḥ sākṣād āṅgirasa ṛṣeḥ svayam, pratyaṅgirasakalpena sarvaṁ tat pratibādhate,* iv.40.

### (g) *Locative*

1. Locative with verbs: *āditye' gnau candramasi vṛkṣāgreṣu ca dhārayet,* iii.206.
2. Locative with adjectives and nouns: *tapasyadhyayane yuktaḥ,* i.8; *sa mūḍho gahane pathi,* iii.57; *nitya-naimittike kāmye tritaye tu parāyaṇam,* ii.26.
3. Locative for accusative: *yatrecchej jātavedasi,* ii.79.
4. Locative for instrumental: *sakhidāreṣu saṁvasan,* ii.152.
5. Locative for ablative: *bhayaṁ cāsya na vidyeta nadītīracareṣvapi,* ii.6.
6. The locative absolute is fairly abundant and calls for no remark. But the following is an instance of a locative absolute partly replaced by the instrumental *patraiś ca puṣpaiś ca phalaiś ca toyairakrītalabdhaiś ca sadaiva satsu,* iii.29.

## *B. Compounds*

Under this head, I give some examples of peculiar compound formations or loose construction with compounds: *nārīnaragośānti,* i.97; *indrāṇyā kṛtasaṁvādam,* iii.119; *priyaṅguvaṭanāgānāṁ kaṣayodghṛṣṭakesaram,* iii.123; *nyāyakḷpta,* iii.192; *akrītalabdha,* iii.229; *bhaktyaikalabhya,* iii.229.

## *C. Verb*

### (*a*) *Tenses*

The use of the tenses is regular, but following are some of the noteworthy features. The causative forms are sometimes used for simplex: *jyotsnāṁ...anusevayet*, ii.185; *sarasvatīṁ cārcayeta*, iii. 17. As in the classical Sanskrit, there is no distinction between the imperfect and the perfect. The latter[17] is the least frequent of all. The only example of an aorist is that of an augmentless one, used with prohibitive particle *mā: mā bhūd asya parikṣayaḥ*, iii. 184. The periphrastic future occurs once: *prayāṇakālo bhavitā*, iv.27.

### (*b*) *Modes*

The optative occurs with about 109 roots giving about 150 forms, while the imperative occurs with about 5 roots giving about 6 forms. The precative occurs twice: *indraṁ stūyāt*, i.91; *iśānaṁ tuṣṭūyāt* i.97. The latter form appears to furnish a rare example of a perfect precative.

### (*c*) *Periphrastic verbal expressions*

The periphrastic verbal expressions, involving the use of future participles with the optative forms of *as* is, on the whole, regular: *japyam eva syāt*, iv.53, 76; *tatrāsya bhojanīyaṁ syāt*. iv.83. The simple future is expressed by means of a desiderative adjective with *asmi*: *vivakṣur asmi*, i.1. In *yaḥ karoti sahasraṁ syāt*, iii.137, we seem to have a periphrasis consisting of a finite verb *karoti* with the optative form *syāt* taking the place of an auxiliary.

### (*d*) *Verbal Compounds*

Some rare verbal compounds are shown under this heading. In some cases the prefixes affixed to the roots are clearly pleonastic. Examples are: *saṁpracāṭayet*, ii.39; *pracāṭayet*, ii.49; *saṁprakalpayet*, ii.95; iii.113; iv.47; *adhigacchati*, iii.104; *upoddharet*, iii.126; *pratimuñceta*, iv.37. The following compound verbs are also noteworthy: *praśnaṁ kṛtvā* (*pṛṣṭvā*), ii.171; *cūrnaṁ kṛtvā* (*cūrṇayitvā*), iv.84).

## *D. Sentence-Construcion*

Usual freedom is observable in sentence-construction, though irregularities in the construction are less frequent.

17. An instance of a perfect in the Berlin edition (Be Ed i.20.2-La Ed i.107) is due to Dr. Meyer's emendation. Another instance (Be Ed i.24.3-La Ed i.132-Cr Ed i.130) seems to be a corruption.

1. Abnormal constructions: *apo hiṣṭheti sūktaṁ tu śuddhavayto'-ghamarṣaṇam, śaṁvatyaḥ svastimatyaś ca pāvamānyas tathaiva ca,* i.16; *na rajasvalayā nāryā patitair nāntyajair nṛbhiḥ, na deva-brāhmaṇadviṣṭair nācāryagurunindakaiḥ,* i.20; *yatātmano' pra-mattasya dvādaśāham abhojanam,* i.39. No finite verb seems to occur in the above examples.
2. Peculiar constructions: *upalabhya paraṁ brahma gatiṁ jñātvā bhavec chuciḥ,* iii.204; *gṛhītaṁ yakṣmaṇā darbhān gṛhītvā saṁ-spṛśan japet,* iv.81; *khādirāṇi ca kāṣṭhāni cūrṇaṁ kṛtvā sahām-bhubhiś śodhayīta rasaṁ caisām,* iii.84.
3. Faulty constructions: *yasyās tu gor gomayena guṭikānāṁ sahasraśaḥ hutvā tāṁ gām avāpnoti,* ii.34; *japann imaṁ ṛṣiṁ vipraḥ strī vaśaṁ sādhigacchati,* iii.104.

## *V. Vocabulary*

At the beginning of this chapter[18], I have pointed out a few instances of Prakritisms and Vedisms. Still a fair number of Vedic words remain. They are: *ajāśva* (=Pūṣan), ii.22; *āhanasyā,* iii.126; *ṛtāvṛdhau* (=Mitrāvaruṇau); ii.22; *gharma,* i.126; *nicṛt,* i.73; *babhru* (=Soma), ii.22; *rapas,* i.38.126; iii.15; *ripra,* i.128, 132; ii.172, 183; *Śukra* (adj.) iv.126.

The most remarkable feature of the *Ṛgvidhāna* vocabulary lies in the desiderative formations. The following desideratives occur in the *Ṛgvidhāna.*

Adjectives: *vivakṣu,* i.1; *mumūrṣu,* i.108; *siṣādhayiṣu,* i.120; *titīrṣu,* ii.7; *uttitīrṣu,* ii.136; *prepsu,* iii.195; *ārirādhayiṣu,* iv. 137.

Substantives: *titīkṣā,* i.7; *jugupsita,* i.147; *jijñāsana,* iii.205; *īpsita,* iii.224.

Finite Verbs: *tuṣṭūṣyante,* i.5; *cikīrṣati,* i.142; *titīrṣati,* ii.8.

Participles: *īpsant,* i.114; *ārurukṣant,* iii.43; *vijigīṣant,* iv.75.

Yet another feature of the *Ṛgvidhāna* consists often in the repetition of the same phrases and idioms. Though examples of such repetitions can easily be multiplied, but a few given below:—

*sa sa kāmaḥ samṛddhaḥ syāt,* i.12; iii.213.

18. *Vide Supra* p. 127.

*gṛhāṁś cāpnoty anāmayān*, i.69, 95, 127.
*śirasā dhārayet*, i.80; ii.69; iii.87; iv.92.
*grāhyam atyantayatnena*, iii.191, 216.
*na paśyec chṛuṇuyān na ca*, iii.197, 200

The following are the rare and peculiar words that occur in the *Ṛgvidhāna*: *aṁsutejas*, iv.24; *atistava*, i.132; *anandhatā*, i.106; *astaga*, i.93; *āyus* (*āyuṣya*), iii.43; *indrajāla* (adj.), iv.116; *ṛṣi* (*ārṣa*), i.67, 90, 124; iii.80, 82, 104, 109, 188, 198, 212-213; iv.16. 34-36; *Kṛṣṇajāyā*, iii.107; *kruddhābhicarita*, iv.30; *drāviṇa* meaning 'possessing or bestowing wealth', ii.11; *pratibhākārya*, i.119; *bhasmahoma*, ii.42; *bhumipāśa*, ii.149; Śunaśepha (Śaunaśepha), i.90; *sāyojya*, iv.45; *sārvabhaumam* (*sarvabhūmyām*), ii.41; *saubhātṛkaraṇa*, iv.123; *sṃṛta* (*smṛti*), iv.98).

A comparison of some of the irregular forms and usages, cited in the different heads above with the list of irregularities in the *Bṛhaddevatā* given by Prof. Macdonell,[19] shows conclusively that the *Ṛgvidhāna* stands on an equal footing with the *Bṛhaddevatā* in all respects.

### *VI. Metre*

The *Ṛgvidhāna* is composed for the most part in the Anuṣṭubh metre except for some eight stanzas—occurring mostly in the First[20] and the Fourth[21] Adhyāyas—with different metres. The following remarks are based entirely on the text as constituted by me. At the outset, I may state that the Anuṣṭubh in the *Ṛgvidhāna* is essentially of a later type than the Anuṣṭubh stanzas of the Gṛhyasūtras,[22] and this is shown by the fact that the posterior *pāda* of each hemistich ends iambically,[23] whereas the second foot of the prior *pāda* is ⏑ — — ⏑ in 1237 cases out of a possible 1472. The remaining 235 cases show a much greater variety of form than is allowed in the classical *śloka*, the two epics being excepted. There

19. *Bṛhaddevatā*, Part I, intro. pp. xxvi-xxviii.
20. *Ṛvidh* i.1, 5-7.
21. ibid., iii.224-225, 229-230.
22. Oldenberg, *Gṛhya Sūtras*, Part, II (SBE 30), pp. xi-xiv, xix, xxxv-xxxvi.
23. Exceptions are: i.59d; ii.11b, 22b(hyp.), 28b; iii.126b; iv.57d(hyp.).

are a dozen[24] instances of Anuṣṭubh *pādas*, when they form the first half of a line, consisting of nine or ten syllables.

In 69 cases[25] the prior *pāda* ends in ⏑⏑⏑⏑. I have arranged them below in the order of frequency, and further distributed them as follows:

1. Schema: — ⏑ — — —, ⏑ ⏑ ⏑ : 8
   +6 with caesura after the sixth syllable.
2. Schema: — — ⏑ — ⏑, ⏑ ⏑ ⏑ : 8
   +5 with caesura after the fourth syllable.
3. Schema: ⏑ ⏑ — —, ⏑ ⏑ ⏑ ⏑ : 6
   +4 with caesura after the fifth syllable.
   +3 with caesura after the sixth syllable.
4. Schema: — — — — ⏑, ⏑ ⏑ ⏓ : 7
   +2 with caesura after the fourth syllable.
   +1 with caesura after the sixth syllable.
5. Schema: ⏑ — — — ⏑, ⏑ ⏑ ⏑ ⏓ : 5
   +4 with caesura after the fourth syllable.
   Schema: ⏑ — — ⏑ —, ⏑ ⏑ ⏑ ⏓ : 1
   Schema: — — — ⏑ —, ⏑ ⏑ ⏓ : 1
   Schema: ⏑ ⏑ ⏑ —, ⏑ ⏑ ⏓ : 1[26]
6. Schema: ⏑ — ⏑ —, ⏑ ⏑ ⏑ ⏓ : 5
   +1 with caesura after the fifth syllable.

In 56 cases[27] the prior *pāda* ends in — ⏑ ⏑ ⏓. There are five forms distributed as follows:—

Schema: ⏑ — ⏑ — — ⏑, ⏑ ⏓ : 12
+8 with caesura after the fourth syllable.

24. ii.100c, 130c, 136c, 179c; iii.54c, 71a; iv.57c, 88c, 93a, 112c, 127c, 134a.

25. i.11c, 23c, 40c, 41c, 46c, 52c, 71a, 77a, 113c, 114a, 114c, 115a, 115c, 129a, 138c, 159c, ii.4c, 52c, 69a, 71c, 72c, 74a, 94c, 106a, 153a, 159a, 180c, 186a; iii.7a, 10a, 16c, 19c, 25a, 32a, 59a, 57a, 67c, 77a, 90a, 116a, 120a, 120c, 128c, 153c, 156c, 156a, 172c, 199c; iv.21a, 37a, 41a, 44c, 45c, 50a, 55c, 62a, 72c, 73a, 74c, 76a, 79a, 93c, 98c, 99c, 102a, 104c, 112a, 131c; Phalaśritu, 6a.

26. The last two forms are very rare even in the *Mbh. vide* Hopkins, *op.cit.*, p. 236.

27. i.11a, 51a, 56a, 56c, 101c, 133a, 134a, 135c, 152c; ii.7a, 15c, 24c, 56c, 74c, 75c, 79a, 96a, 105c, 109c, 127a, 141a, 147a, 182c; iii.30c, 31c, 41c, 70a, 85c, 88c, 91c, 93a, 98a, 111c, 101a, 127c, 169c, 187c, 196a, 206c, 219c, 231a; iv.20c, 21c, 27c, 30a, 36a, 66c, 67a, 68a, 82a, 82c, 95c, 117c, 121a, 121c; Phalaśruti 11c.

+6 with caesura after the fifth syllable

Schema: — — ⏑ — —, ⏑ ⏑ ⏓ : 8

+6 with caesura after the sixth syllable

+5 with caesura after the fourth syllable

Schema: — — — —, — ⏑ ⏑ — : 4

+1 with caesura after the fifth syllable

Schema: — ⏑ — —, — ⏑ ⏑ ⏓ : 2

+2 with caesura after the fifth syllable.

Schema: ⏑ — — —, — ⏑ ⏑ ⏓ : 1

+1 with caesura after the sixth syllable.

In 39 cases[28] the prior *pāda* ends in — — — ⏓. There are seven forms distributed as follows:—

Schema: — — ⏑ — —, — — ⏓ : 17

Schema: ⏑ — ⏑ — —, — — ⏓ : 14

+3 with caesura after the sixth syllable.

Schema: — — — —, — — ⏓ : 1

Schema: ⏑ — — —, — — — ⏓: 1

Schema: ⏑ ⏑ ⏑ — —, — — ⏓ : 1

Schema: ⏑ — ⏑ ⏑ —, — — ⏓ : 1

Schema: ⏑ — — ⏑ —, — — ⏓ : 1

In 33 cases[29] the prior *pāda* ends in — ⏑ — ⏓. There are seven forms distributed as follows:

Schema: — — ⏑ —, — ⏑ — ⏓ : 8

+1 with caesura after the fifth syllable.

Schema: ⏑ — ⏑ —, — ⏑ — ⏓: 5

+1 with caesura after the sixth syllable.

Schema: — — — —, — ⏑ — ⏓ : 5

+1 with caesura after the sixth syllable.

Schema: ⏑ — — —, — ⏑ — ⏓ : 4

Schema: — ⏑ — —, — ⏑ — ⏓ : 3

Schema: — — — ⏑ — ⏑, — ⏓ : 2

+1 with caesura after the fourth syllable.

Schema: ⏑ ⏑ — —, — ⏑ — ⏓ : 2

28. i.60a, 63a, 96c, 101a, 146c; ii.1a, 6c, 59a, 60a, 96a, 129a, 134a; iii.8c, 11c, 50a, 51a, 54a, 59a, 75a, 63, 76c, 114a; 114c, 125a, 163a, 164c; 192a; 200a, 201a, 202a, 208a, 218c; iv.6c, 18c, 23c, 43a, 58a, 113a, 125a.

29. i.17c, 59a, 87c, 130; ii.11c, 34a, 91a, 91c, 138c; iii.6c, 17a, 66a, 84a, 103c, 159c, 160a, 192c, 193a, 194c, 203a, 217a; iv.33a, 34c, 48c, 55a, 62c, 86c, 97a, 114c, 118a, 131a, 135a, 142c.

In 13 cases[30] the prior *pāda* ends in ⏑ – ⏑ ⏓. These cases are of utmost importance, as they constitute the majority of the forms even in the Gṛhya Sūtras[31] etc. The classical *śloka*, it may be observed, does not favour a prior pāda ending in iambus. There are nine forms:—

Schema: ⏑ ⏑ – ⏑, ⏑ – ⏑ ⏓ : 3
Schema: – – ⏑ ⏑ ⏑, – ⏑ ⏓ : 2
Schema: – – – –, ⏑ – ⏑ ⏓ : 1
+1 with caesura after the fifth syllable.
Schema: – ⏑ – ⏑ ⏑ –, ⏑ ⏓ : 1
Schema: ⏑ – ⏑ ⏑ ⏑, – ⏑ ⏓ : 1
Schema: ⏑ – ⏑ –, ⏑ – ⏑ ⏓ : 1
Schema: ⏑ ⏑ – ⏑, ⏑ – ⏑ ⏓ : 1
Schema: – ⏑ – – ⏑, – ⏑ ⏓ : 1
Schema: ⏑ – – –, ⏑ – ⏑ ⏓ : 1

In 10 cases[32] the prior *pāda* ends in ⏑ ⏑ – ⏓. There are seven forms, but all the occurrences are sporadic:—

Schema: – – – –, ⏑ ⏑ – ⏓ : 2
Schema: – ⏑ – –, ⏑ ⏑ – ⏓ : 2
Schema: – – ⏑ –, ⏑ ⏑ – ⏓ : 2
Schema: ⏑ ⏑ – –, ⏑ ⏑ – ⏓ : 2
Schema: ⏑ – – ⏑ ⏑ ⏑, – ⏓ : 1
Schema: – – – ⏑ ⏑ ⏑ – ⏓ : 1
Schema: ⏑ – ⏑ ⏑, ⏑ ⏑ – ⏓ : 1

There remains 3 cases[33] of ending in – – ⏑ ⏓, viz.:—

Schema: ⏑ – ⏑ – – –, ⏑ – : 1
Schema: – – ⏑ – –, – ⏑ – : 1
Schema: ⏑ – – – –, – ⏑ – : 1

Out of the eight stanzas, the first four are Triṣṭubh stanzas[34] with four *pādas* of eleven syllables, the last four syllables of which scan – ⏑ – ⏓., whereas the previous syllables are dissimilar save in the two stanzas (i.1.6), where the first and the third *pādas* are identical. The Triṣṭubh stanza (i.5) has one twelve-syllable *pāda*,

30. i.38a; ii.13c, 67a, 87c, 153c; iii.118a, 119a, 158a; iv.25a, 118c, 123c, 125c, 141c.

31. *vide* Oldenburg, *op.cit.*, p. xi-xiv, xix, xxxv-xxxvi.

32. ii.37a, 172c; iv.1c, 3c, 54a, 56a, 60a, 81c, 85a, 89a.

33. iii.97c; iv.52a, 78c.

34. i.1, 5-7.

which, however, is not a Jagatī-pāda, since it has the Triṣṭubh finale.[35] The remaining four stanzas are: two Vasantatilakas (iii. 224, 225) and two Indravajras (iii.229, 230).

The large variety of the Anuṣṭubh forms together with the inter-*pāda* hiatus and its occasional lapses seem to be conclusive evidence of the transitional character of the Anuṣṭubh stanzas in the *Ṛgvidhāna*. The value of all this evidence linguistic and metrical appears to me to be decisive for, and consistent with, the date assigned to it on other grounds in the next chapter.

35. Cp. Edgerton, Epic Triṣṭubhs and its hyper-metric varieties, *JAOS*, Vol. LIX, p. 159. Regarding the metre of the *Bṛhaddevatā*, see Keith, *JRAS*, 1906, pp. 1-10.

CHAPTER IV

# AUTHORSHIP AND DATE

## 1. *Śaunaka, the author of Ṛvidh and other Works*

The known facts about Śaunaka are few, but the early existence of a tradition according to which the *Ṛgvidhāna* was considered either to be a work of his or at least to contain some of his views on the efficacy of the Ṛgvedic Mantras, is indicated by several passages of the work.[1] This tradition is further corroborated by Ṣaḍguruśiṣya in the introductory verses of his commentary entitled *Vedārthadīpikā* to the *Sarvānukramaṇī* of Kātyāyana. The *Vedārthadīpikā* was completed about the year 1187 A.D.[2] As Ṣaḍguruśiṣya's statements possess considerable importance, I give here the passage:[3]

Sa Śaunako munigato śrūyamāṇo mahāyaśāḥ //
dvitīyaṁ maṁḍalaṁ dṛṣṭvā śruta-Bhāratasaṁhitaḥ /
saṁsārābdhimahāpota-Viṣṇudharmapravarttakaḥ //
ekaviṁśatiśākhasya bahvṛcasya maharṣibhiḥ /
kalpitaḥ kalpitāro' bhūd Ṛgveda iva pāragaḥ //
Śākalasya saṁhitaikā Bāṣkalasya tathā' parā /
te saṁhite samāśritya brāhmaṇānyekaviṁśatiḥ //
Etareyaṁ samāśritya tadevānyaiḥ prapūrayan /
Kalpasūtraṁ cakārādyaṁ maharṣigaṇapūjitaḥ //
Śaunakasya tu śiṣyo' bhūd bhagavān Āśvalāyanaḥ /
sa tasmāc chrutasarvajñaḥ sūtraṁ kṛtvā nyavedayat //
prabodhapariśuddhyarthaṁ Śaunakasya priyaṁ tviti /
sahasrakhaṁḍaṁ svakṛtaṁ sūtraṁ brāhmaṇasaṁnibham //
Śiṣy-Āśvalāyaṇa prītyai Śaunakena vipāṭitam /
uktaṁ tat tatkṛtaṁ sūtram asya vedasya cāstv iti //

1. *Ṛvidh* i.2, 143; ii.141; iv.122-123, 139.
2. Macdonell, Kātyāyana's *Sarvānukramaṇī*, p. v.
3. Max Müller, *ASL* (Reprint), 1926, pp. 123-24.

Śaunakīyā daśagranthās tadā Ṛgvedaguptaye /
Ārṣyānukramaṇītyādyā Chāṁdasī Daivatī tathā //
Ṛkpādayor Vidhāne ca[4] Bārhaddaivatam eva ca /
Prātiśākhyaṁ Śaunakīyaṁ smārtaṁ daśamam ucyate //
Sa sūtradaśakam jñātvā tadā sākṛtagotrajñaḥ[5] /
Śaunakasya prasādena karmajñaḥ samapadyata //
Kātyāyanamunir mene trayodaśakam atra tu /
Śaunakīyaṁ ca daśakaṁ tac chiṣyasya trikaṁ tathā //

Ṣaḍguruśiṣya ascribes the following ten works to Śaunaka. They are:— 1. the *Ārṣānukramaṇī*; 2. the *Chaṁdonukramaṇī*; 3. the *Devatānukramaṇī*, 4. the *Anuvākānukramaṇī*, 5. the *Sūktānukramaṇī*, 6. the *Ṛgvidhāna*, 7. the *Pādavidhāna*, 8. the *Bṛhaddevatā*, 9. the *Ṛkprātiśākhya*, and 10. the *Smārta* work. The manuscripts of the *Devatānukramaṇī* and the *Sūktānukramaṇī* are no longer extant, though some quotations from the former work are embedded in the *Vedārthadīpikā* to the *Sarv* (i.165). All other eight works are either published or known to exist in the manuscripts only.

Dr. Meyer[6] alleges that the tenth work, which that scholar equates evidently with the Smārta-sūtra, is said to have been destroyed by Śaunaka himself. This is incorrect in view of the fact that the stanza which alludes to the alleged destruction of the Sūtras composed by Śaunaka actually precedes the stanzas which enumerate the ten works of Śaunaka and as such the tenth work could not have been destroyed. Further on, we are told by Ṣaḍguruśiṣya that Kātyāyana mastered the thirteen works: the ten works of Śaunaka and three works of Āśvalāyana. Prof. Max Müller asks us to believe that "Śaunaka's Śrauta-sūtra could not have been destroyed at the time of Kātyāyana."[7] But this is unnecessary in view of the following facts. First, we have some references to Śaunaka as an authority on the Dharmaśāstra.[8] Secondly, had

4. Mss. read vidhānena and Prof. Max Müller's above conjecture is correct.
5. Mss. read sākṛtagotrajaḥ. Prof. Max Müller's conjecture sākṛtagotrajñaḥ or vyākṛtagotrajñaḥ is not at all happy. It is metrically defective. Possibly the correct reading is Sāṁkṛtyagotrajaḥ.
6. *Op.cit.*, intro. p. ii.
7. Max Müller, *op.cit.*, p. 122.
8. Kane, *HDS*, Vol. I, pp. 132-23 and the footnotes thereon.

Ṣaḍguruśiṣya meant the tenth work to be a Sūtra one, then he would have, of course, used the word *sautram* in the place of *smārtam*. Thirdly, the use of *smārtam* in its eymological sense may refer to some Smṛti attributed to Śaunaka. That the extant Śaunaka-smṛti cannot be a work of Śaunaka is amply clear from its contents. It mentions a very late work like the *Prayogapārijāta*.[9] I have the following suggestion to make on this difficult problem. The word *Śaunakīyam* in the com. of Ṣaḍguruśiṣya can refer to the well-known work of that name and if this identification is correct, then the term Smārtam can refer only to the work *Śaunakīyam* attributed to Śaunaka[10] with which *Ṛvidh* has fourteen full stanzas and about twelve hemistiches in common.[11]

It is, however, to be noted that Śaunaka is a generic name and as such it is impossible to say who the author really was. The expression "śaunakāya namaḥ" occurring at the end of some of the manuscripts is totally misleading and it may lead one to surmise that Śaunaka, to whom the invocation is addressed and the composition of the work is ascribed, cannot be its real author. But such a view is untenable in view of the fact that the above expression is not found in all the manuscripts and its very existence in the archetypal manuscripts remains probematical, if not doubtful. Moreover, it can as well be ascribed to the copyists of mss.

As is well known, Śaunaka himself is cited as an authority in the *Ṛvidh*. Other authorities quoted are: Ṛṣyaśṛṅga (iii.142, 148), Kuśika (ii.20,66), Kauśika (ii.57), Nārada (iii.230), Manu (iv.121), 121), and Viṣṇu-kumāra (iii.230). There is one circumstance about the authorship of our work that needs to be noted. As a rule, the authorities are cited in connection with some peculiar efficacy of the Mantras or of the procedure, as the case may be, but Viṣṇukumāra alone claims that the *arcāvidhi* of Viṣṇu i.e. *Puruṣasūktavidhāna* was composed by him after going through a similar work 'declared by Nārada'.[12] Two explanations are possi-

9. *Ibid.*, p. 642.
10. *Śaunakīyam* (T.S.S., No. CXX), p. i.
11. *vide* Appendix B.
12. Ityevamuktaḥ puruṣasya viṣṇorarcāvidhirViṣṇukumāra-nāmnā / muktyaikamārgapratibodhanāya dṛṣṭvā vidhānaṁ tviha Nāradoktam // *Ṛvidh* iii.230.

ble, viz. that Viṣṇukumāra can be a personal name either of Śaunaka, as the latter name is clearly patronymic, or of the author of the *Puruṣasūktavidhāna*. The second alternative appears more reasonable than the first one which wholly depends on a fortuitous circumstance. Of this, however, further on.

One thing is certain, the author of the *Bṛhaddevatā*—whoever he may be, either Śaunaka himself or a teacher of his school, as Prof. Macdonell[13] puts it—has to be regarded as the author of the *Ṛgvidhāna* also. This conclusion is based on the following facts. First, the *Ṛgvidhāna* shares two and a half stanzas (exclusively of the frequent identity of diction) with the *Bṛhaddevatā*. Secondly, the *Ṛgvidhāna* mentions Stutyādayaḥ[14] in a casual manner, whereas the *Bṛhaddevatā* illustrates them[15] with quotations and same is the case with terms like *āhanasyā*, *sauparṇāni*, etc. The first section of the *Ṛgvidhāna* has purposely, been, made short and concise in order to avoid repetition of the matter already dealt with in the first chapter of the *Bṛhaddevatā*. Thirdly, the linguistic facts[16] conclusively prove that they are the composition of one author.

## 2. *Date of the Ṛvidh*

This presents considerable difficulty, as the problem of the date is closely connected with the problem of earlier and later strata in the extant *Ṛvidh*. However, an attempt is made in the following pages to record evidences, both external and internal, bearing on the problem of the date and while examining the internal evidence, I shall take up the problem of earlier and later strata and other allied problems.

First, the external evidence may be taken up. The earliest reference to Śaunaka as the author of the *Ṛvidh* occurs in the *Vedārthadīpikā* of Ṣaḍguruśiṣya, and for fixing the date of the *Ṛvidh* we need not consider any evidence after the twelfth century. That the complete *Ṛvidh* as we have it today, cannot be later than the

13. *Bṛhaddevatā* attributed to Śaunaka, intro. p. xxiv.

14. Śtutyādayo ye vikārāḥ pradiṣṭās tathārthvādā ṛkṣu sūkteṣu caiva / *Ṛvidh* i.5b.

15. *BD*, i.35-39, 46-58.

16. See Chapter III pp. 127-144 above.

eight century A.D. follows from the fact that it was made to serve as the basis for the parallel or abridged versions of the *Viṣṇudharmottara-* and the *Agni-purāṇas*. Allowing a certain period for the *Ṛvidh* to obtain recognition, we may set the lower limit at the fifth or the sixth century A.D., when the text of the *Ṛvidh* attained more or less the present form. But we can go still further back and can say with some amount of certainty that, with the exception of the sections containing Smṛti and Tantric topics which were undoubtedly added during the early centuries of the Christian era, the *Ur-Ṛgvidhāna* was anterior even to the *Sarvānukramaṇī* of Kātyāyana. As is well known, Kātyāyana had before him the ten works of Śaunaka and that the *Ṛvidh* being one of them naturally assumes prominence, as it may, perhaps, be the source from which Kātyāyana drew his inspiration.

The words '*ṛgvidha*' and '*ṛgvidhāna*' occur in the *Baudhāyana-Dharmasūtra* (1.7.10) and they are translated as "rik-shaped passage" and "a prescription consisting of a rik" by Dr. Bühler. The commentator explains neither *ṛgvidha* nor *ṛgvidhāna*, but refers to the *Taittirīyāraṇyaka* (1.7.1) which, according to him perhaps, is the passage intended by Baudhayana. Prof. Max Müller states that "the term *Ṛgvidhāna* is mentioned in the Taittirīyāraṇyaka."[17] As a matter of fact, that terms does not occur in any edition of the *TĀ* printed so far and it appears to me that Prof. Max Müller was possibly led away by the commentary on the *Bau Dh Su*. I can state this much that the question whether the term '*ṛgvidhāna*' refers to the well-known work of that name or merely "a prescription consisting of a ṛk" may be open to discussion but the fact remains that Baudhāyana knew some work or works dealing with the ritual employment of Ṛks. This evidence is valuable for us, as Baudhāyana has been assigned a date between 500-200 B.C.[18]

As stated earlier, a greater degree of caution is necessary while utilising the internal evidence for purposes of date. In our attempts to distinguish earlier and later strata, we must be guided as far as possible by the parallel or abridged versions as well as by other cognate works of Śaunaka, and before proceeding with

17. Max Müller, *op.cit.*, p. 122.
18. Kane, *HDS*, Vol. I, p. 30.

this, we may examine the chapter-divisions of our work. The division of the *Ṛvidh* into four (or five)[19] chapters is unscientific and arbitrary and further it does not represent the original state of things. Before the introduction of additional matter, the Adhyāyas I and II formed the First chapter of the *Ur-Ṛgvidhāna* and this is proved by the fact that the first Adhyāya of our work ends abruptly and the same topic is continued even to the next Adhyāya also. That the first chapter of the *Ur-Ṛgvidhāna* ended with second Adhyāya of the *Ṛvidh* is proved by another fact, viz. that the eighth Maṇḍala of the *Ṛgveda* is well-nigh over with the concluding stanzas and the subject-matter of the next Maṇḍala is briefly indicated. Likewise, Adhyāyas III and IV formed the second chapter of the *Ur-Ṛgvidhāna*. These considerations show that there was some rearrangement of the chapters of our work.

Now if we examine the *Ṛvidh* according to the principle enunciated in the preceding para, our results will be as follows: The stanzas 21-56 and 72-78 of the first Adhyāya must be regarded as later additions. The first passage (Sts. 27-56), which enumerates the various penances—mostly from the *Manusmṛti*—and teaches the manner of performing them, interrupts unnecessarily the continuity of the text, and has nothing whatsoever to do with the matter in hand except that one should purify oneself before performing any rite. The second passage (Sts. 72-78) on the efficacy of Gāyatrī verse is suspicious, as that topic is dealt with in the next chapter (ii.25-62). Among smaller additions in this chapter stanzas 9, 58 and 87 must certainly be reckoned.

In the second Adhyāya, there is one longer passage (Sts. 25-62) on the *Gāyatrīmantravidhāna* which is replete with repetitions of all sorts. This shows that the passage has been tampered with, though some stanzas may be found in the *Ur-Ṛgvidhāna*. Other probable additions are stanzas 149-152 on the release from Bhūmipāśa and on the sins of cohabiting with the forbidden women.

The contents of more than half of the third Adhyāya must be considered as later additions. The stanzas 21-33 on the expiation of the Brahmahatyā have their correspondences in the Smṛti literature. The next long passage (Sts. 79-114) on the Hṛdyasūkta is

19. Dr. Meyer's Fifth Adhyāya is=Vargas 1-3 of Phalaśruti.

exceedingly suspicious, as that passage is strongly reminiscent of Tantric practices which, though common in the Purāṇas and later works are unknown in the Vedic literature. That the *Ur-Ṛg-vidhāna* contained few hints regarding the Hṛdyasūkta cannot be denied in view of the overwhelming evidence of the *Bṛhaddevatā*[20] and the *Aṣṭādhyāyī*.[21] The last passage (sts. 134-230) on the *Puruṣasūkta-vidhāna* is entirely due to Viṣṇukumāra. The Tantric and the Yogic elements, which it contains, are possibly added during the ninth century A.D. or even later. That the *Puruṣa-sūktavidhāna* did not form part of the *Ṛgvidh* prior to the ninth century A.D. is proved by the fact that the parallel versions are completely silent about it, and the omission of such an important passage in these versions can be explained only on the assumption that it did not occur in the text of the *Ṛvidh* utilised by these versions. This *argumentum ex silentio* is, no doubt, inconclusive by itself, but we are happily in possession of another circumstance which proves that the *Puruṣasūktavidhāna* existed separately before it was incorporated into the text of *Ṛvidh*. The *Viṣṇudharmottara-Purāṇa* has a separate chapter (ii.129) on the glorification of the Puruṣasūkta. Moreover, some mss.[22] of the *Ṛvidh* have the portion of the *Puruṣasūktavidhāna* only.

Except the name, we do not know anything more about Viṣṇukumāra. He refers to Nārada's work on the Viṣṇu-worship which, except for some quotations in the *Smṛticandrikā*,[23] has not come down to us. The *Smṛticandrikā* has been assigned a date not earlier than 1150 A.D.[24] Regarding these quotations Dr. Kane states:[25] "From the fact that early writers like Viśvarūpa, Medhātithi and Vijñāneśvara do not contain a single quotation of Nārada on topics other than that of Vyavahāra, it appears probable that the quotations on Ācāra and Prāyaścitta belong to a later date than the *Nāradasmṛti* on Vyavahāra and either did not exist in the days of Viśvarupa and Medhātithi or had not attained

20. *BD*, vii.117.
21. 4.4.96 and the scholia thereon.
22. Cf. *Alphabetical List of Mss. in the Oriental Inst.* Baroda, Vol. I, pp. 38-39 (Acc. No. 7378).
23. *SC* (Bibliotheca Sanskrita No. 44) II. Ahnika kanda, pp. 532-534.
24. Kane, *op.cit.*, Vol. I, 346.
25. *ibid.*, p. 200.

canonical authority in those days. These considerations show that the *Puruṣasūktavidhāna* belongs to the latest stratum of the *Ṛvidh.* Very likely the *Puruṣasūktavidhāna* which once upon a time existed separately in some manual of Viṣṇu-worship was incorporated into the *Ṛvidh* owing to the fitness of the subject matter.

In the fourth Adhyāya the passage on coronation and other related matters (sts. 106-114) is likewise exceedingly suspicious, as it has nothing to do with the matter treated in the preceding and succeeding stanzas. The long peroration after the fourth chapter, i.e. Phalaśruti, Vargas 1-3 (sts. 1-13) cannot have formed part of the *Ṛvidh* is proved by the fact that these three Vargas are omitted in the calculation of the total Vargas of the *Ṛvidh.* Its apocryphal character is self-evident. Before concluding this topic, I may point out that many of the remaining passages, if not most, belong to the earliest stratum of the *Ṛvidh.* It lies in the very nature of investigations as the preceding that they are not equally secure at all points.

Turning now to the internal evidence, the extant *Ṛgvidhāna* seems to be much older than the *Bṛhad-*(or *Jyeṣṭha-*) *Ṛgvidhāna,* since the latter work employs mostly the hymns of the tenth Maṇḍala, and further the language of the latter work agrees closer with Pāṇini's rules than that of the former work. The occurrence of so many irregularities[26] in the text of the *Ṛvidh* proves clearly that Śaunaka did not follow Pāṇini's grammar and makes it very unlikely that he ever knew it at all. The latter fact is very important for, as stated earlier, Pāṇini betrays his acquaintance with the Hṛdyasūkta and particularly with the ritual aspect of it. The mere acquaintance with the Hṛdyasūkta may not prove much. It only shows that Pāṇini knew the Khila hymn attributed to Ṛṣi Hṛdya. Though the Hṛdyasūkta is employed in ceremonies like marriage, etc.,[27] its use as a propitiatory charm is known only from the *Ṛvidh.* In this connection, it is worthwhile to remember that Pāṇini[28] sanctions the form Hṛdya to denote a charm used for a propitiatory purpose. This circumstance alone would be sufficient to prove that Pāṇini knew some work which employs

26. See Chapter III above pp. 127-140.

27. *ĀGS,* 1.21.7; *Pa GS.,* 1.8.8; 2.2.16; *MGS,* 1.10.13; 22.10; *ŚGS,* 2.4.1; *HGS* 1.5.11.

28. 4.4.96.

the Hṛdyasūkta as a charm and that work cannot be any other than our *Ṛvidh.*

The pre-Pāṇinian character of the work being thus assured, it remains now to consider the ritual facts and the evidence of metre. The ritual facts of the earlier stratum prove that the rites prescribed therein do not differ considerably from that of the Gṛhya ones and that a date later than that of the Gṛhya-sūtras has to be assigned to our work. The case is entirely different with the rites of later stratum for, many of the newly-added rites do not belong to the ancient Brahmanical worship, but to the Purāṇic religion. The metre of the *Ṛvidh* furnishes another argument for its high antiquity. For, the large variety of Anuṣṭubh forms[29] support a date not later than 400 B.C., and we shall not be far from the truth if we place the *Ṛvidh* between 500-400 B.C. The date, thus arrived at, has the additional support of Prof. Macdonell[30] who assigned a date about 400 B.C. to the *Bṛhaddevatā*, a work which is also attributed to Śaunaka.

### 3. *Mātṛsūnu, the commentator of the Ṛvidh*

It is now necessary to say a few words about Mātṛsūnu, the commentator of the *Ṛvidh.* About the home and personal history of our commentator little is known. We know him only from his work which is called *Ṛgvidhānapadapañcikā* or simply *Padapañcikā* by him. Aufrecht[31] ascribes the authorship of the *Subodhapañcikā*, a Vedānta work, to him. The title of both the works show that our commentator had a peculiar fascination for the word "Pañcikā.' It may be observed here that the *Padapañcikā* is not a running commentary which explains every word of the text, but gives mostly explanations of few words or phrases. It dismisses many stanzas which stand in need of elucidation with the remark "Nigadavyākhyātam" or "Nigadam". It should be said to the credit of Mātṛsūnu that he never fails to give the references to the Vedic passages referred to in the text. He mentions

29. See Chapter III pp. 140-144.
30. *BD*, intro. p. xxiii.
31. *Catalogus Catalogorum*, 1891, p. 448.

the following works: *Nirukta* (folios 5b, 15b, 62a);[32] *Ārṣānukramaṇī* (folio 10b); *Śātātapasmṛti* (folio 16a); *Brāhmaṇa* (folio 22b); *Śatapathabrāhmaṇa* (folio 37a); *Bṛhadṛgvidhāna* (folio 41a), *Rahasyopaniṣat Brāhmaṇa* (folio 49a); *Bhagavadgītā* (? folio 50a). In his commentary, he mentions once[33] a vernacular equivalent for a Sanskrit term. In all probability, he was a native of Northern India. The *Śātātapasmṛti* is, no doubt, a late work.[34] In the present state of our knowledge we are not in a position to assign a date either to the *Śātātpasmṛti* or to Mātṛsūnu. Originally, it was my intention to include the *Padapañcikā* as an appendix to this work, but continued study of the commentary convinced me that no satisfactory text could be reconstructed from the only extant manuscript.

32. The folio numbers refer to the manuscript of the *Padapañcikā* belonging to the Oriental Institute, Baroda (No. 12251) and is listed in the *Alphabetical List of Mss. in the Oriental Institute*, Vol. I, pp. 38-39.

33. Baibhītako nāma "*baheḍaka*" ucyate (folio 38b).

34. Kane, *op.cit.*, Vol. I, pp. 128-29.

CHAPTER V

# THE MATERIALS FOR THE EDITION OF THE TEXT

## 1. *The Manuscripts*

### (a) *General account of the manuscripts*

In preparing this edition of the *Ṛgvidhāna* I have utilised three manuscripts of it and a *codex unicum* of a commentary on the *Ṛvidh* entitled *Padapañcikā* by Mātṛsūnu. Besides I have consulted all the three printed editions, viz., the first edited by R. Meyer (designated in the Critical Notes as Be); the second edited by V.L. Pansikar (designated in the Critical Notes at Bo 1); and the third edited by Jagadīśa Śāstrī (designated in the Critical Notes as La). Further I have collated carefully the quotations of the *Ṛvidh* in Sāyaṇa, Ṣaḍguruśiṣya and in the other medieval works like *Nītimañjarī* and *Pūjāprakāśa*. It appears that Sāyaṇa often cites the *Ṛvidh* inaccurately.[1] This may have been due to quoting from memory. The manuscripts collated by me are:—

(1) Ba: a manuscript belonging to the Oriental Institute, Baroda, (No. 12042) listed in the *Alphabetical List of Manuscripts in the Oriental Institute*, Vol. I, pp. 38-39.

(2) Bo 2: a manuscript belonging to the Bhadkamkar Memorial Collection No. 84.17 in the Bombay University Library, briefly described in the *Descriptive Catalogue of Saṁskṛta and Prākṛta Manuscripts* by G.V. Devasthali, p. 261.

(3) Ta: a manuscript belonging to the Tanjore Maharaja Serfoji's Sarasvati Mahal Library and is described at great length in the *Descriptive Catalogue of Sanskrit manuscripts in the TMSSML, TMSSML.*, Vol. III, p. 1244. It was previously listed by Burnell.[2]

1. Compare, for example, Nāsya syād annajo vyādhir viṣam apy amṛtam bhavet, *RV* (VSM), Vol. I, p. 1095 with *Ṛvidh* i.146.

2. *Classified Index to the Sanskrit Mss. in the Palace at Tanjore*, 1880, p. 5.

(4) Cm: a manuscript belonging to the Oriental Institute, Baroda (No. 12251) having only the commentary of Mātṛsūnu on the *Ṛvidh* and is listed in the *Alphabetical List of manuscripts in the Oriental Institute,* Vol. I, pp. 38-39.

(b) *Detailed description of the manuscripts*

Ba

Contents: the *Ṛvidh* in the longer recension. The work is divided into chapters (Adhyāyas) and sections (Vargas): Adhyāya I has thirty-one sections; Adh. II thirty-five sections; Adh. III forty-three sections; Adh. IV twenty-seven sections and is followed by the Phalaśruti having three sections. The text is bounded on both sides by double red lines. Corrections are often noted in the margin against the line of the text preceded by a number of the line, where corrections are to be made. The transposition of either words or syllables is indicated by the use of numerals one and two written directly above the words or syllables to be transposed, the number one being written above the word or syllable to be brought in front. The manuscript is neat, accurate and is somewhat the best among the manuscripts belonging to the longer recension.

Size: 10″ x 4-3/4″
Material: Paper
Folios: 49
Character: Devanāgarī

Date: on folio 49a: Saṁvat 1648 varṣe Kārttika vadi 5 Bhaume

Scribe: adyeha śrīsūryapure / Paṁ° / (Sic) nyāyalīyāt / Gadādhareṇa likhitam // kalyāṇaṁ brūyāt // (*Sic*) duve Sāṁmalata. Kīkā Laghuvīrajī paṭhanārthaṁ ca / Duve Śrī Gadādharanī pustikāte sahi // He seems to have taken great pains in copying the manuscript, for he gives the customary precautions: (*sic*).

Tailād rakṣej jalād rakṣet śrathalabaṁdhanāt /
Parahastagatā rakṣet evaṁ vadati pustikā //
Bhagnapṛṣṭī kaṭi....

The names of the owners are given on folio 1a as:

Duve Sāṁmalakasya
Duve Kahānajīkasya

Peculiarity of spelling: The medial diphthongs, *e*, *o*, *ai* and *au* are not written above the line, but with perpendicular strokes at the side of the consonant as the following examples from the folio 1 b illustrate:

स्वयंभुवे = स्वयंभुाव
विश्वगोप्त्रे = विश्वागाप्त्र
तथैव = ताथेव
शौनकः = ाशोनकः

Another peculiarity is: घ् with आ is written as ध्म ; e.g. folio 1 b: विविघा is written विविध्म

Bo 2

Contents: The *Ṛvidh* in the shorter recension. The work is divided into chapters (Adhyāyas) and sections (Vargas): Adhyāya I has thirty-one sections; Adh. II thirty-five sections; Adh. III forty-three sections; Adh. IV twenty-seven sections and is followed by the Phalaśruti having three sections.

Size: 8-1/4″ x 4″
Material: Paper
Folios: 52
Character: Devanāgarī

Date and Scribe: Not known. It is a very neat and beautifully written manuscript. It has a modern look.

Ta

Contents: The *Ṛvidh* in the shorter recension. The work is divided into chapters (Adhyāyas) and sections (Vargas): Adhyāya I has thirty-one sections; Adh. II thirty-five sections; Adh. III forty-three sections; Adh. IV twenty-eight sections. It may be stated here that the section twentyeight of the Adh. IV is really same as the first section of the Phalaśruti while the remaining two sections of the Phalaśruti are omitted. The total number of the sections are given as 136 in the colophon. Evidently the section twenty-eight was considered as not belonging to the Adh. IV and hence omitted in the final calculation. As the original of the manuscript, kept in the Tanjore Maharaja Serfoji's Sarasvati Mahal Library is not ordinarily lent out, I had no other alternative but to request the Secretary of the above institution to supply me with the transcribed copy of this manuscript copied in the year 1921. The copy was hopelessly bad, though it was checked and corrected in red ink by a different hand.

Size: Not known. But Burnell[3] described it as D (8-3/4″ x 3-3/4″)
Material: Paper
Folio: 35
Character: Devanāgarī

Date: (*sic*) Śrī saṁvat 1694 varṣe Bhādravadi // saṁvat 1693 varṣe bhādrapadamāse Kṛṣṇapakṣe 11 ekādaśi tithau somavāsare
Scribe: (*sic*) adye śrī Vṛddhanagaravāstavyaṁ ābhyantaraṁ nāgarājñātiya yājñika śrī Somayacittam mahāyājñikaśrī 6 //Nānāsutamātāyājñika śrī 6 Rāghavasūnunā likhitam / śubham astu/ Kalyāṇam astu //
Tailād rakṣej jalād rakṣed rakṣec chithilabandhanāt /
Parahastagatā rakṣed evaṁ vadati pustakam //
yājñikaśrī 6 Nānāsuta yājñikaśrī 6 Rāghavasūnunā Bṛhaspatike nyajya khitvā ācāryaśrī 6 Puruṣottamasuta ā o śrīyajñe Kṛṣṇāryena pradattā // śrī Avimuktapārāśyāṁ lyṣitvā // Śrīr astu Kalyāṇam astu //

The owner is not known; but the place of its origin can be Benares. The last line as emended by me will read: Śrī Avimukta Vārāṇasyāṁ likhitvā // Śrīr astu // Kalyāṇam astu //

Peculiarity of spelling: Not known.

## Cm

Contents: The commentary entitled *Padapañcikā* by *M*ātṛsūnu on the *Ṛvidh*. Except for the four verses from the *Ṛgvidhāna* in the beginning it contains only the commentary and no other manuscript is known to exist. It can be regarded as a *codex unicum*. The *Padapañcikā* is also divided into chapters (Adhyāyas) and sections (Vargas). It is carelessly written and full of mistakes

3. *op.cit.*, p. 5.

and lacuna. The total number of verses in the *Ṛvidh* are worked out on folio 1 a.

Size: 8-1/4″ x 4-1/4″
Material: Paper
Folios: 63
Character: Devanāgarī
Date: saṁ // 1887 nā phālguna śuddha 13 gurau likhitam
Scribe and Owner: Not known.

Peculiarity of spelling: It has preserved the old forms side by side with the new ones and hence can belong to the period of transition. It has a modern look.

2. *Printed Edition or Translation*

*Berlin edition (designated as Be)*

The *editio princeps* of the *Ṛgvidhāna* was brought out by Dr. R. Meyer and published at Berlin, 1878. It was offered as a Doctor dissertation. The text constituted by Dr. Meyer with the three available manuscripts—all of them kept in Berlin—is not valuable from the critical point of view for, besides corrupt readings,[4] it has many spurious stanzas which, at best, could have been relegated to the critical notes. Dr. Meyer often emended and rearranged the text against the manuscript authority. The following is the list of emendations carried out in his text of *Ṛvidh* by Dr. Meyer (1) Vidhānāni (for vividhāni) i.12; (2) trivṛta (for trivṛtā) i.53; (3) sa nigacchati (for saṁniyacchati) i.103; (4) jagau (for garbhe) i.105; (5)' ripram (for ripram) i.128; (6) apabhagnāntam (for apabhagnaṁ tam) ii.15; (7) ṛtāvṛdhau (for ṛtāvṛtau) ii.22; (8) vardhāpayet (for varṣāpayet) ii.41; (9) abbrahma (for abrahma) ii.54; (10) phalalāja (for phalalājā) ii.71; (11) niṣpiḍyanniva (for niṣpīṣanniva) ii.89; (12) bibhetu (for bibheta) ii.105; (13) japtvā (for tvetām) ii.119; (14) ajāvikam (for ajāvikān) ii.146;

4. (1) abhyupayāt, i.21; iii.80; (2) tataḥ svaram, i.169; (3) sottāram; ii.3; (4) nadītīracāreṣvapi, ii.6; (5) ripunāśanaḥ, ii.172; (6) ṛcāṁścaiva, iii.13; (7) Khādire sussamiddhe, iii.78; (8) prādakṣiṇyam, iii.167; (9) yatam, iii.174; (10) śucir vāgyataḥ, iii.193; (11) vīrudhaiḥ iv, 59; (12) brahmaṇāgnir iti hutvā, iv.8.8.

(15) viveṣṭitaḥ (for viceṣṭitaḥ) ii.148; (16) lubhyet (for lupyet) ii. 159; (17) vajriṇaḥ (for vajriṇam) ii.170; (18) japato' nnāni (for japato' trāsti) ii.171; (19) dvṛcenaiva (for dvṛcenaitya) ii.183; (20) guḍam (for gurum) iii.87; (21) vai (for vā) iii.90; (22) dīptā (for dīptām) iii.92; (23) pratikṛtiḥ (for pratikṛtim) iii.92; (24) svam (for sa) iii.92; (25) jayaścaiva (for japeccaiva) iii.112; (26) indrāṇyāḥ (for indrāṇyā) iii.119; (27) abhimantryeha (for abhimantrya hi) iii.124; (28) vipravrājinīm (for vipravādinīm) iii.126; (29) āsthāpya (for āsthāya) iii.131; (30-31) dvitīyā strī (for dvitīyāṁ strīm) iii.147; (32-33) pādmam (for pādam) iii.194, 195; (34) abhijijñāsanāt (api jijñāsanāt) iii.205; (35) bhiṣak (for dviṣat) iv.3; (36) japen (for japan) iv.19; (37) hitvā (for hatvā) iv.20; (38) pratimuñceta (for pratimucyeta) iv.37; (39) aṅgiraso' pyṛṣeḥ (for aṅgirā apyṛṣiḥ) iv.40; (40) ṛṣim (for ṛṣiḥ) iv.42; (41) prāyas (for prāptam) iv.44; (42) yanna pānam (for yo'nnāyālam) iv.47; (43-45) pāṭām (for pāṭhām) iv.56, 61, 64; (46) puṣpyantī (for puṣpavatī) iv.93; (47) abhisiñceta (abhiṣicyeta) iv.106; and (48) prayantā (kurute) Phalaśruti st. 10. In the second chapter he had rearranged the text twice: the first after st. 10ab and the second after st. 78ab. Hence a critical edition of the *Ṛgvidhāna* professing to represent the archetype as closely as possible, and based on the manuscript material hitherto not utilised is therefore still a *desideratum*. Further, Dr. Meyer has adopted the longer recension of the *Ṛgvidhāna*, as I shall presently show, does not represent the original text of the *Ṛvidh* at all.

*Bombay edition* (*designated as Bo* 1)

This was published by V.L. Pansikar in his edition of the *Ṛgveda* (1930). It is printed in pp.47-66 of the above work. The editor is completely silent regarding the manuscript or manuscripts utilised in the publication of it. Though the text is a definite improvement upon that of Dr. Meyer's, still it abounds in misprints, wrong transposition of hemistiches and stanzas. Further, the editor has taken the full liberty to correct the text with assigning any reason whatsoever.[5] The text agrees with the shorter recension.

5. Bo 1 alone reads *mahiṣiḥ* whereas all manuscripts read *mahiṣyaḥ* (*Ṛvidh* ii.35).

*Lahore edition (designated as La)*

This is only a transliterated edition of Dr. Meyer's text of the *Ṛvidh* in Devanāgarī characters. It was reprinted from *Oriental College Magazine*, Vol. XVI, No. IV, 1940. The editor has wrongly transcribed few words[6] and the text abounds in misprints. The editor has given pāda-index of all the stanzas in the *Ṛvidh* and he has added another index of the Ṛgvedic hymns referred to in the *Ṛvidh*. Unfortunately, the editor has given wrong references at places.[7] This edition was occasionally consulted by me.

*Translation of the Ṛgvidhāna*

It is truly unfortunate that a person of the eminence of Dr. Gonda should have brought out a translation of the *Ṛgvidhāna*[8] based mainly on the text of Dr. Meyer, when a new critical edition based on the new manuscript material could have rightly been undertaken along with a translation. Dr. Gonda assures us that he had consulted three more manuscripts designated by him as D, E and F, and states that "the collation of the three English manuscripts has not brought to light many new data of importance."[9] But his long array of critical notes[10] appended to his translation belies his above statement. His translation, on the whole, is inaccurate and at times absurd. I have shown the inaccuracies of his translation in the exegetical notes.

3. *Relationship of the manuscripts: two recensions*

The manuscripts fall into two distinct groups. Bo 1, Bo 2, and Ta form one family group and Ba, Be, and La the other. We

6. (1) maṅgalācārya- (for maṅgalācāra-) i.21; (2) sāṁnipātakam (for sāṁnipātikam) i.52; (3) transp. yāni and jagau i.105; (4) śrāddha kāleṣu (for śrāddhakāle tu) i.109; (5) mitabhūn (for mitabhuk) ii.27; (6) cākṣupati (for cākhupati) ii.74; (7) omit agna ii.25.5 (Meyer); (8) vācam (for vāśam) ii.172; (9) vyamocayet (for vyamocayat) iii.27; (10) hīnām (for hīnam) iii.85; (11) bhakṣam (for bhakṣyam) iv.13; (12) Sarvaprāyaścita (for sarvaprāyaścitta) iv.34; (13) bahupaṇīya (for bahupānīya-) iv.93; (14) purā (for puraḥ) iv.96.

7. Cp. *RV* (VSM), Vol. IV, p. 917.

8. *Ṛgvidhāna*, English translation with an introduction and notes by J. Gonda, 1951.

9. *ibid.*, p. 7.

10. *ibid.*, pp. 127-129.

may, for the sake of convenience, call them X and Y. The former representing the shorter recension and the latter the longer one. The differentia between the two recensions lies in the fact that the latter recension has more than the usual number of Ślokas in some Vargas and thereby it is considerably longer than the former. It may be mentioned here that in both the total number of Vargas do not defer and what more the figures indicating the end of the Vargas occur at the same place. The conspectus of the Ślokas in the Vargas of the *Ṛvidh* (Appendix A) gives, no doubt, a fair idea of this intricate problem.

Coming to the shorter recension we find that Bo 1 and Bo 2 agree in most particulars, but there are minor differences between them. One thing is clear: neither can be a direct copy of the other and both must be traced to a common source, i.e. sub-group X. The affinity of the manuscripts comprising this sub-group X is documented by a mass of readings common between them. A few examples will suffice.

i.7 Bo 1, Bo 2 *vividhā*: rest *vidhinā*

i.9 Bo 1, Bo 2 *vaiśyaḥ śūdraḥ*: rest *vaiśyaśūdrau*

i.28 Bo 1, Bo 2 *vidhim*: rest *vidhiḥ*

i.49 Bo 1, Bo 2 *iṣyan*: rest *iṣṭān*

This affinity is found not only in the matter of concordant readings but also in the matter of additional spurious passages which are peculiar to these manuscripts. I may now cite some readings which Bo 1 Bo 2 share with Ta.

i.36 Bo 1 Bo 2 Ta *evam etat*: rest *etam eva*

i.63 Bo 1 Bo 2 Ta *soccair:* rest *uccair*

i.75 Bo 1 Bo 2 Ta *śatruvināśinī*: rest *śatruvināśanī*

i.140 Bo 1 Bo 2 Ta *na cānye:* rest *tathānye*

I may state that Bo 1, Bo 2 and Ta also exhibit numerous differences in their readings: e.g. i.9; 22-23; 26; 28 etc. These agreements and differences show that while Bo 1 Bo 2 and Ta are akin, their text is not identical. As a matter of fact, Ta does not have the additional spurious passages which are either peculiar to Bo 1 Bo 2 or to the longer recension and hence it is the shortest as well as less spurious text of the *Ṛvidh* which we possesses.

Now coming to the manuscripts representing the longer recension, we find that Ba has preserved the text in a much better form than Be. The latter contains additional matter which is not found in Ba, nor in the shorter recension, nor in any manuscripts of the *Ṛvidh* except in some of the Berlin mss. La being a transliterated copy of Be is not valuable from any point of view.

The position of Cm is rather elusive, for the commentary of Māṭrsūnu is a concise one, and as it is unaccompanied by the text—except, of course, the first four verses—hence we cannot state with any degree of certainty as to which recension it originally belonged. The general trend of the commentary is towards the shorter recension.

The following stemma summarizes my conclusions about the relation of the manuscripts to one another:

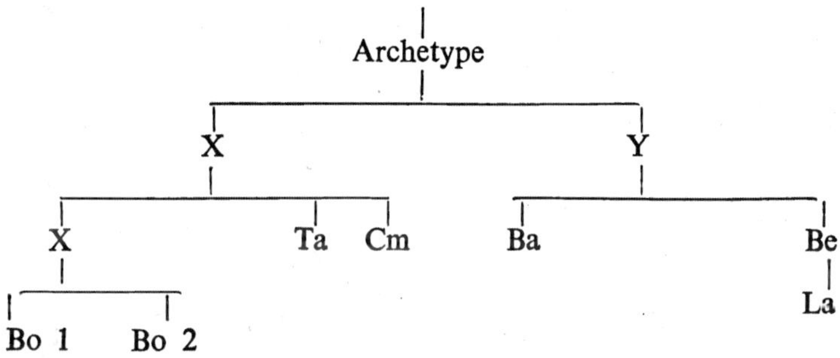


## 4. *Constitution of the text*

For the purpose of this critical edition, three manuscripts—more or less independent—have been directly available. To these three I may add the three manuscripts collated by Dr. Meyer and three more manuscripts collated by Prof. Gonda. Thus, directly or indirectly, the evidence of altogether nine manuscripts of the text and one of the commentary was available to me in the constitution of my text. None of the manuscripts is earlier than 1451 A.D., i.e. the date of a manuscript collated by Dr. Meyer. As stated by me earlier, the difference between the two recensions reduces itself to a few spurious stanzas in the longer recension and a few more in some of the manuscripts (Bo 1, Bo 2) of the shorter recension, Ta as usual representing the shortest version. Thus the principle of selecting one best manuscript as base is obviously inapplicable in this case, for none of the manuscripts transmits the text of the *Ṛvidh* in an uninterpolated state. Nearly half of the text has practically no variants at all, and being handed down uniformly in all the manuscripts, can be regarded as authentic. As for the remaining half, I have put down in the text whatever feature or reading documented uniformly by more or less independent manuscripts, except of course, in the case of palpable corruptions and interpolations which, on the face of it, are very late. Finally, I have cautiously constituted the text of the *Ṛgvidhāna* with the occasional help rendered by the valuable commentary of Mātṛsūnu, and the constituted text may therefore be regarded as more or less settled.

### 5. *Testimonia*

#### (a) *External evidence bearing on the text of the Ṛgvidhāna*

In the case of the *Ṛvidh* we have, fortunately, much evidence outside its own manuscript material. This outside evidence, in the first place, consists mainly in the quotations of the *Ṛvidh* in Sāyaṇa, Ṣaḍguruśiṣya and in the other medieval works like *Nītimañjarī* and *Pūjāprakāśa*. In the second place, there are the parallel or abridged versions of the *Ṛvidh* in the *Viṣṇudharmottara* and *Agni Purāṇas*. These Purāṇas have been assigned to the eighth[11] and the ninth centuries A.D.[12] respectively and as none of the manuscripts of the *Ṛvidh* is earlier than 1451 A.D., hence this external evidence has enabled me, in some cases, to decide on the correct reading. In the third place, the text of the *Ṛgvidhāna* bears an intimate relation to that of the *Śaunakīyam* and the *Bṛhaddevatā*, both of which are attributed to Śaunaka. Finally the commentary of Mātṛsūnu on the *Ṛvidh*. All this has enabled me to emend with certainty few corrupt passages[13] which would have otherwise remained merely conjecture.

#### (b) *Intimate relationship to the version of the Ṛgvidhāna in the Viṣṇudharmottara-Purāṇa*

The relative position of the *Ṛvidh* and the version of it in the

11. Hazra, *Studies in the Upapurāṇas*, Vol. I, p. 209.

12. Hazra, *Studies in the Puranic Records on Hindu Rites and Customs*, p. 138.

13. Examples such are: vaibhītakakṛtaśrucā* (i.77); pramandin* eti (i.123). See the notes on these passages.

*Viṣṇu Dh Pu* induces us to assume that the author of the latter appropriated a large number of stanzas from the former. Further, the latter work claims to be a concise one on 'the sacred precepts of Ṛks'.[14] I have succeeded in identifying some 148 stanzas or portions of stanzas, about one-fifth of the bulk of the former work. The identifications made by me are sufficient for the purpose of illustrating the relation between the two works. In order to show this, evidence of the relation in which the two above works stand towards one another, it will be advisable to give the corresponding passages in parallel columns. I may point out that the *Viṣṇu Dh Pu* has not so far been critically edited, though portions of it have been edited recently.[15] I have utilised the Venkateśvara Steam Press edition, which is full of corrupt readings[16] and I had to retain them unemended.

| *Viṣṇu Dh Pu* ii.123 | *Ṛvidh* |
|---|---|
| 37cd-38ab: Gomūtraṁ gomayaṁ kṣauraṁ dadhi sarpiḥ kuśodakam, ekarātropavāśaś ca kṛchraṁ sāṁtapanaṁ smṛtam / | i.35: Gomūtraṁ gomayaṁ kṣīraṁ dadhi sarpiḥ kuśodakam ekarātropavāśaś ca kṛcchraḥ sāṁtapanaḥ smṛtaḥ // |
| 41: Tryahaṁ sāyaṁ tryahaṁ prātaḥ tryaham adyād ayācitam, tryaḥ paraṁ ca nāśnīyāt prājāpatyaṁ caran dvijaḥ | i.33: Tryahaṁ prātaḥ tryahaṁ sāyaṁ tryaham adyād ayācitam, tryahaṁ paraṁ ca nāśnīyāt prājāpatyaṁ caran dvijaḥ // |
| 53cd-54ab: Yathāśvamedhaḥ kraturāṭ sarvapāpāpanodanaḥ, tathāghamarṣaṇaṁ sūktaṁ sarvakalmaṣanāśam. | iv.121cd-122ab: Yathāśvamedhaḥ kraturāṭ sarvapāpapraṇodanaḥ, tathāghamarṣaṇaṁ sūktaṁ sarvapāpapraṇodanam. |

14. Ṛcāṁ vidhānaṁ kathitaṁ tavaitat, samāsataḥ karmakaraṁ dvijānām, *Viṣṇu Dh Pu* ii.124, 163ab.

15. *Viṣṇudharmottara-Purāṇa*, Third Khaṇḍa, critically ed. by Priyabala Shah, Vols. I-II, 1958-1961.

16. cp. *ibid.*, Vol. I, p. xix.

| *Viṣṇu Dh Pu* ii.124 | *Ṛvidh* |
|---|---|
| 13cd: Śirasā dhārayed vahniṁ yo japet parivatsaram | i.80ab: Śirasā dhārayed agniṁ niyataḥ parivatsaram / |
| 15: Ataḥ paraṁ ṛcaḥ sapta cāgneyyaḥ parikīrttitāḥ tā japan prayato nityamiṣṭān kāmān samaśnute | i.84: Ataḥ paraṁ ṭṛcāḥ sapta vāyvādyā ye prakīrtitāḥ tāñ japan prayato nityamiṣṭān kāmāntsamaśnute |
| 16abc: Medhākāmo japen nityaṁ sadasatpadam ity ṛcam, ambayo yānti yā proktā | i.85c: Medhākāmo japen nityam<br>i.85b: Sadasaspatim ityṛcam<br>i.89a: Ambayo yanti yā proktā |
| 17: Śunaḥśepham ṛṣiṁ tadvat Saṁniruddho'thavā japet mucyate sarvapāpebhyo gadācāpagadī gadan. | i.90: Śunaḥśepam ṛṣiṁ baddhaḥ saṁniruddho'thavā japet, mucyate sarvapāśebhyo gadī cāpy agadī bhavet |
| 18: Yadīcchec chāśvataṁ kāmamindrāt prāptuṁ puraṁdarāt ṛgbhiḥ ṣoḍaśabhiḥ stūyādindram eti dine dine. | i.91: Ya icchec chāśvatān kāman indrāt prāptuṁ puraṁdarāt sa ṣoḍaśabhir evarghbirindraṁ stūyād dine dine. |
| 19ab: Hiraṇyastūpam ityetajjapañ śatrūn prabādhate / | i.92acd: Hairaṇyastūpam indrasya taj japan prayataḥ śatrūnayatnāt pratibādhate |
| 19d: Ye te paktā japan naraḥ | i.95a: Ye te panthā itīmāṁ tu |
| 20abc: Raudrībhiḥ ṣaḍbhir Īśānaṁ stūyād yo vai dine dine caruṁ vā kalpayed raudraṁ | i.96ab: Raudrībhiḥ ṣaḍbhir Īśānaṁ tuṣṭūyād yo dine dine<br>i.98c: Caruṁ vā kalpayed raudram |
| 21ab: Udity udyantam ādityamupatiṣṭhed dine dine | i.99ab: Udity udyantam ādityamupatiṣṭhed dine dine |
| 22: Dviṣantam ity athānarcya dviṣantaṁ ca japan smaret agacchan saptarātreṇa vidveṣam adhigacchati | i.100: Dviṣantam ity athārdharcaṁ yaṁ dviṣyāt taṁ japant smaret āgaskṛt saptarātreṇa vidveṣam adhigacchati |
| 23: Ārogyakāmo rogī ca praskannasyottamaṁ japet uttamas tasya cāva japed vairavināśane | i.101ab: Rogair gṛhīto' rogi ca praskaṇvasyottamaṁ tṛcam /<br>i.102ab: Uttamas tasya cārdharco dviṣaddveṣa iti smṛtaḥ / |

| *Viṣṇu Dh Pu* ii.124 | *Ṛvidh* |
|---|---|
| 24: Udayaty āyur akṣayyaṁ tejo madhyaṁdine japet, astaṁ vrajati sūrye ca dviṣantaṁ pratipāditam | i.103cd-104ab: Udayaty āyur akṣayyaṁ tejo madhyaṁdine japan, astaṁ vrajati sūrye tu dviṣantaṁ pratibādhate |
| 25abc: Nava padyeti sūktāni japañ śatrūn niyacchati ekādaśa suvarṇasya | i.105a: Nava paśveti sūktāni<br>i.105d: śatrūṁś caiva niyacchati<br>i.106ab: Sauparṇāni...ekādaśābhyaset |
| 26a: Ādhyātmikaiḥ ka ity etaj<br>26cd: Āsano rudram ity etad dīrgham āyur avāpnuyāt | i.107a: Ādyātmikīḥ ka ity etā<br>i.108a: Ānobhadrīyam āyuṣyam<br>i.108d: Sarvam āyur avāpnuyāt |
| 27: Tvaṁ someti ca sūktena navaṁ paśyen niśākaram, upatiṣṭhet samitpāṇirvāsāṁsy āpnoty asaṁśayam // | i.110abc: Tvaṁ someti tu sūktena pasyec candram upoditam upatiṣṭhet samitpāṇir<br>i.112c: vāsāṁsy api sa vindeta |
| 28: Āyur ipsann idam iti Kautsasūktaṁ yadābhyaset, apanaḥ śośucad iti stutvā madhye divākaram | i.114ab: Āyur īpsann imam iti kautsaṁ sūktaṁ sadābhyaset<br>i.115cd: Apa naḥ śośucad iti snātvā madhyaṁdine ravau |
| 29: Yathā muṁjād iveṣīkā tathā pāpaṁ pramuṁcati jātavedasa ity etaj japet svastyayanaṁ pathi | i.117: Yathā muñjād iveṣīkā tathā pāpat pramucyate jātavedasa ityādi sadā svastyayane japet |
| 30cd: Vyuṣṭāyāṁ ca tathā rātrāvetad duḥsvapnanāśanam | i.122cd: Vyuṣṭāyāṁ ca japen nityametāṁ duḥsvapnanāśinīm |
| 31: Pramanditeti sūryasya japed garbhavimocanam japann iṁdram iti snāto vaiśvadevaṁ tu saptakam | i.123ab: Pramandineti sūyantyāṁ japed garbhapramocanīm<br>i.124cd: Japannin dram iti snāto vaiśvadevam tu saptakam |
| 32a: Imām iti japan śaśvat | i.127a: Imā iti jāpec chaśvat. |
| 33: Mānas toka iti dvābhyāṁ | i.128cd-129ab: Māno mahāntam |

| *Viṣṇu Dh Pu* ii.124 | *Ṛvidh* |
|---|---|
| trirātropoṣitaḥ śuci, auduṁbarīs tu juhuyāddadhimadhvājyasaṁskṛtāḥ | ityābhyāṁ trirātropoṣitaḥ śuciḥ, auduṁbarīs tu juhuyād dadhimadhvājyasaṁskṛtāḥ |
| 34abc: Chitvā sarvān mṛtyupāśān jived rogavivarijitaḥ, ūrdhvabāhur anenaiva | i.130cd: Chitvā sarvān mṛtyupāśān jived rogair vivarjitaḥ<br>i.130a: ūrdhvabāhur anenaiva |
| 36ab: Citram ityupatiṣṭheta trisaṁdhyaṁ bhāskaraṁ tathā | i.131cd: Citram ity upatiṣṭheta sūktenānena bhāskaram |
| 36d: Prāpnuyāt tu dhanāyuṣī | i.132d: Prāpnoti ca dhanāyuṣī |
| 37abc: Etad duḥsvapnasyeti ca japan prātar dine dine, svapnaṁ dahate kṛtsnam | i.133abc: Adhaḥ svapnasyeti japet prātaḥ prātar dine dine, duḥsvapnaṁ nudate kṣipram |
| 38a: Ubheṣu nāmīti tathā | i.134a: Ubhe punāmīti parā |
| 38cd: Nirvartya paṁcayajñāṁś ca hutvā cāgniṁ kṛtāhnikaḥ | i.135ab: Nirvartya pañcayajñāṁś ca hutvā cāgniṁ kṛtāhnikaḥ |
| 39: Devāsāviti devyedaṁ japan kāmān avāpnuyāt, ātatāyinam āyāṁtaṁ dṛṣṭvā vyāghrādikaṁ naraḥ | i.135cd: Ye devāso divyanayā japan kāmān avāpnuyāt<br>i.138ab: ātatāyinam āyāntaṁ dṛṣṭvā vyāghram atho vṛkam |
| 40ab: Na mā girann iti jāpaṅ stebhya eva pramucyate. | i.138cd: Na mā garann iti japan tebhya eva pramucyate |
| 40c: Kayā śubheti ca japan- | i.143a: Kayā śubheti paiśunyam |
| 41: Imaṁ nu somam ity etat sarvān kāmān avāpnuyāt pitrantvity upatiṣṭheta nityam annam upasthitam | i.144ab: Imaṁ nu somam ity ete dve ṛcau prayato japet<br>i.145ab: Pituṁ nvity upatiṣṭheta nityam annam upasthitam |
| 42: Nāsya syād annato vyādhir viṣam apy annatām iyāt, agne nayeti sūktena pratyṛcaṁ juhuyād ghṛtam | i.146ab: Nāsya syād annajo vyādhirviṣam apy annatām iyāt<br>i.149cd: Agne nayeti sūktena, praty ṛcaṁ juhuyād ghṛtam |

| *Viṣṇu Dh Pu* ii.124 | *Ṛvidh* |
|---|---|
| 43ab: Pakvānnaṁ pratipadyeta kṛtvā cākarma garhitam | i.149ab: Panthānaṁ pratipadyeta, kṛtvā vā karma garhitam |
| 44a: Kaṁkatā ceti sūktena | i.151c: Kaṁkato neti sūktaṁ tu |
| 44c: Yo jāta iti sūktena | i.156a: Yo jāta iti sūktena |
| 45ab: Ye parājann itīmāṁ tu duḥsvapnaśamanāṁ ṛcam | i.161cd: Yo me rājann itīmāṁ tu duḥsvapnaśamanīṁ ṛcam |
| 45c: Ekāmāhamitīyāṁ tu | i.163c: Rākām aham itīmābhiḥ |
| 46abc: Caturdaśīm upoṣyaikāṁ kṛṣṇāsu juhuyād ghṛtam, āttasūktena raudreṇa | i.165abc: Caturdaśīm upoṣyaikāṁ kṛṣṇasya juhuyāc carum, ā te sūktena raudreṇa |
| 47cd: Ābhiṣasyeta yo mohāt kṛtvā vā karma garhitam | i.167cd: Abhiśasyeta yo mohāt kuryād vā karma garhitam |
| 48: Adhvani prasthito yas tu paśyec chakrunum utthitam-apraśaste praśaste vā kanikradam idaṁ japet | i.168cd: Adhvani prasthito yas tu paśyec chakunim utthitam<br>i.169a: Apraśastaṁ praśastaṁ vā<br>i.169cd: Kanikradad itī sūktābhyām |
| 49ab: Aspṛṣṭvaiva ca japtavyaṁ etat taskaramohanam | i.170cd: Apy adṛṣṭvaiva japtavyametat taskaramohanam |
| 49cd: Oṁ ṣvity ṛcam apāṁ madhye japed yo vai nadīṁ taret | ii.7cd: Oṣvity ṛcam apāṁ madhye japed yo vai nadīṁ taran |
| 50: Udvaurmibhir itīmāṁ tu japed rathagatas taran, adhvānaṁ prasthitaś caiva mantrair iti ca saṁsmaret | ii.9: Ud va ūrmir itīmāṁ tu japeta niyataḥ svayam, adhvānaṁ prasthitaś caivam ā mandrair iti saṁsmaret |
| 51a: Sudātāraṁ supuṣṭyarthaṁ | ii.10c: Adātāraṁ supuṣṭārtham |
| 52: Sa sarpīr iti ca japan māsāt taṁ pratipadhyate, yāṇākṣaṁ samabhajyantaṁ dṛṣṭvā durge' dhvani dvija | ii.13cd: Sasarparīr ṛcau japan dvau masau pratipadyate<br>ii.15ab: Yānākṣam apabhagnāntaṁ dṛṣṭvā durge' dhvani dvijaḥ |

| *Viṣṇu Dh Pu* ii.124 | *Ṛvidh* |
|---|---|
| 53: Abhityavasyeti japedṛkṣam akṣabalaṁ dadhat, kṛṣṇapakṣacaturdaśyāṁ trirātropoṣitaḥ śuciḥ | ii.15cd-16ab: Abhi vyayasveti japeddvṛcam akṣabalaṁ dadhat, kṛṣṇapakṣe caturdaśyāṁ trirātropoṣitaḥ śuciḥ / |
| 54: Dakṣiṇāpravaṇe deśe śmaśānasthaḥ samāhitaḥ raktoṣṇīṣyasipāṇiś ca taulākībhyo' nilāśnaḥ | ii.16cd-17ab: Dakṣiṇapravaṇe deśe śmaśānasthaḥ samāhitaḥ, raktoṣṇīṣyasipāṇiśca bailvakedhmo' nilāśanaḥ |
| 55: Saptāhaṁ juhuyāt tailaṁ sārṣapaṁ lavaṇānvitam, samidho rājavṛkṣasya vasiṣṭhe dveṣaṇīḥ paṭhan | ii.17cd-18ab: Saptāhaṁ juhuyāt tailam sārṣapaṁ lavaṇānvitam, samidho rājavṛkṣasya vasiṣṭhadveṣaṇīḥ paṭhan |
| 56: Yaṁ dviṣyāt tasya kṛtvā tu Śamyākenāhṛtaṁ niśi, adhiṣṭhāya ca taṁ kuryādṛgbhiś ca tisṛbhir dvijaḥ | ii.18cd-19ab: Yaṁ dviṣyāt tasya kṛtvā tu śamyākenākṛtiṁ niśi, adhiṣṭhāya ca tāṁ kuryādṛgbhiḥ catasṛbhir dvijaḥ |
| 57: Uddiśya rāma homo' yaṁ saptarātraṁ na jīvati dvāviṁśakaṁ japan sūktam ādhyātmikam anuttamam | ii.19cd: Uddiśya nāma homo' yaṁ saptarātraṁ na jīvati<br>ii.21ab: Dvāviṁśakaṁ japet sūktamādhyātmikam anuttamam |
| 58: Parvasu prayato nityamiṣṭān kāmān samaśnute bṛhaspatiṁ ajāśvaṁ ca satāraṁ babhrum eva ca // | ii.21cd-22ab: Parvasu prayato nityamiṣṭān kāmānt samaśnute, bṛhaspatim ajāśvaṁ ca savitāram babhrum eva ca. |
| 59c: Kṛṇuṣvati japan sūktaṁ | ii.63a: Kṛṇuṣveti japant sūktam. |
| 60: Arātīnāṁ haret prāṇān rakṣāṁsy api ca nāśayet, upatiṣṭheta yo vahniṁ parītya ca dine dine | ii.63cd-64ab: Arātināṁ haret prāṇān rakṣāṁsy api ca nāśayet, upatiṣṭheta yo vahniṁ parītyṛcā dine dine |
| 61abc: Taṁ rakṣati svayaṁ vahnirviśvato viśvatomukhaḥ, ko adyeti ca sūktena | ii.64cd: Taṁ rakṣati svayaṁ vahnirviśvato viśvatomukhaḥ<br>ii.65a: Ko adyeti tu sūktena |

| *Viṣṇu Dh Pu* ii.124 | *Ṛvidh* |
|---|---|
| 62: Kāyeti vāmadevena kuryāt svastyayanaṁ niśi Haṁsaḥ śuciṣad ityetacchucir īkṣan divākaram. | ii.66ab: Kayeti vāmadevyena kuryāt svastyayanaṁ niśi<br>ii.67ab: Haṁsaḥ śuciṣad ity ṛcā śucir īkṣed divākaram |
| 63: Kṛṣiṁ prapadyamānas tu sthālīpākaṁ yathāvidhi, juhuyāt kṣetramadhye tu śunā vāhas tu paṁcabhiḥ. | ii.68: Kṛṣiṁ prapadyamānas tu sthālīpākaṁ yathāvidhi, juhuyād kṣetramadhye tu śunaṁ vāhāś tu pañcabhiḥ. |
| 64: Iṁdrāya ca marudbhyaś ca parjanyāya bhagāya ca, yathāliṁgaṁ tu viharellāṁgalaṁ tu kṛṣīvalaḥ // | ii.69: Yathāliṅgaṁ tu viharellāṅgalaṁ ca kṛṣīvalaḥ, indrāya ca marudbhyaś ca parjanyāya bhagāya ca. |
| 65: Pūṣṇe dhānyāya sītāyai śunāsīram athottaram, gaṁdhamālyopahāraiś ca yajed etāś ca devatāḥ | ii.70ab: Pūṣṇe dhānyāya sītāyai śunāsīram athottaram.<br>ii.71a: Gandhamālyopahāraiś ca<br>ii.70d: Yajed etāś ca devatāḥ |
| 66: Pravāpaṇe pralapane khalasītopahārayoḥ, amoghaṁ karma bhavati vardhate sarvadā kṛṣiḥ | ii.71cd: Pravapaṇe pralavane khalasītopahārayoḥ<br>ii.72cd: Amoghaṁ karma bhavati kṛṣir vardhati sarvadā |
| 67: Kṣetrasya payetat kṣetrāṁ sūryadṛg vindate bhuvam, ākhūtkareṣu caraṇau yajed etena mūṣikām | ii.73a: Kṣeṭrasya patinety etat.<br>ii.73cd: Ikṣetsūryaṁ...vindate kṣetram<br>ii.74abc: Ākhūtkareṣu caruṇā yajed etena mūṣikān, |
| 68a: Citra iṁdreti ca stūyān | Citra id rājety anayā. |
| 68cd: Vijyotiṣyeti jvalayed, yatrecchej jātavedasam. | ii.79ab: Vijyotiṣeti jvalayed yatrechaj jātavedasi |
| 69a: Samudrād iti sūktena | ii.78a: Samudrād iti sūktena |
| 69cd: Viśvāni ca iti dvābhyāṁ ṛgbhyām yo vahnim arcati. | ii.80ab: Viśvāni na iti dvābhyāmṛgbhyāṁ yo vahnim arcati. |
| 70: Sa tarety āpadaḥ sarvā yaś- | ii.80cd: Sa taraty āpadaḥ sarvā |

| *Viṣṇu Dh Pu* ii.124 | *Ṛvidh* |
|---|---|
| aḥ prāpnoti cākṣayam, agre tvam iti ca stutvā dhanam āpnoti vāñchitam. | yaśaḥ prāpnoti cākṣayam. ii.81cd: Agne tvam iti sūktena dhanam āyuś ca vāñchatā. |
| 71a: Uroṣṭa iti sūktena. | ii.82c: Uroṣṭa iti sūktena. |
| 71cd: Prajākāmo yajen nityaṁ varuṇādevasannayā | ii.83ab: Prajākāmo yajen nityaṁ caruṇā devapatnayaḥ |
| 72a: Svastyātreyaṁ japet prātaḥ | ii.85c: Svastyātreyaṁ japen nityam. |
| 72cd: Svasti panthām iti prodya svastimān vrajate' dhvani | ii.87abc: Svasti panthām iti procya svastimān vrajate' dhvani, |
| 73a: Vi jihīṛsurvanasyānte | Vijihīṣva vanaspate. |
| 73c: Striyo garbhapramūḍhāyā | ii.89c: Striyaṁ garbhapramūḍhāṁ vā. |
| 74: Avacchād iti sūktena vṛṣṭikāmaḥ prayojayet, nirāhāraḥ klinnavāsā nacireṇa pravarṣati | ii.90cd-91ab: Acchā vadeti sūktaṁ tu vṛṣṭikāmaḥ prayojayet, nirāhāraḥ klinnavāsā acireṇa pravarṣati |
| 75a: Śriyaḥ paṁcadaśarcaṁ tu | ii.93c: Śriyaḥ pañcadaśarcaṁ ca |
| 75c: Upaitu māṁ devasakha | ii.96c: Upaitu māṁ devasakha |
| 76cd: Manasaḥ kāma ityetāṁ paśukāmo naro japet | ii.97: Manasaḥ kāma ity eṣā paśukāmābhiṣecanī, |
| 77: Kardameneti ca snāyāt prajākāmaḥ śucivrataḥ aśvapūrvām iti snāyāt rājyakāmas tu mānavaḥ | Kardameneti yaḥ snāyāt prajākāmaḥ śucivrataḥ ii.98: Aśvapūrṇām iti snāyāt rājyakāmaḥ śucivrataḥ |
| 78abc: Rohite carmaṇi snāyāt brāhmaṇas tu yathāvidhi, rājā carmaṇi vaiyāghre | rohite carmaṇi snāyāt brāhmaṇas tu yathāvidhi ii.99a: Rājā carmaṇi vaiyāghre |
| 79a: Daśasāhasriko homaḥ | ii.101c: Daśasāhasriko homaḥ |
| 79cd: Apsu vā juhuyād rāma padmāny ayutaśo' gniṣu | ii.105ab: Apsveva juhuyān nityaṁ padmāny ayutaśo nisi |

| | |
|---|---|
| 80cd: ācāra iti sūktena goṣṭhe gāṁ lokamātaram. | ii.112: ā gāva iti sūktena goṣṭhagā lokamātaraḥ, upatiṣṭhed |
| 81ab: Upatiṣṭhed vrajec caiva ya icched gāḥ sadākṣayāḥ | vrajantīś ca ya icchet tāḥ sadākṣayāḥ |
| 82: Upaiteti mṛtī rājño duṁdubhīn abhimantrayet, tejo balaṁ ca prāpnoti śatrūṁś caiva niyacchati | ii.114: Upeti tisṛbhī rājño dundubhīn saṁspṛśed raṇe ojo balam avāpnoti śatrūṁś caiva niyacchati |
| 83: Tṛṇapāṇir japet sūktaṁ rakṣoghnaṁ dasyubhir vṛtaḥ yeke ca mety ṛcaṁ japtvā dīrgham āyur avāpnuyāt | ii.117ab: Tṛṇapāṇir japantsūktaṁ rakṣoghnaṁ dasyubhir vṛtaḥ<br>ii.119a: Ye ke ca jmety ṛcaṁ tvetāṁ<br>ii.119d: dīrgham āyur avāpnuyāt |
| 84a: Yasya naṣṭam bhaved dravyam | ii.121a: Yasya naṣṭaṁ bhavet kiṁcit |
| 84c: Yathāliṅgaṁ tato rāyā | ii.127b: Yathāliṅgam avekṣya vai |
| 86a: Agniṁ nareti sūktena. | ii.130c: So'gniṁ nara iti sūktena |
| 86cd: Prāṇapeti tribhiḥ sūktairdhanam āpnoti cākṣayam | ii.131a: Prāgnaye'tha tribhiḥ sūktaiḥ<br>ii.131d: Dhanaṁ prāpnoti cākṣayam |
| 87a: Abhītayaḥ pragāthena | ii.132a: Abhi tvā yaḥ pragāthena |
| 87c: Śaṁvatī śam na indrāgnī | ii.133a: Śaṁvatīḥ śaṁ na indrāgnī |
| 88: Samudrajyeṣṭheti japet sūktam etaj jayāvaham, vāstoṣpate pratīty etat sūktaṁ vāstoṣpater japet. | ii.136cd: Samudrajyeṣṭhā iti japet sūktam etad bhayāpaham<br>ii.138ab: Vāstoṣpate pratīty etat sūktaṁ vāstoṣpataṁ japet |
| 89: Anīvaheti sūktena bhūtān niḥsvāpayen niśi, saṁbādhe | ii.139b: Amīvaheti sūktena bhūtāni svāpayen niśi |

| *Viṣṇu Dh Pu* ii.124 | *Ṛvidh* |
|---|---|
| viṣame durge baṁdhe vā nigaḍaiḥ kvacit | ii.140ab: Sambādhe viṣame durge baddho vā nirgataḥ kvacit |
| 90a: Palāyitvā gṛhīto vā | ii.140c: Palāyan vā gṛhīto vā |
| 90cd: Trirātraṁ niyatopoṣya śrapayet payasāṁ carum | ii.142: Trirātraṁ niyato'naśnañśrapayet pāyasaṁ carum. |
| 91: Tenāyutaśataṁ pūrṇaṁ juhuyāt tryaṁbaketyṛcā | tenāhutiśataṁ pūrṇaṁ juhuyāt sarpiṣā dvijaḥ |
| Samuddiśya mahādevaṁ jived abdaśataṁ sukhī | ii.143a: Samuddiśya mahādevaṁ |
| | ii.143d: Jived abdaśataṁ sukhī |
| 92: Tac cakṣur ity ṛcā snāta upatiṣṭhed divākaram, udyantaṁ madhyamaṁ caiva dīrgham āyur jijīviṣuḥ | ii.144: Tac cakṣur ityṛcā snāta upatiṣṭhed divākaram udyantaṁ madhyagaṁ caiva dīrgham āyur jijīviṣuḥ |
| 93a: Vyuṣā ity upatiṣṭheta | ii.145c: Vyuṣā ity upatiṣṭheta |
| 93cd: Prāpnuyāt sa hiraṇyādinānārūpadharaṁ bahu | ii.146ab: Prāpnuyāt sa hiraṇyādinānārūpaṁ dhanaṁ bahu |
| 94: Dhruvaṁ sadhyāsu kṣitiṣu japan baddhaḥ pramucyate, | ii.147ab: Dhruvāsu tvāsu kṣitiṣu japan baddhaḥ pramucyate |
| idam āpaḥ pravahata yat kaṁcit duritaṁ punaḥ | ii.153ab: Idam āpaḥ pravahata yat kiñcedam ṛcam punaḥ |
| 95cd: Sūktābhyāṁ para etābhyāṁ hutābhyāṁ bhūtim āpnuyāt | ii.154cd: Sūktābhyāṁ para etābhyāṁ ya icched bhūtim ātmanaḥ |
| 96: Śūktābhyāṁ tisra etābhyāṁ āsyadalpodaka sthitaḥ, | ii.155c: Sūktābhyāṁ tisra etābhyām |
| upatiṣṭhan raviṁ devaṁ pañcarātre gate naraḥ | ii.155a: Āsyadaghnaṁ vigāhyāmbhaḥ |
| | ii.155d: Upatiṣṭhed divākaram |
| | ii.156cd: Pañcarātre vyatite tu, |
| 97b: Mahad varṣam avāpnuyāt | mahadvarṣam avāpnuyāt |
| 97c: Indrā someti sūktaṁ tu | ii.158a: Indrāsometi sūktaṁ tu |
| 98: Yasya lupyed vrataṁ mo- | ii.159: Yasya lupyed vrataṁ mo- |

| *Viṣṇu Dh Pu* ii.124 | *Ṛvidh* |
|---|---|
| hāt vrātyair vā saṁsṛjet saha upoṣyājyasya juhuyāt tvam agne vratapā iti | hāt vrātyair vā saṁspṛśed dvijaḥ upoṣyājyaṁ ca juhuyāt tvam agne vratapā iti |
| 99: Ādityadṛkpramā draujaṁ japtvā vādī jayī bhavet, samagnir agnibhiś ceti prapadyed vāyubhāskarau | ii.160a: Pra samrājam iti tvetaj<br>ii.161d: Kṣipraṁ vādaṁ parājayet<br>ii.162: Śamagnir agnibhiś ceti |
| 100abc: Agniṁ prathamataḥ stutvā mahat kaṣṭāt pramucyate, nahīti ca catuṣkena | prapadyed vāyubhāskarau agniṁprathamataḥ stutvā mahatkṛcpchrāt pramucyate<br>ii.163: Nahīti yaś catuṣkeṇa |
| 101a: Ṛcaṁ japtvā ya ityetat | ii.164a: Tṛc aṁ japtvāyad ity etat |
| 101cd: Prāgbhojanam idaṁ brahma mānavānāṁ maharṣiṇām | ii.167ab: Prāgbhojanam idaṁ brahma mānavānāṁ maharṣiṇām |
| 102abc: Pūrvāhṇe japato nityaṁ tvarthasiddhiḥ parā bhavet, aginety āśvinaṁ sūktam | ii.167cd: Pūrvāhṇe japato nityamarthasiddiḥ parā bhavet<br>ii.168a: Agninety āśvinaṁ sūktam |
| 103a: Samidheti juhoty agnau | ii.169c: Samidheti juhoty agnau |
| 103c: Dvicatvārikaṁ caindraṁ | ii.170c: Dvicatvāriṁśakeneha |
| 104: Nāśaṁ mahīti japtvā ca prāpnoty ārogyam eva ca duḥsvapnaghnāḥ parā japyā naraḥ pāpaiḥ pramucyate | ii.172cd-173ab: Vāśaṁ mahīti ca japtvā prāpnoty ārogyam eva ca, duḥsvapnaghnīḥ parā japtvā prātaḥ pāpaiḥ pramucyate |
| 105abc: Śanno bhaveti dvābhyāṁ tu bhuktvānnaṁ prayataḥ śuciḥ hṛdayaṁ pāṇinā spṛṣṭvā | ii.173cd-174a: Śaṁ no bhavati dvābhyāṁ tu bhuktvānnaṁ prayataḥ śuciḥ, hṛdayaṁ pāṇinā spṛṣṭvā |
| 106cd: Ita ityājyam utpūya juhuyād iṁdram arcayet | ii.175c: Yata ityājyam utpūtam<br>ii.175b: Juhuyḥd indram arcya ca |
| 107cd: Tattvāmandam iti snā- | ii.177ab: Uttvā mandantviti snā- |

| *Viṣṇu Dh Pu* ii.124 | *Ṛvidh* |
|---|---|
| to hutvā śatrūn pramāpayet | to hutvā śatrūn pramāpayet |
| 108: Tānvidyāditya daivatyaṁ japtvā mucyate bandhanāt, yadyāva iti japtvā ca sarvān kāmān samaśnute | ii.178abc: Tyānvity āditya daivatyaṁ sadyo mucyeta bandhanāt, yad dyāveti japen nityam<br>ii.179: Sarvān kāmāntsamaśnute |
| 109abc: Pavitrāṇāṁ pavitraṁ tu pāvamānaṛcaḥ smṛtāḥ vaikhānasa ṛcas triṁśat | iii.icd: Pavitrāṇaṁ pavitraṁ tu pāvamānīr ṛco japet<br>iii.10d: Triṁśad vaikhānasīr ṛcaḥ |
| 110: Ṛcāṁ dviṣaṣṭiḥ proktaṁ copavased ṛṣisattamaiḥ sarvakalmaṣanāśāya pāvanāya śivāya ca | iii.11cd-12ab: Ṛcāṁ dviṣaṣṭiḥ prokteyaṁ pavasvety ṛṣisattamaiḥ sarvakalmaṣanāśāya pāvanāya śivāya ca |
| 111: Svādiṣṭayeti sūktānāṁ saptaṣaṣṭir udāhṛtāḥ daśottarā ṛcaś caitāḥ pāvamānyaḥ śatāni ṣaṭ | iii.12cd-13ab: Svādiṣṭhayeti sūktānāṁ saptaṣaṣṭir ihoditā, daśottarāṇyṛcāṁ caiva pāvamānīḥ śatāni ṣaṭ |
| 112: Etaj juhvañ japaṁś caiva ghoraṁ mṛtyubhayaṁ jayet ādhyātmikaṁ pavitraṁ ca sūktam japtvālpataḥ kvacit | iii.13cd: Etaj juhvañ japaṁś caiva ghoraṁ mṛtyubhayaṁ jayet<br>iii.17cd: Ādhyātmikaṁ pavitraṁ te sūktaṁ japtvāplutaḥ śuciḥ |
| 113: Gatim iṣṭām avāpnoti vindate mahatīṁ śriyam, āpo hiṣṭheti mahataḥ prayuṁjītodakasthitaḥ | iii.18ab: Gatim iṣṭām avāpnoti vindate ceha vṛddhayaḥ<br>iii.19cd: Āpo hiṣṭheti niyataḥ prayuñjīta sadā dvijaḥ |
| 114cd: Upatiṣṭheta rājānaṁ yamasūktena vai dvija | iii.34ab: Upatiṣṭheta rājānaṁ yamaṁ sūktena vai dvijaḥ |
| 115cd: Pareyavāṁsam ityetat sūktam atra prayojayet | iii.35cd: Pareyivāṁsam ityetat sūktam atra prayojayet |
| 116: Parāyuṣaḥ pramīyeta na jātu kathaṁcana mṛtyumeva | iii.36ab: Purāyuṣaḥ pramīyeta na jātu sa kathañcana |

| *Viṣṇu Dh Pu* ii.124 | *Ṛvidh* |
|---|---|
| prapadyeta paraṁ mṛtyor iva dvija | iii.39ab: Mṛtyum eva prapadyeta paraṁ mṛtyo japan dvijaḥ |
| 117a: Vaiśākhyaṁ paurṇamāsyaṁ tu | iii.37c: Vaiśākhyāṁ paurṇamāsyāṁ tu |
| 117: Naktabhojī sadā naraḥ | iii.39c: Naktabhojī mitāhāraḥ |
| 118: Phalāhāro jayen mṛtyuṁ tribhir varṣair sadā naraḥ, daśākṣaraṁ tu śāṁtyarthaṁ bhadraṁ na iti saṁsmaret | iii.40cd: Phalāhāro jayen mṛtyuṁ tribhir varṣair mitāśanaḥ iii.45ab: daśākṣaraṁ tu śāntyarthaṁ bhadraṁ na iti saṁsmaret |
| 119: Phalāhāro bhaven māsaṁ māsān māsaṁ payaḥ pibet, vāyubhakṣo bhaven māsaṁ japann etat sahasraśaḥ | iii.46: Phalāhāro bhaven māsaṁ māsaṁ cāpaḥ pibet tataḥ vāyubhakṣo bhaven māsaṁ japann etat sahasraśaḥ |
| 120: Antardhānam avāpnoti Siddhan paśyati cāraṇān pradeveti niyato japeta marudhanvasu | iii.48a: Antardhānaṁ vrajati iii.47d: Siddhān paśyati cāraṇān iii.49ab: Pradevatreti niyato japeta marudhanvasu |
| 121: Prāṇāntike bhaye prāpte kṣipram āyus tu viṁdati vaibhītakāṁs tu trīn akṣan gaṁdhaissamadhivāsayet | iii.49cd-50ab: Prāṇāntikebhaye prāpte kṣipram ambhaḥ sa vindati, vaibhītakāṁs tu trīn akṣān gandhaiḥ samabhivāsayet |
| 122: Puṣpair avakirec caiva sthāpayitvā vihāyasi, saṁhṛtya pādau tau tatra tiṣṭhed dakṣastutiṁ japet | iii.50cd-51ab: Puṣpair avakirec cainān sthāpayitvā vihāyasi saṁhatya pādau tāṁ rātrīṁ tiṣṭhann akṣastutiṁ japet |
| 123abc: Prāve māsety ṛcāṁ ekāṁ japec ca manasā niśi vyuṣṭāyām udite sūrye | iii.51cd-52a: Prā vepāmā ṛcaṁ tvetāṁ manasaiva japen niśi, vyuṣṭāyām udite sūrye. |
| 124: Abradhnamuṣasānaktetyetat svastyayanaṁ japet, namo mitrasya varuṇasya cakṣuṣeti nityaśaḥ | iii.54: Abudhram uṣāsānaktety ete svastyayane japet, namo mitrasya varuṇasya cakṣasa iti nityaśaḥ |

| *Viṣṇu Dh Pu* ii.124 | *Ṛvidh* |
|---|---|
| 125abc: Tathājyaṁ juhuyān nityaṁ bhītibhyo vipramucyate, devasya rīti nityaṁ tu | iii.55cd: Tayājyaṁ juhuyān nityam enobhyo vipramucyate<br>iii.56a: Divasparīti sūktaṁ tu |
| 126a: Mā pragāmeti mūḍhas tu | iii.57ab: Mā pragāmeti...sa mūḍho... |
| 126cd: Kṣīṇāyur iti manyeta yaṁ kaṁcit suhṛdaṁ priyam<br>127abc: Yat te yamam iti tu snātaḥ tasya mūrdhānam ālabhet sahasrakṛtvā paṁcāhaṁ | iii.58: Kṣīṇāyur iti manyeta yaṁ kañcit suhṛdaṁ priyam yat te yamam iti snātastasya mūrdhānam ālabhet<br>iii.59a: Sahasrakṛtvaḥ pañcāham |
| 128ab: Sruksruve daśamenaiva idhmam audumbaraṁ bhavet | iii.64ab: Sruksruvau camasaś caiva sarvam audumbaraṁ bhavet |
| 129: Paśukāmo gavāṁ goṣṭhe annakāmaś catuṣpathe, pārāvataḥ svastyayanaṁ snātasya vidhīyate | iii.67a: Paśukāmo japed goṣṭhe<br>iii.66a: Catuṣpathe cānnakāma<br>iii.70ab: Parāvataḥ svastyayanaṁ snātakasya vidhīyate |
| 130: Bṛhaspate prathamam iti jñānakāmasya bhārgava, vayaḥ suparṇam ity etāṁ japan vai viṁdate śriyam | iii.71ab: Bṛhaspate prathamam iti nityaṁ jñānastutiṁ japet<br>iii.72cd: Vayaḥ suparṇā ityetāṁ japan vai vindate śriyam |
| 131: Yas te manyo iti sadāmayatnaghnaṁ vidhīyate, haviṣmatīyam abhyasya sarvapāpaiḥ pramucyate | iii.77ab: Yas te manyoiti sadā sapatnaghne tvime japet,<br>iii.132cd: Haviṣpāntīyam abhyasya sarvapāpaiḥ pramucyate |
| 132a: Yā oṣadhīḥ svastyayanaṁ | iii.231a: Yā oṣadhīḥ svastyayanam |
| 132c: Tasya māyā vinaśyeta<br>133: Bṛhaspatiḥ pratīty etad vṛṣṭikāmaḥ prayojayet, sarvatra tu parāśaktirjñeyāpratirathā tathā | iv.1c: Tasyāmayā na bhavanti<br>iv.5ab: Bṛhaspate pratity etadvṛṣṭikāmaḥ prayojayet<br>iv.6ab: Sarvatra tu parā śāntirjñeyo' pratirathas tvṛṣiḥ |
| 134: Bhūtāṁśaṁ kāśyapaṁ | iv.10ab: Bhūtāṁśaṁ kāśyapaṁ |

| *Viṣṇu Dh Pu* ii.124 | *Ṛvidh* |
|---|---|
| nityaṁ prajākāmasya kīrtitam, ahaṁ rudrebhir ity etadvāgmī bhavati mānavaḥ | sūktaṁ prajākāmaḥ sucir japan<br>iv.19ab: Ahaṁ rudrebhir ityetadvāgmī bhavati pūjitaḥ |
| 135b: Jayan rātrīti rātriṣu | iv.21d: Japed rātrīti rātriṣu |
| 136a: Yā kalpayatīti japen | iv.30a: Yāṁ kalpayantīti sadā |
| 136cd: Āyuṣyaṁ caiva varcasyaṁ sūktaṁ dākṣāyaṇaṁ mahat | iv.43ab: Āyuṣyam āyur varcasyaṁ sūktaṁ dākṣāyaṇaṁ mahat |
| 137: Uta devā iti japedāmayaghnaṁ dhṛtavrataḥ agne agnāva ity etaddhanakāmaḥ prayojayet | iv.45cd: Uta devā iti japedāmayāvī yatavrataḥ<br>iv.49ab: Agne acchā vadety etaddhanakāmaḥ prayojayet |
| 138cd: Dviṣantu dhanvinaṁ hutvā dviṣato vindate dhanam | iv.53ab: Dviṣantaṁ dhaninaṁ hatvā dviṣato vindate dhanam |
| 139ab: Ayam agne janiteti japed agniṁ bhaye sati | iv.54ab: Ayam agne jariteti japed agnibhaye sati |
| 140abc: Prātaśca pāṭhayed enaṁ saṁsadi brahmacāriṇām imām iti ca sūktena | iv.61cd: Prātaś ca peṣayedenāṁ saṁsadi brahmacāriṇā<br>iv.63a: Imām iti tu sūktena |
| 141c: Araṇyānīty araṇyeṣu | iv.69c: Araṇyānīty araṇyeṣu |
| 142: Śraddhāsūktaṁ japen nityaṁ śraddhākāmavivardhanam brāhmī yadyasya sūkte dve japeta niyataḥ sadā | iv.70cd: Śraddhāsūktaṁ japen nityaṁ śraddhākāmaḥ samāhitaḥ<br>iv.71cd: Brāhmīm āsādya sūkte dve japeta niyatavrataḥ |
| 143: Śaṁkhapuṣpīṁ tu payasā brāhmīpuṣpāṇi sarpiṣā śatāvarī tu payasā vacām adbhir ghṛtena vā | iv.72cd-73ab: Śaṅkhapuṣpīṁ tu payasā brāhmīpuṣpāni sarpiṣā Śatāvarīṁ tu payasā vacām adbhir ghṛtena vā |
| 144: Sūktābhyāṁ manumantrābhyāṁ caikaikaṁ tryahaṁ pibet śraddhāṁ medhāṁ smṛtiṁ puṣṭim varṇaṁ | iv.73cd: Sūktābhyām anumantry ābhyāmekaikām tu tryahaṁ pibet<br>iv.74ab: Śraddhāṁ medhāṁ |

| *Viṣṇu Dh Pu* ii.124 | *Ṛvidh* |
|---|---|
| lakṣmīṁ ca viṁdati | smṛtiṁ puṣṭiṁ balaṁ lakṣmīṁ ca vindati |
| 145: Śāsanarthañ japannityaṁ saṁgrāme vijigīṣataḥ gṛhītadakṣiṇādarbhān gṛhītvā saṁspṛśej japet | iv.75cd: Śāsa itthā sapatnaghnaṁ saṁgrāmaṁ vijigīṣataḥ<br>iv.81: Gṛhītaṁ yakṣmaṇā darbhān gṛhītvā saṁspṛśan japet |
| 146abc: Muṁcāmi tvā haviṣeti yakṣmānam apakarṣati brahmaṇāgniḥ saṁvidānaṁ | Muñcāmi tvā haviṣeti yakṣmāṇam apakarṣati<br>iv.86c: Brahmaṇāgniḥ saṁvidāna |
| 147: Apehīti japet sūktaṁ sucir duḥsvapnanāśanam devā kapota iti tu kapotasyopaveśane | iv.101cd: Apehīti japet sūktāṁ sucir duḥsvapnanāśanam<br>iv.102ab: Devā kapota iti tu kapotasyopaveśane |
| 148cd: Sapatnaghnaṁ prayuṁjīta ṛṣabhaṁ japahomayoḥ | iv.103ab: Sapatnaghnaṁ prayuñjīta ṛṣabhaṁ japahomayoḥ |
| 149a: Yenedam iti japtvā vai | iv.103c: Yenadam īti vai nityaṁ |
| 149cd: Mayobhūr vāta iti tu gavāṁ svastyayanaṁ param | iv.104cd: Mayo bhūr vāta iti tu gavāṁ svastyayane japet |
| 150: Yavānāṁ ghṛtāktānāṁ gomayāgnau samāhitaḥ, juhuyād goṣṭhamadhye tu dadhimadvājyasaṁskṛtam | iv.105: Yavānāṁ tu ghṛtāktānāṁ kārīṣe' gnau samāhitaḥ, juhuyād goṣṭhamadhye tu dadhimadhvājyasaṁskṛtān |
| 151a: Pataṁtam iti nityaṁ tu | iv.115a: Pataṅgam iti nityaṁ tu |
| 151cd: Śaṁbarīṁ indrajālāṁ vā malām etena dhārayed | iv.116: Śāmbarīm indrajālāṁ vā māyāṁ etena bādhate adṛṣṭā- |
| 152abc: Adṛśyānāṁ ca sattvānāṁ māyām etena bādhate na pratiṣṭheti svastyayanaṁ | nāṁ ca sattvānāṁ māyām etena bādhate<br>iv.118a: Tyamūṣviti svastyayanaṁ |
| 153a: Viṣṇur nyānam·tīmaṁ ca | iv.118a: Viṣṇur yoniṁ nejameṣa |
| 153cd: Mahi tyṛṇāṁ mavosviti pari svastyanaṁ japet | iv.188cd: Mahi trīṇāṁ avo'stviti pathi svastyayane japet |
| 154a: Prāpayed vidviṣadveṣaṁ | iv.119a: Prāgnaye' tha dviṣad- |

| *Viṣṇu Dh Pu* ii.124 | *Ṛvidh* |
|---|---|
| āyaṁ gau saptarājñas tu sarpān etaiḥ prasādhayet | dveṣyaṁ iv.119cd: Āyaṁ gauḥ sārparājñīs tu sarpān etena bādhate |
| 155: Saṁ samid yuvaseccaitat saubhrātṛkaraṇaṁ mahat, tac chaṁyorā vṛṇīmaha japet svastyayanaṁ sadā | iv.123cd: Saṁ samid yuvase vṛṣan saubhrātṛkaraṇaṁ mahat iv. 125cd: Tac chaṁyorā vṛṇīmaha iti svastyayane japet |
| 156ab: Pītṛṇāṁ saṁhitāṁ vidyāt pitṛn prīṇāti vai tathā | iv.130ab: Pitryāṁ tāṁ saṁhitāṁ vidyāt pitṛn prīṇāti caitayā |

### (c) *Intimate relationship to the version of the Ṛgvidhāna in the Agni-Purāṇa*

Now we may turn to the version of the *Ṛvidh* in the Agni-Purāṇa which, as stated by me already earlier,[17] is only a further abridgement of the *Ṛvidh* version in the *Viṣṇu Dh Pu.* This hypothesis rests on the fact that in the second Khaṇḍa of *Viṣṇu Dh Pu*, the principal speaker is Puṣkara, whereas in the *Agni Pu*, Agni, the principal speaker, proposes to report what Puṣkara said to Rāma on "Ṛgyajussāmātharvaṇavidhāna".[18] I may point out that the *Agni Pu* has two stanzas which are not found in the *Viṣṇu Dh Pu* but are found in the *Ṛvidh.*

| *Agni Pu* 259 | *Ṛvidh* |
|---|---|
| 9cd: Śirasā dhārayan vahniṁ yo japet parivatsaram // | i.80ab: Śirasā dhārayed agniṁ niyataḥ parivatsaram / |
| 10cd: Ataḥ param ṛcaḥ sapta vāyvādyā yāḥ prakīrtitāḥ // | i.84: Ataḥ paraṁ tṛcāḥ sapta vāyvādyā ye prakīrtitāḥ / |
| 11: Tā japan prayato nityamiṣṭān kāmān samaśnute med- | tāñ japan prayato nityamiṣṭān kāmānt samaśnute // |

17. *Vide* Chapter I pp. 17-18. Dr. Meyer regards the version of the *Ṛvidh* in the *Agni Pu* as "mutilated and summarised one" (*vide* his *Praefatio*, p. xxxii).

18. Agniruvāca—Ṛgyajussāmātharvaṇavidhānaṁ Puṣkaroditam /
bhuktimuktipradaṁ japyāddhomād rāmāya tad vade //
*Agni Pu* 259.1

| *Agni Pu* 259 | *Ṛvidh* |
|---|---|
| hākāmo japen nityaṁ sadas-aspam iti tryṛcam // | i.85c: Medhākāmo japen nityaṁ<br>i.85b: Sadasaspatimity ṛcam |
| 12a: Ambayo yantimāḥ proktā | i.89a: Ambayo yanti yā proktā |
| 12cd: Śunaḥśepam ṛṣiṁ bad-dhaḥ saṁniruddho' thavā japet | i.90: Śunaḥśepaṁ ṛṣiṁ baddhaḥ saṁniruddho' thavā japet |
| 13: Mucyate sarvapāpebhyo gadī vāpy agado bhavet, ya icchac chāśvataṁ kāmaṁ mitraṁ prājñaṁ puraṁdaram | mucyate sarvapāśebhyo gadī cāpy agadī bhavet<br>i.91: Ya icchec chāśvatān kā-mān indrāt prāptuṁ puraṁ-darāt |
| 14: Ṛgbhiḥ ṣoḍaśabhiḥ kuryād-indrasyeti dine dine hiraṇya-stūpam ity etaj japañ śatrūn prabādhate | sa ṣoḍaśabhir evargbhir in-draṁ stūyād dine dine<br>i.92a: Hairaṇyastūpam indrasya<br>i.92cd: Taj japan...śatrūn...pra-tibādhate |
| 15b: Ye te panthā japan naraḥ | i.95a: Ye te panthā itīmāṁ tu |
| 15cd: Raudrībhiḥ ṣaḍbhir īśā-naṁ stūyād yo vai dine dine | i.96ab: Raudrībhiḥ ṣaḍbhir īśā-naṁ tuṣṭūyād yo dine dine |
| 16a: Caruṁ vā kalpayed raud-raṁ | i.98c: Caruṁ vā kalpayed raud-raṁ |
| 16cd: Udity udyantam ādityam-upatiṣṭhan dine dine | i.99ab: Udity udyantam āditya-mupatiṣṭhed dine dine |
| 17c: Dviṣantam ity athārdhar-cam | i.100a: Dviṣantam ity athārdh-arcaṁ |
| 18abc: Āgaskṛt saptrātreṇa vidveṣam adhigacchati ārōg-yakāmo rogī vā | i.100cd: Āgaskṛt saptarātreṇa vidveṣam adhigacchati //<br>i.101a: Rogair gṛhīto' rogi ca |
| 19: Uttamas tasya cārdharco japed vairivināśane udayaty āyur akṣayyaṁ tejo madh-yaṁ dine japet | i.102ab: Uttamas tasya cārdhar-co dviṣaddveṣa iti smṛtaḥ /<br>i.103cd: Udayaty āyur akṣay-yaṁ tejo madhyaṁdine japan |
| 20: Astaṁ pratigate sūrye dvi- | i.104ab: Astaṁ vrajati sūrye tu |

| *Agni Pu* 259 | *Ṛvidh* |
|---|---|
| ṣantaṁ pratibādhate na vayo neti sūktāni japañ śatrūn niyacchati | dviṣantaṁ pratibhādhate / i.105a: Nava paśveti sūktāni i.105d: Śatrūṁś caiva niyacchati |
| 21a: Ekādaśa suparṇasya | i.106ab: Sauparṇāni...ekādaśa ... |
| 21c: Ādhyātmikīḥ ka ityetā | i.107a: Ādhyātmikīḥ ka ityetā |
| 22: Ānobhadrā ityanena dīrgham āyur avāpnuyāt tvaṁ someti ca sūktena navaṁ paśyen niśākaram | i.108a: Ānobhadrīyam āyuṣyam i.108d: Sarvam āyur avāpnuyāt i.110abc: Tvaṁ someti tu sūktena paśyec candram upoditam upatiṣṭhet samitpāṇir |
| 23: Upatiṣṭhet samitpāṇir-Vāsaṁsy āpnoty asaṁśayam āyur īpsann imam iti kautsaṁ sūktaṁ sadā japet | i.112c: Vāsāṁsyapi sa vindeta i.114ab: Āyur īpsann imam iti kautsam sūktam sadābhyaset |
| 24: Apanaḥ śośucad iti stutvā madhye divākaraṁ yathā muñcati ceṣīkāṁ tathā pāpaṁ pramuñcati | i.115cd: Apa naḥ śośucad iti snātvā madhyaṁdine ravau i.117ab: Yathā muñjād iveṣīkā tathā pāpāt pramucyate |
| 25a: Jātavedasa ityetaj | i.119c: Jātavedasa ity etāṁ |
| 26: Vyuṣṭāyam ca tathā rātryāmetad duḥśvapnanāśanam pramandineti sūyantyā japed garbhavimocanam | i.122cd: Vyuṣṭāyāṁ ca japen nityametāṁ duḥsvapnanāśinīm i.123ab: Pramandine*ti sūyantyāṁ japed garbhapromocanīm |
| 27ab: Japannindram iti snāto vaiśvadevaṁ tu saptakam | i.124cd: Japann indram iti snāto vaiśvadevaṁ tu saptakam |
| 28a: Imām iti japañ śaśvet | i.127ab: Imā iti jāpec chaśvad |
| 28cd: Mā nas toka iti dvābhyāṁ trirātropoṣitaḥ śuciḥ | i.128ab: Mā no mahāntam ity ābhyāṁ trirātropoṣitaḥ śuciḥ |
| 29: Audumbarīś ca juhuyāt samidhaś cājyasaṁskṛtāḥ chitvā sarvāṇ mṛtyupāśāñ jīved rogavivarjitaḥ | i.129ab: Audumbarīs tu juhuyāt dadhimadhvājyasaṁskṛtāḥ i.130cd: Chitvā sarvān mṛtyupāśāñjived rogair vivarjitaḥ |

| *Agni Pu* 259 | *Ṛvidh* |
|---|---|
| 30: Ūrdhvabāhur anenaiva | i.130a: Ūrdhvabāhus tu sūktena |
| 31cd: Citram ity upatiṣṭheta trisaṁdhyaṁ bhāskaraṁ tathā | i.131cd: Citram ity upatiṣṭheta sūktenānena bhāskaram |
| 32cd: Adhaḥ svapneti ca japan prātar madhyaṁ dine dine<br>33a: Duḥsvapnaṁ cārdayet kṛtsnam | i.133abc: Adhaḥ svapnasyeti japet prātaḥ prātar dine dine duḥsvapnaṁ nudate kṣipraṁ |
| 33cd: Ubhe pumān iti tathā rakṣoghnaḥ parikīrtitaḥ | i.134ab: Ubhe punāmīti parā ripughnyas tu prakīrtitāḥ |
| 34abc: Ubhe vāsā iti ṛco japan kāmānavāpnuyāt, tamāgann iti japan | i.135cd: Ye devāso divy anāya japan kāmān avāpnuyāt<br>i.138c: Na mā garann iti japan |
| 35a: Kayā śubheti ca japañ | i.143a: Kayā śubheti paiśunyaṁ |
| 35cd: Imaṁ nu somamityetat sarvān kāmān avāpnuyāt // | i.144a: Imaṁ nu somam ityete<br>i.144c: Sarvān kāmān avāpnoti |
| 36abc: Pitarity upatiṣṭheta nityam artham upasthitam agne nayeti sūktena | i.145abc: Pituṁ nvity upatiṣṭheta nityam annam upasthitam<br>i.149c: Agne nayeti sūktena |
| 37c: Kaṅkato neti sūktena | i.151c: Kaṅkato neti sūktaṁ tu |
| 38a: Yo jāta iti sūktena | i.156a: Yo jāta iti sūktena |
| 39: Yo me rājann itīmāṁ tu duḥsvapnaśamanīmṛcam adhvani prasthito yas tu paśyec chatruṁ samutthitam | i.161cd: Yo me rajann itīmāṁ tu duḥsvapnaśamanīm ṛcam<br>i.168cd: Adhvani prasthito yas tu paśyec chakunim utthitam |
| 40a: Apraśastaṁ praśastaṁ vā | i.169a: Apraśastaṁ praśastaṁ vā |
| 40cd: Dvāviṁśakaṁ japan sūktamādhyātmikam anuttamam | ii.21: Dvāviṁśakaṁ japet sūktamādhyātmikamanuttamam// |
| 41abc: Parvasu prayato nityam- | parvasu prayato nityamiṣṭān |

| *Agni Pu* 259 | *Ṛvidh* |
|---|---|
| iṣṭān kāmān samaśnute<br>kṛṇuṣveti japansūktaṁ | kāmānt samasnute<br>ii.63a: Kṛṇuṣveti japantsūktam |
| 42: Arātīnāṁ haret prāṇān rakṣāṁsy api vināśayet upatiṣṭhet svayaṁ vahniṁ parīty ṛcā dine dine<br>43: Taṁ rakṣati svayaṁ vahnir viśvato viśvatomukhaḥ //<br>haṁsaḥ śuciṣad ityetacchucir īkṣed divākaram // | ii.63cd: Arātīnāṁ haret prāṇān rakṣāṁsy api ca nāśayet<br>ii.64: Upatiṣṭheta yo vahniṁ parīty ṛcā dine dine<br>taṁ rakṣati svayaṁ vahnirviśvato viśvato mukhaḥ<br>i.67cd: Haṁśaḥ śuciṣad ity ṛcā śucir īkṣed divākaram |
| 44: Kṛṣiṁ prapadyamānas tu sthālīpākaṁ yathāvidhi juhuyāt kṣetramadhye tu muniḥ svāhāntapañcabhiḥ | ii.68: Kṛṣiṁ prapadyamānas tu sthālīpākaṁ yathāvidhi / juhuyāt kṣetramadhye tu śunaṁ vāhas tu pañcabhiḥ // |
| 45: Indrāya ca marudbhyas tu parjanyāya bhagāya ca yathāliṅgaṁ tu viharellāṅgalaṁ tu kṛṣīvalaḥ // | ii.69: Yathāliṅgaṁ tu viharellāṅgalaṁ ca kṛṣīvalaḥ / Indrāya ca marudbhyaś ca parjanyāya bhagāya ca // |
| 46: Yukto dhānyāya sītayai śunāsīram athottaram / gandhamālyair namaskārairyajed etāś ca devatāḥ | ii.70ab: Pūṣṇe dhānyāya sītāyai śunāsīram athottaram /<br>ii.71a: Gandhamālyopahāraiśca<br>ii.70d: yajed etāś ca devatāḥ |
| 47: Pravāpane pralavane khalasītāpahārayoḥ amoghaṁ karma bhavati vardhate sarvadā kṛṣiḥ | ii.71cd: Pravapaṇe pralavane khalasītopahārayoḥ<br>ii.72cd: Amogham karma bhavati kṛṣir vardhati sarvadā // |
| 48a: Samudrād iti sūktena | ii.78a: Samudrād iti sūktena |
| 48cd: Viśvāni na iti dvābhyāṁ ya ṛgbhyāṁ vahnim arhati<br>49ab: Sa taraty āpadaḥ sarvā yaśaḥ prāpnoti cākṣayam | ii.80: Viśvāni na iti dvābhyāmṛgbhyāṁ yo vahnim arcati sa taraty āpadaḥ sarvā yaśaḥ prāpnoti cākṣayam |
| 50: Agne tvam iti ca stutvā dhanam āpnoti vāñchitam prajākāmo japen nityam varuṇadaivatatrayam | ii.81cd: Agne tvam iti sūktena dhanam āyuścavāñchatā<br>ii.83ab: Prajākāmo yajen nityaṁ caruṇā devapatnayaḥ |

| *Agni Pu* 259 | *Ṛvidh* |
|---|---|
| 51a: Svastyātreyaṁ japet prātaḥ | ii.85c: Svastyetreyaṁ japan nityaṁ |
| 51cd: Svasti panthā iti procya svastimān vrajate' dhvani // 52abc: Vijihīṣva vanaspate śatrūṇāṁ vyāpitaṁ bhavet striyā garbhapramūḍhāyā | ii.87: Svasti panthām iti procya svastimān vrajate' dhvani vijihīṣva vanaspate tad idaṁ cyāvanaṁ smṛtam ii.89c: Striyaṁ garbhapramūḍhāṁ vā |
| 53: Acchā vadeti sūktaṁca vṛṣṭikāmaḥ prayojayet nirāhāraḥ klinnavāsā na cirena pravarṣati // | ii.90cd-91ab: Acchāvadeti sūktaṁ tu vṛṣṭikāmaḥ prayojayet nirāhāraḥ klinnavāsā acireṇa pravarṣati |
| 54: Manasaḥ kāmam ity etāṁ paśukāmo naro japet kardamena iti snāyāt prajākāmaḥ śucivrataḥ | ii.97: Manasaḥ kāmam ityeṣā paśukāmābhiṣecanī kardameneti yaḥ snāyāt prajākāmaḥ śucivrataḥ |
| 55: Aśvapūrṇām iti snāyāt rājyakāmas tu mānavaḥ rohite carmaṇi snāyādbrāhmaṇas tu yathāvidhi // | ii.98: Aśvapūrṇām iti snāyāt rājyakāmaḥ śucivrataḥ rohite carmaṇi snāyād brāhmaṇas tu yathāvidhi |
| 56a: Rājā carmaṇi vaiyāghre | ii.99a: Rājā carmaṇi vaiyāghre |
| 56c: Daśasāhasriko homaḥ | ii.101c: Daśasāhasriko homaḥ |
| 57: Āgāra iti sūktena goṣṭhe gāṁ lokamātaram upatiṣṭhed vrājec caiva yadīcchet tāḥ sadākṣyāḥ | ii.112: Āgava iti sūktena goṣṭhagā lokamātaraḥ upatiṣṭhed vrajantīś ca ya icchet tāḥ sadākṣayāḥ |
| 58: Upeti tisṛbhī rājño dundubhīn abhimantrayet tejo balaṁ ca prāpnoti śatruṁ caiva niyacchati | ii.114: Upeti tisṛbhī rājño dundubhīn saṁspṛśed raṇe ojo balam avāpnoti śatrūṁś caiva niyacchati |
| 59: Tṛṇapāṇir japet sūktaṁ rakṣoghnaṁ dasyubhir vṛtaḥ ye ke ca jmety ṛcaṁ japtvā dīrgham āyur avāpnuyāt // | ii.117ab: Tṛṇapāṇir japant sūktaṁ rakṣoghnaṁ dasyubhir vṛtaḥ ii.119a: Ye ke ca jmety ṛcaṁ tvetām |

| *Agni Pu* 259 | *Ṛvidh* |
|---|---|
| | ii.119d: Dīrgham āyur avāpnu-<br>yāt |
| 60a: Jīmūtasūktena tathā<br>60c: yathāliṅgaṁ tato rājā | ii.127ab: Jīmūtasūktasya vidhiṁ<br>yathāliṅgam avekṣya vai |
| 61: Prāgnayeti tribhiḥ sūktair-<br>dhanam āpnoti cākṣayam<br>amīvaheti sūktena<br>bhūtāni sthāpayen niśi | ii.131a: Prāgnaye' tha tribhiḥ<br>sūktaiḥ<br>ii.131d: Dhanaṁprāpnoti cāk-<br>ṣayam<br>ii.139ab: Amīvaheti sūktena<br>bhūtāni svāpayen niśi |
| 62: Saṁbādhe viṣame durge<br>baddho vā nirgataḥ kvacit<br>palāyan vā gṛhīto vā<br>sūktam etat tathā japet | ii.140: Sambādhe viṣame durge<br>baddho vā nirgataḥ kvacit<br>palāyan vā gṛhīto vā<br>taskaraiḥ sa japed idam // |
| 63: Trirātraṁ niyatopoṣya<br>śrapayet pāyasaṁ carum<br>tenāhuti śataṁ pūrṇaṁ<br>juhuyāt tryambakety ṛcā // | ii.142: Trirātraṁ niyato'naś-<br>nañśrapayet pāyasaṁ carum<br>tenāhutiśataṁ pūrṇaṁ<br>juhuyāt sarpiṣā dvijaḥ |
| 64: Samuddiśya mahādevaṁ<br>jived abdaśataṁ sukham<br>tac cakṣur ity ṛcā snāta<br>upatiṣṭhed divākaram | ii.143a: Samuddiśya mahāde-<br>vaṁ<br>ii.143d: Jīved abdaśataṁ sukhī<br>ii.144: Tac cakṣur ity ṛcā snāta<br>upatiṣṭhed divākaram |
| 65ab: Udyantaṁ madhyagaṁ<br>caiva dīrgham āyur jijīviṣuḥ | udyantaṁ madhyagaṁ caiva<br>dīrgham āyur jijīviṣuḥ |
| 66abc: Sūktābhyāṁ para evā-<br>bhyāṁ hutābhyāṁ bhutim<br>āpnuyāt<br>indrāsometi sūktaṁ tu | ii.154cd: Sūktābhyāṁ para etā-<br>bhyāṁ ya icched bhūtim<br>atmanaḥ<br>ii.158a: Indrāsometi sūktaṁ tu |
| 67: Yaṣya luptaṁ vrataṁ<br>mohādvrātyair vā saṁsṛjet<br>saha upoṣyājyaṁ sa juhuyāt<br>tvam agne vratapā iti | ii.159: Yasya lupyed vrataṁ<br>mohāt vrātyair vā saṁspṛśed<br>dvijaḥ upoṣyājyaṁ ca juhu-<br>yāt tvam agne vratapā iti |
| 68abc: Adityety ṛcaṁ samrā- | ii.160a: Pra samrājam iti tvetaj |

| *Agni Pu* 259 | *Ṛvidh* |
|---|---|
| jaṁ japtvā vāde jayī bhavet mahīti catuṣkeṇa | ii.161: Kṣipram vādaṁ parājayet<br>ii.163a: Na hīti yaś catuṣkeṇa |
| 69a: Ṛcaṁ japtvā yadi hyetat | ii.164a: Tṛcaṁ japtvā yad ityetat |
| 70: Vācaṁ mahīti japtvā ca prāpnoty ārogyam eva ca Śaṁ no bhaveti dvābhyāṁ tu bhuktvānnaṁ prayataḥ śuciḥ | ii.172cd: Vāśaṁ mahīti ca japtvā prāpnoty ārogyam eva ca<br>ii.173cd: Śaṁ no bhaveti dvābhyāṁ tu bhuktānnaṁ prayataḥ śuciḥ |
| 71a: Hṛdayaṁ pāṇinā spṛṣṭvā | ii.174a: Hṛdayaṁ pāṇinā spṛṣṭvā |
| 71cd: Uttamedam iti snāto hutvā śatruṁ pramāpayet | ii.177ab: Uttvā mandantv iti snāto hutvā śatrūn pramāpayet |
| 72a: Śaṁ no' gna iti sūktena | ii.179c: Tvaṁ no agna iti sūktena |
| 72c: Kanyā variti sūktena | ii.181c: Kanyā vāriti sūktaṁ tu |
| 73: Yad adya kaccety udite japte vaśyaṁ jagad bhavet yad vāg iti ca japtena vāṇī bhavati saṁskṛtā | ii.182c: Yad adya kaccety udite<br>ii.183b: Vaśyaṁ vā kurute jagat<br>ii.183c: Yad vāg iti dvṛcenaiva<br>ii.184a: Tasya nāsaṁskṛtā vāṇi |
| 74: Vacovidam iti tvetāṁ japan vācaṁ samaśnute pavitrāṇāṁ pavitraṁ tu pāvamānyo hyṛco matāḥ | ii.187cd: Vacovidam iti tvetāṁ japan vācaṁ samaśnute<br>iii.1cd: Pavitrāṇāṁ pavitraṁ tu pāvamānīr ṛco japet |
| 75a: Vaikhānasā ṛcas triṁśat | iii.10d: Triṁśad vaikhānasīr ṛcaḥ |
| 75cd: Ṛco dviṣaṣṭiḥ proktāś ca parasyety ṛṣisattama | iii.11cd-12ab: Ṛcāṁ dviṣaṣṭiḥ prokteyaṁ pavasvety ṛṣisattamaiḥ |
| 76: Sarvakalmaṣanāśāya pāvanāya śivāya ca svādiṣṭhayeti sūktānāṁ saptaṣaṣṭir udāhṛtā | Sarvakalmaṣanāśāya pāvanāya śivāya ca<br>iii.12cd-13ab: Svādiṣṭhayeti sūktānāṁ saptaṣaṣṭir ihoditā |

| *Agni Pu* 259 | *Ṛvidh* |
|---|---|
| 77: Daśottarāṇyṛcaś caitāḥ pāvamānyaḥ śatāni ṣat / etaj japaṁś ca juhyac ca ghoraṁ mṛtyubhayaṁ jayet | daśottarāṇya ṛcāṁ caiva pāvamānīḥ śatāni ṣaṭ / iii.13cd: Etaj juhvañ japaṁś caiva ghoraṁ mṛtyubhayaṁ jayet |
| 78cd: Pra devatreti niyato japec ca marudhanvasu | iii.49ab: Pra devatreti niyato japeta marudhanvasu |
| 79: Prāṇāntike bhaye prāpte kṣipram āyus tu vindati prāvepām ity ṛcaṁ ekām japec ca manasā niśi | iii.49cd: Prāṇāntike bhaye prāpte kṣipram ambhaḥ sa vindati<br>iii.51cd: Prā vepā mā ṛcaṁ tvetāṁ manasaiva japen niśi |
| 80a: Vyuṣṭāyām udite sūrye | iii.52a: Vyuṣṭāyām udite sūrye |
| 80c: Mā pragāmeti mūḍhaś ca | iii.57ab: Mā pragāmeti...sa muḍho... |
| 81: Kṣiṇāyuriti manyeta yaṁ kaṁcit suhṛdaṁ priyam yat te yamam iti snātas tasya mūrdhānam ālabhet // | iii.58: Kṣīṇāyur iti manyeta yaṁ kañcit suhṛdaṁ priyam yat te yamam iti snātas tasya mūrdhānam ālabhet |
| 82a: Sahasrakṛtvaḥ pañchāham | iii.59a: Sahasrakṛtvaḥ pañcāhaṁ |
| 82c: Idam ittheti juhuyāt | iii.62a: Idam ittheti mantro'yaṁ |
| 83: Paśukāmo gavāṁ goṣṭhe arthakāmaś catuṣpathe / vayaḥ suparṇā ity etāṁ japan vai vindate śriyam // | iii.67a: Paśukāmo japed goṣṭhe<br>iii.66a: Catuṣpathe cānnakāma<br>iii.72cd: Vayaḥ suparṇā ity etāṁ japan vai vindate śriyam |
| 84ab: Haviṣyantiyam abhyasya sarvapāpaiḥ pramucyate / | iii.132cd: Haviṣpāntīyam abhyasya sarvapāpaiḥ pramucyate |
| 85a: yā oṣadhayaḥ svastyayanaṁ | iii.231a: Yā oṣadhīḥ svastyayanaṁ |
| 85cd: Bṛhaspate atīty etadvṛṣṭikāmaḥ prayojayet // | iv.5ab: Bṛhaspate pratīty etadvṛṣṭikāmaḥ prayojayet |
| 86: Sarvatreti parā śāntirjñeyāpratirathas tathā / | iv.6ab: Sarvatra tu parā śāntirjñeyo' pratirathas tvṛṣiḥ |

| *Agni Pu* 259 | *Ṛvidh* |
|---|---|
| sūktaṁ saṁkāśyapaṁ nityaṁ prajākāmasya kīrtitam// | iv.10ab: Bhūtāṁśaṁ kāśyapaṁ sūktaṁ prajākāmaḥ śucir japan |
| 87ab: Ahaṁ rudrebhir ity etadvāggmī bhavati mānavaḥ | iv.19ab: Ahaṁ rudrebhir itytadvāgmī bhavati pūjitaḥ / |
| 87d: Japan rātrīti rātriṣu | iv.21d: Japed rātrīti rātriṣu |
| 88c: Kalpayantīti ca Japan | iv.30a: Yāṁ kalpayantīti sadā |
| 89: Ayuṣyaṁ caiva varcasyaṁ sūktaṁ dākṣāyaṇaṁ mahat | iv.43ab: Āyuṣyam āyur varcasyaṁ sūktaṁ dākṣāyaṇaṁ mahat |
| uta devā iti japedāmayaghnaṁ dhṛtavrataḥ | iv.45cd: Uta devā iti japedāmayāvī yatavrataḥ |
| 90abc: Ayam agne jarīty etajjaped agnibhaye sati | iv.54ab: Ayam agne jariteti japed agnibhaye sati |
| araṇyānīty araṇyeṣu | iv.69c: Araṇyānīty araṇyeṣu |
| 91a: Brāhmīm āsādya sūkte dve | iv.71c: Brāhmīm āsādhya sūkte dve |
| 92abc: Śāsa itthā sapatnaghnaṁ saṅgrāmaṁ vijigīṣataḥ | iv.75cd: Śāsa itthā sapatnaghnaṁ saṁgrāmaṁ vijigīṣataḥ |
| brahmaṇāgniḥ saṁvīdānam | iv.86c: Brahmaṇāgniḥ saṁvīdāna |
| 93: Apehīti japet sūktaṁ śucir duḥsvapnanāśanam | iv.101cd: Apehīti japet sūktaṁ śucir duḥsvapnanāśanam |
| yenedam iti vai japtvā | iv.103c: Yenedam iti vai nityaṁ |
| samādhiṁ vindate param // | iv.104ab: Samādhiṁ...vindate... |
| 94: Mayobhūr vāta ityetad gavāṁ svastyayanaṁ param | iv.104cd: Mayo bhūr vāta iti tu gavāṁ svastyayane japet |
| śāṁbarīm indrajālaṁ vā māyām etena vārayet | iv.116ab: Śāṁbarīm indrajālāṁ vā māyām etena bādhate |
| 95abc: Mahi trīṇām avo'stiriti pathi svastyayanaṁ japet | iv.118cd: Mahi trīṇām avo'stviti pathi svastyayane japet |
| prāgnaye vidviṣan dveṣyam | iv.119a: Prāgnaye'tha dviṣaddveṣyaṁ |

The fact revealed by the versions in the *Viṣṇudharmottara* and *Agni Purāṇas* is that the authors of these works have freely drawn on the *Ṛvidh* for we find in these texts many stanzas of the *Ṛvidh* unaltered, besides others which are only slightly altered, but the variants are somewhat less and the better one is sometimes found in the *Viṣṇu Dh Pu* version and sometimes in the *Agni Pu.* The chief value of these versions lies exactly in the fact that they precede the known date of the manuscripts by several centuries and are of considerable importance for critical purposes.

Now coming to the relationship of the *Ṛgvidhāna* to the other allied works of Śaunaka, I have to state that it has fourteen full stanzas and about twelve hemistiches in common with the *Śaunakīyam.* This number would, no doubt, be considerably swelled by a comparison of the remaining passages in which the diction is slightly modified. With the *Bṛhaddevatā* it shares two and a half stanzas. I have collected all this common or borrowed matter in Appendix B.

### 6. *Emendations*

The text, as it has been constituted by me, contains about eighteen emendations and this comes to about one emendation for every forty stanzas of the text. Almost all the emendations are concerned with one letter or two of a few isolated words; but, by no means, with whole passages. Whenever I had an occasion to add or alter even a single letter without the authority of any of the manuscripts of the *Ṛvidh* I have inserted an asterisk above the emended syllable of the text and I have given my full reasons for it in the notes. I have given preference to exegesis over emendation and I have suggested a couple of emendations in the notes leaving the concerned text, of course, unemended. In this connection I can only recall the valuable and wholesome advice of Dr. R.G. Bhandarkar who observes:[19] 'Even in the case of corrupt texts conjectural restoration ought to be resorted to only in cases in which the conjecture is happy and carries conviction with it. European scholars, I am sorry to say, indulge too frequently in it, especially in Vedic Literature, when often they are

19. See his edition of the *Mālati-Mādhava* (Bombay 1905), Preface, pp. vi-vii.

not in circumstances to make a happy conjecture. It is not to be denied that some of the conjectures are striking and hit at the truth; but there are others which are simply gratuitous and provoking.'

Following is the list of emendations carried out in my text of *Ṛvidh*: (1-2) abhyupayant*, i.21, iii.80; (3)—srucā*, i.77 (4) dhyāta* mātraḥ, i.82; (5) pra mandine*ti, i.123; (6) tuṣṭvā* ca*, i.130; (7) apabhagnān*tam, ii.15; (8) ṛtāvṛdha*u, ii.22; (9) niṣpe*kṣ*yanniva, ii.89; (10) ajāvikam*, ii.146; (11) dīptā*, iii.92; (12) pratikṛtiḥ*, iii.92; (13) tanvaḥ* iii.125; (14) vipravrā*jinīm, iii.126; (15) rātris*amahitaḥ iv.24; (16) pratimuñc*eta, iv.37; (17) aṅgirasa* ṛṣ*eḥ, iv.40; and (18) abhisiñceta, iv.106. Half of my emendations (items 7-8, 10-12, 14, 16-18) were taken over from Dr. Meyer's text. Of the remaining half, three emendations: two (items 4 and 13) proposed by Prof. Gonda and one (item 9) conjectured by Prof. Macdonell were taken over from their respective works[20] and the rest was conjectured by me alone. In framing emendations of my own as well as in estimating the value of those of others I have been guided by the considerations not only of palaeography but also of the special features of the style and the context.

### 7. *Ṛgvidhāna and its sources*

The main source from which the *Ṛvidh* drew its Mantra-material is, of course, the *Ṛgveda-Saṁhitā.* It presupposes the vulgate text of the *RV* because of the overwhelming majority of hymns of this Saṁhitā are quoted in Pratīkas. Besides hymns from the *RV*, there are 26 hymns or parts of hymns which are found in the Khila collection of the *RV.* A full analysis of the Mantras occurring in the *Ṛvidh* has been given above.[21]

In the Chapter IV, I had an occasion to discuss about the earlier and later strata in the *Ṛvidh* and in that connection I had pointed out the Smṛti-material which the *Ṛvidh* contains was possibly interpolated during the early centuries of the Christian era. Eighteen stanzas of the *Ṛvidh* can be traced to the *Manusmṛti* which is evidently the source. They are: (1) *Ṛvidh* i.9 (=*Manu* 11.34); (2) *Ṛvidh* i.33 (=*Manu* 11.211); (3) *Ṛvidh* i.34 (=*Manu* 11.213),

20. Gonda, *Ṛvidh* trans. pp. 21 and 85. Macdonell, *Sarv* p. 182.
21. pp. 27-89 *supra.*

(4) *Ṛvidh* i.35 (=*Manu* 11.212); (5) *Ṛvidh* i.37 (=*Manu* 11.214); (6) *Ṛvidh* i.39 (=*Manu* 11.215); (7) *Ṛvidh* i.40 (=*Manu* 11.216); (8) *Ṛvidh* i.41 (=*Manu* 11.217); (9) *Ṛvidh* i.42 (=*Manu* 11.219); (10) *Ṛvidh* i.43 (=*Manu* 11.218); (11) *Ṛvidh* i.44 (=*Manu* 11.220); (12) *Ṛvidh* i.45 (nearly=*Manu* 11.221); (13) *Ṛvidh* i.58 (=*Manu* 11.229); (14) *Ṛvidh* iii.14 (nearly=*Manu* 11.253); (15) *Ṛvidh* iii.42 (nearly=*Manu* 6.22cd-23ab); (16) *Ṛvidh* iii.44 (nearly=*Manu* 9.60); (17) *Ṛvidh* iii.143 (=*Manu* 3.263) and (18) *Ṛvidh* iv.121cd-122 (=*Manu* 11.260).

In the same Chapter, I have drawn attention to the fact that the *Puruṣasūktavidhāna* was written by one Viṣṇukumāra (*vide* p. 147ff) after going through a similar work composed by Nārada and that the entire section belongs to the later stratum. Fortunately, the *Smṛticandrikā*[22] preserves few quotations from Nārada's work. These quotations reveal that Viṣṇukumāra's indebtedness to Nārada's work goes beyond mere condensation of the matter contained in the latter's work. As a matter of fact, Viṣṇukumāra appears to borrow passages after passages unaltered from Nārada's work. In order to show this evidence of borrowing, I propose to give the corresponding passages of both the works in parallel columns.

| *SC* | *Ṛvidh* |
|---|---|
| tac cārcanaṁ Nāradenoktam— | |
| Imam arthaṁ purā pṛṣṭo | |
| Nārado bhagavān ṛṣiḥ / | |
| naranārāyaṇābhyāṁ ca | |
| tair munīndraiś ca saṅgataiḥ // | |
| Śṛṇvantu munayas samyak | |
| puruṣottamapūjanam / | |
| yat kṛtvā munayas sarve | yat kṛtvā munayaḥ sarve |
| brahmanirvāṇam āpnuyuḥ //... | brahmanirvāṇam āpnuyuḥ // |
| Kuryād ārādhanaṁ viṣṇor- | |
| devadevasya cakriṇaḥ | devadevasya cakriṇaḥ // |
| apsv agnau hṛdaye sūrye | Apsv agnau hṛdaye sūrye |
| sthaṇḍile pratimāsu ca // | Sthaṇḍile pratimāsu ca / |
| Ṣaṭsveteṣu hares samyag | ṣaṭsveteṣu hareḥ samyag- |
| arcanaṁ munibhis smṛtam / | arcanaṁ munibhiḥ smṛtam // |

22. *SC* (Bibliotheca Sanskrita No. 44) ii.Āhnikakāṇḍa, pp. 532-534.

| | |
|---|---|
| agnau kriyāvatāṁ devo<br>divi devo manīṣiṇām //<br>Pratimāsv alpabuddhīnāṁ<br>yogināṁ hṛdaye hariḥ / | Agnau kriyāvatāṁ devo<br>divi devo manīṣiṇām /<br>pratimāsv alpabuddhīnāṁ<br>yogināṁ hṛdaye hariḥ // |
| āpo hyāyatanaṁ tasya<br>tasmāt tāsu sadā hariḥ /<br>tasya sarvagatatvāc ca<br>sthaṇḍile bhāvitātmanām // | Āpo hyāyatanaṁ tasya<br>tasmāt tāsu sadā hariḥ /<br>tasya sarvagatatvāc ca<br>sthaṇḍile bhāvitātmanām // |
| Ṛgvede pauruṣaṁ sūktam<br>arcitaṁ guhyam uttamam / | |
| ānuṣṭubhasya sūktasya<br>triṣṭubantasya devatā<br>Puruṣo yo jagad bījam<br>ṛṣir nārāyaṇas smṛtaḥ / | Ānuṣṭubhasya sūktasya<br>triṣṭubantasya devatā /<br>puruṣo yo jagad bijam-<br>ṛṣir nārāyaṇaḥ smṛtaḥ // |
| prathamāṁ vinyased vāme<br>dvitīyāṁ dakṣiṇe kare //<br>Tṛtīyāṁ vāmapāde tu<br>caturthīṁ dakṣiṇe tathā / | Prathamāṁ vinyased vāme<br>dvitīyāṁ dakṣiṇe kare /<br>tṛtīyāṁ vāmapāde tu<br>caturthīṁ dakṣiṇe nyaset // |
| pañcamīṁ vāmajaṅghāyāṁ<br>dakṣiṇasyāṁ tathottarām //<br>Saptamīṁ vāmakaṭyāṁ tu<br>dakṣinasyāṁ tathāṣṭamīm / | Pañcamīṁ vāmajānuni<br>saṣṭhīṁ vai dakṣiṇe nyaset /<br>Saptamīṁ vāmakaṭyāṁ tu<br>aṣṭamīṁ dakṣiṇe kaṭau // |
| navamīṁ nābhimadhye tu<br>daśamīṁ hṛdi vinyaset //<br>Ekādaśīṁ kaṇṭhadeśe<br>dvādaśīṁ vāmabāhuke / | Navamīṁ nābhimadhye tu<br>daśamīṁ hṛdaye nyaset /<br>ekādaśīṁ kaṇṭhadeśe<br>dvādaśīṁ vāmabāhuke // |
| trayodaśīṁ dakṣiṇe tu<br>āsyadeśe caturdaśīm //<br>Akṣṇoḥ pañcadaśīṁ nyasya<br>ṣoḍaśīṁ murdhni vinyaset / | Trayodaśīṁ dakṣiṇe ca<br>āsye caiva caturdaśīm /<br>akṣṇoḥ pañcadaśīṁ caiva<br>ṣoḍaśīṁ mūrdhni vinyaset // |
| yathātmati[23] tathā deve<br>nyāsakarma samācaret //... | yathā dehe tathā deve<br>nyāsaṁ kṛtvā vidhānataḥ // |
| Ādyayāvāhayed devamṛcā | Ādyayāvāhayed devamṛcā |

23. Possibly a printing error for the correct reading: yathātmani.

| *SC* | *Ṛvidh* |
|---|---|
| tu puruṣottamam // | tu puruṣottamam / |
| Dvitīyayāsanaṁ dadyāt<br>pādyaṁ caiva tṛtīyayā / | dvitīyayāsanaṁ dadyāt<br>pādyaṁ caiva tṛtīyayā // |
| caturthyārghyaṁ pradātavyaṁ<br>pañcamyācamanīyakam //<br>Ṣaṭhyā snānaṁ prakurvīta<br>saptamyā vastram eva ca / | Arghyaṁ caturthyā dātayaṁ<br>pañcamyācamanīyakam /<br>ṣaṣṭhyā snānaṁ prakurvīta<br>saptamyā vastram eva ca // |
| Yajñopavītam aṣṭamyā<br>navamyā gandham eva ca //<br>daśamyā puṣpadānaṁ syād<br>ekādaśyā tu dhūpakam / | Yajñopavītam aṣṭamyā<br>navamyā cānulepanam /<br>puṣpaṁ daśamyā dātavyam-<br>ekādaśyā tu dhūpakam // |
| dvādaśyā ca tathā dīpaṁ<br>trayodaśyā caruṁ tathā<br>Caturdaśyā namaskāraṁ<br>pañcadaśyā pradakṣiṇam /... | Dvādaśyā dīpakaṁ dadyāt<br>trayodaśyā nivedanam /<br>caturdaśyā namaskāraṁ<br>pañcadaśyā pradakṣiṇam // |
| Snāne vastropavīte ca<br>carāvācamanīyakam /...<br>Tataḥ pradakṣiṇaṁ kṛtvā<br>nārāyaṇam anāmayam //... | Snāne vastre ca naivedye<br>dadyād ācamanīyakam /<br>Tataḥ pradakṣiṇāṁ kṛtvā<br>nārāyaṇam anāmayam / |

Dheyassadā savitṛmaṇḍalamadhyavartī
nārāyaṇassarasijāsanasanniviṣṭaḥ /
keyūravān makarakuṇḍalavān kirīṭī = iii.224
hārī hiraṇmayavapurdhṛtaśaṅkhacakraḥ //

The very first stanza quoted from *SC* tells us that the worship of Viṣṇu with the Puruṣasūkta was originally communicated by Nārada to Nara and Nārāyaṇa. This fact is very important, for without it we cannot explain the queer vocative case in the *Ṛvidh* iii.155. As the entire section on the *Puruṣasūktavidhāna* is concoctive in nature, it is not unlikely that this stanza (*Ṛvidh* iii.155) like the rest, was borrowed from Nārada's work.

Now turning our attention to the eulogium on Viṣṇu (*Ṛvidh* iii.174-185), we find that it agrees closely with the first part of the *jitaṁ te stotra* in the *Pañcarātrasaṁhitā*,[24] and further the first

24. Quoted in the *Bṛhatstotraratnākara*, Part I, NSP, 1952, pp. 56-63.

stanza is found in the *Mbh* 12.336. 42cd-43ab. The question naturally arises as to who borrowed from whom. This question cannot be settled with certainty at present for only few texts of the Viṣṇuite Pāñcarātra sect have been published. According to Prof. Winternitz,[25] the earliest *Pāñcarātrasaṁhitās* date from the 5th-9th century A.D. In this connection it is worth-while to remember that the eulogium on Viṣṇu forms a part of the *Puruṣa-sūktavidhāna* which as we have seen above belongs to the later stratum of the *Ṛvidh* and is concoctive.

| *Pañcarātrasaṁhitā* | *Ṛvidh* |
|---|---|
| Jitaṁ te puṁḍarīkākṣa<br>namaste viśvabhāvana /<br>namaste' stu hṛṣīkeśa<br>mahāpuruṣapūrvaja //1// | Jitaṁ te puṇḍarīkākṣa<br>namas te viśvabhāvana /<br>namaste' stu hṛṣīkeśa<br>mahāpuruṣa pūrvaja // |
| Devānāṁ dānavānāṁ ca<br>sāmānyam adhidaivatam /<br>sarvadā caraṇadvaṁdvaṁ<br>vrajāmi śaraṇaṁ tava //2// | Devānāṁ dānavānāṁ ca<br>sāmānyam adhidaivatam /<br>sarvadā caraṇadvandvaṁ<br>vrajāmi śaraṇaṁ tava // |
| Ekas tvaṁ asi lokasya<br>sraṣṭā saṁhārakas tathā /<br>adhyakṣaś cānumantā ca<br>guṇamāyāsamāvṛtaḥ //3// | Ekas tvam asi lokasya<br>sraṣṭā saṁhārakas tathā /<br>avyaktaś cānumantā ca<br>guṇamāyāsamāvṛtaḥ // |
| Saṁsārasāgaraṁ ghoram<br>anantakleśabhājanam /<br>tvām eva śaraṇaṁ prāpya<br>nistaranti manīṣiṇaḥ //4// | Saṁsārasāgaram ghoram-<br>anantaṁ kleśabhājanam /<br>tvām eva śaraṇaṁ prāpya<br>nistaranti manīṣiṇaḥ // |
| Na te rūpaṁ na cākāro<br>nāyudhāni na cāspadam /<br>tathāpi puruṣākāro<br>bhaktānāṁ tvaṁ prakāśase //5// | Na te rūpam na cākāro<br>nāyudhāni na cāspadam /<br>tathāpi puruṣākāro<br>bhaktānāṁ tvaṁ prakāśase // |
| Naiva kiñcit parokṣaṁ te<br>pratyakṣo' si na kasyacit /<br>naiva kiñcid asiddhaṁ te<br>na ca siddho' si kasyacit //6// | Naiva kiñcit parokṣaṁ te<br>pratyakṣo' si na kasyacit /<br>naiva kiñcid asādhyaṁ te<br>na ca sādhyo' si kasyacit // |

25. *Op.cit.*, p. 590.

| | |
|---|---|
| Kāryāṇāṁ kārāṇaṁ pūrvaṁ<br>vacasāṁ vācyam uttamam /<br>yogānāṁ paramāṁ siddhiṁ<br>paramaṁ te padaṁ viduḥ //7// | Kāryāṇāṁ kāraṇaṁ pūrvaṁ<br>vacasāṁ vācyam uttamam /<br>yogināṁ paramāsiddhiḥ<br>paramaṁ te padaṁ viduḥ // |
| Ahaṁ bhīto' smi deveśa<br>saṁsāre' smin bhayāvahe /<br>pāhi māṁ puṁḍarīkākṣa<br>na jāne śaraṇaṁ param //8// | Ahaṁ bhīto' smi deveśa<br>saṁsāre' smin mahābhaye /<br>trāhi māṁ puṇḍarīkākṣa<br>na jāne paramaṁ padam // |
| Kāleṣv api ca sarveṣu<br>dikṣu sarvāsu cācyuta /<br>śarīre ca gatau cāpi<br>vartate me mahad bhayam //9// | Kāleṣv api ca sarveṣu<br>dikṣu sarvāsu cācyuta /<br>śarīre ca gataś cāsi<br>vartate me mahadbhayam // |
| Tvatpādakamalād anyan<br>na me janmāntareṣv api /<br>nimittaṁ kuśalasyāsti<br>yena gacchāmi sadgatim //10// | Tvatpādakamalād anyan<br>na me janmāntareṣv api /<br>[Cp. Bo 1.2: nimittaṁ kuśala-<br>syāsti yena gacchāmi sadgatim//] |
| vijñānaṁ yad idaṁ prāptaṁ<br>yad idaṁ sthānam arjitam /<br>janmāntare'pi me deva<br>mā bhūt tasya parikṣayaḥ //11// | vijñānaṁ yad idaṁ prāpya<br>yad idaṁ sthānam arjitam //<br>Janmāntare'pi me deva<br>mā bhud asya parikṣayaḥ / |
| Durgatāv api jātāyāṁ<br>tvadgato me manorathaḥ /<br>yadi nāśaṁ na vindeta<br>tāvatāsmi kṛtī sadā //12// | durgatāv api jātasya<br>tvadgato me manorathaḥ //<br>Yadi nāśaṁ na vindeta<br>tāvatāsmi kṛtī sadā |
| Na kāmakaluṣaṁ cittaṁ<br>mama te pādyoḥ sthitam /<br>kāmaye vaiṣṇavatvaṁ tu<br>sarvajanmasu kevalam //13// | [Cp. Bo 1: Akāmakaluṣaṁ cit-<br>taṁ mama te pādayoḥ sthitam/]<br>kāmaye viṣṇupādau tu<br>sarvajanmasu kevalam // |

The question which of the two passages is the original one, need not detain us long. Considering the style of the contents of the *Puruṣasūktavidhāna*, I am inclined to believe that Viṣṇū-kumāra did not compose most of them but extracted them either from the work of Nārada or from the *Pañcarātrasaṁhitā*.

Such are the materials and other accessory literature which I have utilised for the establishment of a correct and a critical text of the *Ṛgvidhāna*.

CHAPTER VI

# RÉSUMÉ

In the preceding pages, I have discussed about the nature of the Vidhāna texts and the essential features of the teaching of the *Ṛgvidhāna.* Incidently I have referred to the circumstances under which these works originated and the influence they exercised on the religious life of the people. The analysis of the contents and of the subject matter has yielded a fairly good picture of the superstitions, taboos, religious and magical practices of that period of which we have, unfortunately, few records. The traditions vouched by Ṣaḍguruśiṣya declares that Śaunaka wrote the ten works in order to preserve the *Ṛgveda* (Ṛgvedaguptaye) and this fact is proved by the works themselves. The *Ṛvidh* was written by him with the express purpose of proving the efficacy of the Ṛgvedic Mantras in the accomplishment of various objects of desire with least effort. The other works of Śaunaka concern, more or less, with the traditional text of the *RV.* We have seen as to how the hymns or verses rubricated in the *Ṛvidh* are those which are familiar enough to any performer of the Śrauta or Gṛhya rites and further the majority of the Ṛgvedic Mantras in the *Ṛvidh* are either misunderstood or half-understood or not understood at all. As is well known, the *Ṛvidh* does not add anything new to our knowledge of the Vedic Mythology since its purpose is not to give us mere description of deities regarding their appearance or habits but to impress upon our mind the importance of their relation to the human beings and the good which a human being can derive from them. The author of the *Bhagavadgītā* has also emphasised the same idea in the eleventh stanza of the Third Adhyāya: *Devān bhāvayatā'nena te devā bhāvayantu vaḥ / paras-paraṁ bhāvayantaḥ śreyaḥ param avāpsyatha //*

My study on the *Ṛgvidhāna* discloses the following important facts:

(1) that it records the tradition prevalent among the Ṛgvedins about the employment of the Ṛgvedic Mantras—without much

care for their sense—for the attainment of worldly or spiritual gains just by means of muttering them. This tradition may be the cause of the distinction between the Vaidikas and the Paṇḍitas;

(2) that the Vidhāna literature arose out of a real need to simplify the Śrauta and Gṛhya rites with the help of magic;

(3) that it is, in fact, a continuation of the earlier literature on ritual and in this latter aspect it is intimately connected with the Kalpa and with the Anukramaṇīs as far as the sequence of the hymns from the Vedic Saṁhitās to which they belong is concerned;

(4) that the Mantras occurring in the *Ṛvidh* can be traced either to the vulgate text of the *Ṛgveda-saṁhitā* or to the Khila collection thereof;

(5) that the linguistic features, metre, etc. conclusively prove that the *Ṛvidh* is a fairly old work which can be assigned a date between 500-400 B.C.; and

(6) that the *Ṛvidh* is a genuine composition of Śaunaka, the author of the *Bṛhaddevatā* and other works.

## Appendix A

## CONSPECTUS OF THE ŚLOKAS IN THE VARGAS OF THE *ṚGVIDHĀNA*

*Adhyāya I*

| *Varga* | *Ba* | *Be* | *Bo*1 | *Bo*2 | *Ta* | *Cm* | *Critical Ed* |
|---|---|---|---|---|---|---|---|
| 1st | 6 | 6 | 6 | 6 | 6 | 6 | 6 |
| 2nd | 5 | 5 | 5 | 5 | 5 | 5 | 5 |
| 3rd | 5 | 5 | 5 | 5 | 5 | 5 | 5 |
| 4th | 5 | 5 | 5 | 5 | 5 | 5 | 5 |
| 5th | 5 | 5 | 5 | 5 | 5 | 5 | 5 |
| 6th | 5 | 5 | 5 | 5 | 5 | 5 | 5 |
| 7th | 5 | 5 | 6 | 6 | 5 | 5 | 5 |
| 8th | 5 | 5 | 5 | 5 | 5 | 5 | 5 |
| 9th | 5 | 5 | 5 | 5 | 5 | 5 | 5 |
| 10th | 5 | 5 | 5 | 5 | 5 | 5 | 5 |
| 11th | 5 | 5 | 5 | 5 | 5 | 5 | 5 |
| 12th | 5 | 5 | 5 | 5 | 5 | 5 | 5 |
| 13th | 5 | 5 | 5 | 5 | 5 | 5 | 5 |
| 14th | 5 | 5 | 5 | 5 | 5 | 5 | 5 |
| 15th | 7 | 7 | 7 | 7 | 7 | 7 | 7 |
| 16th | 5 | 5 | 5 | 5 | 5 | 5 | 5 |
| 17th | 8 | 10 | 10 | 10 | 10 | 9 | 8 |
| 18th | 7 | 7 | 7 | 7 | 7 | 7 | 7 |
| 19th | 5 | 5 | 5 | 5 | 5 | 5 | 5 |
| 20th | 5 | 5 | 5 | 5 | 5 | 5 | 5 |
| 21st | 5 | 5 | 5 | 5 | 5 | 5 | 5 |
| 22nd | 7 | 7 | 7 | 7 | 7 | 7 | 7 |
| 23rd | 7 | 7 | 7 | 7 | 7 | 7 | 7 |
| 24th | 5 | 5 | 5 | 5 | 5 | 5 | 5 |
| 25th | 7 | 7 | 7 | 7 | 7 | 7 | 7 |
| 26th | 6 | 6 | 6 | 6 | 6 | 6 | 6 |
| 27th | 5 | 5 | 5 | 5 | 5 | 5 | 5 |

| Varga | Ba | Be | Bo1 | Bo2 | Ta | Cm | Critical Ed |
|---|---|---|---|---|---|---|---|
| 28th | 5 | 5 | 5 | 5 | 5 | 5 | 5 |
| 29th | 5 | 5 | 5 | 5 | 5 | 5 | 5 |
| 30th | 5 | 5 | 5 | 5 | 5 | 5 | 5 |
| 31st | 5 | 5 | 5 | 5 | 5 | 5 | 5 |
| | 170 | 172 | 173 | 173 | 172 | 171 | 170 |
| | | | *Adhyāya II* | | | | |
| 1st | 5 | 5 | 5 | 5 | 5 | 5 | 5 |
| 2nd | 6 | 6 | 6 | 6 | 6 | 6 | 6 |
| 3rd | 5 | 5 | 5 | 5 | 5 | 5 | 5 |
| 4th | 5 | 5 | 5 | 5 | 5 | 5 | 5 |
| 5th | 3 | 3 | 3 | 3 | 3 | 3 | 3 |
| 6th | 5 | 5 | 5 | 5 | 5 | 5 | 5 |
| 7th | 5 | 5 | 5 | 5 | 5 | 5 | 5 |
| 8th | 5 | 5 | 5 | 5 | 5 | 5 | 5 |
| 9th | 5 | 5 | 5 | 5 | 5 | 5 | 5 |
| 10th | 6 | 6 | 6 | 6 | 6 | 6 | 6 |
| 11th | 5 | 5 | 5 | 5 | 5 | 5 | 5 |
| 12th | 7 | 7 | 7 | 7 | 7 | 7 | 7 |
| 13th | 7 | 7 | 7 | 7 | 7 | 7 | 7 |
| 14th | 5 | 5 | 5 | 5 | 5 | 5 | 5 |
| 15th | 7 | 7 | 7 | 7 | 7 | 7 | 7 |
| 16th | 5 | 5 | 5 | 5 | 5 | 5 | 5 |
| 17th | 6 | 6 | 6 | 6 | 6 | 6 | 6 |
| 18th | 5 | 5 | 5 | 5 | 5 | 5 | 5 |
| 19th | 5 | 5 | 5 | 5 | 5 | 5 | 5 |
| 20th | 5 | 5 | 5 | 5 | 5 | 5 | 5 |
| 21st | 6 | 6 | 6 | 6 | 6 | 6 | 6 |
| 22nd | 6 | 6 | 6 | 6 | 6 | 6 | 6 |
| 23rd | 5 | 5 | 5 | 5 | 5 | 5 | 5 |
| 24th | 5 | 5 | 4 | 4 | 5 | 5 | 5 |
| 25th | 5 | 11 | 5 | 5 | 5 | 5 | 5 |
| 26th | 5 | 5 | 5 | 5 | 5 | 5 | 5 |

| Varga | Ba | Be | Bo1 | Bo2 | Ta | Cm | Critical Ed. |
|---|---|---|---|---|---|---|---|
| 27th | 5 | 5 | 5 | 5 | 5 | 5 | 5 |
| 28th | 5 | 5 | 5 | 5 | 5 | 5 | 5 |
| 29th | 5 | 5 | 4 | 5 | 5 | 5 | 5 |
| 30th | 5 | 5 | 5 | 5 | 5 | 5 | 5 |
| 31st | 7 | 7 | 7 | 7 | 7 | 7 | 7 |
| 32nd | 5 | 5 | 5 | 5 | 5 | 5 | 5 |
| 33rd | 5 | 5 | 5 | 5 | 5 | 5 | 5 |
| 34th | 5 | 5 | 5 | 5 | 5 | 5 | 5 |
| 35th | 7 | 7 | 7 | 7 | 7 | 7 | 7 |
| | 188 | 194 | 186 | 187 | 188 | 188 | 188 |

*Adhyāya III*

| Varga | Ba | Be | Bo1 | Bo2 | Ta | Cm | Critical Ed. |
|---|---|---|---|---|---|---|---|
| 1st | 5 | 5 | 5 | 5 | 5 | 5 | 5 |
| 2nd | 6 | 6 | 6 | 6 | 6 | 6 | 6 |
| 3rd | 6 | 6 | 6 | 6 | 6 | 6 | 6 |
| 4th | 7 | 7 | 6 | 6 | 6 | 6 | 6 |
| 5th | 5 | 5 | 5 | 5 | 5 | 5 | 5 |
| 6th | 5 | 5 | 5 | 5 | 5 | 5 | 5 |
| 7th | 6 | 6 | 6 | 6 | 6 | 6 | 6 |
| 8th | 6 | 6 | 6 | 6 | 6 | 6 | 6 |
| 9th | 5 | 5 | 5 | 5 | 5 | 5 | 5 |
| 10th | 5 | 5 | 5 | 5 | 5 | 5 | 5 |
| 11th | 5 | 5 | 5 | 5 | 5 | 5 | 5 |
| 12th | 5 | 5 | 5 | 5 | 5 | 5 | 5 |
| 13th | 5 | 5 | 5 | 5 | 5 | 5 | 5 |
| 14th | 7 | 7 | 7 | 7 | 7 | 7 | 7 |
| 15th | 5 | 5 | 5 | 5 | 5 | 5 | 5 |
| 16th | 5 | 5 | 5 | 5 | 5 | 5 | 5 |
| 17th | 5 | 5 | 5 | 5 | 5 | 5 | 5 |
| 18th | 5 | 5 | 5 | 5 | 5 | 5 | 5 |
| 19th | 5 | 5 | 5 | 5 | 5 | 5 | 5 |
| 20th | 5 | 5 | 5 | 5 | 5 | 5 | 5 |
| 21st | 5 | 5 | 5 | 5 | 5 | 5 | 5 |
| 22nd | 5 | 5 | 5 | 5 | 5 | 5 | 5 |

| *Varga* | *Ba* | *Be* | *Bo*1 | *Bo*2 | *Ta* | *Cm* | *Critical Ed.* |
|---|---|---|---|---|---|---|---|
| 23rd | 5 | 5 | 5 | 5 | 5 | 5 | 5 |
| 24th | 5 | 5 | 5 | 5 | 5 | 5 | 5 |
| 25th | 6 | 6 | 6 | 6 | 6 | 6 | 6 |
| 26th | 5 | 5 | 5 | 5 | 5 | 5 | 5 |
| 27th | 5 | 5 | 5 | 5 | 5 | 5 | 5 |
| 28th | 5 | 5 | 5 | 5 | 5 | 5 | 5 |
| 29th | 6 | 6 | 6 | 6 | 6 | 6 | 6 |
| 30th | 6 | 6 | 6 | 6 | 6 | 6 | 6 |
| 31st | 10 | 10 | 6 | 6 | 6 | 6 | 6 |
| 32rd | 7 | 7 | 7 | 7 | 7 | 7 | 7 |
| 33rd | 6 | 6 | 7 | 7 | 6 | 6 | 6 |
| 34th | 6 | 6 | 7 | 6½ | 6 | 6 | 6 |
| 35th | 6 | 6 | 7 | 6 | 6 | 6 | 6 |
| 36th | 5 | 5 | 5 | 5 | 5 | 5 | 5 |
| 37th | 5 | 5 | 5 | 5 | 5 | 5 | 5 |
| 38th | 5 | 5 | 5 | 5 | 5 | 5 | 5 |
| 39th | 5 | 5 | 5 | 5 | 5 | 5 | 5 |
| 40th | 7 | 7 | 6 | 7 | 7 | 7 | 7 |
| 41st | 5 | 5 | 5 | 5 | 5 | 5 | 5 |
| 42nd | 3 | 3 | 3 | 3 | 3 | 3 | 3 |
| 43rd | 5 | 5 | 4 | 5 | 5 | 5 | 5 |
| | 236 | 236 | 232 | 232½ | 231 | 231 | 231 |

*Adhyāya IV*

| | | | | | | | |
|---|---|---|---|---|---|---|---|
| 1st | 5 | 5 | 5 | 5 | 5 | 5 | 5 |
| 2nd | 5 | 5 | 5 | 5 | 5 | 5 | 5 |
| 3rd | 5 | 5 | 5 | 5 | 5 | 5 | 5 |
| 4th | 7 | 7 | 7 | 7 | 7 | 7 | 7 |
| 5th | 5 | 5 | 5 | 5 | 5 | 5 | 5 |
| 6th | 5 | 5 | 5 | 5 | 5 | 5 | 5 |
| 7th | 5 | 5 | 5 | 5 | 5 | 5 | 5 |
| 8th | 5 | 5 | 5 | 5 | 5 | 5 | 5 |
| 9th | 6 | 7 | 6 | 6 | 6 | 6 | 6 |
| 10th | 5 | 5 | 5 | 5 | 4 | 5 | 5 |

| | *Ba* | *Be* | *Bo*1 | *Bo*2 | *Ta* | *Cm* | *Critical Ed.* |
|---|---|---|---|---|---|---|---|
| 11th | 7 | 7 | 7 | 7 | 7 | 7 | 7 |
| 12th | 5 | 5 | 5 | 5 | 5 | 5 | 5 |
| 13th | 5 | 5 | 5 | 5 | 5 | 5 | 5 |
| 14th | 5 | 5 | 5 | 5 | 5 | 5 | 5 |
| 15th | 5 | 5 | 5 | 5 | 5 | 5 | 5 |
| 16th | 5 | 5 | 5 | 5 | 5 | 5 | 5 |
| 17th | 5 | 5 | 5 | 5 | 5 | 5 | 5 |
| 18th | 5 | 5 | 5 | 5 | 5 | 5 | 5 |
| 19th | 5 | 5 | 5 | 5 | 5 | 5 | 5 |
| 20th | 5 | 5 | 5 | 5 | 5 | 5 | 5 |
| 21st | 5 | 5 | 5 | 5 | 5 | 5 | 5 |
| 22nd | 5 | 5 | 5 | 5 | 5 | 5 | 5 |
| 23rd | 5 | 5 | 5 | 5 | 5 | 5 | 5 |
| 24th | 5 | 6 | 6 | 6 | 5 | 6 | 5 |
| 25th | 6 | 6 | 6 | 6 | 6 | 6 | 6 |
| 26th | 5 | 5 | 5 | 5 | 5 | 5 | 5 |
| 27th | 6 | 6 | 6 | 6 | 6 | 6 | 6 |
| 28th | .. | .. | .. | .. | 5 | .. | .. |
| | 142 | 144 | 144 | 143 | 146 | 143 | 142 |

| | *Phalaśruti* (=Meyer's *Adhyāya V*) | | | | | | |
|---|---|---|---|---|---|---|---|
| 1st | 5 | 5 | 5 | 5 | .. | 5 | 5 |
| 2nd | 5 | 5 | 5 | 5 | .. | 5 | 5 |
| 3rd | 3 | 3 | 3 | 3 | .. | 3 | 3 |
| | 13 | 13 | 13 | 13 | .. | 13 | 13 |

## Appendix B

# RELATION OF *ṚGVIDHĀNA* TO OTHER TEXTS

## 1. *ŚAUNAKĪYAM*

| *Śaunakīyam I* | *Ṛvidh* |
|---|---|
| 1.138: Yathāśvamedhaḥ kraturāṭ sarvapāpāpanodanaḥ, tathāghamarṣaṇaṁ sūktaṁ sarvapāpāpanodanam | iv.121cd-122ab: Yathāśvamedhaḥ kraturāṭ sarvapāpapraṇodanaḥ, tathāghamarṣaṇaṁ sūktaṁ sarvapāpapraṇodanam |
| 2.4ab: Śaṁvatyā svastimatyā ca pāvamānyais tathaiva ca | i.16cd: Śaṁvatyaḥ svastimatyaś ca pāvamānyais tathaiva ca |
| 4.17c: Anaśnantsaṁhitāmetāṁ | =i.69a |
| 11.10: Ādyayāvāhayed devam ṛcā tu puruṣottamam, dvitīyayāsanaṁ dadyāt pādyaṁ caiva tṛtīyayā | =iii.162 |
| 11.11: Arghyaṁ caturthyā dātavyaṁ pañcamyācamanīyakam, ṣaṣṭhya snānaṁ prakurvīta saptamyā vastram eva ca | =iii. 163 |
| 11.12: Yajñopavītam aṣṭamyā navamyā gandham eva ca, puṣpaṁ daśamyā dātavyam ekādaśyā tu dhūpakam | iii.164: Yajñopavītam aṣṭamyā navamyā cānulepanam, puṣpaṁ daśamyā dātavyamekādaśyā tu dhūpakam |
| 11.13: Dvādaśyā dīpakaṁ dadyāt trayodaśyā naivedyakam, caturdaśyā namaskāraṁ pañcadaśyā pradakṣiṇam | iii.165: Dvādaśyā dīpakaṁ dadyāt trayodaśyā nivedanam, caturdaśyā namaskāraṁ pañcadaśyā pradakṣiṇam |

| *Śaunakīyam I* | *Ṛvidh* |
|---|---|
| 11.16b: Dīrgham āyur avāpnuyāt | =i.94d, ii.119d |
| 14.15cd: Devāḥ kapota ityetat kapotāveśane bhavet | iv.102ab: Devāḥ kapota iti tu kapotasyopaveśane |
| 18.8: Enam kṛtyā na hiṁsanti kruddhābhicaritāḥ paraiḥ pratyaṅgirasakalpena tadvido' bhicaret punaḥ | iv.30cd-31ab: Nainaṁ kṛtyā nihiṁsanti kruddhābhicaritāni ca yam aṅgirasakalpais tu tadvido' bhicaranti saḥ |
| 18.9: Pratyaṅgirasa kalpena sadyastāṁ pratibādhate, pratyaṅgirasavidvāṁstu na riṣyeddhi kathañcana | iv.31cd-32ab: Pratyaṅgirasa kalpena sarvāṁstān pratibādhate. Pratyaṅgirasavidvāṁstu na riṣyeta kadācana |
| 19.5d: upatiṣṭhed vibhāvasum | =ii.111c: |
| 20.1cd: Kṛṣṇapakṣe caturdaśyāṁ trirātropoṣitaḥ śuciḥ | =ii.16ab: |
| 20.2: Dakṣiṇāpravaṇe deśe śmaśāne dakṣiṇāmukhaḥ, raktoṣṇīṣyasipāṇiś ca raktamālānulepanaḥ | ii.16cd-17: Dakṣiṇapravaṇe deśe śmaśānasthaḥ samāhitaḥ // raktoṣṇīṣyasipāṇiś ca bailvakedhmo' nilāśanaḥ |
| 20.5cd: Saptāhaṁ juhuyāt tailaṁ sārṣapaṁ lavaṇānvitam | saptāhaṁ juhuyāt tailaṁ sārṣapaṁ lavaṇānvitam |
| 20.6b: Vasiṣṭhadveṣaṇīṁ paṭhan | ii.18b: Vasiṣṭhadveṣaṇīḥ paṭhan |

| *Śaunakīyam II* | *Ṛvidh* |
|---|---|
| 1.30ab: Ātvāhārṣam antaredhītyathainam anumantrayet | iv.114cd: Ātvāhārṣam antaredhītyathainam abhimantrayet |
| 2.6cd-7: Prācyāṁ tvā diśi vasavo abhiṣiñcantu puṣṭaye dakṣiṇasyāṁ diśi rudrā devā abhiṣiñcantu śreyase, pratīcyāṁ diśi ādityā abhiṣiñcantu tejase | iv.112-113: Prācyāṁ tvā diśi vasavo abhiṣiñcantu tejase, dakṣiṇasyāṁ tvā diśi rudrā abhiṣiñcantu vṛddhaye Pratīcyāṁ tvā diśyādityā abhiṣiñcantu puṣṭaye, |

| *Śaunakīyam II* | *Ṛvidh* |
|---|---|
| 2.8.ab: Uttarasyāṁ diśi Viśve devā abhiṣiñcantu vṛddhaye | Viśve devā udīcyāṁ tu abhiṣiñcantu śreyase |
| 4.7bcd: Tiṣyeṇa śravaṇena vā aindrasāvitrapauṣṇeṣu rohiṇyām uttareṣu vā | iv.106bcd: Tiṣyeṇa śravaneṇa vā pauṣṇasāvitrasaumyāśvī-rohiṇīṣūttarāsu ca |
| 15.4cd-5: Esābhisaṁhitā devaiḥ sarvabrahmamayī śubhā | i.73ab: Eṣā hi sammitā vedaiḥ sarvabrahmamayī nicṛt |
| Ugreṇa tapasā dṛṣṭā Viśvāmitreṇa dhīmatā, homāṁśca japayajñāṁśca nityaṁ kurvīta caitayā | = i.73cd-74ab |
| 15.6: Sarvakāmasamṛddhya-rthaṁ paraṁ brahmaitad ucyate, eṣaiva pratilomoktā jape śatruvināśinī | i.74cd-75ab: Sarvakāmasamṛd-dhyarthaṁ paraṁ brahmedam ucyate. Eṣaiva pratilomoktā pacchaḥ śatruvināśinī |
| 15.7: Akṣarapratilomeyam-abhicāreṣu śasyate, akṣarapratilomeyaṁ yasmin yujyeta karmaṇi | = i.75cd-76ab |
| 15.8: tad amoghaṁ vijānīyād-etaddhi brahmaṇo balam | = i.76cd |
| vyāghātakedhmasamidho yo'kṣara pratilomayā | i.77: Vyāghātakedhmasamidho akṣarapratilomayā |
| 15.9: juhuyāt sārṣapaṁ tailaṁ vibhītakakṛtasrucā, | juhuyāt sārṣpaṁ tailaṁ vaibhītakakṛtasrucā* |
| punaḥ saṁpīḍayec chatrūn varṇaśaś ca pramāpayet | i.87cd: Pacchaḥ saṁpīḍayec chatrūn varṇaśaś ca pramā-payet |
| 21.20d: Nārāyaṇam anāmayam | = iii.191b, 192d: |

## 2. *BṚHADDEVATĀ*

| *BD* | *Ṛvidh* |
|---|---|
| i.1a: Mantradṛgbhyo namas-kṛtvā | i.1b: Namaskṛtvā mantradṛg-bhyaḥ |
| Samāmnāyānupūrvaśaḥ | = i.2b: |

| *BD* | *Ṛvidh* |
| --- | --- |
| vii.21c: Daśākṣaraṁ tu śāntyarthaṁ | =iii.45a: |
| vii.123c: Sūryāyai bhāvavṛttaṁ tu | =iii.115c: |
| viii.7a: Bṛhaspate pratīty etad (A) | =iv.5a: |
| viii.92cd-93ab: Yathāśvamedhaḥ kraturāṭ | iv.121cd-122ab: Yathāśvamedhaḥ kraturāṭ |
| sarvariprapraṇodanaḥ | sarvapāpapraṇodanaḥ |
| tathāghamarṣaṇaṁ sūktaṁ | tathāghamarṣaṇaṁ sūktaṁ |
| sarvariprapraṇodanam | sarvapāpapraṇodanam |

# PART

# II

## *Ṛgvidhāna: Text and Translation*

# अथ ऋग्विधानम्

## प्रथमोऽध्यायः

स्वयम्भुवे ब्रह्मणे विश्वगोप्त्रे नमस्कृत्वा मन्त्रदृग्भ्यस्तथैव ।
विवक्षुरस्म्यृग्विधानं पुराणं पुरादृष्टमृषिभिर्मन्त्रदृग्भिः ॥१॥
मन्त्रेभ्यो मन्त्रदृग्भ्यश्च समाम्नायानुपूर्वशः ।
कर्मणामृषिदृष्टानां विधिं प्रोवाच शौनकः ॥२॥
ऋषिभिर्विविधा मन्त्रा दृष्टा दृष्टप्रयोजनाः ।
प्रयोजनाय चोद्दिष्टास्तस्मिँस्तस्मिन् प्रदर्शिताः ॥३॥
नानार्थानि च कर्माणि शान्तिपुष्ट्याश्रयाणि च ।
सिद्धयश्च तपोमूलाः श्रद्दधानस्य कुर्वतः ॥४॥
स्तुत्यादयो ये विकाराः प्रदिष्टास्तथार्थवादा ऋक्षु सूक्तेषु चैव ।
यैर्यैः कामैर्ऋषिर्देवताश्च तुष्टूष्यन्ते ताञ्शृणुध्वोच्यमानान् ॥५॥
आयुः स्वर्गो द्रविणं सूनवश्च चतुर्विधं प्रोक्तमाशास्यमग्रे ।
अन्ये कामाः शतशः संप्रदिष्टाः संस्तुवद्भिर्ऋषिभिर्देवताश्च ॥६॥ ॥१॥
सिद्धा मन्त्रा विधिना ब्राह्मणस्य फलं यच्छन्ति विधिवत्प्रयुक्ताः ।
सत्यं तेषां साधनं संयमश्च शमस्तितिक्षानसूया दमश्च ॥७॥
तस्माद्द्विजः प्रशान्तात्मा जपहोमपरायणः ।
तपस्यध्ययने युक्तो भवेद्भूतानुकम्पकः ॥८॥
क्षत्रियो बाहुवीर्येण तरेदापदमात्मनः ।
धनेन वैश्यशूद्रौ तु जपहोमैर्द्विजोत्तमः ॥९॥
तपसा स्वर्गमाप्नोति तपसा विन्दते महत् ।
तपोयुक्तस्य सिध्यन्ति कर्माणि नियतात्मनः ॥१०॥
विद्वेषणं संवननं विषघ्नं रोगनाशनम् ।
येन येनार्थमृषिणा यदर्थं देवताः स्तुताः ॥११॥ ॥२॥
स स कामः समृद्धश्च तेषां तेषां तथा तथा ।
तानि कर्माणि वक्ष्यामि विविधानि च कर्मणाम् ॥१२॥
पुरश्चरणमादौ तु कर्मणां सिद्धिकारकम् ।
स्वाध्यायाभ्यसनस्यादौ प्राजापत्यं चरेद्द्विजः ॥१३॥

केशश्मश्रुलोमनखान्वापयित्वाप्लुतः शुचिः ।
तिष्ठेदहनि रात्रौ तु शुचिरासीत वाग्यतः ॥१४॥
सत्यवादी पवित्राणि जपेद् व्याहृतयस्तथा ।
ओंकाराद्यास्तु ता जप्त्वा सावित्रीं च तदित्यृचम् ॥१५॥
आपो हि ष्ठेति सूक्तं तु शुद्धवत्योऽघमर्षणम् ।
शंवत्यः स्वस्तिमत्यश्च पावमान्यस्तथैव च ॥१६॥ ॥३॥
सर्वत्रैतत्प्रयोक्तव्यमादावन्ते च कर्मणाम् ।
आसहस्रादाशताद्वा दशान्तमथवा जपेत् ॥१७॥
ओंकारं व्याहृतीस्तिस्रः सावित्रीमथवायुतम् ।
तर्पयित्वाद्भिराचार्यानृषींश्छन्दांसि देवताः ॥१८॥
प्रपद्येत विरूपाक्षं रौद्रं मन्त्रगणं जपन् ।
अनार्यैर्न च भाषेत न शूद्रैर्नापि गर्हितैः ॥१९॥
न रजस्वलया नार्या पतितैर्नान्त्यजैर्नृभिः ।
न देवब्राह्मणद्विष्टैर्नाचार्यगुरुनिन्दकैः ॥२०॥
न मातृपितृविद्विष्टैर्नावमन्येत कञ्चन ।
मङ्गलाचारयुक्तः स्यात्त्रिरह्नोऽभ्युपयन्नपः* ॥२१॥ ॥४॥
अन्ते द्वादश रात्रस्य स्थालीपाकं प्रकल्पयेत् ।
अग्नये चाथ सोमाय तृतीयां च तयोः सह ॥२२॥
वैश्वदेवीं च रौद्रीं च जुहुयादुत्तरे ततः ।
अवसानस्य पतये तथानुमतयेऽपि च ॥२३॥
धन्वन्तरय इत्यन्या गन्धर्वाप्सरसामपि ।
दशमी ब्राह्मणस्पत्या परा तु ब्रह्मणे स्मृता ॥२४॥
सरस्वत्यै तथा विष्णोरन्त्या सौविष्टकृत्यपि ।
आज्याहुतय एवादौ स्थालीपाके हुते पुनः ॥२५॥
हुत्वाग्निं तर्पयेद्विप्रान् पितृभ्यश्च प्रकल्पयेत् ।
ततः शेषं विधानेन शुचिर्भुञ्जीत वाग्यतः ॥२६॥ ॥५॥
कृच्छ्राणामेष सर्वेषां विधिरुक्तोऽनुपूर्वशः ।
प्राजापत्यातिकृच्छ्रस्य तथा सांतपनस्य च ॥२७॥
पराकस्य च कृच्छ्रस्य विधिश्चान्द्रायणस्य च ।
एकेन शुद्धिमाप्नोति द्वाभ्यां पापैः प्रमुच्यते ॥२८॥
त्रिभिः सिध्यन्ति मन्त्राश्च मुच्यते चोपातकैः ।
चतुर्भिर्भ्रूणहत्यायास्तथैवायाज्ययाजनात् ॥२९॥
पञ्चभिः पातकैः सर्वैर्दुष्कृतैश्च प्रमुच्यते ।

तप्तकृच्छ्रेण सर्वाणि पापानि प्रतिबाधते ॥३०॥
चान्द्रयणं सहाद्यन्तमेभिः कृच्छैः समं स्मृतम् ।
त्रिभिश्चान्द्रायणैः पूतो ब्रह्मलोकं समश्नुते ॥३१॥ ॥६॥
अष्टाभिर्देवताः साक्षात्पश्येत वरदास्तथा ।
छन्दांसि दशभिर्ज्ञात्वा सर्वान्कामान्त्समश्नुते ॥३२॥
त्र्यहं प्रातस्त्र्यहं सायं त्र्यहमद्यादयाचितम् ।
त्र्यहं परं च नाश्नीयात्प्राजापत्यं चरन् द्विजः ॥३३॥
एकैकं ग्रासमश्नीयात्त्र्यहाणि त्रीणि पूर्ववत् ।
त्र्यहं चोपवसेदन्त्यमतिकृच्छ्रं चरन् द्विजः ॥३४॥
गोमूत्रं गोमयं क्षीरं दधिसर्पिः कुशोदकम् ।
एकरात्रोपवासश्च कृच्छ्रःसांतपनः स्मृतः ॥३५॥
एतमेव त्र्यहैर्युक्तं महासांतपनं विदुः ।
उपवासस्तु सप्ताहं शिशुसांतपनं स्मृतम् ॥३६॥ ॥७॥
तप्तकृच्छ्रं चरन् विप्रो जलक्षीरघृतानिलान् ।
प्रतित्र्यहं पिबेदुष्णान्त्सकृत्स्नायी समाहितः ॥३७॥
नियतस्तु पिबेदपः प्राजापत्यविधिः स्मृतः ।
यतिकृच्छ्रं वदन्त्येतद्रूपसामपनोदनम् ॥३८॥
यतात्मनोऽप्रमत्तस्य द्वादशाहमभोजनम् ।
पराको नामकृच्छ्रोऽयं सर्वपापापनोदनः ॥३९॥
एकैकं ह्रासयेत्पिण्डं कृष्णे शुक्ले च वर्धयेत् ।
उपस्पृशँस्त्रिषवणमेतच्चान्द्रायणं व्रतम् ॥४०॥
एतमेव विधिं कृत्स्नमाचरेद्यवमध्यमे ।
शुक्लपक्षादिनियतः चरँश्चान्द्रायणव्रतम् ॥४१॥ ॥८॥
चतुरः प्रातरश्नीयाद्द्विप्रः पिण्डान् कृताह्निकः ।
चतुरोऽस्तमिते सूर्ये शिशुचान्द्रायणं स्मृतम् ॥४२॥
अष्टावष्टौ समश्नीयात्पिण्डान् मध्यंदिने स्थिते ।
नियतात्मा हविष्यस्य यतिचान्द्रायणव्रतम् ॥४३॥
यथाकथञ्चित्पिण्डानां तिस्रोऽशीतीः समाहितः ।
मासेनाश्नन् हविष्यस्य चन्द्रस्यैति सलोकताम् ॥४४॥
एतद्रुद्रास्तथादित्या वसवश्चाचरन् व्रतम् ।
सर्वाकुशलमोक्षाय मरुतश्चर्भुभिः सह ॥४५॥
यावकः सप्तरात्रं तु पातव्यो नियतात्मना ।
स्थानासनत्रिषवणैर्जपता पावनानि च ॥४६॥ ॥९॥

एकैकं सप्तरात्रेण पुनाति विधिवत्कृतः ।
त्वगसृक्पिशितास्थीनि मेदो मज्जानमेव च ॥४७॥
एकैकं सप्तरात्रं तु त्वगादीनां विशोधनम् ।
एभिर्व्रतैर्विपूतात्मा कुर्यात्कर्माण्यतन्द्रितः ॥४८॥
इष्टान्कामान्ततः सर्वानवाप्नोति न संशयः ।
कणपिण्याकतक्राणामेकैकं शोधनं भवेत् ॥४९॥
शुद्धात्मा कर्म कुर्वीत सत्यवादी जितेन्द्रियः ।
एवं शुद्धस्य कर्माणि मन्त्रैर्वक्ष्यामि तद्यथा ॥५०॥
त्रिरात्रमेवोपवसेदादितः सर्वकर्मणाम् ।
त्रीणि नक्तानि वा कुर्यात्ततः कर्म समारभेत् ॥५१॥ ॥१०॥
नित्यप्रयोगिणां चैव प्रयोगादौ व्रतं त्र्यहम् ।
उपरिष्टादुपवसेत्कृत्वा वा सांनिपातिकम् ॥५२॥
आयुष्याण्येव कर्माणि मन्त्रयुक्तः समारभेत् ।
शंवत्यः स्वस्तिमत्यश्च जपेत त्रिवृता ऋचः ॥५३॥
अरण्ये चोदिते सूर्ये दिशं प्राप्यापराजिताम् ।
प्राचीमथोत्तरां वापि शुचौ देशे समाहितः ॥५४॥
सवासाः सशिरस्कोऽप्सु स्नात्वाभ्युक्ष्य जपेद्द्विजः ।
शुद्धवत्यस्तथाब्वत्यः पावमान्योऽघमर्षणम् ॥५५॥
एवं त्रिराप्लुत्य शुचिः प्राणायामान्समाचरेत् ।
त्रीन् षडष्टौ द्वादश वा षोडशाष्टादशापि वा ॥५६॥ ॥११॥
आशताद्वायमेत्प्राणाञ्जपन् ब्रह्माघमर्षणम् ।
यावद्वा मनसस्तुष्टिस्तावत्प्राणान्समायमेत् ॥५७॥
यथा यथा मनस्तस्य दुष्कृतं कर्म गर्हति ।
तथा तथा शरीरं तत्तेनाधर्मेण मुच्यते ॥५८॥
प्राणायामैर्दग्धदोषः शुक्लाम्बरधरः शुचिः ।
यथाविध्यप आचम्य आरोहेद्दर्भप्रस्तरम् ॥५९॥
पवित्रपाणिः कृत्वा तु उपस्थं दक्षिणोत्तरम् ।
दिशोरेवान्तरं प्रेक्ष्यानिमिषं छाद्य चक्षुषी ॥६०॥
ओंकारं व्याहृतीस्तिस्रः सावित्रीं च तदित्यृचम् ।
मनसैता अनुद्रुत्य वेदादिं समुपक्रमेत् ॥६१॥ ॥१२॥
मन्द्रमेव पठेत्प्रातरुच्चैर्मध्यंदिने पठेत् ।
उच्चैरेवापराह्णे तु संध्याकाल उपारमेत् ॥६२॥
ब्राह्मे मुहूर्ते चोत्थाय त्रिराप्लुत्य पठेद्द्विजः ।

मध्यमां वृत्तिमास्थाय न द्रुतां न विलम्बिताम् ॥६३॥
पूर्वां संध्यां जपँस्तिष्ठेदुपासीत च पश्चिमाम् ।
न चान्तरा व्याहरेत विरमेद्वा कथञ्चन ॥६४॥
विरमेद्ब्राह्मणे प्राप्ते कामंतेन तु संवदेत् ।
शूद्रं दृष्ट्वैव संप्राप्तं नाधीयीत कथञ्चन ॥६५॥
आग्नेयं सूक्तमाद्यं तु मुख्यं ब्रह्मर्षिसम्मतम् ।
रायस्पोषकरं धन्यं जपन् विप्रोऽर्थमाप्नुयात् ॥६६॥ ॥१३॥
ऋषिं सर्वमिदं जप्त्वा सपुत्रं नियतः शुचिः ।
संहिताफलमाप्नोति ऋग्वेदस्य न संशयः ॥६७॥
एकादशगुणं ह्येतज्जपन् ब्रह्म सनातनम् ।
सर्वान्कामानवाप्नोति पापैश्च परिमुच्यते ॥६८॥
अनश्नन्संहितामेतां प्रातः प्रातर्दिने दिने ।
आयुर्विद्यां धनं पुत्रान् गृहाँश्चाप्नोत्यनामयान् ॥६९॥
एतद्ब्रह्मजपञ्छूद्रान्नेक्षेतान्याँश्च तद्विधान् ।
प्रेक्ष्याचम्योदकं पूतः पश्येद्गामग्निभास्करौ ॥७०॥
मन्द्रं जपो दश गुण उपाँशु स्याच्छतान्वितः ।
सहस्रं मानसं विद्यादेष जप्यविधिः स्मृतः ॥७१॥ ॥१४॥
आदावेव तु सावित्र्या कर्म कुर्वीत शान्तये ।
पुष्टये धनलाभाय पशुलाभाय भूतये ॥७२॥
एषा हि सम्मिता वेदैः सर्वब्रह्ममयी निचृत् ।
उग्रेण तपसा दृष्टा विश्वामित्रेण धीमता ॥७३॥
होमाँश्च जपयज्ञाँश्च नित्यं कुर्वीत चैतया ।
सर्वकामसमृध्यर्थं परं ब्रह्मेदमुच्यते ॥७४॥
एषैव प्रतिलोमोक्ता पच्छः शत्रुविनाशिनी ।
अक्षरप्रतिलोमेयमभिचारेषु शस्यते ॥७५॥
अक्षरप्रतिलोमेयं यस्मिन्युज्येत कर्मणि ।
तदमोघं विजानीयादेतद्वै ब्रह्मणो बलम् ॥७६॥
व्याघातकेध्मसमिधो अक्षरप्रतिलोमया ।
जुहुयात्सार्षपं तैलं वैभीतककृतस्रुचा* ॥७७॥
य इच्छेत्पीडनं शत्रोरपिवोच्चाटनं पुनः ।
पच्छः संपीडयेच्छत्रून् वर्णशश्च प्रमापयेत् ॥७८॥ ॥१५॥
ऋग्वेदाद्यस्य सूक्तस्य विधिं वक्ष्याम्यतः परम् ।
यथा ऋषिर्मधुच्छन्दाः कर्मैतेनाकरोत्पुरा ॥७९॥

शिरसा धारयेदग्निं नियतः परिवत्सरम् ।
चतुर्थप्राणकालीयो हुतशिष्टमदन् हविः ॥८०॥
जुह्वत्त्रिरुपतिष्ठेत सत्यवादी दिने दिने ।
व्रतकाले तु संप्राप्त आग्नेयं निर्वपेच्चरुम् ॥८१॥
अनग्नौ *ध्यातमात्रोऽग्निर्व्रतान्तेऽस्योपतिष्ठति ।
दहेयमिति यं चेच्छेत्तं दहत्येव पावकः ॥८२॥
अप्स्वप्यग्निर्ज्वलत्येव तद्व्रतस्य महात्मनः ।
समर्धयति तं चेष्टैः कामैर्वह्निः प्रयत्नतः ॥८३॥ ॥१६॥
अतः परं तृचाः सप्त वाय्वाद्या ये प्रकीर्तिताः ।
ताञ्जपन्प्रयतो नित्यमिष्टान्कामान्समश्नुते ॥८४॥
मेधातिथावृषौ पुनः सदसस्पतिमित्यृचम् ।
मेधाकामो जपेन्नित्यं जुहुयाच्चाज्यमेतया ॥८५॥
स्योनेति पृथिवीं नित्यं स्नात्वा विप्रः शुचिर्जपेत् ।
विन्दते महतीं भूमिमसपत्नामकण्टकाम् ॥८६॥
इदं विष्णुरितीमाभिः पञ्चभिः श्राद्धकर्मणि ।
अङ्गुष्ठमन्ने वगाह्य तेन रक्षांसि बाधते ॥८७॥
सप्तजन्मकृतं पापं कृत्वा चाभक्ष्यभक्षणम् ।
तद्विष्णोरित्यपां मध्ये सकृज्जप्त्वा विशुध्यति ॥८८॥
अम्बयो यन्ति या प्रोक्ता नवर्चस्त्वभिषेचनीः ।
आयुष्यास्ताः परिप्रोक्ता भैषज्याः पापमोचनीः ॥८९॥
शुनः शेपमृषिं बद्धः संनिरुद्धोऽथवा जपेत् ।
मुच्यते सर्वपाशेभ्यो गदी चाप्यगदी भवेत् ॥९०॥
य इच्छेच्छाश्वतान्कामानिन्द्रात्प्राप्तुं पुरंदरात् ।
स षोडशभिरेवर्ग्भिरिन्द्रं स्तूयाद्दिने दिने ॥९१॥ ॥१७॥
हैरण्यस्तूपमिन्द्रस्य सूक्तं कर्माभिसंस्तवम् ।
तज्जपन्प्रयतः शत्रूनयत्नात्प्रतिबाधते ॥९२॥
आकृष्णेनेत्यृचा त्वेव यो नित्यं सूर्यमर्चति ।
प्रातर्मध्येऽस्तगं वापि स जीवेदगदः सुखी ॥९३॥
आकृष्णेनेत्यृचं त्वेकां ध्यायन्निशि दिवौकसः ।
अग्नौ हुत्वैतया चाज्यं दीर्घमायुरवाप्नुयात् ॥९४॥
ये ते पन्था इतीमां तु सावित्रीमध्वगोऽभ्यसेत् ।
स्वस्तिमान्व्रजतेऽध्वानं गृहाँश्चाप्नोत्यनामयान् ॥९५॥
सं पूषन्निति यत्सूक्तं घौरः कण्वो जगावृषिः ।

अध्वन्यमेतद्विज्ञेयं परिपन्थ्यपसेधनम् ॥९६॥
रौद्रीभिः षड्भिरीशानं तुष्टूयाद्यो दिने दिने ।
स नारीनरगोशान्तिं शङ्करात्प्राप्नुयात्सदा ॥९७॥
एतेनैव षडर्चेन जुहुयादाज्यमन्वहम् ।
चरुं वा कल्पयेद्रौद्रं भूतिकामोऽथ पर्वसु ॥९८॥ ॥१८॥
उदित्युद्यन्तमादित्यमुपतिष्ठेद्दिने दिने ।
हृद्रोगनाशनं ह्येतत्परमारोग्यवर्धनम् ॥९९॥
द्विषन्तमित्यथार्धर्चं यं द्विष्यात्तं जपन्स्मरेत् ।
आगस्कृत्सप्तरात्रेण विद्वेषमधिगच्छति ॥१००॥
रौगंगृहीतोऽरोगी च प्रस्कण्वस्योत्तमं तृचम् ।
आरोग्यमेतत्प्रयतो जपेन्नित्यमनेकशः ॥१०१॥
उत्तमस्तस्य चार्धर्चो द्विषद्द्वेष इति स्मृतः ।
यं द्विष्यात्तमभिध्यायेद् दृष्ट्वा चैनं जपेदिदम् ॥१०२॥
आगस्कृच्चेत्त्रिरात्रेण विद्वेषं संनियच्छति ।
उदयत्यायुरक्षय्यं तेजो मध्यंदिने जपन् ॥१०३॥ ॥१९॥
अस्तं व्रजति सूर्ये तु द्विषन्तं प्रतिबाधते ।
ओजस्तेजस्तथारोग्यं द्विषद्द्वेषं प्रकीर्तितम् ॥१०४॥
नव पश्वेति सूक्तानि यानि गर्भे पराशरः ।
अरातीनां हरेत्प्राणाञ्छत्रूंश्चैव नियच्छति ॥१०५॥
सौपर्णानि पवित्राणि सूक्तान्येकादशाभ्यसेत् ।
वाञ्छन् पुत्रान्पशून् वित्तं स्वर्गमायुरनन्धताम् ॥१०६॥
आध्यात्मिकीः क इत्येता जपंस्तु सुसमाहितः ।
प्राप्नुयात्स परं धाम विश्वं ज्योतिः सनातनम् ॥१०७॥
आनोभद्रीयमायुष्यं वैश्वदेवं जपन्मुनिः ।
मुमूर्षुरपि जप्त्वैतत्सर्वमायुरवाप्नुयात् ॥१०८॥ ॥२०॥
पितॄणां श्राद्धकाले तु मध्वित्येतत्तृचं जपेत् ।
अघोराः पितरस्तस्य विशन्ति ज्योतिरुत्तमम् ॥१०९॥
त्वं सोमेति तु सूक्तेन पश्येच्चन्द्रमुपोदितम् ।
उपतिष्ठेत्समित्पाणिर्मासि मासि नवं नवम् ॥११०॥
तं मासं तस्य दुःखं हि न जातु त्रिविधं भवेत् ।
गोतमेन पुरा दृष्टं मृत्योर्नाशनमात्मनः ॥१११॥
उद्यन्तमुपतिष्ठेत पूर्णं चैतत्समाहितः ।
वासांस्यपि स विन्देत चन्द्रस्यैति सलोकताम् ॥११२॥

धनकामो जपेन्नित्यमेता इति तु नित्यशः ।
स्नात्वा शुचिस्तु नियत इष्टं धनमवाप्नुयात् ॥११३॥ ॥२१॥
आयुरीप्सन्निममिति कौत्सं सूक्तं सदाभ्यसेत् ।
आज्याहुतिश्च जुहुयात्प्रत्यृचं वाग्यतःशुचिः ॥११४॥
जपेदाप्लुत्य नियतः स साक्षादापदं तरेत् ।
अप नः शोशुचदिति स्नात्वा मध्यंदिने रवौ ॥११५॥
शुद्धिकामो यताहारः प्रत्यृचं जुहुयाद्घृतम् ।
समिधोऽन्वहमष्टौ वा सूक्तमेतदघापहम् ॥११६॥
यथा मुञ्जादिवेषीका तथा पापात्प्रमुच्यते ।
जातवेदस इत्यादि सदा स्वस्त्ययने जपेत् ॥११७॥
दुर्गे पथि प्रयातस्य नास्यारिभ्यो भयं भवेत् ।
राजकार्येऽश्वयूथे वा अभिशस्तो ऽप्यनेकधा ॥११८॥
अशक्ये प्रतिभाकार्ये भये प्राणान्तिकेऽपि वा ।
जातवेदस इत्येतां जपंस्तेभ्यः प्रमुच्यते ॥११९॥
सिषाधयिषुरर्थं च प्रस्थितो मनसा जपेत् ।
सिद्धार्थः स्वस्तिमानेति प्रमीयेत न चाध्वनि ॥१२०॥ ॥२२॥
कृतार्थः स्वगृहान्गाच्छन्नेतामेव सदाभ्यसेत् ।
उदिते सवितर्येतां जपेदस्तंगते तथा ॥१२१॥
अहः स्वस्त्ययनं प्राता रात्रिस्वस्त्ययनं निशि ।
व्युष्टायां च जपेन्नित्यमेतां दुःस्वप्ननाशिनीम् ॥१२२॥
प्रमन्दिने* ति सूयन्त्यां जपेद्गर्भप्रमोचिनीम् ।
इन्द्रं च मनसा ध्यायेन्नारी गर्भं प्रमुञ्चति ॥१२३॥
आपत्सु सर्वकामो वा त्रितं नित्यं जपेदृषिम् ।
जपन्निन्द्रमिति स्नातो वैश्वदेवं तु सप्तकम् ॥१२४॥
मुच्यते जुह्वदाज्यं तु विश्वस्मादेव सोंऽहसः ।
शन्तातीयं परं सूक्तं पञ्चविंशकमुत्तमम् ॥१२५॥
नासत्यौ तु नमस्कृत्वा परामृद्धिमवाप्नुयात् ।
घर्मसंस्तवनं सूक्तं रपसश्च प्रमोचनम् ॥१२६॥
इमा इति जपेच्छश्वद्रौद्रं सूक्तं द्विजः शुचिः ।
आयुर्विद्यां धनं पुत्रान् गृहाँश्चाप्नोत्यनामयान् ॥१२७॥ ॥२३॥
वीरेष्वपत्यगोष्ठेषु दुःस्वप्ने रिप्रमातमनः ।
मा नो महान्तमित्याभ्याँ त्रिरात्रोपोषितः शुचिः ॥१२८॥
औदुम्बरीस्तु जुहुयाद्दधिमध्वाज्यसंस्कृताः ।

सूक्तेन जुहुयादाज्यमादावन्ते च कर्मणाम् ॥१२९॥
ऊर्ध्वबाहुस्तु सूक्तेन तुष्ट्वा* च* शतशो भवम् ।
छित्वा सर्वान्मृत्युपाशाञ्जीवेद्रोगैर्विवर्जितः ॥१३०॥
तिष्ठन्नुद्यन्तमादित्यं समित्पाणिः शुचिः सदा ।
चित्रमित्युपतिष्ठेत सूक्तेनानेन भास्करम् ॥१३१॥
अतिस्तवेन चैतेन नित्यं मध्यंदिने रविम् ।
गृणन्नपोहते रिप्रं प्राप्नोति च धनायुषी ॥१३२॥ ॥२४॥
अधः स्वप्नस्येति जपेत्प्रातः प्रातर्दिने दिने ।
दुःस्वप्नं नुदते क्षिप्रं न चास्याभोजनाद्भयम् ॥१३३॥
उभे पुनामीति परा रिपुघ्न्यस्तु प्रकीर्तिताः ।
ता जपन्हन्ति रक्षांसि सपत्नाँश्च नियच्छति ॥१३४॥
निर्वर्त्य पञ्चयज्ञाँश्च हुत्वा चाग्निं कृताह्निकः ।
ये देवासो दिव्यनया जपन्कामानवाप्नुयात् ॥१३५॥
इन्द्राविष्णू नमस्कृत्य विष्णोर्नुकमिति त्रिभिः ।
समित्पाणिः शुचिर्भूत्वा उपतिष्ठेद्दिने दिने ॥१३६॥
धर्मं बुद्धिं धनं पुत्रानारोग्यं ब्रह्मवर्धनम् ।
प्राप्नोति च परं स्थानं ज्योतीरूपं सनातनम् ॥१३७॥
आततायिनमायान्तं दृष्ट्वा व्याघ्रमथो वृकम् ।
न मा गरन्निति जपँस्तेभ्य एव प्रमुच्यते ॥१३८॥
त्रिरात्रोपोषितो रात्रौ जपेदासूर्यदर्शनात् ।
आप्लुत्य प्रयतः सौरीरुपतिष्ठेद्दिवाकरम् ॥१३९॥ ॥२५॥
नैनं पश्यन्ति वै चौरास्तथान्ये पापवृत्तयः ।
एकःशतानि त्रायेत तस्करेभ्यश्चरन्पथि ॥१४०॥
स्तेयं कृत्वा द्विजो मोहात्त्रिरात्रोपोषितः शुचिः ।
सूक्तं जप्त्वास्यवामीयं क्षिप्रं मुच्येत किल्बिषात् ॥१४१॥
ज्ञातिपुत्रसुहृन्मित्रैर्यश्च राज्यं चिकीर्षति ।
नित्यं स नियतो भूत्वा सूक्तं तु मनसा जपेत् ॥१४२॥
कया शुभेति पैशुन्यं कृत्वाचार्यनृपद्विजैः ।
श्रुत्वा पररहस्यं तु गुरोरप्याह शौनकः ॥१४३॥
इमं नु सोममित्येते द्वे ऋचौ प्रयतो जपेत् ।
सर्वान्कामानवाप्नोति न किञ्चित्पातकं भवेत् ॥१४४॥
पितुं न्वित्युपतिष्ठेत नित्यमन्नमुपस्थितम् ।
पूजयेदशनं नित्यं भुञ्जीयादविकुत्सितम् ॥१४५॥ ॥२६॥

नास्य स्यादन्नजो व्याधिर्विषमप्यन्नतामियात् ।
विषं च पीत्वैतत्सूक्तं जपेत विषनाशनम् ॥१४६॥
नावाग्यतस्तु भुञ्जीत नाशुचिर्न जुगुप्सितम् ।
दद्याच्च पूजयेच्चैव जुहुयाच्च शुचिः सदा ॥१४७॥
क्षुद्भयं नास्य किञ्चित्स्यान्नान्नजं व्याधिमाप्नुयात् ।
उत्पथप्रतिपन्नो यो भ्रष्टो वापि पथः क्वचित् ॥१४८॥
पन्थानं प्रतिपद्येत कृत्वा वा कर्म गर्हितम् ।
अग्ने नयेति सूक्तेन प्रत्यृचं जुहुयाद्घृतम् ॥१४६॥
जपँश्च प्रयतो नित्यमुपतिष्ठेत चानलम् ।
स्नात्वा जपेदनर्वाणं नमस्कृत्य बृहस्पतिम् ॥१५०॥ ॥२७॥
वीरान्धनं च प्राप्नोति सुश्लोक्यं च नियच्छति ।
कङ्कतो नेति सूक्तं तु विषार्तः प्रयतो जपेत् ॥१५१॥
विषं न क्रमते चास्य सर्पाद्दृष्टिविषादपि ।
यत्कीटलूतासु विषं दंष्ट्रिवृश्चिकजं च यत् ॥१५२॥
मौलं च कृत्रिमं चैव जपन्त्सर्वं व्यपोहति ।
धर्मं बुद्धिं धनं पुत्रान् सौभाग्यं ब्रह्मवर्चसम् ॥१५३॥
आरोग्यं पुष्टिमायुष्यं पशून् विद्यां महद्यशः ।
त्रिरात्रोपोषितः स्नातः प्रयतः चरितव्रतः ॥१५४॥
प्राणायामशतं कृत्वा उपतिष्ठेच्छतक्रतुम् ।
एकाहं क्षुरसंयुक्तः पादौ संधाय वाग्यतः ॥१५५॥ ॥२८॥
यो जात इति सूक्तेन ऋषिं गृत्समदं स्मरन् ।
शतकृत्वो जपेदेतदिन्द्रश्रेष्ठेति चान्ततः ॥१५६॥
एकाहाल्लभते वित्तं द्व्यहात्सिद्धिमनुत्तमाम् ।
अहोभिस्त्रिभिरारोग्यं चतुर्भिरशनं बहु ॥१५७॥
पञ्चभिर्ब्रह्मवर्चस्यं षड्भिरायुः सुखावहम् ।
सप्तभिस्तनयान्पुष्टिमष्टभिः प्राप्नुयाद्यशः ॥१५८॥
प्रियो भवति चेन्द्रस्य प्रियं धाम स गच्छति ।
रिपुघ्नं दस्युशमनं रायस्पोषकरं परम् ॥१५६॥
गणानामिति यत्सूक्तं तज्जपेत्सुखवर्धनम् ।
संध्ययोः प्रयतस्त्वेतज्जपेन्नित्यं बृहस्पतिम् ॥१६०॥ ॥२६॥
उपतिष्ठेत सूक्तेन सर्वकामसमृद्धये ।
यो मे राजन्नितीमां तु दुःस्वप्नशमनीमृचम् ॥१६१॥'
जप्त्वा नाशयति क्षिप्रं दुःस्वप्नं ब्राह्मणः शुचिः ।

अहोरात्रमुपोष्यैकं नियतो ब्रह्मवित्तमः ॥१६२॥
प्रजार्थं जुहुयादाज्यं चरुं वा पयसि श्रितम् ।
राकामहमितीमाभिः षष्ठ्यां शुक्लस्य पञ्चभिः ॥१६३॥
हविःशेषं स्वयं प्राश्य विन्दते महतीं प्रजाम् ।
व्याधिना योऽभिभूतः स्याद्घोरेण प्राणहारिणा ॥१६४॥
चतुर्दशीमुपोष्यैकां कृष्णस्य जुहुयाच्चरुम् ।
आ ते सूक्तेन रौद्रेण प्रत्यृचं वाग्यतः शुचिः ॥१६५॥ ॥३०॥
पूर्वमाज्याहुतीर्हुत्वा अथोपस्थाय शङ्करम् ।
हविःशेषेण वर्तेत एकान्तरमतन्द्रितः ॥१६६॥
पूर्णे मासि जयेन्मृत्युं रोगेभ्यश्च प्रमुच्यते ।
अभिशस्येत यो मोहात्कुर्याद्वा कर्म गर्हितम् ॥१६७॥
स्नात्वा भुञ्जञ्जपेदप्सु अम्बीत्यृचमतन्द्रितः ।
अध्वनि प्रस्थितो यस्तु पश्येच्छकुनिमुत्थितम् ॥१६८॥
अप्रशस्तं प्रशस्तं वा स्थित्वैक्ष्य प्रयतो जपेत् ।
कनिक्रददिति सूक्ताभ्यामुपतिष्ठेत्कृतस्वरम् ॥१६९॥
शकुनिं वायसं वापि मृगं दंष्ट्रिणमेव च ।
अप्यदृष्टैव जप्तव्यमेतत्तस्करमोहनम् ॥१७०॥
एतत्तस्करमोहनम् ॥ ॥३१॥

इत्यृग्विधाने प्रथमोऽध्यायः ॥

## द्वितीयोऽध्यायः

कल्याणवादी वान्यो वा न वा रौति न दृश्यते ।
जपेदेव नमस्कृत्य सिद्धार्थः सन् निवर्तते ॥१॥
न तस्यास्ति भयं किञ्चिद्दस्युभ्योऽध्वनि वा क्वचित् ।
तरत्यपि च दुर्गाणि स्वस्तिमाँश्च सुखीभवेत् ॥२॥
यस्य भुक्तं न जीर्येत न तिष्ठेद्वा कथञ्चन ।
ध्यात्वा सोऽत्तारमन्नस्य अग्निरस्मीत्यृचं जपेत् ॥३॥
विश्वामित्रस्य संवादं नद्यतिक्रमणे जपेत् ।
आप्लुत्याचम्य विधिवदुदकस्याञ्जलिं क्षिपेत् ॥४॥
नमःस्रवद्भ्यइत्येतद्यो नित्यं हि समाचरेत् ।
तं नद्यःस्रोतसः पान्ति स्वं पुत्रमिव मातरः ॥५॥ ॥१॥
भयं चास्य न विद्येत नदीतीरचरेष्वपि ।
जलचरेभ्यो भूतेभ्यः शीतोष्णैर्न च बाध्यते ॥६॥
पूर्णां तितीर्षुः सरितं रमध्वमिति संस्मरेत् ।
श्रो ष्वित्यृचमपां मध्ये जपेद्यो वै नदीं तरन् ॥७॥
स शीघ्रं तीरमाप्नोति गाधं वा विन्दते द्विजः ।
युक्तेनैव रथेनाशु योऽपां पारं तितीर्षति ॥८॥
उद्व ऊर्मिरितीमां तु जपेत नियतः स्वयम् ।
अध्वानं प्रस्थितश्चैवमामन्द्रैरिति संस्मरेत् ॥९॥
कार्याण्यशेषतः कृत्वा पुनरायाति वै गृहम् ।
अदातारं सुपुष्टार्थं सर्वदाविष्टचेतनम् ॥१०॥
हत्वा तद्धनमन्विच्छेत्किं ते कृण्वन्तीति स्मरन् ।
इन्द्रापर्वतेति सूक्तमायुष्यं द्राविणं स्मृतम् ॥११॥ ॥२॥
वागिन्द्रियप्रमूढो यो न विद्यां प्रतिपद्यते ।
इन्द्रियार्थान्यथार्थान्वा यो न वेत्ति कथञ्चन ॥१२॥
विद्या वाधिगता यस्य प्रणश्येत पुनः पुनः ।
ससर्परीरृचौ जपन्द्वौ मासौ प्रतिपद्यते ॥१३॥
अनसा संप्रयातस्तु स्थिरौ गावाविति स्मरेत् ।
चतस्रः कुशलेनैति सिद्धार्थः स्थिरयानगः ॥१४॥
यानाक्षमपभग्नान्तं* दृष्ट्वा दुर्गेऽध्वनि द्विजः ।

अभि व्ययस्वेति जपेद् द्वृचमक्षबलं दधत् ॥१५॥
कृष्णपक्षे चतुर्दश्यां त्रिरात्रोपोषितः शुचिः ।
दक्षिणप्रवणे देशे श्मशानस्थः समाहितः ॥१६॥ ॥३॥
रक्तोष्णीष्यसिपाणिश्च बैल्वकेध्मोऽनिलाशनः ।
सप्ताहं जुहुयात्तैलं सार्षपं लवणान्वितम् ॥१७॥
समिधो राजवृक्षस्य वसिष्ठद्वेषणीः पठन् ।
यं द्विष्यात्तस्य कृत्वा तु शम्याकेनाकृतिं निशि ॥१८॥
अधिष्ठाय च तां कुर्यादृग्भिश्चतसृभिर्द्विजः ।
उद्दिश्य नाम होमोऽयं सप्तरात्रं न जीवति ॥१९॥
वसिष्ठानन्ततो हन्ति ब्रह्मैतत्कुशिकोदितम् ।
नास्य कश्चिदवध्योऽस्ति जपतो जुह्वतोऽपि वा ॥२०॥
द्वाविंशकं जपेत्सूक्तमाध्यात्मिकमनुत्तमम् ।
पर्वसु प्रयतो नित्यमिष्टान्कामान्समश्नुते ॥२१॥ ॥४॥
बृहस्पतिमजाश्वं च सवितारं बभ्रुमेव च ।
ऋतावृधौ* दिने दिने तृचैः पञ्चभिरन्वहम् ॥२२॥
बृहस्पत इति पञ्चाहं प्रत्यृचं जुहुयाद्घृतम् ।
हुत्वाग्निमर्चयित्वा तु गन्धमाल्यैः सधूपकैः ॥२३॥
ता एव देवताः पञ्च कामैरर्चन्ति पञ्चभिः ।
रत्नैरपत्यैः पशुभिर्मखैर्दीर्घेण चायुषा ॥२४॥ ॥५॥
अथ वेदादिगीतायाः प्रसादजननं विधिम् ।
गायत्र्याः संप्रवक्ष्यामि धर्मकामार्थमोक्षदम् ॥२५॥
नित्ये नैमित्तिके काम्ये त्रितये तु परायणम् ।
गायत्र्यास्तु परं नास्ति इहलोके परत्र च ॥२६॥
मेध्यान्नमितभुग्मौनी त्रिःस्नानार्चनतत्परः ।
जपेल्लक्षत्रयं धीमाननन्यमानसक्रियः ॥२७॥
कर्मभिर्योजयेत्पश्चात्क्रमशःस्वेच्छयापि वा ।
यावत्कार्यं स कुर्वीत न लोपेत्तावत्तद्व्रतम् ॥२८॥
आदित्यस्योदये स्नात्वा सहस्रं प्रत्यहं जपेत् ।
आयुरारोग्यमैश्वर्यं धनं च लभते ध्रुवम् ॥२९॥ ॥६॥
त्रिरात्रोपोषितः सम्यग्घृतं हुत्वा सहस्रशः ।
सहस्रलाभमाप्नोति हुताशे खादिरेन्धने ॥३०॥
पालाशसमिधां चैव घृताक्तानां हुताशने ।
सहस्रलाभमाप्नोति राहुसूर्यसमागमे ॥३१॥

हुत्वा तु खादिरे वह्नौ सघृतं रक्तचन्दनम् ।
सहस्रं हेममाप्नोति राहुसूर्यसमागमे ॥३२॥
रक्तचन्दनमिश्रं तु सघृतं हव्यवाहने ।
हुत्वा गोमयमाप्नोति सहस्रं गोधनं द्विजः ॥३३॥
यस्यास्तु गोर्गोमयेन गुटिकानां सहस्रशः ।
हुत्वा तां गामवाप्नोति घृताक्तानां हुताशने ॥३४॥ ॥७॥
यवैरश्वाँस्तिलैर्हस्तीन्महिष्यो यावकैस्तथा ।
शालीताण्डुलहोमेन कन्यालाभमवाप्नुयात् ॥३५॥
जातीचम्पकराजार्ककुसुमानां सहस्रशः ।
हुत्वा वस्त्राण्यवाप्नोति घृताक्तानां हुताशने ॥३६॥
सूर्यबिम्बे जलमध्ये तोयं हुत्वा सहस्रशः ।
सहस्रं प्राप्नुयाद्धैमं रौप्यमिन्दुमये हुते ॥३७॥
अलक्ष्मीपापसंयुक्तो मलव्याधिविनायकैः ।
मुच्येत्सहस्रजप्तेन स्नायाद्यस्तु जलेन वै ॥३८॥
यां दिशं सप्तजप्तेन लोष्टेन संप्रचाटयेत् ।
चौराग्निमारुतोत्थानि भयानि न भवन्ति वै ॥३९॥ ॥८॥
क्षीराहारो जपेल्लक्षमपमृत्युं व्यपोहति ।
घृताशी प्राप्नुयान्मेधां बहुविज्ञानसंचयम् ॥४०॥
हुत्वा वेतसपत्राणि घृताक्तानि हुताशने ।
लक्षाद्वर्षापयेद्देवं सार्वभौमं न संशयः ॥४१॥
लक्षेण भस्म होमस्य कृत्वा ह्युत्तिष्ठते जलात् ।
आदित्याभिमुखः स्थित्वा नाभिमात्रे जले शुचिः ॥४२॥
तिलानां लक्षहोमेन घृताक्तानां हुताशने ।
सर्वकामसमृद्धात्मा परां सिद्धिमवाप्नुयात् ॥४३॥
यवानां लक्षहोमेन घृताक्तानां हुताशने ।
सर्वकामसमृद्धात्मा परं स्थानमवाप्नुयात् ॥४४॥ ॥९॥
घृतस्याहुतिलक्षेण सर्वान्कामानवाप्नुयात् ।
पञ्चगव्याशनो लक्षं जपेज्जातिस्मरो भवेत् ॥४५॥
तदेव ह्यनले हुत्वा प्राप्नोति बहुशो धनम् ।
अन्नाद्यहवनान्नित्यमन्नाद्यं च भवेत्सदा ॥४६॥
जुहुयात्सर्वसाध्यानामाहुत्ययुतसंख्यया ।
रक्तसिद्धार्थकान्हुत्वा सर्वान्त्साधयते रिपून् ॥४७॥
लवणं मधुसंयुक्तं हुत्वा सर्वं वशोभवेत् ।

हुत्वा तु करवीराणि रक्तानि जनयेज्ज्वरम् ॥४८॥
हुत्वा वैभीतकं तैलं देशादेव प्रचाटयेत् ।
हुत्वा तु निम्बपत्राणि विद्वेषं जनयेन्नृणाम् ॥४९॥
रक्तानां तण्डुलानां तु घृताक्तानां हुताशने ।
हुत्वा बलमवाप्नोति शत्रुभिर्न स जीयते ॥५०॥ ॥१०॥
प्रत्यानयनसिध्यर्थं मधुसर्पिः समन्वितम् ।
गव्यं क्षीरं प्रदीप्ते ऽग्नौ जुह्वतस्तत्प्रशाम्यति ॥५१॥
ब्रह्मचारी मिताहारो यः सहस्रत्रयं जपेत् ।
संवत्सरेण लभते धनैश्वर्यं न संशयः ॥५२॥
शमीबिल्वपलाशानामर्कस्य तु विशेषतः ।
पुष्पाणां समिधां चैव हुत्वा हेममवाप्नुयात् ॥५३॥
अब्रह्मत्र्यम्बकादीनां यस्यायतनमाश्रितः ।
जपेल्लक्षं निराहारः स तस्य वरदो भवेत् ॥५४॥
बिल्वानां लक्षहोमेन घृताक्तानां हुताशने ।
परां श्रियमवाप्नोति यदि न भ्रूणहा भवेत् ॥५५॥ ॥११॥
पद्मानां लक्षहोमेन घृताक्तानां हुताशने ।
प्राप्नोति राज्यं निखिलमसपत्नमकण्टकम् ॥५६॥
पञ्चविंशतिलक्षेण दधिक्षीरघृताशनः ।
स्वदेहे सिध्यते जन्तुः कौशिकस्य मतं यथा ॥५७॥
एकाहं पञ्चगव्याशी एकाहं मारुताशनः ।
एकाहं ब्राह्मणान्नाशी गायत्रीजप उच्यते ॥५८॥
शतेन गायत्र्या स्नात्वा शतमन्तर्जले जपेत् ।
शतेनापस्ततः पीत्वा सर्वपापैः प्रमुच्यते ॥५९॥
गोघ्नः पितृघ्नो मातृघ्नो ब्रह्महा गुरुतल्पगः ।
सुवर्णरत्नहारी च यश्च विप्रः सुरां पिबेत् ॥६०॥
अयाज्ययाजनं कृत्वा कृत्वा वा कर्म गर्हितम् ।
न सीदेत्प्रतिगृह्णानो महीमपि ससागराम् ॥६१॥
ये चास्य दुःस्थिता लोके ग्रहाः सूर्यादयो भुवि ।
ते यान्ति सौम्यतां सर्वे शिवा इति न संशयः ॥६२॥ ॥१२॥
कृणुष्वेति जपन्सूक्तं रक्षोघ्नं दस्युभिर्वृतः ।
अरातीनां हरेत्प्राणान्रक्षांस्यपि न नाशयेत् ॥६३॥
उपतिष्ठेत यो वह्निं परीत्यृचा दिने दिने ।
तं रक्षति स्वयं वह्निर्विश्वतो विश्वतोमुखः ॥६४॥

को अद्येति तु सूक्तेन यो नित्यं शक्रमर्चति ।
जपेद्वाथ नमस्कारैः शक्रतो लभते वरान् ॥६५॥
कयेति वामदेव्येन कुर्यात्स्वस्त्ययनं निशि ।
जपेद्वा संधिवेलासु ब्रह्मैतत्कुशिकोदितम् ॥६६॥
हंसः शुचिषदित्यृचा शुचिरीक्षेद्दिवाकरम् ।
अन्तकाले जपन्नेति ब्रह्मणः सद्म शाश्वतम् ॥६७॥
कृषिं प्रपद्यमानस्तु स्थालीपाकं यथाविधि ।
जुहुयात्क्षेत्रमध्ये तु शुनं वाहास्तु पञ्चभिः ॥६८॥
यथालिङ्गं तु विहरेल्लाङ्गलं कृषीवलः ।
इन्द्राय च मरुद्भ्यश्च पर्जन्याय भगाय च ॥६९॥ ॥१३॥
पूष्णे धान्याय सीतायै शुनासीरमथोत्तरम् ।
हुत्वा तु पृथगेतासां यजेदेताश्च देवताः ॥७०॥
गन्धमाल्योपहारैश्च फललाजासुरासवैः ।
प्रवपणे प्रलवने खलसीतोपहारयोः ॥७१॥
एता एव यजेन्नित्यं देवता विधिना शुचिः ।
अमोघं कर्म भवति कृषिर्वर्धति सर्वदा ॥७२॥
क्षेत्रस्य पतिनेत्येतत्क्षैत्रपत्यं तृचं जपेत् ।
ईक्षेत्सूर्यं द्विजो नित्यं विन्दते क्षेत्रमुत्तमम् ॥७३॥
आखूत्करेषु चरुणा यजेदेतेन मूषिकान् ।
चित्र इद्राजेत्यनया स्तुत्वा चाखुपतिं सदा ॥७४॥ ॥१४॥
ब्राह्मणान्भोजयेदत्र कीनाशांश्चैव भोजयेत् ।
अप्रमत्तः शान्तिपरः स्वयमेव कृषिं व्रजेत् ॥७५॥
भूमिभङ्गो गवां हिंसा तृणकीटादिनाशनम् ।
एतेषु यत्कृतं पापं खलदानेन शुध्यति ॥७६॥
धान्यानां विंशकं भागं श्रोत्रियेभ्यो निवेदयेत् ।
विंशकस्य हि दानेन कृषिदोषात्प्रमुच्यते ॥७७॥
समुद्रादिति सूक्तेन यः सदा जुहुयाद्घृतम् ।
पूर्वोक्तेनैव कल्पेन संयतात्मा जितेन्द्रियः ॥७८॥
वि ज्योतिषेति ज्वलयेद्यत्रेच्छेज्जातवेदसि ।
तमग्निः सर्वतः पाति भद्रेण द्रविणेन च ॥७९॥
विश्वानि न इति द्वाभ्यामृग्भ्यां यो वह्निमर्चति ।
स तरत्यापदः सर्वा यशः प्राप्नोति चाक्षयम् ॥८०॥
हुत्वा वह्निरूपस्थेयः प्राणार्थं हव्यवाहनः ।

अग्ने त्वमिति सूक्तेन धनमायुश्च वाञ्छता ॥८१॥ ॥१५॥
यइच्छेद्विविधं वित्तं सत्त्वं चानुपमं महत् ।
उरो ष्ट इति सूक्तेन उपतिष्ठेच्छतक्रतुम् ॥८२॥
प्रजाकामो यजेन्नित्यं चरुणा देवपत्नयः ।
उपहृत्योपहारं च शेषं भुञ्जीत वाग्यतः ॥८३॥
उच्छिष्टं च प्रदातव्यं भार्यायै पुत्रमिच्छता ।
धेन्वाः सरूपवत्सायाः पयसा साधयेच्चरुम् ॥८४॥
अनुरूपां प्रजामाशु लभते नात्र संशयः ।
स्वस्त्यात्रेयं जपेन्नित्यं प्रातः प्रातर्द्विजः शुचिः ॥८५॥
एतत्स्वस्त्ययनं पुण्यं सर्वकल्मषनाशनम् ।
सुहृदं ज्ञातिनं चैव गच्छन्तमनुमन्त्रयेत् ॥८६॥ ॥१६॥
स्वस्ति पन्थामिति प्रोच्य स्वस्तिमान्व्रजतेऽध्वनि ।
विजिहीष्व वनस्पते तदिदं च्यावनं स्मृतम् ॥८७॥
यं च्यावयितुकामः स्याच्च्यावयेत्तमिदं जपन् ।
द्विषन्तं वा पदाक्रम्य भूमौ पांसुमयीं कृतिम् ॥८८॥
निष्पेक्ष्य* न्निव संग्रामाच्च्यवते नात्र संशयः ।
स्त्रियं गर्भप्रमूढां वा पाययेदनुमन्त्रितम् ॥८९॥
उदकं च्यावनेनैव गर्भोऽधः च्यवते सुखम् ।
अच्छा वदेतिसूक्तं तु वृष्टिकामः प्रयोजयेत् ॥९०॥
निराहारः क्लिन्नवासा अचिरेण प्रवर्षति ।
हुत्वायुतं वैतसीनां क्षीराक्तानां हुताशने ॥९१॥
महद्वर्षमवाप्नोति सूक्तेनाच्छावदेन हि ।
य इच्छेद्वरदां देवीं श्रियं नित्यं कुले स्थिताम् ॥९२॥ ॥१७॥
स शुचिः प्रयतो भूत्वा जुहुयादाज्यमन्वहम् ।
श्रियः पञ्चदशर्चं च श्रीकामः सततं जपेत् ॥९३॥
आवाहयेच्छ्रियं पद्मे पञ्चभिःकनकेऽपि वा ।
उपहारानुपहरेच्छुक्लान्भक्षान्पयो दधि ॥९४॥
स्थालीपाकं च शालीनां पयसा संप्रकल्पयेत् ।
चान्द्रायणकृतात्मा तु प्रपद्येत्प्रयतः श्रियै ॥९५॥
सर्वौषधीभिः फाण्टाभिः स्नात्वाद्भिः पावनैरपि ।
उपैतु मां देवसख इति राज्ञोऽभिषेचनी ॥९६॥
मनसः काममित्येषा पशुकामाभिषेचनी ।
कर्दमेनेति यः स्नायात्प्रजाकामः शुचिव्रतः ॥९७॥ ॥१८॥

अश्वपूर्णामिति स्नायाद्राज्यकामः शुचिव्रतः ।
रोहिते चर्मणि स्नायाद्‌ब्राह्मणस्तु यथाविधि ॥९८॥
राजा चर्मणि वैयाघ्रे क्षत्रियस्त्वथ रौरवे ।
बस्तचर्मणि वैश्यस्तु होमः कार्यस्त्वनन्तरम् ॥९९॥
चन्द्रामिति तु पद्मानि जुहुयात्सर्पिषा द्विजः ।
आदित्यवर्ण इत्यनया बिल्वहोमो विधीयते ॥१००॥
बिल्वेध्म एव वाग्निः स्यात्स्थालीश्च जुहुयाद्‌द्विजः ।
दशसाहस्त्रिको होमः श्रीकामः प्रथमो विधिः ॥१०१॥
हुत्वा तु प्रयुतं सम्यगनन्तां विन्दते श्रियम् ।
अयुतं शतकृत्वस्तु हुत्वा शुक्लानि सर्पिषा ॥१०२॥ ॥१९॥
अनन्तामव्यवच्छिन्नां शाश्वतीं विन्दते श्रियम् ।
अशक्तौ जप एवोक्तो दशसाहस्त्रिको वरः ॥१०३॥
जप्त्वा नु प्रयुतं सम्यगनन्तां विन्दते श्रियम् ।
अयुतं शतकृत्वस्तु जप्त्वा श्रियमुपाश्नुते ॥१०४॥
अप्स्वेव जुहुयान्नित्यं पद्मान्ययुतशो निशि ।
दृष्ट्वा श्रियं तूपरमेत्किलासत्वाद् बिभेत वै ॥१०५॥
बिल्वाशी बिल्वनिलयो जुह्वद्बिल्वानि सर्पिषा ।
एकविंशतिरात्रेण परां सिद्धिं नियच्छति ॥१०६॥
येन येन च कामेन जुहोति प्रयतः श्रियै ।
पद्मान्यथापि बिल्वानि स स कामः समृद्धचति ॥१०७॥ ॥२०॥
न जातु कृपणार्थाय श्रियमावाहयेत्क्वचित् ।
न यत्किञ्चनकामेन होमः कार्यः कथञ्चन ॥१०८॥
महद्वा प्रार्थ्यमानेन राज्यकामेन वा पुनः ।
वाचः परं प्रार्थयिता यत्नाद्युक्तःश्रियं यजेत् ॥१०९॥
अग्निरेत्विति सूक्तेन जुहुयादाज्यमन्वहम् ।
श्रोजस्विनीमवाप्नोति प्रजां धर्मवतीं शुभाम् ॥११०॥
अच्छा न इत्यृचा दीप्तमुपतिष्ठेद्विभावसुम् ।
प्रज्ञां प्राप्य जयेच्छत्रूंस्तरते दुरितानि च ॥१११॥
आ गाव इति सूक्तेन गोष्ठगा लोकमातरः ।
उपतिष्ठेद्व्रजन्तीश्च य इच्छेत्ताः सदाक्षयाः ॥११२॥
त्वामिद्धीति प्रगाथेन उपतिष्ठेच्छतक्रतुम् ।
मध्याह्ने संध्ययोश्चैव जपन्धनमवाप्नुयात् ॥११३॥ ॥२१॥
उपेति तिसृभी राज्ञो दुन्दुभीन् संस्पृशेद्रणे ।

ओजो बलमवाप्नोति शत्रूंश्चैव नियच्छति ॥११४॥
पाणिना तृणमादाय यज्ञायज्ञेति योऽभ्यसेत् ।
सोऽधीतस्यास्य सूक्तस्य फलं प्राप्नोति नातृणः ॥११५॥
सूक्तान्ते च तृणं त्वग्नाविरिणे वोदकेऽपि वा ।
निक्षिपेत्तत् प्रयत्नेन त्यक्त्वान्यत्र भयावहम् ॥११६॥
तृणपाणिर्जपन्सूक्तं रक्षोघ्नं दस्युभिर्वृतः ।
न भयं विन्दते किञ्चिद्रक्षोभ्योऽरिभ्य एव च ॥११७॥
गृहात्प्रपद्यमानस्तु पन्थानं धनकाम्यया ।
जपेत्सोऽध्वनि यत्नेन अपि पन्थामिति व्रजन् ॥११८॥
ये के च ज्मेत्यृचं त्वेतां ध्यायन्निशि दिवौकसः ।
अग्नौ हुत्वैतया चाज्यं दीर्घमायुरवाप्नुयात् ॥११९॥ ॥२२॥
वयमुत्वेति सूक्तं तु पौष्णं द्रविणवर्धनम् ।
नित्यं जपेच्छुचिर्भूत्वा धनं विन्दत्यभीप्सितम् ॥१२०॥
यस्य नष्टं भवेत्किञ्चिद्द्रव्यं गौर्द्विपदं धनम् ।
नश्येद्वाध्वनि यो मोहात्संपूषन् स जपेन्निशि ॥१२१॥
इयमित्येतवाद्यन्तं सूक्तं सारस्वतं द्विजः ।
नित्यं जपेच्छुचिर्भूत्वा वाग्मी भवति बुद्धिमान् ॥१२२॥
सं वामिति तु यत्सूक्तमष्टर्चं त्रैष्टुभं स्मृतम् ।
तज्जपन्प्रयतो नित्यमिष्टान्कामान्त्समश्नुते ॥१२३॥
योऽद्रिभित्तु यत्सूक्तं तत्सपत्ननिबर्हणम् ।
बृहस्पतिं नमस्कृत्वा सपत्नान्स्तृणुते बहून् ॥१२४॥ ॥२३॥
एनस्वी वाभिशस्तो वा कृत्वा वा कर्म गर्हितम् ।
सोमारौद्रं जपेत्सूक्तं कृत्स्नमेनो व्यपोहति ॥१२५॥
जुहुयाद्वा य एताभिर्ऋग्भिर्नित्यं धृतव्रतः ।
वारुणेभ्यो स पाशेभ्यो मुच्यते शं तथाप्नुयात् ॥१२६॥
जीमूतसूक्तस्य विधिं यथालिङ्गमवेक्ष्य वै ।
ऋग्भिः कर्माणि कुर्वीत रथाङ्गानां यथाविधि ॥१२७॥
संग्रामं तु प्रयातस्य राज्ञश्चैतत्प्रयोजयेत् ।
सर्वाण्यङ्गानि रथ्यांश्च सदश्वांश्चानुमन्त्रयेत् ॥१२८॥
यमेव देशं गच्छेत शत्रुं वाप्यनुमन्त्रितः ।
नाजित्वा विनिवर्तेत परं हि ब्रह्मणो बलम् ॥१२९॥ ॥२४॥
पुत्रानायुरथारोग्यं य इच्छेदव्ययं सुखम् ।
सोऽग्निं नर इति सूक्तेन जुहुयादाज्यमन्वहम् ॥१३०॥

प्राग्नयेऽथ त्रिभिःसूक्तैः संध्ययोर्जपमारभेत् ।
न रक्षोभ्यो भयं वेत्ति धनं प्राप्नोति चाक्षयम् ॥१३१॥
अभि त्वा यः प्रगाथेन नित्यमर्चति वज्रिणम् ।
स श्रियं विपूलां भुङक्ते प्राप्नोति च धनायुषी ॥१३२॥
शंवतीः शंनइन्द्राग्नीइत्येते सततं जपेत् ।
न रक्षोभ्यो न भूतेभ्यो व्याधिभ्यो वा भयं भवेत् ॥१३३॥
निवेष्टुकामो रोगार्तो भगसूक्तं सदाभ्यसेत् ।
निवेशं विन्दते क्षिप्रं रोगेभ्यश्च प्रमुच्यते ॥१३४॥ ॥२५॥
इमा इति जपेन्नित्यं रौद्रं सूक्तं द्विजः शुचिः ।
तज्जपन्प्रजया वित्तैः स्वयं चैव न रिष्यति ॥१३५॥
उत्तितीर्षुरपो यस्तु शङ्केत्स्रोत्यासमागमे ।
समुद्रज्येष्ठा इति जपेत्सूक्तमेतद्भयापहम् ॥१३६॥
आदित्यदैवते सूक्ते रिपुघ्ने रोगनाशने ।
जपेत्प्रातः शुचिर्भूत्वा रिपुरोगैः प्रमुच्यते ॥१३७॥
वास्तोष्पते प्रतीत्येतत्सूक्तं वास्तोष्पतं जपेत्
स्नातः कृत्वा वैश्वदेवं परं ब्रह्मेदमुच्यते ॥१३८॥
अमीवहेति सूक्तेन भूतानि स्वापयेन्निशि ।
न हि प्रस्वापनं किञ्चिदीदृशं विद्यते क्वचित् ॥१३९॥ ॥२६॥
सम्बाधे विषमे दुर्गे बद्धो वा निर्गतःक्वचित् ।
पलायन्वा गृहीतो वा तस्करैः स जपेदिदम् ॥१४०॥
अमीवहा विश्ववतीमुद्धृत्यान्याः प्रयोजयेत् ।
सूक्तमेतज्जपेत्सर्वमिति मन्येत शौनकः ॥१४१॥
त्रिरात्रं नियतोऽनश्नञ्छ्रपयेत्पायसं चरुम् ।
तेनाहुतिशतं पूर्णं जुहुयात्सर्पिषा द्विजः ॥१४२॥
समुद्दिश्य महादेवं त्र्यम्बकं त्र्यम्बकेत्यृचा ।
एतत्पर्वशतं कृत्वा जीवेदब्दशतं सुखी ॥१४३॥
तच्चक्षुरित्यृचा स्नात उपतिष्ठेद्दिवाकरम् ।
उद्यन्तं मध्यगं चैव दीर्घमायुर्जिजीविषुः ॥१४४॥ ॥२७॥
रात्र्या अपरकाले य उत्थाय प्रयतः शुचिः ।
व्युषा इत्युपतिष्ठेत षड्भिः सूक्तैः कृताञ्जलिः ॥१४५॥
प्राप्नुयात्स हिरण्यादि नानारूपं धनं बहु ।
गाअश्वान्पुरुषान्धान्यं स्त्रियो वासांस्यजाविकम्* ॥१४६॥
ध्रुवासु त्वासु क्षितिषु जपन्बद्धः प्रमुच्यते ।

तिष्ठन्नाप्सौ जपेदेनां विपाशः संप्रपद्यते ॥१४७॥
अहोरात्रं स्थितश्चैवमनश्नन्त्स्याद्विचेष्टितः ।
अयः पाशः स्फुटन्त्यस्य दारुपाशास्तथैव च ॥१४८॥
स्योनेति पृथिवीं देवीं प्रपद्येन्नियतः सदा ।
जपेदेनां च तत्रापि भूमिपाशात्प्रमुच्यते ॥१४९॥ ॥२८॥
यत्किञ्चित्पातकं कुर्यात्कर्मणा मनसा गिरा ।
यत्किञ्चेदं वरुणेति ऋचं जप्त्वा प्रमुच्यते ॥१५०॥
अगम्यागमने चैतत्प्रायश्चित्तं विधीयते ।
अन्यत्र गुरुतल्पाच्च तस्मात्पापात्प्रमुच्यते ॥१५१॥
द्वादशाहमभुञ्जानः स्वगोत्रागमने जपेत् ।
अर्धमासमभुञ्जानः सखिदारेषु संवसन् ॥१५२॥
इदमापः प्रवहत यत्किञ्चेदमृचं पुनः ।
इति चैता जपेदपः प्रविश्यैतेषु कर्मसु ॥१५३॥
इन्द्राविष्णू नमस्कृत्य जुहुयादाज्यमन्वहम् ।
सूक्ताभ्यां पर एताभ्यां यइच्छेद्भूतिमात्मनः ॥१५४॥ ॥२९॥
आस्यदघ्नं विगाह्याम्भः प्राङमुखः प्रयतः शुचिः ।
सूक्ताभ्यां तिस्र एताभ्यामुपतिष्ठेद्दिवाकरम् ॥१५५॥
अनश्नता तु जप्तव्यं वृष्टिकामेन यत्नतः ।
पञ्चरात्रे व्यतीते तु महद्वर्षमवाप्नुयात् ॥१५६॥
योऽरिभिः प्रतिपद्येत अभिशस्येत वा मृषा ।
उपोष्यैकं त्रिरात्रं स जुहुयादाज्यमन्वहम् ॥१५७॥
इन्द्रासोमेति सूक्तं तु जपेच्चैतच्छतावरम् ।
किञ्चिद्दद्याद्द्विजेभ्योऽन्ते स्तृणुते सर्वशात्रवान् ॥१५८॥
यस्य लुप्येद्व्रतं मोहाद्व्रात्यैर्वा संस्पृशेद्द्विजः ।
उपोष्याज्यं च जुहुयात्त्वमग्ने व्रतपा इति ॥१५९॥ ॥३०॥
प्र सम्राजमिति त्वेतज्जपन्नीक्षेद्दिवाकरम् ।
उद्यन्तमुपतिष्ठेत स्नात्वा स्नात्वा दिने दिने ॥१६०॥
अभियुक्तो भवेद्यस्तु विवदेद्वापि केनचित् ।
निर्जित्य सगणाञ्छत्रून्क्षिप्रं वादं पराजयेत् ॥१६१॥
शमग्निरग्निभिश्चेति प्रपद्येद्वायुभास्करौ ।
अग्निं प्रथमतः स्तुत्वा महत्कृच्छ्रात्प्रमुच्यते ॥१६२॥
नहीति यश्चतुष्केण स्नात्वा वै प्रातरुत्थितः ।
द्वौ मासावुपतिष्ठेत स त्रायति भयात्स्वयम् ॥१६३॥

तृचं जप्त्वाऽऽयदित्येतत्स्नात्वाभ्यर्च्य पुरंदरम् ।
प्राप्नुयान्मानसान्कामान्त्संपूज्य वसुरोचिषः ॥१६४॥
आद्यानि त्रीणि सूक्तानि पञ्च चाग्रे बृहान्निति ।
षट् तथान्त्यानि सूक्तानि अग्निं नर इतोति च ॥१६५॥
प्रकृतानीति चाध्यायं भोजनात्प्राक् पठेदिदम् ।
सर्वान्कामानवाप्नोति मुच्यते सर्वकिल्बिषैः ॥१६६॥ ॥३१॥
प्राग्भोजनमिदं ब्रह्म मानवानां महर्षिणाम् ।
पूर्वाह्णे जपतो नित्यमर्थसिद्धिः परा भवेत् ॥१६७॥
अग्निनेत्याश्विनं सूक्तं चतुर्विशकमन्वहम् ।
जपेत्प्रातः शुचिर्भूत्वा नासत्यावर्च्य सुव्रतः ॥१६८॥
स प्राप्नुयात्परामृद्धिं द्रविणं चोर्जमेव च ।
समिधेति जुहोत्यग्नौ सूक्तेन प्रत्यृचं घृतम् ॥१६९॥
स सिद्धिमतुलां प्राप्य समानां जीवते शतम् ।
द्विचत्वारिंशकेनेह सूक्तेनाऽऽघेति वज्रिणम् ॥१७०॥
सख्यं लब्ध्वा महेन्द्रेण सपत्नान्त्स्तृणुते बहून् ।
प्राश्नीयाज्जपतोऽन्नास्ति प्रश्नं कृत्वा प्रमाणतः ॥१७१॥ ॥३२॥
तस्मात्पूर्वाह्णिकोऽध्यायः स्मृतोऽयं रिप्रनाशनः ।
वाशं महीति च जप्त्वा प्राप्नोत्यारोग्यमेव च ॥१७२॥
दुःस्वप्नघ्नीः परा जप्त्वा प्रातः पापैः प्रमुच्यते ।
शं नो भवेति द्वाभ्यां तु भुक्त्वान्नं प्रयतः शुचिः ॥१७३॥
हृदयं पाणिना स्पृष्ट्वा ज्योग्जीवेदगदः सुखी ।
यतो भयं विजानीयात्तस्यां दिशि यतव्रतः ॥१७४॥
शुचौ देशेऽग्निमाधाय जुहुयादिन्द्रमर्च्य च ।
यत इत्याज्यमुत्पूतं षड्भिर्गन्धान्निवेद्य च ॥१७५॥
पायसं दधिमन्थं वाऽपूपान्वाप्युपहारयेत् ।
अहोरात्रमुपोष्यैकं तिलान्वा घृतमेव वा ॥१७६॥ ॥३३॥
उत्त्वा मन्दन्त्विति स्नातो हुत्वा शत्रून्प्रमापयेत् ।
बद्धो वाप्यवरुद्धो वा वाग्यतः प्रयतो जपेत् ॥१७७॥
त्यान्वित्यादित्यदैवत्यं सद्यो मुच्येत बन्धनात् ।
यद्द्यावेति जपेन्नित्यं प्रगाथं नियतः शुचिः ॥१७८॥
स कीर्तिमतुलां प्राप्य सर्वान्कामान्त्समश्नुते ।
त्वं नो अग्न इति सूक्तेन हुत्वा चर्याग्निं घृतेन तु ॥१७९॥
पालितो विभ्वतो दीप्त्या प्राप्नुयाद्वह्निना रयिम् ।

आ तू सूक्तेन सततं धनं याचेत्पुरंदरम् ॥१८०॥
प्रसमित्याणये तस्मै धनं यच्छति वृत्रहा ।
कन्या वारिति सूक्तं तु सततं नियतो जपेत् ॥१८१॥ ॥३४॥
त्वग्दोषिणीं तथालोम्नीं क्षिप्रं तस्मात्प्रमोचयेत् ।
यदद्य कच्चेत्युदिते रवौ स्तुत्वा पुरंदरम् ॥१८२॥
गृणन्नपोहते रिप्रं वश्यं वा कुरुते जगत् ।
यद्वागिति द्वृचेनैत्य गौरीं योऽर्चति सुव्रतः ॥१८३॥
तस्य नासंस्कृता वाणी मुखादुच्चरते क्वचित् ।
बण्महाँ इति दृष्ट्वार्कमुपतिष्ठेद् द्वृचं पठन् ॥१८४॥
ब्रुवन्नप्यनृतां वाणीं लिप्यते नानृतेन सः ।
पूर्णे चन्द्रमसि ज्योत्स्नामियं येत्यनुसेवयेत् ॥१८५॥
चन्द्रदृष्टिस्त्वनिमिषो वर्चस्वी दृष्टिमान्भवेत् ।
प्रजा हेति जपन्स्नात्वा न योनिं प्रतिजायते ॥१८६॥
मातेति गामुपस्पृश्य जपन् गास्तु समश्नुते ।
वचोविदमिति त्वेतां जपन् वाचं समश्नुते ॥१८७॥
पावमानं परं ह्येतन्नवमं मण्डलं जपेत् ।
स्नात्वा शुचिः शुचौ देशे सपवित्रः सकाञ्चनः ॥१८८॥
सपवित्रः सकाञ्चनः ॥ ॥३५॥

इत्यृग्विधाने द्वितीयोऽध्यायः ॥

## तृतीयोऽध्यायः

स्वादिष्ठयेति गायत्रीः पावमानीर्जपेद्द्विजः ।
पवित्राणां पवित्रं तु पावमानीर्ऋचो जपेत् ॥१॥
प्रयतोऽप्सु निमज्याशु सर्वपापैः प्रमुच्यते ।
एतासां कीर्तनं पुण्यं स्मरणं धारणं तथा ॥२॥
याथातथ्येन च ज्ञात्वा ब्रह्मलोकं समश्नुते ।
एतेषां तु यथोक्तानां गुणवद्यद्यदुत्तरम् ॥३॥
कीर्तनात्तु भवेत्पूतः स्मरणात्स्मरते परम् ।
धारणाद्ब्रह्मतामेति पूतात्मा विजितेन्द्रियः ॥४॥
याथातथ्येन च ज्ञात्वा ब्रह्मणो विन्दते पदम् ।
श्रावयेद्दैवताकृत्ये ब्राह्मणान्भुञ्जतोऽग्रतः ॥५॥ ॥१॥
प्रीणाति देवतां तच्च समर्धयति कर्म च ।
पित्र्ये पितॄन् प्रीणयन्ति श्राविताः प्रयतात्मना ॥६॥
कृत्वा दोषान्सुमहतोऽप्यपेयादीन् प्रपीय च ।
जप्त्वा तरत्समन्दीयं प्रविश्यापः त्र्यहाच्छुचिः ॥७॥
अक्षय्यं च भवेद्दत्तं पितृभ्यः परमं मधु ।
यः पावमानीरध्येति पूतात्मा विजितेन्द्रियः ॥८॥
तस्य कामदुधा भूत्वा उपतिष्ठन्ति धेनवः ।
आयुर्बलं यशो वित्तं प्रजां कीर्तिमनामयम् ॥९॥
स्वाध्यायपुण्यमतुलं पूतः प्राप्नोति चाक्षयम् ।
अशक्तस्तु जपेद्युक्तः त्रिंशद्वैखानसीर्ऋचः ॥१०॥
सप्तर्षिभिश्च याः प्रोक्ताः पवित्रस्य च याः पराः ।
ऋचां द्विषष्टिः प्रोक्तेयं पवस्वेत्यृषिसत्तमैः ॥११॥ ॥२॥
सर्वकल्मषनाशाय पावनाय शिवाय च ।
स्वादिष्ठयेति सूक्तानां सप्तषष्टिरिहोदिता ॥१२॥
दशोत्तराण्यृचां चैव पावमानीः शतानि षट् ।
एतज्जुह्वञ्जपँश्चैव घोरं मृत्युभयं जयेत् ॥१३॥
व्याधिभ्यः परिमोक्षं च लभते नात्र संशयः ।
प्रतिगृह्याप्रतिग्राह्यं भुक्त्वा चान्नं विगर्हितम् ॥१४॥
जपँस्तरत्समन्दीयं प्रविश्यापः त्र्यहाच्छुचिः ।

पावमानं परं ह्येतत्रपसामपनोदनम् ॥१५॥
प्राणानायम्य च ध्यायेदन्ते देवान्पितॄन्नृषीन् ।
उपोष्याज्यं च जुहुयादग्निं सोमं च पूजयेत् ॥१६॥
सरस्वतीं चार्चयेत पयोऽम्बुमधुसर्पिषा ।
आध्यात्मिकं पवित्रं ते सूक्तं जप्त्वाप्लुतः शुचिः ॥१७॥ ॥३॥
गतिमिष्टामवाप्नोति विन्दते चेह वृद्धयः ।
नानानमिति सूक्तानि अन्तकाले जपेत्सकृत् ॥१८॥
जप्त्वा चैव परं स्थानममृतत्वं च गच्छति ।
आपो हिष्ठेति नियतः प्रयुञ्जीत सदाद्विजः ॥१९॥
स्नानार्थं शुद्धिकामस्तु जपेत त्रिः समाहितः ।
अप्सुचैव निमज्जित्वा त्रिः पठेत्सुसमाहितः ॥२०॥
ब्रह्महा तु कपालेन खट्वाङ्गी चीरसंवृतः ।
चरेद्द्वादश वर्षाणि स्वकर्म परिकीर्तयन् ॥२१॥
अजपन्मनसैवैतदापोहिष्ठेति संस्मरेत् ।
ऊर्ध्वं तु पञ्चमाद्वर्षाज्जपेदेव सहस्रशः ॥२२॥
अपरस्तु त्रिसाहस्रो जपः स्यात्प्रत्यहं सदा ।
पूर्णे तु द्वादशे वर्षे ब्रह्महा विप्रमुच्यते ॥२३॥ ॥४॥
समेत्य ब्राह्मणा ब्रूयुरथ तं चरितव्रतम् ।
अचरितं भवेत्किञ्चिद् मिथ्यावादी पतेः पुनः ॥२४॥
दशावरान् दश परान् हन्यास्त्वमनृतं वदन् ।
ओं भो इति वदेद्विप्रैरनुज्ञातः शुचिर्व्रजेत् ॥२५॥
स्थालीपाकं च कुर्वीत सोऽग्नय व्रतचारिणे ।
एवं स मुच्यते पापात्सावित्रीं प्रतिपद्य च ॥२६॥
ब्रह्महा तु पुरा शक्रस्त्वाष्ट्रंहत्वा त्वृषिं प्रभुम् ।
सिन्धुद्वीपस्तमेताभिरभिषिच्य व्यमोचयत् ॥२७॥
ब्रह्मस्वं च गुरोर्द्रव्यं स्तेयं कृत्वा जपन्निमाः ।
अनेनैव विधानेन षड्भिर्वर्षैः प्रमुच्यते ॥२८॥ ॥५॥
ब्रह्महा च सुरापश्च नियमेन जपन्निमाः ।
अनेनैवोपचारेण ब्रह्मघ्न इव मुच्यते ॥२९॥
ब्राह्मणस्य रुषोद्यम्य जपेदेता निपात्य च ।
त्र्यहं निपात्योपवसेदेकाहमवगूर्य च ॥३०॥
शोणितं तु प्रहारेण उत्पाद्य स कथञ्चन ।
त्रिरात्रमेवोपवसेज्जपेदेताः प्रसाद्य तम् ॥३१॥

प्रातरुत्थाय सततं कुर्यान्मार्जनमात्मनः ।
रात्रौ कृतस्य पापस्य अविज्ञातस्य निष्कृतिः ॥३२॥
सायं च नित्यमेताभिः कुर्यान्मार्जनमात्मनः ।
दिवा कृतस्य पापस्य अविज्ञातस्य निष्कृतिः ॥३३॥ ॥६॥
उपतिष्ठेत राजानं यमं सूक्तेन वै द्विजः ।
स्थालीपाकं च कुर्वीत पक्षयोर्यमदैवतम् ॥३४॥
अष्टम्यां च चतुर्दश्यां यजेत हविषा यमम् ।
परेयिवांसमित्येतत्सूक्तमत्र प्रयोजयेत् ॥३५॥
पुरायुषः प्रमीयेत न जातु स कथञ्चन ।
प्रीयतेऽस्य यमो राजा स्मृतिं चान्ते प्रयच्छति ॥३६॥
धर्मराजाय स्वाहेति मन्त्रान्ते जुहुयाद्धविः ।
वैशाख्यां पौर्णमास्यां तु कर्म नित्यं प्रयोजयेत् ॥३७॥
अयने पर्वसु स्नात्वा यः प्रदद्यात्तिलोदकम् ।
यमाय सगणायैव तद्भयं न स विन्दति ॥३८॥
मृत्युमेव प्रपद्येत परं मृत्यो जपन्द्विजः ।
नक्तभोजी मिताहारः परिसंवत्सरं सदा ॥३९॥ ॥७॥
नैनं पुरायुषो मृत्युर्नयते ससुतप्रजम् ।
फलाहारो जयेन्मृत्युं त्रिभिर्वर्षैर्मिताशनः ॥४०॥
षष्ठे काले तु भुञ्जीत फलं मूलमथापि वा ।
स्थानासनाभ्यां विहरेदुदके शिशिरे वसेत् ॥४१॥
ग्रीष्मे पञ्चतपास्तु स्याद्वर्षास्वभ्रावकाशकः ।
एवं युक्तो जयेन्मृत्युं रोगेभ्यश्च प्रमुच्यते ॥४२॥
भ्रातुर्भार्यामपुत्रस्य सन्तानार्थं मृते पतौ ।
देवरोऽन्वारुरुक्षन्तीमुदोर्ष्वेति निवर्तयेत ॥४३॥
ऋतुकाले तु संप्राप्ते घृताभ्यक्तोऽथ वाग्यतः ।
एकमुत्पादयेत्पुत्रं न द्वितीयं कथञ्चन ॥४४॥
दशाक्षरं तु शान्त्यर्थं भद्रं न इति संस्मरेत् ।
नित्यं जपेच्छुचिर्भूत्वा मानसं विन्दते सुखम् ॥४५॥ ॥८॥
फलाहारो भवेन्मासं मासं चापः पिबेत्ततः ।
वायुभक्षो भवेन्मासं जपन्नेतत्सहस्रशः ॥४६॥
मनसैवास्य सिध्यन्ति सर्वकामाः समीहिताः ।
दिव्यान्पश्यति गन्धर्वान्सिद्धान्पश्यति चारणान् ॥४७॥
अन्तर्धानं व्रजत्यस्माल्लोकादाकाशगो भवेत् ।

दूरात्पश्यति दूराच्च शृणोति परमेष्ठिवत् ॥४८॥
प्र देवत्रेति नियतो जपेत मरुधन्वसु ।
प्राणान्तिके भये प्राप्ते क्षिप्रमम्भः स विन्दति ॥४९॥
वैभीतकाँस्तु त्रीनक्षान्गन्धैः समभिवासयेत् ।
पुष्पैरवकिरेच्चैनान्स्थापयित्वा विहायसि ॥५०॥ ॥९॥
संहृत्य पादौ तां रात्रीं तिष्ठन्नक्षस्तुतिं जपेत् ।
प्रा वेपा मा ऋचं त्वेतां मनसैव जपेन्निशि ॥५१॥
व्युष्टायामुदिते सूर्ये जपन्नादेवनं व्रजेत् ।
एतामेव जपेन्नित्यं जयत्यन्यैर्न जीयते ॥५२॥
यमेव जेतुमिच्छेत स्पृष्ट्वा मूर्धनि तं जपेत् ।
सूक्तशेषं जयत्यन्याञ्जीयते न स केनचित् ॥५३॥
अबुध्रमुषासानक्तेत्येते स्वस्त्ययने जपेत् ।
नमो मित्रस्य वरुणस्य चक्षस इति नित्यशः ॥५४॥
अस्यैव चोत्तमर्गेका ययैनोभ्यः प्रमुच्यते ।
तयाऽऽज्यं जुहुयान्नित्यमेनोभ्यो विप्रमुच्यते ॥५५॥ ॥१०॥
दिवस्परीति सूक्तं तु जपेच्छ्रद्धासमन्वितः ।
सर्वत्र लभते श्रद्धां श्रद्धाकामः समाहितः ॥५६॥
मा प्र गामेति च जपेत्स मूढो गहने पथि ।
स्वस्तिमानेति पन्थानं विन्दते च परं सुखम् ॥५७॥
क्षीणायुरिति मन्येत यं कञ्चित्सुहृदं प्रियम् ।
यत्ते यममिति स्नातस्तस्य मूर्धानमालभेत् ॥५८॥
सहस्रकृत्वः पञ्चाहं जपेदायुर्लभेत सः ।
घृतेन सिन्धुद्वीपस्य सूक्तेनैनं प्रलेपयेत् ॥५९॥
संविशञ्छयने नित्यमेतं मन्त्रं जपेत वै ।
पुत्रान्भार्यां प्रियं चान्यमात्मानं संस्पृशेत्ततः ॥६०॥ ॥११॥
जीवावृत्तिं प्रयुञ्जीत नित्यमेतां घृतेन तु ।
श्रोतांस्यभ्यज्य सर्वाणि सुखी भवति विज्वरः ॥६१॥
इदमित्थेति मन्त्रोऽयं सहस्रसनिरुच्यते ।
अर्धमासं हविष्यान्नमर्धमासं पयः पिबेत् ॥६२॥
उपोष्य चापरं पक्षमरण्ये स्थण्डिले शुचौ ।
औदुम्बरेध्मं प्रज्वाल्य जुहुयात्पावके घृतम् ॥६३॥
स्रुक्स्रुवौ चमसश्चैव सर्वमौदुम्बरं भवेत् ।
हुत्वाहुतिसहस्रं तु तेन कामेन युज्यते ॥६४॥

अमोघमेव कर्मैतज्जानीयात्सिद्धिमेव तु ।
व्यर्थमप्यर्धमेवैतत्फलस्यास्य प्रयच्छति ॥६५॥ ॥१२॥
चतुष्पथे चान्नकाम आदित्याभिमुखो घृतम् ।
जुहुयाद्धनकामस्तु सहस्रं भोजयेद्द्विजान् ॥६६॥
पशुकामो जपेद्गोष्ठे जुहयाद्वाप्युपोषितः ।
विधिनानेन नियतः सहस्रं विन्दते पशून् ॥६७॥
लोहलोहितहेमानां कारयेत्त्रिवृतं मणिम् ।
सहस्रं समिधां चैव संपाताभिहुत्तु भवेत् ॥६८॥
कृत्वा सहस्रसंपातं शिरसा धारयेत्तु तम् ।
पाणिना वा शुचिर्भूत्वा सहस्रानुचरो भवेत् ॥६९॥
परावतः स्वस्त्ययनं स्नाग़तकस्य विधीयते ।
स्वर्गकामश्च तं नित्यं जपेत नियतव्रत : ॥७०॥ ॥१३॥
बृहस्पते प्रथममिति नित्यं ज्ञानस्तुतिं जपेत् ।
ज्ञानवान्भवति श्रीमानानन्तां विन्दते श्रियम् ॥७१॥
अलक्ष्मीनाशनार्थं तु पयोभक्षो भवेद्द्विजः ।
वयः सुपर्णा इत्येतां जपन्वै विन्दते श्रियम् ॥७२॥
तमसा प्रावृतो यस्तु मन्येतात्मानमात्मनि ।
अश्रिया वाप्यथाविष्टो जपन्नेतां प्रमुच्यते ॥७३॥
अक्षिणी प्रातरुत्थाय विमृजीतैतया सदा ।
चक्षुष्मान्भवति श्रीमानलक्ष्मीं च प्रबाधते ॥७४॥
न तं विदाथेत्येतां तु जपन्विप्रः समाहितः ।
विहाय कल्मषं सर्वं ब्रह्माभ्येति सनातनम् ॥७५॥
अनया पर्वसु स्नात्वा यः प्रदद्यात्तिलोदकम् ।
यमाय सगणायैव तद्भूयं न स विन्दति ॥७६॥
यस्ते मन्यो इति सदा सपत्नघ्ने त्विमे जपेत् ।
घृतेनाभिहुतं द्वाभ्यां धारयेदायसं मणिम् ॥७७॥ ॥१४॥
जुहुयादायसं शङ्कुमाभ्यामेव चतुर्दशीम् ।
खादिरेध्मसमिद्धेऽग्नौ सपत्नान्प्रतिबाधते ॥७८॥
यथा हि परमं ब्रह्म गुह्यं पावनमद्भु तम् ।
तथा संवननं हृद्यं नह्यस्माद्विद्यते परम् ॥७९॥
उपोष्य द्वादशाहानि जपन्नेतमृषिं सदा ।
तन्मनाः प्रयतः स स्यान्निरह्नोऽभ्युपयन्नपः* ॥८०॥
अन्ते तु द्वादशाहस्य शुचौ देशे समाहितः ।

पुंसः प्रतिकृतिं कुर्याद्भूमौ पांसुमयीं तथा ॥८१॥
तस्या हृदयदेशं तु समाक्रम्य जपेदृषिम् ।
अमोघं कर्मजानीयावहोरात्रे गते सति ॥८२॥ ॥१५॥
त्र्यहेण धनिनं वैश्यं चतूरात्रेण क्षत्रियम् ।
राजानं पञ्चरात्रेण षड्रात्रेण द्विजोत्तमम् ॥८३॥
तपस्विनं सप्तरात्राज्जयेद्‌यु ञ्जीत चैव तम् ।
अपि वोपोषितः स्नातो जपेदेतत्सदा स्थितः ॥८४॥
यइच्छेदात्मनः कर्तुं हीनं तु परिवर्जयेत् ।
सहस्रसंपातहुतं बिल्वानां चूर्णमावयेत् ॥८५॥
उदपाने वशं नेतुं तं जनं क्षिप्रमानयेत् ।
मातर्यात्मनि पुत्रेषु पितृभ्रातृसुहृत्सु च ॥८६॥
हृद्यमेतत्प्रयुञ्जीत शिरसा धारयेद्गुरुम् ।
सुमित्रं तु परिष्वज्य मूर्धन्याघ्राय चात्मजम् ॥८७॥ ॥१६॥
हृद्यमेतत्प्रयुञ्जीत शान्त्यर्थाय सुखाय च ।
असंसिद्धे संवनने पांसुप्रतिकृतिं पथि ॥८८॥
प्रज्वाल्य जुहुयादग्निं घृतेन ब्राह्मणो यदि ।
क्षत्रियस्य तु तैलेन सार्षपेण विशामपि ॥८९॥
आयसीं वा प्रतिकृतिमग्निमध्ये निधापयेत् ।
तां च प्रज्वलितां मत्वा जुहुयात्तन्मनाः शुचिः ॥९०॥
उग्रेण मनसा हन्यात्क्रुद्धश्च जुहुयाद्घृतम् ।
यथा यथा प्रज्वलिते हूयते जातवेदसि ॥९१॥
दीप्ता* प्रतिकृति* विप्रस्तथा स वशमेष्यति ।
श्मशानदग्धपांसूनां कुयाद्वेदिं विलक्षणाम् ॥९२॥ ॥१७॥
वैभीतकेध्मे ज्वलिते लोहप्रतिकृतिं न्यसेत् ।
अर्धरात्रे स्थिते तैलं सार्षपं लवणान्वितम् ॥९३॥
तत्र शरमयं कुयात्प्रस्तरं प्रतिलोमतः ।
त्रिषु शङ्कुषु चासीनो जुहुयादुग्रदर्शनः ॥९४॥
मुक्तकेशो वधं प्रेप्सुरचिरेण प्रसाधयेत् ।
अथवाभिचरेदेवं जुहुयादात्मशोणितम् ॥९५॥
वशं नयति राजानं क्षिप्रं जनपदं पुरम् ।
पुष्टिकर्मापि कर्तव्यं हृद्येनोक्तं यतात्मना ॥९६॥
अनागसि न कुर्वीत ब्राह्मणो वधसंयुतम् ।
सरूपवत्सायाश्च गोः पयसा साधयेच्चरुम् ॥९७॥ ॥१८॥

सहस्रसंपातहुतं पाययेद्वत्समग्रजम् ।
सहस्रानुचरो वत्सः स स्याद्गार्गैर्विवर्जितः ।।९८।।
गाश्चैव पाययेत्ताश्च भवन्ति विगतज्वराः ।
पुत्राँश्च प्राशयेन्नित्यं प्रियानन्यांश्च सज्जनान् ।।९९।।
निरामयाश्च स्निग्धाश्च भवन्ति विगतज्वराः ।
स्त्रियं चेदभिमन्येत तस्याः संवननं महत् ।।१००।।
व्रीहीणां नखभिन्नानां तण्डुलान्सूक्ष्मचूर्णितान् ।
सहस्रसंपातहुतान्स्वेदयेत्कुशलोऽग्निना ।।१०१।।
तेन प्रतिकृतिं कुर्यात्तां ध्यात्वा मनसा स्त्रियम् ।
अक्तां सर्षपतैलेन जुहुयादङ्गशश्च ताम् ।।१०२।। ।।१९।।
पादौ प्रथमतश्छिन्द्यात्फडित्यग्नौ निधापयेत् ।
अथ जङ्घे जानुनि च ऊरू बाहू ततः शिरः ।।१०३।।
छित्वा हृदयदेशं तु हृदये स्वे निवेशयेत् ।
जपन्नेतमृषिं विप्रः स्त्री वशं साधिगच्छति ।।१०४।।
नैतत्परिगृहीतासु न साध्वीषु कथञ्चन ।
न धर्मव्रतशीलासु कुर्वीत द्विजसत्तमः ।।१०५।।
कामं परिगृहीतासु हीनवर्णासु यश्चरेत् ।
पतिमस्या गुणीकुर्यात्पूर्वं पश्चात्तु तां स्त्रियम् ।।१०६।।
भुक्त्वा वा पायसं सद्यः छर्दयित्वा निधापयेत् ।
तच्चूर्णं कृष्णजायायै देयं संवननं स्मृतम् ।।१०७।। ।।२०।।
महावृक्षफलान्येवमयुग्मान्यभिमन्त्रयेत् ।
तेषां युग्मानि भुञ्जीत स्वयमर्धानि शेषयेत् ।।१०८।।
तानि दद्याद्यमिच्छेत्तु वशीकर्तुं जपन्नृषिम् ।
सुहृद्भूत्वाऽसुहृद्यस्य देयं संवननं स्मृतम् ।।१०९।।
एकैकमभिरूपं तु हृद्यसूक्ताद्यतः पुनः ।
कर्माणि त्वभिरूपाणि कुर्याद्यस्तुयथेच्छति ।।११०।।
पराकदासस्य विधिं हृद्येनोक्तं विदुर्बुधाः ।
स्त्रीणां संवननं चैतत्पुंसामपि विधीयते ।।१११।।
द्वेष्यं तु ज्ञातिनामेव जपेच्चैव सदा युधि ।
खादिरं कारयेच्छङ्कुं हृदि तं संनिवेशयेत् ।।११२।। ।।२१।।
कृत्वा प्रतिकृतिं पूर्वं पांसुभिर्वाथवा तुषैः ।
इषुमप्यनुमन्त्र्यैव संग्रामं संप्रकल्पयेत् ।।११३।।
रिपुघ्नमेतज्जानीयात्प्रयुक्तमपराजितम् ।

परांकदासद्द्वेष्यार्थं हृद्यं संवननं स्मृतम् ॥११४॥
चिन्तयन्मनसाप्येते सूक्ते सिद्धिं नियच्छति ।
सूर्यायै भाववृत्तं तु श्रावयेत्कन्यकां पिता ॥११५॥
अनुरूपं सुसदृशं भर्तारं तेन विन्दति ।
इमामिति जपेत्कन्या नाभिमालभ्य नित्यशः ॥११६॥
एवमेव जपेद्भर्ता ततो दीर्घायुषौ तु तौ ।
स्नापयेदभिरूपैश्च भ्राता कन्यां पितापि वा ॥११७॥ ॥२२॥
दशपुत्रवती भवेन्न च भर्त्रा वियुज्यते ।
सम्राज्ञीति जपेन्मूर्ध्नि कन्यामालभ्य नित्यशः ॥११८॥
श्वश्रूश्वशुरदेवरैर्ननान्द्रा चापि पूज्यते ।
इन्द्राण्याकृतसंवादं स्नाने सूक्तं प्रयोजयेत् ॥११९॥
नववर्गोत्तमयुतं पतिसौभाग्यपुत्रदम् ।
जलपुष्पोत्करयुते चित्रकुम्भसमावृते ॥१२०॥
कर्तव्योऽत्र तथा यागः सोमगन्धर्ववह्निनाम् ।
भगायाप्सरसां चैव यक्षाधिपतयेऽपि च ॥१२१॥
इन्द्राण्यै देवपत्नीनां रतिप्रद्युम्नयोस्तथा ।
नदीसलिलसंपूर्णैः पञ्चगव्यसमावृतैः ॥१२२॥ ॥२३॥
हुत्वाग्निं स्नापयेत्कन्यां स्थितां देशे तु दक्षिणे ।
प्रियङ्गुवटनागानां कषायोद्घृष्टकेसरम् ॥१२३॥
संपाताभिहुतं कृत्वा सर्वौषधिसमन्वितम् ।
अभिमन्त्र्य हि सूक्तान्ते नवभिस्तु विहीति वै ॥१२४॥
स्थेयाभिरद्भिः पूर्णेन अभिषिञ्चेदुपोषिताम् ।
यः पतिघ्न्यः स्त्रियस्तन्वः* शाम्यन्ते तास्त्वनेन वै ॥१२५॥
स्नापयेदाहनस्याभिर्विद्याद्यां विप्रत्रा* जिनीम् ।
सूक्तावुपोद्धरेदेनं न सेश इति तु द्वृचम् ॥१२६॥
उपदिष्टोऽयमेकेषां पुंसः कर्मणि पौरुषे ।
रक्षोहणं वाजिनमित्येतद्रक्षोहणं जपेत् ॥१२७॥ ॥२४॥
अग्निं प्रज्वाल्य चैतेन उपतिष्ठेत नित्यशः ।
आज्याहुतीश्च जुहुयात्तेन रक्षांसि बाधते ॥१२८॥
एतद्रक्षोहणं शान्तिः परमैषा प्रकीर्तिता ।
हविष्पान्तीयमित्येतत्सूक्तमत्र प्रयोजयेत् ॥१२९॥
गर्हिताञ्चाधयोगे च हविष्पान्तीयमभ्यसेत् ।
पवित्रं परमं ह्येतद्ध्यातव्यं चाभीक्ष्णशः ॥१३०॥

आदित्ये दृष्टिमास्थाय षण्मासान्नियतोऽभ्यसेत् ।
देवयानं स पन्थानं पश्यत्यादित्यमण्डले ॥१३१॥
विद्या वैश्वानरी चास्य स्वकायस्था प्रकाशते ।
हविष्पान्तीयमभ्यस्य सर्वपापैः प्रमुच्यते ॥१३२॥
इन्द्रं स्तवेति सूक्तं तु जपेच्छत्रुनिबर्हणम् ।
पवित्राणां पवित्रं तु गुह्यं पावनमद्भुतम् ॥१३३॥ ॥२५॥
शुक्लपक्षे शुभे वारे सुनक्षत्रे सुगोचरे ।
द्वादश्यां पुत्रकामाय चरुं कुर्वीत वैष्णवम् ॥१३४॥
दंपत्योरुपवासः स्यादेकादश्यां सुरालये ।
ऋग्भिः षोडशभिः सम्यगर्चयित्वा जनार्दनम् ॥१३५॥
चरुं पुरुषसूक्तेन श्रपयेत्पुत्रकाम्यया ।
प्राप्नुयाद्वैष्णवं पुत्रमचिरात्सन्ततिक्षमम् ॥१३६॥
द्वादश द्वादशीः सम्यक्पयसा निवर्पेच्चरुम् ।
यः करोति सहस्रं स्याद्याति विष्णोः परं पदम् ॥१३७॥
हुत्वाग्निं विधिवत्सम्यगृग्भिः षोडशभिर्बुधः ।
कृताञ्जलिपुटो भूत्वा स्तवं ताभिः प्रयोजयेत् ॥१३८॥ ॥२६॥
केशवं मार्गशीर्षे तु पौषे नारायणं स्मृतम् ।
माधवं माघमासे तु गोविन्दं फाल्गुने तथा ॥१३९॥
चैत्रे चैव तथा विष्णुं वैशाखे मधुसूदनम् ।
ज्येष्ठे त्रिविक्रमं विद्यादाषाढे वामनं विदुः ॥१४०॥
श्रावणे श्रीधरं विद्याद्धृषीकेशं ततः परे ।
आश्विने पद्मनाभं तु दामोदरं च कार्तिके ॥१४१॥
द्वादशैतानि नामानि ऋष्यशृङ्गोऽब्रवीन्मुनिः ।
पूजयेन्मासनामभिः सर्वान्कामान्त्समश्नुते ॥१४२॥
आयुष्मन्तं सुतं सूते यशो मेधा समन्वितम् ।
धनवन्तं प्रजावन्तं धार्मिकं सात्त्विकं तथा ॥१४३॥ ॥२७॥
समिधोऽश्वत्थवृक्षस्य हुत्वाग्निं जुहुयात्पुनः ।
उपस्थानं हुताशस्य ध्यात्वार्च्य मधुसूदनम् ॥१४४॥
हविर्होमं ततः कुर्यात्प्रत्यृचं वाग्यतः शुचिः ।
सूक्तेन जुहुयादाज्यमादावन्ते च पूर्ववत् ॥१४५॥
हविःशेषं नमस्कृत्वा नारी नारायणं पतिम् ।
भक्षयित्वा हविःशेषं लब्धाशीः संविशेत्क्षपाम् ॥१४६॥
ततस्तु कर्म कृत्वेदं कर्तव्यं द्विजतर्पणम् ।

द्वितीयां स्त्रीं निवर्तेत यावद्गर्भं न विन्दति ॥१४७॥
अपुत्रा मृतपुत्रा वा या च कन्यां प्रसूयते ।
क्षिप्रं सा जनयेत्पुत्रमृष्यशृङ्गो यथाब्रवीत् ॥१४८॥ ॥२८॥
अर्चनं संप्रवक्ष्यामि विष्णोरमिततेजसः ।
यत्कृत्वा मुनयः सर्वे ब्रह्मनिर्वाणमाप्नुयुः ॥१४९॥
अप्स्वग्नौ हृदये सूर्ये स्थण्डिले प्रतिमासु च ।
षट्स्वेतेषु हरेः सम्यगर्चनं मुनिभिः स्मृतम् ॥१५०॥
अग्नौ क्रियावतां देवो दिवि देवो मनीषिणाम् ।
प्रतिमास्वल्पबुद्धीनां योगिनां हृदये हरिः ॥१५१॥
आपो ह्यायतनं तस्य तस्मात्तासु सदा हरिः ।
तस्य सर्वगतत्वाच्च स्थण्डिले भावितात्मनाम् ॥१५२॥
दद्यात्पुरुषसूक्तेन यः पुष्पाण्यप एव वा ।
अर्चितं स्याज्जगदिदं तेन सर्वं चराचरम् ॥१५३॥
आनुष्टुभस्य सूक्तस्य त्रिष्टुबन्तस्य देवता ।
पुरुषो यो जगद्बीजमृषिर्नारायणः स्मृतः ॥१५४॥ ॥२९॥
नारायण महाबाहो शृणुष्वैकमनाः प्रभो ।
वक्ष्ये पुरुषसूक्तस्य विधानं त्वर्चनं प्रति ॥१५५॥
अग्निकार्यं जपविधिं स्तोत्रं चैव सदात्मकम् ।
स्नात्वा यथोक्तविधिना प्राङ्मुखः शुद्धमानसः ॥१५६॥
प्रथमां विन्यसेद्वामे द्वितीयां दक्षिणे करे ।
तृतीयां वामपादे तु चतुर्थीं दक्षिणे न्यसेत् ॥१५७॥
पञ्चमीं वामजानुनि षष्ठिं वै दक्षिणे न्यसेत् ।
सप्तमीं वामकट्यां तु अष्टमीं दक्षिणे कटौ ॥१५८॥
नवमीं नाभिमध्ये तु दशमीं हृदये न्यसेत् ।
एकादशीं कण्ठदेशे द्वादशीं वामबाहुके ॥१५९॥
त्रयोदशीं दक्षिणे च आस्ये चैव चतुर्दशीम् ।
अक्ष्णोः पञ्चदशीं चैव षोडशीं मूर्ध्नि विन्यसेत् ॥१६०॥ ॥३०॥
एवं न्यासविधिं कृत्वा पश्चात्पूजां समारभेत् ।
यथा देहे तथा देवे न्यासं कृत्वा विधानतः ॥१६१॥
आद्ययावाहयेद्देवमृचा तु पुरुषोत्तमम् ।
द्वितीययासनं दद्यात्पाद्यं चैव तृतीयया ॥१६२॥
अर्घ्यं चतुर्थ्या दातव्यं पञ्चम्याचमनीयकम् ।
षष्ठ्या स्नानं प्रकुर्वीत सप्तम्या वस्त्रमेव च ॥१६३॥

यज्ञोपवीतमष्टम्या नवम्या चानुलेपनम् ।
पुष्पं दशम्या दातव्यमेकादश्या तु धूपकम् ।।१६४।।
द्वादश्या दीपकं दद्यात्त्रयोदश्या निवेदनम् ।
चतुर्दश्या नमस्कारं पञ्चदश्या प्रदक्षिणम् ।।१६५।।
स्नाने वस्त्रे च नैवेद्ये दद्यादाचमनीयकम् ।
दक्षिणां तु यथाशक्त्या षोडश्या तु प्रदापयेत् ।।१६६।। ।।३१।।
ततः प्रदक्षिणां कृत्वा जपं कुर्यात्समाहितः ।
यथाशक्ति जपित्वा तु सूक्तं तस्य निवेदयेत् ।।१६७।।
देवस्य दक्षिणे पार्श्वे कुण्डं स्थण्डिलमेव वा ।
कारयेत्प्रथमेनैव द्वितीयेन तु प्रोक्षणम् ।।१६८।।
तृतीयेनाग्निमादध्याच्चतुर्थेन समिन्धनम् ।
पञ्चमेनाज्यश्रपणं चरोश्च श्रपणं तथा ।।१६९।।
षष्ठेनैवाग्निमध्ये तु कल्पयेत्पद्मासनम् ।
चिन्तयेद्देवदेवेशं कालानलसमप्रथम् ।।१७०।।
ततो गन्धं च पुष्पं च धूपदीपनिवेदनम् ।
अनुज्ञाप्य ततःकुर्यात्सप्तम्यादि यथाक्रमम् ।।१७१।।
समिधस्तावतीः पूर्वं जुहुयादभिघारिताः ।
ततो घृतेन जुहुयाच्चरुणा च ततः पुनः ।।१७२।।
एवं हुत्वा ततश्चैव अनुज्ञाप्य यथाक्रमम् ।
अग्नेर्भगवतस्तस्य समीपे स्तोत्रमुच्चरेत् ।।१७३।। ।।३२।।
जितं ते पुण्डरीकाक्ष नमस्ते विश्वभावन ।
नमस्तेऽस्तु हृषीकेश महापुरुषपूर्वज ।।१७४।।
देवानां दानवानां च सामान्यमधिदैवतम् ।
सर्वदा चरणद्वन्द्वं व्रजामि शरणं तव ।।१७५।।
एकस्त्वमसि लोकस्य स्रष्टा संहारकस्तथा ।
अव्यक्तश्चानुमन्ता च गुणमायासमावृतः ।।१७६।।
संसारसागरं घोरमनन्तं क्लेशभाजनम् ।
त्वामेव शरणं प्राप्य निस्तरन्ति मनीषिणः ।।१७७।।
न ते रूपं न चाकारो नायुधानि न चास्पदम् ।
तथापि पुरुषाकारो भक्तानां त्वं प्रकाशसे ।।१७८।।
नैव किञ्चित्परोक्षं ते प्रत्यक्षोऽसि न कस्यचित् ।
नैव किञ्चिदसाध्यं ते न च साध्योऽसि कस्यचित् ।।१७९।। ।।३३।।
कार्याणां कारणं पूर्वं वचसां वाच्यमुत्तमम् ।

योगिनां परमासिद्धिः परमं ते पदं विदुः ॥१८०॥
अहं भीतोऽस्मि देवेश संसारेऽस्मिन्महाभये ।
त्राहि मां पुण्डरीकाक्ष न जाने परमं पदम् ॥१८१॥
कालेष्वपि च सर्वेषु दिक्षु सर्वासु चाच्युत।
शरीरे च गतश्चासि वर्तते मे महद्भयम् ॥१८२॥
त्वत्पादकमलादन्यन्न मे जन्मान्तरेष्वपि ।
विज्ञानं यदिदं प्राप्य यदिदं स्थानमर्जितम् ॥१८३॥
जन्मान्तरेऽपि मे देव मा भूदस्य परिक्षयः ।
दुर्गतावपि जातस्य त्वद्गतो मे मनोरथः ॥१८४॥
यदि नाशं न विन्देत तावतास्मि कृती सदा ।
कामये विष्णुपादौ तु सर्वजन्मसु केवलम् ॥१८५॥ ॥३४॥
पुरुषस्य हरेः सूक्तं स्वर्ग्यं धन्यं यशस्करम् ।
आत्मज्ञानमिदं पुण्यं योगज्ञानमिदं परम् ॥१८६॥
फलाहारो भवेन्मासं पश्यत्यात्मानमात्मनि ।
फलानि भुक्त्वोपवसेन्मासमद्भिश्च वर्तयेत् ॥१८७॥
अरण्ये निवसेन्नित्यं जपन्नेतमृषिं सदा ।
त्रिस्त्रिषवणकालेषु स्नायादप्सु समाहितः ॥१८८॥
आदित्यमुपतिष्ठेत सूक्तेनानेन नित्यशः ।
आज्याहुतोरनेनैव हुत्वैतं चिन्तयेदृषिम् ॥१८९॥
ऊर्ध्वं मासात्फलाहारस्त्रिभिर्वर्षैर्जयेद्दिवम् ।
तद्भक्तस्तन्मना युक्तो दशवर्षाण्यनन्यभाक् ॥१९०॥
साक्षात्पश्यति तं देवं नारायणमनामयम् ।
ग्राह्यमत्यन्तयत्नेन स्रष्टारं जगतोऽव्ययम् ॥१९१॥ ॥३५॥
गृहस्थधर्मे वर्तेत न्यायक्लृप्तः शुचिव्रतः ।
एतं देवं चिन्तयेत नारायणमनामयम् ॥१९२॥
अर्धरात्रे त्यक्तनिद्र उत्थाय शुचिवाग्यतः ।
संप्रसुप्तेषु भूतेषु योगं युञ्जीत योगवित् ॥१९३॥
ऋज्वासीनः समे देशे निवाते शब्दवर्जिते ।
सव्यं पादं दक्षिणस्य जानुनि श्लेषयेत्ततः ॥१९४॥
संहृत्य दक्षिणं पादं सव्ये जानुनि यच्छति ।
ब्रह्माञ्जलिकृतः स्वस्थो योगसम्मीलितेक्षण ः ॥१९५॥
ओमित्युक्त्वा स्वं हृदयं चिन्तयेदविशङ्कितः ।
तत्रात्मानं समादध्यादिन्द्रियाणि मनस्तथा ॥१९६॥ ॥३६॥

न चेद्‌वुध्येत किञ्चान्यन्न पश्येच्छृणुयान्न च ।
न मनस्येद्यदायोगं तदा प्राप्तः स उच्यते ।।१९७।।
हृद्यमेतमृषिमभ्यस्येत्पश्यन्निव यथाश्रुति ।
प्राणानायम्य चासीनो यावत्तं चिन्तयेदृषिम् ।।१९८।।
उच्छ्‌वसिष्यन्नधोनाभि गमयित्वा मनस्तथा ।
उच्छ्‌वसेदेवमसकृत्तन्मना योगमुन्नयेत् ।।१९९।।
एवं हि युञ्जन्त्सामान्यं न पश्येच्छृणुयान्न च ।
तदा शनैर्नयेच्चेतो हृदयादूर्ध्वमेव तु ।।२००।।
समौ तु जत्रू चास्यं च नासिका नयने भ्रुवौ ।
भ्रुवोर्मध्ये परं स्थानं तत्रैतद्धारयेत्स्थिरम् ।।२०१।। ।।३७।।
ललाटदेशे धार्याथ मूर्धानं गमयेत्ततः ।
उच्छ्‌वसंश्च यथाकालं नाभिं गत्वोच्छ्‌वसेत्पुनः ।।२०२।।
एतत्परं स्थानमुक्तं ब्रह्मणः परमात्मनः ।
एवं युक्तो महात्मानमात्मानं प्रतिपद्यते ।।२०३।।
यदि स्यात्सुकृती शुद्धो यदि वा पापकृत्तमः ।
उपलभ्य परं ब्रह्म गतिं ज्ञात्वा भवेच्छुचिः ।।२०४।।
सर्वपापानुबद्धश्चेद्वुद्धैवतत्प्रयतो जपेत् ।
अपि जिज्ञासनादेव गच्छेत परमां गतिम् ।।२०५।।
धारणा तु पृथक्कार्या धर्मेणानेन नित्यशः ।
आदित्येऽग्नौ चन्द्रमसि वृक्षाग्रेषु च धारयेत् ।।२०६।। ।।३८।।
पर्वताग्रे समुद्रे वा यत्र वापि मनो रमेत् ।
न त्वेव विषयान्प्राप्य धारयीत कथञ्चन ।।२०७।।
बह्वत्र दुःखं जानीयात्प्रध्वंसे धारणाकृते ।
धार्मिकाणां कुले शुद्धे योगभ्रष्टोऽभिजायते ।।२०८।।
मूर्ध्नि ब्रह्म यदा विन्देत्तमेव ऋषिसत्तमम् ।
तदामूर्ध्नः परं ज्योतिर्नक्षत्रपथमुन्नयेत् ।।२०९।।
योगी योगेश्वरं प्राप्य निर्द्वन्द्वः परमात्मवित् ।
सर्वत्रैवात्मनात्मानं पश्येदृषिपरायणः ।।२१०।।
जपेच्चैव सदा स्नातः पवित्रमिदमुत्तमम् ।
अपि पातकसंयुक्तः कालेन सुकृती भवेत् ।।२११।। ।।३९।।
तपः परायणो नित्यं सत्यवागनसूयकः ।
जपन्नेतमृषिं विप्रः कालेन स वनी भवेत् ।।२१२।।
येन येन च कामेन जपेदिममृषिं सदा ।

स स कामः समृद्धः स्याच्छ्रद्दधानस्य कुर्वतः ॥२१३॥
होमं वाप्यथवा जाप्यमुपहारमथो चरुम् ।
कुर्वीत येन कामेन तत्सिद्धिमवधारयेत् ॥२१४॥
ज्ञातिश्रैष्ठ्यं महद्वित्तं यशो लोके परां गतिम् ।
पापेन विप्रमोक्षस्तु तत्सिद्धिमवधारयेत् ॥२१५॥
ज्ञानगम्यं परं सूक्ष्मं व्याप्य सर्वमवस्थितम् ।
ग्राह्यमत्यन्तयत्नेन ब्रह्माभ्येति सनातनम् ॥२१६॥
सहस्रशीर्षेति सूक्तं सर्वकामफलप्रदम् ।
वेदगर्भशरीरेण स वै नारायणः स्मृतः ॥२१७॥
ब्रह्मेन्द्ररुद्रपर्जन्या अत्र सूक्ते व्यवस्थिताः ।
अत्रस्थमेतद्द्रष्टव्यं जगत्स्थावरजङ्गमम् ॥२१८॥ ॥४०॥
अनासादयमानोऽपि भक्तिं न परिहापयेत् ।
भक्तानुकंपी भगवाञ्छ्रूयते पुरुषोत्तमः ॥२१९॥
पूजार्थं तस्य देवस्य वन्यान्स्वयमुपार्जितान् ।
आरण्यकविधानेन निर्वपेत्प्रत्यहं चरुम् ॥२२०॥
नारायणाय स्वाहेति मन्त्रान्ते जुहुयाद्धविः ॥
आसहस्रात्ततश्चक्षुर्दिव्यं होतुर्ददाति सः ॥२२१॥
अपि वा चरुसहस्रं तन्त्रेणैकेन निर्वपेत् ।
यावन्तो वापि शक्यन्ते अह्ना सर्वान्त्समापयेत् ॥२२२॥
सहस्रस्येप्सितानां च कामानां लभते फलम् ।
पुरुषायुः समायुक्तः सिद्धो वापि चरेन्महीम् ॥२२३॥ ॥४१॥
ध्येयः सदा सवितृमण्डलमध्यवर्ती नारायणः सरसिजासनसंनिविष्टः ।
केयूरवान्मकरकुण्डलवान्किरीटी हारी हिरण्मयवपुर्धृतशङ्खचक्रः ॥२२४॥
एतत्तु यः पठति केवलमेव सूक्तं नारायणस्य चरणावभिवन्द्य वन्द्यौ ।
पाठेन तेन परमेन सनातनस्य स्थानं जरामरणवर्जितमेति विष्णोः ॥२२५॥
हविषाग्नौ जले पुष्पैर्ध्यानेन हृदये हरिम् ।
यजन्ति सूरयो नित्यं जपेन रविमण्डले ॥२२६॥ ॥४२॥
बिल्वपत्रं शमीपत्रं पत्रं भृङ्गारकस्य च ।
मालतीकुशपद्मं च सद्यस्तुष्टिकरं हरेः ॥२२७॥
यन्नोपपद्यते किञ्चित्तं ध्यायेन्मनसैव तु ।
संपद्यते प्रसादात्तु देवदेवस्य चक्रिणः ॥२२८॥
पत्रैश्च पुष्पैश्च फलैश्च तोयैरक्रीतलब्धैश्च सदैव सत्सु ।
भक्त्यैकलभ्ये पुरुषे पुराणे मुक्त्यै किमर्थं क्रियते न यत्नः ॥२२९॥

इत्येवमुक्तः पुरुषस्य विष्णोरर्चाविधिर्विष्णुकुमारनाम्ना ।
मुक्त्यैकमार्गप्रतिबोधनाय दृष्ट्वा विधानं त्विह नारदोक्तम् ॥२३०॥
या ओषधीः स्वस्त्ययनं जपेत नियतव्रतः ।
ओषधीश्च यजेन्नित्यं षण्मासानेव नित्यशः ॥२३१॥
षण्मासानेव नित्यशः ॥ ॥४३॥

इत्यृग्विधाने तृतीयोऽध्यायः ॥

# चतुर्थोऽध्यायः

इष्ट्वा शरदि वै रुद्रमोषधीश्च यजेत्तथा ।
तस्यामया न भवन्ति तथाजीर्णानि यानि च ॥१॥
श्रियां तु सप्तरात्रेण सप्तकृत्वोऽभ्यसेत्ततः ।
प्रपद्येतौषधीं विप्रः सूक्तमेतज्जपन्त्सदा ॥२॥
द्विषत्क्षेत्राद्विहायध्वमिति विज्ञापयेत च ।
स्वक्षेत्रे वरुणमिष्ट्वा विन्दते द्विषदोषधीः ॥३॥
वृष्टिकामो यताहारः प्रपद्येत बृहस्पतिम् ।
पायसेनोपहारेण होमेन च समन्वितः ॥४॥
बृहस्पते प्रतीत्येतद्वृष्टिकामः प्रयोजयेत् ।
पर्जन्यं च नमस्कृत्वा वृष्टिं विन्दति शोभनाम् ॥५॥ ॥१॥
सर्वत्र तु पराशान्तिर्ज्ञेयोऽप्रतिरथस्त्वृषिः ।
यमेव देशं गच्छेत शत्रुं वाप्यनुमन्त्रितः ॥६॥
नाजित्वा विनिवर्तेत परं हि ब्रह्मणो बलम् ।
सर्वकामैर्जपेदेतत्सर्वकामसमृद्धये ॥७॥
संग्राममभ्युद्यताय राज्ञे चैतत्प्रयोजयेत् ।
सर्वान्विजयते शत्रून्न पराजीयते परैः ॥८॥
पथिस्वस्त्ययनं चैतत्तस्करेभ्यश्चरन्पथि ।
भूतोरगपिशाचेभ्यः सर्वेभ्यः परिरक्षति ॥९॥
भूतांशं काश्यपं सूक्तं प्रजाकामः शुचिर्जपन् ।
अनुरूपां प्रजामाशु लभते नात्र संशयः ॥१०॥ ॥२॥
स्थालीपाकेन नासत्यावश्विनौ तु यजेद्द्विजः ।
अनेनैव तु सूक्तेन हुत्वाश्वाननुमन्त्रयेत् ॥११॥
पायसं कृसरं मांसमोदनं दधिसक्तुकान् ।
कुल्माषांश्च करम्भांश्च फलानि विविधानि च ॥१२॥
चित्रं माल्यं शुभान्गन्धानन्नपानानि यानि च ।
भक्ष्यं भोज्यं च पेयं च समाहृत्योदिते रवौ ॥१३॥
भूतांशमभ्यसेत्तावद्यावदस्तमितो रविः ।
अर्धरात्रे त्वतिक्रान्ते ततोऽश्विभ्यां निवेदयेत् ॥१४॥
दीर्घायुषं सुरूपं च लभेत्पुत्रं सुवर्चसम् ।

रूपवांश्च भवेन्नित्यं भूतांशं यो ऽभ्यसेत्सदा ॥१५॥ ॥३॥
सार्वकामिमित्येतमृषिं विद्याद्विचक्षणः ।
न वा उ देवा इत्येतज्जपेत नियतव्रतः ॥१६॥
अन्नं विन्दति सर्वत्र यत्र यत्रोपतिष्ठति ।
पाप्मोपहतमात्मानं यो मन्येत विचक्षणः ॥१७॥
स जपेन्नियतो भूत्वा लघु मन्येत पाप्मना ।
वाचं प्रपद्येद्वाक्कामो जुह्वदाशु जपन्निमाः ॥१८॥
अहं रुद्रेभिरित्येतद्वाग्मी भवति पूजितः ।
नतमित्यष्टकं सूक्तं वैश्वदेवं जपन्मुनिः ॥१९॥
कृत्स्नं तु कल्मषं हत्वा विश्वैर्देवैः सहासते ।
रात्रीं प्रपद्येत सदा शुचिश्चीर्णव्रतो निशि ॥२०॥
यः कामयेत न पुनर्जायेयमिति योनिषु ।
सहस्रकृत्वो मनसा जपेद्रात्रीति रात्रिषु ॥२१॥
स्थालीपाकेन रात्रीं च यजेताहरहर्निशि ।
तन्मना निशि चासीनस्तिष्ठेदहनि धार्मिकः ॥२२॥ ॥४॥
ऊर्ध्वं संवत्सराच्चैव चरुं पयसि संस्कृतम् ।
सहस्रकृत्वस्त्वेतेन दिवा होमो विधीयते ॥२३॥
जुहुयान्निशि पूर्वस्मिन्भागे रात्रि* समाहितः ।
दिवा चावश्यकं कार्यं छायायामंशुतेजसा ॥२४॥
इति प्रयत आत्मवान्सूक्तं तु मनसा जपेत् ।
संवत्सरे तृतीये तु सर्पिषा साधयेच्चरुम् ॥२५॥
अथास्य वरदा देवी रात्रिर्भवति शर्वरी ।
विज्ञापयति तां देवीं वरदां स्वयमागताम् ॥२६॥
संवत्सर ऋतौ मासि दिवसेऽस्मिन्क्षणेऽपि वा ।
प्रयाणकालो भविता तव वत्सेति वत्सला ॥२७॥ ॥५॥
रात्रीसूक्तं जपन्नेव तं कालं प्रतिपद्यते ।
न योनिं पुनरायाति सर्वपापैः प्रमुच्यते ॥२८॥
ममाग्ने वर्च इत्येतत्सर्वकामैर्जपेद्द्विजः ।
जुह्वदाज्यमनेनैव सर्वान्कामानवाप्नुयात् ॥२९॥
यां कल्पयन्तीति सदा जपेत नियतव्रतः ।
नैनं कृत्या निर्हिसन्ति क्रुद्धाभिचरितानि च ॥३०॥
यमङ्गिरसकल्पैस्तु तद्विदोऽभिचरन्ति सः ।
प्रत्यङ्गिरसकल्पेन सर्वांस्तान्प्रतिबाधते ॥३१॥

प्रत्यङ्गिरसविद्वांस्तु न रिष्येत कदाचन ।
नैनं कृत्या निहिंसन्ति ज्ञाताज्ञातानि वा क्वचित् ॥३२॥ ॥६॥
अजानता जानता वा क्रुद्धेनामर्षितेन वा ।
आक्रुष्टं वा दुरुक्तं वा नैनो लिम्पति तद्विदम् ॥३३॥
एवमेव जपेन्नित्यमृषिं स्वस्त्ययनाय वै ।
सर्वप्रायश्चित्तमेतदभाषत ऋषिः स्वयम् ॥३४॥
स्थावराणां निवेशे तु नगराणां तथैव च ।
ग्रामाणां च गृहाणां च जपेदिममृषिं सदा ॥३५॥
जातरूपमयं विद्वान्कारयेत्त्रिवृतं मणिम् ।
सहस्रसंपातहुतमृषिणा तेन तं ततः ॥३६॥
प्रतिमुञ्चेत* शिरसि ग्रीवायामथवोरसि ।
नैनं कृत्या निहिंसन्ति ज्ञाताज्ञातानि यानि च ॥३७॥ ॥७॥
अनेनैव तु सूक्तेन राज्ञां च समलोहितम् ।
कारयेत मणिं विद्वांस्तावदेवानुमन्त्रणम् ॥३८॥
संग्रामेषु ध्वजाग्राणि वादित्राण्यनुमन्त्रयेत् ।
आसनानि च शय्याश्च यानानि विविधानि च ॥३९॥
तस्याभिचरतः साक्षादाङ्गिरस* ऋषेः* स्वयम् ।
प्रत्यङ्गिरसकल्पेन सर्वं तत्प्रतिबाधते ॥४०॥
अमानुषीर भिचरेत्कृत्याः सूक्तं जपन्निदम् ।
मुच्यते सर्वतोऽनिष्टात्किं पुनर्मानुषाद्भयम् ॥४१॥
तपस्वी नियतो दान्तः प्रयोक्ता चेद्भवेदृषिः ।
सर्वं तरति शान्तात्मा तपो हि सुमहद्बलम् ॥४२॥ ॥८॥
आयुष्यमायुर्वर्चस्यं सूक्तं दाक्षायणं महत् ।
अलङ्कारं हिरण्यं वा प्राप्य दाक्षायणं जपेत् ॥४३॥
प्राप्तं च श्रियमावत्ते बहु चान्नं समश्नुते ।
नासदासीदिति जपेज्जुहुयाद्योगतत्परः ॥४४॥
प्रजापतेस्तु सायोज्यं द्वादशाब्दैः समश्नुते ।
उत देवा इति जपेदामयावी यतव्रतः ॥४५॥
घृतकुम्भं निधायाथ जुहुयाज्जातवेदसि ।
कुम्भात्संपातमन्यस्मिन् कांस्यपात्रे निधापयेत् ॥४६॥
योऽन्नायालं न चान्नं स्यात्स इदं संप्रकल्पयेत् ।
तेनाज्येनाङ्गमभ्यज्य शनकैरन्नभाग्भवेत् ॥४७॥
रोगार्तस्याप्यनेनैव गात्रमङक्त्वा जपेदिदम् ।

अजीर्णाग्नोऽप्यञ्जयीत सुखं भवति तेन ह ॥४८॥ ॥९॥
अग्ने अच्छा वदेत्येतद्धनकामः प्रयोजयेत् ।
नियतः सर्पिषा हुत्वा जपेदयुतशः पुनः ॥४९॥
खादिरीणां हि समिधां जुहुयाद्दशतीर्दश ।
दशकृत्वः सदारेण रायस्पोषेण पुष्यति ॥५०॥
बिल्वोदुम्बरपालाशीस्तथा रौहीतकीश्च याः ।
जुहुयाद्धनकामस्तु रायस्पोषेण पुष्यति ॥५१॥
वैभीतकेध्मो बैल्वकीर्जुहुयादर्धमासभुक् ।
द्विषद्द्वेषेण तस्यान्ते सूक्तमेतत्प्रयोजयेत् ॥५२॥
द्विषन्तं धनिनं हत्वा द्विषतो विन्दते धनम् ।
अथवा जप्यमेव स्याद्रायस्पोषधनार्थिना ॥५३॥ ॥१०॥
अयमग्ने जरितेति जपेदग्निभये सति ।
विधिना तर्पयित्वाग्निं पयोदधि घृतादिभिः ॥५४॥
स्वयं पातुं यावदिच्छेत्तावद्गत्वा चतुर्दिशम् ।
अपामिदं परिणयेत्संततोदकधारया ॥५५॥
उदह्रद इव भूत्वा अग्नेर्भेषजमन्तिकात् ।
अरण्यमेत्य पाठां तु क्रीणीयाद्यवमुष्टिना ॥५६॥
यदि सौम्यसि सोमाय त्वा परिक्रीणाम्योषधिम् ।
यदि वारुण्यसि वरुणाय त्वा परिक्रीणाम्यहं ततः ॥५७॥
वसुभ्योऽथवा रुद्रेभ्य आदित्येभ्योऽथवा पुनः ।
वैश्वदेव्यसि विश्वेभ्यः परिक्रीणाम्यहं ततः ॥५८॥
क्षिप्त्वा सुमनसः पूर्वमोषध्या सह वीरुधि ।
तस्या वीर्यं समादत्ते कर्म यत्र करिष्यति ॥५९॥
तां तु मध्ये निदधीत श्रोषधीनां विहायसि ।
ग्रहणे त्वोषधीनां तु सर्वत्रैष विधिर्भवेत ॥६०॥ ॥११॥
उत्खापयीत तां पाठामिमामिति जपन्निह ।
प्रातश्च पेषयेदेनां संसदि ब्रह्मचारिणा ॥६१॥
तदलाभे व्रतवता कन्यया ब्राह्मणेन वा ।
प्रातः शुचिस्तां घृतेन त्रिः पिबेदनुमन्त्रिताम् ॥६२॥
इमामिति तु सूक्तेन शतकृत्वो दशावरम् ।
सपत्नीं बाधते तेन पतिश्चातीव मन्यते ॥६३॥
पतिस्तु परिजप्यैनां पाठामेतेन वै पिबेत् ।
पयसा सप्तरात्रं तु सपत्नान्प्रतिबाधते ॥६४॥

मूलमन्त्रजपैरन्यैर्या पतिं जेतुमिच्छति ।
अलोका यमलोकस्था मज्जते नरके हि सा ॥६५॥ ॥१२॥
अन्यथा चोपनीतानि चूर्णमूलौषधान्यपि ।
विनाशयेयुः पुरुषं तस्मान्नान्यत्समाचरेत् ॥६६॥
प्रियंवदा भर्तरि या भर्ता यस्याः परायणम् ।
वाक्चैव मधुरा यस्याः पत्युः संवननं महत् ॥६७॥
प्रियं भर्तारमासाद्य पिबेदेवौषधीमिमाम् ।
प्रियंवदां धर्मपरां धर्मपत्नीमनिन्दिताम् ॥६८॥
अवमन्येत यो मोहात्तमाहुः पुरुषाधमम् ।
अरण्यानीत्यरण्येषु जपेत्सूक्तमनेकशः ॥६९॥
अरण्यानीं नमस्कृत्वा सोऽरण्यात्प्रतिमुच्यते ।
श्रद्धासूक्तं जपेन्नित्यं श्रद्धाकामः समाहितः ॥७०॥ ॥१३॥
सर्वत्र लभते श्रद्धां मेधासूक्तं तथैव च ।
ब्राह्मीमासाद्य सूक्ते द्वे जपेत नियतव्रतः ॥७१॥
तां पिबेत्तु यथाशक्त्या त्र्यहात्सिद्धिं नियच्छति ।
शङ्खपुष्पीं तु पयसा ब्राह्मीपुष्पाणि सर्पिषा ॥७२॥
शतावरीं तु पयसा वचामार्द्रां घृतेन वा ।
सूक्ताभ्यामनुमन्त्र्याभ्यामेकैकां तुत्र्यहं पिबेत् ॥७३॥
श्रद्धां मेधां स्मृतिं पुष्टिं बलं लक्ष्मीं च विन्दति ।
सिद्धिं प्राप्नोति च परां दीर्घं चायुः समश्नुते ॥७४॥
अथवा मनसा ध्यायेत्सूक्ते सिद्धिं नियच्छति ।
शास इत्था सपत्नघ्नं संग्रामं विजिगीषतः ॥७५॥ ॥१४॥
प्रयोक्तव्यं तु शुचिना जुहुयात्तत्र सिद्धये ।
अथवा जप्यमेव स्यात्संग्राममभिगच्छतः ॥७६॥
शास इत्थेति यो हन्तुं शत्रून्त्सर्वान्निवारयेत् ।
अलक्ष्मीनाशनार्थं तु जपेन्नित्यं शिरिम्बिटम् ॥७७॥
अपामार्गमयीं शाखां सदर्भां सहवीरुधाम् ।
गृहीत्वात्मानं पावयेदधश्चोर्ध्वं च नित्यशः ॥७८॥
आज्यं चानेन जुहुयात्सहस्रं दशतीर्दश ।
त्र्यहेण नुदते देहादलक्ष्मीं शतवार्षिकीम् ॥७९॥
चान्द्रायणं चरन्नेतत्सूक्तं सिद्धिकरं जपेत् ।
अलक्ष्मीं नुदते देहादपि वर्षसहस्रकीम् ॥८०॥ ॥१५॥
गृहीतं यक्ष्मणा दर्भान् गृहीत्वा संस्पृशञ्जपेत् ।

मुञ्चामि त्वा हविषेति यक्ष्माणमपकर्षति ॥८१॥
समिद्धमग्निं जुहुयादाज्येनैव यथाविधि ।
संपातमाज्ये निनयेत्संपातैश्च पयः पिबेत् ॥८२॥
संपातभाजने सर्पिश्चूर्णं तत्र निधापयेत् ।
तत्रास्य भोजनीयं स्यात्पानीयं चानुमन्त्रितम् ॥८३॥
खादिराणि च काष्ठानि चूर्णं कृत्वा सहाम्बुभिः ।
शोधयीत रसं चेषां मध्वाज्याभ्यां पिबेत्सह ॥८४॥
मुञ्चामि त्वा हविषेति तत्र तत्र प्रयोजयेत् ।
यक्ष्माणमपकर्षन्ति शरीरात्तेन कर्मणा ॥८५॥ ॥१६॥
यस्याः गर्भः प्रमीयेत तत्राग्नौ जुहुयाद्धविः ।
ब्रह्मणाग्निः संविदान इत्याज्येन यथाविधि ॥८६॥
आज्यशेषेण चाभ्यज्य गर्भिणी प्रसवेत्ततः ।
पिबेदेवाज्यशेषं तु जीवंस्तस्याः प्रजायते ॥८७॥
जातानि चेत्प्रमीयेरन्नाज्यं कृत्वानुमन्त्रितम् ।
जुहुयाद्ब्रह्मणाग्निरिति संपातान्निनयेन्मणौ ॥८८॥
मणिं तु त्रिवृति सूत्रे वासयेद्वाससा सह ।
न्यग्रोधशुङ्ग्या तत्र शुक्ललोहितवेष्टितम् ॥८९॥
तं सावित्र्ययुतेनैव अनुमन्त्र्य यथाविधि ।
संपातैरयुतेनैव ब्रह्मणेति च संस्तुतम् ॥९०॥ ॥१७॥
उपरिष्टाच्च सावित्र्या तावदेवानुमन्त्रणम् ।
सर्वैःस्वस्त्ययनैश्चैतज्जपेदभिहुतं मणिम् ॥९१॥
शिरसा धारयेन्नारी प्रयता गर्भिणी सती ।
तृतीये गर्भमासे तु मणिमेतं समासजेत् ॥९२॥
पुष्पवती शरदं नारी गौः सवत्सा वसेद्यथा ।
बहुपानीययवसा वत्सेन पिबता सह ॥९३॥
जातस्य तु कुमारस्य कण्ठे तं मणिमासजेत् ।
आज्यशेषं पुरस्कृत्य तमभ्यज्य कुमारकम् ॥९४॥
हुत्वा स्वस्त्ययनैरेव स्त्री पुमांसं प्रसूयते ।
ऊर्ध्वं वर्षात्स्वस्त्ययनं पुनरेव विधीयते ॥९५॥ ॥१८॥
पुरः स्तनप्रदानात्तं श्रद्धासूक्तेन पाययेत् ।
मेधासूक्तेन चैवैनं पिष्टं व्रीहिमयं चरुम् ॥९६॥
मधुमिश्रं जातरूपं मेधावी तेन जायते ।
शतं वर्षाणि जीवेत् म्रियते न पुरायुषः ॥९७॥

स्मृतमेव तस्य स्यात् षण्मासाच्च ततः परम् ।
आज्यं संस्कृत्य जुहुयादक्षिभ्यां त इति द्विजः ॥९८॥
पाणिना तु घृताक्तेन मूर्धानं संस्पृशेत्ततः ।
कर्णौनेत्रे च छुबुकं नासिके चैव संस्पृशेत् ॥९९॥
एवमेव जपेन्नित्यं यक्ष्मणो विप्रमुच्यते ।
पूर्वोक्तेनैव कल्पेन यक्ष्मनाशनमाचरेत् ॥१००॥ ॥१९॥
होमेन च जपैश्चैव यक्ष्मनाशनमाचरेत् ।
अपेहीति जपेत्सूक्तं शुचिर्दुस्वप्ननाशनम् ॥१०१॥
देवाःकपोत इति तु कपोतस्योपवेशने ।
सूक्तेन जुहुयादाज्यं यमदूतं हि तं विदुः ॥१०२॥
सपत्नघ्नं प्रयुञ्जीत ऋषभं जपहोमयोः ।
येनेदमिति वै नित्यं जपेत नियतव्रतः ॥१०३॥
समाधिं मनसस्तेन विन्दते नैव मुह्यति ।
मयोभूर्वात इति तु गवां स्वस्त्ययने जपेत् ॥१०४॥
यवानां तु घृताक्तानां कारीषेऽग्नौ समाहितः ।
जुहुयाद्गोष्ठमध्ये तु दधिमध्वाज्यसंस्कृतान् ॥१०५॥ ॥२०॥
राजानमभिषिञ्चे*त तिष्येण श्रवणेन वा ।
पौष्णसावित्रसौम्याश्विरोहिणीषूत्तरासु च ॥१०६॥
हुत्वाग्निं राजलिङ्गाभिः सावित्र्या प्रयतः शुचिः ।
महाव्याहृतिभिश्चैव संपाताभिहुतो भवेत् ॥१०७॥
सर्वौषधिरसैः श्लक्ष्णैर्नदीनां सलिलेन च ।
व्याघ्रचर्मण्यथासीनमासन्द्यामभिषिच्य च ॥१०८॥
तिष्ठन्प्रत्यङ्मुखो ब्रूयाज्जय त्वं पृथिवीमिमाम् ।
धर्मस्ते निखिलो राजन् वर्धतां पालयन्प्रजाः ॥१०९॥
वर्धस्व त्वं श्रियै पुष्टयै जयायाभ्युदयाय च ।
राजानः सन्तु ते गोत्रे ततोऽप्रतिरथं जपेत् ॥११०॥ ॥२१॥
वैयाघ्रं तु भवेच्चर्म समिदौदुम्बरी भवेत् ।
त्रिरेनमभिषिच्यैवं दुन्दुभीनभिमन्त्रयेत् ॥१११॥
प्राच्यां त्वा दिशि वसवो अभिषिञ्चन्तु तेजसे ।
दक्षिणस्यां त्वा दिशि रुद्रा अभिषिञ्चन्तु वृद्धये ॥११२॥
प्रतीच्यां त्वा दिश्यादित्या अभिषिञ्चन्तु पुष्टये ।
विश्वेदेवा उदीच्यां तु अभिषिञ्चन्तु श्रेयसे ॥११३॥
अभिषिच्य च राजानमाशीर्भिरभिनन्द्य च ।

आ त्वाहार्षमन्त्रेरधीत्यथैनमभिमन्त्रयेत् ।।११४।।
पतङ्गमिति नित्यं तु जपेदज्ञानभेदनम् ।
मायाभेदनमेतद्धि सर्वमायाः प्रबाधते ।।११५।। ।।२२।।
शाम्बरीमिन्द्रजालां वा मायामेतेन वारयेत् ।
अदृष्टानां च सत्त्वानां मायामेतेन बाधते ।।११६।।
त्यमूष्विति स्वस्त्ययनं जपेत नियतव्रतः ।
पुष्पं दृष्ट्वा तु या गर्भं न गृह्णीयाद्वयोन्विता ।।११७।।
विष्णुर्योनिं नेजमेष योनिं स्पृष्ट्वा ततो जपेत् ।
महि त्रीणामवोऽस्त्विति पथि स्वस्त्ययने जपेत् ।।११८।।
प्राग्नयेऽथ द्विषद्द्वेष्यं जपेद्द्वेषस्य निष्कृतिम् ।
आयं गौः सार्पराज्ञीस्तु सर्पानितेन बाधते ।।११९।।
पवित्राणां पवित्रं तु जपेदेवाघमर्षणम् ।
अपः प्रविश्य यश्चैतत्त्रिः पठेत्सुसमाहितः ।।१२०।। ।।२३।।
यथाश्वमेधावभृथस्तादृशं मनुरब्रवीत् ।
यथाश्वमेधः क्रतुराट् सर्वपापप्रणोदनः ।।१२१।।
तथाघमर्षणं सूक्तं सर्वपापप्रणोदनम् ।
सेनादारणमेतत्स्यान्नैर्हस्त्यमिति शौनकः ।।१२२।।
मनसाध्येयमेतत्तु मन्यते शौनकस्त्वृषिः ।
सं समिद्युवसे वृषन्सौभ्रातृकरणं महत् ।।१२३।।
ज्ञातिभेदे प्रयुञ्जीत न भिद्यन्ते कदाचन ।
कृते भेदे तु संज्ञानमेतत्संधिकरं जपेत् ।।१२४।।
न तत्र भेदो भूयः स्याद्यत्रैतत्सततं जपेत् ।
तच्छंयोरा वृणीमह इति स्वस्त्ययने जपेत् ।।१२५।। ।।२४।।
महानाम्न्यः परं ब्रह्म शुक्रं ज्योतिः सनातनम् ।
सपत्नघ्न्यश्च पुण्याश्च पावमान्यः पराः स्मृताः ।।१२६।।
वृष्टिकामो जपेच्चैता आपो हिष्ठाः सनातनाः ।
श्रोंकारपूर्वा व्याहृतयो मधुच्छन्दस आदितः ।।१२७।।
सूक्तान्यन्ते महानाम्न्यः संहिता सामृता स्मृता ।
अमृतत्वं ययुर्देवाः पूर्वं संहितयानया ।।१२८।।
जेपेदेतां शुचिर्नित्यममृतत्वं स गच्छति ।
अत्रैव त्वावपेन्मध्ये पितृसूक्तान्यनेकशः ।।१२९।।
पित्र्यां तां संहितां विद्यात्पितॄन् प्रीणाति चैतया ।
एवमेव समाहृत्य वासवी संहिता भवेत् ।।१३०।।

रौद्रादित्या वैश्वदेवी यद्देवत्यां च कामयेत् ।
कुर्वीत वास्तुशमनं मध्ये गोष्ठस्य धर्मवित् ॥१३१॥ ॥२५॥
पुष्पैर्गन्धैश्च माल्यैश्च वानस्पत्यैस्तथौषधैः ।
वास्तु सर्वं प्रतिकिरेत्सप्तधान्यैस्तथैव च ॥१३२॥
वास्तोष्पतिं यजेच्चात्र पायसेन बृहस्पतिम् ।
औदुम्बरपलाशैश्च बलिं प्रतिदिशं हरेत् ॥१३३॥
सूर्यो वायुर्यमः पितरो वरुणो निर्ऋतिस्तथा ।
सोमो महेन्द्र इत्येता दिक्षु वै देवताः स्मृताः ॥१३४॥
दद्याद्दानं ब्राह्मणेभ्यः शिवं भवति वास्तुनि ।
प्रतिसंवत्सरं कार्यं गृहे वै गृहमेधिना ॥१३५॥
यद्येवं सविधं चान्यदनुक्तमपि किञ्चन ।
अग्निमिन्द्रमथो वायुं सूर्यमन्याश्च देवताः ॥१३६॥ ॥२६॥
आरिराधयिषुर्यां यामभिधावेत देवताम् ।
अभिरूपेण सूक्तेन यथादिष्टं प्रयोजनम् ॥१३७॥
ऋषीणां मन्त्रदृष्टेन प्रत्यक्षा सिद्धिरिष्यते ।
सर्वत्र दक्षिणां दद्याद्धनं या कर्मसिद्धये ॥१३८॥
न त्वेवादक्षिणं कर्म किञ्चिदस्तीति शौनकः ।
शक्त्या हि पूर्णपात्रेण सम्मिताप्यन्ततो भवेत् ॥१३९॥
तस्मात्स्वल्पापि दातव्या दक्षिणा कर्मसिद्धये ।
ऋषभैकावशा दद्याद्येन वा तुष्यते गुरुः ॥१४०॥
धर्मज्ञे सत्यवादिनि ब्रह्मदानं च दीयते ।
तदिदं परं ब्रह्म गुह्यं पावनमद्भुतम् ॥१४१॥
नाप्रशान्ताय दातव्यं नापुत्रायातपस्विने ।
नासंवत्सरोषिताय नाशिष्यायाहिताय च ॥१४२॥
नाशिष्यायाहिताय च ॥ ॥२७॥

इत्यृग्विधाने चतुर्थोऽध्यायः ॥

## अथ फलश्रुतिः

नराणां भाग्यहीनानामृग्विधानमजानताम् ।
ऋग्वेदः कल्पवृक्षोऽयं फलं नैव प्रयच्छति ॥१॥
रत्नगर्भ इवावास ऋग्वेदः प्रतिभाति मे ।
ऋग्विधानप्रदीपेन विना नैव प्रकाशते ॥२॥
रत्नाकर इवोदार ऋग्वेदोऽत्यन्तदुस्तरः ।
ऋग्विधानमहापोतं विना नैव फलप्रदः ॥३॥
निधानं सर्वरत्नानामृग्वेदो ब्रह्ममन्दिरम् ।
ऋग्विधानविधानेन ध्रुवमेतदवाप्यते ॥४॥
ऋग्वेदः पठितोऽप्येष नृणां भवति निष्फलः ।
ऋग्विधानं विना तस्मादध्येयं तत्प्रयत्नतः ॥५॥ ॥१॥
सूक्ततत्त्वार्थकथनमृग्विधानमवैति यः ।
ऋग्वेदो जायते तस्य प्रसादोत्फुल्लमानसः ॥६॥
आयुष्यं संपदो मूलं सर्वकल्मषनाशनम् ।
ऋग्विधानाभ्यनुष्ठानं शुभ्रकीर्तिकरं परम् ॥७॥
ऋविधानेन संयुक्तमृग्वेदं वेत्ति यो द्विजः ।
धर्मार्थकाममोक्षाणामाश्रयः स भवेद्ध्रुवम् ॥८॥
वेदेषु प्रथमो वेद आयुर्वेदनिधिः प्रभुः ।
ऋग्विधानसदाभ्यासादतीव परितुष्यति ॥९॥
शत्रुनाशं मनस्तुष्टिं सुहृज्जनसमागमम् ।
ऋग्वेदः कुरुते नित्यमृग्विधानेन तोषितः ॥१०॥ ॥२॥
ऋग्वेदं वेत्ति यः साङ्गमृग्विधानरतः सदा ।
मनोरथादप्यधिकं भवेत्तस्य समीहितम् ॥११॥
कुले जन्मनि शीले वा प्रज्ञायामुद्यमेऽपि वा ।
ऋग्विधानपरिज्ञानादुशन्ति चरितार्थताम् ॥१२॥
तुष्यन्ति देवताः सर्वाः संपद्यन्ते विभूतयः ।
दुराधयः प्रणश्यन्ति नित्यमृग्विधिपाठिनाम् ॥१३॥

इत्यृग्विधानं समाप्तम् ॥

## APPARATUS CRITICUS

### *Adhy. I*

5d) **Bo** 1.2 tuṣṭūyante
7d) **Bo** 1.2 vividhā
9c) **Bo** 1.2 vaiśyaḥ śūdraḥ
12a) **Be** samṛddhiś ca
d) **Be** vidhānāni (conj.)
19b) **Be** japet
21c) **La** maṅgalācārya-
d) **Be** 'bhyupayāt; **Bo** 1 'bhyudayāt
22d) **Bo** 1 tṛtīyā
23d) **Bo** 1.2 vaiśvadevī ca raudrī ca
24a) **Be Bo** 2 ityanyām
c) **Ta** daśamīm
26a) **Ba** devān; **Bo** 1.2 vidvān
28b) **Bo** 1.2 vidhim
33d) **Ta** caret
34b) **Ba** pūrvataḥ
d) **Ta** caret
34 After 34, **Bo** 1.2 ins.
1* Amāvāsyāṁ na bhuñjīta hyeṣa cāndrāyaṇo vidhiḥ /
Kukkuṭāṇḍa pramāṇaṁ tu grāsaṁ kuryād atandritaḥ //
36a) **Bo** 1.2 **Ta** evam etat
38a) **Bo** 1.2 āpaḥ
b) **Be**—vidhiṁ smaran
d) **Bo** 1 rahasām
39a) **Ba** jitātmanaḥ
d) **Ba Bo** 1.2 praṇodanaḥ
41d) **Ta** cāndrāyaṇam
43d) **Bo** 2 **Ta** cāndrāyaṇam
44c) **Ba** haviṣyānnasya māsena
45c) **Ba Bo** 1.2 **Ta** Sarve' kuśala-
d) **Bo** 1.2 caturbhiḥ
46a) **Ba Bo** 1.2 **Ta** saptarātreṇa

d) **Bo** 1 pāvamāny ṛcaḥ
49a) **Bo** 1.2 iṣyan
50b) **Be** yatendriyaḥ
d) **Be** yad yathā
52d) **La** sāṁnipātakam
53d) **Be** trivṛta ṛcaḥ; **Ta** niyatavrataḥ
54a) **Bo** 1.2 **Ta** vodite
56d) **Ba Ta** vā (for ca)
58b) **Ta** garhitam
60ab) **Ba** kṛtvāntarupastham; **Bo** 1 **Ta** kṛtvā tūpasthaṁ vai
c) **Ta** prokṣya
62c) **Bo** 1.2 **Ta** soccaiḥ
63a) **Be** utthāya
66c) **Bo** 1.2 rāyaspoṣaṁ dhuram
66 After 66, **Bo** 2 ins. iti paribhāṣā
72d) **Ba Bo** 1.2 **Ta** paśukāmāya
73a) **Bo** 1 saṁhitā devaiḥ
74d) **Bo** 1.2 parabrahmedam
75b) **Bo** 1.2 śatruvinaśinī
77ab) **Ba Bo** 2 **Ta** samidho' kṣara-; **Bo** 1 samidho hyakṣara-
d) **Ba Bo** 2 -kṛtasruvaḥ; **Bo** 1 **Ta**—kṛtasrucaḥ; **Be**—kṛtā srucaḥ
78 After 78, **Bo** 1 ins. iti paribhāṣā; **Ta** arddho' dhyāyaḥ
91a) **Bo** 1.2 **Ta** juhvaṁstrir upatiṣṭhaṁśca
82a) All mss dhyānamātraḥ
87c) **Bo** 1 vagāhyet
87 After 87, **Be Bo** 1.2 **Ta** ins.

2* Aṅguṣṭamātro bhagavān viṣṇur paryaṭate mahīm /
rākṣasānāṁ vadhārthāya tac chrāddhe prahariṣyati //

3* Akṣayyaṁ ca bhaved annaṁ śraddhābhakti samanvitam /
tasmācchrāddheṣu sarveṣu aṅguṣṭhagrahaṇam smṛtam //

89b) **La** tvabhiṣecaṇīḥ
90b) **Ba** japan
d) **Bo** 1 cāpyagado bhavet
91a) **Ba** śāśvataṁ kāmam
b) **Bo** 1 prāpsye

92d) **Bo** 1.2 pratibādhyate
94a) **Ba Bo** 1.2 tvetām (for tvekām)
97c) **Bo** 1 sa nārīsahitaḥ; **Bo** 2 sanārīsanaraḥ
98c) **Bo** 1 ca (for vā)
103b) **Be** sa nigacchati (conj.)
104b) **Bo** 1.2 pratibādhyate
105b) **Be** yāni jagau; **La** transp. yāni and jagau
108d) **Ta** dīrgham (for sarvam)
109a) **La** śrāddhakāleṣu tu (hyp.)
110a) **Bo** 1 ca (for tu)
111c) **Bo** 1.2 gautamena
112c) **Ba** tu (for sa)
116a) **Bo** 1.2 śucikāmo jitā-
117d) **Ba** transp. sadā and japet
119a) **Bo** 1 aśakto' pra-; **Bo** 2 aśaktye' pra-
120a) **Ba Be Bo** 2 sisādha-; **Bo** 2 tu (for ca)
121a) **Ba** Kṛtārthas tu (for Kṛtārthaḥ sva-)
123a) **Ba** pramandina iti sūyantyām; **Be** pramandina ityasūtyām; **Bo** 1 pramandine' prasūyantyām; **Bo** 2 pramandina ityasūyantyām
125a) **Bo** 1.2 juhuyād ājyam
126d) **Bo** 1.2 **Ta** sarvapāpaiḥ pramucyate
127b) **Ba** sanātanam (for dvijaḥ śuciḥ)
128a) **Bo** 1 vitaṣvapatya-; **Bo** 2 viveṣvapatya- (Both corrupt)
b) **Bo** 1 'tivram; **Bo** 2 'tipram
129a) **Bo** 1 ca (for tu)
130b) **Ba Be Bo** 1.2 **Ta** tuṣṭāva
132b) **Be** ravau
c) **Bo** 1.2 gṛṇāno' pohate
133c) **Ba** kṛtsnam (for kṣipram)
134a) **Be** purā (for parā)
135a) **Bo** 1.2 nivartya
c) **Ba** devāsa ityanayā
136cd) **Ba Bo** 2 **Ta** bhūtvopatiṣṭhet; **Bo** 1 bhūtvopatiṣṭhet tu
137b) **Bo** 1.2 dharmavardhanam
139c) **Ta** sauraiḥ
140a) **Bo** 1.2 paśyanti taskarā nainam
b) **Bo** 1.2 **Ta** na cānye
145d) **Be** avikutsayan

148c) **Ba Ta** utpathaḥ
151b) **Bo** 1 suślokyāṁ kīrtim ṛcchati
c) **Bo** 1.2 yatsūktam (for sūktaṁ tu)
152c) **Be**—luṭāsu; **Ta**—lutāsthi-
153d) **Bo**.1.2 dhanavardhanam
155ab) **Ba Bo** 2 Kṛtvopatiṣṭhet; **Bo** 1 Kṛtvopatiṣṭheta
c) **Ba Bo** 1.2 **Ta** Karasaṁyuktaḥ
156c) **Ba** japec caitad
d) **Bo** 1.2—śreṣṭhāni (for—śreṣṭheti)
160c) **Ba** caitat (for tvaitat)
163b) **La** śṛtam
167d) **Ba** Kṛtvā vā (for Kuryād vā)
168ab) **Ba** apsvambītyṛcam
d) **Be** śakunam
169b) **Ba Bo** 1 sthitvekṣya
d) **Be** tataḥ svaram
170b) **Ba** vā (for ca)

*Adhy. II*

2b) **Bo** 1 na (for vā)
3cd) **Ba** so'ttāram annasyāgniḥ; **Bo** 1 So'ṁtaram annasyāpy agniḥ;
**Bo** 2 Sorttaramannasya agniḥ; **Ta** Saunnāram annasya agniḥ
6b) **Bo** 1.2 vaneṣvapi (for—careṣvapi); **Be**—cāreṣvapi
7a) **Ba** titīṛṣṇuḥ
8b) **La** gāḍham
10-11 **Be** transp 10cd and 11cd
11b) **Ba** kṛṇvanti tā japet; **Bo** 1 Kṛṇvanty ṛcaṁ japet; **Bo** 2 Kṛṇvanty ṛcaṁ japan
13c) **Ba Bo** 2 japet; **Bo** 1 japtvā
14d) **Ba** kṛtārthaḥ (for siddhārthaḥ); **Bo** 1 sthirayānagaḥ (for -guḥ)
15a) **Ba** api bhajyaṁ tam; **Bo** 1.2 apabhagnaṁ tam
d) **Bo** 1 **Ta** ṛcam (for dvṛcam)
20b) **Bo** 1.2 brahma tat (for brahmaitat)
21a) **Ba** japan
22b) **Be** babhruṁ ca
c) **Ba Bo** 1.2 **Ta** ṛtāvṛtau

cd) **Bo** 1.2 dinetyṛcaiḥ
23d) **Bo** 1 Sudhūpakaiḥ
24a) **Bo** 1.2 etāvat (for tā eva)
c) **Ta** putraiḥ
25b) **Bo** 1.2 prasāra-
26c) **Bo** 1 ca (for tu)
27a) **La**—mitabhūn
28c) All mss na kurvīta
d) **Bo** 1 tāval luṁpen na
30c) **Bo** 1.2 sahasram
d) **Bo** 1.2 rāhusūryasamāgame
31c) **Bo** 1.2 sahasram
32a) **Bo** 1.2 khādiram
c) **Be** sahasra-
35a) **Bo** 1 gajān
b) **Bo** 1 mahiṣīḥ
c) **Bo** 1.2 śālitaṇḍula-
36a) **Bo** 1.2 —raktārka-
38a) **Ba Ta** alakṣmīḥ
b) **Bo** 1.2 **Ta**—vināśakaiḥ
39b) **Bo** 1 saṁpracārayet
41b) **Be La** ghṛtāktānām
c) **Be La** vardhāpayet (conj.)
49b) **Bo** 1 pracārayet
53d) **Bo** 1.2 hemam
54a) **Be** abbrahma- (conj.)
56c) **Bo** 1.2 akhilam
58ab) **Ba**—gavyāśyekāham; **Bo** 1—gavyāśī hyekāham
62d) **Bo** 1 Śivāyeti
65b) **Bo** 1 śaktim
d) **Bo** 1 śaktitaḥ
67c) **La** japann iti
71b) **Be** phalalāja- (conj.)
c) **Ba** pravāpane; **Bo** 1.2 pralāpane; **Bo** 1 praṇayane; **Bo** 2 praṇavane
72d) **Ba** bhavati
73b) **Bo** 1 **Ta** kṣetrapatyam
74b) **Bo** 1.2 **Ta** mūṣakān
76a) **Bo** 1.2 bhūmibhaṅge

78 After 78ab, **Be** reads 79cd
80b) **Be** arcayet
81a) **Ba Bo** 1.2 vahnim upasthāya; **Ta** vahnirupasthāya
b) **Ta** prāṇarthe; **Ba Bo** 1.2 havyavāhanam
d) **Ba Ta** āyuṣyam icchatā
82cd) **Ba** sūktenopatiṣṭhet; **Bo** 1 sūktena hyupatiṣṭhet
85a) **Bo** 1 asyām (for āśy)
d) **Ba** transp dvijaḥ and śuciḥ
86c) **Bo** 1 jñātijam
88d) **Ta** kṛtī; **Ba** tathā (for kṛtim)
89a) **Ba Bo** 1.2 **Ta** niṣpīṣanniva; **Be** niṣpīḍyanniva (conj.)
91b) **Bo** 1 hyacireṇa
94b) **Bo** 1.2 kanyake
95a) **Bo** 1 sthālīpācitaśālīnām
d) **Bo** 1 śriyam
98a) **Bo** 1 aśvapūrvām
c) **Bo** 1.2 lohite
99a) **Bo** 1.2 rājakarmaṇi
101b) **Ba** sthālīm
103d) **Bo** 1.2 daśa sāhasrikāvaraḥ
105d) **Be** kilāsitvād bibhetu vai
106b) **Bo** 1.2 juhvan
108a) **Ba Bo** 1.2 Kṛpaṇo'rthāya
110a) **Bo** 1.2 agne tvaṣṭarca-
111c) **Ba Bo** 1 prajām
112b) **Bo** 1 gotragā
113ab) **Ba** pragāthenopatiṣṭhet; **Bo** 1 pragāthena hyupatiṣṭhet
116b) **Bo** 1.2 codake
d) **Bo** 1 **Ta** tyakte (for tyaktvā)
117c) **Ba Be Bo** 1.2 vindate; **Be** kvacit (for kiñcit)
118cd) **Ba** yatnenāpi; **Bo** 1 yatnena nāpi
119a) **Be** japtvā (conj.)
c) **Bo** 1 **Ta** tayā (for etayā)
121b) **Bo** 1.2 godvipadam
112d) **La** vāṅmī
123b) **Bo** 1 matam
125b) **Bo** 1 vigarhitam
126) **Bo** 1.2 omit
127d) **Bo** 1 svasyāṁgānām

131c) **Bo** 1 vaiti; **Bo** 2 veti
131 After 131, **Be** ins.

4* Aṣṭāvaṣṭau tathā cāṣṭāv ṛgityeva tripādikam /
akārādihakārāntaṁ jale sthitvā drutam japan //
5* Upapātakakoṭīnāṁ brahmahatyāyutāni ca /
bhrūṇahatyā kṛtaṁ pāpaṁ tatkṣaṇādeva naśyati //
6* Agniṁ dūtaṁ puro dadhe agne rakṣā no aṁhasaḥ /
adābhyena śociṣāgnā agna agna ihāvase //

132 After 132, **Be** ins.
7* Vasiṣṭhena purā gītā mahad adbhutamārjanam /
Viśvāmitrābhicāreṣu mahad rakṣo nivāraṇam //
8* yaḥ prātar iti sūktaṁ tu strīkāmaḥ satataṁ japet /
labhate sadṛśīṁ kanyāṁ dīrghamāyuḥ svarūpiṇīm //
9* Uttarasyādyam ācāryo juhyuyād vāstukarmaṇi /
Snātaḥ kṛtvā vaiśvadevaṁ paraṁ brahmedam ucyate //

133a) **Be** śaṁvatī
b) **Bo** 1 ityetām
134a) **Ba** niveśakāmaḥ
d) **Ba** prajñāṁ ca draviṇaṁ bahu
135d) **Ba Bo** 1.2 **Ta** tariṣyati
136b) **Bo** 1.2 srotyāḥ; **Ta** sindhu-
cd) **Bo** 1.2 ityetaj japet sūktam
137c) **Bo** 1.2 paṭhet
138b) **Ba Bo** 1.2 vāstoṣpatim japan (**Ba** japet)
140d) **Bo** 1.2 sañjapet
141b) **Ba** parā japet
c) **Bo** 1 manveti; **Bo** 2 manyeti
146c) **Bo** 1.2 aśvāṁśca (for gā aśvān); **Be** puruṣam; **Ba Ta** kanyām (for dhānyam)
d) All mss ajāvikān
147d) **Ta** piśācaḥ (for vipāśaḥ); **Ba** saṁprajāyate; **Bo** 2 **Ta** saṁpramucyate (both for saṁprapadyate)
148b) **Be** viveṣṭitaḥ (conj.)
150 **Bo** 1 omit
152b) **Be** Svagotra-; **Ta** sagotrā-
d) **Ba Bo** 1 saṁviśan
153c) **Bo** 1.2 āpaḥ
154d) **Bo** 1 bhūmim

157ab) **Ba** pratipadyetābhiśasyeta; **Bo** 1 Saṁpratipradyetābhiśasyeta
158d) **La** sarvaśāstravān
159a) **Be** lubhyet (conj.)
162b) **Ba** pūjayet (for prapadyet)
163c) **Bo** 1 bhūmāv- (for māsāv-)
167b) **Bo** 1.2 mānavāt tu
d) **Bo** 1.2 sadā (for parā)
169a) **Ba Be** prāpnuyāt paramām ṛddhim
170d) **Bo** 1 śukrenādy-; **Bo** 2 śuktanādy-; **Be** vajriṇaḥ (conj.)
171c) **Be** 'nnāni (conj.)
d) **Bo** 1.2 vidhāntaḥ
172b) **Be** ripu-; **Ta** riṣṭa- (both for ripra-)
c) **La** vācam (for vāśam); **Bo** 1 transp mahīti and ca
174a) **Bo** 1 hṛdya (for hṛdayam)
b) **Ta** sa (for jyok)
176b) **Bo** 1 yūṣān; **Bo** 2 pūṣān (both for 'pūpān); **Bo** 1.2 **Ta** vābhyupahārayet
d) **Ta** ca...ca (for vā)
178c) **Bo** 1.2 yadyāvas tu
180a) **Bo** 1 dīptāt (for dīptyā)
b) **Bo** 1 vahnito (for vahninā)
183a) **Ta** kṣipram (for ripram)
c) **Ba** dvṛceneha; **Be** dvṛcenaiva
184b) **Bo** 1 uccāryate; **Bo** 2 uccarite
d) **Bo** 1 ṛcam (for dvṛcam); **Ba** japan (for paṭhan)
185b) **Bo** 1.2 na liṁped anṛtena
d) **Be** anuṣevayet
186c) **Ba** naraḥ (for japan)
d) **Be** pratipadyate
187b) **Ba Ta** japan yo (**Ta** japan vai) gām upāśnute
188b) **Bo** 1.2 paṭhet

*Adhy. III*

3a) **Be** tu
4c) **Bo** 1 brahmāṇam; **Bo** 2 brahmaṇām
6a) **Bo** 1.2 śaśvat (for tac ca)
b) **Bo** 1.2 vā (for ca)

8a) Bo 1.2 bhaved annam
9ab) **Ba** bhūtvopatiṣṭhanti; **Bo** 1 bhūtvopatiṣṭhanti ca
10a) **Bo** 1.2 svādhyāyam (for svādhyāya-)
11a) **Ta** sapta ṛṣibhiḥ (hyp.)
13a) **Be** ṛcāṁś caiva
c) **Bo** 1.2 japen mantram (for japaṁścaiva)
d) **Bo** 1.2 haret (for jayet)
15d) **Bo** 1 rahasām (for rapasām)
16a) **Ba** cādhyāyet
b) **Ta** antye
17a) **Be** cārcayīta
d) **Bo** 1.2 punaḥ (for suciḥ)
18b) **Bo** 1 siddhayaḥ
cd) **Bo** 1 sūktānyattat; **Bo** 1 sūktānyatat (both corrupt)
18 After 18 ab, **Ba Be** ins.
10* Maṇḍalaṁ pāvamānaṁ tu japet lakṣam[1] upoṣitaḥ /
nāśayed brahmahatyām vai Vasiṣṭhavacanaṁ yatha /
[1 **Ba** pakṣam]
20d) **Ba Bo** 1.2 tu (for su-)
22b) **Ba** saṁsmaran
d) **Ba** japec caiva
23d) **Bo** 1 brāhmaṇo; **Bo** 2 brahmaṇā
24a) **Be Bo** 2 brāhmaṇān
c) **Bo** 1 ācaritam
d) **Be Bo** 1.2 **Ta** patet
25b) **Bo** 1.2 svam (for tvam)
27d) **La** vyamocayet
28a) Bo 1.2 gurudravyam
31d) **Ba** japed etā; **Bo** 1 japetāpi; **Bo** 2 japed etāni (hyp.)
32cd) **Ba Bo** 2 pāpasyāvijñātasya; **Bo** 1 pāpasyāvijñātasyāpi; **Ta** pāpasyāvijñātasya ca
33cd) **Ba Bo** 2 pāpasyāvijñātasya; **Bo** 1 pāpasyāvijñātasyāpi; **Ta** pāpasyāvijñātasya ca
34b) **Ba Bo** 1 **Ta** yamasūktena
c) **Bo** 1.2 tu (for ca)
36c) **Bo** 1 prīyet tasya
d) **Bo** 1.2 mṛtim
37c) **Bo** 1 vaiśākhapaurṇamāsyām
38d) **Be** vindate

39a) **Bo** 1 nityam (for mṛtyum)
40a) **Bo** 1 purāyuṣān
c) **Bo** 1.2 japan
d) **Bo** 1.2 tribhir varamitāśanaḥ
41b) **Bo** 1.2 phalamulam
d) **Bo** 1 vasan; **Bo** 2 vasat
44a) **Ta** ca tasya tu (for tu saṁprāpte)
b) **Ta** ha (for 'tha)
d) **Ba** transp na and dvitīyam
45a) **Bo** 1.2 daśārakṣamtu
50b) **Ba** gandhaiś ca parivāsayet
c) **Bo** 1.2 caivam (for cainān)
51c) **Ba Bo** 1.—metyṛcam (for—mārcam)
52a) **Bo** 1.2 vyuṣāyām
d) **Bo** 1.2 annair na (for anyair na)
57b) **Ta** saṁmūlhaḥ
c) **Bo** 1.2 vrajate 'dhvānam (for eti panthānam)
58d) **Ta** mūrdhani saṁspṛśet
59d) **Bo** 1 sūktena ca (for sūktenainam)
60b) **Bo** 1.2 etan mantram
c) **Ta** vānyam (for cānyam)
d) **Bo** 1.2 **Ta** ca (**Ta** vā) samālabhet
62b) **Ba Ta** sahasram (for sahasra-)
64a) **Bo** 1.2—srucau camasāḥ
c) **Ba** ājyāhu-
d) **Ba** yojayet
65a) **Bo** 1 ābhogam
c) **Ba Bo** 2 **Ta** apyaratham; **Bo** 1 avyaratham
67c) **Bo** 1.2 tena (for 'nena)
68c) **Bo** 1.2 sahasrasa- (for sahasraṁ sa-)
69a) **Bo** 1.2 hutvā (for kṛtvā)
b) **Bo** 1.2 dhārayeta tām
c) **Bo** 1.2 nityam (for bhūtvā)
70d) **Ba** japet tu; **Ta** yajeta
72b) **Bo** 1.2 naraḥ; **Ta** tataḥ
73c) **Bo** 1.2 **Ta** vāpi saṁyuktaḥ
74d) **Bo** 1 lakṣmīścāpi pravardhate; **Bo 2** lakṣmīś ca pravardhate
75a) **Bo** 1 ca (for tu)

76d) **Bo** 1.2 transp. na and sa
77c) **Be** cābhyām
78c) **Be** khādire susamiddhe
80d) **Ba Be Bo** 2 **Ta** 'bhyupayāt; **Bo** 1 'bhyudayāt
81d) **Bo** 1 Kṛtī, **Bo** 2 kṛtam (both for tathā)
84a) **Bo** 1.2 tapasvinaḥ
b) **Bo** 1.2 japet
d) **Ba** japeccaitatt (for japed etat)
85a) **Bo** 1.2 **Ta** Vaśam ānetum
b) **La** hīnām
87b) **Be** dhārayed guḍam (conj.); **Bo** 1 dhārayeta tam; **Bo** 2 dhārayettu sam; Ta dhārayet tu tam
89c) **Bo** 1.2 kṣatriyas tvatha
d) **Bo** 1 viśo'pi (for viśām api)
90a) **Be** vai (for vā)
91a) **Bo** 1.2 mahasā (for manasā)
92a) All mss dīptām pratikṛtim
b) **Be** svam (for sa)
93a) **Ba Bo** 2 **Ta** prajvalite (hyp.)
95b) **Be** prasādayet
c) **Bo** 1.2 enam (for evam)
96d) **Bo** 1.2 hṛdyenaiva
97a) **Ba Ta** Kartavyam
b) **Ba Ta** brāhmaṇaiḥ
c) **Ba** Sarūpavatsāyā goś caiva (hyp.); **Bo** 1 transp ca and goḥ
98b) **Bo** 1 pāyase (for pāyayet)
99c) **Bo** 1.2 prārthayet (for prāsayet)
104c) **Bc** imam (for etam)
106c) **Ba** tasyāḥ (for asyāḥ); **Bo** 1.2 kurvan (for kuryāt)
107c) **Bo** 1 Kṛtya- (for Kṛṣṇa)
108d) **Ba Ta** śeṣayet
112b) **Be** jayaś caiva (for japeccaiva)
114c) **Bo** 1 -preṣyārtham (for-dveṣyārtham)
115a) **Bo** 1.2 mansaivetat
b) **Bo** 2 sūkasi- (for sūkte si-)
116a) **Ba** tu (for su)
117b) **Bo** 1.2 dīrghāyuḥ saṁbhavet tataḥ
c) **Ba** tu (for ca)

118a) **Bo** 1.2 yāvat (for bhavet)
b) **La** bhartā
119b) **Ba** nanāndrādibhiḥ; **Be** vāpi (for cāpi)
c) **Be** indrānyāḥ (conj.)
121a) **Ba** yathā (for tathā)
d) **Ta** yajñā- (for yakṣā-)
122c) **Bo** 1 -pūrṇe; **Ta** -pūrṇais taiḥ
d) **Ba** citrakumbhasa- (for pañcagavyasa-); **Bo** 1—yute (for -vṛtaiḥ)
124c) **Be** adhimantryeha; **Bo** 1 abhimantrya ca
d) **Bo** 1 ca stuvīta (for tu vihīti)
125a) **Bo** 1 etābhiḥ (for stheyābhiḥ)
ab) **Ba** pūrṇenābhiṣiñcet
c) All mss tanvyaḥ
d) **Bo** 1 nāsthitena (for tāstvanena)
126a) **Ba Bo** 1.2 āhanasyādbhiḥ
b) **Bo** 1.2 **Ta** vidyāyām (for vidyādyām); All mss vipravādinīm
128ab) **Ba** caitenopatiṣṭheta
129c) **Bo** 1.2 etat tu (for ityetat)
130a) **Ba** garhitādyādya-; **Bo** 1-2 garhitānāttṛ-
d) **Be** apyabhīkṣṇaśaḥ
131a) **Be** āsthāpya (conj.)
b) **Bo** 1.2 bhavet (for 'bhyaset)
133c) **Bo** 1 ca (for tu)
137b) **Ba** sādhayet (for nirvapet)
c) **Bo** 1.2 hayastha (for sahasra); **Ba** sa (for syāt)
138a) **Ta** vidhitaḥ
b) **Be** dvijaḥ
d) **Ba** stuvan (for stavam)
139b) **Bo** 1 tathā (for smṛtam)
d) **Bo** 1 punaḥ (for tāthā)
141d) **Ba Ta** tu (for ca)
143b) **Bo** 1.2 parāmedhā- (for yaśo medhā-)
146d) **Ta** laghvāśī (for labdāśīḥ)
147a) **Bo** 1.2 transp Karma and kṛtvedam
c) **Be** dvitīyā strī
d) **Bo** 1 ca (for na)
148b) **Ba Bo** 1 kanyāḥ

152d) **Ta** bhāvitātmanaḥ
154c) **Bo** 1 'tha (for yaḥ)
155b) **Bo** 1.2 śṛṇuṣvaikaṁ mahāprabho
156b) **Bo** 1 tadātmakam
158c) **Bo** 1.2 vāmakukṣau
159a) **Ba Bo** 1.2 nābhideśe
160ab) **Ba** bāhau mukhadeśe; Be bāhāvāsye caiva
161 After 161, **Ba** Be ins.
11* Mantranyāsaṁ purā kṛtvā svadehe devatāsu ca /
gāyatryoṁkāranyastāṅgaḥ pujayed viṣṇumavyayam //
12* Ucchvāsāvāhane[1] na staḥ sthirāyām uddhavārcane /
asthirāyāṁ vikalpaḥ syāt sthaṇḍile tu bhaved dvayam //
13* Ucchvāsāvāhane[1] na staḥ sthāvare vai yathā tathā /
śāligrāmārcenaiva hyāvāhanavisarjane //
14* Śāligrāme tu bhagavān ādibhūto yathā hariḥ /
na tathānyatra sūryādau vaikuṇṭhe vāpi sarvagaḥ //
[1 **Ba** Udvāsāvāhane]
163d) **Bo** 1 saptamyām astram (for saptamyā vastram); **Bo** 1.2 tu (for ca)
166c) **Bo** 1 yathāśakti
166 **Bo** 1 transp 166[ab] and 166[cd]
167a) **Be** prādakṣiṇyam
d) **Bo** 1 tasmai (for tasya)
169a) **Bo** 1.2 tṛtīyayā
b) **Bo** 1.2 Caturthyā ca
c) **Bo** 1.2 pañcamyā
170b) **Be** pādmam (conj.)
174a) **Be** yatam
c) **Bo** 1 Subrahmaṇya namaste' stu
174 After 174, **Bo** 1.2 ins.
15* Namo hiraṇyagarbhāya pradhānāvyktarūpiṇe /
Oṁ namo vāsudevāya śuddhajñānasvarūpiṇe //
176c) **Bo** 1 adhyakṣah (for avyaktaḥ)
177c) **Be** tvam eva
180c) **Bo** 1.2 paramām (**Bo** 2 paramam) siddhim
d) **Bo** 1 vindati paramaṁ vidaḥ
181d) **Bo** 1 śaraṇaṁ param (for paramaṁ padam)
182c) **Be** jagataḥ (conj.); **Bo** 1 vigate; **Bo** vāpi (for cāsi)

183c) **Bo** 1 prāptam (for prāpya)
183 After 183[ab], Bo 1.2 ins.
16* Nimittaṁ kuśalasyāsti yena gacchāmi sadgatim /
184c) **Be** jñātasya
185a) **Bo** 1 nāthaṁ ca (for nāśaṁ na)
185 After 185[ab], **Bo** 1 ins.
17* Akāmakaluṣaṁ cittam mama te pādayoḥ sthitam /
186d) **Be** yogadhyānam
186 After 186, **Bo** 1 ins.
18* Ityevam anayā stutyā stutvā devaṁ dine dine /
Kiṁkarosmīti cātmānam devāyaiva nivedayet //
188c) **Ba**—kāle tu (for-Kāleṣu)
191d) **Bo** 1.2 tvaṣṭāram
192b) **Ba Bo** 1.2-vṛttaḥ (for kḷptaḥ); **Bo** 1 samāhitaḥ (for śucivrataḥ)
c) **Bo** 1.2 etad evam (for etaṁ devam)
193b) **Be** śucir vāgyataḥ
c) **Bo** 1 sūteṣu (for bhūteṣu)
194b) **Bo** 1.2 nirvāte (for nivāte)
c) **Be** pādmam (conj.); **Bo** 1 dakṣiṇasyām (for dakṣiṇasya)
195a) **Be** pādmam (conj.)
196a) **Ba** sve hṛdaye
b) **Bo** 1.2 -kutsitaḥ (for -śaṅkitaḥ)
197a) **Bo** 1.2 na ca (for na cet)
c) **Bo** 1 sadā (for yadā)
198a) **Ba Be** abhyaset
b) **Bo** 1 iva (for eva)
199a) **Be** adhonābhim; **Bo** 1 adhanābhi
c) **Ba** ucchvasec caivam
200b) **Bo** 1.2 yuñjyāt; **Ta** yujyamānasya; **Ba** Sonyanyan (for sāmānyam)
c) **Ba** jayeccetaḥ; **Bo** 1 niyaccheta
201a) **Ba** jaṁttu; **Bo** 1.2 jānū; **Ta** jaṁtū
202d) **Bo** 1 nābhitaścocchva-; **Bo** 2 nābhitatvocchva-
203c) **Bo** 1 mahātmā san (for mahātmānam)
203d) **Bo** 1.2 mahātmānaṁ prapadyate
205a) Ba 'nuviddaḥ; Bo1 'va baddhaḥ
b) **Ba** hṛdye
c) **Be** abhiji- (for api ji-)

d) **Bo** 1.2 gacchate (for gaccheta)
206a) **Bo** 1.2 dhāranāt tu pṛthak kuryāt
208b) **Bo** 1 maraṇe sati
209a) **Bo** 1.2 sa vindeta (for yadā vindet)
b) **Bo** 1 Sa eva ṛṣisattamaḥ
212d) **Ba** sukṛtī (for sa vanī)
212 **Bo** 1 omit
214a) **Bo** japyam
b) **Ba** anuttamam (for atho carum)
215c) **Be** jñānena vipramokṣaṁ ca
216b) **Bo** 1.2 vyavasthitam (for avasthitam)
219a) **Bo** 1 ataḥ saṁpaṭhamā- (for anāsādayamā-)
b) **Bo** 1.2 parihārayet (for parihāpayet)
220b) **Bo** 1 vanāt svayam upāhṛtāt
222a) **Ba** tu (for vā); **Bo** 1.2 -sāhasram
223d) **Bo** 1 Ta vā vicaret (for vāpi caret)
226d) **Be** japyena; **Bo** 1 japanti; **Bo** 2 **Ta** japeta
228a) **Bo** 1 yatraitat paṭhyate
b) **Bo** 1 tad (for tam)
c) **Bo** 1.2 saṁpādya tat prasādāc ca
229d) **Bo** 1 tu (for na)
231 **Bo** 1 omit

### *Adhy. IV*

Note: **Bo** 1 regards *Rvidh* iii.231 as the first verse of this chapter.

1a) **Bo** 1 dṛṣṭvā
c) **Bo** 1 na bhavanty āmayās tasya
d) **Bo** 1—jīrṇādikāni ca (for -jīrṇāni yāni ca)
2b) **Ba Bo** 1.2 **Ta** samāhitaḥ
3a) **Bo** 1.2 labdhām (for 'yadhvam)
b) **Be** vijñāpayīta
c) **Bo** 1 caruṇeveṣṭvā; **Bo** 2 caruṇām iṣṭvā
d) **Be** bhisag- (conj.) for dviṣad-
4a) **Bo** 1.2 jitā- (for yata-)
5c) **Be** namaskṛtya
6a) **Ba** Sarvatraiva (for sarvatra tu)
b) **Ba** jñeyā

8a) **Bo** 1 abhyudyāto vā
b) **Bo** 1 rājā (for rājñe)
9b) **Ba** ca rakṣati (for caran pathi)
10a) **Be Bo** 1 bhūtāṁśasya ṛṣeḥ
11b) **Ba** Sadā (for dvijaḥ)
c) **Be** anenaivopacāreṇa; **Ta** anenaivopahāreṇa
12a) **Be** Kṛśarā- (for kṛsaram)
13a) **Bo** 1.2 citramālyaśu- (for citraṁ mālyaṁ śu-)
15a) **Be** sarūpam
16a) **Be** sarvakāmikam
18d) **Bo** 1 hunet
19d) **Be** japen muniḥ
20a) **Be** hitvā (conj.)
c) **Bo** 1 prapadye manasā (for prapadyeta sadā)
d) **Bo** 1.2 parṇavrataḥ (for cīrṇavrataḥ)
22c) **Ta** cāsīta (for cāsīnaḥ)
23b) **Be** transp bhāge and rātri; **Ba** rātriḥ; **Bo** 1 rātrau; **Bo** 2 rātrim; **Ta** rātrīm
c) **Bo** 1.2 cāviśpatim (for cāvaśyakam)
25a) **Ba** atipra—**Bo** 1 pratipra- (both for its pra-)
26c) **Be Bo** 1 vijñāpayīta
29c) **Bo** 1.2 juhvannājyam (for juhvad ājyam)
31a) **Ba** pratyaṅgi-; **Bo** 1.2 yamāṅgi-
b) **Ba** 'bhicaran punaḥ; **Bo** 1 'bhicareta saḥ
32d) **Be** yāni ca (for vā kvacit)
33b) **Bo** 1 -dharṣi- (for -marṣi-)
c) **Ba** ākṛṣṭam (for ākruṣṭam)
d) **Bo** vindati (fcr limpati)
34a) **Be** etam eva
c) **La** -prāyaścitam
35a) **Bo** 1.2 niveśeṣu (for niveśe tu)
d) **Bo** 1 japeta tam (for japed imam)
37a) All mss pratimucyeta
38b) **Ba** tu (for ca)
40b) **Ba Bo** 2 **Ta** aṅgirā apyṛṣiḥ; **Bo** 1 aṅgirarṣirapi
41b) **Ba Be** Kṛtyāsūktam; **Ta** japet (for japan)
42b) **Be** ṛṣim (conj.)
43b) **Ba** tathā (for mahat)
44a) **Be** prāyaḥ (conj.) for prāptam

44 After 44[ab], **Be** ins.
19* Bhāvavṛtte pare sūkte saptarce pāvane japet /
prajāpatiṁ namaskṛtvā sarvān kāmān avāpyate //
45a) **Bo** 1.2 sāyujyam
46a) **Be** kāṁsye pātre; **Ba** transp kāṁsye and pātre
47a) **Be** yan na pānam (conj.); **Bo** 1 yo'nnārthyalam
b) **Bo** 1 -kāśayet (for—kalpayet)
48c) **Bo** 1 ajīrṇānnotthaṁ jayīta
d) **Ba Bo** 1.2 **Ta** vijvaraḥ
50a) **Bo** 1.2 Khādirāṇām
51a) **Bo** 1.2 -pālāśaiḥ
b) **Bo** 1 rohitakaiś ca yaḥ
c) **Bo** hotavyā dhanakāmena
52a) **Bo** 1 vaibhītakedhmair bailvaiś ca
b) **Bo** 1 ardhamāsakam (for ardhamāsabhuk)
56a) **Bo** 2 uta hṛda
ab) **Ba** bhūtvāgneḥ; **Bo** 1 bhūtvāpyagneḥ
c) **Be** pāṭām (conj.)
58a) **Bo** 1.2 vasubhyaś cātha
59b) **Be Bo** 1.2 virudhaiḥ
60ab) **Ba** nidadhītauṣadhīnām; **Bo** 1 Saṁdadhītauṣadhīnām ca
61a) **Be** pāṭām (conj.)
64a) **Ba** Ta parijapyaitām
b) **Be** pāṭām (conj.)
c) **Ba** Bo 1.2 saptarātrena (for saptarātraṁ tu)
66a) **Be** vopanītāni
d) **Be** anyam (for anyat)
68c) **Bo** 1 suśīlām ca (for dharmaparām); **Ta** dharmaratām
70b) **Ba** araṇyāt; **Bo** 1 āraṇyān; **Be** 1.2 pratibādhate
71d) **Ta** japed ayutaśaḥ punaḥ
64c) **Bo** 1.2 **Ta** paramām (for ca parām)
d) **Ba Bo** 1.2 omit ca
76b) **Bo** 1.2 siddhayaḥ
77b) **Bo** 1 tāṁstu (for sarvān); **Bo** 1 vibādhate; Bo 2 nibādhate
78b) **Ba** sahavīruṇam; **Be** sahavīraṇām; **Bo** 1.2 sahavirudhaiḥ;
**Ta** sahavīraṇaiḥ
80a) **Ba** caranneva (for carannetat)
c) **Bo** 1 alakṣmīḥ
84a) **Be** tu (for ca)

c) **Be** sādhayīta
85c) **Be Bo** 2 apakarṣati
d) **Bo** 1 śarīrārogyaka- (for śarīrāt tena ka-)
88c) **Be** brahmāgnir iti hutvā
89a) **Ba Ta** trivṛtisūtrena (for tu trivṛti sūtre); **Bo** 1.2 trivṛte sūtre
90ab) **Ba Bo** 2 -yutenaivānumantrya; **Be**—yutenātha anumantrya; **Bo** 1 -yutenaivānumantryātha
91a) **Ba** tu (for ca)
c) **Bo** 1.2 caiva (for caitat)
93a) **Ba** puṣpitā; **Be** puṣpyanti (conj.); **Ta** puṣpatī; **Bo** 1 param (for śaradam)
b) **Bo** 1 caret (for vaset)
c) **La** bahupaṇī- (for bahupānī-)
96a) **La** purā; **Bo** 1.2 punaḥ; **Bo** 1.2—dānārtham (for -dānāt tam)
c) **Bo** 1 caivaitat (caivainam)
d) **Bo** 1.2 **Ta** kṛtam (for carum)
97d) **Ba Ta** kadācana (for purāyuṣaḥ)
99c) **Bo** 1 cubukam; **Ta** cibukam
d) **Bo** 1 nāsikām
100a) **Be** etad eva
c) **Ta** pūrvoktena vidhānena
d) **Ta** ārabhet
101a) **Bo** 1 homaiś caiva (for homena ca)
d) **Ba Ta** ṛṣiḥ (for śuciḥ)
102b) **Bo** 1.2 **Ta** praveśane
d) **Bo** 1.2 ha (for hi)
104d) **Bo** 1 svastyayanam
105a) **Be** yāvāṁścaiva ghṛtābhyaktān
106a) All mss abhiṣicyeta
d) **Bo** 1.2 **Ta** -rohiṇyām
108d) **Be** tam (for ca)
109d) **Be** pālaya (for pālayan)
110a) **Bo** 1.2 vardha tvaṁ ca
b) **Ba** dharmāya vijayāya ca
111c) **Ba** trir evam (for trir enam); **Ba** abhiṣicyainam; Ta abhiṣicyeta
112b) **Bo** 1 hyabhiṣiñcantu

113b) **Ta** tuṣṭaye (for puṣṭāye)

cd) **Ba** tvabhisiñcantu

114b) **Ta** abhiṣicya (for abhinandya)

115a) **Bo** 1.2 vai nityam (for nityaṁ tu)

118d) **Bo** 1 svastyayanam

119b) **Ba** baddhasya; Bo 1.2 dviṣyasya; Ta vadhasya

120c) **Bo** 1.2 āpaḥ

d) **Bo** 1.2 paṭheta samāhitaḥ (for paṭhet susamāhitaḥ); **Ba Ta** paṭhed aghamarṣaṇam

121a) **Bo** 1.2 athā- (for yathā-)

d) **Ba Bo** 1.2 -praṇodanaḥ (for 'panodanaḥ)

121 After $121^{ab}$, **Be Bo** 1.2 ins.
20* Apsu caiva nimajjitvā triḥ paṭhed aghamarṣaṇam /
yathāśvamedhāvabhṛtha evaṁ tad ṛṣir abravīt //

122b) **Ba Bo** 1.2 -praṇodanam (for 'panodanam)

123a) **Ba** 'dhyayane tattu (for dhyeyam etat tu)

124c) **Ba Ta** 'pi (for tu)

125d) **Be Bo** 1 svastyayanam

127a) **Bo** 1.2 haitāḥ

128c) **Bo** 1.2 vedāḥ (for devāḥ)

129a) **Be** japan; **Bo** 1.2 enām (for etām)

b) **Ba** ca (for sa)

c) **Bo** 1.2 tu japet (for tvāvapet)

130d) **Bo** 1.2 vāsasī

132c) **Bo** 1 pravikiret; **Ta** pratigiret

d) **Ba Ta** Saptadhānyam

133c) **Be** -pālāśais tu

134c) **Be** ityete

d) **Bo** 1.2 **Ta** digdevatāḥ

135b) **Bo** 1 vāstviti

136a) **Bo** 1.2 nānyat (for cānyat)

137a) **Bo** 1.2 arirādhayiṣur yo yām

b) **Be** abhidhāveta tāṁ ca tām; **Bo** 1 abhidhatte tathātra tām

138b) **Bo** 1.2 pratyakṣāt

d) **Ta** annam (for dhanam)

139c) **Ba** tu (for hi)

141a) **Ba** transp. dharmajñe and satyavādini

b) **Bo** 1 pradīyate (for ca dīyate)

*Phalaśruti*

3c) **Bo** 1.2 -mahāpūtam
d) **Bo** 1.2 phalapradam; **Ta** prakāśate
5a) **Be** hyeṣa ('pyeṣa)
6d) **Ba Be Bo** 2 prasādāt phu- (for prasādotphu-)
7d) **Bo** 1 śubham (for śubhra-)
9c) **Bo** 1 -nasya cābhyā- (for -nasadābhyā-)
10a) **Bo** 1 -nāśamana- (for -nāśaṁ mana-)
c) **Be** prayantā (conj.)
12b) **Ba** prajñāyāvadyam eva ca; **Ba** vā (for 'pi)

# ṚGVIDHĀNA

## TRANSLATION AND NOTES

### ADHYĀYA I

1. With obeisance to the self-existent Brahmā, the protector of the World [and] also to the seers of Mantras,[a] I am desirous of declaring[b] the ancient precept concerning the Ṛks (Ṛgvidhāna) which was formerly determined [lit. seen] by the sages who saw the Mantras.

(a) *namaskṛtvā mantradṛgbhyaḥ* occurs in the *BD*.1.1a.

(b) *vivakṣur asmi = yakṣyāmi.*

2. From the Mantras as well as from the seers of [those] mantras, Śaunaka declared,[a] in the sequence of the traditional text[b] [i.e. *Ṛgveda*], the precept of rites which were determined by the sages.

(a) The verb is in the past tense.

(b) *Samāmnāyānupūrvaśaḥ* occurs in the *BD*.i.1b.

3. Several Mantras having tangible purposes, were seen by the sages and were shown [and] explained for a [definite] purpose in those[a] [Mantras],

(a) *tasmiṁs tasmin* scil. *mantre*, but Prof. Gonda translates it as "under their respective headings."

4.[a] and the rites with many objects relating to pacification and prosperity, and [the supernormal] attainments founded on Tapas [belong] to the faithful performer.

(a) Mātṛsūnu has not commented on the preceding three stanzas but he has the following comment to make on this stanza: *darśitaṁ tapasaḥ prādhānyaṁ śraddhayāśceti samastārthaḥ* ||

5. The modifications [rather, varieties] such as praise and etc.

which are ordained, likewise statements of an object in verses and hymns and with what desires the gods wish to be praised by the sages—hear them being told [by me].

The commentary on the first hemistich runs as follows: *Stuty arthavādamantrarūpo vedas tatra yā ṛcaḥ / yāni ca sūktāni teṣu stutyādayo ye vikārāḥ pradiṣṭāḥ / kvacit stutiḥ kvacid āśīḥ kvacit karaṇatvaṁ kvacit kriyamāṇānuvāditā evam ādi stutyādivikārān śṛṇuṣveti saṁbaṁdhaḥ //* The definition of the Veda given by Mātṛsūṇu is different from the one given usually. Cp. *Āp. Yaj. Par.* Sūtra, xxxi and Sāyaṇa's intro. to the *Ṛgveda* (VSM), Vol. I, p. 3. Possibly *vikārāḥ* 'modifications' may mean *prakārāḥ* 'varieties' *vide BD.*i.34-40: *mantrā nānāprakārāḥ syuḥ ...stutiḥ praśaṁsā* and etc. *...evaṁ prakṛtayo mantrāḥ sarvavedeṣu sarvaśaḥ //*

6. The fourfold to be wished for[a]—[long] life, heaven, wealth and sons—has been stated at first. Other desires by hundreds are indicated by the sages, who praised the gods.

(a) Mātṛsūnu glosses *āśāsya* by *āśaṁsanīya*, but Prof. Gonda translates it as 'prayer'. The end of the Varga is here marked by 1 in Ba Ta.

7. The Mantras, when perfected by the correct method and employed according to the precept, impart the [desired] result to the Brāhmaṇa.[a] Truth is a means[b] of achieving them as also self-control, tranquility, endurance, freedom from envy and equanimity.

(a) Prof. Gonda has misunderstood the term Brāhmaṇa.
(b) The predicative noun *sādhanam* agrees with the preceding word *satyam*, though followed by three masculine and two feminine nouns.

8. Therefore a twice-born person who is composed in mind; [should be] zealously engaged in muttered prayers and burnt-offerings; [and being] intent upon Tapas and [Veda-] study, [he] should be compassionate towards living beings.

Mātṛsūnu has the following comment: *tasmād dvija iti / tasmāt pūrvāni(ṇi) sādhanāni dvijaḥpraśāṁtātmeti nigadavyākhyātam //*

9. A Kṣatriya should overcome his miseries by the strength of his arms; a Vaiśya and a Śūdra, by their wealth; but the best of the twice-born, by muttered prayers and burnt-offerings.

Identical with the *Manusmṛti*, xi.34.

10. By Tapas one attains heaven, by Tapas one obtains power (*mahat*).[a] The rites of a person who is fully devoted to Tapas and self-controlled, succeed.

(a) Prof. Gonda is wrong in translating *mahat* by "greatness". Cp *Ṛvidh* iv.42d: *tapo hi sumahad balam* //

11. With whatever [desired] object[s, such as]: the causing of hostility, propitiating, counteracting of poison, removing of disease, [and] for what purpose the gods are praised by the sages—

Mātṛsūnu: *vidveṣaṇādayo'rthā uktā teṣvatipratipreteṣu (abhipreteṣu)* yat kāma ṛṣi[r*] gāthāṁ (yāṁ yāṁ)* devatāṁ stauti / etad asmiṁ śloke uktam / vakṣyamāṇena ślokena kṛiyāsaṁbaṁdhaḥ //*

The end of the Varga is here marked by 2 in Ba Ta.

12. that desire of those [objects] accordingly [becomes] fulfilled and I shall teach those various (*vividhāni*)[a] performances of rites.

(a) Dr. Meyer's text shows the reading *vidhānāni* which, I think, is merely a conjecture of his, unsupported by the authority of mss.

13. The preparatory restraint is efficacious at the beginning of rites [and] a twice-born person should perform the *prājāpatya*[a] at the commencement of self-reading (*svādhyāya*).

(a) The penance *prājāpatya*, which is one of the *Kṛcchras*, is described below *Ṛvidh* i.33 = *Manusmṛti*, xi.211.

14. After having the hairs on the head, beard and body shorn [and having] the nails [trimmed] and having bathed, one, [on becoming] pure, should stand during the day and remain seated at night, pure [and] restrained in speech.

The terms *tiṣṭhet* and *āsīta* correspond to *sthānāsana* in *Ṛvidh* i.46 and iii.41, cp. *Manu.* xi.224a; *Mbh.* xii. 165.59a.

15. One, truth-speaking, should mutter the purificatory texts[a] and the mystical utterances.[b] Having muttered them beginning with syllable Oṁ and the Sāvitrī verse beginning with *Tat* [*RV*. 3.62.10].

(a) Mātṛsūnu explains *pavitrāṇi* by *pāvamānasūktāni.*

(b) *vyāhṛtayaḥ*, nominative for accusative.

16. And, the hymn beginning with Apo hi ṣṭhā [*RV*.10.9], [the verses] having the word '*Śuddha*' [*RV*.8.96.7-9], the Aghamarṣaṇa hymn [*RV*.10.190], [the verses] having [the word] '*Śaṁ*' [*RV*. 7.35], and those having [the word] *Svasti* [*RV*.1.89.6 or *RV*.5.51. 11-15] and likewise the Pāvamāni hymns [*RV.Kh*.iii.10 or *RV*. 9.1-67]—[these should be muttered].

The end of the Varga is here marked by 3 in Ba Ta.

17. This[a] [rather, these] should always be employed at the beginning and the end of [all] rites. Upto a thousand times or a hundred [times] or as far as ten times, one should mutter.

(a) We can rightly expect here *etāni* in the place of *etat*. But Mātṛsūnu explains *etat* by *prāguktaṁ japyaṁ mantrajātam.*

18. The syllable Oṁ, the [first] three mystical utterances [and] Sāvitrī [-verse] ten thousand times. Having satiated by offering water to the teachers, the sages, the metres, [and] the gods—

Sts. 17cd-18ab refer to the rhythmic repetition of Sāvitrī i.e. the famous verse addressed to the Sun [*RV*.3.62.10] to the required number of times according to one's ability Cp. the verse of Hārita quoted by Viśvarūpa on *Yaj*.i.25: *Devī sahasraśīrṣā tu śatamadhyā daśāvarā / japed ataḥ sahasrāntāṁ śatamadhyāṁ daśāvaram //*

19. one should resort to Virūpākṣa, muttering the group of Mantras relating to Rudra. And one should not speak with the non-Aryans nor with the Śūdras, nor with the censured [people]—

Mātṛsūnu: *tataḥ prapadyeta virūpākṣam anusmaret rudram anugacchet / kiṁ kurvan ityāha / raudraṁ mantragaṇaṁ japet / katamam ityucyate / kad rudrāya* [*RV*.1.43], *imā rudrāya* [*RV*.1. 114], *ā te piter* [*RV*.2.33], *imā rudrāya sthiradhanvane* [*RV*.7.46] *ityanyaccaitat kuryāt | anāryair aśiṣṭair na saṁbhāṣen na ca rudraira* (*śūdrair*)* *na cānvair vigarhitaiḥ kutsai* -(*kutsitai-*) *riti* || Prof. Gonda misunderstood the term '*raudraṁ mantragaṇam.*'

20. nor with the menstruating woman, nor with men who are outcasts [and] low-born,[a] nor with those who dislike gods and brāhmaṇas, nor with those who revile spiritual guides and elders.

(a) For the term *antyaja*, see Kane, *HDS*, Vol. II, p. 70.

21. Nor with those who dislike their parents [and] one should not despise anyone. Being attended with auspicious ceremonies, [one should] approach[a] the water [i.e. for bathing] thrice a day.

(a) The mss. read, for metrical reasons, *abhyupayāt* for *abhyupeyāt*, but I have corrected it to *abhyupayant*. Its correctness is proved by the parallel passage of the *Manusmṛti* 11.259b. The end of the Varga is marked here by 4 in Ba Ta.

22. At the end of a period of twelve days, one should prepare a *sthālīpāka* [and offer oblations] to Agni, and then to Soma and the third [oblation] to both [the gods] together,

Mātṛsūnu: *anta iti* | *dvādaśarātrikā prājāpatyaḥ kṛcchre uktas tasyānte samāptau sthālīpākaṁ kuryāt* | *tasya devatāḥ paṭhanti* | *agnaye somāyāgni somābhyām iti* || A *sthālīpāka* is an offering at which rice cooked in a pot is offered in the fire, *vide ĀGS*, 1.10.1 ff.

23. And then next one should offer [oblations dedicated] to the All-gods, to Rudra, to Avasānasya Pati[a] [= Sadasaspati], and also to Anumati,

(a) Prof. Gonda is wrong in translating this expression by "the lord of Death". Mātṛsūnu: *avasānasya pataye tathānumatayeti cetau* (*caitau*)* *devatāpadanirdeśāviti* ||

24. [and yet] another [oblation] to Dhanvantari, [the oblations] also to the Gandharvas and the Apsarasas,[a] the tenth [oblation dedicated] to Brahmaṇaspati, and (*tu*) the following[b] is declared to Brahmā

(a) *gandharvāpsarasām*, genitive for dative.

(b) Mātṛsūnu: *parātu ekādaśī brahmaṇa smṛtā āhutiḥ* ||

25. [and oblations] to Sarasvatī, likewise to Viṣṇu, [and] the last [oblation dedicated] to Agni Sviṣṭakṛt.[a] At first the oblations of clarified butter[b] [have to be offered], but when *sthālīpāka* is burnt as a sacrificial offering.

(a) The *mantra* with which the offering to Agni Sviṣṭakṛt is made is given in the *ĀGS*. 1.10.22.

(b) Mātṛsūnu: *ājyāhutaya evādau sthālipākasya prakalpayet | mahāvyāhṛtibhiḥ sūtrāntaradṛṣṭatvāt* ||

26. One should gladden the Brāhmaṇas after having poured [again oblations of clarified butter] into the fire and prepare [offerings] to the manes; then, one who is pure and restrained in speech, should partake of the remnants according to the rule.

Mātṛsūnu: *pūrvoktābhir devatābhir agniṁ hutvā tatra parisamāpya tato brāhmaṇa bhojanaṁ kuryāt | pitṛbhyaś ca śrāddhaṁ kuryāt | tataś ca hutaśeṣaṁ bhojanavidhinā śucir bhūtvā kṛtamauno bhuṁjītati* || The end of the Varga is here marked by 5 in Ba Ta.

27. The rule of all penances (Kṛcchra)[a] is declared in due order: [the rule] of the Prājāpatya [-kṛcchra][b] and the Atikṛcchra[c] and likewise [the rule] of the Sāṁtapana,[d]

(a) vide Kane, *HDS*, Vol. IV, pp. 132-134.

(b) *ibid.*, p. 145 and *Ṛvidh* i.33 below.

(c) *ibid.*, p. 130 and *Ṛvidh* i.34 below.

(d) = *Mahāsāṁtapana*, *ibid.*, p. 147, and *Ṛvidh* i.35 below.

28. and [the rule] of Parākakṛcchra,[a] and the rule of Cāndrāyaṇa.[b] By [the performance of] one [Kṛcchra] a person obtains [bodily] purity, by two [Kṛcchras] a person is released from sins.[c]

(a) *vide*, Kane, *HDS*, Vol. IV, p.143 and *Ṛvidh* i.39 below.

(b) *ibid.*, p.134-138 and *Ṛvidh* i.40-44.

(c) *pāpaiḥ pramucyate*, instrumental for ablative.

29. By three [Kṛcchras], the Mantras become perfected and a person is released from minor sins[a] (Upapātaka) by four [Kṛcchras], from the murder of a learned Brāhmaṇa and likewise from [sins incurred by] sacrificing for unworthy persons.

(a) *mucyate copapātakaiḥ*, instrumental for ablative.

30. By five [Kṛcchras] a person is released from all Pātakas and evil deeds. A person wards off all sins by the [performance of] Tapta-kṛcchra.

If the first hemistich of this stanza is regarded as the continuation of the preceding one, then the translation would be: "[and] a person is released from five [Mahā-pātakas and all evil deeds."

31. A Cāndrāyaṇa [performed] at the beginning and end [of any rite] is declared to be equal to these [five Kṛcchras]. A person purified by the three Cāndrāyaṇas attains the world of Brahmā.

Mātṛsūnu: *Cāṁdrāyaṇa*[*ṁ**] *kṛcchrāṇām ādyaṁtayor anuṣṭhīyamānaṁ* (*mānam*)* *mahācāṁdrāyaṇaṁ bhavati / tat tu paṁcānāṁ kṛcchrāṇāṁ yat phalaṁ tat tulyaphalaṁ bhavati / tisṛbhiḥ cāṁdrāyaṇaiḥ pūto brahmalokaṁ prāpnotītyarthaḥ //* Prof. Gonda translates *cāndrāyaṇam sahādyantam* by "a complete Cāndrāyaṇa." The end of the Varga is here marked by 6 in Ba Ta.

32. By eight [Cāndrāyaṇas] one sees the gods who are ready to fulfil requests in person. One obtains all desired objects after having known the metrical canons (*chandāṁsi*) by ten [Cāndrāyaṇas.]

Mātṛsūnu: *mahācāndrāyaṇakṛtaṁ tasyaitat saṁkhyānuṣṭhāne etat phalami* [*ti*]* *ślokārthaḥ / aṣṭābhiś cāndrāyaṇa*[*ir**] *devatāḥ pratyakṣa kṛtaḥ paśyati varadā etā bhavanti / daśabhis tu gāyatryādīni chaṁdāṁsi jñātvā pratyakṣaṁ dṛṣṭvā teṣaṁ anuṣṭhānena japahomādinā sarvān kāmān prāpnoti / pādādyavivakṣita iti //*

33. A twice-born person, who performs the Prājāpatya[—kṛcchra], should eat in the morning for three days [and] in the evening for [next] three days [and eat the food given] unasked for [the following] three days and he should not eat [anything] during the subsequent period of three days.

Identical with the *Manusmṛti*, 11.211.

34. A twice-born person, who performs the Atikṛcchra, should

partake of one morsel of food only for three periods of three days as above and he should fast during the final period of three days.

Identical with the *Manusmṛti*, 11.213.

35. [Subsisting on the five products of cow]: urine, dung, milk, curd, ghee [and] Kuśa water (*kuśodaka*) and fasting for one [day and] night—[this] is called a Sāṁtapana-kṛcchra.

Identical with the *Manusmṛti*, 11.212abc.

36. And the same [Kṛcchra] having three days [at a time for each of the six ingredients and a fast for three days], they consider a Mahā-Sāṁtapana [-kṛcchra], but fasting for seven days [continuously] is called Śiśusāṁtapana.

The explanation which commentary gives of this stanza can hardly be accepted: *etam eva tryahair yuktam iti paṁcagavyaprāśanaṁ bhaṇyate / trīṇyahāny ekabhaktavidhinā / trīṇi naktavidhinā / trīṇy ayācitavidhinā upavāsatrayaṁ cen mahāsāmtapanam...tantrābhiprāyeṇoktaḥ / apare tvāhuḥ / sapta rātreṇa sāṁtapanaṁ bhavati / tathaiva tryahaṁ gomūtraṁ gomayaṁ tryahaṁ dadhi tryahaṁ ghṛtaṁ kuśodakam prāta*[*ḥ**] *snāyād aham upayased evaṁ bhayati.* Regarding *mahāsāṁtapana* see *Śaṅkhasmṛti* XVIII. 9 and *Bau DS.*, iv.5.17. The śiśusāṁtapana is same as the Mahāsāṁtapana in *Yaj.*3.315. As for Prof. Gonda's translation, less said is better. The end of the Varga is here marked by 7 in Ba Ta.

37. A Brāhmaṇa, who performs Taptakṛcchra and who is steadfast, should drink hot water, hot milk, hot ghee, [and inhale] hot vapour, each [at a time] for three days [continuously] and bathe once [a day].

Identical with the *Manusmṛti*, 11.214.

38. [According to] the rule of Prajāpati declared [above],[a] a restrained person should drink water[b] [in the place of food]. They call this Yatikṛcchra which wards off infirmities (*rapas*).[c]

(a) I have translated according to the commentary, which has the following note: *prājāpatyavidhināpaḥ pibet.*

(b) The text has *apaḥ*, perhaps we ought to read *āpaḥ* (mss. Bo 1.2). The latter reading is definitely preferable, as it avoids a diiambus. For the use of *āpas* as accu. see Whitney 393a.

(c) Mātṛsūnu quotes *Nirukta* iv.21: *rapo ripram iti pāpanāmānī bhavataḥ.*

39. A twelve-days fast, [which is laid down] for a self-restrained and vigilant person is called Parākakṛcchra which wards off all guilt.

Identical with the *Manusmṛti* 11.215.

40. [If] a person reduces [his food daily by] one mouthful during the dark half [of the month] and increases [likewise] during the bright half [of the month] and touching water at the time of each *savana* [i.e. bathes thrice daily]—this is called a Cāndrāyaṇa.

Identical with the *Manusmṛti* 11.216. The *cāndrāyaṇa*, which is described above, is known as the *pipīlikāmadhya* in contradistinction to the *yavamadhya*, which is described in the next verse.

41. A self-governed person should observe the same rule with regard to the Yavamadhya [-cāndrāyaṇa] which begins with the first day of the bright half [of the month].

Identical with the *Manusmṛti* 11.217. The end of the Varga is here marked by 8 in Ba Ta.

42. A Brāhmaṇa, who has performed daily ceremonies should eat four morsels [of food] in the morning, four after sun-set [for two fortnights]—this called the Śiśucāndrāyaṇa.

Identical with the *Manusmṛti* 11.219abd.

43. A self-controlled person should eat eight morsels at a time of sacrificial food, when the mid-day reigns, [for two fortnights]—[this is called] Yaticāndrāyaṇa.

Identical with the *Manusmṛti* 11.218ab.

44. In whatever manner a person who is steadfast and who eats thrice eighty morsels of sacrificial food in a month, attains to identity of world of the moon.

Identical with the *Manusmṛti* 11.220.

45. The [eleven] Rudras, likewise the [twelve] Ādityas and the [eight] Vasus and the Maruts with the Ṛbhusp erformed this penance for the sake of release frcm all that is inauspicious.

Identical with the *Manusmṛti* 11.221abc. The mss. Be.Cm. have the correct reading: *sarvākuśalamokṣāya*.

46. The barley gruel should be sucked in for a week by a self-controlled person who mutters purificatory verses, alternatively standing and sitting and at the time of each *savana*[a] [i.e. while bathing].

(a) *Sthānāsanatriṣavaṇaiḥ*, instrumental for locative of time. The end of the Varga is here marked by 9 in Ba Ta.

47. [The above penance] performed according to the rule purifies, within a week, successively skin, blood, flesh, bones, fat and marrow.

Mātṛsūnu: *ṣaḍ ete śarīradhātava* [*ḥ**] *tvagādyekaikaṁ saptarātreṇa yāvako bhuktaḥ śodhayati.*

48. The purification of skin etc. [takes place] successively within a week[a]. A person, who is thoroughly purified by these observances and alert, should perform rites:

(a) The text has *saptarātram tu,* perhaps we ought to read here *saptarātreṇa*, as required by Pāṇini 2.3.6.

49. then he obtains undoubtedly all favourite and desired objects. [Each ingredient] amongst the broken grain,oil-cake and butter-milk [if consumed] successively can be a means of purifying [the body].

The commentary on the second hemistich runs as follows: *kaṇapiṇyākatakrāṇaṁ ekaikaṁ bhakṣitaṁ kāyaśodhanaṁ bhavati* //

50. A pure-minded and truth-speaking person who has restrained the senses should perform a rite and with reference to a person thus (*evam*) purified, I will declare the manner in which the rites [are to be performed] by Mantras.

Mātṛsūnu: *evam adhastanaṁ śodhanaṁ parāmṛśyate / tena*

*pariśodhitaśarīrasya maṁtrair yad yathā karma kartavyaṁ tad yathā vakṣyāmi* ||

51. At the commencement of all rites, one should fast for three days or take food at night (*nakta*)[a] for three days: then one should start the rite.

(a) *Nakta* primarily denotes the period of time when the stars begin to appear and secondarity means taking food at *nakta* time. The end of the Varga is here marked by 10 in Ba Ta.

52. At the commencement of a [religious] practice, a three-days-penance [is laid down] for a regular ritual practician or one should fast later on, after performing a Sāṁnipātika [-rite].[a]

(a) Mātṛsūnu: *Saṁ* (*Sāṁ*) *nipātikaṁ naimittikam ucyate* || Cp. the com. on the *Go. GS.*4.5.13: *sānnipātikam aniyatanimittam ucyate.*|

53. A person who is adept in Mantras[a] should start the rites which bestow long life and mutter [the verses] having [the word] Śam [*RV.*7.35] and those having [the word] Svasti [*RV.*1.89.6 or *RV.*5.51.11-15] and the Trivṛt[b] verses.

(a) Mātṛsūnu: *vrataniyamaiḥ sādhitā mantrā yena sa mantrayukta ity ucyate.* Prof. Gonda translates Mantrayukta by "being attentive on mantras."

(b) According to Sāyaṇa on the *Aitareya-brāhmaṇa* [3.42], the Trivṛt-stoma consists of three tristiches from three different sūktas [*RV.*9.11.1-3; 64.23-30; 66.10-12] and it is chanted in three *paryāyas* (sections). The first *paryāya* of three verses are taken from the first verse of each sūkta, the second from second verses and the third from the third verses.

54. Having arrived at the north-eastern direction or the eastern [direction] or the northern [direction] in a forest, when the sun has arisen [and having] settled on a pure spot,

Mātṛsūnu: *araṇyc gatvā prācīṁ vā pūrvāṁ diśaṁ gatvā uttarās-āgā* (sic) *tāsu dikṣu śucau deśe sthitaḥ* | *kṛtasamādhikarma samārabhed iti saṁbaṁdhaḥ* ||

55. a twice-born person should mutter [the verses] having [the

word] Śuddha [*RV*.8.95-7-9] likewise [the verses] having [the word] Āp [*RV*.10.9], the Pāvamanī hymns [*RV.Kh*.iii.10 or *RV*.9.1-67] and the Aghamarṣaṇa hymn [*RV*.10.190], after having immersed in water with clothes and head-gear on and sprinkling [the spot after coming out of water].

The commentary on the first hemistich runs as follows: *tāsu dikṣu yuktāśraye kaścii jalāśayo bhavati tasmiṁt* (*tasmint*)* *sacailaṁ snānaṁ kṛtvā / tatas taṁ pradeśam abhukṣya japed vakṣyamāṇā ṛcāḥ //*

56. [On becoming] pure after having immersed [in water] thrice, one should exercise three *prāṇāyāmas* or six, eight or twelve, sixteen or eighteen [*prāṇāyāmas*].

The end of the Varga is here marked by 11 in Ba Ta.

57. While muttering the sacred text of Aghamarṣaṇa [*RV*. 10.190], one should restrain the breath[a] upto a hundred [*prāṇāyāmas*]; or one should restrain as much of one's breath to one's heart's content.

(a) Mātṛsūnu explains *āyamet prāṇān* by *prāṇāyāmān kuryāt*.

58. In proportion as his heart repents of his evil deeds, even so far is his body released from that guilt.
Identical with the *Manusmṛti* 11.229.

59. A person who has burnṭ his blemishes by *prāṇāyāmas* who has worn white garments and who is pure should sit on a sacrificial seat of *kuśa* grass after sipping the water according to the rule.

Mātṛsūnu: *prāṇāyāmān kṛtvā śuklāni vāsāṁsi paridhāyāpa ācamya śucir bhūtvā darbhaprastaram ārohati /*

60. Holding the *darbha* grass in hand, making a lap by bending his legs so that the right leg lies uppermost, covering (*chādya*)[a] the eyes and looking at the horizon without winking.

(a) Mātṛsūnu notices a different reading: *prachādya* which is not found in any mss. of the *Ṛvidh*.

61. The syllable *oṁ*, the three Vyāhṛtis and the Sāvitrī verse

beginning with *Tat* [*RV*.3.62.10]—these being run over in reciting mentally, one should commence the Veda [-study] and etc.

The end of the Varga is marked here by 12 in Ba Ta.

62. In the morning one should recite in a low tone and in a high tone at midday and in the afternoon and at the twilight-time one should cease.

Mātṛsūnu: *vāṁchitasya paṭhanavidhir ucyate | maṁdram eveti ||*

63. Having got up at the hour sacred to Brahmā and having immersed in water thrice, a twice-born person should recite [the Veda], after having resorted to the mode of reciting in a medium speed, neither too quickly, nor [too] slowly.

(a) It is defined as: *rātreś ca paścime yāme muhūrto yas tṛtīyakaḥ | sa brāhma iti vikhyāto vihitaḥ saṁprabodhane ||* Sumantu quoted in *Āhnikatattva*, p.326.

64. One should remain standing[a] while muttering the morning Saṁdhyā and perform the evening Saṁdhyā [in a sitting posture] and in between (*antarā*) [the two Saṁdhyās], one should neither utter a word, nor desist from the [recitation of the Veda] on any account.

(a) Cp. Medhātithi on *Manu*. 2.101: *japasya tu guṇatvaṁ śatrantatvāj japater lakṣanatvāgamāt | adhikārasaṁbaṁdhaś ca sthānāsanayor eva ||*

65. One should pause, when a Brāhmaṇa has arrived and one may converse with him freely; scarcely having seen a Śūdra approaching, one should not study on any account.

Mātṛsūnu: *paṭhato' yaṁ niyama ucyate | brāhmaṇe śrotriye āgate pāṭham upasaṁharet tena brāhmaneṇa saha kiṁcid yathāprāptaṁ vadet | virāme āgneyasūktam | śudraṁ tvāsannaṁ dṛṣṭvā pāṭham upasaṁhared iti niyamaḥ ||*

66. Having muttered the first hymn [*RV*.1.1] which is dedicated to Agni and which is pre-eminent [and] approved by the Brahmanical sages and which is productive of wealth and prosperity and is auspicious, a Brāhmaṇa obtains [his] object.

The end of the Varga is here marked by 13 in Ba Ta.

67. Having muttered all [the hymns having Madhucchandas as] the Ṛṣi [*RV*.1.1-10] along with his son [*RV*.1.11], a person who is restrained and pure undoubtedly obtains the fruit of [the complete recitation of] the *Ṛgveda-saṁhitā*.[a]

(a) *ṛgvedasya saṁhitāphalam* is an example of a word (*ṛgveda-sya*) agreeing with the prior member of a compound.

68. Having muttered[a] this eternal sacred text eleven times,[b] one obtains all desired objects and is freed from sins.

(a) Mātṛsūnu glosses *japant* by *japtvā*.
(b) Mātṛsūnu explains *ekādaśaguṇam* by *ekādaśāvartitam*, but Prof. Gonda takes it as an adj. qualifying *brahman*.

69. [Having muttered], without eating, this collection [of eleven hymns] in the morning every day, one obtains [long] life, wealth, sons and a healthy housewife.[a]

(a) I have ventured, differing from Prof. Gonda ("a house, that suffers no loss") to translate *anāmayān gṛhān* in accordance with the meaning attributed to *gṛha* (pl. wife) in the lexicons. Cp. *MW*. *s.v*. *gṛha*.

70. Whilst muttering this sacred text, one should not look at the Śūdras, and other men of that kind [and if perchance] looked at [them, one, on becoming] pure after sipping water, should look at [auspicious objects such as][a] a cow, a fire or the Sun.

(a) Cp. *AV.Par*. iv.1.23: *Proktāni maṅgalānyaṣṭau brāhmaṇo gaur hutāśanaḥ / bhumiḥ siddhārthakāḥ sarpiḥ śamī vrīhiya-vau tathā //*

71. Muttering in a low tone is ten times [superior to aloud], inaudibly uttered a hundred times [superior to the former] and one should regard the mentally revolved one to be a thousand times [superior to both]—this is declared to be the precept regarding the Japa.[a]

(a) Japa is of three kinds *vācika, upāṁśu* and *mānasa, vide Smṛticandrikā* II, p.394; *trividho japayajñaḥ syāt tasya bhe-daṁ nibodhata / vācikākhya upāṁśuś ca mānasas trividhaḥ smṛtaḥ / trayāṇāṁ japayajñānaṁ śreyān syād uttarottaram iti / atra-Hārītaḥ—Uccais tvekaguṇaḥ prokto dhyānād daśaguṇaḥ smṛtaḥ / upāṁśuḥ syāc chataguṇaḥ sahasro mānasaḥ smṛtaḥ //* Cp. *Manu* 2.85. The end of the Varga is here marked by 14 in Ba Ta.

72. At first, with the Sāvitrī verse [*RV*.3.62.10], one should perform the rite for the sake of pacification (*śānti*)[a] for obtaining prosperity, for acquiring wealth and cattle [and] for [attaining] power.

(a) *Śānti* is a rite intended to avert an impending misfortune.

73. Verily, this Nicṛt[a] [verse] which belongs to all the sacred texts[b] and is consistent with the Vedas has been seen by the wise Viśvāmitra by means of severe asceticism.

(a) The metre of the Sāvitri verse [*RV*.3.62.10] is *gāyatrī* and we are told here that it is *nicṛt* i.e. the *gāyatrī* metre with the syllable less. Possibly the author of the work counted the syllables of *vareṇyam* as three instead of four.
(b) Cp. *Manu*.2.77: *tribhya eva tu vedebhyaḥ pādaṁ pādam adūduhat tad ity ṛco'syāḥ sāvitryāḥ parameṣṭhī prajāpatiḥ //*

74. And with this [verse], one should always perform Homas and muttered prayers as a religious sacrifice for the sake of fulfilling all wishes [since] this is said to be the best sacred text.

Mātṛsūnu: *ye kecit sāmānyavihitā homā japa yajñās ca te sarve "tat savitur vareṇyam"* [*RV*.3.62.10] *ity etayā gāyatryā kartavyaḥ / Kiṁ kāraṇam ity ucyate / sarvakāmasamṛdhyarthaṁ gāyatryākhyam idam ucyate yad iti //*

75. [When] uttered foot by foot[a] in the inverted order, this indeed, is destructive of enemies [and] this inverted order of syllables [of Sāvitri] is recited in the exorcising [rites.][b]

(a) For the formation of *pacchaḥ* see Whitney 1106a. Prof. Gonda has omitted this word in his translation.
(b) Mātṛsūnu explains *abhicāreṣu* by *abhicārakeṣu* and supplies *karmasu* to the latter.

76. One should regard that [rite as] infallible in which rite this

inverted order of syllables [of Sāvitrī] is employed—this, indeed, [is] the power of the sacred text.

Identical with the *Śaunakīyam* 2.15. 7cd-8ab.

77. One should offer the fuel-sticks and the fuel of *vyāghātaka*-wood[a] along with [the Sāvitri verse] in the inverted order of syllables and [offer] mustard oil with the offering ladle made of Vibhītaka-wood.[b]

(a) According to lexicons the term *vyāghāta, rājavṛkṣa* and *śamyāka* are synonyms, *vide* the quotation in *kṣīrataraṅginī on Amara* 2.4.23.

(b) The mss. have corrupt readings: *vaibhītaka kṛtasrucaḥ* (Bo 1 Ta; °sruvaḥ Ba Bo 2) and *vaibhītakakṛtā srucaḥ* Be. I have corrected the reading to *vaibhītakakṛtasrucā* and its correctness is proved by the parallel passage of the *Śaunakīyam* [2.15.9ab].

78. Whoever wishes to annoy [his] foe or also to make [him] depart from [a place or an occupation] can, by *pādas*, oppress the foes and can, by syllables, annihilate [them].

Mātṛsūnu: *yaḥ kaścic chatroḥ pīḍanam icched ātmanaḥ purato vā uccāṭanam icchet sa pādaviparītayā karma kuryāt / yas tu śatru [ṁ]* mārayitum icchet sa varṇaviparītayā karma kuryāt //* The end of the Varga is here marked by 15 in Ba Ta.

79. Henceforth, I shall declare the rule regarding the first hymn of the *Ṛgveda* [1.1] and in what manner the Ṛṣi Madhucchandas performed the rite with this[a] hymn in days of old.

(a) Mātṛsūnu supplies *sūktena* to *etena.*

80. A person who is restrained should honour[a] the fire for a full year while subsisting on the residue of the burnt-offering belonging to the time of the fourth *prāṇa*[b] [=*prāṇāgnihotra* i.e. taking food during the evening *prāṇāgnihotra* of every second day of a person's fasting].

(a) The phrase *śirasā dhārayet* in the secondary sense occurs also below (iii.87). It occurs twice in the primary sense (iii.69;iv.92).

(b) I take *caturthaprāṇakālīya* to mean *caturthaprāṇāgnihotra-kālīya* which is same as *caturthakālīya* in the Smṛti literature. Cp. *Manu.*11.110. Mātṛsūnu, no doubt, refers to *prāṇāgnihōtra*, but he understands the *caturthaprāṇa* to be the fourth vital breath (*udāna*) and he has ignored the last member of the compound. Prof. Gonda renders it by "during the fourth part of a prāna."

81. Offering [oblations] thrice every day, a truth-speaking person should worship [the fire]. The time of vow[a] having arrived, one should offer an oblation of rice etc. dedicated to Agni.

(a) Mātṛsūnu explains *vratakāle* by *bhojanakāle*.

82. The fire, when it is merely meditated upon on a substance other than fire, waits upon him at the end of the vow and the fire, indeed, burns that person whom he wishes thus (iti): 'I shall burn [him]'.

As is well known, the Mss. confuse the letters *t* and *n*, hence I have corrected *dhyānamātra* to *dhyātamātra*.

83. Verily the fire burns even in water by [the might of] that eminent vow[a] and the fire zealously fulfils him with [all] favourite and desired objects.

(a) Mātṛsūnu supplies *prabhāvāt* to *tadvratasya mahātmanaḥ*. The end of the Varga is here marked by 16 in Ba Ta.

84. Next to this, the seven strophes of tristiches which are revealed as beginning with [the deities] Vāyu etc. [*RV.*1.2-3] and a person who is piously disposed obtains [all] favourite and desired objects [after having] often muttered them.

Mātṛsūnu: *prathamasūktasya vidhir uktaḥ / ataḥ paraṁ dvitīya-tṛtīyayor vidhir ucyate / tato* (*tayo*) **reka* [*ṁ**] *navarcam apara* [*ṁ*]* *dvādaśarcam etena sapta tṛcā bhavaṁti / tathā ca praüga-śastraṁ brāhmaṇe uktam / navarcaṁ dvādaśarcaṁ ca tadeka-viṁsatir iti tāḥ sapta tṛcā japa* [*n*]* *nityaṁ suci*[*ḥ*]* *prayataḥ sarvān kāman avāpno*[*tī*]**ti samastārthaḥ //*

85. Further in [the hymn of] Ṛṣi Medhātithi,[a] [there is] a verse beginning with *Sadasaspatim* [*RV.*1.18.6]. One who is desirous of

intelligence should often mutter [it] and offer an oblation of clarified butter with this verse].

(a) The text has *medhātithau ṛṣau.* Cp. *BD.*i.58 and the note thereon.

86. A Brāhmaṇa [on becoming] pure after having taken a bath, should often mutter [the verse], beginning with *Syonā*[*RV.*1.22.15] towards the Earth:[a] [then] he obtains huge landed property, unrivalled and free from difficulties.

(a) *pṛthivīm scil. uddiśya.*

87. Having plunged the thumb into the food along with the [recitation of] five [verses] beginning with *Idaṁ viṣṇuḥ* [*RV.*1.22.17-21], a person repels the *rakṣas* by that [performance] during the Śrāddha-rite.

The present stanza itself appears to be exceedingly suspicious (*videsupra* p.150) and even more so are the two stanzas inserted after this stanza in Be, Bo 1.2, Ta. These two stanzas are evidently late interpolations, as shown by the following: (1) these stanzas are omitted by the earliest ms. Ba consulted by me. The mss. DEF of Prof. Gonda also does the same (*vide Ṛvidh.* trans. by J. Gonda, p.127); (2) the nature of their contents reveals that these were borrowed from some Smṛti text. Cp. the verses from the *Yamasmṛti* quoted by Apārka on *Yaj.* i.238; (3) The vulgate text has ten stanzas for this Varga, a figure which in itself is suspicious and extremely doubtful. The normal number of *ślokas* in a Varga is five and by no means can it exceed seven or eight *ślokas* (Appendix A). The way in which these interpolated stanzas should be dealt with has caused me much anxious thought and finally I have decided to relegate them to the *apparatus criticus.*

88. Having muttered once [the verse] beginning with *Tad viṣṇoḥ* [*RV.*1.22.20] in the midst of water, one becomes thoroughly cleansed of the sin committed during the seven [previous] existences and [the sin arising from] eating forbidden food.

The general rule stated by *Svidh.*i.5.13; *Manu* 11.160 and others is that one should not eat forbidden food, if eaten, one shall perform *prāyaścitta.*

89. The nine verses beginning with *Ambayo yanti* [*RV*.1.23.16-24], which are laid down as belonging to the sprinkling ceremony,[a] are declared to be conducive to long life, curative[b] and liberating from sins.

(a) *abhiṣecanīḥ* = *abhiṣecanīyāḥ.*
(b) *bhaiṣajyāḥ* = *bheṣajyāḥ.*

90. A person who is bound or held fast should mutter [the hymn(s) having] Śunasepha as the Ṛṣi[a] [*RV*.1.24-30]: then he is released from all fetters and he who is sick becomes healthy.[b]

(a) Śunasepham ṛṣim = *Śaunasepham.*
(b) *agadin.* Possibly *agadī bhavet* is a verbal compound, see Whitney 1094.

91. He who wishes to obtain every-lasting objects of desire from Indra, the destroyer of forts should praise [him] daily with the sixteen verses[a] [*RV*.1.28-29].

(a) Mātṛsūnu: "*yatra grāvā pṛthubudhna*" [*RV*.1.28.1-9] *ityādyā nava* "*yacciddhi satyasomapā* [*RV*.1.29.1-7] *ityādyāḥ sapta evaṁ ṣoḍaśaitā ṛcaḥ* // But Prof. Gonda takes 'the sixteen verses' to be *RV*.1.30.1-16. The end of the Varga is here marked by 17 in Ba Ta. This is the longest Varga in the vulgate see above. i.87n.

92. He who is piously disposed should mutter[a] Hiraṇyastūpa's hymn [*RV*.1.32] which is a high praise of Indra's deeds: [then] he drives back his enemies with the least effort.

(a) Mātṛsūnu glosses *japan* by *japet.*

93. Whoever continually worships the sun with the verse beginning with *Ākṛṣṇena* [*RV*.1.35.2] in the morning [or when the sun is] in the middle or even [at the time of] setting [of the sun] will remain healthy[a] and happy.

(a) Mātṛsūnu explains *agadaḥ* by *arogaḥ.*

94. Having meditated on the gods [with] the single verse begin-

ning with *Ākṛṣṇena* [*RV*.1.35.2] at night and offered with this [verse] an oblation of clarified butter into the fire, one obtains long life.

Mātṛsūnu's comment is not available on this stanza. Possibly the curt remark *spaṣṭaḥ* occurring after his comment to the next stanza strictly applies to this stanza.

95. A wayfarer should recite [the verse] which is addressed to the sun and which begins with *Ye te panthāḥ* [*RV*.1.35.11]; faring well he proceeds on his way and he obtains a healthy house-wife.[a]

(a) The phrase which has occurred earlier (i.69), is, no doubt, corrupt here, though the general sense is not doubtful. The context requires that we should read here: *gṛhaṁ cāpnoty ānamayaḥ* and the translation is such a case would be: "Being free from disease he goes to his house".

96. One should regard the hymn beginning with *Saṁ pūṣan* [*RV*.1.42] which the Ṛṣi Ghaura Kāṇva sang. to be fit for speeding up a journey[a] [as it] wards off adversaries on the way.

(a) Mātṛsūnu explains *adhvanyam* by *adhvani hitaṁ pathigacchatāṁ pathyam.*

97. Whoever praises[a] [the god] Īśāna daily with the six verses addressed to Rudra [*RV*.1.43] will always obtain pacification in respect of women, men and cattle.

(a) The text has *tuṣṭūyāt*, a rare form of perfect precative. A clean emendation would be: *tu stūyat.* Mātṛsūnu glosses *tuṣṭūyāt* by *stauti.*

98. He who is desirous of power should offer oblation of clarified butter with these six verses daily or prepare a Caru dedicated to Rudra during the new or full moon days.[a]

(a) Mātṛsūnu explains *parvasu* by *parvakāleṣu paurṇamāsyāmavāsyādiṣu.* The end of the Varga is here marked by 18 in Ba Ta.

99. One should worship the rising sun [with the verse] beginning with *Ud u* [*RV*.1.50] daily. Verily this [hymn] is destructive of the heart-disease[a] and conducive to excellent health.

(a) According to *Sarv.* (i.50), the last three verses [i.e. RV.1.50. 11-13] are declared to *rogaghna upaniṣat* but *Ṛvidh.* (i.99) and *BD*.iii.113 declare them to directed against the heart-disease. cp. *RV*.1.50.11cd: *hṛdrogaṁ mama sūrya harimāṇam ca nāśaya* //

100. Having muttered the half-verse beginning with *Dviṣantam* [*RV*.1.50.13cd] one should think of him whom one hates; [then] the evil-doer obtains enmity within a week.

Mātṛsūnu: *dviṣantaṁ ṛcaḥ / atraiva sūkte "dviṣantam mahyam"* [*RV*.1.50.13cd] *saptarātreṇa āgaskṛt pāpakārī dveṣakārī praguṇo bhavatīti* //

101. A piously disposed person should regularly and repeatedly mutter the last three verses of Praskaṇva [*RV*.1.50.11-13], [when] he is seized by diseases as well as when he is healthy[a] [for] this [is] healthful.

(a) The text has '*arogī*' which is explained as *vimuktarogo* by Mātṛsūnu.

102. And the last half-verse of his[a] [i.e. Praskaṇva's] is called the hostility to enemies (*dviṣad-dveṣa*).[b] One should think of him whom one hates and mutter this [half-verse] on seeing him.

(a) Mātṛsūnu supplies *praskaṇvasya* to *tasya*. But Prof. Gonda translates it as 'of that'.
(b) cp. *BD*.iii.114c: *ardharce tu dviṣaddveṣaḥ* //

103. If he [is] an evil-doer [then] within three days[a], one restrains his hatred. Having muttered it when [the sun] rises,[b] [he obtains] an undecaying life, [spiritual] lustre when midday reigns,

(a) Mātṛsūnu glosses *trirātreṇa* by *trirātrābhyaṁtare*.
(b) He supplies *āditye* to *udayati*. The end of the Varga is here marked by 19 in Ba Ta.

104. but when the sun sets, he wards off his hater. Vigour, [spiritual] lustre likewise health [and] hostility to enemies—[these have been] explained.[a]

(a) The verbal adjective *prakīrtitam* agrees with *dviṣad dveṣam*. We can naturally expect here *prakīrtitāni*.

105. One can cause death to one's foes and can suppress one's enemies [with] the nine hymns beginning with *Paśvā* [*RV*.1.65-73] which [were seen by] Parāśara[a] [while he was] in the womb.

(a) Mātṛsūnu supplies *gṛhītavān* = *dṛṣṭavān* to Parāśara.

106. He who longs for sons, cattle, wealth, heaven, [long] life, [and] unimpaired eyesight should recite the eleven purifying Sauparṇa hymns [*RV.Kh*.i.2-12].

Identical with the *Suparṇādhyāya* 1.1. Dr. Meyer is of the opinion that the *Suparṇ.* is the source of the above stanza, but it can as well be the other way. The commentary on the first hemistich runs as follows: *Śaścad vivāsaścitāgner ayaṁtīty evam ādīni sauparṇāni nilāni* (*khīlāni*)* *śucīni pavitrāṇyekādaśa sūktāni* // The text of mantra quoted by Mātṛsūnu is, no doubt, corrupt but it is clearly identical with the *BD*.iii.118d: *śaśvaddhi vām iti*, if we only remember that the letters *s* and *ś*, *c* and *v*, *dv* and *ddh* are confused in the mss. In the Kashmir ms. the first Sauparṇa khila has fourteen verses, the first line being *śaśvan nāsatyā vuvayor mahitvam.* It may, however, be noted that the text of Sauparṇa hymns is extant in a single ms., and as such the variant readings in the *Ṛvidh.* com. and the *BD* must remain uncorroborated.

107. A person who is steadfast will attain the highest, all-brilliant [and] eternal abode, after having muttered those [verses] which relate to the supreme spirit[a] and which begins with *Ka* [*RV*.1.84.16-18].

(a) The text has *ādhyātmikī*.

108. An ascetic should mutter[a] [the hymn] Ānobhadrīya [*RV*. 1.89] which is addressed to the All-gods and which is conducive to long life. Having muttered this even a person who is about to die[b] will obtain a full [span of] life.

(a) Mātṛsūnu glosses *japan* by *japet*.
(b) Prof. Gonda connects this with the ascetic. The end of the Varga is here marked by 20 in Ba.Ta.

109. A person should mutter the three verses[a] beginning with Madhu [*RV*.1.90.6-8] at the time of worship of the departed ances-

tors: [then] his ancestors having a placed appearance enter [the abode] of highest light.

(a) The procedure of *śrāddha* prescribed by Yajñavalkya (*vide Yaj* 1.226-249) contains a direction to mutter these three verses.

110. One should look at the moon, when it is about to be visible, with the hymn beginning with *Tvam soma* [*RV*.1.91]; [and one] holding fuelsticks in the (right) hand should worship[a] the new moon every month:

(a) Mātṛsūnu explains *upatiṣṭhet* by *upasthānaṁ kuryāt.*

111. [then] during that month one will never have the three-fold miseries[a] [for] Gotama saw his own annihilation from Yama.

(a) According to Mātṛsūnu, they are *ādhidaivika, ādhibhautika* and *ādhyātmika.*

112. A person who is steadfast should worship the moon, when it rises as well as when it is full, [with] this [hymn], then he will even obtain clothes[a] and obtain identity of world of the moon.

(a) Mātṛsūnu explains *vāsāṁsi* by *vastrāṇi.* But Prof. Gonda translates it by "residences" !

113. A person who desires wealth and who is restrained should always mutter [the hymn] beginning with *Etā* [*RV*.1.92] on becom ing pure after a bath [then] he will obtain the wealth wished for[a].

(a) Mātṛsūnu explains *iṣṭam* by *yathepsitam.* The end of the Varga is here marked by 21 in Ba Ta.

114. A person who wishes to obtain [long] life[a] should often recite the hymn which belongs to Kutsa and which begins with *Imam* [*RV*.1.94] and one who is reserved in speech and pure should offer oblations of clarified butter with each verse.

(a) Mātṛsūnu explains *āyur īpsant* by *āyuḥkāmaḥ.*

115. He who is restrained[a] should mutter [this hymn] after having immersed [in water], then he will actually overcome misfortune. Having taken a bath, when the sun is at the midday, [with the hymn] *Apa naḥ śośucat* [*RV*.1.97],

(a) Mātṛsūnu glosses *niyataḥ* by *niyamena* !

116. verse by verse, one who desires ritual purity and who is temparate in food should offer either ghee or eight fuel-sticks [for] this hymn [is] eradicative of evil,

Mātṛsūnu: *ātmanaḥ śuddhikāmo yayā'nvaham aṣṭāv aṣṭau samidho juhuyāt / Kiṁ karaṇam ity ucyate / ya etat sūktam aghāpaham iti //*

117. and one is released from sin just as a reed from its sheath. One should often mutter [the verses] beginning with *Jātavedase* [*RV*.1.99] etc. at the blessing ceremony (svastyayana)[a].

(a) Mātṛsūnu explains it by *svastyayanakarmaṇi.*

118. When about to proceed on an inaccessible path, there is no fear for him from enemies, either in a state-affair or among a troop of [wild] dogs[a] [or when one is] sinful in various ways,

(a) The text has *śvayūthe.* Can it be *aśvayūthe* with the initial *a* elided after *e* of *rājakārye?*

119. [or when engaged] in a bold deed[a] which is impracticable or even in a peril endangering life—from these, one is released after having muttered this [verse] beginning with *Jātavedase* [*RV*. 1.99.1].

(a) Mātṛsūnu explains *pratibhākārya* by *ojasvikārya.*

120. While starting [on a journey], a person who wishes to achieve an object[a] should mentally mutter it. Being successful he fares well and he does not perish on the way.

(a) I have corrected *sisādhayiṣu* to *siṣādhayiṣu.* The end of the Varga is marked here by 22 in Ba Ta.

121. One should often recite[a] this [verse] while returning to one's house after having attained one's object. One should mutter this [verse], when the sun has risen, as well as when it has set.

(a) Mātrsūnu explains *abhyaset* by *japann āgacchet.*

122. [It becomes] a blessing for the day [when it is muttered] in the morning and a blessing for the night [when it is muttered]

in the evening and at day-break one should often mutter this [verse] which is destructive of evil dreams.

The translation follows Mātṛsūnu's commentary.

123. When [a woman is] about to bring forth, one should mutter [the verse] which sets free the unborn child (*garbha*) and which begins with *Pra mandine* [*RV*.1.101.1] and one should [also] mentally meditate on Indra, [then] that woman will deliver the child.

The first *pādā* is read differently by the mss. and the root of trouble appears to me to be the double-sandhi (*pramandineti* = *pramadine iti*) which possibly goes to the archetype. The correctness of my emendation is corroborated by the parallel versions of *Viṣṇudharmottara-* and *Agni-Purāṇas* also *vide supra* pp. 167 and 183 resp.

124. In misfortunes, or when one is desirous of possessing everything, one should often mutter [the hymn having] Trita as the Ṛṣi [*RV*.1.105]. Having muttered the seven-versed [hymn] which is addressed to the All-gods and which begins with *Indram* [*RV*. 1.106] after taking a bath [at midday],[a]

(a) Mātṛsūnu supplies *madhyaṁdine* to *snātaḥ*.

125. and having offered an oblation of clarified butter, one is released from all distress. The next hymn [*RV*.1.112] which has [the word] Śaṁtāti[a] and which consists of twenty-five verses [is] excellent,

(a) The formation of the term *śaṁtātīya* is regular and in accordance with Pāṇini 5.2.59, whereas the formation of the term *śaṁtātīya* which often occurs in the *Gṛhyasūtras* and elsewhere with reference to *RV*.7.35 is uncertain. Cp. the scholium on *ĀGS*.2.8.13.

126. the hymn which is a praise of the hot milk oblation and which is eradicative of infirmities[a] [should be muttered] then one will obtain the highest prosperity after having adored the Aśvins (*nāsatyau*).

(a) See i.38 above and note (c).

127. A pure Brāhmaṇa should frequently mutter the hymn which is addressed to Rudra and which begins with *Imā* [*RV*.1.114], then he obtains a [full] life, knowledge, wealth, sons and a healthy housewife.[a]

(a) See i.69 above and note (a). The end of the Varga is here marked by 23 in Ba Ta.

128. [Having perceived] the impurity of self [persisting?] on heroic sons, grandsons, cow-pens and in a dream, one who is pure and who has fasted for three nights should, with the two [verses] beginning with *Mā no mahāntam* [*RV*.1.114.7-8],

Both the text and the scanty commentary on the first hemistich of this stanza are corrupt.

129. offer the Udumbara [fuel-sticks] sanctified by curds, honey and clarified butter [and likewise] with the [complete][a] hymn one should offer an oblation of clarified butter at the beginning and end of [other] rites.[b]

(a) Mātṛsūnu supplies *samastena* to *sūktena*.
(b) Mātṛsūnu supplies *anyeṣām* to *karmaṇām*.

130. Having praised[a] with uplifted arms, [the god] Bhava, a hundred times by means of [this] hymn,[b] one who is free from diseases will live long after having cut asunder all the nooses of death.

(a) Sense as well as construction require that we should emend *tuṣṭāva* to *tuṣṭvā ca*. The emendation is palaeographically sound *vide* i.106.
(b) Mātṛsūnu: "*īmā rudrāya*" [*RV*.1.114] *ityanenaiva sūktena ūrdhvabāhur bhūtvā śataśo ye* [*yo*]* *bhavaṁ rudraṁ stauti bahukālaṁ jīvati rogavarjita iti* ||

131. In a standing posture, a person who holds fuel-sticks in [the right] hand and who is pure should often worship the rising sun, the resplendent one,[a] with hymn beginning with *Citram* [*RV*. 1.115],

(a) As the term *āditya* is synonymous with *bhāskara*, hence the latter term has been translated in its etymological sense.

132. and with the same high-praise, one removes infirmity and obtains wealth and [long] life after having often invoked [the sun], when it is at the midday.

The end of the Varga is here marked by 24 in Ba Ta.

133. One should mutter [the verse] beginning with *Adhaḥ svapnasya* [*RV*.1.120.12] in the morning every day, [then] he dispels evil dreams and there is no fear for him by reason of fasting [for want of food].

Mātṛsūnu: "*adhaḥ svapnasya nirvide* [*RV*.1.120.12] *ity etāṁ ṛcaṁ japan prātar ahanyahani duḥsvapnakṛtaṁ doṣaṁ nāśayati* | *bhojanaṁ na cotpadhyate tataś ca kṣudhayā na piḍyata iti* ||

134. The subsequent (*parā*) [verses, rather the hymn] beginning with *Ubhe punāmi* [*RV*.1.133] are announced as destructive of enemies. Having muttered them one kills[a] the demons and suppresses one's rivals.

(a) Mātṛsūnu explains *hanti* by *nikṛṁtati*.

135. A person who performs the daily ceremonies will obtain desired objects[a] after having accomplished the five [daily] sacrifices and having-offered [an oblation] into the fire while muttering [the verse] *Ye devāso divi* [*RV*.1.139.11].

(a) Mātṛsūnu supplies *abhipretān* to *kāmān*.

136. On becoming pure, a person who holds fuel-sticks in [the right] hand should daily worship [the deities] Indra and Viṣṇu, after obeisance, with the three[a] [Mantras] beginning with *Viṣṇor nu kam* [*RV*.1.154.1-3]:

(a) *tribhiḥ scil. mantraiḥ*.

137. [then] one will obtain Dharma, intelligence, wealth, sons, the increase of Brahman and the highest abode[a] of eternal light.

(a) *paraṁ sthānam*. cp. *RV*.1.154.5d: *viṣṇoḥ pade parame madhva utsaḥ* ||

138. Having perceived an incendiary[a] approaching or a tiger or

a wolf one is rescued from them by means muttering[b] [the verse] beginning with *Na mā garan* [*RV*.1.158.5].

(a) For the term *ātatāyin* see Kane, *HDS*, Vol. III, pp.517-18.
(b) Mātṛsūnu glosses *japan* by *japāt*.

139. After fasting for three, days, one should mutter during the [whole] night until the sun appears [on the horizon, then] after having immersed [in water], one should worship the sun with the verses addressed to Sūrya.[a]

(a) *Saurīḥ scil. ṛcaḥ* accusative for instrumental, but Mātṛsūnu explains it by *sauryaiḥ sūktaiḥ* (*RV*.1.50, 115 etc.). But Dr. Meyer refers to *RV*.1.164.46-47 and Prof. Gonda to *RV*. i.164.44, 51-52 as the text of the Saurī verses. The end of the Varga is here marked by 25 in Ba Ta.

140. Neither the thieves nor others of bad conduct see him while proceeding on a way, [he] alone [unaided] rescues[a] hundred persons from the robbers.

(a) The text has, for metrical reasons, the ungrammatical form *trāyeta*. Grammatical accuracy has probably been sacrificed to the exegencies of the metre. Mātṛsūnu glosses it by *rakṣayati*.

141. Having committed a theft out of infatuation, a twice-born person fasting for three days and pure will quickly be freed from [his] guilt after having muttered the hymn *Asyavamīya* [*RV*.1.164],

Mātṛsūnu: *yasyājñānataḥ pramādād abuddhipūrvakaṁ suvarṇa-haraṇaṁ saṁpadyate tasyaitad rahasyaprāyaścittam ucyate / tri-rātram upoṣya tato "asya vāmasya palitasya hotur* [*RV*.1.164] *ityeta* (*etad*)* *dvāpaṁcāśad ṛcaṁ sūktam japet / tata*[ḥ]* *steya-kṛtā* (*kṛtād*)* *doṣāt pramucyate* //

142. and whoever wishes to establish a kingdom [along][a] with kinsmen, sons, friends and allies should mentally and often mutter the hymn[b] after becoming restrained.

(a) I supply *sārdham* to *jñātiputrasuhṛnmitraiḥ*, but Mātṛsūnu supplies the word *stūyamānaḥ*. The term *jñātiputra* can also be resolved as a tatpuruṣa-compound and the translation in such a case would be "sons of agnate relatives."

(b) Prof. Gonda takes "the hymn" to be *RV*.i.165. But Mātṛsūnu, with whom I concur, takes it to be *Āsyavamīya* [*RV*. 1.164] which is treated in the preceding stanza. It is most unlikely that our author would dispose off the enigmatic hymn [*RV*.1.164] with a single stanza.

143. [One should] mutter the hymn beginning with *Kayā śubhā* [*RV*.1.165] after having culminated one's spiritual guides, kings and brāhmaṇas, but Śaunaka declared [it] even [in the case of] hearing an important secret[a] of [or rather concerning] one's spiritual guide.

(a) The term *pararahasyam* can also be resolved as a *tatpuruṣa*-cpd., and the translation of the second hemistich in such case would be "but Śaunaka declared [it in the case of] hearing other's secret, [and] even [a secret] of one's spiritual guide." The translation implies a reading, *paraṁ rahasyam.*

144. A piously disposed person should mutter these two verses beginning with *Imaṁ nū somam* [*RV*.1.179.5-6], [then] he will obtain all objects of desire [and] there can be no sin[a] whatsoever.

(a) Mātṛsūnu paraphrases *pātakam* by *duṣkṛtam.*

145. One should often worship the food which is served with the hymn beginning with *Pituṁ nu* [*RV*.1.187] and should often honour and eat the undespised food.

Mātṛsūnu: "*pituṁ nu stoṣam*" [*RV*.1.187] *ityevat(etad)* daśarcaṁ sūktam anena sūktena bhojanārtham annam upasthitaṁ bhojanakartum (kartā)* upatiṣṭhet tata*[ḥ]* *stūyāt tatas tad annaṁ sarvān doṣān pramuṁcati / bhuktaṁ vā* [na]* *duḥkhakaraṁ bhavatiti //* The end of the Varga is here marked by 26 in Ba Ta.

146. For him [there] can be no disease arising from food [and] even poison is reduced to a consumable state.[a] One should mutter this hymn which is destructive of poison after having drunk poison [through mistake].

(a) Prof. Gonda renders *annatām* as 'food'.

147. And one should not eat while one is unrestrained in speech,[a] nor when one is impure, nor [eat] disgusting food, and on becoming pure one should always give food, honour it and offer [oblations into the fire].

(a) Mātṛsūnu understands *avāgyataḥ* to be genitive singular and in order to bring out some sense he had to supply *annam* to it. All this is unnecessary.

148. For him there can be[a] no fear whatsoever from hunger [and] one will not suffer any disease arising out of food. A person who has entered upon a wrong path or who has deviated from the right path somewhere,

(a) Mātṛsūnu paraphrases *syāt* by *bhavati.*

149. or who has done an ignominious deed will arrive at the right path, when he offers ghee, verse by verse, [into the fire] with the hymn beginning with *Agne naya* [*RV*.1.189].

Mātṛsūnu: *paṁthānam iti* / "*agne naya supathā rāye asmān*" [*RV*.1.189] *ity asya pūrvaṁ suktaṁ tasya vidhāne pūrvam eva phalaṁ paṭhitaṁ paścāt vidhānam* / *tataḥ prathamaṁ tad vidhānamucyate* / *paścāt phalaṁ dṛśyate* / *paṁthā dvividhaḥ* / *eko deśakṛtaḥ paṁthā aparaḥ karmaṇām anuṣṭhānena kṛtaḥ* / *tayoḥ prabalito* (*pracalito*)* *yaḥ so'gne naya supathā* [*RV*.1.189] *ityanena sūktena pratyṛcam ājyaṁ juhuyāt* //

150. A piously disposed person should worship the fire after having muttered [the hymn] always. Having taken a bath one should mutter the hymn beginning with *Anarvāṇam* [*RV*.1.190] after bowing to Bṛhaspati:

The commentary on the second hemistich runs as follows: "*anarvāṇaṁ vṛṣabhaṁ maṁdrajihvam*" [*RV*.1.190] *ityetad aṣṭarcaṁ bārhaspatyaṁ sūktaṁ tad etat snātvā śucir bhūtvā japet sa bṛhaspatim* / *anusmareti* // The end of the Varga is here marked by 27 in Ba Ta.

151. [then] he obtains heroic sons and wealth and attains fame.[a] A piously disposed person should mutter the hymn beginning with *Kaṁkato na* [*RV*.1.191] when he is afflicted by poison:

(a) Mātṛsūnu paraphrases *suślokyaṁ ca niyacchati* by *sukīrtitvam ca prāpnoti.* Prof. Gonda renders it as 'one preserves one's fame'.

152. then the poison does not take effect, even if it comes from a serpent that poisons by mere look.[a] The poison which is in worms and spiders and which arises out of hyenas and scorpions,

(a) *dṛṣṭiviṣāt* lit. 'from a serpent which has poison in its eyes.'

153. and which comes from roots and artificial—all [that], he heals [by] muttering. Dharma, intelligence, wealth, sons, good fortune, spiritual lustre,

The st. 153cd-154ab, which is a faint repetition of the st.137 above, is regarded as interpolated by Prof. Gonda. Here we have the *phala* without any *vidhāna* nor any *pratīka* whatsoever. Moreover, Mātṛsūnu has commented on this stanza.

154. health, prosperity, longevity, cattle, knowledge [and] high fame. A piously disposed person who has observed a vow after having taken a bath and fasted,

Constructionally this stanza is joined to the next, which contains the main verb.

155. should worship Śatakratu after having performed a hundred breathing exercises. Having placed the feet joined together and holding a dagger [in hand][a] a person who is restrained in speech for a day [should]—

(a) Prof. Gonda renders it as "furnished with a razor." I am not certain what he means thereby. The term *kṣurasaṁyukta* occurs in *Svidh.* 2.5.5 and Sāyaṇa glosses it by *kṣuraṁ dhārayan.* The end of the Varga is here marked by 28 in Ba. Ta.

156. keep in mind the *ṛṣi* Gṛtsamada by means of the hymn beginning with *Yo jāta* [*RV*.2.12] and should mutter this [hymn] a hundred times[a] as well as [the verse] beginning with *Indra-śreṣṭha-* [*RV*.2.21.6] at the end.

(a) Mātṛsūnu explains *śatakṛtvas* by *anekaśas.*

157. One obtains wealth within a day (*ekāhāt*)[a] the highest success within two days, health within three days, plenty of food within four[b] [days],

(a) The instrumental expresses the notion registered by Pāṇini 2.3.6.
(b) *caturbhiḥ scil. ahobhiḥ.*

158. the spiritual lustre within five[a] [days], delightful life within six [days], sons and prosperity within seven [days] and one will obtain fame within eight [days],

(a) *pañcabhiḥ scil. ahobhiḥ.*

159. and one becomes a favourite of Indra and departs to his favourite abode. Destructive of enemies, subjugative of robbers, highly productive of wealth and prosperity,

Mātṛsūnu: *ripughnam iti sārddham / "gaṇānāṁ tvā gaṇapatiṁ havāmahe* [*RV*.2.23] *iti tad ekonaviṁśarcaṁ sūktaṁ bārhaspatyaṁ tasyāyam itiṣṭayo ripughnam ityādikaḥ //*

160. [is] the comfort-increasing hymn beginning with *Gaṇānāṁ* [*RV*.2.23] which one should mutter. A piously disposed person should often mutter this [hymn addressed to] Bṛhaspati[a] during the time of twilights,

(a) *bṛhaspatim = bārhaspatyam* cp. Com. on st. 159 above. But Prof. Gonda makes a mistake by connecting the word with the next stanza. The end of the Varga is here marked by 29 in Ba Ta.

161. [and] worship [the sun] with the hymn [*RV*.2.28] for the sake of fulfilment of all desired objects. The verse beginning with *Yo me rājan* [*RV*.2.28.10] [is] subjugative of evil dreams—

Mātṛsūnu: *upatiṣṭhe* [*ti*]* / "*idam kaver ādityasya svarāja* [*RV*. 2.28] *ity ekādaśarcaṁ sūktam anena sūktenādityam upatiṣṭheta samṛdhyartham / asminneva sūktena* (*sūkte*)* "*yo me rājan yujyo vā sakhā va* [*RV*.2.28.10] *itīyaṁ duḥsvapnanāśanī*[*ṛk*]* //

162. muttering[a] [this]—a pure Brāhmaṇa quickly destroys an evil dream. After having fasted for a day and night, a person who

is restrained and who is the best among those who know the Brahman—

(a) Mātṛsūnu paraphrases *japtvā* by *japant*.

163. should offer oblations of clarified butter or a Caru mixed[a] with milk, for the sake of progeny, with these five [verses] beginning with *Rākām aham* [*RV*.2.32.4-8] on the sixth day of the bright [fortnight]:

(a) The metre requires that we should read here *śritam* (mss. Ba Ta) instead of *śṛtam* (mss. Ba Bo 1.2.)

164. [then] he obtains prolific[a] progeny, after having eaten the residue of burnt-offering himself. A person who is overcome by a violent disease which threatens [his] life,

(a) Mātṛsūnu glosses *mahatīm* by *śobhanām*.

165. being restrained in speech and pure, should offer a Caru, verse by verse, with the hymn addressed to Rudra viz. *Ā tē* [*RV*. 2.33] after having fasted on a fourteenth [day] of the dark [fortnight].

The end of the Varga is here marked by 30 in Ba Ta.

166. At first, having offered oblations of clarified butter and then, having worshipped Śaṅkara, a person who is vigilant should subsist on the residue of burnt-offering every other [day i.e. with an interval of one day].

Mātṛsūnu: *pūrvāddham* (*pūrvam*)* *iti sārddham* / *anenaiva* "*ā te pitar marutāṁ sumnam* [*RV*.2.33] *etyādinā* (*ityādinā*)* *sūktenaikāṁtariṣvahastu* (*aikāntariteṣvahassu*)* *pratyṛcaṁ prathamājyāhutir* (*prathamam ājyāhutīr*)* *hutvā* / *tataḥ samastena sūktena śaṁkarasyopasthānaṁ kuryāt* // Prof. Gonda renders *ekāntaram* as 'every other meal'!

167. When a month is completed [in the above manner], he will overcome death and he is released from diseases. Whoever is blamed, out of infatuation, or whoever does an ignominous deed—

Mātṛsūnu: *evaṁ māsaṁ yāvad ekāṁtaritaṁ kuryāt* / *caruśrapaṇaṁ ca kṛtvā hutvā havi*[*ś*]* *śeṣeṇa vartate* / *evam anālasyo bhūtvā māsena mṛtyuṁ jayati* / *rogebhyaś ca pramuṁcata iti* //

168. should, while in water, mutter the verse beginning with *Ambi* [*RV*.2.41.16] becoming vigilant after having taken a bath and fasted. He who, while proceeding on a way sees an ominous bird[a] swooping on [him],

(a) The manuscript evidence is in favour of the reading *śakuni* which is practically same as *śakuna* but with a clear reference to divination.

169. should [remain] piously disposed and mutter after having stood and ascertained [as to whether it is] an inauspicious [bird] or an auspicious one and with the two hymns [*RV*.2.42-43, the first one] beginning with *Kanikradat* [*RV*.2.42], he should worship that which made the noise,[a]

(a) *Kṛtasvaram* construes with *śakunim̐ vāyasam̐* etc. in the next stanza.

170. [whether it is] a bird or a crow, an animal or a serpent, and even without seeing [them] this [hymn] which perplexes robbers should be muttered.

The end of the Varga is here marked by 31 in Ba Ta and the last *pāda* is repeated in Ba Bo 2 Cm. It is the universal practice of the ancient writers to repeat the last line of a chapter in order to mark its end. Cp. Mātṛsūnu: *dvirabhyāso' dhyāyasamāptisūcanārthaḥ śiṣṭācārāthaś ca tad ācaraṇam̐ cāyuṣyam iti* ||

## ADHYĀYA II

1. Whether it [is] a being that utters auspicious sound or whether it is another being or yet another which neither shrieks nor is it seen, [in any case], he should mutter after bowing [then] he returns [home] successful.

Mātṛsūnu believes that this stanza refers to enemies. But this is hardly possible, as the present stanza is only a continuation of the last stanza of the previous chapter.

2. [There] is no fear whatsoever for him from robbers anywhere on his way; he surmounts difficulties [and] he fares well and is[a] happy.

(a) The verb *bhavet* agrees with *svastimān* and *sukhī*, hence *sukhībhavet* can be regarded as an instance of a mere collocation and not a full-fledged verbal compound.

3. One whose consumed food is neither digested nor does it cease in any way, should mutter the verse beginning with *Agnirasmi* [*RV*.3.26.7] after having meditated upon the eater of food [i.e. Agni].[a]

(a) Prof. Gonda renders 'getting rid of the food.' But the idea is common. Cp. *BG*.15.14: *ahaṁ vaiśvānaro bhūtvā prāṇīnāṁ deham āśritaḥ / prāṇāpanasamāyukto pacāmy annaṁ caturvidham //*

4. One should mutter the dialogue of Viśvāmitra[a] [with the rivers i.e. *RV*.3.33] when one crosses over a river. Having bathed and sipped [water] according to the precept, one should let go a handful of water [into the river].

(a) Cp. *Saṁvādo nadībhir viśvāmitrasya*, *Sarv*.iii.33; *BD*.iv.-105ff.

5. The rivers, like mothers their own son, protect him, who regularly performs this [rite] after having muttered 'homage to the streams", from the torrent,[a]

(a) Prof. Gonda renders 'streams'. The end of the Varga is here marked by 1 in Ba Ta.

6. and [there] can be no fear for him even from [the beings] which move about on the banks of rivers[a] nor from the beings which live in water nor is he oppressed by cold and heat.[b]

(a) The text has *nadītīracareṣu*, locative for ablative, but Prof. Gonda renders '(when travelling) on ways at the bank of rivers.'

(b) *śītoṣṇaiḥ* = *śitoṣṇābhyām*.

7-8. Whoever wishes to cross a flooded river should remember fully [the verse] *Ramadhvam* [*RV*.3.33.5] and in the midst of water while crossing the river he should mutter the verse *Oṣu* [*RV*.3.33.9]: [then] he reaches [the other] bank quickly or [that] Brāhmaṇa finds a ford. Whosoever wishes to cross over quickly to the other side of the water with a yoked chariot,

Mātṛsūnu glosses *gādham* by *svalpodaka prādeśam* (*pradeśam*)*.

9. being restrained, should mutter himself (*svayam*) this [verse] *Udva urmir* [*RV*.3.33.13]. Likewise [a person] who has set on a journey[a] should remember fully [the hymn] beginning with *Ā mandrair* [*RV*.3.45]:

(a) The text has *adhvānaṁ prasthitaḥ*. For a different idiom see above i.168: *adhvani prasthitaḥ*.

10. [then] he returns home again, after having accomplished his business. [A person] who is not liberal [but] has abundant riches and whose mind is always engrossed [with wealth]:

Constructionally, the second hemistich is joined to the first hemistich of the next stanza, which contains the main verb. Dr. Meyer, however, wants to read the hemistich 11cd after 10ab and hence he had to rearrange the text.

11. one should endeavour to obtain his wealth, after murdering and recollecting [the verse] *Kiṁ te kṛṇvanti* [*RV*.3.53.14]. The wealth-bestowing hymn beginning with *Indrāparvata* [*RV*.3.53] is declared to be conducive to long life.

The end of the Varga is here marked by 2 in Ba Ta.

12. One whose organ of speech is stupified [and hence] cannot obtain the right knowledge or whoever does not know in any way the objects of senses as they really are,

The commentary on the second hemistich runs as follows: *iṁdrīyārthān yathārthān yo na jānāti śabdārthaṁ vā yo na budhyatīrtyarthaḥ* //

13. or the knowledge which was acquired by him is lost again and again, he obtains it in two months, after having muttered the two verses [beginning with] *Sasarparī* [*RV*.3.53.15-16].

Mātṛsūnu paraphrases *praṇaśyeta* by *vismarati.*

14. Proceeding with a cart, one should recollect the four [verses] beginning with *Sthirau gavau* [*RV*.3.53.17-20]: [then] he, [being] successful and having sturdy oxen, returns happily.[a]

(a) Prof. Gonda renders *kuśalenaiti* 'he goes in good condition.'

15. A Brāhmaṇa having perceived the axle of the cart with its end broken off, while [journeying] in a difficult route, should mutter the two verses *Abhi vyayasva* [*RV*.3.53.19-20] which give strength to the axles.

Prof. Gonda translation of the first hemistich is inaccurate.

16. On the fourteenth day of the dark fortnight, a person who is pure and steadfast, having fasted for three days and remaining on a cremation ground sloping towards the south—

Mātṛsūnu: *Kṛṣṇapakṣa iti / asminn eva sūkte* "*iṁdrotibhir bahulābhir no adya*" [*RV*.3.53.21-24] *etāś catasra ṛcaḥ paṭhyante / vasiṣṭhadveṣiṇyo nāmakā adhikṛtyedam ucyate ślokacatuṣṭayam / prathamaśloke puraścaraṇam uktam / kṛṣṇapakṣe caturdaśyām ityādi tato anantaraṁ vidhānam uktam* // The end of the Varga is here marked by 3 in Ba Ta.

17. wearing a red headgear, and having a sword in hand,[a] with fuel-sticks belonging to the Bilva-tree, living on air [i.e. fasting], should for seven days offer mustard-oil mixed with salt,

(a) Mātṛsūnu explains *asipaṇiḥ* by *gṛhītakhaḍgaḥ, gṛhītakṣurikaḥ.*

18. [and] fuel-sticks of *rājavṛkṣa,*[a] whilst reciting those [verses

i.e. *RV*.3.53.21-24], which express hatred for the Vasiṣṭhas. At night, having made an image of him, whom one hates, out of the Śamyāka-wood,[b]

(a) Mātṛsūnu glosses *rājavṛkṣaḥ* by *vaibhītakaḥ*, but according to *Yādavaprakāśa* it is synonymous with *vyāghāta-tree*. See *Vaijayantīkośa* edited by G. Oppert, p.282 (line 40) and the next note.

(b) See above i.77, note (a).

19. and having tread on it, a twice-born person should perform the sacrifice with the four verses [*RV*.3.53.21-24]. This Homa [is to be] aimed at (*uddiśya*) the name—he [the victim] will not survive a week.

Mātṛsūnu: *adhiṣṭhāya ca taṁ puruṣaṁ pādenākṛṣyābhyas tata etābhiś catasṛbhir ṛgbhir homaṁ kuryāt | dveṣy asya nāmoccārayitvā tato'sau dveṣyaḥ saptarātram api na jīvati ||*

20. This spell i.e. Brahman communicated by Kuśika kills in the end [all] the Vasiṣṭhas. There is nothing inviolable to him while he mutters and offers oblation [with it].

Prof. Gonda's rendering of the second hemistich is as follows: 'Nobody is safe from him when he mutters (it) and offers oblations.'

21. A restrained person should regularly mutter the pre-eminent *ādhyātmika* hymn consisting of twenty-two verses [i.e. *RV*. 3.55] on the new or full moon days: [then] he obtains all favourite desires.

Mātṛsūnu: *Dvāviṁśakam iti* | "*imaṁ mahe vidathyāya śūṣam* [*RV*.3.55] *iti ta* (*tad*)* *dvāviṁśaṛcaṁ sūktaṁ ādhyātmikam anuttam | tat parvasu pauṛnamāsyādiṣu japyam etaj japan iṣṭān kamān āpnotiti ||* The end of the Varga is here marked by 4 in Ba Ta.

22. [One should] daily [worship the deities], Bṛhaspati, Ajāśva [i.e. Puṣan], Saviṭr, Babhru [i.e. Soma], and Ṛtāvṛdhas [i.e. Mitra and Varuṇa] with the five sets of tristiches every day.

The text refers to the *RV*.3.62.4-18.

23. One should, verse by verse, offer ghee [with the verse] beginning with *Bṛhaspate* [*RV*.3.62.4-6] for five days. Having offered oblations into the fire and having honoured [them] with sandal wood paste and garlands together with incense.

Prof. Gonda renders *gandha* 'fragrances.'

24. Those five deities confer five benefits: riches, progeny, cattle, festivities and long life.

The end of the Varga is here marked by 5 in Ba Ta.

25. Now I shall declare the precept productive of favour regarding the Gāyatrī-verse which is chanted at the commencement of the Vedas and which bestows *dharma*, *artha*, *kāma* and *mokṣa*.

Mātṛsūnu: *atha vedādīti gāyatryā vargapaṁcakam ||*

26. In the triad of obligatory, occasional and optional [ceremonies there exists], no doubt, a final aim but (*tu*) there is nothing beyond the Gāyatrī-verse either in this world or in the next.

Prof. Gonda has not brought out the force of particle *tu* in his translation of this stanza.

27. A wise person who eats sparingly the sacrificial food,[a] who keeps silence, who is eagerly engaged in ablutions and prayer thrice [a day] should, exercising undivided attention, mutter [it] three hundred thousand times.

(a) *medhyānna*: same as *haviṣya*, i.43-44 above.

28. A person can combine the [mutterings] with the [other] rites, either gradually or according to his wish and his observance would not break as long as he performs what ought to be done (*kāryam*).

The use of *yāvat...na......tāvat...nā* in the vulgate text is unparalleled, and the emendation suggested: *yāvat...sa** is palaeographically sound.

29. Having taken a bath at the rising of the sun, one should mutter [it] a thousand times every day; [then] he surely obtains long life, health, power and wealth.

The end of the Varga is here marked by 6 in Ba Ta.

30. Having duly fasted for three days and having offered ghee by thousands into the fire [which is lit with] the fuel-sticks belonging to the Khādira-wood, one obtains a thousandfold gain.

The last *pāda* in Bo 1.2 is *rāhusūryasamāgame*, doubtless owing to the succeeding stanzas (31-32) which have that *pāda* at the end.

31. [Having offered] the fuel-sticks of the Palāśa[a] anointed with ghee into the fire at the conjunction of the Rāhu and the sun, one obtains a thousandfold gain.

(a) *Palāśa* designates the tree Butea frondosa. Regarding its use see *AV.P.*XXVI.5.1a: *puṣṭikāmaḥ palāśasya.*

32. Having offered the red-sandal-wood pieces anointed with ghee into the fire [which is lit with] Khādira-wood at the conjunction of the Rāhu and the Sūrya, one obtains a thousand gold [pieces].[a]

(a) Prof. Gonda renders 'a thousand (fold) gold'.

33. Having offered the cowdung mixed with red sandalwood pieces and ghee into the fire, a twice-born person obtains a wealth consisting of a thousand cows.

(a) Prof. Gonda renders 'a thousand herds of cows'.

34. He acquires that cow, whose cowdung balls anointed with ghee [were] offered into the fire by thousands.

The sense is obvious, but the anacoluthic construction is a bit difficult. The end of the Varga is here marked by 7 in Ba Ta.

35. One will obtain horses by [the offering of] barley corns: elephants by [offering of] sesamum-seeds; likewise she-buffalos by [the offering of] barley-meal and the acquisition of a virgin [wife] by the offering of the *śāli* rice grains.

(a) *hastīn* = *hastinaḥ*.
(b) *mahiṣyaḥ* = *mahiṣīḥ*.

36. Having offered the flowers of the Jāti, the Campaka, the Rājārka anointed with ghee- into the fire by thousands, one obtains clothes.

(a) *ghṛtāktānāṁ jāticaṁpakarājārkakusumānām*, genitive for accusative.

37. Having offered water into the orb of the sun [reflected] in the water by thousands, one will obtain a thousand gold [pieces], silver [pieces] when offered into [the orb of] the moon.

(a) lit. 'full of moon' (*indumaya*).

38. Whoever is possessed of evil fortune and sin is released from the impurity, disease, and Vināyakas—while he takes a bath with the water over which [the Gāyatrī-verse] is muttered a thousand times.

(a) For the term *vināyakas*, see Kane, *HDS*, Vol. II, p.214.

39. The direction in which one dismisses—a clod of earth over which [the Gāyatrī-verse] is muttered seven times—will have no dangers arising out of thieves, fire and wind.

(a) *saṁpracāṭayet*, a rare verbal compound. From the ritual point of view *saṁpracārayet* (ms. Bo 1) appears to be a preferable reading. The end of the Varga is here marked by 8 in Ba Ta.

40. Subsisting on milk, one should mutter [the Gāyatrī verse] a hundred times: [then] he wards off accidental death. Consuming ghee, one obtains a retentive faculty consisting of much understanding[a].

(a) Prof. Gonda renders 'a large quantity' of intellect'.

41. Having offered leaves of the rattan smeared with ghee into the fire, he causes, no doubt, the rain to fall over the whole expanse of earth[a] by means of a hundred thousand [oblations].

(a) I surmise that *sārvabhaumam* should mean *sarvabhūmyām*.

42. By [offering] a hundred thousand oblations of ash, an evil spirit (Kṛtyā) arises from the water. A pure person standing in water reaching up to the navel and facing the sun.

The second hemistich is too compressed for clear construction.

43. By offering a hundred thousand oblations of sesamum seeds

anointed with ghee into the fire, a person [being] endowed with all desired objects, will obtain the highest success.

Prof. Gonda connects the first hemistich with the preceding stanza.

44. By offering a hundred thousand oblations of barley-corn anointed with ghee into the fire, a person [being] endowed with all desired objects, will obtain the highest abode.

This stanza with its repetition of previous ideas and words can hardly be authentic. The end of the varga is here marked by 9 in Ba Ta.

45. One will obtain all desired objects by means of a hundred thousand oblations of ghee. Subsisting on the five products of the cow, one should mutter [the Gāyatrī verse] a hundred thousand [times: then] he recollects previous births.[a]

(a) Prof. Gonda's reference to *AV.P.* LXII.2.13 is wrong and misleading.

46. Having offered the same[a] [viz. the five products of the cow] into the fire, one acquires much wealth. By means of offering food, etc. regularly, there would always be [plenty of] food, etc.

(a) Prof. Gonda explains it by 'objects of value, movable property, etc.' !

47. [For the sake of] accomplishing everything,[a] one should offer oblations upto the number of myriad. Having offered red mustard seeds [into the fire], one subdues all enemies.

(a) *Sarvasādhyānām scil. kṛte.*

48. Having offered salt with honey, he subdues[a] everything Having offered red Karavīra [flowers], he can cause fever [to his adversaries].

(a) For the formation of *Vaśībhavet*, see Whitney, 1094.

49. Having offered oil to the Vibhītaka wood [into the fire], a person can expel[a] [his enemy] from his country. By offering leaves of the *nimba*, a person can create hostility among men.

(a) *pracāṭayet*, a rare verbal compound.

50. Having offered reddened rice grains anointed with ghee into the fire, a person obtains vigour; [and] he cannot be vanquished by his enemies.

The end of the Varga is here marked by 10 in Ba Ta.

51. That[a] [i.e. vigour] becomes allayed [rather, settled] to a person who, for the sake of success in the restoration [of it], offers cow's milk mixed with honey and clarified butter into the well-lit fire.

(a) *tat scil. balam* from the st. 50 above.

52. Remaining celibate and moderate in food he who mutters [the Gāyatrī verse] three thousand [times] undoubtedly obtains wealth and power within a year (*saṁvatsareṇa*)[a]

(a) The instrumental expresses the notion registered by Pāṇini 2.3.6.

53. Having offered flowers and fuel sticks of the *Śamī*, the *bīlva*, the *palāśa* and especially that of the *arka*, one will obtain gold [pieces].

(a) *puṣpāṇāṁ samidhām*, genitive for accusative.

54. That [deity], in whose sanctuary—of A[a] [i.e. Viṣṇu], Brahmā, Tryambaka [i.e. Śiva]—a person having resorted to and remaining abstemious mutters the Gāyatrī-verse a hundred thousand times—will be ready to fulfil wishes.

(a) The text has *abrahmatryambakādīnāṃ*, but Dr. Meyer conjectures *abbrahmatryambakādīnām*. Neither Dr. Meyer's conjecture nor Prof. Gonda's translation gives a good sense here.

55. By offering a hundred thousand oblations of *bilvas* anointed with ghee, one will obtain the highest fortune, [if] [only] he is not a *bhrūṇahan*.

The end of the Varga is here marked by 11 in Ba Ta.

56. By offering a hundred thousand oblations of lotuses anoin-

ted with ghee into the fire, one acquires an entire (*nikhila*)[a] kingdom without a rival and free from difficulties.

(a) Mss. Bo 1.2. read *akhila*.

57. Subsisting on curds, milk and ghee, a person attains perfection in his very body by means of two million and five hundred thousand [mutterings], such is the opinion of Kauśika.

The translation of the stanza is tentative. Cp. Gāyatrī-sādhana in the *Yajurmañjarī* (p. 60): *dadhikṣīraghṛtāharaḥ pañcaviṁśatilaksajapena viśvāmitra iva dehasiddhiṁ labhate* ||

58. Subsisting on the five products of a cow for one day, living on air [i.e. fasting] for one day, eating food given by Brāhmaṇas for one day—this is called the Gāyatrī-japa.

The hiatus between the first and second padas is original, though Bo 1, removes it with the insertion of the particle *hi*.

59. Having taken a bath along with [the muttering of] the Gāyatrī-verse a hundred times, one should mutter a hundred times inside the water, then having sipped water with a hundred, one is freed[a] from all sins

(a) the verb *pra muc* governs instrumental, besides ablative.

60. [Likewise] the killer of a cow, a patricide, a matricide, the killer of a Brāhmaṇa, the person who violates his teacher's bed, the robber of gold and gems and a Brāhmaṇa who drinks spirituous liquor[a] [are freed]

(a) *Surā*, i.e. spirituous liquor extracted from rice, to drink which is considered a heinous crime.

61. Having performed a sacrifice for unworthy persons or having done a contemptible deed, one should not become dejected even [while] accepting land- [gift] together with oceans.

The second hemistich is nearly identical with the *AV.P.* XLI.3. 11ab.

62. And those planets in the sky the sun and others which are badly situated for him on earth, will all become auspicious and gentle; there is no doubt.

Cp. *AV.P.*XLI.3.11cd-12ab: *ye cāsya viṣamāḥ kecid divi sūryādayo grahāḥ / te cāsya saumyā jāyante śivāḥ sukhakarāḥ sadā* // The end of the Varga is here marked by 12 in Ba Ta.

63. When surrounded by robbers he who mutters the demon-destroying hymn beginning with *Kṛṇuṣva* [*RV*.4.4], will take away the life of [his] adversaries and will also destroy the demons.

Mātṛsūnu: "*Kṛṇuṣva*" [*RV*.4.4] *iti sūktaṁ jāpann ājyam āhitaṁ juhuyāt pratyṛcaṁ tataḥ śatrūṇāṁ prāṇān uddharati rakṣāṁsi ca nivārayatīti* //

64. From every direction (*viśvataḥ*) the Vahni facing all sides (*viśvatomukhaḥ*) himself protects him, who worships the fire with the verse beginning with *Pari* [*RV*.4.9.8] every day.

Mātṛsūnu: "*Pari te dūḷabho ratha*" [*RV*.4.9.8] *ityanayā ṛcā yo agner ahanyahani upasthānaṁ karoti tam agniḥ sarvato mukhaḥ sarvebhyo bhayebhyo rakṣati* //

65. Whoever regularly worships Śakra with the hymn beginning with *Ko adya* [*RV*.4.25] or mutters with obeisances will obtain favours from Śakra.

Mātṛsūnu: *anena sūktena yo nityam iṁdraṁ stauti / athavā ya etat sūktaṁ pratyṛcaṁ namaskarair japati sa śreṣṭān agniṣṭomādikratuphalaṁ* (?) *labhate prāpnoti* //

66. One should perform a blessing ceremony at night with [the hymn seen by] Vāmadeva[a] beginning with *Kayā* [*RV*.4.31] or one should mutter it at twilight times [for] this spell, ie, Brahman is communicated by Kauśika.

(a) For the formation of *vāmadevya*, see Pāṇini 4.2.9.

67. A person [on becoming] pure should look at the sun with the verse beginning with *Haṁsaḥ śuciṣat* [*RV*.4.40.5] and having muttered it at the time of death, a person goes to the eternal abode of Brahmā.

The commentary on the second hemistich runs as follows: *yas tvaṁtakāle imām ṛcaṁ japati brahmaṇaḥ śāśvataṁ sadma sthānaṁ prāpnoti* //

68. He who betakes himself to agriculture should, according to the precept, offer a *sthālīpāka* in the midst of the field with the five verses [beginning with] *śunaṁ vāhāḥ* [*RV*.4.57.4-8]—

Mātṛsūnu: *Kṣetra* (*Kṣetrasya*)* *patinā vayam* [*RV*.4.57] *ityaṣṭarcaṁ sūktaṁ tatra caturthīprabhṛtibhiḥ paṁcabhir ṛgbhiḥ pratyṛcaṁ juhuyāt* / *tata ṛṣiḥ* (*kṛsiḥ*)* *suṣṭhu saṁpadyata iti* //

69-70. [which] should be distributed according to the characteristic mark, and the farmer, having offered [oblations] separately to these: the plough, Indra, the Maruts, Parjanya, Bhaga, Puṣan, the corn, the furrow and at last to Śunāsīra, should worship these deities.

The translation follows Mātṛsūnu's commentary. The end of the Varga is marked after st. 69 by 13 in Ba Ta.

71-72. One should regularly according to the precept, worship the same deities with sandal wood paste, garland, oblation, fruit, fried grains, spirituous liquor and light intoxicant at the [time of] sowing and mowing [and at the time of] offerings to the granary and the furrow: [then] the rite becomes infallible [and] the harvest thrives well.[a]

(a) Mātṛsūnu paraphrases *vardhati* by *saphalā bhavati*.

73. One should mutter the tristich beginning with *Kṣetrasya patinā* [*RV*.4.57.1-3] addressed to the lord of the field and a Brāhmaṇa should regularly look at the sun: [then] he obtains a preeminent[a] field.

(a) Mātṛsūnu glosses *uttamam* by *śobhanam*.

74. With this [tristich], one should worship the moles on molehills with an oblation of rice after having praised the lord of the moles with the [verse] beginning with *Citra id rājā* [*RV*.8.21.18] always.

The end of the Varga is here marked by 14 in Ba Ta.

75. At this place (*atra*), one should feed Brāhmaṇas and the cultivators. Being vigilant and intent on pacificatory ceremonies, one should proceed oneself to the cultivation.

Mātṛsūnu: *atreti kṛṣi karma kṣetram ucyate / tatra brāhmaṇān bhojayet / Kīnāśāṁś ca bhojayet, Kīnāśā balivardadayo* (?) *bhaṇyaṁte/ evam apramattaḥ śāṁtiparo bhūtvā svayam eva kṛṣiṁ vrajet //*

76. Whatever sin committed in these [acts:] breaking of the soil, harming cows, destroying grass, worms etc. is absolved by the gift of a granary[a] [to a Brāhmana].

(a) Prof. Gonda renders 'by the gift to the threshing floor.'

77. One should offer the twentieth part of the total grain [harvested] to the learned Brāhmaṇas (*śrotriya*), [for] by the gift of the twentieth part, one is released from the guilt of ploughing.

None of the Dharmaśāstras appear to prescribe the above rule.

78. Whoever is controlled in mind and has the senses under his control, offers ghee with the hymn beginning with *Samudrāt* [*RV*.4.58] always according to the aforesaid precept—

Here we have the *pratīka* and the *vidhāna*, but no *phala*. Dr. Meyer wants to read the hemistich 79cd after 78ab and hence he had to rearrange the text for the second time. The weight of the manuscript evidence and Mātṛsūnu's commentary favour the text adopted.

79. [with the verse] beginning with *Vijyotiṣā* [*RV*.5.2.9] he can kindle a fire [even] on Jātaveda[a] [if] he so desires. The fire protects him from all sides with good fortune and wealth.

(a) Mātṛsūnu *jātavedasi* by *agnau.*

80. Whoever worships the fire with the two verses beginning with *Viśvāni na* [*RV*.5.4.9-10], overcomes all misfortunes and obtains imperishable fame.

Mātṛsūnu: "*viśvāni na*" [*RV*.5.4.9-10] *ityābhyāṁ dvābhyām ṛgbhyāṁ yo vahnim agnim arcati stauti sa taraty āpadaḥ sarvā yaśaḥ prāpnoti cākṣayam iti //*

81. Having offered [oblations] with hymn beginning with *Agne tvam* [*RV*.5.24], the fire—the bearer of oblations [to gods]—should for the sake of long life be worshipped by a person who desires wealth and long life.

The end of the Varga is here marked by 15 in Ba Ta.

82. Whosoever wishes to have manifold (*vividham*) wealth, inherent power [both] great and incomparable, should worship Śatakratu with the hymn beginning with *Uroṣṭa* [*RV*.5.38].

(a) Mātṛsūnu reads *vipulam* for *vividham.*

83. A person who is desirous of progeny should regularly worship the wives of gods- with an oblation of rice. [Being] restrained in speech, he should, after having presented oblations, partake of the residue.

(a) The text has *devapatnayaḥ* for *devapatnīḥ*. Mātṛsūnu quotes *RV*.5.46.7-8 as used in the above rite.

84. The left-over should be given to the wife by a person who is desirous of a son. He should prepare a oblation of rice with the milk of a cow which has a calf of the same outward appearance:[a]

(a) Mātṛsūnu glosses *sarūpavatsāyāḥ* by *samānarūpa vatsāyāḥ*.

85. [then] he obtains, quickly no doubt, an offspring resembling [him]. A twice-born person, [on becoming] pure, should mutter [the hymns having] Svastyātreya [as the seer i.e. *RV*.5.50-51] every morning.

Mātṛsūnu: "*viśvo devasya netur*" [RV.5.50.1] *ity etat sūkta-dvayaṁ svastyātreyam ucyate* ||

86. This [is] an auspicious blessing which destroys all stains, and [with it] one bids farewell with blessing a friend or relative who sets out [on a jcurney].

The end of the Varga is here marked by 16 in Ba Ta.

87. A person fares well on his way after having [duly] recited[a] [the verse] beginning with *Svasti panthām* [*RV*.5.51.5]. [The verse beginning with] *Viji hīṣva vanaspate* [*RV*.5.78.5]: this is declared to be [a spell] which causes a expulsion.

(a) Prof. Gonda connects the gerund with the preceding stanza.

88. [Whilst] muttering this [verse], one expels him—or an

enemy—whom one wishes to banish after having tread upon an image (*kṛti*)[a] of sand on the ground:

(a) *Kṛti* = *ākṛti.*

89. [then his adversary feeling], as if crushed, retires, no doubt, from the battle. One shall cause a benumbed woman about to bring forth a child to drink the consecrated—

I have adopted Prof. Macdonell's conjecture: *niṣpekṣyanniva vide* the *Ṛgvidhāna* quoted in Ṣaḍguruśiṣya (*Sarv.* p.123). The mss. have the corrupt reading: *niṣpīṣanniva.*

90. water: [then] the child comes out[a] easily by means of the ejective [spell]. A person who is desirous of rain should employ the hymn beginning with *Acchā vada* [*RV*.5.83]—

(a) Mātṛsūnu glosses *adhaś cyavate* by *nirgacchati.*

91. while he fasts and wears wet cloths. It will soon rain. Having offered ten thousand fuel-sticks or rattan smeared with milk into the fire,

Mātṛsūnu: *yo vṛṣtikāma ādravāsā nirāhāra etat sūktaṁ japati tasya devaḥ śighraṁ pravarṣati | hutvāyutam iti ||*

92. one obtains ample rain by means of the hymn designated *Acchā vada* [*RV*.5.83]. Whosoever wishes to have the wish-fulfilling goddess Śrī always to remain in his family—

The end of the Varga is here marked by 17 in Ba Ta.

93. should, on becoming pure, and piously disposed, offer clarified butter daily and whoever is desirous of fortune continuously mutters the fifteen verses belonging to Śrī [*RV.Kh*.ii.6].

The stanza is identical with the sixteenth verse of the Śrīsūkta *vide RV.* (Aundh) p. 373.

94. With the first five [verses] one should invoke Śrī [mounted] on a lotus or on a gold [pedestal] and offer white victuals, milk, curds as oblations.

Mātṛsūnu: *ā vāhayeti | śrīyaṁ āvāhayatyeva śriyaṁ padme sthitāṁ kanake'pi vā sthitām iti sambaṁdhaḥ | paṁcaprathamābhir ṛgbhir "hiraṇyavarṇām hariṇīm* [*RV.Kh*.ii.6] *ityādyābhiḥ* *tataḥ upāhārān upahare* [*c*]* *chuklān puṣpavilepanādin* (*ādīn*)* *atha bhakṣān api śubhe copahārān payo dadhi śālibhakṣādīn tata* [*ḥ*]* *sthālīpākam iti* //

95. And he should prepare a *sthālipāka* of superior rice [boiled] with milk and having disciplined himself with a *cāndrāyaṇa*,[a] he should, [on becoming] piously disposed, resort[b] to Śrī—

(a) For the term *cāndrāyaṇa*, see i.40-41 above.
(b) The verb *pra pad* governs dative, besides accusative.

96. having taken a bath with holy waters and with the infusion of herbs of all sorts. [The verse] *Upaitu māṁ deva sakha* [*RV.Kh*.ii. 6.7] belongs to the sprinkling ceremony of a king.

Mātṛsūnu: *Sarvauṣadhībhiḥ phāṇṭa*[*ḥ*]* *kvāthitam īsaghṛtam* (*īṣadghṛtam*)* *ucyate* / "*upaitu māṁ devasakha* [*RV*.Kh.ii.6.7) *iti abhisecanā snāpanītyarthaḥ* //

97. [The verse] *Manasaḥ kāmam* [*RV.Kh*.ii.6.10] belongs to the sprinkling ceremony of a person who is desirous of cattle. A well-behaved person who is desirous of progeny should take a bath [whilst muttering the verse] beginning with *Kardamena* [*RV.Kh*. ii.6.11].

The end of the Varga is here marked by 18 in Ba Ta.

98. A well-behaved person who is desirous of a kingdom should take bath [whilst muttering the verse] beginning with *Aśvapurṇām* [*RV.Kh*.ii.6.3]. But a Brāhmaṇa should, according to the precept, take bath [while seated] on a red skin [of an ox][a]

(a) Mātṛsūnu glosses *rohite carmaṇi* by *rakte ānaduhe carmaṇi*.

99. [While] a king, on the skin of tiger; a Kṣatriya, on [the skin of] a Ruru-deer, but a Vaiśya, on the skin of a goat, [and] a sacrifice has to be performed immediately thereafter.

The commentary on the second hemistich runs as follows: *homaś ca sarvair yathā kathaṁcit kartavyaḥ* //

100. A twice-born person should offer lotuses along with clarified butter [whilst muttering the verse] beginning with *Candrām* [*RV.Kh*.ii.6.5]. A sacrifice consisting of *bilvas* is laid down[a] with this [verse] *Ādityavarṇe* [*RV.Kh*.ii.6.6].

(a) Prof. Gonda renders 'is performed.'

101. The fire should be [lit up with] *bilva*-fuel-sticks and a twice-born person should offer a pot [of mess]. The sacrifice consists of ten thousand [oblations is laid down] as the foremost rule[a] for a person who is desirous of fortune.

(a) Mātṛsūnu paraphrases *prathamo vidhiḥ* by *prathamakalpa.*

102. One obtains boundless fortune, after having correctly offered a hundred thousand oblations and having offered white [victuals] with clarified butter, a hundred times ten thousand—

The end of the Varga is here marked by 19 in Ba Ta.

103. one obtains fortune which is boundless, perpetual and eternal. The muttering [of the hymn] ten thousand times is declared to be the best in [cases] of inability.

Mātṛsūnu: *evaṁ bilvahome sarvāhutiḥ saṁkhyā pradarśitā / phalaṁ ca pradarśayati / aśaktau japa evokto daśasāhasriko varaḥ //*

104. Having correctly muttered a hundred thousand [times], one obtains boundless fortune and having muttered a hundred times ten thousand, one comes into the possession of vast fortune.

This stanza with its repetition of ideas and words from st. 102 can hardly be authentic.

105. One should regularly offer lotuses, by myriads, into the water at night and should cease after visualising Śrī, [for], one should be afraid of the state of a leper.

Mātṛsūnu: *aśveti* (*apsveti*)* *trayaṁ nigadavyākhyātam //*

106. A person who eats *bilvas,* who lives amidst *bilva*-shelter and who offers *bilvas* with clarified butter obtains highest success within twentyone days (*ekaviṁśatirātreṇa*).[a]

(a) The instrumental expresses the notion registered by Pāṇini 2.3.6.

107. That very desire, with which a piously-disposed person offers lotuses or *bilvas* to Śrī, becomes fulfilled.

The end of the Varga is here marked by 20 in Ba Ta.

108. One should not, at any time, invoke Śrī for the sake of [obtaining] a mean object[a] and a sacrifice should never be done by a person who is desirous of anything whatever.

(a) Prof. Gonda renders 'for the sake of a miser.'

109. Rather [the sacrifice should be done] by a person who aspires for a vast [wealth] or again by a person who is desirous of a kingdom. A person who strives after [something] surpassing speech should diligently worship Śrī.

Prof. Gonda makes a mistake by connecting the first hemistich with previous stanza which has a negative import. Further that scholar has committed a serious blunder in translating *vācaḥ param* by 'highest degree of speech.'

110. A person should daily offer clarified butter with the hymn beginning with *Agnir etu* [*RV.Kh.*ii.11]: [then] he obtains a noble offspring devoted to Dharma and virtuous.

Mātṛsūnu: *agnir iti dvayaṁ nigadam* //

111. One should worship the blazing fire with the verse beginning with *Accha na* [*RV.*6.2.11]: [then] having obtained intelligence, one can conquer one's enemies and can surmount [all] difficulties.

The reading *prajām* found in mss. Ba, Bo 1, Cm and mss. AC. of Dr. Meyer is evidently corrupt.

112. Whoever wishes always to have the mothers of the world[a] [i.e. cows] everlasting should worship them with the hymn beginning with *Āgāva* [*RV.*6.28] while they are in the cowpen (*goṣṭhagah*)[b] as well as while they are roaming.

(a) *lokamātaraḥ*, nom. for acc.
(b) I was tempted to emend *goṣṭhagāḥ* in the text to *goṣṭhe gāḥ*, since a substantive was required for *lokamātaraḥ*. Cp. the parallel version in the *Viṣṇudharmottara-Purāṇa: goṣṭhe gāṁ lokamātaram*. (*vide supra* p. 173)

113. One should worship Śatakratu with [the hymn in] pra-

gātha [-metre] beginning with *Tvām iddhi* [*RV*.6.46]: [then] one obtains wealth, after having muttered [it] at noon and at the twilight-times.

The end of the Varga is here marked by 21 in Ba Ta.

114. In a battle, one should touch the large kettle-drums for the sake of a king with the three [verses beginning with] *Upa* [*RV*.6.47.29-31]: then [that king] obtains vigour and strength and [finally] subdues enemies.

Prof. Gonda renders *saṁspṛṣet* 'sprinkle', but cp. *ĀGS*. 3.12.17: *upaśvāsaya pṛthivīm uta dyām iti tṛcena duṁdubhim abhimṛśet.*

115. Whoever recites [the hymn beginning with] *Yajñā-yajñā* [*RV*.6.48] after having taken [a bunch of] grass in hand, obtains the fruit of the recitation of this hymn, [but] not he who has no grass [in hand].

(a) Prof. Gonda renders the fourth pāda thus: 'he will (always) be in possession of grass' ! It would be worthwhile to quote the comments of Mātṛsūnu on the fourth pāda: *agṛhīte tṛṇe'sya sūktasyādhyayanaphalaṁ na prāpyate* ||

116. And at the end of the hymn [-recital], he should throw the grass into the fire, or in an inhospitable region or into the water, after having diligently abandoned that fearful [thing] elsewhere.-

(a) Prof. Gonda, however, renders the second hemistich thus: "having, by applying himself to that , left behind elsewhere what is fearful.'

117. One having grass in hand should mutter[a] this Rakṣoghna-hymn [when] surrounded by Dasyus: [then] there can be no fear whatsoever [for him] from Rakṣas and adversaries.

(a) I have translated as if the text has *japet* instead of *japant*. The former reading is found in Ṣaḍguruśiṣya.

118. When one is about to set out on a journey from home [and] while proceeding on a way, one with a desire for wealth should diligently mutter [the verse] beginning with *Api panthām* [*RV*.6.51.16].

Observe the hiatus between the third and the fourth padas. It is scrupulously avoided in mss Ba Bo 1.

119. One obtains a long life after having meditated upon the gods at night [with] the verse beginning with *Ye ke ca jmā* [*RV*. 6.52.15] and offered clarified butter with it.

The end of the Varga is here marked by 22 in Ba Ta.

120. On becoming pure, one should regularly mutter the hymn beginning with *Vayam u tvā* [*RV*.6.53] which is addressed to Pūṣan and which increases wealth: [then] one obtains the desired wealth.

Mātṛsūnu's commentary to this and the following stanzas is broken.

121. He whose possessions: a cow, a man,[a] money, be somehow lost or whoever loses his way out of infatuation should mutter [the hymn beginning with] *Saṁ pūṣan* [*RV*.6.54] at night.

(a) Note the use of *dvipadam*, acc., among the prevailing nominatives. It can as well be corrected to *dvipadaḥ* without spoiling the metre.

122. On becoming pure, a twice-born person should regularly mutter the complete[a] hymn which is addressed to Sarasvatī and which [begins with] *Iyam* [*RV*.6.61].

(a) Prof. Gonda renders *ādyanta* 'at the beginning and end of the rite, but it can resolved thus: *āditaḥ antaparyantam* lit. from the beginning to end, i.e. complete. See, however, *MW*, *ādyanta.*

123. A person who is ritually pure[a] obtains favourite objects of desire after having regularly muttered that hymn which is declared as consisting of eight verses in Triṣṭubh-metre and which begins with *Sam vām* [*RV*.6.69].

(a) Prof. Gonda renders *prayataḥ* 'well-prepared.'

124. The hymn which begins with *Yo adribhit* [*RV*.6.73] is destructive of rivals [and] one lays low many rivals after having respectually saluted Bṛhaspati.

The end of the Varga is here marked by 23 in Ba Ta.

125. When one is either wicked or sinful or has done an ignominious deed, should mutter the hymn addressed to Soma and Rudra [*RV*.6.74]: [then] one dispels all wickedness.

The commentary of Mātṛsūnu on the first hemistich runs as follows: *yaḥ kaścid virūpaṁ karma karoti sa etaj japitvā tato* (*tataḥ*)* *pāpaṁ nāśayati* //

126. [Being] intent upon his vow, whoever regularly offers [oblations into the fire] with these verses becomes free from the fetters of Varuṇa and obtains happiness.

Mātṛsūnu: *Yas tvanena sūktenājyaṁ juhoti sa vāruṇebhyaḥ pāśebhyo mucyate sukhaṁ ca prāpnoti / śam iti sukhanāmeti //*

127. Having pondered over the precepts of the Jīmūta-sūkta [i.e. *RV*.6.75] according to the characteristic marks, one should, according to the rule, perform the rites for the [various] parts of the chariot with the verses [of the above hymn].

Mātṛsūnu: *asmin sūkte pratyṛcaṁ yasya rathāṁgasya liṅgaṁ śrūyate tattad rathāṁgam uddiśya tayā ṛcā homaḥ kartavyaḥ / tad rathāṁgaṁ saṁgrāmakāle dṛḍhaṁ bhavati //*

128. one should employ this [hymn] for the sake of a king who has gone to war [and] one should consecrate all the parts [of the chariot], the chariot-horses and noble horses.

Mātṛsūnu: *Saṁgrāmakāle etat sūktaṁ japet / pratyṛcaṁ yathāliṁgaṁ rathāṁgāni sārathiṁ yoddhāram aśvān saṁnāhanādīni cānumaṁtrayed iti //*

129. A [king] duly consecrated will never return without having conquered [that] country or [that] enemy towards which he proceeds [for conquest], since this [hymn represents] the highest power of the spell i.e. Brahman.

Mātṛsūnu: *yaṁ śatruṁ deśaṁ cāṇumaṁtrito gacchet tatra śatruṁ jitvā nivartate na parājīyata iti //* The end of the Varga is here marked by 24 in Ba Ta.

130. Whoever wishes to have sons, [long] life, health and ever-

lasting pleasure should daily offer [oblations of] clarified butter with the hymn beginning with *Agniṁ nara* [*RV*.7.1].

Mātṛsūnu: *ya icchet putrādīni somena* (*so'nena*)* *sūktena pratidinam ājyaṁ juhuyāt | tatas tasya putrādayo bhavatīti ||*

131. At both the twilight-times, one should commence the muttering of the three hymns beginning with *Prāgnaye* etc. [*RV*. 7.5-7]: [then] he knows not fear from Rakṣas and obtains everlasting wealth.

After St.131, Berlin ed. has three more stanzas which are found only in ms. A of Dr. Meyer. None of the other mss. consulted by Dr. Meyer, Prof. Gonda and myself have them, hence these stanzas (Nos. 4*, 5*, and 6*) have been relegated to the critical apparatus.

132. Whoever regularly worships Vajrin with [the verse in] Pragātha [–metre beginning with] *Abhitvā* [*RV*. 7.32.22-23] enjoys abundant fortune, obtains wealth and [long] life.

Again, after St. 132, Berlin ed. has three more stanzas (No. 7*, 8*, 9*). See my remarks under St. 131 above.

133. One should continually mutter these [two hymns]: *śaṁvatī* [*RV.Kh*.ii.13 and] *Śaṁ na indrāgnī* [*RV*.7.35]: [then] there can be no fear either from Rakṣas or from spirits, or from diseases.

Mātṛsūnu: *Śaṁvatīḥ śaṁ na indrāgnītyādi ya etā ṛco nityaṁ japati tasya rakṣoghnā* (?) *dibhyo bhayaṁ na bhavatīti ||*

134. Whoever wishes to settle in life should always recite the hymn addressed to Bhaga [*RV*.7.41]. [If he] is afflicted with a disease, [then] he quickly settles in life and is freed from diseases.

The end of the Varga is here marked by 25 in Ba Ta.

135. A twice-born person who is pure should regularly mutter the hymn which is addressed to Rudra and which begins with *Imā* [*RV*.7.46]. Having muttered that [hymn], he suffers no harm in [respect of] progeny, wealth, and self.

The mss. consulted by me have the corrupt reading: *tariṣyati* for the correct one: *na riṣyati.* The latter reading is supported by mss. utilised by Dr. Meyer and Prof. Gonda and is, moreover, confirmed by Mātṛsūnu's paraphrase: *na vinaśyati.*

136. While passing out of water, [a person] who is apprehensive at the confluence of streams should mutter this fear-removing hymn beginning with *Samudrajyēṣṭhā* [*RV*.7.49].

Mātṛsūnu: *mahānandīsaṁgame uttiryaṇāṇo* (*uttīryamāṇo*)* *bibheti sa etat sūktaṁ japet tato nadīpāraṁ gacchatīti* //

137. In the morning, [a person] on becoming pure should mutter the two hymns which have Ādityas as the deity [*RV*. 7.51-52] and which destroy the enemies[a] and diseases: [then] one gets rid of enemies and diseases.

(a) All mss. read *ripughne,* but in the first stanza of *RV*.7.51.1, Adityas are requested to make the worshipper 'sinless and free' Could the reading be *ripraghne*? See however, St. 172 note (a) below.

138. One should mutter the hymn which is addressed to Vāstoṣpati and which begins with *Vāstoṣpate prati* [*RV*.7.54] after having taken a bath and performed the Vaiśvadeva [-sacrifice] this is called the highest spell i.e. Brahman.

(a) The text has *vāstoṣpatam,* a form which violates Pāṇini 4.1.85.

139. With the hymn beginning with *Amīvahāḥ* [*RV*.7.55], one can put [all] living beings to sleep at night for a soporific [text] like this, is found no where else.

The end of the Varga is marked here by 26 in Ba Ta.

140. One should mutter the [following text] in case of distress in an inaccessable defile when one is imprisoned or caught by robbers while proceeding somewhere or while escaping [from them].

Prof. Gonda translates the stanza thus: 'In case if distress, at an impassable bad road, or when one, after having been confined, goes away somewhere, or in running away, or when one has been caught by robbers, one must mutter this (sūkta viz.).' This is far from satisfactory.

141. After having omitted [the verse which begins with] *Amīvahāḥ* containing [the word] *Viśva* [i.e. *RV*.7.55.1], one should employ the rest [i.e. *RV*.7.55.2-8], but Śaunaka holds the view[a] that one should mutter the entire hymn.

(a) The text has *manyeta* for *manyate*. Grammatical accuracy has probably been sacrificed to the exegencies of the metre.

142-143. After having fasted for three days, a twice-born person who is restrained should cook an oblation of rice with milk and offer a full hundred oblations with clarified butter in honour of Tryambaka Mahādeva with the verse beginning with *Tryambakam* [*RV*.7.59.12]. After having performed this [rite] on full and new-moon days [upto] a hundred, he will live happily for hundred years.

Mātṛsūnu: *trirātramiti dvayam* / "*yaṁ trāyadhva idaṁ*" [*RV*. 7.59] *iti dvādaśarcaṁ tatrāṁtyā ṛg*(*ṛk*)* *khailikyā* / "*tryambakaṁ yajāmahety eṣā tām adhi*° *te* / *trirātropoṣyetādi* / *parvakāle paurṇamāsyām amāvāsyāyāṁ ca raudraṁ pāyasaṁ caruṁ śrapayitvā'nayā ṛcā āhutiśataṁ juhuyāt* / *parvāṇāṁ śataṁ yāvat* / *tato'bdaśatam sukhaṁ sa jīvatīti* //

144. After having taken a bath, a person desirous of living a long life should, with the verse beginning with *Taccakṣuḥ* [*RV*. 7.66.16], worship the sun when it rises and when it is in the meridian (*madhyaga*).

The end of the Varga is here marked by 27 in Ba Ta.

145. A person who is piously-disposed and pure should worship [Uṣas] with the six hymns beginning with *Vyuṣā* [*RV*.7.75-80], after having got up at the latter part of the night and having cupped the hands reverentially (*kṛtāñjali*)—

Mātṛsūnu: "*vyuṣā ā vo divijā ṛtena*" [*RV*.7.75] *ityaṣṭarcaṁ sūktam* / "*udu jyotir amṛtaṁ visvajanyam*" [*RV*.7.76] *iti sapatarcaṁ sūktaṁ* / "*upo ruruce yuvatir na yoṣā*" [*RV*.7.77] *iti saḷrcaṁ sūktam* / "*prati ketavaḥ prathamā adṛśran*" [*RV*.7.78] "*vyuṣā āvaḥ pathyājanānām*" [*RV*.7.79] *iti paṁcarce sūkte* / "*prati stomebhir* *uṣasaṁ vasiṣṭhā* [*RV*.7.80] *iti tṛcaṁ sūktaṁ etāṇi ṣaṭ sūktāny adhikṛtyedam ucyate / rātryā aparakāle ya ityādi ślokadvayam paṭhitaṁ prāpnoti / ya etai* [ḥ]* *ṣaḍbhiḥ sūktaiḥ upasthānaṁ karoti sa hiraṇyādi prāpnuyāt //*

146. [then] he will obtain manifold wealth [consisting of] gold etc., kine, horses, men, corn, women, clothes, goats and sheep.[a]

(a) All the mss. have the corrupt reading *ajāvikān*. Dr. Meyer emends it to *ajāvikam* which is grammatically correct. See Pāṇini 2.4.18.

147. A person imprisoned is released after having muttered [the verse beginning with] *Dhruvāsu tvāsu kṣitiṣu* [*RV*.7.88.7]. One should mutter this [verse] while standing: [then] one becomes freed from fetters.

Mātṛsūnu: *dhruvāsu tvetyevamādi / anayā baṁdhapāśebhyaḥ pramucyate iti tasmād etām divā rātrau ca japed iti //*

148. Having fasted, [whoever] stands motionless[a] for a day and night in this manner can have his iron fetters burst and likewise the wooden shackles.

(a) The text has *viceṣṭitaḥ* = *niśceṣṭaḥ*, hence Dr. Meyer's conjecture: *viveṣṭitaḥ* is unnecessary.

149. A person who is restrained should always attend upon the goddesses Earth [with the verse] beginning with *Syonā* [*RV*. 1.22.15] and should also recite this [verse] on that occasion: [then] he is released from the Bhūmipāśa.[a]

(a) The exact meaning of the term is uncertain. The end of the Varga is here marked by 28 in Ba Ta.

150. Whatever sin one commits in deed, thought [and] speech, one is released [from that], after having muttered the verse beginning with *Yat kiñcedaṁ varuṇa* [*RV*.7.89.5].

Prof. Gonda translates the first hemistich thus: 'whatever crime one performs with deed, mind or voice'!

151. And this[a] expiation is laid down in case of illicit intercourse with a forbidden woman other than a teacher's wife [and] one is released from this sin.

(a) Prof. Gonda possibly takes the term *etat* to mean *ṛcam* or how else can we understand his translation of the first hemistich: 'And this is (also) enjoined as an expiation in case of illicit sexual intercourse'?

152. One should mutter [the following verse] in case of sexual intercourse with a Sagotrā-woman after fasting for twelve days and in case of cohabitation with a friend's wife after fasting for half-a-month.

Mātṛsūnu: *dvādaśāheti / etad api "yat kiṁcedam"* (*RV*.7.89.5] *ityasyaiva prāyaścittavidhānam iti //* Mātṛsūnu failed to understand the force of *eteṣu karamasu* in the next stanza.

153. In [all] these performances, one should mutter these [verses]: *Idam āpaḥ pravahata* [*RV*.1.23.22-24]; *Yat kiñcedam* [*RV*.7.89.5] after having immersed in water.

Mātṛsūnu: *idameti / "idam āpaḥ pravahata* [*RV*.1.23.22-24] *iti ṭṛco" yat kiṁcedaṁ varuṇetīyam ṛk etāś catasra ṛca udake praviśya japet tataḥ sarvasmāt pāpāt pramucyata iti //* Prof. Gonda refers only to *RV*.1.23.22 and 7.89.5 and hence his remark 'These (stanzas): plural in the text.'

154. With obeisance to Indra and Viṣṇu a person desiring power (*bhūti*) for himself should daily offer [oblations of] clarified butter with the two hymns [beginning with] *Paraḥ* [*RV*.7.99-100].

Mātṛsūnu: *iṁdrāviṣṇviti / "paro mātrayā tanvā vṛdhāna"* [*RV*. 7.99] *"nū marto dayate saniṣyann* [*RV*.7.100] *iti saptarce sūkte adhikṛtyedaṁ ucyate indrāviṣṇu namaskṛtyetyādi //* The end of the Varga is here marked by 29 in Ba Ta.

155. [A person] who is piously-disposed, pure and facing the east, should worship the sun with the two hymns [beginning with] *Tisra* [*RV*.7.101-102] after having immersed in water upto the mouth.

Mātṛsūnu: *āsyadaghneti / "tisro vācaḥ pravada jyotir agrā"* [*RV*.7.101] *iti ṣaḷṛcaṁ sūktam / "parjanyāya pragāyata"* [*RV*. 7.102] *iti tṛcaṁ sūktam ityete adhikṛ° te / āsyadaghnā (āsyada-*

*ghnaṁ)* vigāhyāṁbha ityādi / mukhamātram udakam avatīrya tato'nena sūktadvayena ādityopasthānaṁ kuryād iti //*

156. [The above pair of hymns] should diligently be muttered[a] by a fasting person desiring rain: [then] he will obtain much rain after a lapse of five days.

(a) *japtavyam scil. sūktadvayam*, but Prof. Gonda supplies 'it'.

157. Whoever is either held[a] or accused wrongly by enemies should daily offer [oblations of] clarified butter [into the fire], after having fasted for a period of three days—

(a) Prof. Gonda renders 'wronged'.

158. and should mutter this hymn beginning with Indrā-somā [*RV*.7.104] at least a hundred times and should give something to Brāhmaṇas at the end: [then] he slays all [his] enemies.

Mātṛsūnu: *ya eta [c]* chatakṛtvo japati sa śatrūn nikṛṁtatīti //*

159. One whose observance is disturbed out of infatuation, or [when] a Brāhmaṇa comes into contact with Vrātyas, should offer [oblations of] clarified butter [into the fire with the verse] beginning with *Tvam agne vratapā* [*RV*.8.11].

The end of the Varga is here marked by 30 in Ba Ta.

160. One should behold the sun while muttering this [hymn] beginning with *Pra samrājam* [*RV*.8.16] and should daily worship [the sun] when it rises, after having taken a bath.

Mātṛsūnu: *prasamrājam iti tvaṁ tadityāṁdi (tvetadityādi)* / ādityaṁ paśyati tatsūktaṁ japet //*

161. He who has been accused or with whomsoever he disputes, he will quickly overcome[a] the dispute after having won over his enemies with their followers.

(a) *parājayet*, Par. for Atm. Both the text and the commentary on this stanza are corrupt.

162. One should resort to Vāyu and Bhāskara [with the verse] beginning with *Śamagnir agnibhiḥ* [*RV*.8.18.9]: [then] one is released from a great difficulty. After having praised Agni at first—

Mātṛsūnu: *Śamagnir iti* / *...anayā ṛcāgniṁ prathamata*[ḥ]* *stutvā tato bhāskaraṁ sūryaṁ tato mahato duḥkhāt pramucyata iti* //

163. with [the hymn] consisting of four verses beginning with *Nahi* [*RV*.8.30], and worships Agni for two months, after getting up early in the morning and having taken a bath, protects himself from danger.

The translation follows Mātṛsūnu's commentary: *nahīti yaś catuṣkeṇetyādi* / *anena ṛkcatuṣṭayena prāvarddhvau* (*prātar dvau*)* *māsau japtenātmānaṁ mahato bhayāt trāyati* //

164. Having muttered this tristich beginning with *Āyat* [*RV*. 8.34.16-18] having taken a bath and adored Puraṁdara, one obtains [all] objects of desire conceivable[a] after having honoured Vasurocis.

(a) Prof. Gonda's rendering : 'wishes sprung from one's mind' is too literal.

165-166. The first three hymns [i.e. *RV*.1.1-3] and the five [hymns] beginning with *Agre bṛhan* [*RV*. 10.1-5], likewise the last six hymns [i.e. *RV*.10.186-191] and [the hymn] beginning with *Agniṁ nara* [*RV*.7.1] and the chapter (Adhyāya)[a] beginning with *Pra kṛtāni* [*RV*. 8.32-45]—these one should recite before the meals: [then] one obtains all objects of desire and one gets rid of all sins.

(a) *Ṛvidh*., mainly, follows the division of *RV*. into Maṇḍalas and Sūktas, but here as well as in St. 172 below the Adhyāya-division is clearly referred to. Dr. Meyer is wrong in stating that *Ṛvidh* ignores Aṣṭaka-division (*vide Ṛvidh. Praefatio* p. xi). The end of the Varga is here marked by 31 in Ba Ta.

167. The highest accomplishment of an object belongs to him [who] regularly mutters this spell i.e. Brahman of the great sages amongst men in the forenoon before his meal.

Mātṛsūnu: *prāg bhojaneti* / *asyaiva sūktasyāyaṁ japa iti* //

168. A strict observant of a vow (*suvrata*)[a] on becoming pure should daily mutter the hymn of Aśvins which consists of twenty-

four verses and which begins with *Agninā* [*RV*.8.35] in the morning after having adored the Nāsatyas:

(a) Mātṛsūnu glosses it by *sukarmā, śobhanāuṣṭhānarataḥ.*

169-170. [then] he obtains the highest power, possession and energy. Whoever offers [oblations of] ghee into the fire verse by verse with the hymn beginning with *Samidhā* [*RV*.8.44] lives a hundred years after having attained unequalled success. [Having praised] Vajrin[a] with the hymn which consists of fortytwo verses and which begins with *Ā ghā* [*RV*.8.45]—

(a) *Vajriṇam scil. stutvā.* Neither Dr. Meyer's conjecture: *vajriṇaḥ* nor Prof. Gonda's translation of it, give a good sense.

171. one vanquishes many rivals after having obtained the friendship of Mahendra. One must eat after having enquired of mutterer, [for] there may be[a] [something worthwhile asking for] according to the rules (*vidhāntaḥ*).[b]

(a) The text has '*trāsti=atra bhavet scil. kiñcit pṛṣṭavyam.* Dr. Meyer conjectures: '*nnāni.*

(b) Prof. Gonda conjectures: '*vidhānataḥ.* The second hemistich is corrupt though general sense is not doubtful. Possibly the second hemistich as well as the first hemistich of the next stanza belong rather to the Varga 31 above than to this. The end of the Varga is here marked by 32 in Ba. Ta.

172. Therefore this chapter [i.e. *RV*.8.32-45] which relates to the forenoon is declared to be destructive of sins.[a] One gains health after having muttered [the hymn of] Vaśa [i.e. *RV*.8.46) and[b] the [one] beginning with *Mahī* [*RV*.8.47].

(a) Dr. Meyer reads: *ripunāśanaḥ* for *ripranāśanaḥ.* Mss. often confuse the sub-script r-sign and u-sign. Here, of course, it is *ripranāśanaḥ.* Cp. St.166d: *mucyate sarva kilbiṣaiḥ* and Mātṛsūnu: *Vāśam* iti / "*tvāvataḥ purūvaso*" [*RV*. 8.46] *iti trayastriṁśadṛcaṁ sūktaṁ vāśam ucyate / tathā "mahi vo mahatām ava*" [*RV*.8.47] *ity aṣṭādaśarcaṁ sūktaṁ tadadhi*° *te / vāśam mahī*[*ti*]* *ca japtvetyādi / etat sūktaṁ*(*ete sūkte*)* *pāpanāśanam*(*pāpanāśane*)* *ārogyakaraṇaṁ* (*ārogyakaraṇe*)* *ceti* //

(b) The particle *ca*, disturbs the metre, but if it is transposed to the end of the pāda (so Bo 1) for the sake of metre, then we are left with one hymn only i.e. *RV*.8.47.

173. Having muttered the final verses (i.e. *RV*.8.47.14-18) which are destructive of evil dreams in the morning, one is released from sins. With the two verses beginning with *Śaṁ no bhava* [*RV*. 8.48.4-5], a person who is piously disposed and pure, after having eaten the food—

Mātṛsūnu: *duḥsvapneti nigadam* /

174-175. [should] touch his heart with the hand: [then] he will live long, healthy and happy. Having established fire on a clean spot in that direction from whence he comprehends danger, a person who is firm of purpose should with the six verses beginning with *Yata* [*RV*.8.61.13-18] offer clarified butter which is sanctified[a] after having adored Indra and presented sandalwood paste [to him].

(a) Sanctification is usually done by waiving a lighted *darbha* grass over the clarified butter.

176. [And] in addition he should present an oblation of rice boiled in milk (*pāyasa*), or a beverage obtained from churning (*dadhimantha*) or cakes. Having fasted for one day and night [and] offered the sesamum-seeds or ghee—

The end of the Varga is here marked by 33 in Ba Ta.

177. [into the fire] with [the hymn] beginning with *Uttvā mandantu* [*RV*.8.64], a person who has taken a bath destroys his enemies. A person who is restrained in speech and piously disposed should, when imprisoned or shut up [in a cell], mutter—

Prof. Gonda regards the first hemistich as an independent unit, but it is constructionally connected with the second hemistich of the preceding stanza.

178. [the hymn] which has Ādityas as its deity and which begins with *Tyānnu* [*RV*.8.67]: [then] he is immediately released from bondage. A person who is restrained and pure should regularly mutter the [strophe in] Pragātha [-metre] beginning with *Yad dyāvā* [*RV*.8.70.5-6]:

Mātṛsūnu's commentary on the second hemistich runs as follows: *yad dyāveti* / "*yo rājā carṣaṇīnām*" [*RV*.8.70] *iti paṁcadaśarcaṁ sūktaṁ tatrāyaṁ pragāthaḥ pathyate* / "*yad dyāva indra te śatam* [*RV*.8.70.5-6] *iti tad*⁰ *te* / *yad dyāva iti pragātham ityādi* / *anena japtena siddhim atulāṁ prāpya sarvān kāmān avāpnotīti* //

179. [then] he attains all objects of desire, after having gained unequalled fame. [Whoever] having adored Agni with the hymn beginning with *Tvaṁ no agne* [*RV*.8.71] offers ghee [into the fire]—

(a) Prof. Gonda renders: 'Having sacrificed with the sūkta "thou us, Agni", and having honoured the fire with ghee'.

180. gains possession through Agni, [he being] protected from all sides by splendour. One should continually ask Puraṁdara for wealth with hymn [beginning with] *Ā tū* [*RV*.8.81]:

Mātṛsūnu's commentary on the second hemistich runs as follows: "*ā tū na iṁdra kṣumaṁtam*" [*RV*.8.81] *iti aṣṭarcaṁ sūktaṁ tad*⁰ *te* / *ā tū sūktenetyādi* / *hastau saṁhatau kṛtvānena sūktenemdram dhanaṁ yācet* //

181. [then] Vṛtrahan gives (*yacchati*)[a] wealth to him who holds the best fuel-stick in hand (*prasamitpāṇi*). A person who is restrained should continually mutter the hymn beginning with *Kanyā vār* [*RV*.8.91]:

(a) Dr. Meyer finds a *tmesis, pra...yacchati*! See his *Ṛvidh. Praefactio* p.x. The end of the Varga is here marked by 34 in Ba Ta.

182. [then] he causes [a woman] who suffers from skin-disease and hairless to be freed from that [disease]. Having praised Puraṁdara with the [verse] beginning with *Yadadya kacca* [*RV*.8.93.4] at day-break—

Mātṛsūnu's commentary on the first hemistich runs as follows: *tvag iti* / *anenādhastanena sūktena japtena tvagdoāṭṣ pramucyata iti* //

183. he removes sin (*ripra*)[a] [by] invoking or he subjugates the world. He who is a strict observant of a vow, worships the god-

dess Gaurī [i.e. Vāk][b] with the distich beginning with *Yad vāk* [*RV*.8.100.10-11], after entreating[c] [her]—

(a) Prof. Gonda renders 'enemy'. Same trouble *ripra:ripu*!
(b) *Sarv*.viii.100: *upāntye vācyau* i.e. 'penult-distich is addressed to Vāk'. Gaurī is a synonym of Vāk (*Nigh*.1.11).
(c) The text has *etya*. Dr. Meyer emends it to *eva*.

184. his mouth will not utter any unrefined speech. After seeing the sun one should worship it whilst muttering the two verses beginning with *Baṇ mahām̐* [*RV*.8.101.11-12]:

185. [then] one is not tainted by untruth even if one [intends] to speak untruth. On a full moon [day] one should betake[a] oneself to the moon-light with the [verse] beginning *Iyaṁ yā* [*RV*.8.101-13]—

(a) Mātṛsūnu glosses *anusevayat* by *niṣevate*.

186. whilst gazing at the moon without winking: [then] one becomes possessed of lustre and sight. [A person] who has taken bath [should] mutter the [verse] beginning with *Prajā ha* [*RV*. 8.101.14]: [then] he will have no rebirth.

Prof. Gonda translates the first hemistich thus: '(then) one will become 'moon-looking' (like the moon or lovely to the sight), not winking (watchful), vigorous, in the possession of sight (intelligence)'!

187. Gently touching a cow one [should] mutter the [verse] beginning with *Mātā* [*RV*.8.101.15]: [then] one obtains kine. One obtains [gracious] speech by muttering the [verse] beginning *Vocovidam* [*RV*.8.101.16].

Mātṛsūnu's commentary on the first hemistich runs as follows: *māteti gāmiti* / "*prajā ha tisro atyāyam īyur*" [*RV*.8.101.14] *ityasyā eva uparitanā ṛk* "*mātā rudrāṇāṁ duhitā vasūnām* [*RV*. 8.101.15] *iti tām*[0] *te* / *māteti gām upaspṛśyetyādi* / *yo gavām* (*gām*)* *upaspṛśya japati tasya bahvyo gāvo bhavatīti* (*bhavantīti*)* //

188. [On becoming] pure after taking a bath, one having [a bunch of] Darbha (*sapavitra*)[a] [and a] gold [-piece in hand] should

mutter this excellent ninth Maṇḍala which relates to the Purifying Soma.

(a) Prof. Gonda renders: 'Strainer'. The end of the Varga is here marked by 35 in Ba Ta and further these mss. repeat that last *pāda* of the *adhyāya* in accordance with the usage of Vedic works.

## ADHYĀYA III

1. A twice-born person should mutter the Gāyatrī-verses which relate to the purifying Soma and which begin with *Svādiṣṭhayā* [*RV*.9.1-67]. He should mutter the verses dealing with the Purifying Soma [which are] the holy among the holies.

The translation follows the Mātṛsūnu's commentary: *Svādiṣṭhayeti / caturdaśottaraṁ śuktaśataṁ pāvamānamaṁḍalaṁ "Svādiṣṭhayā madiṣṭhayārabhya (madiṣṭhayetyārabhya)**" *yat te rāja[ñ]* chṛtaṁ havir* [*RV*. 9.1-114] *ityevaṁ aṁtaṁ tasya samastasya sāmānyamadhyayanam uktam adhunā saptaṣaṣṭīnāṁ pavamānasūktānām viśeṣato vidhānam ucyate / tad adhikṛtyedam ārabhyate svādiṣṭhayeti gāyatrīr ityādi / Svādiṣṭhayetyevam ādyā ṛcaḥ pāvamānīr ityeva[ṁ]* saṁjñakā gāyatrīchaṁdasthā japan dvijo nityaṁ pavitrāṇām sarveṣām api pavitrataraṁ tad yat pāvamānīr ṛco'tastaj japed iti saṁbaṁdhaḥ //* Prof. Gonda renders *pavitrāṇāṁ pavitram* by 'the pre-eminent means of purification'.

2. Immersing in waters, a piously disposed person is released from all sins. Recitation[a] of these [verses] is [considered to be] meritorious, likewise recollection and retention [of them] in memory.

(a) Mātṛsūnu glosses *kīrtanam* by *pāṭhaḥ*.

3. And having known [them] properly one attains the abode of Brahmā. But among those that are declared [i.e. Recitation, Recollection and Retention in memory] whatever is subsequent is effective [than the preceding].

Prof. Gonda renders the second hemistich thus: 'And these above mentioned (stanzas are characterised by) any extremely excellent (property):'. The learned Professor has, evidently, missed the point.

4. By recitation one becomes pure by recollection one remembers what is the Highest and by retention in memory, a person

who is pure-minded and who has subdued all organs of sense attains the oneness with Brahmā.

Mātṛsūnu: *eteṣāṁ guṇavadyad[yad]* uttaram iti uktaṁ ca viśe-ṣataḥ sādhikurvann āha / Kīrtanāt tu- ya iti //*

5. And after having known [them] one attains the abode of Brahmā. In the worship of gods,[a] one must have [these verses] recited in the presence of Brāhmaṇas enjoying the feast.

(a) Mātṛsūnu glosses *devatākṛtye* by *devakārya*, but Prof. Gonda renders 'to the image of the god (?)'. The end of the Varga is marked here by 1 in Ba Ta.

6. And that [recitation] pleases the godhead and causes the rite to prosper. [These purifying verses], when recited in the Pitrya[a] [rite] by a person who is piously disposed, gladens the manes.

(a) Mātṛsūnu glosses *pitreye* by *pitṛkarmaṇi*.

7. A person, even if he has committed very great sins and has imbibed[a] [drinks] that ought not to be drunk and so on, becomes pure in three days after having muttered the [hymn] *Taratsamandīya* [*RV*.9.58] while immersing in water.

(a) The text has *prapīya*, a form which violates Pāṇini 6.4.69.

8-9. And [whatever] offered to the manes becomes everlasting and exceedingly delightful.[a] The cows which yield all objects desire wait upon him who, being pure in mind and having the organs of sense under control, recites the verses relating to the Purifying Soma. Long life, Strength, renown, wealth, progeny, fame, health—[b]

(a) Prof. Gonda renders 'and (by doing so) an undecaying, excellent sweet drink will be given to the ancestors'. Prof. Gonda makes a mistake by connecting this hemistich with the preceding stanza i.e. St.7, but it is intimately connected with St. 6, though St.7 a late intruder, intervenes.

(b) Constructionally, this hemistich is joined to the next which contains the main verb.

10. unequalled and unfailing merits of Veda study—[these] a person who is pure obtains. A person who is incapable [of reciting these verses relating to the Purifying Soma] but who is diligent should mutter the thirty verses of Vaikhānasas[a] [*RV*.9.66]—

(a) Regarding Vaikhānasas, see Ṣaḍguruśiṣya's commentary on *Sarv*.ix.66.

11. and [those] which are proclaimed by the Seven Sages [*RV*.9.67.1-21] and [those] of Pavitra [*RV*.9.67.22-32] which are subsequent [to them]—these sixty-two verses beginning with *Pavasva* [*RV*.9.66-67] are proclaimed by the excellent sages—

The end of the Varga is marked here by 2 in Ba Ta.

12. for the destruction of all sins, for purification and for auspiciousness. In this[a] [work, the first] sixty-seven hymns beginning *Svādiṣṭhayā* [*RV*.9.1-67] are treated [so far].

(a) The text has *iha* which is rendered by Prof. Gonda as 'With this (exposition)'.

13. [The verses] relating to Purifying Soma comprise six hundred and ten verses and one will overcome the violent fear of death by muttering and by offering [with these verses]—

This verse is identical with verse 19 of *RV.Kh*.iii.10. See *RV*. (*VSM*), Vol.IV, 947.

14. and will undoubtedly obtain complete release from disease. Accepting [gifts] that ought not to be accepted[a] and eating forbidden food—

(a) This prohibition applies only to the gifts given by a prohibited person and not to the gifts themselves.

15. one becomes pure in three days after having muttered the [hymn] *Tarat samandīya* [*RV*.9.58][a] while immersing in water. The [hymn] relating to Purifying Soma which is subsequent (i.e. *RV.Kh*.iii.10][b] is destructive of infirmities (*rapas*).

(a) The ritual use of Taratsamandīya-hymn, coming as it does after the employment of *RV*.9.67, appears to be an afterthought if we regard the traditional order of stanzas in the text of *Ṛvidh* as perfect. On an earlier occasion I had pointed out that St.7 which also concerns with the Taratsamandīya-hymn interrupts the connection between St.6 and St.8ab. A re-arrangement of stanzas 7-15 seems necessary. According to this new arrangement, St.7 will have hemistiches 8ab and 7ab; St.8, hemistiches 7cd and 14cd; St.9, hemistiches 15ab and 8cd; St. 15, hemistiches 14ab and 15cd; and the intervening stanzas have to be renumbered accordingly.

(b) The text probably refers to the Khila hymn which comes after *RV*.9.67 in the Kashmir Khila collection. For details see note under the next stanza.

16. Restraining the breath, one should meditate on gods, manes, and sages and in the end offer [oblations of] clarified butter after fasting and adoring Agni and Soma.

This stanza as well as the first hemistich of the next stanza are strongly reminiscent of verse 16 of *RV.Kh*.iii.10. *Vide RV* (*VSM*), Vol.IV, p.947. See also St. 13 above. We may possibly be correct in assuming that *Ṛvidh* is aware of the Khila-text of Pāvamāna-hymn.

17. And one should worship Sarasvatī with [offering of] milk, water, honey and ghee. One on becoming pure after taking a bath [should] mutter the hymn [beginning with] *Pavitraṁ te* [*RV*. 9.83]:

The end of the Varga is here marked by 3 in Ba Ta.

18. [then] one attains a favourite refuge [in the next world] and acquires prosperity here. At the time of death one should always mutter the hymns beginning with *Nānānam* [*RV*.9.112-114].

Mātṛsūnu: *gatīti sārddham / eta*[*c*]* *chucir bhūtvā yo nityaṁ jāpati tasyāṁtakāle iṣṭā śobhanā gatir bhavati / iha loke mahatī ca vṛddhir bhavatīti / nānānam iti //* After St. 18ab, Dr. Meyer's text has two additional hemistiches which are found in the text of his ms. C. But they are found in the margin of his ms. B and in *Secunda manu* of his ms. A.

19-20. And one attains the highest abode and immortality after having muttered [them]. A twice-born person who is restrained should always employ [the hymn] beginning with *Āpo hi ṣṭhā* [*RV*.10.9] at the time of bathing (*snānārtham*).[a] But a person who is desirous of purity and who is steadfast should mutter [it] thrice and [being] very intent he should recite [it] thrice while immersing in water.

(a) I have followed Mātṛsūnu who explains it by *snānakāle*.

21-22. A Brāhmaṇa-slayer covering himself with a bark-cloth and having a skull and foot of a bedstead [in each hand] should go about declaring his deed for twelve years [and] should mentally recollect this [hymn] beginning with *Āpo hi ṣṭha* [*RV*.10.9] without pronouncing but after the fifth year he should mutter [it] by thousands (*sahasraśas*).[a]

(a) Prof. Gonda renders it 'a thousand times.'

23. And there should always be an additional muttering of three thousand times daily, and when the twelfth year is complete a Brāhmaṇa-slayer is freed [from his guilt].

The end of the Varga is here marked by 4 in Ba Ta.

24. The Brāhmaṇas after assembling together should address him who has observed the vow thus: "If there be anything left undone, [thou], speaking falsely will sin[a] again—

(a) Though most of the mss. read: *patet* and only Ba: *patēḥ*, I have chosen the latter reading, as it is impossible to construe the former, and moreover the former appears to be an early corruption due to anticipation helped by the confusion between the *upadhmānīya-sign* which optionally replaces the *visarga* before labial surds and the letter *t*. It can be illustrated thus: पतेः पुनः पते⌣पुनः पतेत्पुनः ॥

25. Thou, speaking untruth, wilt kill ten later [generations of

your family] and ten preceding [ones]". [Then] he must say: "Oṁ bhoḥ"[a] and after being thus allowed by the Brāhmaṇas he on becoming pure should mutter [the aforesaid hymn],

(a) The expression *oṁ bhoḥ* is a sign of assent on the part of the accused who readily admits that he has fully carried out the expiatory rite.

26. and he should prepare a *sthālīpāka* for the vow-fulfilling Agni and thus he is released from guilt and he regains[a] the Sāvitrī [i.e. the well-known verse addressed to Savitṛ, *RV*.3.62.10].

(a) The idea seems to be that a Brāhmaṇa-slayer loses his Sāvitrī and that he can regain it only after performing an expiatory-rite. Prof. Gonda, however, renders the second hemistich thus: 'And in this way he gets rid of sin, when he has resorted to the Sāvitrī'!

27. After having killed the powerful sage Tvāṣṭra, Śakra [became] formerly a Brāhmaṇa-slayer[a] [and] Sindhudvīpa freed him [from that guilt] after sprinkling him with these [verses].

(a) The term *brahmahā* is applied to Śakra i.e. Indra because Tvāṣṭra is said to have been well-versed in the Vedas.

28. After having stolen the possessions of a Brāhmaṇa, and the property of a preceptor, one is released [from sin] within six years after muttering these [verses] according to the [aforesaid] precept.

The end of the Varga is here marked by 5 in Ba Ta.

29. A Brāhmaṇa-slayer who is also a drinker of *surā*[a] [should] invariably mutter these [verses] according to the [aforesaid] practice: [then] he is released [from sin] like a Brāhmaṇa-slayer.

(a) i.e. spiritous liquor extracted from rice, to drink which is considered a heinous crime.

(b) Prof. Gonda renders *niyamena* 'under fixed restrictions'.

30. Having raised [one's fist or stick] in a fit of anger towards a Brāhmaṇa, one should mutter these [verses] after overthrowing him and should fast for three days after his defeat and for one day after assailing him.

Mātṛsūnu: *brāhmaṇeti / upapātakasaṁbaṁdham api prāsaṁga* (?) *evoktaṁ tad api paṭhita siddham eva / ruṣā krodha ucyate tad vaśād vastumuṣṭyā* (?) //

31. One who has caused [a Brāhmaṇa's] blood to flow should fast for three days after pacifying him and should mutter these [verses].

Mātṛsūnu: *Śoṇitam iti / etad api paṭhitasiddham eva //*

32. Getting up always in the morning one should sprinkle oneself [with water, for this is] an expiation for the unintentional sin committed at night.

The manuscript consulted by me contract the word *pāpasya avijñātasya* in the text to *pāpasyāvijñātasya* and insert a particle to make up the deficiency of metre. I have preferred the reading with hiatus. Same is the case with the next stanza (See Critical Notes p. 269).

33. One should sprinkle oneself [with water] along with these [verses] regularly in the evening [for this is] an expiation for the unintentional sin committed during day-time.

The end of the Varga is here marked by 6 in Ba Ta.

34. A Brāhmaṇa should wait upon king Yama with the hymn [addressed to him][a] and one should prepare a *sthālīpāka* dedicated to Yama as the deity during the bright and dark fortnights.

(a) i.e. *RV*.10.14 which is otherwise known as *Yamasūkta*. See *Yaj*.3.2. The mss. consulted by me read *Yamasūktena*, but I prefer to follow Dr. Meyer, whose text reads *yamaṁ sūktena* because none of the Dharmaśāstras seem to prescribe this hymn for the purpose of waiting upon a king. We can also supply *adhastanena* to *sūktena*.

35. And on the eighth and fourteenth [lunar days] he should worship Yama with an offering and in this case he should employ the hymn beginning with *Pareyivāṃsam* [*RV*.10.14]:

Mātṛsūnu: *aṣṭamyāṁ ca caturdaśyāṁ cā'nenaiva sūktena yamaṁ pūjayed iti //*

36. [then] he will never die before [the full] duration of life. Yama is pleased with him and he gives a [good] recollection,[a] when the end is near (ante).

(a) Prof. Gonda renders 'memory' and adds 'viz. of past births'.

37. Exclaiming (iti): "Dharmarājāya svāhā", he should offer oblation at the end of [each] formula and should regularly perform the rite on the full moon day [of the month] of Vaiśākha.

Mātṛsūnu's commentary on this stanza is full of lacuna.

38. Whoever offers water mixed with sesamum to Yama and his followers after taking a bath on the two solstices and on the full and new moon days will have no fear from them.

Mātṛsūnu: *ayaneti / Kaiścid anyair ṛṣiḥ paṭhayate sa ca pāṭhe siddha eveti // //* Possibly the commentary, as it is, is misplaced and the latter part of it may belong to the next stanza. In such a case, *ṛṣiḥ* may possibly be a variant reading for *dvijaḥ*.

39. Regularly eating at the Nakta [–time] and sparing in diet for one full year, a twice-born person should resort to Mṛtyu by muttering [the hymn beginning with] *Paraṁ mṛtyo* [*RV*.10.18]:

The end of the Varga is here marked by 7 in Ba Ta.

40. [then] Mṛtyu does not take away that person who is possessed of sons and offspring before the [full] duration of life. Subsisting on fruits and sparing in diet a person can conquer death within three years (*tribhiḥ varṣaiḥ*)[a]

(a) Prof. Gonda renders 'in (after) three years'. See, however, Pāṇini 2.3.6.

41. At the sixth [meal-] time [i.e. in the evening of the third day] one must eat fruit or even a [bulbous] root, pass the time standing [during the day] and sitting [during the night], and remain in water during cold season.

Prof. Gonda renders the second hemistich thus: 'one must alternatively stand, sit down and move on; one must dwell in cool water'!

42. During summer, one must expose oneself to the heat of five fires, [have] the clouds as the only shelter[a] during rainy season [and being] thus diligent one conquers death and is released from diseases.

(a) Prof. Gonda renders 'one must live under the open sky (exposing oneself) to rain'.

43. With the [verse] beginning with *Udīrṣva* [*RV*.10.18.8], a brother-in-law should prohibit the wife of [his] issueless brother,[a] for the sake of progeny, from ascending [the funeral pyre] when [her] husband is dead.

(a) The text has *bhrātur bhāryām aputrasya,* an example of loose construction.

44. And smearing himself with ghee and controlling his speech, he [i.e. brother-in-law] should at the proper time after menses beget one son, but on no account a second [one].

Mātṛsūnu introduces commentary with the words: *adhunā niyoga ucyate* //

45. One should mentally recollect the ten-syllabled [formula] beginning with *Bhadraṁ na* [*RV*.10.20.1] for sake of pacification and regularly mutter [it] on becoming pure: [then] one attains mental ease.

Mātṛsūnu: *daśākṣaraṁ tu śāṁtyartham ityādi* / *idaṁ daśākṣaraṁ pādam ātmanaḥ śāṁtyartham nityam anusmaret* / *nityeva* (*nityam eva*) *śucir bhūtvā japet tato mānasaṁ sukhaṁ prāpnoti* // The end of the Varga is here marked by 8 in Ba Ta.

46. [While] muttering this [formula] by thousands,[a] a person should subsist on fruit for one month, drink water only for [the next] one month [and] subsist on air for [another] one month.

(a) Prof. Gonda renders 'a thousand times'.

47. To such a person, all objects of desire longed for are ful-

filled by [mere] wish, [and] he sees heavenly host, the Gandharvas, the Siddhās and the Cāraṇas.

Prof. Gonda renders the first hemistich thus: 'only in thought. (Then) all the wishes he strives after are fulfilled to him:'

48. He vanishes from this world, moves through the atmosphere, sees and hears from afar like Brahmā.

Prof. Gonda renders this stanza thus: 'He disappears (i.e. becomes able to disappear at will) he becomes (able to depart) from this world through the atmosphere. He sees from afar and he hears from afar like one who stands in the highest place (i.e. like a supreme deity)'.

49. When a mortal fear presents [itself] in a sandy desert, a person who is restrained should mutter the [hymn] beginning with *Pra devatrā* [*RV*.10.30]: [then] he quickly finds water.

Mātṛsūnu: *pradevatreti niyata ityādi / marudhanvā nāma niruko* (*nirudako*)* *deśa ucyate / tatraitat sūktaṁ japati yaḥ kṣipram āpo labhyante* (?) *nirudake' pi deśa iti //*

50. One must have the three dice of Vibhītaka [-nut] scented with fragrances, and cover them with flowers after placing them in a terrace.

The end of the Varga is here marked by 9 in Ba Ta.

51. Bringing the feet together and remaining in an upright position during that night one should mentally mutter the verse in praise of dice,[a] viz. that beginning with *Prā vepā mā* [*RV*.10.34.1] at night,

(a) cp. *Sarv.* (x.34): *prā vepāḥ ṣaḷūnā maujavān vā' kṣo' kṣakṛṣipraśaṁsā cā'kṣakitavanimdā ca //*

52. and when [the night] has passed away (*vyuṣṭāyām*)[a] and the sun has arisen, he should mutter [this verse] even while proceeding to the place of gambling and regularly muttering this [verse] only, he wins [and he] is not vanquished by others.

(a) Mātṛsūnu supplies *rātrau*.

53. Touching the head of that person[a] whom one wishes to vanquish, whilst muttering the rest of the hymn, one vanquishes others [and one] is not vanquished by anyone.

(a) Mātṛsūnu supplies *dyūtakāram.*

54. One should mutter the two [hymns] beginning with *Abudhram* [*RV*.10.35] and *Uṣāsānaktā* [*RV*.10.36] at the blessing ceremony [and] constantly [mutter the hymn] beginning with *Namo mitrasya varuṇasya cakṣase* [*RV*.10.37]

The second hemistich is tagged on to the first one without any apparent purpose.

55. Of this [latter hymn, i.e. *RV*.10.37] there [is,] one verse which comes last (*uttamā*);[a] with that [verse], with which one is freed from sins, one should regularly offer clarified butter: [then] one is released from sins.

(a) i.e. *RV*.10.37.12, but Mātṛsūnu takes *RV*.10.36.14 as the verse intended to be employed in the above rite. Prof. Gonda renders *uttamā* 'best', though he refers to the same verse like me. The end of the Varga is here marked by 10 in Ba Ta.

56. A person endowed with religious faith[a] should mutter the hymn beginning with *Divaspari* [*RV*.10.45]: [then that person] who is desirous of religious faith and who is steadfast wins religious faith everywhere.

(a) Mātṛsūnu explains *śraddhā* by *abhilāṣaḥ* and further on gives *āstikyam* as one of its characteristics.

57. He who is perplexed[a] in an impenetrable path should mutter [the hymn] beginning with *Mā pra gāma* [*RV*.10.57]: [then] he fares well on his way and obtains highest pleasure.

(a) The word *mūḍhaḥ* occurs in *AGS*.3.7.9: *Saṁpūṣan viduṣeti naṣṭam adhijigamiṣan muḷho* (v.1. *mūḍho*)*vā* // Dr. Meyer reads *samūḍhaḥ* but suggests *saṁmūḍhaḥ*, a reading which is found in some of the mss. consulted by Prof. Gonda.

58. [whilst muttering the hymn] beginning with *Yat te yamaṁ* [*RV*.10.58] one should, after bathing, touch the head of some dear friend regarding whom one might think thus: "[He is] diminishing in vital power".

Mātṛsūnu: *kṣiṇāyur iti manyetetyādi / yaṁ kaṁcit suhṛdam abhīṣṭam atikṛśaṁ vyādhigṛhītam dṛṣṭvā kṣīṇāyur asāv ityevaṁ manye [ta]* jānīyāt / tasyā'nena sūktena snātvā śucir bhūtvā śirasi spṛśet tato' sau dīrghāyur bhavatīti //*

59. One should mutter [this hymn] a thousand times for five days: [then] he will obtain [a prolonged] life [and further] along with the [recital of] Sindhudvīpa's hymn [*RV*.10.9] one should anoint him with ghee.

Mātṛsūnu has the following comment to make regarding this stanza: *adhastān mūrdhābhimarśanam uktam iha tu japam ucyate //*

60. [While] reclining on a couch one should mutter this formula[a] [and] then one should touch one's sons, wife, any other amiable person and oneself.

(a) Possibly the text has in view *RV*.10.59.4. Cf. *Sarv* (X.59): *caturthyām somaṁ cā'stuvan mṛtyor apagamanāya.* But Mātṛsūnu refers to the earlier hymn. The end of the Varga is here marked by 11 in Ba Ta.

61. One should regularly employ this *jīvāvṛtti*[a] after anointing all apertures of one's body with ghee: [then] one becomes happy and free from fever.

(a) Possibly here also the text has in view *RV*.10.60.7-12. Cp. *Sarv* (X.60): *parābhiḥ subandhor jīvam āhvayan.* Mātṛsūnu also refers to the same verses quoting a few words *jīvātave na mṛtyave*'. The word *jivāvṛtti* occurs in *BD* vii.85.

62. The formula beginning with *Idam ittha* [*RV*.10.61.1] is declared as one which bestows a thousand. [Subsisting on] sacri-

ficial food for half a month, one must drink milk for a half a month.

Mātṛsūnu: *idam icheti (ittheti)* caturaḥ / "idamitthā raudraṁ gūrtavacā"* [*RV*.10.61.1] *iti saptaviṁśatyṛcaṁ sūktam / tatrādyāmṛcam adhikṛtyedam ucyate / idam ittheti maṁtro' yam ityādi / ayaṁ prathamamaṁtraḥ sahasrasani* [*ri*]**tyanavā saṁjñā bhaṇyate savanir nāma dānaṁ tad anena prakāram anena maṁtreṇa labhyata iti //*

63. After fasting for another fortnight, one should offer [oblations of] ghee into the fire, after setting on fire the fuel-sticks of Udumbara-wood[a] on a consecrated ground in a forest.

(a) Udumbara (Ficus glomerata) is used for ritual purposes of varied kinds. See, however *AV.Par*.26.5.1c: *udumbarasya vittārthī.*

64. All [sacrificial utensils like] the *sruk*,[a] the *sruva*, and the *camasa* should be of Udumbara-wood, and one gets one's object of desire after offering a thousand oblations.

(a) The *sruk* is a large ladle meant for offering, whereas the *sruva* is a small one which is used for dipping. See Kane, *HDS*, Vol.II, pp.984-85.

65. The rite [is][a] indeed infallible and one will surely experience success [for] this [rite], even though half [done]- and aimless, gives the desired fruit to him.

(a) Scil. *bhavati* cp. above ii.72c: *amoghaṁ karma bhavati.*
(b) Scil. *Kṛtam*. But Prof. Gonda connects *ardham* with *phalasya* and renders 'the half of the fruit'! The end of the Varga is here marked by 12 in Ba Ta.

66. While facing the sun one desiring food should offer [oblations of] ghee on a cross-road and one desiring wealth should feed a thousand Brāhmaṇas.

Prof. Gonda renders the second hemistich thus: 'let (the man) who wishes wealth feed brahmans a thousand times'.

67. One desiring cattle should mutter [it] in the cow-pen[a] or even offer [oblations in that place] after fasting according to the

precept: then that person who is restrained obtains a thousand heads of cattle.

(a) *goṣṭhe*, placed as it is between *japet* and *juhuyāt*, construes with both. See below iv.105c: *juhuyād goṣṭhamadhye tu.*

68-69. One must prepare a triple amulet made of iron, copper and gold and pour over it the residue of a thousand burnt fuel-sticks. One, on becoming pure, should wear it on the head or on the hand after the pouring of a thousand [oblations]: then one will have a thousand followers.

Mātṛsūnu: *tatas taṁ maṇiṁ śarīrasthaṁ dhārayet* //

70. For a Snātaka, [the hymn beginning with] *Parāvataḥ* [*RV.* 10.63] is prescribed at the blessing ceremony and one who is desirous of heaven and who is regular in one's observances should regularly mutter it.

Mātṛsūnu: *parāvataḥ svastyayanam ityādi / etat sūktam japyam snāta[ka]*sya vihitaṁ gṛhasthasya ca svargakāmasyeti //* The end of the Varga is here marked by 13 in Ba Ta.

71. One should regularly mutter [the hymn in] praise of knowledge beginning with *Bṛhaspati prathamam* [*RV.*10.71]: [then] one becomes a possessor of knowledge [and] beauty [and] obtains everlasting fortune.

Mātṛsūnu: *bṛhaspate prathamam ityādi / jñānapraśaṁsārtham idaṁ sūktam taj jñānārthaṁ śrīkāmaś ca japet / tataś ca jñānavān bhavati / anaṁtāṁ ca śriyaṁ prāpnotiti //*

72. Whilst muttering this [verse] beginning with *Vayaḥ suparṇā* [*RV.*10.71.2], a twice-born person must subsist on milk [alone] in order to destroy misfortune, [and] he will surely obtain fortune [also]

Mātṛsūnu: *alakṣmī naśanārtham ityādi / payobhakṣo "vayaḥ suparṇā* [*RV.*10.71.2] *ityetām japan alakṣmīr nāśayate śriyaṁ ca labhata iti //*

73. Whoever considers himself (*ātmānam*) [as if] covered with mental darkness or engrossed in the self (*ātmani*) with misfortune is freed after muttering this [verse].

Mātṛsūnu: *tamaseti / aśrīrūpeṇa tamasā ya ātmānaṁ prāvṛtaṁ manyeta so'pyetām eva ṛcaṁ japet ||* Prof. Gonda, however, renders this stanza thus: 'But he who, being wrapped in mental darkness, regards his person to be in the Self, is, even, if he is subject to ill-luck, freed (from it) by muttering this (stanza)'.

74. Getting up in the morning one should wipe off one's eyes always with this [verse: then] one becomes a possessor of good sight [and] beauty and wards off misfortune.

Mātṛsūnu: *ahar ahaśca prātar utthāya anayā ṛcā akṣiṇī saṁmārjayed iti | tataś ca cakṣuṣmān śrīmāṁś ca bhavati ||*

75. A twice-born person who is steadfast attains the eternal [abode of] Brahmā by muttering the [verse] beginning with *Na taṁ vidātha* [*RV.*10.82.7] after leaving aside all stains.

Mātṛsūnu's commentary on this stanza is not found and in its stead we find a long quotation from *Bṛhadṛgvidhāna.* Since it has nothing to do either with the preceding stanzas or with the succeeding ones, I presume it to be misplaced.

76. With this [verse] whoever offers water mixed with sesamum to Yama and his followers after taking a bath on the full and new moon days will have no fear from them.

This stanza is practically same as the one occurred earlier (iii.38).

77. 'One should always mutter the two [hymns] which are destructive of enemies [and] which begin with *Yas te manyo* [*RV.* 10.83-84] and wear an iron amulet over which [the residue of] an oblation of ghee has been poured along with the [muttering of the] two [hymns].

The end of the Varga is here marked by 14 in Ba Ta.

78. On the fourteenth (lunar day] one should with the same two [hymns] offer an iron pin into a fire kindled with Khādira-fuel: [then] one wards off one's rivals.

Mātṛsūnu: *juhuyād iti | etā[bhyā]*m eva sūktābhyāṁ caturdaśyāṁ lohamayaṁ kīlamayaṁ juhuyāt | kathaṁbhūte' gnāv ityucyate | khādiredhmasamiddhe khādiredhmaprajvalite tataḥ sapatnān pratibādhata ityetayor api maṇi śaṁkoḥ phalam iti ||*

79. The propitiatory [hymn of] *Hṛdya* [*RV.Kh*.iii.15] is mysterious, pure [and] wonderful like the highest Brahman for there is nothing beyond this.

This is the first of the two khilas which in the Kashmir Khila collection comes after *RV*.10.84. Mātṛsūnu is not aware of this Khila and Prof. Gonda is silent here. See, however, iii.109 below.

80. Fasting for twelve days whilst muttering [the hymn of] this Ṛṣi [i.e. Hṛdya] always, a piously disposed person should be absorbed in mind by that (*tanmanāḥ*) after approaching water [i.e. for bathing] thrice a day.

Prof. Gonda renders the first hemistich thus: 'Having fasted for twelve days and muttering always (the sūktas of) this ṛṣi'. Evidently he takes 'the sūktas' to be *RV*.10.83-84!

81. [After having] settled on a pure spot[a] at the end of twelve days : one should make an image of a man, made of sand on the ground.

(a) Prof. Gonda renders 'on a pure spot and concentrated', but the phrase has occurred earlier. See i.54 above.

82. After having trodden upon the heart-region[a] of that [image], one should mutter [the hymn of this] Ṛṣi :- [then] one will experience [this] rite as infallible when a day and a night have passed.

(a) The text has *hṛdayadeśam*. Prof. Gonda renders (the spot of) the heart'. Brackets are unnecessary.
(b) Prof. Gonda renders 'should mutter (the Sūktas of) the ṛṣi'. Evidently *RV*.10.83-84! The end of the Varga is here marked by 15 in Ba Ta.

83-84. One can win over a rich Vaiśya within three days, a Kṣatriya within four days, a king within five days, the best among the twice-born within six days and an ascetic after seven days and one can control him as well. Or else, one should always stand [and] mutter this [hymn] after fasting and bathing.

Mātṛsūnu: *tryaheṇeti / pūrvoktena vidhinā pratikṛtim pādenāvaṣṭabhyaitat sūktadvayaṁ japanīyam / tata iyatā kālena jayate jitaṁ vasaṁtaṁ vaśībhūtaṁ bhunaktīti ślokārthaḥ /* Mātṛsūnu paraphrased *bhuñjīta* by *bhunkati*. Prof. Gonda renders 'one will use (this person's) services'.

85. Whoever wishes to have for himself [a person under subjection] should avoid a low [one]. One should pour the powder of *bilvas*, over which the residue of a thousand oblations has been poured—

Mātṛsūnu: *śeṣaṁ spaṣṭam* //

86-87. into the well in order to bring him under control: [then] he will quickly bring that person [under his control]. One should employ this [hymn of] Hṛdya[a] on one's own mother, sons, father and on brothers and friends. In the case of parents (*guru*)- one should honour them highly [when employing it] but (*tu*) in the case of friends [one should employ it] after embracing them and in the case of one's son after kissing his head.

(a) Prof. Gonda explains it as 'a Vedic mantra used to effect the subjection of a rival or enemy'!

(b) Neither Meyer's conjecture (*guḍam* for *gurum*) nor Prof. Gonda's rendering: 'one shall (a lump of) sugar on the head' gives a good sense. The end of the Varga is here marked by 16 in Ba Ta.

88-89.[a] one should employ this [hymn of] Hṛdya for the sake of pacification and ease. When the propitiatory rite has failed, one should, after setting on fire the image of sand on the way, offer [oblations] into the fire with ghee if [he is] a Brāhmaṇa, but with mustard-oil in the case of a Kṣatriya as well as of a Vaiśya.

(a) Mātṛsūnu: *hṛdyety arddham / asamiti sarddharm / yadi pūrvoktena vidhinā saṁvananaṁ na siddhyeta / sādhyasya gachato yatra tu pradeśe padaṁ sthāpitaṁ dṛśyate tasya pāṁsu māṣya-cūrṇasya godhūmacū* [*ṛna*]**sya ca madhye prakṣipya mardayitvā pratikṛtiṁ putralakaṁ* (*puttalikām*)* *kuryāt taṁ* (*tāṁ*)* *ghṛtenābhyajya juhuyāt ghṛtenaiva saha pratyaṁgaṁ kha* [*ṁ*]**ḍayitvā* (*yadi*)* *brāhmaṇaḥ sādhyaḥ / yadi kṣatriyo vaiśyo vā sādhyaḥ tataḥ sārṣapeṇa tailenainam avajuhuyāt* (*d*)* *iti* //

(b) The construction is disturbed, the genitives in the second hemistich does not agree with the conjunction *yadi*.

90. Or one should place an iron image into the fire and on becoming pure and absorbed in mind by that, offer [oblations over it when one considers it ablaze.

Mātṛsūnu: *āyasī* [*ti*]* *sārddham / prakṣipet taṁ sādhyaṁ manasi kṛtvā' mūko'yam anenābhiprāyeṇa ca tataḥ sūktena ghṛtam juhuyāt //*

91-92.[a] one should strike [the image] with ferocious mind and getting angry should offer ghee [into the fire]. In whatever manner the glittering image is sacrificed into the fire [by] a Brāhmaṇa (*vipra*), in like manner that person comes under his control. One should make an unusual sacrificial altar out of cemetery-burnt sands.

(a) Mātṛsūnu: *tasyopari yadi tu kruddha* [ḥ] *sādhakas tatas tu tām pratighātayet / mitrayet* (?) */ yatheti / yathā ca pra* [*ti*]* *kṛtis tapyate tathā sādhyo vaśyo bhavatīti / Śmaśānetyarddham //*

(b) Construction requires that we should read here *vipreṇa* instead of *vipraḥ*. Could it be *sa vipraḥ* 'that twice-born person'?

See, however, St.104cd below. The end of the Varga is here marked by 17 in Ba Ta.

93-95. One should place the metallic image into [the fire] kindled with the Vaibhītaka-wood. When it is midnight, one having a fierce appearance with hair dishevelled, sitting on three stakes and desiring the death [of one's rival] should prepare a seat, full of arrow-heads [kept] invertedly in that place and offer the mustard-oil with salt: [then] one will reduce [him] to subjection in no time. Or one should go on exorcising [one's rival] with spells in this manner and offer one's blood:

Mātṛsūnu: *baibhīti sārddhadvayam / athavā'yaṁ prakāraḥ / yasmin pratikṛti-homo kartum ichati tadā tasmin pradeśe śmaśānabhumidagdhamṛttikām ānīya tāṁ cūrṇayitvā taiḥ pāṁsubhir vedīṁ kṛtvā tasya veder dakṣiṇāpathe' gniṁ vidadhyāt tataḥ śaramayena barhiṣā stad* (*tad*)* *abhimukhaṁ staraṇaṁ kuryāt tato vaibhītakhedhmaḥ parivayaś* (*paricayaś*)* *ca kartavyaḥ / tatra vaibhītakedhme prakalpitedhme lohamaya* (*lohamayīṁ*) *pratikṛtiṁ nidadhyāt tato' rddharātravelāyāṁ ugradarśanaḥ kruddhaḥ san kruddharūpaḥ sārṣapatailaṁ lavaṇānvitam etābhyāṁ sūktābhyāṁ juhuyāt sadyamāraṇe apsu / tataḥ sādhyo vaśyo bhavati / athaveti / evaṁ vābhicāraṁ kuryāt sādhyaṁ dhyāyann ātmaśoṇitam ābhyāṁ sūktābhyāṁ juhuyāt tato vaśaṁ nayati rājānaṁ kṣipraṁ janapadaṁ puram iti //*

96. [then] one quickly brings under subjection a king, a country [and] a town. The rite for prosperity which was declared by the self-restrained [Ṛṣi] Hṛdya should also be performed.[a]

(a) Prof. Gonda renders the second hemistich thus: 'A rite for (the attainment of' prosperity (as) taught by the hṛdyam, must also be performed by (a person) who controls his soul and spirit'. Obviously, Prof. Gonda connect s*yatātmanā* with *kartavyam.*

97. A Brāhmaṇa must not perform [any rite] connected with murder against a sinless [person]. One should prepare a pap with the milk of a cow having a calf of the same colour [as the cow].

Mātṛsūnu's commentary on the second hemistich runs as follows: *atha gavāṁ puṣṭikarmocyate / sarūpavatsāyā* [*go*]**ś caiva payasā sādhyec* carum // The third *pāda* of this stanza is Major Ionic. The simplest way to restore it would be reading: *goś ca sarūpavatsāyāḥ*. Possibly the author wanted *goḥ* to be as near as possible to *payasā.* The end of the Varga is here marked by 18 in Ba Ta.

98. One must cause the first-born calf to drink [that] over which the residue of a thousand oblations has been poured: [then] that calf will have a thousand companions and be free from diseases.[a]

(a) The text has *rogair vivarjitaḥ* instead of a compound (*rogavi*°).

99. Likewise, one must cause the cows to drink: [they] also become free from fevers (*vigatajvara*)- and one must regularly feed [one's] sons and other amiable and good people:

(a) Prof. Gonda renders 'free from diseases'.

100. [then] they become healthy, affectionate and free from

fevers. If one longs for a woman: [then the following rite] makes her highly propitious.[a]

(a) Prof. Gonda renders the second hemistich thus: 'If one puts one's mind upon a woman: (this is) a mighty mean to win her'.

101. A person who is an expert (*kuśala*)[a] should by means of fire soften the fine particles of rice grain unhusked with nails, over which the residue of a thousand oblations has been poured:

(a) Prof. Gonda renders 'Being in good condition'!

102. With that [substance] one must prepare an image after visualising that woman in one's mind and offer, member by member, that [image] anointed with mustard-oil.

The end of the Varga is marked here by 19 in Ba Ta.

103. One must tear off the feet first exclaiming (iti): *phaṭ* and then put them into the fire, then the shanks, the knees, the thighs and then the head,

Mātṛsūnu: *pāda iti / strīvaśīkaraṇam ucyate / strīṇāṁ nakhacīrṇair* (?) *atuṣīkṛtānāṁ* (*nistuṣī kṛtānāṁ*?) *tamḍulānāṁ cūrnaṁ kārayitvā tato' gniṁ prajvālyābhyāṁ sūktābhyāṁ ājyāhutisahasraṁ juhuyāt / tasmin cūrṇe saṁpātaṁ kṛta* (*kṛtvā*)* *cūrṇam uṣṇodakenāgninā* [*vā*] *svedayet / nipuṇaḥ kartā tatas tena cittena sādhyāṁ striyaṁ manasā dhyāya* (*dhyātvā** or could it be *adhyāya*?) *pratikṛtiṁ kuryāt tāṁ ca sārṣapatailenābhyaktā pada* (*pāda*)* *prabhṛty avayavānāṁ* (*avayavān*)* *khaṁḍayitvā 'nena sūktadvayena juhuyāt / phaṭ svāhety aṁtataḥ kṛtvā hṛdayaṁ tu khaṁḍayitvā" tmahṛdaye niveśya tato juhuyāt / sā strī vaśyā bhavatīti //*

104. and after cutting off the heart-region [of that image], one must place it on one's heart. A Brāhmaṇa, after muttering [the hymn of] this Ṛṣi [Hṛdya], obtains that woman under [his] control.[a]

(a) The translation implies a change of construction in the fourth *pāda*, though the sense is obvious. Prof. Gonda however, renders 'a brahman (must) mutter (the text of) this ṛṣi: (thus) that woman comes into (his) power'. Evidently,

Prof. Gonda regards *adhi* in *adhigacchati* as pleonastic and takes *japant*=*japet*.

105. The best among the twice-born must not direct [this rite] towards married [women], nor towards faithful [women], nor towards [women having] a virtuous and religious character.

Mātṛsūnu: *naitat parīti / yāsu strīṣvetad vaśīkaraṇam prayojyṁ tad api ślokokta iti //*

106. Rather (*kāmam*) whoever acts towards low-caste married women should first reduce her husband to subjection and afterwards that woman.

Mātṛsūnu: *kāmam iti / striyām etad vaśīkaraṇaṁ na prayoktavyam ityetad ayuktam / pūrvam asyāḥ patim guṇīkuryāt vaśī kūryāt / paścāt striyam iti / etac ca saṁvananaṁ kuryāt(d)* **yo 'nyastrīgāmī ata evoktaṁ hīnavarṇāstri* (*hīnavarṇāsu*)* *yaś cared iti //* Prof. Gonda renders the second hemistich thus: 'Should first submit her (sic!) husband and afterwards he should place (the image of) that woman (on the fire)'.

107.[a] One should preserve the [remains of] milk-porridge after taking it in and vomitting it immediately and that powder [prepared out of milk-porridge], when given to a low-caste woman (*kṛṣṇajāyā*), is declared to be propitious.

(a) Mātṛsūnu: *bhuktveti / bhuktvā vā pāyasaṁ samyag iti / vaśīkaraṇasya prakarāṁtaram ucyate / pāyasaṁ bhuktvā tataḥ chardiḥ kuryāt tatas tatra ye taṁḍūlā[s] tān uddhāpayitvā peṣayitvā cūrṇaṁ kārayet / taṁ* (*tac*)* *cūrṇaṁ hīnajātiyāyai dadyād abhyāṁ sūktābhyām abhimaṁtraitastribhis* (?) *tataḥ sā vaśībhavatīti //* Mātṛsūnu reads *samyak* for *sadyaḥ*.

(b) Prof. Gonda renders 'a wicked wife (?). The end of the Varga is here marked by 20 in Ba Ta.

108. In a like manner one should charm an odd number of fruits of a Mahāvṛkṣa and spare [those forming] half, after eating oneself the pairs among them.

Mātṛsūnu: *etāt prakārāṁtaram [a]vaśiṣyate / mahāvṛkṣo vaṭas tān vauduṁbarādbibhayāni* (?) *viṣamasaṁkhyākāni ābhyāṁ sūktābhyām anumaṁtrayet tataḥ saṁkhyākāny arddhāni śoṣitāni kṛtvā sādhyāni tato vaśyo bhavati* ||

109. And one should give them [to him] whom one wishes to bring under control, whilst muttering [the hymn of this] Ṛṣi [Hṛdya]. It is declared to be propitious when given to a friend who has turned out to be an enemy.

Prof. Gonda has appended a long note on *hṛdyasūktam* without being aware of the fact that the *viniyoga* of the Hṛdyasūkta actually began with the St.79.

110. As every single (*ekaikam*)[a] [Mantra] from the Hṛdyasūkta is congruous (*abhirūpam*)- [with the rite] hence anybody can perform congruous rites according to his wish.

(a) Prof. Gonda connecting *ekaikam abhirūpam* with preceding stanza, renders this stanza thus: 'must be performed and further the mantra (s) to be used to the effect the subjection of an enemy (hṛdyam) and so on. If anybody performs suitable rites according to his wish,–'

111. The wise men know the sacred precept [concerning the hymn] of Parākadāsa [*RV.Kh.*iii.16 and that] declared by Hṛdya, and it is propitious for women and it is likewise laid down for men also.

The *hṛdyasūkta* which is treated so far in the first of the two hymns inserted after *RV.*10.84, the second one being the hymn attributed to Parākadāsa which is spelled as Parāgadāsa by *khilānukramaṇī.*

112. But [the text[a] designated as] *dveṣyam* [is laid down] for kinsmen and one should always mutter [it] in the battle. One must have a pin made of Khādira-wood and one must fix it in the heart [of]

(a) I follow Mātṛsūnu who refers to some khila hymns which are designated as *dūṣyam*, *dveṣyam* and *jayyam* (see under the next stanza. The end of the Varga is here marked by 21 in Ba Ta.

113. an image prepared previously out of sand or husks and arrange a [mock] battle [with it] after charming an arrow.

Mātṛsūnu: *Kṛtveti / dūṣyaṁ dveṣyaṁ jayyam ityetāni khilasūktanāmāni tair nānārūpāni vihitāni asādhyāni svārūpa* (?) *kartavyam* (?) / *tad yathā parākasya dāsyasya vaniva* (?) *strīṇāṁ nīcapuruṣāṇāṁ ca hṛdyasūktena karma kartavyam* / *dveṣa sūktam anujñātānāṁ karma kartavyam* // *japa* (*jayya*?) *sūktena tu saṁgrāme śatrūṇāṁ karma kartavyam iti* //

114. one must consider this [hymn] as destructive of enemies and invincible when employed against Parākadāsa's enemies[a] [and it] is declared to be dear to the heart [and] propitious.

(a) Prof. Gonda renders 'parākadāsa (by name), aiming at enemies'.

115. One obtains success after mentally pondering over these two hymns. A father must relate the evolutionary [hymn] of Sūrya [i.e. *RV*.10.85] to [his] daughter:

Mātṛsūnu: *sūryāyai bhāvavṛttaṁ tvityādi* / *etat sūktam sūryāyāṁ* (*sūryāyāḥ*)* *bhāvavṛttam ucyate* / *tat pitā vivāhakāle kanyakāṁ śrāvayet* / *tataḥ śobhanaṁ patīṁ labhata iti* //

116. [then] she conformably obtains a suitable husband by that [rite].[a] Touching her navel a girl must constantly mutter [the verse] beginning with *Imāṁ* [*RV*.10.85.45]

(a) Prof. Gonda renders 'by that she obtains a worthy and similar husband'.

117. [And] the husband must likewise mutter it: [then] both of them [will be] long-lived. A brother or a father must sprinkle the girl whilst [muttering] congruous [mantras]:

The end of the Varga is here marked by 22 in Ba Ta.

118. [then] she will have ten sons and she will not be separated[a] from her husband. One should constantly mutter [the verse] beginning with *Samrājñī* [*RV*.10.85.46] after touching the head [of one's] girl:

(a) Mātṛsūnu paraphrases *viyujyate* by *viyogo na jāyate*.

119. [then] she is honoured by her parents-in-law and also by her husband's brothers and sisters. One should employ the hymn which is a dialogue conducted by Indrāṇī.[a] [*RV*.10.86] at the sprinkling ceremony.

(a) Dr. Meyer reads *indrāṇyāḥ kṛtasaṁvādam* for *indrāṇyākṛta*°, an anomalous compound, which is found in all mss.

120. [The hymn] which consists of nine excellent sections[a] and which bestows a happy union with husband and sons.[b] [In a place] endowed with heaps of aquatic flowers and surrounded with speckled water-jars—

(a) Possibly the text has in view *RV*.10.85 which consists of nine Vargas. Prof. Gonda renders 'concerned with the nine chiefs of a class'. Dr. Meyer regards it as an astronomical term, see *Ṛvidh. Praefatio*, p.xviii.
(b) The first hemistich, as it is, is rather misplaced. Its proper place would be after St. 115ab. above.

121. a sacrifice should be performed there, for Soma, the Gandharvas, and Vahni,[a] also for Bhaga, the Apsarases,[a] and also for the Lord of Yakṣas,

(a) *Somagandharvavahninām...apsarasām*, genitive for dative.

122. for Indrāṇī, for the wives of gods, as well as for Rati and Pradyumna. With [jar-]full of river water [and] of five products of a cow (samāvṛta)[a]

(a) lit. 'covered with the five products of a cow'. The end of the Varga is here marked by 23 in Ba Ta.

123-124. One must cause a girl to bathe while she stands on a place in the south, after offering [oblations] into the fire. Having poured the residue into the decoction of Priyaṅgu, Vaṭa and [Pun] nāga, rubbed over with [Nāga–] kesara and filled with all-herbs, one [should] at the end of the hymn [i.e. *RV*.10.85] consecrate [it] with the nine [verses] beginning with *Vi hi* [*RV*.10.86-1-9].

Prof. Gonda's rendering of Sts.122-24 is as follows: 'to Indrāṇī, the Wives of the gods and to Rati and Pradyumna.

After having offered in the fire (oblations] which are richly furnished with the water of a river and which are filled up with the five products of the cow, one must cause a girl to bathe while she is on a spot in the South, after having poured over (her) hair, which (first) has been rubbed over with a decoction of priyaṅgus, Indian fig-trees and nāgas,– with leavings (refuse matter) and filled it up with all kinds of medicinal herbs. After having charmed it at the end of the sūkta with the nine (stanzas beginning with) 'away, indeed',

125. [and] sprinkle, [her] who had fasted, with [jar–]full of water kept overnight (*stheya*): [then] those bodily marks which are husband-killing are allayed by this [rite].

The translation implies the obvious emendation *tanvaḥ* (for *tanvyaḥ*). Cp. Mātṛsūnu: *strīṇāṁ tisras tanva* [ḥ] *patighnā* [ḥ] *paṭhya* [*n*]*te* //

126. [She] whom one finds to be cohabiting [with others? Vipravrājinī][a] must be sprinkled [with waters] to the accompaniment of the Āhanasyā [–Verses *RV.Kh.*v.22 and further] one must select the distich beginning with *Na Seśa* [*RV.*10.86.16-17.][b]

(a) I have adopted the reading conjectured by Dr. Meyer.
(b) The second hemistich, as it is, is rather misplaced. Its proper place would be after St.119cd.

127.[a] This [hymn i.e. *RV.*10.86] is prescribed by some [teachers], for men, in a rite for regaining virility (*pauruṣe karmaṇi*). One should mutter the [hymn] beginning with *Rakṣohaṇaṁ vājinam* [*RV.*10.87],

(a) *upetyarddham* / *ayam ity adhataḥ* (*adhastanaḥ*)* *snānavidhi* [ḥ]* *parāmṛśyate* / *upadiṣṭo' yam ekeṣāṁ ācāryāṇāṁ matena puṁsake pauruṣe karmaṇi pramādā* [*dā*]**v iti* //
(b) Prof. Gonda renders 'in connection with the manly act'! The end of the Varga is here marked by 24 in Ba Ta.

128. and constantly worship Agni, after kindling it, with this hymn and offer oblations of clarified butter: [then] repels evil demons (Rakṣas) with that [rite],

Mātṛsūnu: *agnim iti* / "*rakṣohaṇaṁ vājinam ā jigharmi*" [*RV.*

10.87] *iti paṁcaviṁśaty ṛcaṁ sūktaṁ tad⁰ te / rakṣohaṇaṁ vājinam ity etad api sūktaṁ nityajapyaṁ ghātanārtham rakṣasāṁ / agniṁ prajvālya tenopasthānaṁ kartavyam / anenaivājyahutī [r]* juhuyāt tato rakṣāṁsi pratibaṁdhata (pratibādhata)* iti //*

129. [for] the pacificatory rite regarding this demon-destroying hymn is declared to be the highest. One should employ the Haviṣpāntīya-hymn [*RV*.10.88] in case of—

Mātṛsūnu: *etad iti / nigadavyākhyātam etad iti //*

130. sins [arising out of] forbidden food and recite the Haviṣpāntīya- [hymn] for (*hi*) this [hymn] is sacred as well as excellent, and should perpetually be meditated upon.[a]

(a) Prof. Gonda renders the second hemistich thus: 'one shall perpetually meditate on this eminent means of purification'.

131. A restrained person gazing at the sun should recite [this hymn] for six months: [then] he sees the way leading to the gods in the orb of the sun,

Mātṛsūnu: *ādityam īkṣyate (īkṣate)* saṇmāsaṁ yāvat sa ādityamaṁḍale devayānaṁ paśyati //*

132. and the knowledge of the Highest self (Vaiśvānarī Vidyā)[a] which abides in his body becomes manifest. One gets rid of all sins after reciting the Haviṣpāntīya [-hymn].

(a) see *Chāndogyopaniṣat*, 5.11-24, and Śaṅkara's comments thereon. Cp. the fourth pāda of this stanza with *Ch.Up.* 5.24.3: *Sarve pāpmānaḥ pradūyante.*

133. One should mutter the hymn destructive of enemies, which is [the most] sanctified among sanctified [texts][a] mystic, purifying and wonderful and which begins with *Indraṁ stava* [*RV*.10.89].

(a) Prof. Gonda renders 'the most excellent means of purification'. The end of the Varga is here marked by 25 in **Ba Ta.**

134. On an auspicious day, the twelfth lunar day, during the

bright fortnight, under an auspicious asterism [and planetary] position, one should prepare a rice-mess dedicated to Viṣṇu for the sake of a person desiring a son.

Mātṛsūnu: *Śuklapakṣe śubhe vāretyādi paṭhitasiddham / carviti yo' dhastāc carur uktas taṁ puruṣasūktena śrapayed ityayam asyārthaḥ* //

135. There must be a fast for the married couple on the eleventh lunar day at the temple. After properly adoring Janārdana with the sixteen verses.[a]

(a) Constructionally this hemistich is joined to the next, which contains the main verb.

136. One desiring a son must boil the rice-mess [accompanied] by the Puruṣasūkta [*RV*.10.90]: [then] he will soon obtain a son who is devoted to Viṣṇu (Vaiṣṇava)[a] and who is fit for lineage.

(a) Regarding *vaiṣṇava* in the above sense, see Pāṇini 4.3.95.

137. One should offer rice-mess together with (*samyak*) milk for twelve twelfth [lunar days]. Whoever is able to perform [upto] a thousand [oblations] will attain the highest abode of Viṣṇu.

Mātṛsūnu: *dvādaśeti / dvādaśīvidhānokto dvādaśa ityucyate / taṁ dvādaśyāṁ [(dvādaśyāṁ)] payasā caruṁ kuryāt / yāvat sahasraṁ carūṇāṁ pūrṇaṁ syāt tato' nuṣṭhāna* (?) *viṣṇulokaṁ gachatīti ślokārthaḥ* //

138. Offering [oblations] into the fire, according to the rule, together with (*samyak*) the sixteen verses, a wise person should after joining the palms of hands pronounce the praise with those [verses].

The end of the Varga is here marked by 26 in Ba Ta.

139-141. Keśava[a] is declared [to be the name of Viṣṇu] in [the month of] Mārgaśīrṣa; Nārāyaṇa, in [the month of] Pauṣa; but Mādhava, in the month of Māgha; likewise Govinda in [the month of] Phālguna; and likewise Viṣṇu in [the month of] Caitra; Madhusūdana in [the month of] Vaiśākha; one must know [the name to be] Trivikrama in [the month of] Jyeṣṭha; [but] they know [the name to be] Vāmana in [the month of] Āṣāḍha; [further] one must know [the name to be] Śrīdhara, in the month of Śrāvaṇa; then Hṛṣīkeśa in the next one [i.e. Bhādrapada]; but Padmanābha in [the month of] Āśvina; and Dāmodara in [the month of] Kārttika.

(a) Prof. Gonda supplies '(He shall praise)' before Keśava.

142. These twelve names, Ṛṣi Ṛṣyaśṛṅga has proclaimed. One should adore [Viṣṇu] with the [aforesaid] names of months: [then] one will acquire all objects of desire.

Dr. Meyer regards Ṛṣyaśṛṅga as the author of Vargas 26-28. See his Preface to *Ṛvidh.* p.*V*.

143. One will beget a long-lived son possessing fame and intelligence, rich, prolific in progeny, religious and virtuous.

Identical with *Manu* 3.263 (except for the transposition of *dharmikam* and *sāttvikam*). The end of the Varga is here marked by 27 in Ba Ta.

144. Offering fuel-sticks of Aśvattha-wood, one should again offer [oblations of clarified butter] into the fire and [perform] the worship of Agni, after meditating and adoring Madhusūdana.

Mātṛsūnu: *Samiddheti* (*Samidheti*)* / *asmiñ carau juhuyād āśvatthīḥ samiddaḥ kartavyaḥ* (?) *tās caivam aṣṭottaraprabhṛti hotavyāḥ / hutvā cāgnir* (*cāgner*)* *upasthānaṁ kartavyaṁ nārāyaṇaṁ manasā dhyāyan* //

145. A person who is controlled in speech and who is pure should then perform a sacrifice consisting of burnt-offering, verse by verse with the hymn and offer [oblations of] clarified butter, as above, at the beginning and end.

Mātṛsūnu: *havir iti / upasthānad anaṁtaraṁ havir homaṁ kuryāt / anenaiva pratyṛcaṁ vagyataḥ śucir iti viśeṣaṇena homānaṁtaram ājyaṁ juhuyāt haviḥ śeṣaṁ ca prāśayet pūrvavad iti* //

146. Saluting Lord Nārāyaṇa and eating the residue of burnt-offerings, a woman who has received blessings should cohabit at night [with her husband].

Mātṛsūnu: *haviḥ śeṣam iti / putrakāmānāṁ strīṇāṁ haviḥ śeṣam prāśayet / ayaṁ viśeṣaḥ* //

147. But after performing this rite, the satiation of the Brāhmaṇas should be brought about: [then it] withholds a second female [issue] till [a woman] ceases to conceive.[a]

(a) Prof. Gonda renders the second hemistich thus: 'As long as she is not with child, a second wife shall retreat'!

148. She who is childless or whose children are deceased or who gives birth to a female issue, will soon bring forth a son because Ṛṣyaśṛṅga has declared [it].

The end of the Varga is here marked by 28 in Ba Ta.

149. I shall [now] declare [the precept concerning] the worship of Viṣṇu whose glories are boundless, after performing which all the sages will attain the highest beatitude.

Mātṛsūnu: *adhunā arcanavidhir ucyate / tatrā'yaṁ graṁthaḥ / arcanaṁ saṁpravakṣyāmīti //*

150. In water, in fire, in the heart, in the sun, in the altar (*sthaṇḍila*)[a] and in idols—in these, the worship of Hari has rightly been declared by sages.

(a) A *sthaṇḍila* is the raised mound, four fingers high, which is used as the altar for the Gṛhya ceremonies.

151. For the ritualists, the god is in the fire; for the intellectuals [it is] in the heaven; for the dull-witted ones, [it is] in idols; but for the yogins Hari [is present] in the heart.

Cf. *Apsu devā manuṣyāṇāṁ divi devā manīṣiṇām / kāṣṭhaloṣṭheṣu mūrkhāṇāṁ yuktasyātmani devatā //* Śātātapa quoted in *Āhnikaprakāśa*, p.382.

152. Water is His abode:[a] therefore Hari [is] always [present] in it. By reason of His omnipresence, [He is present] in the altar for those whose thoughts are fixed in the supreme soul.

(a) Cp. *Manu* 1.10: *āpo nārā iti proktā āpo vai narasūnavaḥ / tā yadasyāyanaṁ pūrvaṁ tena nārāyaṇaḥ smṛtaḥ //*

153. The whole universe consistingof movable and immovable [things] is adored by him[a] who offers flowers or water with the Puruṣasūkta.

(a) Prof. Gonda omits 'by him' in his rendering.

154. The deity of this hymn which is [mostly] in Anuṣṭubh [-metre] and which ends with the Triṣṭubh [-metre] is the Puruṣa, who is the originator of the universe and the *ṛṣi* is declared to be Nārāyaṇa.

The end of the Varga is here marked by 29 in Ba Ta.

155-156. Attentively listen, O Lord Nārāyaṇa, the long-armed one! I will expound the Puruṣasūktavidhāna with regard to the worship, the fire-rite, the rule [s] concerning the muttering, and the hymn of praise possessing the nature of true existence. A person who is pure in mind [should] face the east after bathing according to the aforesaid rule.

Mātṛsūnu: *nārāyaṇeti / ayaṁ nārāyaṇasya saṁbodhanārtha-ślokaḥ //*

157-160. One should direct the first [verse] towards the left [hand]; the second, towards the right hand; the third, towards the left foot; and one should direct the fourth towards the right [foot]; the fifth, towards the left knee and one should direct the sixth towards the right [knee]; the seventh, towards the left hip; and the eighth, towards the right hip, the ninth, towards the interior of the navel; and one should direct the tenth towards the heart; the eleventh, towards the throat-region; the twelfth, towards the left arm; the thirteenth, towards the right [arm]; the fourteenth, towards the mouth; the fifteenth, towards the eyes and one should direct the sixteenth towards the crown of the head.

The end of the Varga is here marked by 30 in Ba Ta.

161. Performing in this manner the Nyāsa-precept [on oneself], [one should] perform the *nyāsa* on the deity in such a way according to the rule, just as [it was done] on the body and commence the [regular] worship afterwards.

Mātṛsūnu: *evam iti / pūrvam ṛgbhiḥ prāyeṇa strīliṁganirdēśaḥ kṛtā* [*a*]**dhunā maṁtrābhiprāyeṇa puṁlliṁganirdeśān kṛtvā yāni vastūni kartavyāni tāni darśayati yathākramam //* After the above stanza, ms Ba has four additional stanzas in its text, whereas the Berlin mss have them in the margin. Dr. Meyer has put these stanzas within brackets in his constituted text, but I have relegated them to the critical apparatus.

162-166. one should invoke Puruṣottama by means of the first verse [i.e. *RV.* 10.90.1] and give a seat by means of the second [i.e. *RV* 10.90.2] and water for washing the feet by means of the third [i.e. *RV.*10.90.3] *arghya* should be offered by means of the fourth [i.e. *RV.*10.90.4] [and] water meant for sipping (*ācamanīyaka*) by means of the fifth [i.e. *RV.*10.90.5]. One should perform the ablution (*snāna*) by means of the sixth (i.e. *RV.* 10.90.6] [and give] cloth by means of the seventh [i.e. *RV.*10.90.7]. The sacred thread (Yajñopavīta) should be offered by means of the eighth [i.e. *RV.*10.90.8], sandal wood paste (Anulepana)[a] by means of the ninth [i.e. *RV.*10.90.9] flower by means of the tenth [i.e. *RV.*10.90.10] and incense by means of the eleventh [i.e. *RV.* 10.90.11]. One should offer a lighted lamp by means of the twelfth [i.e. *RV.*10.90.12] food offering (*nivedana*)[b] by means of the thirteenth [i.e. *RV.*10.90.13], salutation by means of the fourteenth [i.e. *RV.*10.90.14], [and] circumambulation by means of the fifteenth [i.e. *RV.*10.90.15]. At [the time of] ablution, [offering of] a cloth, and food offering, one should [invariably] offer water meant for sipping [to the deity]. One should according to one's ability offer the sacrificial fee (*dakṣiṇā*) by means of the sixteenth [i.e. *RV.*10.90.16].

(a) Same as *gandha* see above ii.23, 71, *passim*.
(b) *nivedana* is used in the sense of *naivedya*. The end of the Varga is here marked by 31 in Ba Ta.

167. A steadfast person should mutter [the hymn] after performing a circumambulation and make an offering of the hymn [-recital] to Him after muttering it according to his ability.[a]

(a) Prof. Gonda renders the second hemistich thus: 'Having muttered the sūkta according to one's ability one shall present (the sacrificial gifts) to him'.

168. On the right side of the deity one must prepare a kuṇḍa or an altar by means of the first [verse][a] and sprinkling [of it] by means of the second [verse].

(a) Prof. Gonda supplies '(turn)'.

169. One should deposit the fire[a] by means of the third [verse], the act of kindling by means of the fourth [verse], the heating of clarified butter as well as the cooking of rice-mess by means of the fifth [verse].

(a) Prof. Gonda renders 'one shall add fuel to the fire'!

170. One should [mentally] design a lotus [-shaped] seat [for the deity] in the midst of fire and meditate thereon the chief god among gods whose spendour is equal to the destructive fire at the end of the world.

Mātṛsūnu: *adhunā ṣaṇṇām ṛcaṁ viniyoga* [ḥ]* *krameṇocyate* / *devasyetyādi sārddhatrayam* //

171. Then sandal wood paste, flower, incense, lighted lamp and food-offering [should be offered], after requesting [the principal deity, i.e. Viṣṇu] and then one should in due order perform [the following] by means of [the verse] beginning with the seventh onwards.

Mātṛsūnu: *anviti dvayam* / *tataḥ saptamī prabhṛtibhir yathākramaṁ daśa samidho juhuyāt* //

172. One should offer so much of fuel-sticks as are previously (*pūrvam*)[a] sprinkled [with clarified butter and] then one should alternatively offer ghee and food-offering again and again.

(a) Prof. Gonda connects *pūrvam* with *juhuyāt*.

173. Offering [oblations] in this manner and then requesting [Agni] in due order, one should utter [the following] hymn of praise.

Mātṛsūnu: *yathākramam eva* / *evaṁ yathākramam* / *sa ca ājyaṁ caru* [*ṁ*] *hutvā* / *paryukṣya tato' gniṁ kṣamāpayet* / *kṣamāpya tataḥ* / *agner iti sārddhakam* / *tato'gnisannidhau stotraṁ paṭhet* //
The end of the Varga is indicated by 32 in Ba Ta.

174. [May] thou excell [*jitam*] O Lotus-eyed one! Salutation

to thee, O all-creator! Salutation to thee, O Hṛṣīkeśa;, primaeval Supreme Spirit!

(a) Dr. Meyer has chosen the corrupt reading *yatam* which is found in his ms. B, but his mss. AC as well as mss. DEF (consulted by Prof. Gonda) have uniformly *jitam*. Prof. Gonda, however, sticks to the former reading and renders '(It has been) offered'.

175. [Thou art] the Presiding deity common to [both] gods and demons[a] and I always take refuge in thy pair of feet.

(a) Prof. Gonda renders the first hemistich thus: 'Universal and common Supreme deity of gods and dānavas'.

176. Thou, [being] one, art the creator and annihilator of the world as well as the unmanifest and the consentor [though] enveloped by the illusion of the [three] *guṇas*.[a]

(a) They are *sattva*, *rajas* and *tamas*.

177. The wise, on attaining the refuge in thee along, cross over the awful and endless (*anantam*)[a] ocean of existence which is a [veritable] receptacle of afflictions (*kleśabhājanam*).

(a) Prof. Gonda connects *anantam* with *kleśabhājanam*.

178. [Even though ther is] no colour, nor form, nor weapons, nor abode for thee, still thou appearest in human form to thy devotees (*bhaktānām*)[a]

(a) Observe the use of genitive with root *prakāś*.

179. [There is] nothing invisible to thee [though] thou art not visible to anyone and nothing impossible to thee [though] thou are not amenable to anyone else.

The end of the Varga is here marked by 33 in Ba Ta.

180. [Thou art] the prime cause for the necessary results [i.e. created beings], the highest object of speech among the words, the highest attainment for the Yogins and they declare thy abode as the highest.

Prof. Gonda renders the first hemistich thus: 'Of the occupations (works) the first cause, of the words the highest which is to be expressed'!

181. I am afraid of this formidable existence (Saṁsāra), O chief among the gods! Protect me, O Lotus-eyed one!, [for] I do not know [thy] highest abode.

Mātṛsūnu: *Kāryetyādi ṣaṭ / etad api stotraṁ paṭhitasiddhaṁ japyam eveti //*

182-185. Thou pervadest, O Acyuta!, in all periods and in all directions [and even] in [my] body. A great fear is (in store] for me even in my future lives since there is no refuge] other than thy lotus-like feet. After gaining this discernment and acquiring this abode, let this not fail me, O Lord! even in my next life [for this] wish of mine, who am born in misfortune, belongs to Thee. I shall always remain contented with that much provided it [discernment or abode] does not get lost [for] I exclusively pine indeed for the twain feet of Viṣṇu in all [future] lives.

The end of the Varga is here marked by 34 in Ba Ta.

186. The hymn of the Puruṣa [in praise] of Hari is conducive to heaven and wealth and productive of fame [for] this is [in itself] the sacred knowledge of the soul and the highest knowledge of Yoga.

Mātṛsūnu: *asyaiva sūktasya praśaṁsā stutiparaḥ śloko'yam //*

187. One should subsist on fruits for one month: [then] one sees one's self in the Self. One should fast after eating fruits and subsist on water for one month.

Mātṛsūnu: *adhunā' syaiva sūktasya japakaraṇe kartu...māhā / phalāhāra iti trayam //*

188-189. A steadfast person should perpetually remain in a forest whilst muttering the [hymn] of this Ṛṣi always, and bathe thrice in water at the time of three ablutions. One should continually worship the sun with this hymn and direct one's thoughts towards [the hymn of] this Ṛṣi, after offering oblations of clarified butter with it.

Mātṛsūnu: *etad anuṣṭhānam uktam asyaiva tat phalaṁ vakṣyamāṇam //*

190-191. Subsisting on fruits after one month, one will win heaven within three years but one who is devoted to him, who is absorbed in mind by him, and who worships none else for twelve years sees before one's eyes the god Nārāyaṇa, who is free from illness, who could be grasped only by excessive diligence and who is the immutable creator of the world.

Mātṛsūnu: *ūrdhvam ityādi dvayam / ...muktam / tatā ūrdhvaṁ yadi trīṇi varṣāni tasyānuṣṭhānaṁ karoti / tataḥ svargam jayati / yadi tu bhaktiyogād daśavarṣāṇi tasyānuṣṭhānaṁ kuryāt tato' kṣayam avyayaṁ sarvalokasṛṣṭāraṁ nārāyaṇaṁ pratyakṣeṇaiva paśyatīti //* The end of the Varga is here marked by 35 in Ba Ta.

192. A person who is equipped with righteousness and who is virtuous in his conduct should remain in the duty of a householder (*gṛhastha-dharma*) and direct [his] thought towards the god Nārāyaṇa who is free from illness

Mātṛsūnu: *ataḥ paraṁ dhyāyanavidhir ucyate / gṛhasthadharme vartamāno ananyanityanyāyavṛtaḥ* (?) *san śucir bhūtvā etadeva nārāyaṇaṁ ciṁtayed iti ślokārthaḥ //*

193. A restrained person who is pure in speech[a] and who is conversant with Yoga should, on getting up at midnight after leaving aside sleep, immerse in deep meditation when all living beings are fast asleep.

(a) Prof. Gonda following Dr. Meyer's text reads śucir vāgyataḥ, a reading which is metrically defective, and renders 'pure and restrained in speech (silent)'.

194-196. A person sitting straight on a levelled spot which is sheltered from the wind and free from sounds, should then connect the left foot on to the right knee [so as to rest on it], and draw up the right foot after bringing it on to the left knee. A person who is self-possessed and whose eyes are closed in deep meditation should, on joining the hollowed hands in token of homage, direct [his] thoughts towards the heart, after utter the [mystic] syllable *oṁ*, and intently fix his self, sense organs and mind in that place [i.e. heart].

The end of the Varga is here marked by 36 in Ba Ta.

197. When a person does not mentally perceive, nor see, nor hear anything else, nor has anything in mind, then he is said to have achieved Yoga (*yogaṁ prāptaḥ*)[a]

(a) Prof. Gonda connects *yogam* with *manasyet* and renders the second hemistich thus: 'when one has no longer (any) reflection about yoga, then one is said to have achieved (the god)'. I follow Mātṛsūnu who paraphrases *yōgaṁ prāptaḥ* by *prāptayogaḥ*.

198. One should recite [the hymn of] this Ṛṣi in one's heart as if seeing it [there] just as in the sacred text [and so long] direct one's thought towards the Ṛṣi as long as one [remains] seated after controlling the breaths.

Mātṛsūnu: *hṛdyeti / hṛdaya etat sūktaṁ nityaṁ ciṁtayet / yathāsya paṭhah śrūyate / tathā rūpaṁ paśyan ciṁtayed ityarthaḥ / prāṇeti / prāṇāyāmasya* (?) *prānān āyamya tāṁ* (?) *kṛtvā / āsīno bhaved yāvat tam ṛṣiṁ ciṁtayet / yāvat tāvat sūktam abhyased ityarthaḥ //*

199. Breathing out and causing the mind to go below thc navel, one who is absorbed in mind by it should repeatedly breath out [and thus] lead out yoga.

Mātṛsūnu: *u*[*c*]**chveti / pūrvakāle prāṇeṣvāyateṣu uchvāsasyatum* (*ucchvasitum*)* *i*[*c*]**chatā tme vo bhāge* (*nabher adhobhāge*)* *manaḥ kṛtvā punaḥ punar u*[*c*]**chvased yāvat svasthībhūtaḥ / tataḥ svasthībhutās tanmanā evaṁ bhūtva yogam unnayet / yogam utsṛjed ityarthaḥ //*

200-201. Concentrating in this manner one should neither see nor hear [anything] insignificant[a] [and] then gradually lead the mind above the heart whilst holding straight th collar-bones, the mouth, the nose and the eyes and firmly fix it there, the highest place between the eye-brows.

(a) Prof. Gonda renders 'the equilibrium (?)'. The end of the Varga is here marked by 37 in Ba Ta.

202-203. Fixing [it] upon the forehead region and breathing

out in due time, one should cause [it] to go to the crown of the head and breath out after reaching the navel again. This [i.e. the crown of the head][a] is declared to be the highest abode of Brahmā, the Supreme Spirit. Thus a diligent person attains the Highest Self in his self.

(a) But Mātṛsūnu understands it to be 'the forehead' (*lalāṭa-deśa*). See, however, St.209 below.

204-205. Even if one be a virtuous and pure person or a great sinner [still] one becomes pure on attaining the Highest Self after knowing the means (*gati*). A person who is piously disposed should mutter this [hymn] if he knows that he is tied to all sorts of sins: [then] he attains the highest refuge even by reason of a mere desire of knowing [it].[a]

(a) Prof. Gonda following Dr. Meyer's text reads *abhijijñā-sanāt* (for *api jijñāsanāt*) and renders 'because of the very wish to possess supernormal knowledges'.

206-208. The steady abstraction of mind (*dhāraṇā*) should separately and continuously be practised according to this [afore-said] practice and one must fix [it] upon [objects like] the sun, the fire, the moon and on the tree-tops, on the mountain-top or on the sea or in whichever [place] one's mind is pleased, but on attaining the objects of the senses he should by no means fix it [upon them, for] in this matter one must be aware of much uneasiness. [But] when an utter destruction caused by the *dhā-raṇā* [takes place], a person who has fallen from the practice of Yoga is reborn in a pure family[a] of virtuous people.

(a) Prof. Gonda renders 'In an impure family'! Possibly he read *Kule' śuddhe* instead of *Kule śuddhe*. Cp., however, *BG*.6.41cd: *śucīnām śrīmatāṁ gehe yogabhraṣṭo' bhijāyate*. After St.206, the end of the Varga is marked by 38 in Ba Ta.

209. When one finds the Highest Self in the crown of the head, then the highest light [i.e. the Supreme Spirit] will lead away the best one among the sages from the crown of the head to the starry path.

Prof. Gonda renders this stanza thus: 'When one finds Brahman in the skull, one shall lead the best of sages upwards from the skull towards the highest light, towards the starry sky'.

210. On attaining the Lord of Yoga, the Yogin, who is devoted to the Ṛṣi [Nārāyaṇa, becomes] indifferent to the pairs of opposites and possessed of the [knowledge of the] Supreme Spirit and he himself sees the Self everywhere.

Mātṛsūnu: *yogīti / yogī yogeśvaraṁ dṛṣṭvā nirdvaṁdvo vai tadā bhavet / vītarāgatayā / kiṁ kāraṇam ityucyate / sarveti / sa yatra vātmanātmānaṁ paśyet sarvagatam etat sūktam dhyānaparāyaṇa* (?) *iti //*

211. After bathing one should always mutter this excellent and sanctified [hymn]: [then] one, even though possessed of sins becomes virtuous in course of time.

The end of the Varga is here marked by 39 in Ba Ta.

212. A Brāhmaṇa who is devoted to *tapas*, who is truth-speaking and who is free from malice becomes an ascetic in course of time after muttering [the hymn of] this Ṛṣi

Mātṛsūnu: *tapa iti / tapaḥ parāyaṇas tapaś cārītayāyuktaḥ* (?) *san satyavāganasūyakaḥ śraddhālur etat sūktaṁ japan mahāpātaka saṁyukto' pi kālena° dityarthaḥ //*

213-214. That very object of desire, with which object of desire in view one always mutters [the hymn of] this Ṛṣi, becomes fulfilled to the faithful performer. With whatever object of desire one performs a sacrifice or a muttered prayer, food-offering or rice-mess, that [object of desire] must one regard as fulfilled.

Mātṛsūnu: *yeneti dvayam paṭhitasiddhaślokāḥ //*

215. Superiority among one's kindred,[a] much wealth, fame in [this] world, the highest refuge [in the next world] and deliverance from sin—that [rather, these] must one regard[b] as fulfilled.

(a) Prof. Gonda renders 'Superiority as to knowledge'!

(b) Mātṛsūnu paraphrases *avadhārayet* by *cetasi saṁkalpayet.*

216. [After muttering this hymn] one attains the Highest self attainable by knowledge, utmost subtle, which abides after pervading everything, and can be grasped by excessive diligence and which is eternal.

Mātṛsūnu: *jñāneti triḥ / etat sūktaṁ japann īdṛśaṁ puruṣaṁ dhyāyed ityarthaḥ //*

217. The hymn which bestows the [desired] fruit of all objects of desire and which begins with *Sahasraśīrṣā* [*RV*.10.90 should be muttered for] He (Supreme spirit) indeed is declared to be Nārāyaṇa by the whole body of [sacred texts with] the Vedas as [their] source.[a]

(a) Prof. Gonda renders 'through the person of Vedagarbha' and connects it with the first hemistich.

218. [The deities] Brahmā, Indra, Rudra and Parjanya abide in this hymn and one must regard the universe consisting of both immovable and movable [beings] as abiding in this [hymn].

The end of the Varga is here marked by 40 in Ba Ta.

219. One must not in any case lessen Bhakti even if one does not [fully] accomplish [one's object, for] the Highest Person, the Divine One is known to be sympathetic to His devotees.

Mātṛsūnu: *anāseti / asādanam iha japānuṣṭhānam abhipretam tathā kurvann api nārāyaṇasyāya* (?) *bhaktiṁ na tyajet / kiṁ kāraṇam ityucyate / bhaktānukamiti* (*bhaktānukaṁpīti*)* *//*

220. According to the forest-precept (*āraṇyakavidhāna*) one should, for the worship of that god, offer a rice-mess [consisting of grains of the wild rice[a] which are grown in forest [and which are] self-procured.

(a) Cp. *Manu*.6.11b: *munyannaiḥ svayamāhṛtaiḥ.*

221-223. Exclaiming (*iti*): "Nārāyaṇāya svāhā" one should, at the end of [each] Mantra, offer oblations upto a thousand (ones): then He gives a supernatural vision to the sacrificer, or offer a thousand [oblations of] rice-mess in one uninterrupted series (*tantra*) or complete all [such oblations] as can be [offered] in the course of a day: [then] one acquires the [desired] fruit of countless objects of desire longed for or even one may roam over the earth after [becoming] a Perfected one with a full duration of life.

The end of the Varga is here marked by 41 in Ba Ta.

224. Nārāyaṇa should always be meditated upon, [He] who abides in the midst of the orb of the sun, who is seated on the lotus-[shaped] seat, who possesses bracelets, ear-rings shaped like a *makara*, a diadem and a necklace, whose body has a golden hue [and] who holds a couch shell and a discus (*dhṛtaśaṅkhacakraḥ*)[a].

(a) Dr. Meyer's text reads *ghṛta*—which is possibly due to mistranscription. Prof. Gonda proposes to read *dhṛta*—instead of *ghṛtā*, but all this is unnecessary in view of the fact that mss. often confuse the subscript *dh* and *gh*.

225. After adoring the adorable feet of Nārāyaṇa, whoever merely recites this hymn [of praise][a] attains the abode of the everlasting Viṣṇu, free from old age and death, by means of that excellent recitation

(a) i.e. the stanza which immediately precedes the present one. Prof. Gonda, however, renders 'this sūkta in its entirety'.

226. The wise regularly worship Hari by means of a burnt-offering in the fire, by means of flowers in the water, by means of meditation in the heart and by means of a muttered prayer in the orb of the sun.

The end of the Varga is here marked by 42 in Ba Ta.

227. A *bilva* leaf, a *śamī* leaf, a leaf of the *bṛṅgāraka*, and [flowers of] the jasmine *kuśa* and lotus—[all this is] instantly gratifies Hari.

(a) The predicative noun *tuṣṭikaram* agrees with the nearest subject *mālatīkuśapadmam* and is left to be understood with rest.

228. When [anything] whatsoever is not obtained, one must mentally meditate on Him [for everything] turns out well[a] by the grace of Cakrin (i.e. Viṣṇu), the god of gods.

(a) Prof. Gonda renders 'one obtains it'.

229. When [the means of gratification such as] leaves, flowers, fruits and water which [can be] obtained free (*akrītalabdha*) are always existent[a] and when the Primaeval Person who is attainable by mere devotion [is in existence], why no effort is made for the sake of deliverance [from births and deaths]?

(a) The first hemistich contains a locative absolute construction, which is partly replaced by the instrumental. Prof. Gonda renders the first hemistich thus: 'With leaves, flowers, fruits and (presents consisting of) water which have got without buying them among those who are always punctual (and respectable).

230. The precept concerning the worship of Viṣṇu has thus been declared [by a person] named Viṣṇukumāra in order to teach the sole path [leading] to deliverance,[a] after perusing the precept taught by Nārada in this matter (*iha*).

(a) *muktyaikamārga*—(from *muktyai ekamārga–* to *muktyāyekamārga–* or *muktyā ekamārga*) is an instance of double Sandhi.

231. A person who is regular in his observances should mutter the benedictory [hymn beginning with] *Yā oṣadhīḥ* [*RV*.10.97] and constantly worship the herbs daily for six months at a stretch (eva).

Mātṛsūnu: "*yā oṣadhīḥ pūrvā jātā*" [*RV*.10.97] *iti trayoviṁsatyṛcaṁ tad-te | paṭhitasiddham | tṛtīyo' dhyāyaparisamāptāv iti | śiṣṭācāras tadācaraṇaṁ cāyuṣyam iti ||* The end of the Varga is here marked by 43 in Ba Ta.

## ADHYĀYA IV

1. In the autumn one should worship the herbs after offering [an oblation dedicated] to Rudra: [then] diseases do not overcome him nor any indigestive troubles whatsoever.

Mātṛsūnu: *iṣṭveti* / "*yā oṣadhīḥ pūrvā jātā*" [*RV*.10.97] *ity etat sūktaṁ prakṛtaṁ tat saṁgham* (*saṁbandham*)* *idam ucyate* / *śaradi nanvābhir auṣadhībhiḥ rudradaivatyaṁ caruṁ kuryāt* / *tataḥ yā oṣadhya* (?) *praty ṛcaṁ homaṁ kut* (*kuryāt*)* / *evaṁ rudrayāge kṛte oṣadhiyoge oṣadhīṣu sādhyamānāsu rōgā na bhavaṁtīti ślokārthaḥ* //

2. A Brāhmaṇa should repeatedly perform the rite seven times in the course of a week and resort to the herb whilst always muttering this hymn [*RV*.10.97],

Mātṛsūnu: *kriyām tu-* / *pūrvoktā*[*ṁ*] *kriyāṁ rudrātmikā* [*ṁ*] *saptarātra* [*ṁ*] *satvakṛto* (*saptakṛtvo*)' *bhyāsaṁ kuryāt* (*d*)* *ityarthaḥ* / *tataḥ prapadyetauṣadhī* [*ṁ*] *vipreti proktaṁ prārabhyeta* / *sūktasyādyāṁ ṛcaṁ japet* / *sadā sarvakālam iti tat puraścaraṇam iti* //

3. and request thus (*iti*): "may you [,the herbs] come to this place from region of [our] haters": [then] he obtains the herbs of his haters—after offering [an oblation dedicated] to Varuṇa.

(a) Prof. Gonda renders (then) the physician (will doubtless) find herbs', though he states that he has "adopted the reading of the Mss. *dviṣadoṣadhīḥ*". Dr. Meyer's text shows *bhiṣag oṣadhīḥ*, the reading, which I think is merely a conjecture, unsupported by the authority of the mss.

4-5. An abstemious person who is desirous of rain should resort to Bṛhaspati after equipping [himself], with Pāyasa as food-offering and a burnt-offering, and employ this [hymn] beginning with *Bṛhaspate prati* [*RV*.10.98] after saluting Parjanya: [then] he obtains excellent rain.

Mātṛsūnu: *bṛhaspatidevatākaṁ pāyasaṁ caruṁ kuryāt* / *par-*

*janyaṁ ca namaskṛtvā tato vṛṣṭiṁ dhyāyan* "*bṛhaspate prati me devatām ihi* [*RV*.10.98] *ityetat sūktaṁ japet* / *tato vṛ*[*ṣṭiṁ*] *labhata iti* // The end of the Varga is here marked by 1 in Ba Ta.

6-7. Everywhere [the hymn of] the Ṛṣi Apratiratha [*RV*.10.103] should be recognised as an excellent pacification. A [king] duly consecrated will never return without having conquered [that] country or [that] enemy towards which he proceeds [for conquest], since [this hymn represents] the highest power of Brahman. One desiring all objects of desire should mutter this [hymn] for the fulfilment of all [those] objects of desire.

Mātṛsūnu: *Sarvatreti* / "*āśuḥ śiśāno vṛṣbho na bhīma* [*RV*. 10.103] *iti trayodaśarcaṁ sūktam apratirathasaṁjñaṁ liṅgitam* / *tad*° *te* / *sarvatra tu parā śāṁtir ityādi ślokadvayaṁ paṭhitasiddham* //

8. One should employ this [hymn] for the sake of a king who is proceeding to a battle: [then] he [viz. the king] conquers all his enemies [and] is not defeated by his adversaries.

Mātṛsūnu: *Sāṁgrāmam iti* / *etad api ślokadvaya* [*ṁ*?] *paṭhitasiddham* //

9. Whilst journeying on a path, this [hymn] is a benediction for the path [since] it protects[a] [him] from all robbers, evil beings, snakes and fiends.

(a) Prof. Gonda renders 'one defends (oneself and others)'.

10. A person, who is desirous of progeny and who is pure, quickly obtains a progeny resembling [him], after muttering the hymn of Bhūtāṁśa Kāśyapa [i.e. *RV*.10.106]. There is doubt about that.

Mātṛsūnu: "*ubhā u nūnaṁ tad idarthayethe*" [*RV*.10.106] *ityekādaśarcaṁ sūktam adbhutāṁsaḥ* (*bhūtāṁśaḥ*)* *Kāśyapa ṛṣis tena liṁgitam* / *tadadhi*° *te* / *bhūtāṁśaḥ kāsyapa ityādinā paṭhitasiddhaślokaḥ* // The end of the Varga is here marked by 2 in Ba Ta.

11. A Brāhmaṇa should worship the Nāsatyas, the Aśvins, with

a *sthālīpāka* and consecrate the horses with this hymn after offering [them].

Mātṛsūnu: *sthālīpākeneti* / *nāsatyā* [*va*]**śvinau daivatyaṁ sthālīpākaṁ juhuyād anena sūktena aśvān apy anumaṁtrayed anenaiva sūkteneti* //

12-14. After having collected when the sun has risen [the things] such as *pāyasa*, a mixed dish (*kṛsara*), meat, porridge. curds, a barley meal, sour gruel, a dish of parched grains, various fruits, a variegated garland, auspicious fragrances, and whatever food or drinks [which are meant either to be masticated [or] eaten [or] drunk, one should recite [the hymn of] Bhūtāṁśa until the sun has set and offer [them] to the Aśvins when the midnight is over.

Mātṛsūnu: *pāyasam ityādi catuḥ* / *dadhiś ca saktavaś ca pṛthag bhūtaṁ sad gīyate* (*nīyate*)* *kara* [*mbha*]**s tu tadeva dyāmiśram* (*vyāmiśram*) *avaśiṣtaṁ pāṭhasiddham iti* //

15. Whoever constantly recites [the hymn of] Bhūtāṁśa, will obtain a long lived, handsome and lustrous son and possessing graceful appearance always.

The end of the Varga is here marked by 3 in Ba Ta.

16-20. A wise must regard [the hymn of] this Ṛṣi as one which bestows all objects of desire. A person who is regular in his observances should mutter this [hymn] beginning with *Na vā u devāḥ* [*RV*.10.117]: [then] he obtains food in all [those] places towards which he proceeds. A wise man who regards himself as affected by evil should, on becoming restrained, mutter [this hymn: then] he may think lightly of the evil. A person desiring speech should resort to the [Goddess of ] Speech whilst quickly offering [with, and] muttering these [verses of] this [hymn] beginning with *Ahaṁ rudrebhiḥ* [*RV*.10.125]: [then] he becomes eloquent [and] honoured. A sage [who] mutters the eight-versed hymn which is addressed to the all-gods and which begins with *Na tam* [*RV*.10.126] dwells in the company of all-gods (*Viśvedevaiḥ saha*)[a] after destroying all stains. A person who is pure and who has observed a vow should always resort to the [Goddess of] Night

(a) Prof. Gonda renders 'competes with 'all the gods'! Both Dr. Meyer and Prof. Gonda punctuate *viśvadevaiḥ sahāsate* as *viśvedevaiḥ sa hāsate*. Dr. Meyer regards *hās* as a Vedic root, *vide* his *praefaṭio* to *Ṛvidh.* p.xi f.n. That Prof. Gonda blindly follows the lead of Dr. Meyer is amply clear from the inclusion of *hās* among the "List of Remarkable Words in the *Ṛgvidhāna*" (vide *Rvidh.* trans. p.126).

21-22. Whoever wishes thus (*iti*): "I would never be reborn again in wombs," should mentally mutter [the hymn] beginning with *Rātrī* [*RV.*10.127] a thousand times during nights, and worship [the Goddess] Night with a *sthālīpāka* every day at night and on becoming pious he must stand during the day and sit absorbed by that [hymn] during the night.

The end of the Varga is here marked by 4 in Ba Ta.

23. After a full year, a sacrifice is prescribed wherein one must offer an oblation of rice cooked in milk a thousand times by means of that [hymn] during the day.

Prof. Gonda renders this stanza thus: 'And after a year (the person performing this rite) should offer an oblation (*caru*) prepared in milk—a thousand times a burnt-offering is performed by means of that by day—'.

24. Being intent upon the [Goddess] Night one must offer [oblations into the fire] during the first part of the night, but during the day [the Homa] should invariably be done by means of a sunlit [fire] (*aṁśutejasā*) in a shady place.

As the mss are not unanimous with regard to the reading of the second *pāda,* I had to recourse to a minor emendation. Both the text and the scanty commentary on this stanza are corrupt.

25. In this manner (*iti*) a person who is ritually pure and composed should mentally mutter [this] hymn and prepare an oblation of rice with clarified butter in the third year.

Mātṛsūnu: *ity evaṁ prayata ātmavān sūktaṁ homāṁte etad eva sūktaṁ japed iti / saṁvatsareti / tṛtīye tu saṁvatsare ghṛta* [(*ṁ*)] *saṁ militaṁ caruṁ juhuyāt / anenaiva sūktena rātrau ca pūrvoktakāle avaśyakaṁ* (*āvaśyakaṁ*)* *kṛtveti //*

26-27. Then Śarvarī, the goddess of Night, becomes ready to fulfil his wishes. To that goddess who grants wishes and who has come of her own accord, he makes the [following] request [with which] the Loving one (Vatsalā) [concurs and speaks] thus: "O child! thy time for departure [from this world] will occur on [such-and-such] year, season, month, day and such-and-such moment."

The end of the Varga is here marked by 5 in Ba Ta.

28. He awaits the [proper] time whilst muttering this very hymn addressed to the [goddess of] Night and he never undergoes [a rebirth] again in the womb and he gets rid of all sins.

(a) Prof. Gonda renders 'should reach'.

29. A twice-born person desiring all objects of desire should mutter this [hymn] beginning with *Mamāgne varcaḥ* [*RV*.10.128] after offering clarified butter along with this very [hymn: then] he will obtain all objects of desire.

Mātṛsūnu: *mamāgne varca ityādi / etat sūktaṁ sarvakāmikaṁ (sārvakāmikāṁ) sarveṣu kāmeṣv abhipreteṣu japyam / anenaiva sūktena pratyṛcaṁ ya ājyahomaṁ karoti sa yena yena kāmena karoti sa sa kāmaḥ samṛdhyatīti ślokārthaḥ //*

30. A person who is regular in his observances should always mutter [the hymn] beginning with *Yāṁ kalpayanti* [*RV.Kh*.iv.5]: then evil spirits[a] and fierce incantations do not injure him.

(a) Cp. *Khilānukramaṇī*: *yām, catvāriṁśat pratyaṅkṛtyānāśanam āśīḥ, paṅktyantam.*

31-32. He, on whom the experts cast a charm by means of the Aṅgirasa-texts, wards off all that by means of the Pratyaṅgirasa-text, and he who is conversant with the Pratyaṅgirasa-text will never suffer [any] wrong [for] neither the evil-spirits (*kṛtyā*) nor [imprecations either] known or unknown[b] injure him anywhere.

(a) Mātṛsūnu notices a different reading *yāni* (for *yam*) which is not found in any mss. of the *Ṛvidh.*

(b) Prof. Gonda commits a mistake by connecting *jñātājñātāni* with *Kṛtyāḥ*. He renders this hemistich thus: 'Enchantments do not injure him, be they known (perceived) or unknown (unexpected)'. The end of the Varga is here marked by 6 in Ba Ta.

33. No evil contaminates an expert [in the Pratyaṅgirasa-text] if he be cursed or harshly addressed either by a known or unknown [person] or by a wrathful or an impatient [person].

Mātṛsūnu: *ajānateti | paṭhitasiddhaślokaḥ ||*

34. Similarly one should mutter the [hymn of this] Ṛṣi for the sake of benediction. [Moreover] the Ṛṣi himself has proclaimed this hymn as a general expiation [for all kinds of sin].

(a) Prof. Gonda renders the first hemistich thus: 'one should constantly mutter (the sūkta of) this ṛṣi to be a benediction'.

35. One should always mutter [the hymn of] this Ṛṣi at the [time of] establishing a real estate,[a] towns, villages and houses.

(a) Prof. Gonda renders 'in a place in the mountains'!

36-37. An expert must prepare a triple amulet made of gold over which the residue of a thousand oblations has been poured by means of [the hymn of] that Ṛṣi[a] and fasten[b] [it] to the head, neck or breast: [then] neither evil spirits nor [imprecations] whatsoever [either] known or unknown injure him.

(a) The reading of Ba: *ṛṣiṇā' nena* appears to be definitely preferable here.

(b) I follow Dr. Meyer. My mss., however, read *pratimucyeta.* The end of the Varga is here marked by 7 in Ba Ta.

38. An expert should for the sake of kings prepare an amulet made out of equal parts of metals[a] [such as gold, silver, copper, iron and lead] and the consecration by means of this very hymn [shall be] of the extent [aforesaid].

(a) Prof. Gonda renders 'made of a uniformly red colour'.

39. One should consecrate the tops of standards, musical instruments, seats, couches and various vehicles at the [time of] hostile encounters.

Mātṛsūnu: *Saṁgrāma iti paṭhitasiddhaślokaḥ* //

40. Notwithstanding that the Ṛṣi Aṅgirasa himself is openly engaged in casting a charm on him he wards off all that by means of the Pratyaṅgirasa-text.

As the mss, are not unanimous with regard to the reading of the second *pāda,* I had to recourse to a minor emendation which is palaeographically sound. ऋषि: the reading of most of the mss., would be easy corruption of ऋषे: spelt according to the older characters. Without being aware of this fact, Dr. Meyer has, correctly, emended the reading *ṛṣiḥ* to *ṛṣeḥ* in order to get over the difficult construction.

41. Whilst muttering this hymn one must cast a charm on the unhuman evil spirits (*amānuṣīḥ kṛtyāḥ*):- [then] one is released from an unwelcome object: what to say of a fear from a human being?

(a) I have adopted this reading only on the strength of the mss. Bo 1.2 and I may include the ms. F (of Prof. Gonda) which also reads *kṛtyāḥ*. My reasons are as follows: (1) the *khilānukramaṇī* designates this hymn as *pratyaṅkṛtyānāśanam* and not *kṛtyāsūktam*; (2) the adj. *amānuṣīḥ* requires some noun to qualify. Prof. Gonda also does likewise both in his translation and notes.

42. If the agent be a Ṛṣi who is devout, restrained and mild, [then that] calm-minded [person] overcomes everything, for *tapas* [is in itself] a very great power.

Prof. Gonda renders this stanza thus: 'If one will practice austerities, be self-governed, restrained, (and) use (the sūkta of) the ṛṣi, one overcomes all (evil), (all influences which disturb) one's soul's happiness are) allayed; for austerity (tapas) is a very great power'. The end of the Varga is here marked by 8 in Ba Ta.

43. The excellent hymn of Dākṣāyaṇas [beginning with] *Āyuṣyam* [*RV.Kh.*iv.6] is conducive to [spiritual] lustre and long life. One should mutter [the hymn of] Dākṣāyaṇas after obtaining either ornaments or gold.[a]

(a) Prof. Gonda renders the second hemistich thus: 'Let (a man) provide himself with a golden amulet and mutter the Dākṣāyaṇa-text'.

44. It adds grace to [the wealth] obtained (*prāptam*)- and one gains much food. Being intent upon the *yoga*, one should mutter [the hymn] beginning with *Nāsad āsīt* [*RV*.10.129] and offer [oblations with it]:

(a) Dr. Meyer's text shows *prāyaḥ*, the reading which I think is merely a conjecture, unsupported by the authority of mss. Prof. Gonda renders the first hemistich thus: 'Then he is likely to receive the gifts of fortune and he gains much good'.

45-46. [then] one attains communion (*sāyojya*)[a] with Prajāpati within twelve years. When afflicted with indigestion, a person observing vows should mutter [the hymn] beginning with *Uta dēvāḥ* [*RV*.10.137] and offer [ghee] into the fire after keeping a jar of ghee [nearby, and] have that residue from that jar deposited in another brazen vessel.

(a) It is recorded by *MW* in a passage from the *MaitrīUp*. (4.1.4) but the editions of it published by the Ānandāśrama and the Vaidika Saṁśodhana Maṇḍala uniformly read *sāyujyam*.

47. And when there is not enough food he, who is competent for eating food[a] should perform this [rite] after smearing his body with that [residue of] clarified butter: [then] he will gradually be adapted to food.

(a) Dr. Meyer corrects *yo' nnāyālam* to *yan na pānam*. Is this correction necessary?

48. One should mutter this [hymn] after anointing the body of a diseased person with self-same [residue of the clarified butter] and one whose food remains undigested should also anoint [oneself with it]: then one fares well by that.

The end of the Varga is here marked by 9 in Ba Ta.

49. One desiring wealth should on becoming restrained employ

this (hymn beginning with *Agne acchā vada* [*RV*.10.141] and mutter [it] by myriads again and again, after offering [oblations] with the clarified butter.

Mātṛsūnu: *agne acchā vadetyādi / niyata iti / niyataḥ saṁyato bhūtvā tato' nena sūktena pratyṛcam ājyahomaṁ kṛtvā tato' yutamayutaṁ japet / daśadaśasahasrāṇīty arthaḥ //*

50. One should offer a thousand fuel-sticks of Khādira-wood [into the fire] ten times: [then] one along with wife, will prosper by an increase of property.

Mātṛsūnu: *khādireti / tato' nena sūktena khādirāṇāṁ samidhāṁ daśa daśa-sahasrāṇi juhuyāt / tato rāyaspoṣeṇa puṣṭo bhavatīti //*

51. One desiring wealth should offer [fuel-sticks of] the *bilva-*, *udumbara-*, *palāśa-*, and *rohitaka*-trees; [then] one will prosper by an increase of property.

(a) The text has *bilvodumbarapālāśīḥ,* a form which offends Pāṇini 4.3.136.

52-53. One eating for half-a-month should offer [fuel-sticks of] Vibhītaka- and Bilva- trees by means of the [half-verse designated as] Dviṣaddveṣa [= *RV*.1.50.13cd] and at the end of that, one should employ this hymn; [then] one will gain the wealth of that rich enemy whose death one has caused. Rather [this hymn] should be muttered by one desiring increase of property and wealth.

The end of the Varga is here marked by 10 in Ba Ta.

54-55. When there is fear from fire, one should mutter [the hymn] beginning with *Ayam agne jaritā* [*RV*.10.142] after satiating the fire with milk, curds, ghee and so on, in strict accordance with rule, and lead around muttering the verse beginning with *Apām idam* [*RV*.10.142.7] to the accompaniment of a continuous stream of water whilst proceeding as much in [all the] four directions as one wishes to protect oneself.

Mātṛsūnu: *ayam agne jaritetyādi / agnibhaye sati pradīpanādau "agne" etat sūktaṁ tato parām eva* (?) *bhavatti / vidhineti / tarpayitvāgni* [*ṁ*] *payodadhighṛtādibhir dravyaiḥ svataḥ svakī-*

*yasya nivāsasya rakṣaṇīyasya caturdiśam gatvā etat sūktaṁ japet / japtvā caitat sūktaṁ tato vakṣyamāṇaṁ kuryād iti / apām idam iti / "apāmidam nyayanam* [*RV*.10.142.7] *ity anayā ṛcā agni* [*ṁ*] *parito navad* (*nayed*)* *veṣayet* (?) //

56-58.[a] Then that stream of water becomes, as it were, a pool of water (*udahrada*)[b], [then] one [possesses] a healing power from Agni. Having come to a forest one should purchase [the plant] *pāṭhā* with a handful of barley [whilst muttering the following *mantras*:] "If thou belongest to Soma, I purchase thee, herb, for Soma. If then belongest to Varuṇa, then I purchase thee for Varuṇa [and one should repeat likewise] for the Vasus, or for the Rudras or also for the Ādityas. "[If] thou belongest to the all-gods, then I purchase thee for the all [-gods].[c]"

(a) Mātṛsūnu: *Saṁtataṁ vā'chinnadhārayā tatas tayā dhārayodahrada iva bhūtvā' gner bhaṣajaṁ kṛiyate / tathā' ṁtikād agnir ajanad* [? cp. *RV* (Aundh) Pariśiṣṭa No.30.2cd: *antikām agnim ajanya dūrvādaḥ śaśahāgamat*] *itīmām ṛcaṁ japet / araṇyeti / "imāṁ khanāmyoṣadhim"* [*RV*.10.145] *iti ṣaḍṛcaṁ sūktaṁ tad*° *te / aranyaghāḍham* (?) *krīṇīyād iti / araṇyaṁ gatvā tatra tāmoṣadhīstām* (?) *kṛīṇīyād yavamuṣṭinā yavamuṣṭi* (?) *anenāraṇyānyā-devatāyaḥ sakāśad iti / yadīti / etair maṁtrair oṣadhiparikaryaḥ kartavyaḥ / ete cāpi paṭhita siddhamaṁtrā iti / vasv iti otair maṁtrair oṣadhipari krayaḥ / ete cāpi paṭhitasiddhamaṁtrā iti* //,

(b) Cp. *RV*. (Aundh) Pariśiṣṭa No. 30. 1cd: *utahrado hi no dhiyo' gnir dadātu bheṣajam* //

(c) Prof. Gonda renders 'for them all'. But I supply *devebhyas* to *viśvebhyas*. Instances like the present one are by no means rare in the *Bṛhaddevatā*. See Macdonell's translation and notes to *BD*.ii.12.

59. Having, at first, cast flowers with the herb on the shrub (*virudhi*)[a] one extracts the efficacy of that [plant in that place] where one intends to perform the rite.

(a) I have adopted this reading only on the strength of the mss. Ba Ta. The Berlin ed. reads *vīrudhaiḥ* which is also the reading of Bo 1.2. Neither Dr. Meyer nor Prof. Gonda seem to be aware of any variant reading.

60. One should place it amidst the herbs in an open space. In the matter of gathering herbs this precept [invariably] applies at all times.

The end of the Varga is here marked by 11 in Ba Ta.

61-63. One must dig up [the plant] *pāṭhā* whilst muttering [the hymn] beginning with *Imāṁ* [*RV*.10.145] and at morn have it crushed, in the sacrificial session, by one practicising chastity and in absence of such a one either by one performing vows, or by a virgin, or by a Brāhmaṇa. On becoming pure in the morning a woman should drink it thrice together with ghee, [it] which is duly consecrateed a hundred times or ten times at least by means of the hymn beginning with *Imām* [*RV*.10.145]: then she wards[a] off a co-wife by that [rite] and her husband will value [her] highly.

(a) Mātṛsūnu glosses *bādhate* by *abhibhavati.*

64. The husband on his part (*tu*), should for one week drink the [efficacy of] *pāṭhā* together with milk, after muttering over it by means of this[a] [hymn]: then he wards off rivals.

(a) But Mātṛsūnu supplies *vidhānena* to *anena.*

65. She who wishes to win over [her] husband by means of other roots, formulas and muttering [than those given above], having no abode [but] living in Yama's world, sinks into the hell.

The end of the Varga is here marked by 12 in Ba Ta.

66. [Since] the pulverized roots and herbs when employed in a different manner might ruin a person, hence one must not perform any [thing], other [then what is prescribed]

Prof. Gonda renders this stanza thus: 'Also ground roots and herbs which are prescribed in a different manner might ruin a man; one should, therefore, not perform another (rite)'.

67-70. She, who speaks kindly to her husband, whose highest object in life is her husband and whose speech is melodious—[this in itself] is highly propitious to her husband—should, on attaining an affable husband drink [the efficacy of] this herb. Whoever, out of delusion, reproaches a lawfully wedded wife, who speaks kindly, religious and irreproachable, him, they call the vilest among men. Whoever repeatedly mutters the hymn beginning with *Araṇyāni* [=*RV.*10.146] in forests is freed from it [rather, them] after saluting the Goddess of Forest (Araṇyāni]. A steadfast person desiring religious faith (śraddhā) should constantly mutter the Śraddhā-sūkta [=*RV.*10.151]

The end of the Varga is here marked by 13 in Ba Ta.

71-73. He obtains religious faith everywhere [and he should mutter] likewise the Medhā-sūkta [=*RV.Kh.*iv.8]. A person who is regular in his observances should, on attaining the [plant] *brāhmī*, mutter [these] two hymns and drink [the efficacy of] it as far as possible: [then] he obtains success after three days. [Boiling] the *śaṅkhapuṣpi* with milk, the Brāhmī-flowers with ghee, the *śatāvarī* with milk and the *vacā* with water or ghee—[these] one should drink one by one for three days after consecrating [them] with these two hymns.

Mātṛsūnu: *Sarvatreti / paṭhita siddhaḥ / brāhmīti / Śraddhāmedhāsūkte prakṛte / te adhikṛ[tyadam ucya]*te / brāhmīm āsādyety āsane sthāpanam ucyate / prapaṇa vo vāco samarthaḥ? / brāhmīm oṣadhī[ṁ] prāpya sthāpayitvā' bhīṣṭapradeśe tatas tad abhimukha etat sūktadvyaṁ japet / śraddhākhyaṁ medhākhyam iti ca / tām iti / tatas teṣām peṣayitvā saṁskṛtya pibet / yathā śaktyā trīṇyahānī tataḥ śraddhām eva prāpnotīti / śaṁkheti śārddhadvyaṁ paṭhita siddham etad iti //*

74-75. One obtains religious faith, intelligence, memory, vigour, strength and fortune. [Moreover] one attains highest success and enjoys a long life. Rather one should mentally meditate on [these] two hymns: [then] one obtains success. [The hymn] which is destructive of rivals and which begins with *Śāsa itthā* [*RV.*10.152] should, for the sake of one desiring success in a battle—

Mātṛsūnu: *atheti / athavaite pūrvoktē sūkte dve manasaiva nityaṁ dhyāyed anusmaret / tataḥ siddhiḥ prāpnotīti / śāsety arddham / "śāsa itthā mahāṁ asi"* [*RV.*10.152] *iti paṁcarcaṁ sūktaṁ tada*° *te / śāsa itthā sapatnaghnam ityādi / prayoktavyam iti vakṣyamāṇāyaḥ kriyāyāḥ saṁbaṁdham iṣṭaṁ paṭhitam iti //*
The end of the Varga is here marked by 14 in Ba Ta.

76-77. be employed by a pure person and he should, for the sake of success, sacrifice there. Rather [the hymn] beginning with *Śāsa itthā* [*RV*.10.152] should for the sake of one proceeding to a battle be muttered [by him] who [desires] to kill: [then] he wards off all enemies. For the removal of misfortune, one should regularly mutter [the hymn of] Śrīmbiṭha [*RV*.10.155]

Mātṛsūnu: *prayokteti / etat sūktaṁ śucinā japyaṁ saṁgrāma-jayārthaṁ cānena sūktena pratyṛcam ājyam agnau juhuyāt / atheti paṭhitasiddham / alakṣmīm iti /* "*arāyi kāṇe*" [*RV*.10.155] *iti paṁcarcaṁ sūktam śira* (*śirim*)* *biṭhinā* (?) *dṛṣṭam / tada*] *te / alakṣmīnāśanārtham tu ityādi paṭhitasiddham //*

78[a]. Holding a branch of the apāmārga together with *kuśa* grass (*sadarbhām*) and shrub (*sahavīrudhām*)[b] [in one's hand] one should constantly purify oneself [with it] up and down.

(a) Mātṛsūnu: *apeti / apāmārgaśākthā* [*ṁ*] *darbha-sahitaṁ vīruṇisahitāṁ gṛhītvā*" *tmānam ahar ahar* "*arāyi kāṇe*" [*RV*. 10.155] *ity anena pāvayet //*

(b) I have adopted this reading (which is found in Prof. Gonda ms. E as a "stop-gap", though the weight of the ms. evidence favours either *sahavīruṇam* (Ba Cm) or *sahavīrudhaiḥ* (Bo 1.2; so Prof. Gonda's ms. D). Other readings are: *sahavīranaiḥ* (Ta; so Dr. Meyer's ms. B) and *sahavīraṇām*, the reading which Dɪ. Meyer has adopted in his text is found in his ms. C. All the latter readings appear to be corrupt.

79-80. And one should offer clarified butter a hundred thousand times[a] by means of this [hymn]: [then] within three days one removes from one's person the misfortune of a hundred years. While performing the Cāndrāyaṇa- [Vrata], one must mutter this hymn which is productive of success: [then] one removes from one's person the misfortune even of a thousand years.

(a) Prof. Gonda renders 'a thousand times thousand (offerings)! The end of the Varga is here marked by 15 in Ba Ta.

81[a]. One should mutter [the hymn] beginning with *Muñcāmi* [*RV*.10.161] while holding a bunch of *kuśa* and sprinkling [him] who is seized by consumption [with it][b] [then] one removes the consumption.

(a) Mātṛsūnu: *gṛhītaṁ yakṣmaṇetyādi / etat sūktam japan rājaya kṣmagṛhītaṁ darbhaiḥ saṁspṛśya japet tato rājayakṣmāṇaṁ nāśayatīti ślokārthaḥ //*

(b) Prof. Gonda renders the first hemistich thus: 'Having taken a bunch of sacrificial grass one should sprinkle (a person) who is seized by consumption and mutter'.

82. One should in accordance with the precept offer clarified butter into the fire which has been kindled, pour out the residue on the clarified butter and drink milk [along] with the residues.

Mātṛsūnu: *samiddheti / anenaiva suktenājyam agnau juhuyāt / ghṛtena saṁpātam asminn ājye ninayet tena saha pibet yakṣmagṛhitaḥ tato yakṣmāṇam apanayatīti //*

83. He [a consumptive patient] finds his consecrated eatables and drinkable in that vessel of residues where ghee and powder [of the Khādira wood] have been placed.

Prof. Gonda renders this stanza thus: 'In the vessel of the residues (one shall) pour ghee (sarpis) and there one shall preserve (the) pounded stuff (flour): there will be one's consecrated eatables and drinkables'. Mātṛsūnu's commentary on the stanza runs as follows: *Saṁpāta iti / saṁpātabhājane yat sarpiḥ saṁlagnaṁ tatra vakṣyamāṇaṁ khādiracūrṇam prakṣipet / prakṣipya cānena sūktenānumaṁtritam upayojayet / sato* (*tato*)* *rājayakṣmāṇaṁ nāśayati / yathā cūrṇaṁ tathānyad apy aśata* (*aśana*)* *pānīyādikaṁ tasminn eva bhājane sthitam anumaṁtritam upabhoktavyam iti //*

84. Having ground the Khādira wood to powder, one should, with water, filter the efficacy of those [fine particles of Khādira wood] and drink it together with honey and clarified butter.

Mātṛsūnu: *khādireti / tasminneva bhājane khādirāṇi kāṣṭhāni ślakṣnāni saṁcūrṇayitvodake prakṣipet tataḥ karpaṭādau nisvātūyatta* (?) *evaṁ rasa śodhanaṁ kṛtvā tatra madhu ghṛtam ca prakṣipya tatas tat pibet //*

85. One should employ [the hymn] beginning with *Muñcāmi tvā* [*RV*.10.161] in those various cases. They [experts] remove the consumption from the body by means of that rite.

Mātṛsūnu: *tata* (*tato*)* *yakṣmāṇaṁ nāśayatīti* / *tatra caivaṁ kṣīmāṇe saṁcūrṇena rasasādhane pāne ca pratipatti* (?) *etat sūktaṁ prayojayed ityarthaḥ* / *śeṣaṁ paṭhitasiddham eveti* // The end of the Varga is here marked by 16 in Ba Ta.

86. One should, [for the sake] of an aborting woman offer a burntoblation with the clarified butter into the fire, in accordance with the precept, [by means of the hymn] beginning with *Brahmaṇāgniḥ saṁvidāna* [*RV*.10.162].

Prof. Gonda renders this stanza thus: 'A woman whose embryo might come to naught shall, under those circumstances, pour a burnt-offering into the fire, with clarified butter, in accordance with the ritual precepts, (whilst pronouncing the sūkta beginning with) "Agni, joining Brahma".'

87. Let a pregnant woman bring forth [her child] after anointing herself with the remnant of the clarified butter and also drink the remnant of the clarified butter: then her [child] will be born alive.

Mātṛsūnu: *ājyaśeṣeneti* / *hutaśeṣaṁ cājyaṁ saṁghya tasmiṁścid* (?) *bhājanādu tena mūḍhagarbha garbhiṇīṁ abhyaktāṁ kuryāt tasyā* [*h*]* *sūkhena prasavo bhavati* / *tad evājyaṁ yad api tām* (?) *garbhaṇī prāśayet* / *tatas tasya* (?) *jīved garbho bhavet* (?) *iti* //

88-90. If [children] die [after they] were born, one should, after consecrating the clarified butter, offer [it into the fire by means of the hymn] beginning with *Brahmaṇāgniḥ* [*RV*.10.162], pour the residue on an amulet and fumigate (?) [it, to wit:] the amulet, [which is fixed] on a threefold thread together with a cloth, [which is made] out of the sheath of a young bud of a Nyagrodha tree, and which is wrapped up with white and red (thread?], [should be] praised [by means of the hymn] beginning with *Brahmaṇā* [*RV*.10.162], after consecrating it ten thousand times with the Sāvitrī [-verse, i.e. *RV*.3.62.10] in accordance with the precept, [and pouring over it] the residue of ten thousand [oblations].

The translation follows Mātṛsūnu's commentary: *jāteti / pratitajāni* (?) *garbharūpāṇi pramīyeran tata ājyaṁ saṁskṛtyānumaṁtrya ca "brahmaṇāgniḥ saṁvidāna"* [*RV*.10.162] *ity anena sūktena tato juhuyāt / anenaiva hutaśeṣasya taṁ ca saṁpātamaṇau ninayet / iti maṇim iti / maṇis tu nyagrodha śṛṁgatayā* (?) *kartavyaḥ / śuklalohitasūtraveṣṭita iti / trivṛtena* (*trir vṛttena*?)* *ca taṁtuke sūtre āsakte sa ca vasasā paridhānīyena sahaikatra vāsanīyo rātrim ekām iti / taṁ sāvitreyeti tatas taṁ maṇiṁ gāyatrīṇām daśabhiḥ sahasrair niṣiktaṁ kuryāt / "brahmaṇāgniḥ saṁvidānaḥ"* [*RV*.10.162] [(*ityagniḥ saṁvidāna*)] *ityanena cānumaṁtritaṁ kuryāt / ayutenaiveti //* The end of the Varga is here marked by 17 in Ba Ta.

91-92.[a] And further on, the consecration with Sāvitrī [-verse] and with all benedictory verses [shall be] of this extent [i.e. ten thousand] and one must [invariably] mutter this [hymn].[b] A woman who is piously disposed should, when she is pregnant, wear this amulet, which is duly invoked on the head and fasten the amulet [to neck] in the third month of her pregnancy.

(a) Mātṛsūnu: *upeti / yathā purāstāt homānumaṁtraṇe maṇer evaṁ upariṣṭād api sāvitryā daśasahasram anumaṁtraṇaṁ kartavyam / na kevalaṁ sāvitryā' pi vā' nyair ai svastyayanaiḥ / "svasti no iṁdro"* [*RV*.1.89.6] *"svasti no mimītām"* [*RV*.5.51.11] *ityādyair api / siraseti / evam etam anumaṁtritaṁ maṇiṁ garbhiṇī nārī śirasā vahet / śirasi badhnīyād ity arthaḥ //*

(b) Prof. Gonda renders this stanza thus: 'And afterwards this (Sūkta shall be muttered together with the Sāvitrī—this is really a consecration—and with all benedictions (svastyayana-)'.

93. When menses [reappear after] a year,[a] a woman must [till then] remain in the condition of a cow possessing a calf, with much to be drunk and eaten, together with the young suckling one.

(a) Though the reading *śaradam* gives one syllable too much to the line, it is probably original, as the rhythm at the end of the pāda is normal (∪——). Both the text and the scanty commentary are corrupt.

94-95. When a boy has been born, one must fasten the amulet to his neck, after honouring the residue of the clarified butter, anointing the boy [with it], and offering [oblations into the fire] to the accompaniment of the benedictory verses. [In this manner], a woman brings forth a male child. A blessing ceremony is again prescribed after one year.

Mātṛsūnu: *ājyaśeṣaṁ saṁpātasaktaṁ puraskṛtvā yata* (?) *sthāpayitvā tena kumāram abhyajya tato vakṣmāṇam iti / hutveti / ārājya* (?) *kumārakaṁ tatas taṁ maṇiṁ nidhāya svastyayanaiḥ sūktaiḥ pratyṛcam ājyahomaṁ kṛtvā saṁpatair niṣicya saṁprati svastyayanai[s] tat karma kṛtvā kumārasya maṇibaṁdhanaṁ kuryāt / trimāsikasya jātasya tataḥ prativarṣamevam svaitat [(karma kṛtvā)] kuryād upanayanakālaṁ yāvat //* The end of the Varga is her marked by 18 in Ba Ta.

96-98. Before the breast-feeding one must cause him [i.e. the child] to lick an oblation consisting of rice meal mixed with honey [and rubbed with] gold by means of the Śraddhā- and Medhā-sūktas [i.e. *RV*.10.151 and *RV*.*Kh*.iv.8]: [then that child] becomes intelligent by that [rite], lives a hundred years and dies not before the [full] duration of life, [besides] there would be retentive memory to him after six months. Afterwards, a twiceborn person should, after purifying the clarified butter, offer [oblations into the fire, by means of the hymn] beginning with *Akṣibhyāṁ te* [*RV*.10.163].

Mātṛsūnu: *punar iti medhājananakarmocyate / puna[ḥ]* stanapradānā tham ityādi / puna* [ḥ] *stanapradānartham yāvan māta pravartate / tāvad evaitaj jātamātramāṇavaje* (?) *karma / madhunā saha suvarṇaṁ peṣayitvā vrīhipiṣṭaṁ ca tatra prakṣipya śraddhāsūktena ca kumārakaṁ pāyayet tēna medhāvī bhavatīti dīrghāyuś ca bhavatīti / smṛtam iti / smṛtaṁ smaraṇam ucyate / tac cānena karmaṇā tasya māṇavakasya ṣaṇmāsāt bhavati / tataḥ param iti vakṣyamāṇena saṁbaṁdhaḥ / ājyam iti / "akṣibhyāṁ te nāsikābhyām"* [*RV*.10.163] *iti ṣaḍṛcaṁ sūktaṁ tada*° *te / ājyaṁ saṁskṛtyetyādi / tato medhājananakarmaṇaḥ parata ājyaṁ pratyṛcam iti //*

99-100. Then with the hand smeared with ghee one should touch his head, ears and eyes and touch his chin and likewise his two nostrils and constantly mutter in this manner: [then] that child] is freed from consumption. [Thus] one should undertake the removal of consumption by means of the aforesaid ritual precept.

Mātṛsūnu: *pānīti* / "*akṣibhyaṁ te*" [*RV*.10.163] *ityanena yaḥ kṛtahomas tadanaṁtaraṁ ghṛtābhyaktābhyāṁ hastābhyāṁ hastābhyām maṇāvakasya saṁspṛśet tatha karṇau netre ca* / *cibukaṁ hanur ucyate* / *tadvan nāsikāṁ cānena sūkteneti* / *evamevāti* / *nigada vyākhyā tam etat* / *purveti* / "*gṛhītaṁ yakṣmaṇ-a darbhān gṛhitve*" [*Ṛvidh*.iv.81] *ti prakṛtim* (*prakṛtam*) "*muñcāmi tvā haviṣa jīvanāya kam*" [*RV*.10.161] *ityanena sūktena vadya nānakasemoktaṁ* (*yadyan nānākarmoktam*)* *tad* "*akṣibhyāṁ te nāsikābhyām*" [*RV*.10.163] *iti anenā pi kṛiyata iti ślokārthaḥ* // The end of the Varga is here marked by 19 in Ba Ta.

101. One should undertake the removal of consumption by means of burnt-offerings and mutterings. One should, on becoming pure, mutter the hymn which is destructive of evil dreams [and which] begins with *Apehi* [*RV*.10.164].

Mātṛsūnu: *homa iti* / "*akṣibhyām te*" [*RV*.10.163] *iti prakṛtaṁ tasyaitat saṁbadhyate* / *asya sūktena pāpi* (*va'pi*)* *ca pūrvoktavad yakṣmanāśanaṁ kartaryam iti* / *api iti* / "*apehi manasaspate*" [*RV*.10.164] *iti paṁcarcaṁ sūktam tada*° *te* / *apehītyādi paṭhita siddham* //

102. When a pigeon excretes[a] [on a house], one should offer clarified butter by means of the hymn beginning with *Devāḥ kapota* [*RV*.10.1965] for they regard it as a messenger of Yama.

(a) Prof. Gonda renders 'should a dove alight'.

103-105. One should employ [the hymn] which is destructive of rivals [and which begins with] *Ṛṣabham* [*RV*.10.166] at the [time of] mutterings and burnt-offerings. A person who is regular in observances should regularly mutter [the hymn] beginning with *Yenedam* [*RV*.*Kh*.iv.11]: [then] he obtains concentration of the mind by means of that [hymn] and does not get perplexed. A steadfast person should mutter [the hymn] beginning with *Mayobhūrvāto* [*RV*.10.169] at the blessing ceremony for cows and offer barley corns anointed with ghee and purified by means of curds, honey and clarified butter into the fire [lit. with] cow-dung cakes, when he is in the midst of the cow-stall.

The end of the Varga is here marked by 20 in Ba Ta.

106. One should anoint (*abhiṣiñceta*)[a] under the [asterism] Tiṣya or Śravaṇa or also under the [asterism] presided by Pūṣan [Revatī], that by Savitṛ [Hastā] that by Soma [Mṛgaśiras] and that by the Aśvins [Aśvinī] and under the [asterism] Rohinī as well as under [those asterisms which are preceded by] Uttarā[b].

(a) I follow Dr. Meyer. My mss. except Cm. read *abhiṣicyeta*.
(b) They are *uttarāphālgunī*, the twelfth lunar mansion consisting of two stars; *uttarāṣāḍhā*, the twenty-first lunar mansion consisting of three stars; and *uttarābhādrapadā*, the twentysixth lunar mansion consisting of two stars.

107. After offering [oblations] into the fire with [the verses] possessing royal tokens, let a king who is piously-disposed and pure be poured over with the residue by means of the Sāvitri [-verse] and the Mahāvyāhṛtis.

*Hutveti / tatrābhiṣekasya pūrvam ayam doṣaḥ (homaḥ)* kartavyaḥ / rājya-(rāja)*. liṁgābhir iti / "yo rājā carṣaṇīnām"* [*RV*. 8.70.1] *ityādibhiḥ sāvitrīṁ ca vyāhṛtibhiś ca saṁpātād rājñaḥ śirasi ninīya yatrāṁtaṁ vidheyam //*

108-110. Having anointed him, who is seated on a tiger's skin [placed] on a stool (*āsandī*), by means of the fine sap of all sorts of herbs and the water taken from [various] rivers, one should, while standing and facing the west, pronounce [the following]: "Conquer thou this earth! Let thy virtues increase by protecting thy subjects! May thou prosper unto good fortune, prosperity, victory and success! Let there be [always] kings in your lineage!" and then mutter the [hymn of] Apratiratha [viz. *RV*.10.103].

Mātṛsūnu: *Sarvauṣadhir iti / taṁ rājānaṁ vyāghracarmā* [*c*]* *chāditāmāsaṁdyāṁ pīṭhikāyāmudumbaraśākhyām upaveśya tataḥ sarvauṣadhirasaiḥ ślakṣṇaiḥ piṣṭair upalepyodvartayet / uddhṛtena nadīsalilena śirasi abhiṣiñcet / prāpayet / "ā tvā harṣam aṁtaredhi"* [*RV*.10.173] *ity etat sūktaṁ japann iti tiṣṭhati /* [*n*]*etāni āśīḥ padāni brūyāt / vardha tvaṁ catrate tyuktvā / tato* *khe "āśuḥ śiśāno vṛṣabho na bhīma* [*RV*.10.103] *ity etat sūktam apratiratha-saṁjñaṁ jāpet* // The end of the Varga is here marked by 21 in Ba Ta.

111. The skin [used in this ceremony] should be that of a tiger [and] the fuel-stick[s] that of a Udumbara-tree.[a] After having anointed him thrice; one should consecrate the kettle-drums.

(a) Prof. Gonda renders (rather literally) the first hemistichthus: 'And the skin shall come from a tiger, the fuel from Udumbara'.

112-114. "Let the Vasus anoint thee for the benefit of heroic lustre in the eastern quarter! Let the Rudras anoint thee for the benefit of success in the southern quarter! Let the Ādityas anoint thee for the benefit of prosperity in the western quarter! Let the all-gods anoint [thee] for the benefit of auspicious result!" One should consecrate a king by means of [the hymn] beginning with *Ā tvā hārṣam antar edhi* [*RV*.10.173], after anointing and pleasing him with [numerous] benedictions.

Mātṛsūnu: *prācyam iti / taṁ rājānaṁ maṁtreṇābhimaṁtraṇād anaṁtaram etāny apy āśīḥ yadanye* (*padāni*)* *ca paṭhed iti paṭhitasiddham etat* //

115. One should constantly mutter [the hymn] which is destructive of illusion (*ajñānabhedana*) and which begins with *Pataṅgam* [*RV*.10.177]. This hymn is, indeed, destructive of sorcery (*māyābhedana*) and repels all sorts of sorceries.

The end of the Varga is here marked by 22 in Ba Ta.

116. One should, by means of this [hymn], prevent the magic [from operating], be it that of Śambara or Indrajāla. [Likewise] one should, by means of this [hymn], ward off the magic caused by unseen beings.

Mātṛsūnu: *Śāṁbarīṁ iṁdrajālām iti / sa ca rājñe māyāvino lokadaṁbhakābhramanāya* (?) *ceṁdrajālikās tadīyāṁ māyāmanena japtena bādhata iti* //

117-118. A person who regular in his observances should mutter the benedictory [hymn] beginning with *Tya mūṣu* [*RV*.10.178].

After touching the limbs [of that woman], who [though] matured and menstruating, cannot conceive, one should mutter [the hymns beginning with] *Viṣṇur yonim* [*RV*.10.184], and] *Nejameṣa* [*RV. Kh*.iv.13 respectively]. One should mutter [the hymn] beginning with *Mahi trīṇām avo'stu* [*RV*.10.185] at the blessing ceremony for the path (*pathisvastyayana*).

Mātṛsūnu: *tyamūṣviti* / "*tya mūṣu vājinaṁ devajūtam*" [*RV*. 10.178] *iti tṛcaṁ sūktam tada*° *te* / *tyamūṣviti svastyayanam ityādi paṭhita siddham* / *puṣpam iti* / "*viṣṇur yoniṁ kalpayatu*" [*RV*.10.184] *iti tṛcaṁ sūktam tada*° *te* / *puṣpaṁ dṛṣṭvā ca yā garbham ityādi* / *yasyāḥ striyaḥ pratimāsaṁ rajo dṛśyate garbhasrāvaḥ saṁbhavati tasyā anena sūktena yonimabhimaṁtrya tato garbhaṁ sambhavatīti* / *mahīti* / "*mahitrīṇām avo'stu* [*RV*.10.185] *iti paṭhitasiddham* //

119. One should, in order to do away with enmity, mutter the hymn which is hostile to enemies and which begins with *Prāgnaye* [*RV*.10.187]. One wards off snakes by means of this [hymn, verses of which] are addressed to Sarparājñī and which begins with *Āyaṁ gauḥ* [*RV*.10.189].

Mātṛsūnu: *prāgnaye tu dviṣa* [*d*]* *dveṣyam ityādi* / *yo dveṣyaṁ dveṣṭum i*[*c*]**chati sa caitat sūktaṁ nityam japet tathā dveṣopaśam* (*dveṣopaśamaṁ*) *yā* [(*ṁ*)] *it* / *avaśyaṁ vaśīkaroti niyatasya* (?) *niṣkṛtir iti* / *āyaṁ gaur iti* / "*āyaṁ gauḥ praśnir akramīt*" [*RV*.10.189] *i*[*ti*]* *tṛcaṁ sūktaṁ tada*° *te* / "*āyaṁ gauḥ sārparājñīstv ityādi* / *anena japtena sarpabhayaṁ na bhavatīti* //

120. One should mutter [the hymn of] Aghamarasaṇa [*RV*. 10.190] which is the [most] sanctified among the sanctified [hymns] and whoever, on becoming steadfast, recites it thrice after immersing in water, [obtains desired result]

Mātṛsūnu: *pavitreti* / "*ṛtaṁ ca satyaṁ cābhīddhāt*" [*RV*.10.190] *ity ṛcaṁ trirāvṛtya asdyo' ghamarṣaṇa* [*ṁ*]* *sūktaṁ tada*° *te* / *pavitrāṇāṁ pavitraṁ tviti paṭhitasiddham* / *āpa iti* / *tasya vakṣyamāṇaṁ phalaṁ bhavatīti vākyaśeṣaḥ* // The end of the Varga is here marked by 23 in Ba Ta.

121-122. comparable to that of a final purificatory bath in the Aśvamedha [ceremony], for, Manu has declared thus (*iti*): "Just as the Aśvamedha, the chief amongst the sacrifices, removes all sins even so the hymn of Aghamarṣaṇa removes all sins." [The hymn] beginning with *Nairhastyam* [*RV.Kh.V.*2] is a means of routing an army—so says (*iti*) Śaunaka.

Mātṛsūnu: *yatheti / seneti / "nairhastyaṁ senā-dāraṇam"* [*RV. Kh.*V.2] *iti khilaṁ navarcaṁ sūktam tada*° *te / senādāranam etasmād ityādi / etasmād aghamarṣaṇād anaṁtaram etat sūktaṁ śaunakācāryeṇoktam iti //*

Mātisūnu notices a different reading: *etasmāt* (for *etat syāt*) which is not found in any mss. of the *Ṛvidh.*, but which appears to be definitely preferable because it controverts the view expressed by Macdonell in *BD*, Part II. p.320.

123. Further Śaunaka opines that it should mentally be meditated upon. [The hymn beginning with] *Saṁsamid yuvase vṛṣan* [*RV.*10.191] is highly conducive to fraternity.

Mātṛsūnu: glosses *Saubhātṛkaraṇam* by *sasnehakaraṇam.*

124-125. One should employ it in case of dissension among the kindred: [then] they never become disunited at any time. But when the dissension is complete, one should mutter this [hymn] which brings about reconciliation [and which begins with] *Saṁjñānam* [*RV.Kh.V.*1]: then there would not be [any further] dissension in that place where one constantly mutters this hymn. One should, at the [time of] blessing ceremony, mutter [the hymn] beginning with *Tac chaṁyorā vṛṇīmahe* [*RV.Kh.V.*1.5 = V.3.7].

The end of the Varga is here marked by 24 in Ba Ta.

126. The Mahānāmnī [-verses (*RV.Kh.V.*4) representing] the highest Brahman, the eternal resplendent light, [should be muttered. The verses] belonging to Purifying Soma, which are declared as subsequent (*parā*), are destructive of rivals and are auspicious [besides].

The translations follows Mātṛsūnu's commentary: *mahānāmnīti / "vidā maghavan vidā gātu"* [*RV.Kh.*V.4] *ityādi khilapaṭhitā mahānāmnī ucyate / mahānāmnyaḥ paraṁ brahmetyādi / etāvatī japyāḥ / puṇya iti sapatnaghnya iti / "pāvamānyaḥ"* (*pāvamanīḥ*)* *svastyovanīr* [*RV.Kh.*iii.10] *ityādyāḥ parā pāvamānya ucyaṁte //*

127-131. One desiring rain should mutter these eternal [verses beginning with] *Āpo hiṣṭha* [*RV*.10.9]. The mystical utterances preceded by *oṁ* at the beginning, the [ten] hymns of Maducchandas, the Mahānāmnī [-verses] at the end—this is declared to be Amṛtā-saṁhitā, by means of which the gods previously attained immortality and whoever constantly mutters this [*saṁhitā*], on becoming pure, will attain immortality. Let a person frequently insert the hymns addressed to the manes in the midst of this [aforesaid collection]—this one should know as the Pitryā-saṁhita and with it one [should] propitiate one's manes. Compiling in this way one can have a Vāsavī-Saṁhitā, Raudrī–, Ādityā–, Vaiśvadevī– [saṁhitās] [or] one relating to whichever divinity one desires. A person conversant with religious duties should perform a pacificatory ceremony for the foundation in the midst of the cow-shed.

Mātṛsūnu: *Oṁkāreti | oṁkārapurvā vyāhṛtayaḥ | tathā "agnimīḷe purohitam"* [*RV*.1.1-10] *ityādīni madu* [*c*]**caṁdasadṛṣṭāni daśa sūktāni | tathā pāvamānya ṛcaḥ "pāvamanīḥ svastyayanīḥ* [RV.Kh.iii.10] *ityādyās tatvasūktāyaṁte* (?) *mahānāmnya saṁjñikā ityamṛtaṁ* (*amṛtā*) *saṁhitocyate | atīvapuṇyāḥ pavitrā japyā iti | amṛteti | anayā purvoktayā saṁhitayā devā amṛtatvaṁ yayuḥ prāptā ityarthaḥ | anye' pyenaṁ śucir nityam japenāmṛtatvaṁ ga* [*c*]**chatīti | atraiveti | atraivāsyāya cāmṛtasaṁhitāyā* (?) *madhye pitṛsūktāni catu*[ḥ]* *paṁcāśad adhyāye* [i.e. *RV*. 10.6-18] *paṭhitāni | "aṁgiraso naḥ pitaro navagvā"* [*RV*.10.14.6] *ityevamādīni prakṣipet tataḥ sā pitryā saṁhitā bhavati | tā japet prīṇātīti | evameveti | evam eva yadvā pitṛdevatyām anyatamasaṁhitāyāṁ pitṛdaivatyeṣu prakṣiteṣu tathābhūte tathā vasudevatyeṣvaiṁdreṣu prakṣipteṣu vāsavī aiṁdrīsaṁhitā bhavati | yathā aiṁdrī tathā raudryādyā' pi bhavatīti | yaś caivam utpādyotpādya yāni yayā karmāṇi abhipretāni tayā japtavyā* (?) *kartavyāni ||* The end of the Varga is here marked by 25 in Ba Ta.

132. One should scatter flowers, sandal-paste, garlands, fruits of large trees, herbs and likewise the seven kinds of grains (*saptadhānya*)[a] on the whole foundation.

(a) Prof. Gonda refers *Bṛh-Up* 6.3.13, where "ten cultivated kinds of grains" are enumerated. We need not take the number 'seven' very seriously. The systematic classification of grain was attempted only later. See *Bhāvaprakāśa* Pt.I, p.495: *Śālidhānyaṁ vrīhidhānyaṁ śūkadhānyaṁ tṛtīyakaṁ / śimbīdhānyaṁ kṣudradhānyam ityuktaṁ dhānya-pañcakam //*

133. One should sacrifice Vāstoṣpati and Bṛhaspati with the *pāyasa* and with [the fuel-sticks of] *udumbara-* and *palāśa-*trees[a] and present a *bali* in every direction in that place.

(a) Prof. Gonda renders 'with fruits of the udumbara and the palāśa'. Mātṛsūnu supplies *samidbhis* to *audumbarapalāśais.*

134. Sūrya [the sun], Vāyu [wind], Yama, Pitṛs, Varuṇa, Nirṛti, Soma and Indra—these deities are declared as [stationed] in the [eight] directions.

Mātṛsūnu: *Sūryo vāyur iti / prācyādiṣu dikṣu etā yathākramaṁ devatā* [ḥ]* *smṛtās tāsu tāsveva dikṣu sthitāḥ pujanīyā iti // Ṛvidh.* gives the guardians of the directions in an unsystematic manner, besides omissions and additions. See, however, *Amara*, 1.70.

135-136. One should give a donation to the Brāhmaṇas in order that there may be well-being in one's establishment. [This rite] should be performed every year by the householder in his house [and one should], according to the precept, [perform] any other [rite] even if it has not been proclaimed. Agni, Indra and also Vāyu, Sūrya and the other deities–

The end of the Varga is here marked by 26 in Ba Ta.

137. to whomsoever [deity], a person who is desirous of worshipping might approach, [that person will], by means of the congruous hymn, [achieve] the purpose as enjoined [by the sages]. Mātṛsūnu's commentary on the second hemistich runs as follows: *abhīti / yathāpaṭhitaṁ sūkte maṁtraliṁgābhirūpeṇa sūktena yathā devatārādhanaṁ kartavyam / yathādiṣṭaṁ prayojanam ṛṣibhir maṁtradṛgbhir madhu* [*c*]* *chaṁdā prabhṛti*[*bhi*]**s tat siddhyartham iti ślokārthaḥ* // Prof. Gonda renders this stanza thus: 'one should quickly approach that very (divinity), of whichsoever one endeavours to gain the favour, with a cor-

responding sūkta, which has been divulged by means of (or: in) the mantras of the ṛṣis.'

138. The success as [it is] revealed in the Mantras (*mantra-dṛṣṭena*), is laid down as immediate in the case of sages.[a] One should in every case give a sacrificial fee (*dakṣiṇā*) or wealth for the accomplishment of a rite.

(a) Prof. Gonda renders the first hemistich thus: (with such an application as has been enjoined (by the authorities); (then success is regarded as instantaneous'.

139. Śaunaka [holds] that there is hardly any rite whatsoever without a sacrificial fee. As far as possible there should at least be [a sacrificial fee] commensurate with a full vessel [of grain] at the end [of a rite][a]

(a) Prof. Gonda renders the second hemistich thus: '(A donation presented) according to one's ability will, indeed, in the end (prove to) be like a full vessel of value'. Mātṛsūnu's commentary on the same runs as follows: *Śaktyeti / yathā kaṁcit karmaśaṁmataḥ* (?) *samāptau svaśaktyāpekṣayā pūrṇapātratulyāpi dakṣiṇā dātavyā //*

140. Therefore a sacrificial fee, even though little, should be given for the successful accomplishment of a rite. One should give [ten cows] with a bull as the eleventh or that by which one's preceptor is satisfied.

Mātṛsūnu's commentary on the second hemistich runs as follows: *ṛṣabheti / svaśaktyā śaktyapekṣayākāmya* [(*vat*)] *karmasu yatra viśeṣadakṣiṇā ma* (*na*)* *paṭhitā danu* (*dhenu*)* *ṛṣabhaikādaśa mayā dātavyā yena vā dānena gurus tuṣyati tad dātavyaṁ karmaphala siddhvartham iti ślokārthaḥ //*

141-142. [Just as] the gift of the knowledge of Brahman is imparted to one who is conversant with religious duties and who is truth-speaking, in like manner this [work] which is mysterious purifying and wonderful [like] the highest Brahman should not be given to one who is not peaceful, nor to one who is sonless, nor to one who has not practised *tapas*, nor to one who has not remained for one year [under his preceptor], nor to one who is not fit to be taught as well as to one who is hostile [to his preceptor].

Mātṛsūnu: *tad iti / tad idam ṛgvidhānagraṁthākhyaṁ paraṁ brahmetyādi paṭhitasiddhaḥ / nāpraśāṁtāyeti / etad brahmā' praśāṁtātmani yatheṣṭācāriṇe na dātavyam / putrāya* (?*putravate*) *yaśasvine tapasvine dātavyaṁ nānyasmani* / ? *naca saṁvatsaro na ca uśitāya ārādhanaṁ akurvataḥ / ityṛgvidhāne mātṛsūnu viracite* (?) *paṁcikāyāṁ caturtho' dhyāyaḥ samāptaḥ //* The end of the Varga is here marked by 27 in Ba Ta. The last *pāda* is repeated in Ba only.

## ATHA PHALAŚRUTIḤ[a]

1. The *Ṛgveda* which is comparable to a heavenly tree that bestows all benefits [or which is a veritable tree consisting of ritual precepts] does not yield the desired result to luckless men bereft of the knowledge of the *Ṛgvidhāna.*[b]

(a) I follow the practice of most of my mss (Ba Bo 1.2), but Dr. Meyer designates it as "Paṇcamo' dhyāyaḥ".

(b) Mātṛsūnu: *nārāṇām ityādi vargadvayaṁ* (?) *paṭhitaśiddha ślōkaḥ* 13 //

2. The *Ṛgveda* appears to me like an abode which holds precious gems and which does not become visible without [the aid of] a lamp, to wit: the *Ṛgvidhāna* (*ṛgvidhānapradīpenā*)[a].

(a) Resolve: *ṛgvidhāna eva pradīpāḥ, ṛgvidhānapradīpaḥ, tena.*

3. Like a great ocean [or like a munificent source of precious gems] the *Ṛgveda* which [is] exceedingly sacrosanct [or invincible] does not yield any desired result without [the aid of] a ship, to wit: the *Ṛgvidhāna* (*ṛgvidhānamahāpotaṁ*).[a]

(a) Resolve: *ṛgvidhāna eva mahāpotaḥ, taṁ vinā* (or *tena vinā*).

4. The *Ṛgveda* which is a sanctuary of Brahmā[a] and which is a divine treasure of all precious gems is certainly attained by means of the precepts of the *Ṛgvidhāna.*

(a) Could it be *Brahman* 'sacred text'?

5. The *Ṛgveda* recited without the *Ṛgvidhāna* remains fruitless: therefore it [i.e. the *Ṛgvidhāna*] should diligently be studied.

The end of the Varga is here marked by 1 in Ba Ta.

6. The *Ṛgveda* becomes favourably disposed towards him who knows the *Ṛgvidhāna* which unfolds the true object of the hymns.

Prof. Gonda renders this stanza thus: 'who understands the Ṛgvidhāna, the account of the exact meaning of the sūktas, for him he mind of the Ṛgveda is full-blown, because of the serenity and kindness of its disposition' !

7. The religious practice[a] of he *Ṛgvidhāna* is, conducive to long life, the basis of good fortune and a means of destroying all stains. [Moreover] it is highly productive of splendid fame.

(a) The text has °*abhyanuṣṭhāna* which is same as °*anuṣṭhāna.*

8. A twice born person who knows the *Ṛgveda* together with the *Ṛgvidhāna*, certainly becomes a repository of *dharma*, *artha*, *kāma* and *mokṣa*[a].

(a) Prof. Gonda renders the second hemistich thus: 'dharma, artha, kāma and mokṣa will certainly be inherent (received)'!

9. The first amongst the Vedas, [i.e. *Ṛgveda*], which is the abode of Āyurveda[a] and which is powerful is extremely pleased with the constant recitation of the *Ṛgvidhāna.*

(a) An *upaveda* of *Ṛgveda*. Cp. *Caranavyūha*: *Sarveṣām eva vedānām upavedā bhavanti ṛgvedasyāyurvedopavedaḥ* etc.

10. The *Ṛgveda*, when gratified always by means of the *Ṛgvidhāna*, accomplishes (*kurute*)[a] the destruction of enemies and the mental ease arising from the union with friends.

(a) I have adopted this reading on the strength of the mss. Ba Bo 1.2, but Dr. Meyer adopts an inferior reading: *prayantā.* The end of the Varga is here marked by 2 in Ba Ta.

11. The [object of] desire of whomsoever knowing the *Ṛgveda* with all its [six] auxiliaries and always devoted to the *Ṛgvidhāna* turns out well, even beyond his wishes.

Prof. Gonda renders this stanza thus: 'Of (that man) who knows the Ṛgveda with all its aṅgas and is always intent upon the Ṛgvidhāna, all endeavours will be successful, even beyond his wishes'.

12. They long for the attainment of their aim[a] in matter of lineage, birth, conduct, knowledge and of industry by means of the thorough knowledge of the *Ṛgvidhāna.*

(a) Prof. Gonda renders 'people have command of successfulness'.

13. All deities are satisfied, the supernormal powers are accomplished [or successful] and the mental uneasiness vanish to those who regularly recite the Ṛgvidhi[a] [i.e. the *Ṛgvidhāna*].

(a) Prof. Gonda renders 'the Ṛgveda' ! The end of the Varga is not marked in any of the mss accessible to me.

# BIBLIOGRAPHY

I. Vedic Texts, Purāṇas, and other original sources arranged alphabetically:—


Agni-Purāṇa (Ānandāśrama Sanskrit Series No.41), Poona, 1900.

Aitareya Āraṇyaka edited by A.B. Keith, Oxford, 1909.

Aitareya Brāhmaṇa with the commentary of Sāyaṇācārya (Ānandāśrama Sanskrit Series No.32) edited by Kāśināth Śāstri Agashe, Pts. I-II, Poona, 1931.

Aṣṭādhyāyī of Pāṇini.

Āśvalāyana Gṛhya Sūtra edited by A.F. Stenzler, Leipzig, 1864.

Āśvalāyana Śrauta Sūtra (Ānandāśrama Sanskrit Series No.81) edited by Ganeśa Śāstri Gokhale, Poona, 1917.

Ātharvaṇa Jyotiṣam edited by Bhagavad Datta, Lahore, 1924.

Atharvaveda Saṁhitā edited by S.D. Satavalekar, Aundh, 1943.

Atharvaveda Saṁhita tr. by W.D. Whitney (Reprint), Delhi 1962.

Baudhāyana Dharma Sūtra edited by A. Chinnasvāmi Sāstri, Benares, 1934.

Bhagavadgītā (P.O.S. No.1) edited by D.V. Gokhale, Poona, 1950.

Bṛhaddevatā (H.O.S. Nos. 5 & 6) edited by A.A. Macdonell, Pts. I-II, Cambridge, 1904.

Bṛhatstotraratnākara edited by N.R. Acarya, Pt. I, Bombay, 1952.

Gṛhya Sūtras tr. by H. Oldenberg, Pts. I-II, Oxford, 1866, 1892.

Hymns of the Atharvaveda tr. by M. Bloomfield, Oxford, 1897.

Kauśika Sūtra edited by M. Bloomfield, New Haven, 1890.

Mānavagṛhyasūtra (G.O.S. No.35) edited by R.H. Śāstri, Baroda, 1926.

Manusmṛti with the commentary of Kullūkabhaṭṭa edited by V.L. Pansikar, Bombay, 1925.

Muṇḍakopaniṣat (P.O.S. No.5) edited by S.S. Phatak, Poona, 1925.

Nirukta of Yāska edited by L. Sarup, Bombay, 1927.

Nyāyamañjarī of Dyā Dviveda, Benares, 1933.

Pāraskaragṛhyasūtra edited by M.G. Bakre, Bombay, 1917.

Pariśiṣṭas of the Atharvaveda edited by G.M. Bolling and J. Van Negalein, Leipzig, 1909.
Ṛgvedaprātiśākhya with the commentary of Uvaṭa, Benares, 1903.
Ṛgveda Saṁhitā edited by S.D. Satavalekar, Aundh, 1940.
Ṛgveda Saṁhitā with the commentary of Sāyaṇācārya (V.S.M.), Vols. I-IV, Poona, 1933-1951.
Ṛgvidhānam edited by R. Meyer, Berlin, 1878.
Ṛgvidhānam edited by J. Śāstri, Lahore, 1940.
Ṛgvidhāna tr. by J. Gonda, Utrecht, 1951.
Ṣaḍviṁśa-brāhmaṇa edited by J. Vidyasagar, Calcutta, 1881.
Ṣaḍviṁśa-brāhmaṇa tr. by W.B. Bollee, Utrecht, 1956.
Sāmavidhānabrāhmaṇa with the commentary of Sāyaṇācārya edited by A.C. Burnell, London, 1873.
Śāṅkhāyana Gṛhya Sūtra edited by S.R. Sehgal Delhi, 1960.
Śāṅkhāyana Śrauta Sūtra edited by A. Hillebrandt, Calcutta, 1888.
Śāṅkhāyana Śrauta Sūtra tr. by W. Caland, Nagpur, 1953.
Sarvānukramaṇī edited by A.A. Macdonell, Oxford, 1886.
Śaunakīyam (T.S.S. No. 120), Trivandrum, 1935.
Śikṣāsaṅgraha, Benares, 1893.
Smṛticandrikā of Devaṇṇabhaṭṭa, Pt. II, Mysore, 1914.
Śuklayajurvidhānasūtra edited by A.S. Vare, Bombay, 1943.
Vaitāna Śrauta Sūtra edited by R. Garbe, London, 1878.
Viṣṇudharmottara-Purāṇa (Venkatesvara Press Edition) Bombay, V.S. 1969 = Saka 1834.
Vīṣṇudharmottara-Purāṇa edited by P. Shah, Vols. I-II, Baroda, 1958-1961.
Vīramitrodaya (Chowkhamba edition), Benares, 1906-37.
Yājñavalkyasmṛti with the commentary of Aparāditya (Ānandāśrama Sanskrit Series No.46), Vols. I-II, Poona, 1903.

II. Other Books chiefly consulted:—

Alphabetical Index of Sanskrit Mss. in the University Mss. Library, Vol. I, Trivandrum, 1957.
Alphabetical List of Mss. in the Oriental Institute, Vol. I, Baroda, 1942.
Catalogus Catalogorum by T. Aufrecht, Vols. I-III, Leipzig, 1891-1903.

Catalogue of the Sanskrit and Prakrit Mss. in the Library of the India Office, Vol. II, Pts. I-II, London, 1935.
Classified Index to the Sanskrit Mss. in the Palace at Tanjore, London, 1880.
Descriptive Catalogue of the Government Collection of Mss. deposited at the Deccan College, Vol. I, Bombay, 1916.
Descriptive Catalogue of Mss. on the Central Library, Vol. I: Vedic, Baroda, 1925.
Descriptive Catalogue of Sanskṛta and Prākṛta Mss. in the Library of the University of Bombay by G.V. Devasthali, Vols. I-II, Bombay, 1944.
Descriptive Catalogue of Sanskrit Mss. in the TMSSML, Vols. I-XIX, Srirangam, 1928-34.
Epic triṣṭubh and its hypermetric varieties by F. Edgerton (in JAOS, Vol.LIX, pp. 159-194).
Great Epic of India by E.W. Hopkins, New Haven, 1920.
History of Ancient Sanskrit Literature by F.W. Muller (Pāṇini Office Reprint), 1926.
History of the Dharmaśāstra by P.V. Kane, Vols. I-V, Poona, 1930-62.
History of the Indian Literature by M. Winternitz tr. by Mrs. S. Ketkar, Vol. I, Calcutta, 1927.
Religion and Philosophy of Vedas and Upanisads (H.O.S. Nos. 31-32) by A.B. Keith, Pts. I-II, London, 1925.
Religions of India by A. Barth, tr. by J. Wood, 5th Edition, London, 1921.
Sanskrit-English Dictionary by M. Monier-Williams Rev. Ed., London, 1899.
Sanskrit Grammar by W.D. Whitney, London, 1950.
Studies in the Puranic Records on Hindu Rites and Customs by R.C. Hazra, Dacca, 1940.
Studies in the Upapurāṇas by R.C. Hazra, Vol. I, Calcutta, 1958.

## ABBREVIATIONS

| | |
|---|---|
| *AA* | Aitareya Āraṇyaka |
| *AB* | Aitareya Brāhmaṇa |
| *Agni Pu* | Agni Purāṇa |
| *ĀGS* | Āśvalāyana Gṛhyasūtra |
| *ĀJ* | Ātharvaṇa Jyotiṣa |
| *Amara* | Amarakoṣa of Amarasiṁha |
| *Āp.Yaj.Par* | Āpastambīya Yajña Paribhāṣa Sūtra |
| *ASL* | Ancient Sanskrit Literature by M. Müller (Reprint) |
| *ĀSS* | Āśvalāyana Śrauta Sūtra |
| *AV* | Atharvaveda |
| *AVP.* or *Par.* | Atharvaveda Pariśiṣṭa |
| *Bau DS* | Baudhāyana Dharma Śūtra |
| *BD* | Bṛhad-devatā |
| *HDS* | History of Dharma-Śāstra by P.V. Kane |
| *HGS* | Hiraṇyakeśī Gṛhya Sūtra |
| *HIL* | History of Indian Literature by M. Winternitz |
| *JAOS* | Journal of the American Oriental Society |
| *JRAS* | Journal of Royal Asiatic Society of Gr. Britain and Ireland |
| *Kauś* | Kauśika Sūtra |
| *KGS* | Kauśītakī Gṛhya Śūtra |
| *Manu* | Manusmṛti |
| *Mbh* | Mahābhārata |
| *MGS* | Mānava Gṛhya Sūtra |
| *Mu Up* | Muṇḍaka Upaniṣad |
| *MW* | Monier William's Sanskrit-English Dictionary (New Ed. 1899) |
| *Nigh.* | Nighaṇṭu of Yāska |
| *Pa GS* | Pāraskara Gṛhya Sūtra |
| *Pāṇini* | Pāṇini's *Aṣṭādhyāyī* |
| *RPV* | Religion and Philosophy of Vedas and Upaniṣads by AB Keith |
| *Ṛvidh* | Ṛgvidhāna |
| *RV Prati* | Ṛgveda Prātiśākhya |

| | |
|---|---|
| *Sad.Br.* | Ṣaḍviṁśa Brāhmaṇa |
| *Sarv.* | Sarvānukramaṇī of Kātyāyana |
| *SC* | Smṛticandrikā of Devaṇṇabhaṭṭa |
| *ŚGS* | Śāṅkhāyana Gṛhya Sūtra |
| *ŚŚS* | Śāṅkhāyana Śrauta Sūtra |
| *Svidh* | Sāmavidhāna Brāhmaṇa |
| *TA* | Taittirīya Āraṇyaka |
| *Viṣṇu Dh.Pu* | Viṣṇu-Dharmottara-Purāṇa |
| *Whitney* | Whitney's Sanskrit Grammar (2nd ed. 1889) |
| *Yaj* | Yājñavalkya Smṛti |
| *Yvidh* | Yajurvidhāna Sūtra |

# INDEX OF VERSES IN ṚGVIDHĀNA

# INDEX